Encyclopedia of
EDUCATION
LAW

Editorial and Advisory Boards

Encyclopedia of
EDUCATION LAW

2

Charles J. Russo
University of Dayton
Editor

Los Angeles • London • New Delhi • Singapore

A SAGE Reference Publication

For information:

 SAGE Publications, Inc.
2455 Teller Road
Thousand Oaks, California 91320
E-mail: order@sagepub.com

SAGE Publications Ltd.
1 Oliver's Yard
55 City Road
London, EC1Y 1SP
United Kingdom

SAGE Publications India Pvt. Ltd.
B 1/I 1 Mohan Cooperative Industrial Area
Mathura Road, New Delhi 110 044
India

SAGE Publications Asia-Pacific Pte. Ltd.
33 Pekin Street #02-01
Far East Square
Singapore 048763

Printed in the United States of America.

Library of Congress Cataloging-in-Publication Data

Encyclopedia of education law / editor, Charles J. Russo.
    p. cm.
Includes bibliographical references and index.
ISBN 978-1-4129-4079-5 (cloth)
    1. Educational law and legislation—United States—Encyclopedias. 2. Educational law and legislation—United States—Cases.
3. Educational law and legislation—United States—History. 4. Education—United States—Encyclopedias. I. Russo, Charles J.

KF4117.E53 2008
344.73'0703—dc22   2008001210

This book is printed on acid-free paper.

08   09   10   11   12   10   9   8   7   6   5   4   3   2   1

Publisher:	Rolf A. Janke
Acquisitions Editor:	Diane McDaniel
Assistant to the Publisher:	Michele Thompson
Developmental Editor:	Diana E. Axelsen
Reference Systems Manager:	Leticia Gutierrez
Production Editor:	Kate Schroeder
Copy Editors:	Carla Freeman, Cate Huisman
Typesetter:	C&M Digitals (P) Ltd.
Proofreaders:	Kevin Gleason, Penny Sippel
Indexer:	Julie Grayson
Cover Designer:	Michelle Kenny
Marketing Manager:	Amberlyn Erzinger

Contents

List of Entries

Reader's Guide

Biographies

Alito, Samuel A., Jr.
Black, Hugo L.
Brennan, William J.
Breyer, Stephen G.
Burger, Warren E.
Darrow, Clarence S.
Douglas, William O.
Frankfurter, Felix J.
Ginsburg, Ruth Bader
Jefferson, Thomas
Kennedy, Anthony M.
Marshall, John
Marshall, Thurgood
O'Connor, Sandra Day
Rehnquist, William H.
Roberts, John G., Jr.
Scalia, Antonin
Souter, David H.
Stevens, John Paul
Thomas, Clarence
Warren, Earl

Collective Bargaining

Agency Shop
Arbitration
Closed Shop
Collective Bargaining
Grievance
Impasse in Bargaining
Mediation
Open Shop
Unions

Concepts, Theories, and Legal Principles

Assault and Battery, Civil
Attorney Fees
Authority Theory
Bureaucracy
Civil Law
Civil Rights Movement
Common Law
Consent Decree
Contracts
Copyright
Critical Theory
Defamation
Deposition
Disparate Impact
Dual and Unitary Systems
Due Process
Educational Malpractice
Equal Protection Analysis
Fair Use
False Imprisonment
Federalism and the Tenth Amendment
Fraud
Hearsay
Immunity
In Loco Parentis
Intellectual Property
Interrogatory
Negligence
Parens Patriae
Precedent
Preventative Law
Regulation
Remedies, Equitable Versus Legal

Educational Equity

Governance Issues

Litigation[†]

Collective Bargaining

Curricular Governance Issues

[†]The entry "U.S. Supreme Court Cases in Education" provides an overview of key decisions in education law. In addition, the encyclopedia contains 180 entries on specific cases, which are listed below according to their subject matter. Thirty-five of these are followed by entries consisting of case excerpts. To avoid excessive duplication, case excerpts are not listed in this section of the Reader's Guide. See Reader's Guide section "Primary Sources: Excerpted U.S. Supreme Court Landmark Cases" for these entries.

*An asterisk indicates that the case was not a U.S. Supreme Court ruling.

Religion in Public Schools

Special Education and Rights of Disabled Persons

Statutes and Treaties

LAMB'S CHAPEL V. CENTER MORICHES UNION FREE SCHOOL DISTRICT

In disputes over the question of separation of church and state, the use of school facilities by religious groups has been an issue numerous times. The landmark case of *Lamb's Chapel v. Center Moriches Union Free School District* (1993) set a broad precedent for the use of public school facilities by outside groups, including religious organizations. In a rare unanimous decision, the U.S. Supreme Court ruled that a school board's denial of school facility use to a religious group violated the group's First Amendment guarantee to free speech.

Facts of the Case

Lamb's Chapel arose where a New York state law allowed school boards to permit a wide variety of groups to use their facilities and property for a wide array of outside purposes, including social, civic, and recreational meetings and entertainment. However, the law did not include the use of meetings for religious purposes.

A local church twice requested to use school facilities at Center Moriches Union Free School District, outside of school hours, to show a 6-hour video series dealing with parenting issues that centered on Christian family values. Board officials denied the church's request on both occasions, claiming that the film was "church related."

When the church and its pastor sued the board for violating the Free Speech Clause of the First Amendment of the U.S. Constitution, a federal trial court granted its motion for summary judgment. The court maintained that since the school's facilities were only a limited public forum, the board's denials of the group's request to use them for religious activities were, in fact, viewpoint neutral. The Second Circuit affirmed in favor of the board.

The Court's Ruling

On further review, the U.S. Supreme Court reversed in favor of the religious organization, on the basis that the board's denial of its request to use school facilities solely because the group planned to show a film with a religious basis did, indeed, violate the church's free speech rights as protected by the First Amendment. The Court explained that since the facilities were used by other non-school-related groups for functions during nonschool hours, the board had in effect established a "limited public forum."

The Court added that since there was no apparent threat of violence or disruption for allowing the group to use school facilities, the request to use district facilities should likely have been granted. The Court thus found that insofar as the only reason the board rejected the organization's request was solely that the group was of a religious nature, denying it access for this reason was a violation of the "viewpoint neutrality" standard that requires state agencies to exhibit neither a positive nor negative attitude toward religion.

By allowing school facilities to be used by civic and social groups, such as the Boy Scouts or Girl Scouts, the Supreme Court was of the opinion that school boards such as the one in Center Moriches establish a "limited public forum" and cannot then deny similar access or facility use to religious groups or organizations. The Court reasoned that opening school doors for some groups but not specifically for religious groups violates both the notion of viewpoint neutrality and their rights to free speech as protected by the First Amendment, even if this speech has its basis in religion or is made for religious purposes.

Likewise, the Court observed that allowing a group to use school facilities for religious purposes does not imply that school or board officials promote or establish religion. In fact, the Court pointed out that the use of facilities does not imply that a meeting (or movie, as in the case at bar) is a school-sponsored or school-endorsed event, because while such a gathering is not necessarily closed to the public, there is nothing to suggest that the board has established an open forum for the use of its facilities.

As the Supreme Court noted in *Lamb's Chapel,* and reiterated almost a decade later in *Good News Club v. Milford Central School* (2001), if the message being delivered by the use of school facilities is appropriate (which the movie on child rearing and family values was), then a government-sponsored agency such as a school board cannot discriminate solely on the basis of the religious nature of the messenger.

Stacey L. Edmonson

See also First Amendment; *Good News Club v. Milford Central School;* Religious Activities in Public Schools

Legal Citations

Good News Club v. Milford Central School, 21 F. Supp. 2d 147 (N.D.N.Y. 1998); *aff'd,* 202 F.3d 502 (2d Cir. 2000, *rev'd*); 533 U.S. 98 (2001). *Lamb's Chapel v. Center Moriches School District,* 508 U.S. 384 (1993).

LAU V. NICHOLS

At issue before the U.S. Supreme Court in *Lau v. Nichols* was whether a school system is required to provide a program to address the language problems of non-English-speaking students. In this civil rights class action suit, the Court ruled that school districts receiving federal funds must act to correct students' linguistic deficits to ensure they receive an equal education. The decision, based on the Civil Rights Act of 1964, failed to specify what kinds of remedies were required. This entry describes the case, the decision, and its impact on education.

Facts of the Case

Kinney Kinmon Lau and other non-English-speaking Chinese students sought to compel the San Francisco Unified School District (SFUSD) to provide all non-English-speaking Chinese students with bilingual compensatory education in the English language. The non-English-speaking Chinese students claimed that the SFUSD violated their rights under the Fourteenth Amendment Equal Protection Clause, Section 601 of the Civil Rights Act of 1964, the California Constitution, and provisions of the California Education Code.

According to the Equal Protection Clause, states are prohibited from denying any person equal protection of the laws. In *Brown v. Board of Education of Topeka* (1954), the Supreme Court relied on the Equal Protection Clause in reasoning that "separate but equal" educational facilities were unconstitutional. In the *Lau* case, a federal trial court determined that the SFUSD satisfied students' rights to an education and to equal educational opportunities; it denied relief to the non-English-speaking Chinese students. Interpreting *Brown* as mandating the provision of education on equal terms, the trial court concluded that the board did not violate the Equal Protection Clause, because officials provided the students with equal educational opportunities when they received the same education that was available to all other students in the SFUSD.

In 1973, the Ninth Circuit affirmed that the SFUSD did not violate either the equal protection rights of non-English-speaking Chinese students or Section 601 of the Civil Rights Act of 1964. The Ninth Circuit court focused extensively on distinguishing the facts and decision in *Lau* from those in *Brown*. Insofar as the SFUSD had not directly or indirectly caused the language deficiencies, the Ninth Circuit found that the requisite discriminatory state action was absent. The Ninth Circuit explained that there were neither constitutional nor statutory mandates requiring the SFUSD to provide special remedial programs to students who were disadvantaged.

The Court Ruling

The Supreme Court granted certiorari because of the public importance of the issue in *Lau v. Nichols*. The Court decided that since the students could not read or speak English proficiently, the SFUSD had denied them their right to equal educational opportunities as required by Section 601 of the Civil Rights Act of 1964. Consistent with the Court's approach of seeking to avoid constitutional grounds in reviewing disputes, Section 601 of the Civil Rights Act was the sole basis on which it resolved *Lau*. According to Section 601, individuals may not be discriminated against based on race, color, or national origin in any program or activity receiving federal financial assistance.

The Department of Health, Education and Welfare (HEW) clarified this section of the Civil Rights Act of 1964 based on its duty to promulgate regulations prohibiting discrimination in school systems that receive federal financial assistance. In 1968, HEW issued a guideline directing school systems to provide students of a particular race, color, or national origin with an opportunity to obtain the same education that was available to all students. In 1970, HEW issued a second guideline, which specifically imposed upon federally funded school systems the responsibility of rectifying students' linguistic deficiencies to make instruction accessible for these students. These two guidelines attempted to clarify the responsibility of school systems to educate students in a nondiscriminatory fashion as required under Section 601 of the Civil Rights Act. In *Lau*, the Court pointed out both that HEW had authority to regulate the Civil Rights Act and that school boards were contractually obligated to comply as a condition of receiving federal funds.

Lau influenced state and federal policies that impacted the development of bilingual education programs in many school districts. For example, soon after *Lau*, Congress enacted the Equal Educational Opportunity Act (EEOA) of 1974 and the Bilingual Education Act of 1974. Thus, *Lau* signifies a fundamental turning point that reaffirmed the rights of non-English-speaking students to be free from discriminatory practices in educational programs and services.

Although *Lau* had a significant impact on the education of non-English-speaking students, the Court failed to adopt specific remedies to redress the school board's discriminatory practices. As a result, the Court did not deliver a clear mandate to the SFUSD or to other school systems regarding the provision of specific programs or services that would satisfy the obligation to educate non-English-speaking students in a nondiscriminatory fashion pursuant to Section 601 of the Civil Rights Act of 1964. Consequently, policy debates to determine appropriate programs for non-English-speaking students have been and will continue to be waged in school systems, state legislatures, and Congress.

Susan C. Bon

See also Bilingual Education; *Brown v. Board of Education of Topeka*; *Brown v. Board of Education of Topeka* and Equal Educational Opportunities; Civil Rights Act of 1964; English as a Second Language

Legal Citations

Brown v. Board of Education of Topeka I, 347 U.S. 483 (1954).
Brown v. Board of Education of Topeka II, 349 U.S. 294 (1955).
Equal Educational Opportunity Act of 1974, 20 U.S.C. § 1703(f).
Lau v. Nichols, 483 F.2d 791 (9th Cir. 1973); 414 U.S. 563 (1974).
Section 601 of the Civil Rights Act of 1964, 42 U.S.C. § 2000d.

LEAGUE OF UNITED LATIN AMERICAN CITIZENS (LULAC)

Responding to a long history in which their people have been at best ignored and at worst suffered discrimination, Mexican American citizens have formed numerous civil rights organizations, typically in cities, to work to improve the conditions facing them. Perhaps the most notable of these civil rights organizations is the League of United Latin American Citizens (LULAC), with approximately 115,000 members in over 700 councils in the United States and Puerto Rico. Since its founding in 1929, LULAC has been an active advocacy organization dedicated to defending and protecting the rights of Hispanics, including their right to education.

Background

American history textbooks rarely recount the lives of the people who lived in Texas and California before and after these areas were incorporated into the United States during the early and mid-19th century. Typical history texts fail to mention that Mexican American citizens had to endure numerous forms of discrimination. In many places, they were barred from voting because they did not know English and were also deprived of English language instruction. Further, if they were allowed to vote, they had to pay a "poll tax."

Similarly, Mexican Americans were not allowed to serve on juries. If their children were able to attend a school, they attended segregated "Mexican schools," which had poorly prepared teachers and deplorable physical facilities. Finally, many private businesses posted signs stating "No Mexicans Allowed."

Emerging out of such conditions was LULAC, created in Corpus Christi, Texas, on February 17, 1929, when the local chapter of the Order of the Sons of America, the Knights of America of San Antonio, and the League of Latin American Citizens of South Texas united into one organization. The convention adopted as the organization's motto "All for One and One for All," as a constant reminder of the trials of unification and as basis for all LULAC's future activities. According to LULAC's mission statement, its goal is to advance the economic condition, educational attainment, political influence, health, and civil rights of the Hispanic population of the United States.

Civil Rights Litigation

LULAC has been involved in a number of cases at the state and federal levels that led to changes in laws affecting Mexican Americans. In the earliest case, *Mendez v. Westminster* (1947), an en banc panel of the Ninth Circuit held that the segregation of Mexican and Mexican American students into separate "Mexican schools" was unconstitutional.

Seven years later, LULAC spearheaded a successful effort in *Hernandez v. Texas* (1954), a dispute that involved a Mexican American who was tried and convicted for murder by an all-Anglo jury. Insofar as Mexican Americans had not served on a jury in Texas for 25 years, the plaintiff claimed that they had been discriminated against as a class. In writing the Supreme Court's unanimous opinion, Chief Justice Earl Warren explained as follows:

> When the existence of a distinct class is demonstrated, and it is shown that the laws, as written or as applied, single out that class for different treatment not based on some reasonable classification, the guarantees of the Constitution have been violated. (*Hernandez v. Texas*, p. 478)

Two civil rights laws, Title VI of the Civil Rights Act of 1964 and the Equal Educational Opportunity Act (EEOA) of 1974, and the Supreme Court ruling in *Lau v. Nichols* (1974) afforded LULAC additional legal bases and precedents for bringing suits to protect Mexican American interests. Subsequently, in *Castaneda v. Pickard* (1981), parents of Mexican American students in Texas alleged that the instructional practices of the schools that their children attended violated their rights.

The Fifth Circuit established a three-pronged test in evaluating the claim: first, boards must use research-based programs viewed as sound by experts; second, boards must make adequate resources to implement programs; and, third, boards must evaluate programs and modify them if they fail to produce acceptable results. The Office for Civil Rights adopted this prong test for English Language Learning Classes, and LULAC has used the precedent to bring other suits involving the education of Mexican American students.

Two cases from Texas reached dissimilar results for Mexican Americans. In the first, *Plyler v. Doe* (1982), the Supreme Court ruled that a law denying a free public education to children whose parents were undocumented violated the Equal Protection Clause of the Fourteenth Amendment. Conversely, a year later, in *Martinez v. Bynum* (1983), the Court upheld a residency law that did not permit a minor to live apart from his parents in order to attend a public school tuition free, because the sister with whom he lived refused to become his legal guardian.

LULAC initiated a suit against the Florida State Department of Education concerning the education provided to Hispanic students (*LULAC v. Florida Board of Education*, 1990), leading to a consent decree between the parties. Pursuant to this consent decree, Florida agreed to comply with the federal and state laws and judicial order addressing the education of limited-English-proficient (LEP) students. The consent decree provided for specific actions by the state in educating the students and preparing the teachers who would instruct the LEP children. Even so, on January 13, 2003, LULAC alleged that the state violated Section IV of the agreement. The Florida State Board of Education approved a mediation agreement on August 19, 2003, that required school administrators and guidance counselors to earn 60 hours of in-service in English for Speakers of Other Languages (ESOL); teachers who passed the ESOL test also had to complete 120 hours within a 3-year period.

LULAC was also involved in a political gerrymandering case from Texas that alleged that Hispanics would not be fairly represented because of the way the district was redrawn after the 2000 census. In *League of United Latin American Citizens v. Perry* (2006), the Supreme Court ordered the lower court to remedy the situation by redrawing district lines.

Robert J. Safransky

See also Civil Rights Movement; *Lau v. Nichols; Martinez v. Bynum; Plyler v. Doe*

Legal Citations

Castaneda v. Pickard, 648 F.2d 989 (5th Cir. 1981).
Equal Educational Opportunity Act of 1974, 20 U.S.C. § 1703(f).
Hernandez v. Texas, 347 U.S. 475 (1954).
Lau v. Nichols, 483 F.2d 791 (9th Cir. 1973); 414 U.S. 563 (1974).

League of United Latin American Citizens v. Perry, 548 U.S. 399 (2006).
LULAC v. Florida Board of Education, C.A. # 90–1913-M (S.D. Fla. 1990).
Martinez v. Bynum, 461 U.S. 321 (1983).
Mendez v. Westminster School District of Orange County, 64 F. Supp. 544 (D.C. Cal. 1946), aff'd, 161 F.2d 774 (9th Cir. 1947).
Plyler v. Doe, 457 U.S. 202 (1982).
Title VI of the Civil Rights Act of 1964, 42 U.S.C. § 2000d.

LEAST RESTRICTIVE ENVIRONMENT

One of the key mandates of the Individuals with Disabilities Education Act (IDEA) is that all students with disabilities are to be educated in the *least restrictive environment* (LRE). This requirement applies across the continuum of placement alternatives that a school board needs to maintain under the statute.

In particular, the IDEA requires states, and consequently school boards, to set up procedures ensuring that students with disabilities are educated to the maximum extent appropriate with children who do not have disabilities. The IDEA further directs that students with disabilities be placed in special classes or separate facilities, or otherwise be removed from the general education environment only when the nature or severity of their disabilities is such that instruction in general education classes cannot be achieved satisfactorily, even with supplementary aids and services. The IDEA's LRE provisions relate to students who attend private schools, institutions, or other care facilities at public expense in addition to those who attend special education programs within the public schools. The IDEA's LRE provisions are so intertwined with the statute's requirement to provide a free appropriate public education that one is rarely mentioned without reference to the other.

Required Inclusion

In *Board of Education of the Hendrick Hudson Central School District v. Rowley* (1982), the U.S. Supreme Court stated that an appropriate education is one that is formulated pursuant to all of the IDEA's procedures and is sufficient to confer some educational benefit on a student with disabilities. The Court added that the program provided to a student in a special education placement who attends school in a regular classroom setting should enable the child to achieve passing marks and advance from one grade to the next.

In determining the least restrictive setting for a given student, school officials need to consider a variety of factors, including the student's educational needs and social needs. Initial guidance in this regard was provided by several high-profile court cases. In two of these cases, federal appellate courts directed school boards to place students with disabilities in regular settings, as opposed to segregated special education classrooms. In both disputes, the courts insisted that educators must consider a variety of factors when formulating the LRE for children with disabilities.

In a case from New Jersey, *Oberti v. Board of Education of the Borough of Clementon School District* (1993), the Third Circuit adopted a two-part test, originally outlined by the Fifth Circuit in litigation from Texas (*Daniel R. R. v. State Board of Education,* 1989), for evaluating compliance with the IDEA's LRE mandate. The first component of the test asks whether the child in question can be educated satisfactorily in a regular classroom with the use of supplementary aids and services. The second element of the test, which is applicable when a placement outside of the general education setting is necessary, asks whether the child will be placed to the maximum extent appropriate with children who are not disabled.

The Ninth Circuit in *Sacramento City Unified School District Board of Education v. Rachel H.* (1994), a dispute from California, summarized the pronouncements of several courts when it stated that school officials must consider four factors in making LRE placements: the educational benefits of placing children with disabilities in regular classrooms, the nonacademic benefits of such placements, the effect that the presence of students with disabilities would have on teachers and other children in a class, and the costs of inclusionary placements. Each of these factors must be taken into account when placing students with disabilities in any educational program.

Approved Exceptions

Included in both the *Oberti* and *Rachel H.* opinions is the principle that school authorities must make reasonable efforts to place students with disabilities in inclusive settings by providing them with supplementary aids and services to ensure their success prior to considering more restrictive placements. Despite the emphasis on inclusion, not all students with disabilities are best placed in general education classes. Due to the nature or severity of their disabilities, many students are better served in more restrictive settings. Courts will approve segregated settings over parental objections when individualized educational (IEP) teams can show that students with disabilities cannot function in regular classrooms or will not receive educational benefit in such settings, even with the addition of supplementary aids and services (*Beth B. v. Van Clay,* 2002; *Clyde K. v. Puyallup School District No. 3,* 1994; *Capistrano Unified School District v. Wartenberg,* 1995). In one such situation, the federal trial court in New Hampshire recognized that an IEP calling for inclusion in some subjects was not suitable for a 15-year-old student who was reading on a first-grade level (*Manchester School District v. Christopher B.,* 1992).

In essence, a placement in the general education setting should be the placement of choice, and a segregated setting should be considered only if a fully inclusive placement has failed despite the best efforts of educators or there is overwhelming evidence that it is not reasonable.

Allan G. Osborne, Jr.

See also *Board of Education of the Hendrick Hudson Central School District v. Rowley;* Free Appropriate Public Education; Inclusion

Legal Citations

Beth B. v. Van Clay, 282 F.3d 493 (7th Cir. 2002).
Board of Education of the Hendrick Hudson Central School District v. Rowley, 458 U.S. 176 (1982).
Capistrano Unified School District v. Wartenberg, 59 F.3d 884 (9th Cir. 1995).
Clyde K. v. Puyallup School District No. 3, 35 F.3d 1396 (9th Cir. 1994).
Daniel R. R. v. State Board of Education, 874 F.2d 1036 (5th Cir. 1989).
Individuals with Disabilities Education Act, 20 U.S.C. §§ 1400 *et seq.*
Manchester School District v. Christopher B., 807 F. Supp. 860, (D.N.H. 1992).

Oberti v. Board of Education of the Borough of Clementon School District, 995 F.2d 1204 (3d Cir. 1993).

Sacramento City Unified School District Board of Education v. Rachel H., 14 F.3d 1398 (9th Cir. 1994), *cert. denied,* 512 U.S. 1207 (1994).

LEAVES OF ABSENCE

School boards and other employers offer an array of leaves, including sick leave, emergency leave, personal leave, vacation, jury duty leave, Family and Medical Leave Act (FMLA) leave, and sabbatical leave. Leaves of absence are generally granted through federal or state statutes to state, local, and federal employees, including school employees. Leave categories are either unpaid or paid leave for employees meeting eligibility requirements, which usually address length of service. Labor agreements generally contain specifics for local education systems requirements, along with school board policy, for paid and unpaid leaves and must be in compliance with state and federal statutes.

Unpaid Leaves

The FMLA ensures eligible employees up to 12 work weeks unpaid leave within a 12-month period for one or more of the following reasons: the birth and care of the newborn child of the employee; placement with the employee of a son or daughter for adoption or foster care; caring for an immediate family member identified as a spouse, child, or parent with a serious health condition; or taking medical leave when the employee is unable to work because of a serious health condition. To be eligible, employees must have been employed by the employer for at least 12 months and for at least 1,250 hours of service during the 12-month period immediately preceding the commencement of the leave. FMLA's "serious health condition" is defined in state statutes or labor agreements. Benefits continue while employees are on approved FMLA leave. Employees may elect to use (or boards may require the use of) available, accrued paid vacation, personal, or medical/sick leave for all or part of the maximum 12-week period of medical leave. Special rules apply to school employees who wish to take FMLA leave at or near the end of an academic year.

Maternal/paternal/parental leave for birth, adoption, or child care is unpaid leave when school employees have utilized other forms of paid leaves available to them through statutes. The FMLA allows for up to 12 work weeks of unpaid leave for maternal/paternal/parental leave.

Guidelines for educational/professional leave and sabbatical vary by state and district. The purpose of these leaves is to permit educational professionals to study, and typically this is limited to no more than 1 academic year to eligible employees. In states that offer this as a form of paid leave, it is generally based on a formula of no more than one half of an individual's annual salary

Overused sick leave occurs when school employees have used all available sick leave. If sick leave banks are not available, employees would then be on unpaid leave.

Personal leaves may be granted through labor agreements and can be both paid and unpaid if employees have used their available days. Eligibility perimeters are typically set forth in school board policies or collective bargaining agreements. Personnel who are on unpaid leaves may be granted the opportunity to retain insurance benefits by personally paying the premiums.

Military leave is addressed in both state and federal law. Under this leave, school boards must grant their employees defense service leave to fulfill their military obligations.

Paid Leaves

Most paid leaves are short term and range from a few days to a few weeks. Generally, benefits continue while school employees are on paid leaves.

Sick leave is used for employees' medical examinations and treatments or occurs due to the physical inability to work because of personal illness or the illness or death of an immediate or close family member. In many states, school employees earn 1 day of sick leave for each month that they are on the job. State statutes usually grant school boards the authority to establish policies that allow for portions of accrued sick leave to be used for personal reasons.

Illness-in-the-line-of-duty leave is paid leave for school employees who are absent from their duties on account of personal injuries received in the discharge of their jobs or having contracted illness from a contagious or infectious disease. Personal injury claims, which are usually handled through worker's compensation laws, vary according to state laws. Depending on state law, employees (or their estates) may have to forfeit their benefits if their injuries or deaths result from willful misconduct or from intoxication.

Maternity leave is considered a short-term disability and can be paid leave if teachers use their accrued vacation and personal leave. Discrimination on the basis of pregnancy, childbirth, or other related medical conditions is considered unlawful sex discrimination under the terms of the Pregnancy Discrimination Act, as incorporated into Title VII of the Civil Rights Act of 1964.

Jury duty leave for the majority of employers is paid leave if employees are summoned to serve on juries or are subpoenaed as witnesses, but not as defendants or plaintiffs in litigation. School boards typically require employees to submit copies of the summonses or subpoenas to their supervisors.

Vacation leave is normally earned according to a formula based on days/hours worked. It is usually earned by school employees on 12-month contracts.

Paid holidays are addressed in both federal and state statutes. In states where school employees operate under collective bargaining agreements, designated paid holidays are negotiated and may be celebrated on dates other than the public holiday date as set by the state. Holidays are part of the total contractual days. For example, in Florida, teachers work 196 to 198 days (180 instructional days), including six paid holidays and the remainder designated as work days or professional development.

Darlene Y. Bruner

See also Collective Bargaining; Family and Medical Leave Act; Title VII

Legal Citations

Family and Medical Leave Act, 29 U.S.C. §§ 2611 *et seq.*
Pregnancy Discrimination Act, incorporated in Title VII, 42 U.S.C. 2000e(k).

Lee v. Weisman

Prayer as a long-standing tradition in many public school graduation ceremonies came under the scrutiny of the Supreme Court in *Lee v. Weisman* (1992). The Court ruled that having the school principal select a clergyman to deliver a prayer at graduation violated the Establishment Clause's prohibition against state involvement in establishing religion.

Facts of the Case

A public middle school in *Lee* had a practice of selecting clergy to deliver a graduation invocation and benediction graduation. Clergy who were interested in participating in graduation ceremonies had only to contact the middle school principal who was in charge of graduation. The principal in *Lee* selected a rabbi to deliver the prayers, provided him with a pamphlet containing guidelines for the composition of public prayers at civic ceremonies, and advised him that the prayers should be nonsectarian.

The invocation and benediction delivered by the rabbi had two references to "God" and one to "Lord" (*Lee,* p. 581). Attendance at the middle school graduation was voluntary. Those attending the graduation at issue in *Lee* stood for the Pledge of Allegiance and remained standing for the rabbi's invocation and, at the end of the graduation, stood again for the benediction.

A parent of a middle school student challenged, under the Establishment Clause, the use of prayer at graduation. Although the parent was unsuccessful in securing a preliminary injunction prohibiting the use of the prayers at his daughter's graduation, the federal trial court in Rhode Island subsequently found the prayers unconstitutional under the second part of the three-part *Lemon v. Kurtzman* (1971) test, which prohibits government interaction with religion that has the impermissible effect of advancing religion. The First Circuit affirmed, also on the basis of *Lemon.*

The Court's Ruling

The Supreme Court affirmed in *Lee* that the practice of prayer at the public school graduation ceremony violated the Establishment Clause. Critical to the Court's analysis was the involvement of the principal in selecting the person to deliver the prayers, wherein the Court perceived "the potential for divisiveness over the choice of a particular member of the clergy to conduct the ceremony" (*Lee,* p. 587). Despite what the Court characterized as the "good-faith attempt by the school" (p. 589) to eliminate sectarianism from the prayers, the Court was of the opinion that "our precedents do not permit school officials to assist in composing prayers as an incident to a formal exercise for their students" (p. 590).

In reaching its holding, the Court took issue with the school's position that attendance at graduation was voluntary, with the observation that graduation is a rite of passage in which those closest to students "celebrate success and express mutual wishes of gratitude and respect" (*Lee,* p. 596). According to the Court, compelling graduates and their families to make a choice between missing graduation or attending graduation and feeling compelled to stand for a religious part of the ceremony with which they disagree amounts to a kind of psychological coercion that leaves them "with no alternative but to submit" (p. 597).

In the end, the Court found the prayer exercises a violation of the Establishment Clause "because the State has in every practical sense compelled attendance and participation in an explicit religious exercise at an event of singular importance to every student, one the objecting student had no real alternative to avoid" (*Lee,* p. 598).

Justice Scalia wrote a scathing dissent, observing that the majority's opinion in *Lee* "lays waste a tradition that is as old as public-school graduation ceremonies themselves" (p. 632). Nevertheless, *Lee* has not been overturned. *Lee* resulted in cases where school officials sought to circumvent the Court's decision by permitting students to decide whether a prayer was permissible at a school event and then by changing a prayer to a student message. The notion was that student votes would have avoided the problem in *Lee,* in which a school official selected the person to pray, and the use of the student message was thought desirable to allow for secular content while avoiding the religious connotation of a prayer.

Eight years after *Lee,* in *Santa Fe Independent School District v. Doe* (2000), the Supreme Court invalidated the use of a student message prior to every home football game despite a two-step process whereby students would first vote on whether to have a message and then vote on the student who would deliver the message. The Court pointed out that student-initiated and student-led messages did not amount to private speech because they were delivered over the school's public address system on government property at a government-sponsored, school-related event and because the school's tradition would encourage a message that was religious in nature.

On the other hand, the Eleventh Circuit, in *Adler v. Duval County School Board* (2000), reached a conclusion just the opposite of *Santa Fe,* finding that student-initiated and student-led messages at graduations constituted private speech and were not so entwined with governmental policies or so impregnated with governmental character as to become subject to the constitutional limitations placed on state action.

Ralph D. Mawdsley

See also *Lemon v. Kurtzman;* Prayer in Public Schools; Religious Activities in Schools; *Santa Fe Independent School District v. Doe*

Legal Citations

Adler v. Duval County School Board, 206 F.3d 1070 (2000).
Lee v. Weisman, 505 U.S. 577 (1992).
Lemon v. Kurtzman, 403 U.S. 602 (1971).
Santa Fe Independent School District v. Doe, 530 U.S. 290 (2000).

Lee v. Weisman (Excerpts)

In Lee v. Weisman *the Supreme Court decided that school sponsored prayer at a graduation ceremony violated the Establishment Clause not only because educational officials were involved in selecting who would pray but also because prayer may have psychologically coerced those who did not wish to participate.*

Supreme Court of the United States

LEE

v.

WEISMAN

750 U.S. 577

Argued Nov. 6, 1991.

Decided June 24, 1992.

Justice KENNEDY delivered the opinion of the Court.

School principals in the public school system of the city of Providence, Rhode Island, are permitted to invite members of the clergy to offer invocation and benediction prayers as part of the formal graduation ceremonies for middle schools and for high schools. The question before us is whether including clerical members who offer prayers as part of the official school graduation ceremony is consistent with the Religion Clauses of the First Amendment, provisions the Fourteenth Amendment makes applicable with full force to the States and their school districts.

I

A

Deborah Weisman graduated from Nathan Bishop Middle School, a public school in Providence, at a formal ceremony in June 1989. She was about 14 years old. For many years it has been the policy of the Providence School Committee and the Superintendent of Schools to permit principals to invite members of the clergy to give invocations and benedictions at middle school and high school graduations. Many, but not all, of the principals elected to include prayers as part of the graduation ceremonies. Acting for himself and his daughter, Deborah's father, Daniel Weisman, objected to any prayers at Deborah's middle school graduation, but to no avail. The school principal, petitioner Robert E. Lee, invited a rabbi to deliver prayers at the graduation exercises for Deborah's class. Rabbi Leslie Gutterman, of the Temple Beth El in Providence, accepted.

It has been the custom of Providence school officials to provide invited clergy with a pamphlet entitled "Guidelines for Civic Occasions," prepared by the National Conference of Christians and Jews. The Guidelines recommend that public prayers at nonsectarian civic ceremonies be composed with "inclusiveness and sensitivity," though they acknowledge that "[p]rayer of any kind may be inappropriate on some civic occasions." The principal gave Rabbi Gutterman the pamphlet before the graduation and advised him the invocation and benediction should be nonsectarian.

Rabbi Gutterman's prayers were as follows:
"INVOCATION
"God of the Free, Hope of the Brave:
"For the legacy of America where diversity is celebrated and the rights of minorities are protected, we thank You. May these young men and women grow up to enrich it.

"For the liberty of America, we thank You. May these new graduates grow up to guard it.

"For the political process of America in which all its citizens may participate, for its court system where all may seek justice we thank You. May those we honor this morning always turn to it in trust.

"For the destiny of America we thank You. May the graduates of Nathan Bishop Middle School so live that they might help to share it.

"May our aspirations for our country and for these young people, who are our hope for the future, be richly fulfilled.

AMEN"
"BENEDICTION
"O God, we are grateful to You for having endowed us with the capacity for learning which we have celebrated on this joyous commencement.

"Happy families give thanks for seeing their children achieve an important milestone. Send Your blessings upon the teachers and administrators who helped prepare them.

"The graduates now need strength and guidance for the future, help them to understand that we are not complete with academic knowledge alone. We must each strive to fulfill what You require of us all: To do justly, to love mercy, to walk humbly.

"We give thanks to You, Lord, for keeping us alive, sustaining us and allowing us to reach this special, happy occasion.

AMEN"

The record in this case is sparse in many respects, and we are unfamiliar with any fixed custom or practice at middle school graduations, referred to by the school district as "promotional exercises." We are not so constrained with reference to high schools, however. High school graduations are such an integral part of American cultural life that we can with confidence describe their customary features, confirmed by aspects of the record and by the parties' representations at oral argument. In the Providence school system, most high school graduation ceremonies are conducted away from the school, while most middle school ceremonies are held on school premises.... The parties stipulate that attendance at graduation ceremonies is voluntary. The graduating students enter as a group in a processional, subject to the direction of teachers and school officials, and sit together, apart from their families.

We assume the clergy's participation in any high school graduation exercise would be about what it was at Deborah's middle school ceremony. There the students stood for the Pledge of Allegiance and remained standing during the rabbi's prayers. Even on the assumption that there was a respectful moment of silence both before and after the prayers, the rabbi's two presentations must not have extended much beyond a minute each, if that. We do not know whether he remained on stage during the whole ceremony, or whether the students received individual diplomas on stage, or if he helped to congratulate them.

The school board (and the United States, which supports it as *amicus curiae*) argued that these short prayers and others like them at graduation exercises are of profound meaning to many students and parents throughout this country who consider that due respect and acknowledgment for divine guidance and for the deepest spiritual aspirations of our people ought to be expressed at an event as important in life as a graduation. We assume this to be so in addressing the difficult case now before us, for the significance of the prayers lies also at the heart of Daniel and Deborah Weisman's case.

B

Deborah's graduation was held on the premises of Nathan Bishop Middle School on June 29, 1989. Four days before the ceremony, Daniel Weisman, in his individual capacity as a Providence taxpayer and as next friend of Deborah, sought a temporary restraining order

in the United States District Court for the District of Rhode Island to prohibit school officials from including an invocation or benediction in the graduation ceremony. The court denied the motion for lack of adequate time to consider it. Deborah and her family attended the graduation, where the prayers were recited. In July 1989, Daniel Weisman filed an amended complaint seeking a permanent injunction barring petitioners, various officials of the Providence public schools, from inviting the clergy to deliver invocations and benedictions at future graduations. We find it unnecessary to address Daniel Weisman's taxpayer standing, for a live and justiciable controversy is before us. Deborah Weisman is enrolled as a student at Classical High School in Providence and from the record it appears likely, if not certain, that an invocation and benediction will be conducted at her high school graduation.

The case was submitted on stipulated facts. The District Court held that petitioners' practice of including invocations and benedictions in public school graduations violated the Establishment Clause of the First Amendment, and it enjoined petitioners from continuing the practice. The court applied the three-part Establishment Clause test set forth in *Lemon v. Kurtzman.*...

On appeal, the United States Court of Appeals for the First Circuit affirmed.... We granted certiorari and now affirm.

II

These dominant facts mark and control the confines of our decision: State officials direct the performance of a formal religious exercise at promotional and graduation ceremonies for secondary schools. Even for those students who object to the religious exercise, their attendance and participation in the state-sponsored religious activity are in a fair and real sense obligatory, though the school district does not require attendance as a condition for receipt of the diploma.

This case does not require us to revisit the difficult questions dividing us in recent cases, questions of the definition and full scope of the principles governing the extent of permitted accommodation by the State for the religious beliefs and practices of many of its citizens.... We can decide the case without reconsidering the general constitutional framework by which public schools' efforts to accommodate religion are measured. Thus we do not accept the invitation of petitioners and *amicus* the

United States to reconsider our decision in *Lemon v. Kurtzman*. The government involvement with religious activity in this case is pervasive, to the point of creating a state-sponsored and state-directed religious exercise in a public school. Conducting this formal religious observance conflicts with settled rules pertaining to prayer exercises for students, and that suffices to determine the question before us.

The principle that government may accommodate the free exercise of religion does not supersede the fundamental limitations imposed by the Establishment Clause. It is beyond dispute that, at a minimum, the Constitution guarantees that government may not coerce anyone to support or participate in religion or its exercise, or otherwise act in a way which "establishes a [state] religion or religious faith, or tends to do so." The State's involvement in the school prayers challenged today violates these central principles.

That involvement is as troubling as it is undenied. A school official, the principal, decided that an invocation and a benediction should be given; this is a choice attributable to the State, and from a constitutional perspective it is as if a state statute decreed that the prayers must occur. The principal chose the religious participant, here a rabbi, and that choice is also attributable to the State. The reason for the choice of a rabbi is not disclosed by the record, but the potential for divisiveness over the choice of a particular member of the clergy to conduct the ceremony is apparent.

Divisiveness, of course, can attend any state decision respecting religions, and neither its existence nor its potential necessarily invalidates the State's attempts to accommodate religion in all cases. The potential for divisiveness is of particular relevance here though, because it centers around an overt religious exercise in a secondary school environment where, as we discuss below, subtle coercive pressures exist and where the student had no real alternative which would have allowed her to avoid the fact or appearance of participation.

The State's role did not end with the decision to include a prayer and with the choice of a clergyman. Principal Lee provided Rabbi Gutterman with a copy of the "Guidelines for Civic Occasions," and advised him that his prayers should be nonsectarian. Through these means the principal directed and controlled the content of the prayers. Even if the only sanction for ignoring the instructions were that the rabbi would not be invited back, we think no religious representative who valued his or her continued reputation and effectiveness in the community

would incur the State's displeasure in this regard. It is a cornerstone principle of our Establishment Clause jurisprudence that "it is no part of the business of government to compose official prayers for any group of the American people to recite as a part of a religious program carried on by government," and that is what the school officials attempted to do.

Petitioners argue, and we find nothing in the case to refute it, that the directions for the content of the prayers were a good-faith attempt by the school to ensure that the sectarianism which is so often the flashpoint for religious animosity be removed from the graduation ceremony. The concern is understandable, as a prayer which uses ideas or images identified with a particular religion may foster a different sort of sectarian rivalry than an invocation or benediction in terms more neutral. The school's explanation, however, does not resolve the dilemma caused by its participation. The question is not the good faith of the school in attempting to make the prayer acceptable to most persons, but the legitimacy of its undertaking that enterprise at all when the object is to produce a prayer to be used in a formal religious exercise which students, for all practical purposes, are obliged to attend.

We are asked to recognize the existence of a practice of nonsectarian prayer, prayer within the embrace of what is known as the Judeo-Christian tradition, prayer which is more acceptable than one which, for example, makes explicit references to the God of Israel, or to Jesus Christ, or to a patron saint. There may be some support, as an empirical observation . . . that there has emerged in this country a civic religion, one which is tolerated when sectarian exercises are not. If common ground can be defined which permits once conflicting faiths to express the shared conviction that there is an ethic and a morality which transcend human invention, the sense of community and purpose sought by all decent societies might be advanced. But though the First Amendment does not allow the government to stifle prayers which aspire to these ends, neither does it permit the government to undertake that task for itself.

The First Amendment's Religion Clauses mean that religious beliefs and religious expression are too precious to be either proscribed or prescribed by the State. The design of the Constitution is that preservation and transmission of religious beliefs and worship is a responsibility and a choice committed to the private sphere, which itself is promised freedom to pursue that mission. It must not be forgotten then, that while concern must be given to define the protection granted to an objector or a dissenting nonbeliever, these same Clauses exist to protect religion from government interference. James Madison, the principal author of the Bill of Rights, did not rest his opposition to a religious establishment on the sole ground of its effect on the minority. . . .

These concerns have particular application in the case of school officials, whose effort to monitor prayer will be perceived by the students as inducing a participation they might otherwise reject. Though the efforts of the school officials in this case to find common ground appear to have been a good-faith attempt to recognize the common aspects of religions and not the divisive ones, our precedents do not permit school officials to assist in composing prayers as an incident to a formal exercise for their students. And these same precedents caution us to measure the idea of a civic religion against the central meaning of the Religion Clauses of the First Amendment, which is that all creeds must be tolerated and none favored. The suggestion that government may establish an official or civic religion as a means of avoiding the establishment of a religion with more specific creeds strikes us as a contradiction that cannot be accepted.

The degree of school involvement here made it clear that the graduation prayers bore the imprint of the State and thus put school-age children who objected in an untenable position. We turn our attention now to consider the position of the students, both those who desired the prayer and she who did not.

To endure the speech of false ideas or offensive content and then to counter it is part of learning how to live in a pluralistic society, a society which insists upon open discourse towards the end of a tolerant citizenry. And tolerance presupposes some mutuality of obligation. It is argued that our constitutional vision of a free society requires confidence in our own ability to accept or reject ideas of which we do not approve, and that prayer at a high school graduation does nothing more than offer a choice. By the time they are seniors, high school students no doubt have been required to attend classes and assemblies and to complete assignments exposing them to ideas they find distasteful or immoral or absurd or all of these. Against this background, students may consider it an odd measure of justice to be subjected during the course of their educations to ideas deemed offensive and irreligious, but to be denied a brief, formal prayer ceremony that the school offers in return. This argument cannot prevail, however. It overlooks a fundamental dynamic of the Constitution.

The First Amendment protects speech and religion by quite different mechanisms. Speech is protected by ensuring its full expression even when the government participates, for the very object of some of our most important speech is to persuade the government to adopt an idea as its own. The method for protecting freedom of worship and freedom of conscience in religious matters is quite the reverse. In religious debate or expression the government is not a prime participant, for the Framers deemed religious establishment antithetical to the freedom of all. The Free Exercise Clause embraces a freedom of conscience and worship that has close parallels in the speech provisions of the First Amendment, but the Establishment Clause is a specific prohibition on forms of state intervention in religious affairs with no precise counterpart in the speech provisions. The explanation lies in the lesson of history that was and is the inspiration for the Establishment Clause, the lesson that in the hands of government what might begin as a tolerant expression of religious views may end in a policy to indoctrinate and coerce. A state-created orthodoxy puts at grave risk that freedom of belief and conscience which are the sole assurance that religious faith is real, not imposed.

The lessons of the First Amendment are as urgent in the modern world as in the 18th century when it was written. One timeless lesson is that if citizens are subjected to state-sponsored religious exercises, the State disavows its own duty to guard and respect that sphere of inviolable conscience and belief which is the mark of a free people. To compromise that principle today would be to deny our own tradition and forfeit our standing to urge others to secure the protections of that tradition for themselves.

As we have observed before, there are heightened concerns with protecting freedom of conscience from subtle coercive pressure in the elementary and secondary public schools. Our decisions in *Engel v. Vitale* and *School Dist. of Abington* recognize, among other things, that prayer exercises in public schools carry a particular risk of indirect coercion. The concern may not be limited to the context of schools, but it is most pronounced there. What to most believers may seem nothing more than a reasonable request that the nonbeliever respect their religious practices, in a school context may appear to the nonbeliever or dissenter to be an attempt to employ the machinery of the State to enforce a religious orthodoxy.

We need not look beyond the circumstances of this case to see the phenomenon at work. The undeniable fact is that the school district's supervision and control of a high school graduation ceremony places public pressure, as well as peer pressure, on attending students to stand as a group or, at least, maintain respectful silence during the invocation and benediction. This pressure, though subtle and indirect, can be as real as any overt compulsion. Of course, in our culture standing or remaining silent can signify adherence to a view or simple respect for the views of others. And no doubt some persons who have no desire to join a prayer have little objection to standing as a sign of respect for those who do. But for the dissenter of high school age, who has a reasonable perception that she is being forced by the State to pray in a manner her conscience will not allow, the injury is no less real. There can be no doubt that for many, if not most, of the students at the graduation, the act of standing or remaining silent was an expression of participation in the rabbi's prayer. That was the very point of the religious exercise. It is of little comfort to a dissenter, then, to be told that for her the act of standing or remaining in silence signifies mere respect, rather than participation. What matters is that, given our social conventions, a reasonable dissenter in this milieu could believe that the group exercise signified her own participation or approval of it.

Finding no violation under these circumstances would place objectors in the dilemma of participating, with all that implies, or protesting. We do not address whether that choice is acceptable if the affected citizens are mature adults, but we think the State may not, consistent with the Establishment Clause, place primary and secondary school children in this position. Research in psychology supports the common assumption that adolescents are often susceptible to pressure from their peers towards conformity, and that the influence is strongest in matters of social convention. To recognize that the choice imposed by the State constitutes an unacceptable constraint only acknowledges that the government may no more use social pressure to enforce orthodoxy than it may use more direct means.

The injury caused by the government's action, and the reason why Daniel and Deborah Weisman object to it, is that the State, in a school setting, in effect required participation in a religious exercise. It is, we concede, a brief exercise during which the individual can concentrate on joining its message, meditate on her own religion, or let her mind wander. But the embarrassment and the intrusion of the religious exercise cannot be refuted by arguing that these prayers, and similar ones to be said in the

future, are of a *de minimis* character. To do so would be an affront to the rabbi who offered them and to all those for whom the prayers were an essential and profound recognition of divine authority. And for the same reason, we think that the intrusion is greater than the two minutes or so of time consumed for prayers like these. Assuming, as we must, that the prayers were offensive to the student and the parent who now object, the intrusion was both real and, in the context of a secondary school, a violation of the objectors' rights. That the intrusion was in the course of promulgating religion that sought to be civic or nonsectarian rather than pertaining to one sect does not lessen the offense or isolation to the objectors. At best it narrows their number, at worst increases their sense of isolation and affront.

There was a stipulation in the District Court that attendance at graduation and promotional ceremonies is voluntary. Petitioners and the United States, as *amicus,* made this a center point of the case, arguing that the option of not attending the graduation excuses any inducement or coercion in the ceremony itself. The argument lacks all persuasion. Law reaches past formalism. And to say a teenage student has a real choice not to attend her high school graduation is formalistic in the extreme. True, Deborah could elect not to attend commencement without renouncing her diploma; but we shall not allow the case to turn on this point. Everyone knows that in our society and in our culture high school graduation is one of life's most significant occasions. A school rule which excuses attendance is beside the point. Attendance may not be required by official decree, yet it is apparent that a student is not free to absent herself from the graduation exercise in any real sense of the term "voluntary," for absence would require forfeiture of those intangible benefits which have motivated the student through youth and all her high school years. Graduation is a time for family and those closest to the student to celebrate success and express mutual wishes of gratitude and respect, all to the end of impressing upon the young person the role that it is his or her right and duty to assume in the community and all of its diverse parts.

The importance of the event is the point the school district and the United States rely upon to argue that a formal prayer ought to be permitted, but it becomes one of the principal reasons why their argument must fail. Their contention, one of considerable force were it not for the constitutional constraints applied to state action, is that the prayers are an essential part of these ceremonies because for many persons an occasion of this significance lacks meaning if there is no recognition, however brief, that human achievements cannot be understood apart from their spiritual essence. We think the Government's position that this interest suffices to force students to choose between compliance or forfeiture demonstrates fundamental inconsistency in its argumentation. It fails to acknowledge that what for many of Deborah's classmates and their parents was a spiritual imperative was for Daniel and Deborah Weisman religious conformance compelled by the State. While in some societies the wishes of the majority might prevail, the Establishment Clause of the First Amendment is addressed to this contingency and rejects the balance urged upon us. The Constitution forbids the State to exact religious conformity from a student as the price of attending her own high school graduation. This is the calculus the Constitution commands.

The Government's argument gives insufficient recognition to the real conflict of conscience faced by the young student. The essence of the Government's position is that with regard to a civic, social occasion of this importance it is the objector, not the majority, who must take unilateral and private action to avoid compromising religious scruples, hereby electing to miss the graduation exercise. This turns conventional First Amendment analysis on its head. It is a tenet of the First Amendment that the State cannot require one of its citizens to forfeit his or her rights and benefits as the price of resisting conformance to state-sponsored religious practice. To say that a student must remain apart from the ceremony at the opening invocation and closing benediction is to risk compelling conformity in an environment analogous to the classroom setting, where we have said the risk of compulsion is especially high. Just as in *Engel v. Vitale* and *School Dist. of Abington v. Schempp*, where we found that provisions within the challenged legislation permitting a student to be voluntarily excused from attendance or participation in the daily prayers did not shield those practices from invalidation, the fact that attendance at the graduation ceremonies is voluntary in a legal sense does not save the religious exercise.

. . . .

We do not hold that every state action implicating religion is invalid if one or a few citizens find it offensive. People may take offense at all manner of religious as well as nonreligious messages, but offense alone does not in every case show a violation. We know too that sometimes to endure social isolation or even anger may be the price of conscience or nonconformity. But, by any reading of our cases, the conformity required of the student in this case was too high an exaction to withstand the test of the Establishment Clause. The prayer exercises in this case are especially improper because the State has in every practical sense compelled attendance and participation in an explicit religious exercise at an event of singular importance to every student, one the objecting student had no real alternative to avoid.

Our jurisprudence in this area is of necessity one of line-drawing, of determining at what point a dissenter's rights of religious freedom are infringed by the State. "The First Amendment does not prohibit practices which by any realistic measure create none of the dangers which it is designed to prevent and which do not so directly or substantially involve the state in religious exercises or in the favoring of religion as to have meaningful and practical impact. It is of course true that great consequences can grow from small beginnings, but the measure of constitutional adjudication is the ability and willingness to distinguish between real threat and mere shadow."

Our society would be less than true to its heritage if it lacked abiding concern for the values of its young people, and we acknowledge the profound belief of adherents to many faiths that there must be a place in the student's life for precepts of a morality higher even than the law we today enforce. We express no hostility to those aspirations, nor would our oath permit us to do so. A relentless and all-pervasive attempt to exclude religion from every aspect of public life could itself become inconsistent with the Constitution. We recognize that, at graduation time and throughout the course of the educational process, there will be instances when religious values, religious practices, and religious persons will have some interaction with the public schools and their students. But these matters, often questions of accommodation of religion, are not before us. The sole question presented is whether a religious exercise may be conducted at a graduation ceremony in circumstances where, as we have found, young graduates who object are induced to conform. No holding by this Court suggests that a school can persuade or compel a student to participate in a religious exercise. That is being done here, and it is forbidden by the Establishment Clause of the First Amendment.

For the reasons we have stated, the judgment of the Court of Appeals is

Affirmed.

Citation: *Lee v. Weisman*, 505 U.S. 577 (1992).

LEMON V. KURTZMAN

Lemon v. Kurtzman (1971), or *"Lemon I,"* is best known for its three-part test, which the Supreme Court created to be used in evaluating whether government action violates the Establishment Clause; this provision prohibits the government from making laws "respecting an establishment of religion." The three parts of the *"Lemon* test" are that (1) a statute or program must have a secular legislative purpose, (2) its principal or primary effect must be one that neither advances nor inhibits religion, and (3) it must not foster an excessive government entanglement with religion (*Lemon,* pp. 612–613). This entry examines the background of that decision and succeeding rulings.

The Original Cases

Lemon I involved jointure of two separate cases interpreting statutes in Rhode Island and Pennsylvania that provided funds and materials for religious schools. The case from Rhode Island addressed the constitutionality of a Salary Supplement Act enacted in 1969 that provided for a 15% salary supplement to be paid to teachers in nonpublic (including religious) schools at which the average per-pupil expenditure on secular education was below the average in public schools. For teachers in nonpublic schools to be eligible for the supplement, they had to teach only courses offered in the public schools, use only materials that were used in the public schools, and agree not to teach courses in religion.

The case from Pennsylvania involved a constitutional challenge to the state's Nonpublic Elementary and Secondary Education Act, passed in 1968, which authorized reimbursement for specific secular subjects and for textbooks and materials used in those courses by nonpublic schools and approved by the superintendent. The law did not allow for any payment for teachers' salaries, textbooks, and instructional materials for any courses containing subject matter expressing religious teaching or the morals or forms of worship of any sect.

Approximately 25% of all elementary students in Rhode Island and 20% in Pennsylvania attended religious schools, virtually all of which were operated by the Roman Catholic Church. Three-judge federal trial courts in Rhode Island and Pennsylvania reached opposite conclusions about the constitutionality of the state statutes, with the court in Rhode Island finding the state's statute a violation of the Establishment Clause. Conversely, the court in Pennsylvania did not think that there was any such violation. On direct appeal to the Supreme Court in *Lemon I,* it struck down both statutes as violating the Establishment Clause.

The Supreme Court held that both statutes violated the third part of the so-called *Lemon* test, namely, that supervision of the nonpublic school support programs authorized by the statutes would excessively entangle the states with the religious schools being served. In both cases, the Court decided that the law violated the Establishment Clause because of the restrictions and surveillance that were necessary to ensure that teachers played a strictly nonideological role and by creating state supervision of nonpublic school accounting procedures to establish the cost of secular as distinguished from religious education.

The Court also determined that political divisiveness along religious lines would likely result, as religious groups benefiting from the successive and probably annual state legislative appropriations would intensify their lobbying efforts for more funding.

Two years after *Lemon I,* the Supreme Court, in *Lemon II* (1973), revisited the case from Pennsylvania after a federal trial court refused to permit reimbursements to be made for the 1970–1971 school year, even though *Lemon I* had not occurred until June 28, 1971. A bare majority of the Supreme Court maintained that the payment of the allocated funds for the 1970–1971 school year would not have substantially undermined the constitutional interest at stake and that the denial of the payment would have serious financial consequences on private schools that relied on the agreement.

Worth noting is that the attorney successfully representing the interests of the religious schools in *Lemon II* was William Ball, the same attorney who, in another U.S. Supreme Court case during the previous year, defended two Amish fathers from a truancy charge in *Wisconsin v. Yoder* (1972).

The *Lemon* Test

The *Lemon* three-part test became a prominent feature in the 1970s, as the Supreme Court and lower courts used it in a variety of cases to invalidate state efforts to assist religious schools (see *Committee for Public Education & Religious Liberty v. Nyquist,* 1973; *Meek v. Pittenger,* 1975; and *Wolman v. Walter,* 1977). However, beginning with *Mueller v. Allen,* in 1983, the Court began relaxing *Lemon I*'s stranglehold on public assistance of religious schools by relying on a neutrality test. In addition, Justice O'Connor, in her concurring opinion in *Lynch v. Donnelly* (1976), suggested a new two-part endorsement test that became a staple in Establishment Clause analysis. The two parts of the endorsement test are a *secular government purpose* (virtually unchanged from the first part of the *Lemon I* test) and a *reasonable objective observer* test as to whether state involvement with religion would be perceived as endorsing or sponsoring religion.

In addition to *Lemon I,* neutrality, and endorsement tests, the Supreme Court had over the years referenced three other tests: divisiveness (*Meek v. Pittenger,* 1975, p. 375), coercion (*Lee v. Weisman,* 1992, p. 588), and historical intent (*McCreary County v. American Civil Liberties Union,* 2005, pp. 2748–2749). Even so, the use of these other tests has not eliminated judicial reliance on the *Lemon I* test, much to the chagrin of some justices. In his memorable, concurring opinion in *Lamb's Chapel v. Center Moriches Union Free School District* (1993), Justice Scalia lamented the resiliency of the *Lemon* test:

> Like some ghoul in a late-night horror movie that repeatedly sits up in its grave and shuffles abroad, after being repeatedly killed and buried, *Lemon* stalks our Establishment Clause jurisprudence once again, frightening the little children and school attorneys of Center Moriches Union Free School District. Its most recent burial, only last Term, was, to be sure, not fully six feet under. (p. 398)

New Standards

As Justice Scalia so eloquently expressed, the *Lemon* test is not dead, but it has survived with a somewhat subdued vitality, as reflected in two recent Supreme Court cases, *McCreary County v. American Civil Liberties Union* (2005) and *Van Orden v. Perry* (2005). While both of these disputes concerned the display of the Ten Commandments on public property and were handed down on the same day, the Court reached opposite results. In *McCreary,* a bare majority of the Court relied on the "purpose" part of the *Lemon* test to invalidate the display of the Ten Commandments in two county courthouses. Despite the presence of other historical documents, the display was arranged in such a manner that juxtaposed the Commandments with other documents, with highlighted references to God as their sole common element. The Court observed that "the display's unstinting focus was on religious passages, showing that the Counties were posting the Commandments precisely because of their sectarian content" (*McCreary,* p. 2739).

Another bare Supreme Court majority in *Van Orden* held that a monument inscribed with the Ten Commandments located on the Texas State Capitol grounds did not violate the Establishment Clause. The Court observed that "whatever may be the fate of the *Lemon* test in the larger scheme of Establishment Clause jurisprudence, we think it not useful in dealing with the sort of passive monument that Texas has erected on its Capitol grounds" (*Van Orden,* p. 2861). Instead, the Court created an historical intent test, noting that in terms of the nation's history, "There is an unbroken history of official acknowledgment by all three branches of government of the role of religion in American life from at least 1789" (*Van Orden,* p. 2861, quoting from *Lynch,* p. 674).

The Court refused to find that the mere presence of the Ten Commandments on government property was sufficient to violate the Establishment Clause, with the Court candidly observing that "since 1935, Moses has stood, holding two tablets that reveal portions of the Ten Commandments written in Hebrew, among other lawgivers in the south frieze [of the Supreme Court Building]" (*Van Orden,* p. 2862). Thus, even though the monument on the grounds of the Texas capitol building had "religious significance . . . the Ten Commandments [also] have an undeniable historical meaning" (p. 2863).

McCreary and *Van Orden* suggest that while the *Lemon* test is a useful instrument for analyzing the relationship between government and religion, it is by no means the only test. The Court's position in *Van Orden* that the *Lemon* test was inappropriate suggests that courts can be more selective when choosing which of the Establishment Clause tests are most appropriate for particular sets of facts.

Ralph D. Mawdsley

See also *Committee for Public Education & Religious Liberty v. Nyquist; Lamb's Chapel v. Center Moriches Union Free School District; Lee v. Weisman; Meek v. Pittenger; Mueller v. Allen;* State Aid and the Establishment Clause; *Wisconsin v. Yoder; Wolman v. Walter*

Legal Citations

Committee for Public Education & Religious Liberty v. Nyquist, 413 U.S. 756 (1973).
Lamb's Chapel v. Center Moriches Union Free School District, 508 U.S. 384 (1993).
Lee v. Weisman, 505 U.S. 577 (1992).
Lemon v. Kurtzman I, 403 U.S. 602 (1971).
Lemon v. Kurtzman II, 411 U.S. 192 (1973).
Lynch v. Donnelly, 465 U.S. 668 (1984).
McCreary County, Kentucky v. American Civil Liberties Union of Kentucky, 545 U.S. 844 (2005).
Meek v. Pittenger, 421 U.S. 349 (1975).
Mueller v. Allen, 463 U.S. 388 (1983).
Van Orden v. Perry, 545 U.S. 677 (2005).
Wisconsin v. Yoder, 406 U.S. 205 (1972).
Wolman v. Walter, 433 U.S. 229 (1977).

Lemon v. Kurtzman (Excerpts)

Lemon v. Kurtzman and its companion case, Earley v. DiCenso, *are the Supreme Court's most important cases on the parameters of permissible state aid to students and their religiously affiliated non-public schools under the Establishment Clause of the First Amendment to the United States Constitution. In creating the so-called tripartite* Lemon *test, which also applies in disputes involving prayer and religious activities in public schools, the Court ruled that interactions between religion and government must have a secular legislative purpose, must have a principal or primary effect that does not advance or inhibit religion, and do not result in excessive entanglement of government in religion.*

Supreme Court of the United States

LEMON

v.

KURTZMAN,

EARLEY

v.

DICENSO

403 U.S. 602

Argued March 3, 1971.

Decided June 28, 1971.

Mr. Chief Justice BURGER delivered the opinion of the Court.

These two appeals raise questions as to Pennsylvania and Rhode Island statutes providing state aid to church-related elementary and secondary schools. Both statutes are challenged as violative of the Establishment and Free Exercise Clauses of the First Amendment and the Due Process Clause of the Fourteenth Amendment.

Pennsylvania has adopted a statutory program that provides financial support to nonpublic elementary and secondary schools by way of reimbursement for the cost of teachers' salaries, textbooks, and instructional materials in specified secular subjects. Rhode Island has adopted a statute under which the State pays directly to teachers in nonpublic elementary schools a supplement of 15% of their annual salary. Under each statute state aid has been given to church-related educational institutions. We hold that both statutes are unconstitutional.

I

The Rhode Island Statute

The Rhode Island Salary Supplement Act was enacted in 1969. It rests on the legislative finding that the quality of education available in nonpublic elementary schools has been jeopardized by the rapidly rising salaries needed to attract competent and dedicated teachers. The Act authorizes state officials to supplement the salaries of teachers of secular subjects in nonpublic elementary schools by paying directly to a teacher an amount not in excess of 15% of his current annual salary. As supplemented, however, a nonpublic school teacher's salary cannot exceed the maximum paid to teachers in the State's public schools, and the recipient must be certified by the state board of education in substantially the same manner as public school teachers.

In order to be eligible for the Rhode Island salary supplement, the recipient must teach in a nonpublic school at which the average per-pupil expenditure on secular education is less than the average in the State's public schools during a specified period. Appellant State Commissioner of Education also requires eligible schools to submit financial data. If this information indicates a per-pupil expenditure in excess of the statutory limitation, the records of the school in question must be examined in order to assess how much of the expenditure is attributable to secular education and how much to religious activity.

The Act also requires that teachers eligible for salary supplements must teach only those subjects that are offered in the State's public schools. They must use 'only teaching materials which are used in the public schools.' Finally, any teacher applying for a salary supplement must first agree in writing 'not to teach a course in religion for so long as or during such time as he or she receives any salary supplements' under the Act.

Appellees are citizens and taxpayers of Rhode Island. They brought this suit to have the Rhode Island Salary Supplement Act declared unconstitutional and its operation enjoined on the ground that it violates the Establishment and Free Exercise Clauses of the First Amendment. Appellants are state officials charged with administration of the Act, teachers eligible for salary supplements under the Act, and parents of children in church-related elementary schools whose teachers would receive state salary assistance.

A three-judge federal court . . . found that Rhode Island's nonpublic elementary schools accommodated approximately 25% of the State's pupils. About 95% of these pupils attended schools affiliated with the Roman Catholic church. To date some 250 teachers have applied for benefits under the Act. All of them are employed by Roman Catholic schools.

The court held a hearing at which extensive evidence was introduced concerning the nature of the secular instruction offered in the Roman Catholic schools whose teachers would be eligible for salary assistance under the Act. Although the court found that concern for religious values does not necessarily affect the content of secular subjects, it also found that the parochial school system was 'an integral part of the religious mission of the Catholic Church.'

The District Court concluded that the Act violated the Establishment Clause, holding that it fostered 'excessive entanglement' between government and religion. In addition, two judges thought that the Act had the impermissible effect of giving 'significant aid to a religious enterprise.' We affirm.

The Pennsylvania Statute

Pennsylvania has adopted a program that has some but not all of the features of the Rhode Island program. The Pennsylvania Nonpublic Elementary and Secondary Education Act was passed in 1968 in response to a crisis that the Pennsylvania Legislature found existed in the State's nonpublic schools due to rapidly rising costs. The statute affirmatively reflects the legislative conclusion that the State's educational goals could appropriately be fulfilled by government support of 'those purely secular educational objectives achieved through nonpublic education. . . .'

The statute authorizes appellee state Superintendent of Public Instruction to 'purchase' specified 'secular educational services' from nonpublic schools. Under the 'contracts' authorized by the statute, the State directly reimburses nonpublic schools solely for their actual expenditures for teachers' salaries, textbooks, and instructional materials. A school seeking reimbursement must maintain prescribed accounting procedures that identify the 'separate' cost of the 'secular educational service.' These accounts are subject to state audit. The funds for this program were originally derived from a new tax on horse and harness racing, but the Act is now financed by a portion of the state tax on cigarettes.

There are several significant statutory restrictions on state aid. Reimbursement is limited to courses 'presented in the curricula of the public schools.' It is further limited 'solely' to courses in the following 'secular' subjects: mathematics, modern foreign languages, physical science, and physical education. Textbooks and instructional materials included in the program must be approved by the state Superintendent of Public Instruction. Finally, the statute prohibits reimbursement for any course that contains 'any subject matter expressing religious teaching, or the morals or forms of worship of any sect.'

. . . . More than 96% of these pupils attend church-related schools, and most of these schools are affiliated with the Roman Catholic church.

Appellants brought this action in the District Court to challenge the constitutionality of the Pennsylvania statute. The organizational plaintiffs-appellants are associations of persons resident in Pennsylvania declaring belief in the separation of church and state; individual plaintiffs-appellants are citizens and taxpayers of Pennsylvania. Appellant Lemon, in addition to being a citizen and a taxpayer, is a parent of a child attending public school in Pennsylvania. Lemon also alleges that he purchased a ticket at a race track and thus had paid the specific tax that supports the expenditures under the Act. Appellees are state officials who have the responsibility for administering the Act. In addition seven church-related schools are defendants-appellees.

A three-judge federal court . . . held that the individual plaintiffs-appellants had standing to challenge the Act. The organizational plaintiffs-appellants were denied standing. . . .

The court granted appellees' motion to dismiss the complaint for failure to state a claim for relief. It held that the Act violated neither the Establishment nor the Free Exercise Clause, Chief Judge Hastie dissenting. We reverse.

II

In *Everson v. Board of Education*, this Court upheld a state statute that reimbursed the parents of parochial school children for bus transportation expenses. There Mr. Justice Black, writing for the majority, suggested that the decision carried to 'the verge' of forbidden territory under the Religion Clauses. Candor compels acknowledgment, moreover, that we can only dimly perceive the lines of demarcation in this extraordinarily sensitive area of constitutional law.

The language of the Religion Clauses of the First Amendment is at best opaque, particularly when compared with other portions of the Amendment. Its authors did not simply prohibit the establishment of a state church or a state religion, an area history shows they regarded as very important and fraught with great dangers. Instead they commanded that there should be 'no law respecting an establishment of religion.' A law may be one 'respecting' the forbidden objective while falling short of its total realization. A law 'respecting' the proscribed result, that is, the establishment of religion, is not always easily identifiable as one violative of the Clause. A given law might not establish a state religion but nevertheless be one 'respecting' that end in the sense of being

a step that could lead to such establishment and hence offend the First Amendment.

In the absence of precisely stated constitutional prohibitions, we must draw lines with reference to the three main evils against which the Establishment Clause was intended to afford protection: 'sponsorship, financial support, and active involvement of the sovereign in religious activity.'

Every analysis in this area must begin with consideration of the cumulative criteria developed by the Court over many years. Three such tests may be gleaned from our cases. First, the statute must have a secular legislative purpose; second, its principal or primary effect must be one that neither advances nor inhibits religion; finally, the statute must not foster 'an excessive government entanglement with religion.'

Inquiry into the legislative purposes of the Pennsylvania and Rhode Island statutes affords no basis for a conclusion that the legislative intent was to advance religion. On the contrary, the statutes themselves clearly state that they are intended to enhance the quality of the secular education in all schools covered by the compulsory attendance laws. There is no reason to believe the legislatures meant anything else. A State always has a legitimate concern for maintaining minimum standards in all schools it allows to operate. As in Allen, we find nothing here that undermines the stated legislative intent; it must therefore be accorded appropriate deference.

In [*Board of Education v.*] *Allen* the Court acknowledged that secular and religious teachings were not necessarily so intertwined that secular textbooks furnished to students by the State were in fact instrumental in the teaching of religion. The legislatures of Rhode Island and Pennsylvania have concluded that secular and religious education are identifiable and separable. In the abstract we have no quarrel with this conclusion.

. . . .

III

In *Walz v. Tax Commission*, the Court upheld state tax exemptions for real property owned by religious organizations and used for religious worship. That holding, however, tended to confine rather than enlarge the area of permissible state involvement with religious institutions by calling for close scrutiny of the degree of entanglement involved in the relationship. The objective is to prevent, as far as possible, the intrusion of either into the precincts of the other.

Our prior holdings do not call for total separation between church and state; total separation is not possible in an absolute sense. Some relationship between government and religious organizations is inevitable. Fire inspections, building and zoning regulations, and state requirements under compulsory school-attendance laws are examples of necessary and permissible contacts. Indeed, under the statutory exemption before us in *Walz*, the State had a continuing burden to ascertain that the exempt property was in fact being used for religious worship. Judicial caveats against entanglement must recognize that the line of separation, far from being a 'wall,' is a blurred, indistinct, and variable barrier depending on all the circumstances of a particular relationship.

This is not to suggest, however, that we are to engage in a legalistic minuet in which precise rules and forms must govern. A true minuet is a matter of pure form and style, the observance of which is itself the substantive end. Here we examine the form of the relationship for the light that it casts on the substance.

In order to determine whether the government entanglement with religion is excessive, we must examine the character and purposes of the institutions that are benefited, the nature of the aid that the State provides, and the resulting relationship between the government and the religious authority. Mr. Justice Harlan, in a separate opinion in *Walz*, echoed the classic warning as to 'programs, whose very nature is apt to entangle the state in details of administration....' Here we find that both statutes foster an impermissible degree of entanglement.

(a) Rhode Island program

The District Court made extensive findings on the grave potential for excessive entanglement that inheres in the religious character and purpose of the Roman Catholic elementary schools of Rhode Island, to date the sole beneficiaries of the Rhode Island Salary Supplement Act.

The church schools involved in the program are located close to parish churches. This understandably permits convenient access for religious exercises since instruction in faith and morals is part of the total educational process. The school buildings contain identifying religious symbols such as crosses on the exterior and crucifixes, and religious paintings and statutes either in the classrooms or hallways. Although only approximately 30 minutes a day are devoted to direct religious instruction, there are religiously oriented extracurricular activities. Approximately two-thirds of the teachers in these schools are nuns of various religious orders. Their dedicated efforts provide an atmosphere in which religious instruction and religious vocations are natural and proper parts of life in such schools. Indeed, as the District Court found, the role of teaching nuns in enhancing the religious atmosphere has led the parochial school authorities to attempt to maintain a one-to-one ratio between nuns and lay teachers in all schools rather than to permit some to be staffed almost entirely by lay teachers.

On the basis of these findings the District Court concluded that the parochial schools constituted 'an integral part of the religious mission of the Catholic Church.'...

The substantial religious character of these church-related schools gives rise to entangling church-state relationships of the kind the Religion Clauses sought to avoid. Although the District Court found that concern for religious values did not inevitably or necessarily intrude into the content of secular subjects, the considerable religious activities of these schools led the legislature to provide for careful governmental controls and surveillance by state authorities in order to ensure that state aid supports only secular education.

The dangers and corresponding entanglements are enhanced by the particular form of aid that the Rhode Island Act provides. Our decisions from *Everson* to *Allen* have permitted the States to provide church-related schools with secular, neutral, or nonideological services, facilities, or materials. Bus transportation, school lunches, public health services, and secular textbooks supplied in common to all students were not thought to offend the Establishment Clause.....

In *Allen* the Court refused to make assumptions, on a meager record, about the religious content of the textbooks that the State would be asked to provide. We cannot, however, refuse here to recognize that teachers have a substantially different ideological character from books. In terms of potential for involving some aspect of faith or morals in secular subjects, a textbook's content is ascertainable, but a teacher's handling of a subject is not. We cannot ignore the danger that a teacher under religious control and discipline poses to the separation of the religious from the purely secular aspects of precollege education. The conflict of functions inheres in the situation.

In our view the record shows these dangers are present to a substantial degree. The Rhode Island Roman

Catholic elementary schools are under the general supervision of the Bishop of Providence and his appointed representative, the Diocesan Superintendent of Schools. In most cases, each individual parish, however, assumes the ultimate financial responsibility for the school, with the parish priest authorizing the allocation of parish funds. With only two exceptions, school principals are nuns appointed either by the Superintendent or the Mother Provincial of the order whose members staff the school. By 1969 lay teachers constituted more than a third of all teachers in the parochial elementary schools, and their number is growing. They are first interviewed by the superintendent's office and then by the school principal. The contracts are signed by the parish priest, and he retains some discretion in negotiating salary levels. Religious authority necessarily pervades the school system.

The schools are governed by the standards set forth in a 'Handbook of School Regulations,' which has the force of synodal law in the diocese. It emphasizes the role and importance of the teacher in parochial schools: 'The prime factor for the success or the failure of the school is the spirit and personality, as well as the professional competency, of the teacher. . . .' The Handbook also states that: 'Religious formation is not confined to formal courses; nor is it restricted to a single subject area.' Finally, the Handbook advises teachers to stimulate interest in religious vocations and missionary work. Given the mission of the church school, these instructions are consistent and logical.

Several teachers testified, however, that they did not inject religion into their secular classes. And the District Court found that religious values did not necessarily affect the content of the secular instruction. But what has been recounted suggests the potential if not actual hazards of this form of state aid. The teacher is employed by a religious organization, subject to the direction and discipline of religious authorities, and works in a system dedicated to rearing children in a particular faith. These controls are not lessened by the fact that most of the lay teachers are of the Catholic faith. Inevitably some of a teacher's responsibilities hover on the border between secular and religious orientation.

We need not and do not assume that teachers in parochial schools will be guilty of bad faith or any conscious design to evade the limitations imposed by the statute and the First Amendment. We simply recognize that a dedicated religious person, teaching in a school affiliated with his or her faith and operated to inculcate its tenets, will inevitably experience great difficulty in remaining religiously neutral. Doctrines and faith are not inculcated or advanced by neutrals. With the best of intentions such a teacher would find it hard to make a total separation between secular teaching and religious doctrine. What would appear to some to be essential to good citizenship might well for others border on or constitute instruction in religion. Further difficulties are inherent in the combination of religious discipline and the possibility of disagreement between teacher and religious authorities over the meaning of the statutory restrictions.

We do not assume, however, that parochial school teachers will be unsuccessful in their attempts to segregate their religious beliefs from their secular educational responsibilities. But the potential for impermissible fostering of religion is present. The Rhode Island Legislature has not, and could not, provide state aid on the basis of a mere assumption that secular teachers under religious discipline can avoid conflicts. The State must be certain, given the Religion Clauses, that subsidized teachers do not inculcate religion—indeed the State here has undertaken to do so. To ensure that no trespass occurs, the State has therefore carefully conditioned its aid with pervasive restrictions. An eligible recipient must teach only those courses that are offered in the public schools and use only those texts and materials that are found in the public schools. In addition the teacher must not engage in teaching any course in religion.

A comprehensive, discriminating, and continuing state surveillance will inevitably be required to ensure that these restrictions are obeyed and the First Amendment otherwise respected. Unlike a book, a teacher cannot be inspected once so as to determine the extent and intent of his or her personal beliefs and subjective acceptance of the limitations imposed by the First Amendment. These prophylactic contacts will involve excessive and enduring entanglement between state and church.

There is another area of entanglement in the Rhode Island program that gives concern. The statute excludes teachers employed by nonpublic schools whose average per-pupil expenditures on secular education equal or exceed the comparable figures for public schools. In the event that the total expenditures of an otherwise eligible school exceed this norm, the program requires the government to examine the school's records in order to determine how much of the total expenditures is attributable to secular education and how much to religious activity. This kind of state inspection and evaluation of the religious content of a religious organization is fraught with the sort of entanglement that the Constitution forbids. It is a relationship pregnant with dangers of excessive government direction of church schools and hence of churches. The Court noted 'the hazards of government supporting churches' in *Walz v. Tax Commission* and we cannot ignore here the danger that pervasive modern governmental power will ultimately intrude on religion and thus conflict with the Religion Clauses.

(b) Pennsylvania program

The Pennsylvania statute also provides state aid to church-related schools for teachers' salaries. The complaint describes an educational system that is very similar to the one existing in Rhode Island. According to the allegations, the church-related elementary and secondary schools are controlled by religious organizations, have the purpose of propagating and promoting a particular religious faith, and conduct their operations to fulfill that purpose. Since this complaint was dismissed for failure to state a claim for relief, we must accept these allegations as true for purposes of our review.

As we noted earlier, the very restrictions and surveillance necessary to ensure that teachers play a strictly non-ideological role give rise to entanglements between church and state. The Pennsylvania statute, like that of Rhode Island, fosters this kind of relationship. Reimbursement is not only limited to courses offered in the public schools and materials approved by state officials, but the statute excludes 'any subject matter expressing religious teaching, or the morals or forms of worship of any sect.' In addition, schools seeking reimbursement must maintain accounting procedures that require the State to establish the cost of the secular as distinguished from the religious instruction.

The Pennsylvania statute, moreover, has the further defect of providing state financial aid directly to the church-related schools. This factor distinguishes both *Everson* and *Allen*, for in both those cases the Court was careful to point out that state aid was provided to the student and his parents—not to the church-related school. In *Walz v. Tax Commission*, the Court warned of the dangers of direct payments to religious organizations. . . .

The history of government grants of a continuing cash subsidy indicates that such programs have almost always been accompanied by varying measures of control and surveillance. The government cash grants before us now provide no basis for predicting that comprehensive measures of surveillance and controls will not follow. In particular the government's post-audit power to inspect and evaluate a church-related school's financial records and to determine which expenditures are religious and which are secular creates an intimate and continuing relationship between church and state.

IV

A broader base of entanglement of yet a different character is presented by the divisive political potential of these state programs. In a community where such a large number of pupils are served by church-related schools, it can be assumed that state assistance will entail considerable political activity. Partisans of parochial schools, understandably concerned with rising costs and sincerely dedicated to both the religious and secular educational missions of their schools, will inevitably champion this cause and promote political action to achieve their goals. Those who oppose state aid, whether for constitutional, religious, or fiscal reasons, will inevitably respond and employ all of the usual political campaign techniques to prevail. Candidates will be forced to declare and voters to choose. It would be unrealistic to ignore the fact that many people confronted with issues of this kind will find their votes aligned with their faith.

Ordinarily political debate and division, however vigorous or even partisan, are normal and healthy manifestations of our democratic system of government, but political division along religious lines was one of the principal evils against which the First Amendment was intended to protect. The potential divisiveness of such conflict is a threat to the normal political process. To have States or communities divide on the issues presented by state aid to parochial schools would tend to confuse and obscure other issues of great urgency. We have an expanding array of vexing issues, local and national, domestic and international, to debate and divide on. It conflicts with our whole history and tradition to permit questions of the Religion Clauses to assume such importance in our legislatures and in our elections that they could divert attention from the myriad issues and problems that confront every level of government. The highways of church and state relationships are not likely to be one-way streets, and the Constitution's authors sought to protect religious worship from the pervasive power of government. The history of many countries attests to the hazards of religion's intruding into the political arena or of political power intruding into the legitimate and free exercise of religious belief.

Of course, as the Court noted in *Walz*, '[a]dherents of particular faiths and individual churches frequently take strong positions on public issues.' We could not expect otherwise, for religious values pervade the fabric of our national life. But in *Walz* we dealt with a status under state tax laws for the benefit of all religious groups. Here we are confronted with successive and very likely permanent annual appropriations that benefit relatively few religious groups. Political fragmentation and divisiveness on religious lines are thus likely to be intensified.

. . . .

V

In *Walz* it was argued that a tax exemption for places of religious worship would prove to be the first step in an inevitable progression leading to the establishment of state churches and state religion. That claim could not stand up against more than 200 years of virtually universal practice imbedded in our colonial experience and continuing into the present.

The progression argument, however, is more persuasive here. We have no long history of state aid to church-related educational institutions comparable to 200 years of tax exemption for churches. Indeed, the state programs before us today represent something of an innovation. We have already noted that modern governmental programs have self-perpetuating and self-expanding propensities. These internal pressures are only enhanced when the schemes involve institutions whose legitimate needs are growing and whose interests have substantial political support. Nor can we fail to see that in constitutional adjudication some steps, which when taken were thought to approach 'the verge,' have become the platform for yet

further steps. A certain momentum develops in constitutional theory and it can be a 'downhill thrust' easily set in motion but difficult to retard or stop. Development by momentum is not invariably bad; indeed, it is the way the common law has grown, but it is a force to be recognized and reckoned with. The dangers are increased by the difficulty of perceiving in advance exactly where the 'verge' of the precipice lies. As well as constituting an independent evil against which the Religion Clauses were intended to protect, involvement or entanglement between government and religion serves as a warning signal.

Finally, nothing we have said can be construed to disparage the role of church-related elementary and secondary schools in our national life. Their contribution has been and is enormous. Nor do we ignore their economic plight in a period of rising costs and expanding need. Taxpayers generally have been spared vast sums by the maintenance of these educational institutions by religious organizations, largely by the gifts of faithful adherents.

The merit and benefits of these schools, however, are not the issue before us in these cases. The sole question is whether state aid to these schools can be squared with the dictates of the Religion Clauses. Under our system the choice has been made that government is to be entirely excluded from the area of religious instruction and churches excluded from the affairs of government. The Constitution decrees that religion must be a private matter for the individual, the family, and the institutions of private choice, and that while some involvement and entanglement are inevitable, lines must be drawn.

The judgment of the Rhode Island District Court in No. 569 and No. 570 is *affirmed.* The judgment of the Pennsylvania District Court in No. 89 is *reversed,* and the case is *remanded* for further proceedings consistent with this opinion.

Citation: *Lemon v. Kurtzman I,* 403 U.S. 602 (1971).

LICENSURE REQUIREMENTS

Teacher licensure is a measure designed to ensure a minimal level of competency for educators. Couched in the definition is the impression that the licensing agency warrants that the educator is qualified. Current licensure, or certificate, practices focus on

ensuring proficiency in subject matter and pedagogy, often by means of testing. In addition, the licensure process allows licensing agencies to examine applications for individuals with prior criminal records. Agencies may require periodic license renewals, continued professional development, and established levels of acceptable behavior for educators to maintain their licenses.

In short, states may impose reasonable restrictions, such as citizenship, loyalty oaths, and residency requirements, as long as these requirements further a legitimate state interest. For example, in *Ambach v. Norwick* (1979), the U.S. Supreme Court held that the New York State's licensure requirement to be a citizen bore a rational relationship to the state's educational goals. New York prohibited noncitizens from obtaining licensure unless the individual indicated intent to become a citizen. The Court noted that the state's interest in promoting civic values was rationally related to the citizenship requirement.

There is no national teacher certification requirement, yet each state has adopted some form of licensure. As a result, there is substantial disparity in the specific rules and procedures among the states, although traditional state licensure schemes are similar. First, state licensing agencies establish standards or minimum guidelines for teacher education colleges within the states. In most instances, the licensing agency is the state's board of education or a professional practices board made up of elected or appointed licensed teachers and administrators. Second, teacher education colleges (and universities) establish programs to meet the minimally established state criteria. Finally, when prospective educators complete the college programs, their institutions recommend the students to the state agencies, which then provide licenses to successful candidates.

Supportive of the licensure process, the No Child Left Behind Act (2002) requires all teachers in the core subject areas to be highly qualified. The U.S. Department of Education defines "highly qualified teachers" as those who possess bachelor's degrees, are licensed by their states, and have demonstrated competency in the core academic areas they teach. Yet empirical studies supporting the efficacy of teacher licensure are scant, at best. There is some evidence that student performance in mathematics is positively associated with teacher licensure. However, studies that explore relationships between licensure and student success in other subject areas are inconclusive.

Standards Movement

The awarding of teacher's licenses based on the completion of state-approved programs was the predominant means of licensing during the early 20th century. By the early 1950s, most states issued licenses based on this model. Citing studies showing the importance of the teacher on student learning, policymakers in the 1980s began to focus on teacher quality. Shifting from the process-oriented emphasis of teacher preparation, states moved to a standards-based emphasis. Influenced greatly by standards developed by the National State Directors of Teacher Education and Certification, most state standards are similar in nature. Due to the similarity of standards, states frequently honor reciprocity agreements.

Affiliated with the standards-based movement, states implemented testing to make certain that licensed teachers met the minimum standards. Teacher testing serves two primary purposes. First, testing provides for an efficient method of evaluating teacher competence. Second, testing enables licensing agencies to focus on standards-related performances, as opposed to process-oriented regulations. Yet due to the pressure to help prospective educators excel on the state-administered tests, teacher testing also had the effect of altering teacher preparation curricula. Many programs adjusted the curricula to (a) align the content of the course work with the standards and (b) adjust course assessment to mimic the state assessment.

Legal challenges to the system of licensure tied to testing have produced few changes. As long as tests maintain content validity, the courts have upheld their use as a prerequisite to licensure.

Adverse Certification Actions

Each state has a method for taking adverse actions against licensed educators. These adverse actions include private reprimands, public reprimands, license suspensions, and license revocations. Using an administrative hearing process, licensing agencies can take adverse actions due to a wide range of improper actions on the part of educators in public schools. The improper actions include ethics violations, contract abandonment, and the violation of state or federal laws.

In sum, states may establish reasonable requirements for licensure as long as they are rationally related to the educational interests of the state. Often, those requirements include minimum levels of educational attainment, minimum age requirements, acceptable criminal records, and adequate performance on measures of academic and pedagogical competence. Continued licensure may be predicated on demonstrated continuing professional growth and adherence to state and federal laws and state educational ethical codes.

Mark Littleton

See also *Ambach v. Norwick;* Drug Testing of Teachers; Educational Malpractice; Highly Qualified Teachers; No Child Left Behind Act

Further Readings

Goldhaber, D., & Brewer, D. (2000). Does teacher certification matter? High school teacher certification status and student achievement. *Educational Evaluation and Policy Analysis, 22,* 129–145.

Kaye, E. A. (Ed.). (2003). *Requirements for certification of teachers, counselors, librarians, administrators for elementary and secondary schools* (68th ed.). Chicago: University of Chicago Press.

Roth, R. A., & Pipho, C. (1990). Teacher education standards. In W. R. Houston, M. Haberman, & J. Sikula (Eds.), *Handbook of research on teacher education* (pp. 119–135). New York: Macmillan.

Legal Citations

Ambach v. Norwick, 441 U.S. 68 (1979).
No Child Left Behind Act, 20 U.S.C. §§ 6301 *et seq.* (2002).

LIMITED ENGLISH PROFICIENCY

All demographers have noted that the United States is clearly experiencing a high growth in students who are English language learners (ELLs). Moreover, almost all researchers predict this trend will continue and increase substantially. How school officials respond to the challenge to meet the needs of students who seek to learn English in an appropriate way will determine much of the future of American education. This entry describes how politics is influencing decisions that schools make in this area.

Bilingual Controversy

Unfortunately, this area of educational praxis is highly politicized and controversial. In American education law and politics, there is no more volatile mix of policy, research, folklore, myth, and xenophobia than in the various state and federal laws and regulations addressing the needs of language minority students attempting to learn English. As a result, even the term *bilingual* has become polemic.

Bilingual is monolithic neither in its meaning nor in the programs it describes. The term is generally used as a label to describe several programs and a group of theories and varied implementation practices to address the needs of ELLs in public education that to some extent utilize the abilities of students with their native languages to facilitate acquisition of the target languages. However, the term *bilingual,* and thus to some extent the methodology it employs, has become politicized. The administration of President George W. Bush has excised the term *bilingual* from almost all documents, and the word is almost nonexistent in the extensive No Child Left Behind Act (NCLB) (2002). The Office for Bilingual Education and Minority Language Affairs of the United States Department of Education has undergone a name and focus change, with the word *bilingual* being excised from its name and focus. Currently, it is called the Office of English Language Acquisition, Language Enhancement, and Academic Achievement for Limited English Proficient Students.

Research Issues

In such a policy environment, it is difficult to conduct, access, and utilize research in meeting the needs of language minority students. Some states have actually outlawed bilingual methods for meeting the needs of ELLs. The laws in these states have declared that immersion or sheltered immersion for a year by waiver, followed by immersion in the target language, is the only worthwhile and certainly the only legally allowable methodology. The first of these was passed by referendum, Proposition 227 in California, followed by similar but increasingly stringent referenda in Arizona and Massachusetts. Totalizing pronouncements in these referenda laws, such as the following from California, have replaced research on language acquisition: "Whereas, young immigrant children can easily acquire full fluency in a new language, such as English, if they are heavily exposed to that language in the classroom at an early age." Such authoritative pronouncements do not necessarily reflect all or even most of the research in this area.

The results of research on bilingual methodologies have, in fact, often contradicted the reasoning behind current administration policy. For example, a recent meta-analytical study combining earlier research regarding the effectiveness of bilingual versus monolingual educational methods, conducted by a panel of researchers selected by the Bush administration, found small to modest gains from bilingual programs. The researchers also discovered that greater gains were revealed in those studies that used random assignment and other more rigorous and effective research designs. However, after seeing the findings, the Bush administration declined to release the report.

Current anti-intellectual or anti-research policy mandates notwithstanding, language minority students still have the bedrock right, based on the classic case of *Lau v. Nichols* (1974), to receive some type of language intervention or program that will enable them to benefit from public education. This seminal case was followed by legislation codifying its holdings in the form of the Equal Educational Opportunity Act. The act requires that equal educational opportunity must not be denied any individual as a result of "the failure by an educational agency to take appropriate action to overcome language barriers that impede equal participation by its students in its instructional programs."

No Child Left Behind

Currently, the impact of the NCLB on ELLs is significant. Other than receiving exemptions for their first year of enrollment in the U.S. education system, such learners are generally required to take the same state assessments required of native-English-speaking students in the third and eighth grades. Officials in local school systems can make some accommodations for ELL students so long as they have not yet attended 3 years of public instruction in the United States.

These accommodations may include options such as small-group administration of examinations, extra time to complete examinations, and simplified instructions. These accommodations may even include native language examinations for reading/language arts assessments for 3 to 5 years if states allow for such modifications. In addition, school officials must assess ELLs annually on their English proficiency in the areas of reading, writing, speaking, and listening in English.

NCLB is salutary because it provides information about the progress of ELLs through the provision of disaggregated data about their performance. Yet since school systems are assessed as failing or not based on how quickly and how many ELLs are moved into the status of "English proficient," the statute forces schools to push students to quickly display minimal English proficiency for their own benefit under the NCLB. This approach ignores theories regarding practices that result in high-level acquisition of English. It is possible that rushing to show low-level proficiency by moving students quickly into English-proficient status, and thus into immersion in English, causes school systems to tend to ignore programs and theories that may require more instructional time but may result in a higher-level acquisition by ELLs of English and academic content at the same time. Due to the NCLB's mandates and the political climate, late transition bilingual and dual-immersion programs may not survive the current policy strife in most states. The net result is that studies of educational and linguistic gains or features of these programs may not be available as a laboratory to compare with the current penchant for short-term basic language proficiency.

Certainly, the coming decade will call for assessment of group outcomes of ELLs in terms of their access to higher education and full participation in the American economy under the current educational policies. It is one thing to be classified quickly as being "proficient" or making "adequate yearly progress" on an average level. It may be very different, and require different methodologies, to be prepared to continue in demanding college preparation and Advanced Placement courses that will enable ELLs to enter and succeed in higher education, and in our increasingly sophisticated economy. The challenge for the future will be whether American education will be allowed to assess and to adapt to achieve the latter long-range goal for ELLs.

Scott Ellis Ferrin

See also Bilingual Education; *Lau v. Nichols*

Further Readings

Ellis, R. (1994). *The study of second language acquisition.* Oxford, UK: Oxford University Press.

Gass, S., & Selinker, L. (2001) *Second language acquisition: An introductory course.* Mahwah, NJ: Lawrence Erlbaum.

Krashen, S., & McField, G. (2005). What works? Reviewing the latest evidence on bilingual education. *Language Learner, 1*(2), 7–10, 34.

Rossell, C. H., & Baker, K. (1996). The educational effectiveness of bilingual education. *Research in the Teaching of English, 30,* 7–74.

Skutnabb-Kangas, T., & Toukomaa, P. (1976). *Teaching migrant children's mother tongue and learning the language of the host country in the context of the socio-cultural situation of the migrant family.* Tamprere, Finland: UNESCO.

Tollefson, J. W. (2002). *Language policies in education: Critical issues.* Mahwah, NJ: Lawrence Erlbaum.

Legal Citations

Equal Educational Opportunity Act of 1974, 20 U.S.C. § 1703(f).

Lau v. Nichols, 483 F.2d 791 (9th Cir. 1973); 414 U.S. 563 (1974).

No Child Left Behind Act, 20 U.S.C. §§ 6301 *et seq.* (2002).

LOCKER SEARCHES

Locker searches are common occurrences in American public schools. The use of locker searches has proliferated in recent years due to continuing threats of drugs and violence. Many school officials view locker searches as an indispensable tool to deter negative behaviors, and on the whole, lower courts seem clearly to side with the efforts of school officials to curb crime by conducting locker searches. While recent acts of violence in schools justify their use, students' privacy interests and school safety should be equally balanced. Although locker searches may represent a minimally intrusive search, their unchecked use could very well weaken students' expectations of privacy. This entry reviews the case law on this issue.

An Early Case on Privacy

In 1985, the U.S. Supreme Court handed down its first decision clarifying the Fourth Amendment rights of students. Although *New Jersey v. T. L. O.* afforded school officials greater flexibility by way of permitting searches of students based on the less rigid "reasonable suspicion" standard (as opposed to the "probable cause" expected of the police), the Court acknowledged that students are entitled to legitimate expectations of privacy.

Justice White, author of the majority in *T. L. O.,* recognized this expectation, writing as follows:

> School children may find it necessary to carry with them a variety of legitimate, noncontraband items, and there is no reason to conclude that they have necessarily waived all rights to privacy in such items merely by bringing them onto school grounds. (p. 339).

Although the presumption that students relinquish all privacy is clearly rebutted, the Court chose not to offer specific implementation guidelines with regard to privacy protection in lockers, desks, or other forms of school property, nor did it place any restrictions on mass suspicionless searches. The Court's refusal to elaborate is not unusual given its usual deference to the expertise of school officials in administrative matters.

In *T. L. O.,* interest groups such as the National School Boards Association (NSBA) rallied in support of school officials' powers in maintaining safety and order through so-called friend-of-the-court briefs. As to lockers, the NSBA contended that since student lockers are neither student domiciles nor "castle[s]," they are not protected by the Fourth Amendment.

Mass Suspicionless Searches

Two subsequent U.S. Supreme Court cases, *Vernonia School District 47J v. Acton* (1995) and *Board of Education of Independent School District No. 92 of*

Pottawatomie County v. Earls (2002), validated the constitutionality of mass suspicionless searches, specifically random drug testing, through a three-part analysis. The analysis involved assessing students' privacy interest, the relative unobtrusiveness of the searches, the severity of the need to justify such a search, and the likelihood that it would achieve its goal.

Lower courts apply similar analyses in justifying mass locker searches. At the same time, there appears to be a fair amount of consensus across lower courts regarding the degree to which privacy in lockers should be afforded. Case law reflects a trend of upholding searches on the basis that doing so is clearly in the best interest of maintaining school safety and order.

Courts typically view mass locker searches as a minimally intrusive method of confronting drug and weapons problems. In *Commonwealth v. Cass* (1998), the Supreme Court of Pennsylvania ruled that a search of 2,000 high school lockers was reasonable at its inception, in light of suspicious activity that included students' use of beepers, students' dilated eyes, and students carrying around large amounts of money, as well as reasonable in scope because of the minor intrusiveness of the type of search.

Similarly, in *State of Iowa v. Marzel Jones* (2003), a scheduled locker cleanout for the purposes of "[ensuring] the health and safety of the students and staff and to help maintain the school's supplies" (p. 144) resulted in the discovery of a blue jacket containing a small amount of marijuana. Initially, the identity of the student to whom the locker was assigned was unknown, but it was later discovered. The student was eventually charged but prevailed in an Iowa district court, which ruled that the evidence was illegally obtained. The Supreme Court of Iowa reversed an earlier decision to the contrary in relying heavily on the three-part test enunciated in *Earls;* the court concluded that school officials acted reasonably under the circumstances.

In re Patrick Y. (2000) may best reflect the state and national press toward school safety. A school security officer obtained a tip that drugs and weapons had been reported in the middle school portion of the campus. After the principal was informed, the security officer was authorized to search all lockers in the middle school campus. A search of a book bag within a locker revealed a knife and pager—both school violations. While the student argued that a lack of reasonable suspicion along with the intrusiveness of a book bag search violated the legitimate expectations of privacy afforded to students in *T. L. O.,* the Court of Appeals of Maryland affirmed a bylaw of the state board of education that students have no reasonable expectation of privacy in temporarily assigned lockers.

Individual Searches

As these cases demonstrate, courts rarely find that mass locker searches undermine the Fourth Amendment. As for individualized searches, the tendency is much the same. In *M. E. J. v. State of Florida* (2002), in which a middle school student smelling of marijuana was loitering in the faculty parking lot, a school official subsequently searched his locker and discovered a knife. Consequently, the student was charged with possession of a weapon on school premises. The student unsuccessfully claimed that school officials violated his Fourth Amendment rights because the suspicion was based on drugs and not the knife. An appellate court affirmed that the knife was legally obtained evidence because educators had already met the standard of reasonable suspicion.

In another case, an appellate court in Ohio upheld an individualized search of two students that yielded a marijuana pipe but censured the school's use of a blanket random locker search as unreasonable, since educators lacked an inadequate basis on which to act (*In re Adam,* 1997).

Mario S. Torres, Jr.

See also Board of Education of Independent School District No. 92 of Pottawatomie County v. Earls; Drugs, Dog Searches for; In Loco Parentis; *New Jersey v. T. L. O.; Vernonia School District 47J v. Acton*

Further Readings

Gregory, G. H., Steinhilber, A. W., & Shannon, T. A. (1984). *Amicus curiae brief for* New Jersey v. T. L. O. (No. 83–712). Alexandria, VA: National School Boards Association.

Stefkovich, J. A., & Torres, M. S. (2003). The demographics of justice: Student searches, student rights, and administrator practices. *Educational Administration Quarterly, 39,* 259–282.

Legal Citations

Board of Education of Independent School District No. 92 of Pottawatomie County v. Earls, 536 U.S. 822 (2002), *on remand,* 300 F.3d 1222 (10th Cir. 2002).

Commonwealth v. Cass, 709 A.2d 350 (Pa. 1998).

In re Adam, 697 N.E.2d 1100 (Ohio Ct. App. 1997).

In re Patrick Y., 746 A.2d 405 (Md. 2000).

M. E. J. v. State of Florida, 805 So. 2d. 1093 (Fla. Dist. Ct. App. 2002).

New Jersey v. T. L. O., 469 U.S. 325 (1985).

State of Iowa v. Marzel Jones, 666 N.W. 2d 142 (Iowa 2003).

Vernonia School District 47J v. Acton, 515 U.S. 646 (1995).

LOCKE V. DAVEY

In *Locke v. Davey* (2004), the U.S. Supreme Court upheld the constitutionality of "no-funding provisions" in Washington State's constitution, as applied to a student who attended a religiously affiliated institution of higher learning. Such no-funding provisions are often referred to as "Blaine Amendments," after Senator James K. Blaine of Maine, who unsuccessfully introduced a constitutional amendment to limit governmental aid to "sectarian" or religious schools in 1876. In *Davey,* however, the Court specifically asserted that the constitutional provision underlying the dispute was not a Blaine Amendment, but rejected the claim that state officials violated the student's First Amendment rights in denying him a scholarship because he wished to study devotional theology.

Facts of the Case

The state of Washington created a scholarship program for low- and middle-income students who had excellent academic credentials. The Promise Scholarship Program provided funds for education-related expenses, including room and board, for eligible students. However, state officials refused to award the scholarship to students who were studying for degrees in theology. Davey, who was pursuing a degree in devotional theology as part of a joint major, challenged

the prohibition of the scholarship for theology majors on the basis that it singled out religion for unfavorable treatment in violation of the First Amendment.

A federal trial court in Washington rejected the student's claim, but the Ninth Circuit reversed in his favor. In so doing, the court cited *McDaniel v. Paty* (1978) for the proposition that the scholarship policy lacked neutrality. In *McDaniel,* the Supreme Court struck down a state constitutional provision from Tennessee that barred ministers or priests from seeking public office. As a result, the Ninth Circuit concluded that the Promise Scholarship Program impermissibly singled out religion for unfavorable treatment.

The Court's Ruling

Reversing in favor of the state, the Supreme Court, in a 7-to-1 opinion authored by Chief Justice Rehnquist, rejected Davey's argument. Instead, the Court held that the state's refusal to grant Davey an award as part of the Promise Scholarship Program did not violate the Establishment, Free Exercise, or Free Speech Clauses of the First Amendment. In reviewing the facts, the Court pointed out that the Promise Scholarship could have been used at any accredited public or private institution of higher education in Washington. However, the Court also pointed out that in an attempt to avoid a conflict with its own constitutional constraints, the state legislature stipulated that student recipients may not be pursuing degrees in theology while receiving the scholarship.

At the heart of its analysis, the Supreme Court declared that nothing in the history or the text of the Washington State Constitution suggested animus toward religion. The Court was of the opinion that since there is "play in the joints" between the Establishment and Free Exercise Clauses, the Establishment Clause permits some state actions that are not required by the Free Exercise Clause. In addition, the Court determined that the nontheology degree provision in the Promise Scholarship Program was an example of just such an instance. The court maintained that unlike *McDaniel,* the scholarship program was constitutionally permissible because it did not require students to choose between governmental service and their religious beliefs.

On the other hand, Justice Scalia's dissent, which Justice Thomas joined, thought that the program should have been vitiated as unconstitutional because it discriminated against religion. In a two-paragraph dissent, Justice Thomas added that he objected to the program's having been applied only to students who wished to study theology.

The upshot of *Davey* is that since it was set in the context of higher education, it is likely to be of limited applicability in elementary and secondary schools, should it be used to challenge choice programs. Of course, the outcome of such challenges may well depend on the wording of state statues and constitutions. At the same time, in states such as Washington with Blaine-type provisions, it remains to be seen whether *Davey* will impact the bounds of permissible aid for students who wish to seek similar scholarships while attending religiously affiliated institutions of higher learning.

Mark Littleton

See also First Amendment; State Aid and the Establishment Clause

Further Readings

Goldenziel, J. (2005). Blaine's name in vain? State constitutions, school choice, and charitable choice. *Denver University Law Review, 83,* 57–99.

Legal Citations

Locke v. Davey, 540 U.S. 712 (2004).
McDaniel v. Paty, 435 U.S. 618 (1978).

Loyalty Oaths

Loyalty oaths are administered as a condition to public employment or entrance into the practice of a given occupation, such as teaching. A teacher loyalty oath is a promise to uphold the constitutions and laws of a jurisdiction. Typically, in cases involving education law, loyalty oaths involve state laws that mandate adherence to the federal and state constitutions and laws. For instance, the language of the oath may state,

I do solemnly swear (or affirm) that I will uphold and defend the Constitution of the United States of America and the Constitution of the State of [insert state name] and that I will oppose the overthrow of the government of the United States of America or of this State by force, violence or by any illegal or unconstitutional method. (*Cole v. Richardson,* 1972)

In many instances, loyalty oaths were passed into law as a reaction to heightened concerns over threats to national security. The balance between the sensitive nature of individual rights and governmental interests limits the acceptable application and wording of loyalty oaths. Stated another way, constitutional protections set parameters regarding to whom loyalty oaths apply and what considerations exist in the crafting of the loyalty oath language.

The difficulty with loyalty oaths rests in the construction of constitutionally permissible language. In other words, questions emerge over how public employers can adopt loyalty oaths that do not offend the constitutional rights of employees. In attempting to address this question, the courts have created constitutional doctrines to assess the legality of loyalty oaths. Through a series of decisions, the Supreme Court established four parameters: Loyalty oaths (1) may not infringe on established constitutional rights, (2) may not prevent or chill protected speech, (3) may not limit associational memberships and activities or presume subscription to beliefs based on associational affiliations, and (4) may not contain vague language so that a person of "common intelligence" cannot decipher their meaning. These parameters are discussed further in this entry.

Established Rights

First, the courts have made it clear that loyalty oaths may not infringe on established constitutional rights. For instance, shortly after the Civil War, early cases in the application of a loyalty oath for public office challenged the constitutionality of its statutory language. One Missouri statute required public officials to attest to never having participated in activities that were connected to actions against the federal or state governments, which would have included actions in support of the Confederates.

The U.S. Supreme Court declared the law unconstitutional because it made once-legal acts illegal retrospectively (i.e., ex post facto laws) while declaring individuals guilty of crimes based on those acts (i.e., bill of attainder), in violation of Article I, Section 9, of the U.S. Constitution. Similarly, in instances of an otherwise constitutionally permissible loyalty oath, the U.S. Supreme Court held that an individual's refusal to take the oath cannot result in a default interpretation that the individual subscribes to the nonsupport of the federal and state constitutions and believes in the overthrow of the government. According to the Court, a default interpretation of an individual's subscription of disloyalty—without an opportunity to explain coupled with the summary dismissal from public employment—violates the individual's due process rights.

Protected Speech

Second, courts have agreed that loyalty oaths may not prevent or chill protected speech. In *Keyishian v. Board of Regents* (1967), a New York state loyalty oath law included a provision through which educators within the state would be removed from their positions if they participated in subversive activities. Pursuant to an internal memo to state employees, examples of subversive activities included "writing of articles, the distribution of pamphlets, the endorsement of speeches made or articles written or acts performed by others" (*Keyishian,* p. 602), whether inside or outside the classroom.

Insofar as these acts of speech and expression are protected for common citizens under the First Amendment, as well as within legitimate educational and scholarly applications under constitutional interpretations of academic freedom, the loyalty oath and its administrative policies classified protected speech as prohibited acts. Consequently, the Supreme Court struck the loyalty oaths down as impermissible under the Constitution.

Associational Memberships

Third, courts have noted that loyalty oaths may not limit associational memberships and activities or presume disloyalty based on associational memberships and activities. Several Supreme Court cases involved challenges to state loyalty oaths that barred individuals from public employment due solely to their associational memberships. Based on a series of cases, the Court, in *Wieman v. Updegraff* (1952), identified three clear problems with this irrefutable categorization of disloyalty based on organizational associations.

In one situation, an individual may associate with an organization that was initially lawful and innocent but later takes on active threats of treason. Similarly, an individual may associate with an organization that had engaged in "subversive" activities but later changed its position and eliminated these activities so it conformed to lawful behavior. Equally notable, an individual's membership by itself cannot determine that the person is aware of the activities and purposes of a group. Indeed, the Court, in *Elfbrandt v. Russell* (1966), even elaborated that mere organizational associations cannot qualify as violations to loyalty oaths. To determine whether one has been disloyal, the Court explained that more evidence is required, such as the individual's subscription to treasonous or seditious acts and demonstrating a specific intent to further a group's unlawful goals.

Vague Language

Fourth, courts have indicated that loyalty oaths may not contain such vague language that its interpretation may deter legitimate acts and seemingly approve unintended, illegal acts. Based on a standard set by the Supreme Court, a person of "common intelligence" must be able to decipher the loyalty oath's meaning. In *Cramp v. Board of Public Instruction* (1961), a Florida loyalty oath law required public employees to attest that they did not and will not "lend . . . aid, support, advice, counsel or influence to the Communist Party" (p. 280). The statutory language included many conceivable acts that some may interpret as acceptable and others may not.

Further, the Court pointed out that the problem becomes more complex when one factors in the recent past. Not long before the case arose, the Communist Party had legal candidates on the ballot, and the Communist Party had legitimately endorsed candidates from other parties. To this end, the Court posed the questions of whether these activities precluded individuals from taking the oath or made oath takers subject to perjury. To the Court, these facts contextualized reasons to explain why misinterpretation occurs easily and questions of constitutional vagueness are asserted in these cases. As such, the Court concluded that interpretations and subsequent behaviors caused by loyalty oaths from an unconstitutionally vague statute subjected individuals to "risk of unfair prosecution and the potential deterrence of constitutionally protected conduct" (*Cramp v. Board of Public Instruction*, p. 279). With these possibilities, the Court struck down loyalty oaths that contained unconstitutionally vague language because they tend to violate the First and Fourteenth Amendments.

Jeffrey C. Sun

See also Due Process; Due Process Rights: Teacher Dismissal; *Keyishian v. Board of Regents;* Pledge of Allegiance; Political Activities and Speech of Teachers

Further Readings

Newsom, N. W. (1954). Teacher loyalty and related issues. *Peabody Journal of Education, 32,* 174–179.
Schrecker, E. W. (1986). *No ivory tower: McCarthyism and the universities.* New York: Oxford University Press.

Legal Citations

Cole v. Richardson, 405 U.S. 676 (1972).
Cramp v. Board of Public Instruction, 368 U.S. 278 (1961).
Elfbrandt v. Russell, 384 U.S. 11 (1966).
Keyishian v. Board of Regents, 385 U.S. 589 (1967).
Wieman v. Updegraff, 344 U.S. 183 (1952).

LULAC

See LEAGUE OF UNITED LATIN AMERICAN CITIZENS (LULAC)

MALDEF

See MEXICAN AMERICAN LEGAL DEFENSE AND
EDUCATIONAL FUND (MALDEF)

MANIFESTATION DETERMINATION

Disciplining students with disabilities is one of the most contentious practices that educators in public schools must face on a regular basis. In 1997, for the first time, and nine years after the Supreme Court's only case involving the disciplining of students with disabilities, *Honig v. Doe* (1988), the Individuals with Disabilities Education Act (IDEA) codified the process by which school officials may discipline students with disabilities. Pursuant to the IDEA's discipline provisions, school officials must engage in multidisciplinary decision-making processes and are prohibited from taking unilateral actions when students with disabilities violate school codes of conduct if there are questions about whether their misbehaviors are manifestations of their disabilities. This entry looks at these *manifestation determinations* and how they are implemented.

What the Law Requires

By definition, *manifestation determinations* are formal inquiries that evaluate whether there are relationships between student disabilities and their misconduct. In effect, teams that have developed the student's individualized education program (IEP) must consider the appropriateness of that program at the time specific behavioral incidents occurred that prompted disciplinary actions, as well as the possible need to change aspects of those programs and whether the behavior of concern resulted from the student's disabilities. At the end of the manifestation determination process, IEP teams must evaluate and decide whether the behaviors of concern are direct manifestations of disabilities that are beyond the student's comprehension and control.

The IDEA mandates manifestation determinations when students with disabilities undergo changes in their educational placement due to suspensions for periods of 10 school days or longer. Such determinations must be made by local educational agencies, parents (or guardians), and relevant members of the IEP team, as determined jointly by the parents and the local educational officials. Although the IDEA encourages parents to have a say in the composition of IEP teams, parents may not prevent specified individuals from participating if educational officials deem the presence of such persons necessary.

Pursuant to the IDEA, teams must conclude that a relationship between disability and misconduct exists if the conduct in question was caused by or had a direct and substantial relationship to the student's disabilities or if the conduct in question was the direct result of the failure of local educational officials to implement the

IEP properly. If either of these circumstances is present, then the behavior is a manifestation of a student's disability. If neither is true, then the behavior is not a manifestation of the student's disability.

How the Law Is Implemented

In situations where the IEP team decides that there was no relationship present, school officials may apply the same disciplinary procedures and severity that they use for students without disabilities. Even so, students with disabilities must continue to receive services consistent with the content of their IEPs. In circumstances where IEP teams are convinced that misconduct was related to student disabilities, school officials may not apply the same disciplinary procedures that they use for children without disabilities. Where manifestations are established, the IDEA requires IEP teams to conduct functional behavioral assessments if they are not already in place or review these assessments and plans if they have already been implemented for students with disabilities, revise the IEPs as necessary to implement behavior intervention plans, and return children to their then-current placements unless their parents and local educational officials agree to changes in placements based on the modifications of the behavioral intervention plans.

The differential application of disciplinary procedures when manifestations are established represents the fundamental belief that students with disabilities should not be treated the same as children without disabilities for behavior that is a function of their disabilities, because their actions are out of their control. The language of IDEA 2004 differs subtly but in meaningful ways from its 1997 predecessor, which required only that IEP teams evaluate simply whether misconduct was a "manifestation of" student disabilities. In contrast, IDEA 2004 directs IEP teams to consider whether misconduct was caused by student disabilities or was the direct result of the failure of local educational officials. The new language essentially places more accountability on students, because IEP teams are unlikely to meet the stringent criteria of evaluating whether misbehavior is a manifestation of students' disabilities.

Students with disabilities may be removed from school for up to 45 school days and placed in appropriate interim alternative placements without manifestation determinations (as long as the same penalties would apply to students who do not have disabilities) under three circumstances: possession of weapons at school or school related functions; knowing possession or use of illegal drugs or selling or soliciting the sale of controlled substances while at school, on school premises, or at school functions; and infliction of serious bodily injury on another person while at school, on school premises, or at school functions. When parents and local educational officials disagree with the decisions of IEP teams, either party may appeal by requesting hearings to challenge their actions. Appeals must be arranged by the educational agency within 20 school days of the date the hearings are requested, and a determination must be made within 10 school days after the hearings are completed. Once parents request appeals, students remain in their then-interim alternative placements pending the outcomes of hearings or until the expiration of their suspensions. The burden of proof at such hearings rests on the parties making the appeals.

Theresa A. Ochoa

See also Behavioral Intervention Plan; Due Process Hearing; *Honig v. Doe;* Individualized Education Program (IEP); Stay-Put Provision

Further Readings

Katsiyannis, A., & Maag, J. W. (2001). Manifestation determination as a golden fleece. *Exceptional Children, 8*(1), 85–96.

Russo, C. J., Osborne, A. G., & Borreca, E. (2005). The 2004 re-authorization of the Individuals with Disabilities Education Act. *Education and the Law, 17*(3), 111–117.

Smith, C. R. (2000). Behavioral and discipline provisions of IDEA '97: Implicit competencies yet to be confirmed. *Exceptional Children, 66*(3), 403–412.

Smith, T. E. C. (2005). IDEA 2004: Another round in the reauthorization process. *Remedial and Special Education, 26*(6), 314–319.

Turnbull, R., Huerta, N., & Stowe, M. (2006). *The Individuals with Disabilities Education Act as amended in 2004.* Upper Saddle River, NJ: Pearson Merrill Prentice Hall.

Legal Citations

Honig v. Doe, 484 U.S. 305 (1988).

Individuals with Disabilities Education Act, 20 U.S.C.
  §§ 1400 *et seq.*

MARBURY V. MADISON

In *Marbury v. Madison* (1803), the fledgling U.S. Supreme Court asserted its authority both to review acts of Congress and to invalidate those acts that conflict with the U.S. Constitution. In a case that depended upon power granted to the Court by Congress over and above what the Constitution provided, the Court emphasized that the Constitution is paramount. At the same time, the Court established itself as the appropriate body to evaluate whether a law either conflicts with or conforms to the Constitution. *Marbury v. Madison* is thus an important case defining the concept of judicial review that is so important in cases relating to schools and many other aspects of American life.

Facts of the Case

The facts in *Marbury* reflect the politics of the day. Thomas Jefferson was elected as the third U.S. president, defeating John Adams in the election of 1800, which was ultimately resolved on February 17, 1801. After losing the election, but before leaving office, President Adams determined to fill a number of judicial vacancies created by the Judiciary Act of 1801 with members of his own Federalist Party. The appointments were made on March 2, 1801, just two days before the expiration of his term, and were approved by the Senate on the next day; and Adams signed the commissions. However, in order for the appointments to be effective, the commissions had to be delivered to those who were appointed. This task was delegated to John Marshall, acting secretary of state and soon to be chief justice of the Supreme Court.

Despite his best efforts, Mr. Marshall was unable to deliver a number of the judicial commissions prior to President Adams's leaving office. When President Jefferson took office on March 4, 1801, he directed his new secretary of state, James Madison, *not* to deliver the remaining commissions for President Adams's "eleventh hour" appointments. Jefferson believed that the commissions, not having been delivered prior to the expiration of President Adams's term, were void.

William Marbury was one of Adams's "midnight appointees" to a newly created justice of the peace position in the District of Columbia. When his commission was not delivered, Marbury sued James Madison. Marbury, taking advantage of a provision in Section 13 of the Judiciary Act of 1789, began an original action in the Supreme Court seeking an order to show cause why a writ of mandamus should not issue. In essence, Marbury was asking the Supreme Court to order the secretary of state to deliver his commission.

Marbury's action raised the issue of whether the Supreme Court had the jurisdiction, or the power, to hear and resolve his case. The U.S. Constitution defines the jurisdiction of the Court in Article III, Section 2, Clause 2:

> In all Cases affecting Ambassadors, other public Ministers and Consuls, and those in which a State shall be a Party, the supreme Court shall have original Jurisdiction. In all the other Cases before mentioned [within the judicial power of the United States], the supreme Court shall have appellate Jurisdiction, both as to Law and Fact, with such Exceptions, and under such Regulations as the Congress shall make.

The Judiciary Act of 1789, and in particular Section 13 of the act, on which Mr. Marbury relied in bringing his action, addressed the jurisdiction of the Supreme Court as follows:

> The Supreme Court shall also have appellate jurisdiction from the circuit courts and courts of the several states, in the cases herein after provided for; and shall have power to issue writs of prohibition to the district courts . . . and writs of mandamus . . . to any courts appointed, or persons holding office, under the authority of the United States.

The constitutional issue in *Marbury* was whether Congress had the authority to expand the Supreme

Court's original jurisdiction. Insofar as Marbury filed his petition for a writ of mandamus directly in the Supreme Court, the justices needed to be able to exercise original jurisdiction over the dispute in order to have the power to hear the case. Marbury argued that Congress granted the Court original jurisdiction over petitions for writ of mandamus by enacting the Judiciary Act of 1789.

The Court's Ruling

The Court rendered its unanimous judgment on February 24, 1803. Chief Justice John Marshall, the same person who was acting secretary of state under President Adams, wrote the opinion for the Court. Essentially, Marshall held that while Madison should have delivered the commission to Marbury, the Supreme Court did not have the authority to issue the requested writ of mandamus. While it was true that Section 13 of the Judiciary Act of 1789 gave the Court the authority to issue writs of mandamus, the Court found that by including Section 13 in the Act, Congress exceeded the authority allotted to the Court under Article 3 of the Constitution. The Court ruled that Congress did not have the authority to modify the Supreme Court's original jurisdiction as defined in the Constitution.

Although Marbury never became a justice of the peace in the District of Columbia, his case gave the Supreme Court an opportunity to establish its power to declare acts of Congress unconstitutional, with extensive consequences.

Jon E. Anderson

See also Marshall, John

Further Readings

Dewey, D. O. (1970). *Marshall v. Jefferson: The political background of Marbury v. Madison.* New York: Knopf.
Haskins, G. L., & Johnson, H. A. (1981). *Foundations of power: John Marshall 1801–1851.* New York: Macmillan.
The Supreme Court Historical Society. (n.d.) *History of the Court: The Marshall Court (1801–1803).* Retrieved February 20, 2007, from http://www.supremecourthistory .org/02_history/subs_history/02_c04.html

Legal Citations

Marbury v. Madison, 5 U.S. (1 Cranch) 137 (1803).

MARSHALL, JOHN (1755–1835)

John Marshall was the longest serving and arguably greatest chief justice of the United States (1801–1835). Marshall was born on September 24, 1755, in what is now Fauquier County, Virginia. As a young man, Marshall fought in the Revolutionary War and served with George Washington at Valley Forge in 1777–1778. During 1780, when the fighting had subsided, he studied law under George Wythe at the College of William & Mary. Following the British surrender at Yorktown, Virginia, in October 1781, Marshall was elected to the Virginia General Assembly. He also began a law practice in Richmond, the new capital of Virginia. He was a delegate to the Virginia Ratifying Convention for the Constitution in 1788 and distinguished himself with a speech defending the proposed federal judiciary.

Following Virginia's ratification of the U.S. Constitution and subsequent establishment of the new national government, Marshall declined various suggestions that he seek election to Congress or some other federal appointment. In 1797, he did accept an appointment from President Adams to be part of a commission negotiating with France. Although the commission failed due to French intrigues and corruption, Marshall established a national reputation by resisting French demands. As a result, Marshall was elected to Congress in 1798 and was appointed secretary of state in 1800. When the chief justice position became vacant and President Adams' first choice declined, the appointment was offered to Marshall. He assumed office one month before President Adams left office.

During Marshall's tenure as chief justice, the fundamental question before the Court, indeed before the nation, was the nature of the more perfect union created by the Constitution of 1787. Many Americans regarded the union as merely a treaty between independent states, each of which was actually an independent country. They saw the national government as nothing more than an early example of the European Union or NATO. It was not sovereign. In sharp contrast, others believed that the union was a distinct nation. The national government, like the states, was a sovereign. Within the spheres of responsibility explicitly assigned by the Constitution, the national government was supreme.

Marshall subscribed to the latter view and, through his extraordinary powers of persuasion, convinced his fellow justices to go along with him. Several of Marshall's opinions form the foundation of modern constitutional law. First and most significantly, in *Marbury v. Madison* (1803), Marshall established the principle of judicial review—the Court could review the constitutionality of an act of Congress. Thus, the Court acquired the right to have the final say as to the meaning of the Constitution and to set aside legislation passed by democratically elected legislators. In *Fletcher v. Peck* (1810), he held that the Contracts Clause of the Constitution forbids the states from rescinding land grants. *McCulloch v. Maryland* (1819) established a broad view of the enumerated powers of the national government. His opinion in *Gibbons v. Ogden* (1824) suggested a broad view of Congress's power to regulate interstate commerce.

Yet, while affirming that the national government was sovereign, he also recognized the sovereignty of the states. The Court's decision in *Barron v. Baltimore* (1833) held that the Bill of Rights limited only the national government, not the states. *Wilson v. Black Bird Creek Marsh Co.* (1829) recognized the right of a state to block a navigable waterway and, thus, regulate interstate commerce.

Marshall's tenure spanned the Adams, Jefferson, Madison, Monroe, Quincy Adams, and Jackson administrations. He died in July 1835.

William E. Thro

Further Readings

Hobson, C. F. (1996). *The great chief justice: John Marshall and the rule of law.* Lawrence: University of Kansas Press.
Simon, J. F. (2002). *What kind of nation: Thomas Jefferson, John Marshall, and the epic struggle to create the United States.* New York: Simon & Schuster.
Stites, F. N. (1981). *John Marshall: Defender of the Constitution.* Boston: Little, Brown.

Legal Citations

Barron v. Baltimore, 32 U.S. (7 Pet.) 243 (1833).
Fletcher v. Peck, 10 U.S. (6 Cranch) 87 (1810).
Gibbons v. Ogden, 22 U.S. (9 Wheat.) 1 (1824).
Marbury v. Madison, 5 U.S. (1 Cranch) 137 (1803).
McCulloch v. Maryland, 17 U.S. (4 Wheat.) 316 (1819).
Wilson v. Black Bird Creek Marsh Co., 27 U.S. (2 Pet.) 245 (1829).

MARSHALL, THURGOOD (1908–1993)

Justice Thurgood Marshall was the first African American appointed to the Supreme Court of the United States. His service there was the capstone on an already noteworthy legal career in which he led the NAACP's battle against segregation, especially in schools. It was his argument on behalf of the plaintiffs that led to the Court's landmark *Brown v. Board of Education of Topeka* ruling. Later, as an associate justice himself, he often raised an eloquent voice on behalf of equity.

Early Years

Born in Baltimore, Maryland on July 2, 1908, Thurgood Marshall was the younger of two sons of William Canfield Marshall and Norma A. Marshall. He received his formative education in the public school system of Baltimore, Maryland. After completing public school, Marshall enrolled in Lincoln University, a public, historically Black university in Oxford, Pennsylvania, where he attempted to study dentistry, but it failed to keep his interest. His academic interest soon changed to law, and he graduated with honors from Lincoln University in 1930.

Marshall's first choice of law schools was the University of Maryland; but his application was denied by the state's segregated system of higher education. Instead, he attended Howard University School of Law in Washington, D.C., where, under the tutelage of law school Dean Charles Hamilton Houston, he graduated in 1933 as class valedictorian.

On graduation, Marshall entered the private practice of law, starting his career as a labor and antitrust lawyer. His early years in Baltimore, Maryland, were arduous and discouraging due to the Depression making profitable cases few and far between. Marshall did not expect to become wealthy in private practice, but did expect to make a modest income. However, during the Depression, even a modest income was difficult to achieve.

The NAACP Years

In 1934, Marshall volunteered his legal services to the local branch of the National Association for the Advancement of Colored People (NAACP). In 1935, he won his first case for the NAACP by persuading the Maryland Court of Appeals to order the University of Maryland Law School to admit its first African American applicant. By 1936, the national NAACP had taken notice of Marshall, and he joined the organization's national legal staff in the role of assistant special counsel to the NAACP. This began Marshall's series of legal battles to persuade the local, state, and federal courts to overrule the "separate but equal" doctrine that the U.S. Supreme Court had enunciated in 1896 in *Plessy v. Ferguson.* Marshall's long association with the NAACP and appointment as assistant special counsel was the beginning of many milestones in his legal career.

Under the direction of Thurgood Marshall, the NAACP's Legal Defense and Educational Fund adopted a strategy of attrition against the concept of separate but equal facilities in education. Beginning with its attack on segregated public professional schools and colleges and proceeding to elementary and high school education, Marshall and his staff sought to erode the basis of discrimination by advocating for equality not only in tangible facilities, but also in intangible factors. Marshall argued before the Supreme Court that it was impossible for a state to provide equality in such intangible features as the prestige of an institution, the quality of faculty, and the reputation of degrees for African Americans in separate schools.

Marshall and the NAACP sought to prove the inconsistency of the separate but equal doctrine itself and compel the Supreme Court to re-examine the constitutionality of the doctrine of separate but equal educational facilities. Turning from specific discrimination to racial segregation, Marshal argued that the doctrine of separate but equal was without legal foundation or social justification. The result of this strategy was the overturning of the separate but equal doctrine in *Brown v. Board of Education of Topeka* (1954).

In the decade following *Brown,* Marshall and the Legal Defense and Educational Fund challenged local and state actions upholding separate but equal policies and practices. They argued that *Brown* had to be construed and applied to other areas of state activity besides education, that the separate but equal policy had no place in the area of legitimate state responsibility, including the use of public facilities. After countless court battles, Marshall grew weary of arguing cases and believed that state legislation was sorely needed to advance equality for all persons.

On the Bench

President John F. Kennedy nominated Thurgood Marshall to the Second Circuit Court of Appeals in New York in 1961. He then received a recess appointment in October 1961, and his nomination was confirmed by the Senate on September 11, 1962. Of the 150 opinions he authored after his appointment to the Second Circuit, not one was overturned. President Lyndon B. Johnson nominated Justice Marshall as solicitor general of the United States on June 13, 1965. He assumed the office of solicitor general on August 24, 1965.

Judge Thurgood Marshall was the first African American to serve as solicitor general of the United States. President Johnson nominated Marshall to the bench of the Supreme Court as associate justice on June 13, 1967. The Senate confirmed his nomination on August 30, 1967; he took the oath of office on October 2, 1967.

Justice Marshall was appointed during Chief Justice Earl Warren's tenure. During this period, Associate Justice Marshall consistently joined with his liberal colleagues on the Supreme Court in most of its 99 opinions. Justice Marshall dissented in 6; concurred in 3; and joined in the majority opinion on

66 cases. He wrote 11 majority opinions in this period. As the Warren Court gave way to the Burger Court (1969–1986), Justice Marshall voted as a dissenter in 754 decisions with opinions and 183 in memorandum decisions, for a total of 937 dissenting votes.

Justice Marshall's service to the government of the United States, like his role as lawyer and judge, was filled with activity. In 1951, he investigated court-martial cases involving African American soldiers in both Japan and Korea. Marshall served as a consultant at the Constitutional Conference of Kenya in London in 1961 and as the U.S. representative to the independence ceremonies of Sierra Leone in 1961. He was also the chief of the U.S. delegation to the Third United Nations Congress on Prevention of Crime and Treatment of Offenders in Stockholm, Sweden, in August 1965. President Harry S. Truman appointed Marshall to represent the United States at the laying of the cornerstone ceremony at the Harry S. Truman Center for the Advancement of Peace. He was a member of numerous boards and the recipient of many prestigious national and international medals, awards, and citations for his tireless pursuits in the field of civil rights.

Suffering from poor health, Justice Thurgood Marshall submitted his resignation from the Supreme Court on June 27, 1991. His career as a justice of the court did not end with his resignation. For a brief period of time, the Court by special order assigned Justice Marshall to perform judicial duties in the Second Circuit in 1992 and to hear cases in the Fourth Circuit. Supreme Court Justice Thurgood Marshall died on January 24, 1993, and is buried in Arlington National Cemetery in Washington, D.C.

Paul Green

See also *Brown v. Board of Education of Topeka; Brown v. Board of Education of Topeka* and Equal Educational Opportunities

Further Readings

Bland, R. W. (2001). *Justice Thurgood Marshall: Crusader for liberalism, his judicial biography (1908–1993)*. Bethesda, MD: Academic Press.

Davis, M. D., & Clark, H. R. (1992). *Thurgood Marshall: Warrior at the bar, rebel on the bench.* New York: Carol.

Smith, J. C. (2003). *Supreme justice: Speeches and writings.* Philadelphia: University of Pennsylvania Press.

Williams, J. (1998). *Thurgood Marshall: American revolutionary.* New York: Random House.

Legal Citations

Brown v. Board of Education of Topeka I, 347 U.S. 483 (1954).
Brown v. Board of Education of Topeka II, 349 U.S. 294 (1955).
Plessy v. Ferguson, 163 U.S. 537 (1896).

Martinez v. Bynum

In *Martinez v. Bynum* (1983), the Supreme Court held that a bona fide residence requirement was a permissible precondition before even a U.S. citizen could demand a state's services such as public education. The Court thus ruled that a child who was a citizen but who did not meet the requirements of Texas's bona fide residence was not entitled to a free public education.

Facts of the Case

Roberto Morales, who was born in McAllen, Texas, was a citizen of the United States. After his birth, Roberto and his parents, Mexican citizens, returned to Mexico, where he lived until he was eight years old. When Roberto turned eight, his mother and father sent him to live with his sister, who had established legal residency in McAllen, Texas. The family's goal was that Roberto would re-enter the United States and live with his sister in order to attend American public schools and to learn English.

Even though Roberto was a citizen, local school board officials denied Roberto a tuition-free education pursuant to a state statute that denied such an education to children who lived apart from their parents or guardians and who were present in districts merely to obtain an education. Roberto's sister filed a lawsuit claiming this statute was unconstitutional, as it violated provisions of the Equal Protection Clause, the Due Process Clause, and the Privileges and Immunities Clause.

The lower courts ruled in favor of the school board on the ground that Texas had a substantial interest in assuring that services intended for the state's residents were provided only to residents.

The Court's Ruling

The sister appealed to the Supreme Court, which deemed it necessary to define two major components of the Texas statute. The first of these components was the issue of whether Roberto lived apart from a parent or guardian. Roberto's sister claimed that her "custody" of Roberto for five years was sufficient to meet the requirement of parent or guardian. However, the Court determined that the wording of the statute deliberately intended that in order to establish residency, a child was required to live with his or her natural parents or with guardians; guardians were defined as persons appointed by the courts or those having lawful control over children with the responsibility to care for their rights and needs. The Court reasoned that while the sister had cared for her brother, her custody did not rise to the level of parenthood or guardianship.

In reviewing the second component of the statute, concerning the need to be present in a district to obtain an education, the Supreme Court pointed out that history revealed that board officials had been liberal in allowing students to attend school without benefit of a parent or guardian if they resided in the district for any reason other than to obtain an education. The Court acknowledged that while the board had, on occasion, granted tuition-free admission to children who were in the district without benefit of a parent or guardian, the

state of Texas (and the McAllen School District) was within its rights to deny a tuition-free education to students who lived in the school district solely to receive a free American education.

Additionally, the Supreme Court was of the opinion that because a public education is not a right guaranteed to individuals by the Constitution, bona fide residence requirements that are clearly defined and uniformly applied further a state's interest in meeting constitutional standards. The Court concluded both that the statute that denied a tuition-free education to students who lived in a school district without parents or a guardian and whose sole purpose was to obtain an education satisfied constitutional standards and that the board was not required to provide tuition-free education.

Brenda Kallio

See also Due Process; Equal Protection Analysis; Parens Patriae; *Plyler v. Doe*

Legal Citations

Martinez v. Bynum, 461 U.S. 321 (1983).
Plyler v. Doe, 457 U.S. 202 (1982).

Martinez v. Bynum (EXCERPTS)

In Martinez v. Bynum, *the Supreme Court upheld the constitutionality of residency laws for school attendance as long as they are clearly defined and uniformly applied.*

Supreme Court of the United States

MARTINEZ

v.

BYNUM

461 U.S. 321

Argued Jan. 10, 1983.

Decided May 2, 1983.

Justice POWELL delivered the opinion of the Court.

This case involves a facial challenge to the constitutionality of the Texas residency requirement governing minors who wish to attend public free schools while living apart from their parents or guardians.

I

Roberto Morales was born in 1969 in McAllen, Texas, and is thus a United States citizen by birth. His parents are Mexican citizens who reside in Reynosa, Mexico. He left Reynosa in 1977 and returned to McAllen to live with his sister, petitioner Oralia Martinez, for the primary purpose of attending school in the McAllen Independent School District. Although Martinez is now Morales's custodian, she is not—and does not desire to become—his guardian. As a result, Morales is not entitled to tuition-free admission to the McAllen schools. Section 21.031(b) and (c) of the Texas Education Code would require the local school authorities to admit him if he or "his parent, guardian, or the person having lawful control of him" resided in the school district, but

§ 21.031(d) denies tuition-free admission for a minor who lives apart from a "parent, guardian, or other person having lawful control of him under an order of a court" if his presence in the school district is "for the primary purpose of attending the public free schools." Respondent McAllen Independent School District therefore denied Morales's application for admission in the fall of 1977.

In December 1977 Martinez, as next friend of Morales, and four other adult custodians of school-age children instituted the present action in the United States District Court for the Southern District of Texas against the Texas Commissioner of Education, the Texas Education Agency, four local school districts, and various local school officials in those districts. Plaintiffs initially alleged that § 21.031(d), both on its face and as applied by defendants, violated certain provisions of the Constitution, including the Equal Protection Clause, the Due Process Clause, and the Privileges and Immunities Clause. Plaintiffs also sought preliminary and permanent injunctive relief.

The District Court denied a preliminary injunction in August 1978. It found "that the school boards ... have been more than liberal in finding that certain children are not living away from parents and residing in the school district for the sole purpose of attending school." App. 20a. The evidence "conclusively" showed "that children living within the school districts with someone other than their parents or legal guardians will be admitted to school if *any* reason exists for such situation other than that of attending school only." *Ibid.* (emphasis in original).

Plaintiffs subsequently amended the complaint to narrow their claims. They now seek only "a declaration that ... § 21.031(d) is unconstitutional on its face," App. 3a, an injunction prohibiting defendants from denying the children admission to school pursuant to § 21.031(d), restitution of certain tuition payments, costs, and attorney's fees. After a hearing on the merits, the District Court granted judgment for the defendants. The court concluded that § 21.031(d) was justified by the State's "legitimate interest in protecting and preserving the quality of its educational system and the right of its own bona fide residents to attend state schools on a preferred tuition basis." In an appeal by two plaintiffs, the United States Court of Appeals for the Fifth Circuit affirmed. In view of the importance of the issue, we granted Martinez's petition for certiorari. We now affirm.

II

This Court frequently has considered constitutional challenges to residence requirements. On several occasions the Court has invalidated requirements that condition receipt of a benefit on a minimum period of residence within a jurisdiction, but it always has been careful to distinguish such durational residence requirements from bona fide residence requirements. In *Shapiro v. Thompson,* for example, the Court invalidated one-year durational residence requirements that applicants for public assistance benefits were required to satisfy despite the fact that they otherwise had "met the test for residence in their jurisdictions." Justice BRENNAN, writing for the Court, stressed that "[t]he residence requirement and the one-year waiting-period requirement are distinct and independent prerequisites for assistance," and carefully "impl[ied] no view of the validity of waiting-period *or* residence requirements determining eligibility to vote, eligibility for tuition-free education, to obtain a license to practice a profession, to hunt or fish, and so forth." In *Dunn v. Blumstein,* the Court similarly invalidated Tennessee laws requiring a prospective voter to have been a state resident for one year and a county resident for three months, but it explicitly distinguished these durational residence requirements from bona fide residence requirements. This was not an empty distinction. Justice MARSHALL, writing for the Court, again emphasized that "States have the power to require that voters be bona fide residents of the relevant political subdivision."

We specifically have approved bona fide residence requirements in the field of public education. The Connecticut statute before us in *Vlandis v. Kline,* for example, was unconstitutional because it created an irrebuttable presumption of nonresidency for state university students whose legal addresses were outside of the State before they applied for admission. The statute violated the Due Process Clause because it in effect classified some bona fide state residents as nonresidents for tuition purposes. But we "fully recognize[d] that a State has a legitimate interest in protecting and preserving ... the right of its own bona fide residents to attend [its colleges and universities] on a preferential tuition basis." This "legitimate interest" permits a "State [to] establish such reasonable criteria for in-state status as to make virtually certain that students who are not, in fact, bona fide residents of the State, but who have come there solely for educational purposes, cannot take advantage of the in-state rates." Last Term, in *Plyler v. Doe,* we reviewed an aspect of ... the statute at issue in this case. Although we invalidated the portion of the statute that excluded undocumented alien children from the public free schools, we recognized the school districts' right "to apply . . . established criteria for determining residence."

A bona fide residence requirement, appropriately defined and uniformly applied, furthers the substantial state interest in assuring that services provided for its residents are enjoyed only by residents. Such a requirement with respect to attendance in public free schools does not violate the Equal Protection Clause of the Fourteenth Amendment. It does not burden or penalize the constitutional right of interstate travel, for any person is free to move to a State and to establish residence there. A bona fide residence requirement simply requires that the person *does* establish residence before demanding the services that are restricted to residents.

There is a further, independent justification for local residence requirements in the public-school context. As we explained in *Milliken v. Bradley*: "No single tradition in public education is more deeply rooted than local control over the operation of schools; local autonomy has long been thought essential both to the maintenance of community concern and support for public schools and to quality of the educational process. . . . [L]ocal control over the educational process affords citizens an opportunity to participate in decision-making, permits the structuring of school programs to fit local needs, and encourages 'experimentation, innovation, and a healthy competition for education excellence.'"

The provision of primary and secondary education, of course, is one of the most important functions of local government. Absent residence requirements, there can be little doubt that the proper planning and operation of the schools would suffer significantly. The State thus has a substantial interest in imposing bona fide residence requirements to maintain the quality of local public schools.

III

The central question we must decide here is whether § 21.031(d) is a bona fide residence requirement. Although the meaning may vary according to context, "residence" generally requires both physical presence and an intention to remain. As the Supreme Court of Maine explained over a century ago: "When . . . a person voluntarily takes up his abode in a given place, with intention to remain permanently, or for an indefinite period of time; or, to speak more accurately, when a person takes up his abode in a given place, without any present intention to remove therefrom, such place of abode becomes his residence. . . ." This classic two-part definition of

residence has been recognized as a minimum standard in a wide range of contexts time and time again.

In *Vlandis v. Kline, supra,* we approved a more rigorous domicile test as a "reasonable standard for determining the residential status of a student." That standard was described as follows: "'In reviewing a claim of in-state status, the issue becomes essentially one of domicile. In general, the domicile of an individual is his true, fixed and permanent home and place of habitation. It is the place to which, whenever he is absent, he has the intention of returning.'" This standard could not be applied to school-age children in the same way that it was applied to college students. But at the very least, a school district generally would be justified in requiring school-age children or their parents to satisfy the traditional, basic residence criteria-*i.e.,* to live in the district with a bona fide intention of remaining there—before it treated them as residents.

Section 21.031 is far more generous than this traditional standard. It compels a school district to permit a child such as Morales to attend school without paying tuition if he has a bona fide intention to remain in the school district indefinitely, for he then would have a reason for being there other than his desire to attend school: his intention to make his home in the district. Thus § 21.031 grants the benefits of residency to all who satisfy the traditional requirements. The statute goes further and extends these benefits to many children even if they (or their families) do not intend to remain in the district indefinitely. As long as the child is not living in the district for the sole purpose of attending school, he satisfies the statutory test. For example, if a person comes to Texas to work for a year, his children will be eligible for tuition-free admission to the public schools. Or if a child comes to Texas for six months for health reasons, he would qualify for tuition-free education. In short, § 21.031 grants the benefits of residency to everyone who satisfies the traditional residence definition and to some who legitimately could be classified as nonresidents. Since there is no indication that this extension of the traditional definition has any impermissible basis, we certainly cannot say that § 21.031(d) violates the Constitution.

IV

The Constitution permits a State to restrict eligibility for tuition-free education to its bona fide residents. We hold that § 21.031 is a bona fide residence requirement that satisfies constitutional standards. The judgment of the Court of Appeals accordingly is

Affirmed.

Citation: *Martinez v. Bynum,* 461 U.S. 321 (1983).

MCDANIEL V. BARRESI

In *McDaniel v. Barresi* (1971), the U.S. Supreme Court was asked to determine whether a school board that was found to have maintained an unconstitutionally segregated system could implement a desegregation plan by affirmatively redrawing geographic attendance zones for the specific purpose of establishing a greater racial balance in its schools. The primary issue in *McDaniel* was whether school officials could constitutionally take race into account when assigning elementary school children to specified schools in order to effectuate a desegregation order. The Supreme Court said yes.

Facts of the Case

The school desegregation plan at issue in *McDaniel* involved reassigning African American students who resided in heavily segregated areas to other school attendance zones, which necessitated that they walk further distances to school or be transported by bus. Opponents contended that the plan violated the Equal Protection Clause of the Fourteenth Amendment by treating students differently based on race, and the plan also violated the Civil Rights Act of 1964, because it required busing students from one school to another school located farther from the students' residence.

On further review of a judgment from the Supreme Court of Georgia, a unanimous U.S. Supreme Court approved the school board's student desegregation assignment plan. Reversing in favor of the proponents of the plan, the Court held that it violated neither the Equal Protection Clause of the Fourteenth Amendment nor the Civil Rights Act of 1964.

The Court's Ruling

The Supreme Court reasoned that the school board acted within its affirmative duty to replace its segregated school system with a unitary racially balanced school system when it established attendance lines and reassigned students based solely on race. While the Equal Protection Clause typically prohibits any disparate treatment on the basis of race, here the Court was of the opinion that the classification was permissible. The Court explained that the formulation of such a remedy for unconstitutional racial segregation invariably required that the students be treated differently based on their races. The Court acknowledged that "any other approach would freeze the status quo that is the very target of all desegregation" (p. 41).

Barresi sets forth parameters within which school boards may exercise discretion in voluntarily desegregating their school systems. The Court, by approving the board's redistricting based on race, granted other boards broad remedial power to desegregate their school systems. The Court first acknowledged this expansive remedial power of school boards to rectify past segregation in *Green v. County School Board of New Kent County* (1968), which permitted school boards to "take whatever steps might be necessary" to eradicate segregation. *McDaniel* is illustrative of this broad remedial power and permits within its purview race-conscious geographical redistricting and busing to desegregate school systems. Prior to this recognition that race could serve as a legitimate factor in reapportioning pupil school attendance to end segregation, such disparate treatment of individuals based solely on race was deemed unconstitutional in violation of the Fourteenth Amendment's Equal Protection Clause. However, it is well established that while school officials must not consider race in providing equal educational opportunity to all students, they may take race into account for the purposes of crafting remedies for historical unconstitutional racial discrimination.

McDaniel is most often cited with respect to the authoritative ability of local school boards to utilize race as a factor in student assignments to specified schools in order to rectify unlawful segregation. Moreover, state school boards have the unequivocal discretion to assign students within their school systems and can consider race in seeking to achieve racial balance. While *McDaniel* stands firm for the proposition that boards may take race into consideration when assigning students in the system to ameliorate the detrimental effects of past segregation, more recent litigation at the Supreme Court posed a somewhat different legal question that was not ultimately resolved.

In *Parents Involved in Community Schools v. Seattle School District No. 1* (2007), a consolidation of suits from Seattle, Washington, and, Louisville Kentucky, a majority of justices on the Supreme Court, in a plurality ruling, struck down race conscious assignment plans. The plurality invalidated the plans, which were designed to achieve racial balance and the benefits of diversity, not only because neither system was operating under desegregation orders (Seattle never had, and the one in Louisville had been terminated), but also because race was the only factor used in student assignments. However, insofar as this judgment was a plurality, questions remain about the constitutionality of the use of race in making student assignments in K–12 public schools.

Aimee R. Vergon

See also *Brown v. Board of Education of Topeka;* Civil Rights Act of 1964; Dual and Unitary Systems; *Green v. County School Board of New Kent County; Parents Involved in Community Schools v. Seattle School District No. 1; Swann v. Charlotte-Mecklenburg Board of Education*

Legal Citations

Brown v. Board of Education of Topeka I, 347 U.S. 483 (1954).
Brown v. Board of Education of Topeka II, 349 U.S. 294 (1955).
Green v. County School Board of New Kent County, 391 U.S. 430 (1968).
McDaniel v. Barresi, 402 U.S. 39 (McDaniel, 1971).
North Carolina Board of Education v. Swann, 402 U.S. 43 (1971).
Parents Involved in Community Schools v. Seattle School District No. 1, 127 S. Ct. 2738 (2007).
Swann v. Charlotte-Mecklenburg Board of Education, 402 U.S. 1 (1971).

McDonnell Douglas Corporation v. Green

In *McDonnell Douglas Corporation v. Green* (1973), the U.S. Supreme Court explained how to prove a case of employment discrimination under Title VII of the Civil Rights Act of 1964 when evidence of discrimination is circumstantial. Rarely do job seekers or employees have direct evidence of discrimination, such as policies that specifically exclude members of

particular races. Recognizing this, in *McDonnell Douglas* the Court provided a framework for proving disparate treatment when circumstantial evidence is all that is available.

Most cases of discrimination filed under Title VII allege disparate treatment discrimination even though the law also covers policies that have a disparate impact. Disparate treatment occurs when employers treat specified job seekers, employees, or particular workers differently on the basis of impermissible factors such as race, religion, or sex. Moreover, disparate treatment is referred to as intentional discrimination, because employers knowingly treat one person, or group of persons, differently than others.

While the *McDonnell Douglas* Court found that a job application may have violated Title VII, the judiciary applies the same framework to other types of discriminatory treatment, including hiring, dismissal, discipline, promotion, and tenure in the educational context. Likewise, although Title VII prohibits discrimination on the basis of race, color, national origin, religion, or sex, the courts employ the same framework in other federal discrimination cases, including age and disability discrimination.

The Initial Decision

At issue in *McDonnell Douglas* was a claim that the plaintiff's former employer relied on racially motivated hiring practices. The suit began after the plaintiff engaged in disruptive and illegal activity due to his having been fired. In a disparate treatment case where only circumstantial evidence is available, the court found, an employee first must establish a prima facie case of discrimination. *Prima facie* means that a court will presume that an employee's discrimination claim is true unless contrary evidence is provided. The employee need only show facts that give rise to an inference of intentional discrimination.

In order to establish a prima facie case of discrimination in hiring, for example, applicants must show that they are members of a protected group covered by the law, applied for an available position, were qualified, and were rejected, and that the job remained open and the employer continued to seek qualified applicants, or the job was filled by someone who was not in a protected group. If job seekers or employees establish prima facie cases and employers do not come up with any nondiscriminatory reasons for their action, then employees will prevail.

After employees or job applicants establish prima facie cases, employers can rebut their claims by articulating legitimate, nondiscriminatory reasons for their employment actions. At the same time, employers do not have to prove these facts; they merely have to offer explanations why plaintiffs were not hired. Once employers offer explanations, it is up to plaintiffs to prove that those justifications were untrue pretexts for discrimination.

Clarifying Cases

The Supreme Court clarified what happens once an employer's justification is proved to be untrue. In *St. Mary's Honor Center v. Hicks* (1993), the Court held that employees or job seekers do not automatically prove their cases of disparate treatment discrimination when they show that the reasons offered by employers for adverse employment actions are mere pretexts. In *Hicks,* the Court expressed its concern that large corporations might not be able to ascertain the exact reason why someone was not hired or promoted or was fired and that in this context an employer's failure to provide the true reason for an employment decision should not automatically impose liability without additional facts. However, in a case in which the individual offering the reason is the same person who made the employment decision, evidence of pretext may be strong circumstantial evidence. There was some confusion in the lower courts that *Hicks* required additional independent evidence of employment discrimination.

In *Reeves v. Sanderson Plumbing Products* (2000), an age discrimination case, the Supreme Court clarified *Hicks* by explaining judges should weigh a number of factors to determine whether discrimination occurred, including the strength of the prima facie case and the fact that an employer's reason for the adverse action was proven to be a mere pretext. Even though employees always bear the burden of proving discrimination, the Court explained in *Reeves* that it did not require additional independent evidence of discrimination.

Karen Miksch

See also Disparate Impact; Equal Employment Opportunity Commission; *Griggs v. Duke Power Company;* Title VII

Legal Citations

Griggs v. Duke Power Company, 401 U.S. 424 (1971).
McDonnell Douglas Corporation v. Green, 411 U.S. 792 (1973).
Reeves v. Sanderson Plumbing Products, 530 U.S. 133 (2000).
St. Mary's Honor Center v. Hicks, 509 U.S. 502 (1993).

MCLAURIN V. OKLAHOMA STATE REGENTS FOR HIGHER EDUCATION

McLaurin v. Oklahoma State Regents for Higher Education (1950), like *Sweatt v. Painter* (1950), is a landmark case in civil rights law that demonstrated that because the "separate but equal" doctrine was eroding, it was not possible to provide a separate but equal education in graduate and professional schools as well as in K–12 education.

Facts of the Case

George McLaurin, an African American man, applied for admission to the all-White University of Oklahoma to obtain a doctoral degree in education. McLaurin was denied admission to the university solely due to his race under a state law that made it a misdemeanor to teach African American and White students in the same facility. When McLaurin pursued legal action to be admitted to the university, a federal court in Oklahoma was of the opinion that the state, through university officials, had the constitutional duty to provide him with the education that was provided for members of other populations.

Further, the court declared that to the extent the Oklahoma statutes denied McLaurin admission, they were unconstitutional and void. Following the litigation, the state legislature amended its statutes to permit the admission of African Americans to institutions of higher learning attended by White students as long as these programs were administered "upon a segregation basis." McLaurin was thus accepted to study at the university.

Once McLaurin began attending classes, he realized that university officials segregated him from the White students. The classes that McLaurin attended were purposely scheduled for classrooms that had adjoining anterooms, in which he was forced to sit. In the library, McLaurin was required to sit at a designated desk on the mezzanine floor, and in the cafeteria, he had to eat at different times than White students. McLaurin objected to this treatment and sought a remedy from the lower federal court. When a federal trial court denied McLaurin's motion for relief on the basis that he was denied equal protection under the law, he appealed to the Supreme Court.

In the interim, university officials adjusted the institution's segregation policies in a very limited way. University officials began allowing McLaurin to sit at a desk in the main classroom, but only in a row designated for African Americans. McLaurin also began to be able to study on the main floor of the library, but he was still only allowed to use specified desks. Similarly, officials allowed him the privilege of being able to eat at the same time as White students, but he was still not permitted to sit at the same tables as those students.

The university contended that these restrictions did not affect McLaurin's ability to study, learn, or interact with other students in preparing for his profession. McLaurin disagreed with the university's position, pressing his claim that officials infringed on his Fourteenth Amendment Equal Protection Rights. The core of his claim was that the restrictions negatively affected his educational achievement and his education was unequal to that of White students.

The Court's Ruling

On further review, the U.S. Supreme Court, in a brief opinion, reversed in favor of McLaurin. In writing for the unanimous court, Chief Justice Fred Vinson stated,

> Those who will come under [McLaurin's] guidance and influence must be directly affected by the education he receives. Their own education and development will necessarily suffer to the extent that his training is unequal to that of his classmates. State-imposed restrictions which produce such inequalities cannot be sustained. (p. 641)

In buttressing the Court's analysis, he added that

the conditions under which [McLaurin] is required to receive his education deprive him of his personal and present right to the equal protection of the laws. . . . We hold that under these circumstances the Fourteenth Amendment precludes differences in treatment by the state based upon race. [McLaurin], having been admitted to a state-supported graduate school, must receive the same treatment at the hands of the state as students of other races. (p. 641)

Viewed together, *McLaurin* and *Sweatt* demonstrated that there were intangible social aspects to education that could never be equal in segregated facilities. Further, these victories in higher education bolstered efforts to focus attention on the inequalities of segregated elementary and secondary public schools. Needless to say, *McLaurin* and *Sweatt* foreshadowed the legal strategy and judicial analysis that would become well known in *Brown v. Board of Education of Topeka* (1954).

Aaron Cooley

See also Brown v. Board of Education of Topeka: Brown v. Board of Education of Topeka and Equal Educational Opportunities; Civil Rights Movement; Fourteenth Amendment; *Plessy v. Ferguson;* Segregation, De Jure; *Sweatt v. Painter*

Further Readings

Klarman, J. (2004). *From Jim Crow to civil rights: The Supreme Court and the struggle for racial equality.* New York: Oxford University Press.

Tushnet, M. (2005). *The NAACP's legal strategy against segregated education, 1925–1950.* Chapel Hill: University of North Carolina Press.

Legal Citations

Brown v. Board of Education of Topeka I, 347 U.S. 483 (1954).
Brown v. Board of Education of Topeka II, 349 U.S. 294 (1955).
McLaurin v. Oklahoma State Regents for Higher Education, 339 U.S. 637 (1950).
Sweatt v. Painter, 339 U.S. 629 (1950).

MEDIATION

Public policy in the United States favors alternative dispute resolution as an effective means of resolving labor disputes instead of litigation. For this reason, the majority of states with collective bargaining agreements between public school teachers and their boards of education mandate the use of formal grievance procedures to settle labor disputes. Three famous U.S. Supreme Court labor cases, referred to as the steelworkers' trilogy (*United Steelworkers of America v. American Manufacturing Company* [1960], *United Steelworkers of America v. Warrior and Gulf Navigation Company* [1960], and *United Steelworkers of America v. Enterprise Wheel and Car Company* [1960]) reflect the connection between federal labor law and state collective bargaining law.

Along with fact-finding and arbitration, mediation is one of the three primary methods of dispute resolution used in the collective bargaining process when parties fail to reach mutually acceptable agreements. The process of mediation involves the use of neutral third-party mediators, who work closely with the parties to facilitate their reaching mutually acceptable agreements; it is regulated by state statute. In practice, individual mediators are chosen either by state labor relations boards or through the mutual agreement of local school boards and the bargaining units of their employees.

In contrast to arbitrators' recommendations, those rendered by mediators are usually not disclosed to the public. At the same time, while the legal authority of mediators is limited, a number of states require that parties exhaust formal mediation efforts before they can proceed to other alternative means of dispute resolution, such as fact-finding, arbitration, or the termination of bargaining altogether.

Labor topics that are often subjects of mediation include those areas that are bargainable subjects under state collective bargaining agreements. In most states, labor issues surrounding wages, hours of employment, and contractual issues related to the terms and conditions of employment represent issues that are subject to mediation if the parties cannot reach agreements under their collective bargaining agreements. If school boards and unions ultimately fail to reach agreement after exhausting the dispute negotiation remedies of mediation, fact-finding, and arbitration, the majority, but certainly not all, of the states that allow bargaining require the parties to maintain the terms and conditions of the previous collective bargaining contract.

Kevin P. Brady

See also Arbitration; Collective Bargaining; Contracts; Impasse in Bargaining; Unions

Further Readings

Brady, K. P. (2007). Bargaining. In C. J. Russo (Ed.), *The yearbook of education law: 2007* (pp. 101–110). Dayton, OH: Education Law Association.

Brady, K. P. (2006). Collective bargaining. In C. J. Russo & R. D. Mawdsley (Eds.), *Education law.* New York: Law Journal Press.

Legal Citations

United Steelworkers of America v. American Manufacturing Company, 363 U.S. 564 (1960).

United Steelworkers of America v. Enterprise Wheel & Car Corporation, 363 U.S. 593 (1960).

United Steelworkers of America v. Warrior & Gulf Navigation Company, 363 U.S. 574 (1960).

MEEK V. PITTENGER

In *Meek v. Pittenger* (1975), the plaintiffs, three individuals and four organizations, filed suit alleging that two Pennsylvania statutes violated the Establishment Clause of the First Amendment by authorizing the use of state purchased books, materials, and equipment in religious schools. One of the statutes, Act 194, authorized commonwealth officials to provide auxiliary services, including counseling, testing, and psychological services, to all children in Pennsylvania's nonpublic schools, free of charge. The other law, Act 195, provided that the commonwealth would loan textbooks, instructional materials, and equipment to these same children.

On direct appeal from a federal trial court in Pennsylvania, the U.S. Supreme Court held that Act 195, only as it relates to the loan of textbooks, did not violate the Establishment Clause. Affirming the constitutionality of the textbook loan statute, the Court referred to *Board of Education v. Allen* (1967), in which the justices upheld a law from New York that required public school authorities to lend textbooks to all students in Grades 7 through 12, including children who attended nonpublic, including religiously affiliated, schools. As in *Allen,* in a manner consistent with the child benefit test, the Court observed that loans of the textbooks were constitutionally acceptable, because they went to the students, not to their nonpublic schools. Further, the Court pointed out that the program withstood constitutional scrutiny insofar as ownership of the textbooks remained with the commonwealth.

Central to the analysis of the application of both Pennsylvania statutes was the three-part test established in *Lemon v. Kurtzman* (1971), which requires governmental action to have a secular legislative purpose and a principal or primary effect that neither advances nor inhibits religion; the action also must not result in excessive entanglement between religion and the government.

In applying this test, the Court concluded that Act 194, and its auxiliary services provision, violated *Lemon's* excessive entanglement prong. More specifically, insofar as the services were to be provided by public employees in the setting of nonpublic schools, the Court was concerned about the possible advancement of religion using public resources. The Court thus determined that the continued surveillance necessary to ensure that the teachers did not further the religious mission of religiously affiliated nonpublic schools violated the Establishment Clause.

Turning to Act 194 and the loan of instructional materials, the Court acknowledged that it resulted in "massive aid provided [to] the church-related nonpublic schools" (p. 635). In finding this act unconstitutional, the Court invalidated provisions that allowed the commonwealth to loan periodicals, films, recordings, and laboratory equipment along with equipment for recording and projecting to nonpublic schools. Although the Court conceded that the aid was secular in purpose, the aid had the primary effect of advancing religion, because it was largely provided on site in religiously affiliated nonpublic schools. In addition, the Court thought that the great amount of aid sent to educational environments where religious instruction was so omnipresent meant that it would have inevitably been used to further the religious missions of the schools in violation of the Establishment Clause.

In *Mitchell v. Helms* (2000), the Supreme Court partially invalidated *Meek*. Holding that governmental funds utilized for the purchase of instructional and educational materials in sectarian schools did not violate the Establishment Clause, the court admitted that, in that respect, *Meek* was no longer good law. However, insofar as *Helms* was a plurality decision, the status of *Meek* and similar loan programs for nonpublic schools is in some doubt.

Mark Littleton

See also Agostini v. Felton; Board of Education v. Allen; Child Benefit Test; Lemon v. Kurtzman; Mitchell v. Helms; Nonpublic Schools; State Aid and the Establishment Clause; Wolman v. Walter; Zobrest v. Catalina Foothills School District

Legal Citations

Board of Education of Central School District No. 1 v. Allen, 392 U.S. 236 (1968).
Lemon v. Kurtzman, 403 U.S. 602 (1971).
Meek v. Pittenger, 421 U.S. 349 (1975).
Mitchell v. Helms, 530 U.S. 793 (2000). reh'g denied, 530 U.S. 1296 (2000), *on remand sub nom. Helms v. Picard,* 229 F.3d 467 (5th Cir. 2000).

MENDEZ V. WESTMINSTER SCHOOL DISTRICT

Called the *Brown v. Board of Education of Topeka* (1954) for Mexican Americans and other Latinos in California, *Mendez v. Westminster School District* (1947) stands out as the case that ended legally sanctioned segregation for Mexican American students. *Mendez* was a test case in which social science data were introduced as evidence showing how Mexican American children developed an inferiority complex caused by racial segregation in schools. At the same time, *Mendez* is additionally noteworthy because it helped to pave the way for the use of a similar line of reasoning in *Brown*.

In a touch of irony, the then-governor of California and later chief justice of the U.S. Supreme Court who authored the unanimous opinion in *Brown*, Earl Warren, took *Mendez* and used it to push laws through the legislature repealing school segregation for Asian and Native American school children.

Facts of the Case

Mexicans lived in California before the Gold Rush days of the mid-19th century. However, the problem of segregation did not arise until 1910, when large numbers of Mexicans began appearing to work in the citrus groves. By 1920, the Mexican population in California had tripled. To the extent that the burgeoning Mexican population created great anxiety among the Anglo communities, social segregation practices soon began appearing that prohibited Mexicans from sitting with Whites in movie theaters and swimming with them in pools. These practices also led to the establishment of segregated housing patterns.

In Orange County, the center of a large citrus industry, Gonzalo Mendez and his wife, Felicitas, who was from Puerto Rico, formed a group to battle against school segregation based on race. In 1945, the plaintiffs filed suit in the federal trial court in Southern California against four school districts (Westminster, Santa Ana, Garden Grove, and El Modena), seeking an injunction that would end racial segregation of the schools.

The Mexican American parents turned to the courts in their attempt to end racial segregation, because their petitions to the boards of education and their superintendents received muted responses. The prevailing belief among educational officials was that the Mexican American children were dirty, unkempt, and not as intelligent as the White students. The "proof" was offered in the familiar IQ test data, which showed that Mexicans were intellectually inferior to Whites. Insofar as IQ scores were considered genetic and not mutable, this difference fueled resistance by White educators to integrating Mexican children in the schools.

The Court's Rulings

At trial, when the school superintendents testified, they portrayed Mexican children as decidedly inferior because of their poor personal hygiene and their language deficits. However, the attorney for the Mendez group fought back by calling in social scientists as expert witnesses who put the question of the need for separate schools clearly in the court's view.

The judge in the trial court took a year to render a judgment. The trial court was then of the opinion that racial segregation was not only unjustifiable under the Constitution of the State of California but was also a clear violation of the Equal Protection Clause of the Fourteenth Amendment. On further review, the Ninth Circuit affirmed in favor of the plaintiffs.

In its analysis, the Ninth Circuit began by pointing out that the trial court properly assumed jurisdiction in Mendez. The court next pointed out that the acts of officials in the state department of education were under the color of state law, meaning that they behaved as if they had the apparent authority to do as they did. The court reasoned that when officials placed children of Mexican descent in segregated schools against their wills, they violated both state law and the Equal Protection Clause, because doing so deprived them of equal protection and of liberty and property without due process of the laws.

Fenwick W. English

See also *Brown v. Board of Education of Topeka; Brown v. Board of Education of Topeka* and Equal Educational Opportunities; Equal Protection Analysis; Fourteenth Amendment; Social Sciences and the Law

Further Readings

Stewart, A. (2003). *Mendez v. Westminster.* The right to an equal education, the responsibility of the state to promote California History Day. Los Angeles, CA: Constitutional Rights Foundation.

Mendez v. Westminster: A look at our Latino heritage. (n.d.) Available from http://www.mendezvwestminster.com

Legal Citations

Brown v. Board of Education of Topeka I, 347 U.S. 483 (1954).

Brown v. Board of Education of Topeka II, 349 U.S. 294 (1955).

Mendez v. Westminster School District of Orange County, 64 F. Supp. 544 (D.C. Cal. 1946), *aff'd,* 161 F.2d 117 (9th Cir. 1947).

MERITOR SAVINGS BANK V. VINSON

Meritor Savings Bank v. Vinson (1986) was the first case wherein the U.S. Supreme Court addressed sexual harassment in the workplace under Title VII. Although *Meritor* did not occur in a school context, it should be of interest to educators at all levels, because the Court established criteria for judging claims that relate to a hostile work environment.

Facts of the Case

Michelle Vinson began working for Meritor Savings Bank in 1974 as a teller-trainee. Her immediate supervisor, Sidney Taylor, was a vice president of the bank. Over the next four years, Vinson was promoted to teller, head teller, and then assistant branch manager. It was undisputed that her promotions were based on merit alone. In 1978, Vinson's employment was terminated for excessive use of sick leave. Vinson then filed suit under Title VII against Taylor and the bank, alleging that she was subject to sexual harassment during her tenure in the job.

At trial, Vinson alleged that she had had sexual intercourse with Taylor on multiple occasions, out of fear of losing her job, and that he fondled her and made suggestive remarks to her any number of times. Taylor denied the allegations in their entirety and argued that Vinson's accusations arose from a business-related dispute. The bank also denied Vinson's allegations while specifically avowing that officials were unaware of Taylor's behavior and that if he acted as Vinson alleged, he did so of his own volition.

The federal trial court for the District of Columbia held that Vinson was not the victim of sexual harassment, because the sexual relationship, if it existed, was voluntary. The District of Columbia Circuit reversed in favor of Vinson on the basis that if Taylor made Vinson's toleration of sexual harassment a condition of her employment, the voluntary nature of the sexual relationship was irrelevant. The court also recognized that there were two categories of actionable sexual harassment under Title VII: harassment that conditions employment benefits on sexual favors (quid pro quo sexual harassment) and harassment that, while not affecting economic benefits, creates a hostile or offensive working environment (hostile work environment harassment). Applying agency principles, the court decided that the bank was absolutely liable for sexual harassment arising from the actions of its supervisor, regardless of whether officials knew or should have known about the harassment.

The Court's Ruling

On further review, the Supreme Court, in an opinion by Justice Rehnquist, affirmed that allegations of sexual harassment under Title VII may include hostile work environment claims and are not limited to economic benefits. The Court thus decided that a claim of "hostile work environment" sex discrimination is actionable under Title VII. At the heart of its analysis, the Supreme Court noted that there are five elements in claims of sex discrimination based on the existence of a hostile work environment, an offense that is ordinarily established by a series of incidents. The criteria can also apply in cases of quid pro quo harassment.

The Court noted that the first element in hostile work environment sex discrimination claims is that plaintiffs must belong to a protected category. Insofar as most suits are filed by women, the Court indicated that this element is satisfied when women file claims. Second, the Court explained that plaintiffs must have been subjected to unwelcome sexual advances. The Court added that the correct inquiry into sexual harassment claims is not based on whether plaintiffs' participation was voluntary but whether it was unwelcome. To this end, the justices were thus satisfied that the trial court had not erred in allowing evidence about Vinson's sexually provocative dress and speech, because such evidence could prove useful in evaluating whether the sexual behaviors at the center of the dispute were welcome or unwelcome.

Third, the Supreme Court indicated that the harassment must have been based on sex. Fourth, the Court was of the opinion that the harassment must have affected a term, condition, or privilege of employment to such a degree that it created a hostile work environment. In other words, the treatment must have been so pervasive as to alter working conditions to the point that, under the totality of the circumstances, it seriously affects plaintiffs' psychological well-being. The fifth element that the Court identified was that employers knew or should have known of the harassment but failed to take prompt remedial action to resolve situations.

Even though the Supreme Court set the standards for evaluating whether hostile work environment harassment occurred, it stopped short of definitely imposing liability on the bank. Insofar as it rejected the appellate panel's disregard for the general principles of agency in imposing absolute liability on the bank for the acts of one of its supervisors, the Court remanded this part of the dispute for further consideration

David L. Dagley

See also Hostile Work Environment; *Robinson v. Jacksonville Shipyards;* Sexual Harassment, Quid Pro Quo; Title VII

Legal Citations

Robinson v. Jacksonville Shipyards, 760 F. Supp. 1486 (M.D. Fla. 1991).
Meritor Savings Bank v. Vinson, 477 U.S. 57 (1986).

MEXICAN AMERICAN LEGAL DEFENSE AND EDUCATIONAL FUND (MALDEF)

The Mexican American Legal Defense and Educational Fund (MALDEF) was incorporated in Texas in 1968. MALDEF was modeled after the National Association for the Advancement of Colored People, Legal Defense Fund (NAACP/LDF) as a civil rights organization to protect the rights of Mexican Americans using the judicial system. MALDEF has evolved from a grassroots first-generation Mexican American legal organization to a diverse, more corporate law firm protecting the rights of all Latino groups. MALDEF's civil rights legal history is grounded in the protection of voting rights, educational rights, employment protections related to national origin and citizenship status, language issues, and hate crimes. MALDEF'S mission is to foster sound public policies, laws, and programs to safeguard the civil rights of all Latinos living in the United States. This entry summarizes its history and achievements.

Background

MALDEF was incorporated by a group of attorneys committed to protecting the civil rights of an emerging, nationally significant population. The early leaders in MALDEF were later appointed by governors and presidents to more globally serve the United States. Among these were James De Anda, who was appointed to serve as a federal judge in the Southern District of Texas; Pete Tijerina, who served in the Texas legislature; Mario Obledo, who was appointed secretary of health and welfare in California; Dan Sosa, who later served as a justice on the Supreme Court of New Mexico; Carlos Cadena, who later became an appellate court judge in Texas; Gregory Luna, who served in the Texas senate; and Alex Armendariz, who became an immigration judge in El Paso. MALDEF's former executive director and its general counsels transitioned into private practice and served on prominent private corporate boards. MALDEF has become a national organization that provides opportunities for service-oriented lawyers to protect the civil rights of its constituents while distinguishing themselves as leaders.

MALDEF was incorporated in Texas but expanded throughout the United States, where significant numbers of Latinos have emerged. Originally headquartered in San Antonio, Texas, the organization expanded to include offices in Los Angeles (now the national headquarters), Chicago, Atlanta, and Washington, D.C. MALDEF operates on a substantial annual budget that is supported by private national fundraising efforts and attorney's fees. Its emerging corporate image is that of a self-sufficient organization that engages in responsible fundraising and meets its management goals. The organization has development efforts to provide ongoing financial and public support.

Original MALDEF litigation focused on education, employment, and police brutality cases of the 1960s and the 1970s. Litigation became more focused under the leadership of Mario Obledo, who targeted Supreme Court cases by filing friend-of-the-court briefs.

School-Related Litigation

The only U.S. Supreme Court case that addresses school finance, *San Antonio Independent School District v. Rodriguez* (1973) directly affected the legal strategy that MALDEF would later use in school finance litigation. Although it was not a MALDEF case, *Rodriguez* was based on the legal theory that school finance was a Fourteenth Amendment equal access issue. However, the Supreme Court ruled that education is not a fundamental right under the federal Constitution. Using *Rodriguez,* the MALDEF legal staff refocused school finance litigation strategies using state constitutions and state courts to file equity finance cases in Texas and other states.

In 1989, MALDEF won a major school finance equity case when the Supreme Court of Texas ruled that because the state's public school financing structure was unconstitutional, the legislature had to formulate an equitable school finance plan. After an intermediate appellate court in Texas reversed in favor of the state, the plaintiffs sought further review. On July 5, 1989, the Supreme Court of Texas, in a unanimous opinion in *Edgewood Independent School District v. Kirby,* reinstated the trial court's opinion, thereby ordering the legislature to implement an equitable school finance system by the start of the 1990–1991 school year. Like a Russian novel, the *Edgewood* litigation continued until May 28, 1998, when the Texas legislature enacted a finance plan that offered property-rich school districts one of five voluntary options to redistribute wealth using a wealth equalization formula.

Rights to an education and educational opportunities are a major litigation area for MALDEF. In *Plyler v. Doe* (1982), the Supreme Court decided that an education statute from Texas violated the Equal Protection Clause of the Fourteenth Amendment; this statute withheld state funds for the education of children who were not "legally admitted" into the United States and authorized local school boards to refuse to enroll these students. *Plyler* confirmed that the Equal Protection Clause applies to all, regardless of whether they are citizens who are subject to the laws of the United States. At the heart of its rationale, the Court acknowledged that children should not have been denied the right to education based on the status of their parents. MALDEF has also litigated cases that prevent school systems from engaging in discrimination in public elementary and secondary education.

As the number of Latino students increases in American public schools, issues of educational equality, adequacy, and barriers to fair and equal education opportunities will continue to be a challenge for MALDEF. There are 41 million Latinos in the United States; they compose 20% of the K–12 student enrollment, include

5.5 million English Language Learning students (ELL), and compose 33% of U.S. children under the age of 18. These numbers suggest a drastic change in the American population that calls for transitional support and protection of the civil rights of a class of people.

Other Actions

Voter rights and participation are two areas in which MALDEF has been involved since 1970. MALDEF joined forces with the Southwest Voter Registration Education Project to litigate voting inequities. The two organizations filed 88 suits and successfully lobbied to ensure that the 1975 extension of the Voting Rights Act of 1965 included Spanish-surnamed citizens in the Southwest. In November 2006, MALDEF defended the voting rights of Latinos in Orange County, California; Tucson, Arizona; and Texas. In an Orange County case, a legislative candidate mailed a letter to 14,000 registered Spanish-surnamed voters. The letter, which was written in Spanish, falsely stated that immigrants were not allowed to vote and that there was no benefit to voting in American elections. While eligible naturalized immigrants may freely participate in American elections, the real intent of the letter was to intimidate Latino voters. MALDEF contacted the attorney general providing notification of the voter intimidation effort and instigated an investigation by the U.S. Civil Rights Division.

In another 2006 U.S. civil rights incident, MALDEF witnessed anti-immigrant activists aggressively intimidating Latino voters at the election polls, pushing a video camera in front of approaching Latino voters and requesting personal information. As it does with most American civil rights incidents, MALDEF refers these incidents to the United States Attorney and the U.S. Office for Civil Rights. In its litigation, MALDEF works cooperatively with organizations such as the NAACP, the ACLU, and the League of United Latin American Citizens (LULAC). In 2006, LULAC and MALDEF worked cooperatively in *League of United Latin American Citizens v. Perry* as Nina Perales, a MALDEF attorney, successfully argued before the Supreme Court that the redistricting plan from Texas amounted to a vote dilution plan in violation of the Voting Rights Act. In addition to these voting rights cases, MALDEF has argued school board and other redistricting claims throughout the United States. In fact, MALDEF attorneys have argued five cases before the Supreme Court.

Augustina H. Reyes

See also Equal Protection Analysis; National Association for the Advancement of Colored People; *Plyler v. Doe; San Antonio Independent School District v. Rodriguez;* U.S. Supreme Court Cases in Education

Further Readings

Casey, T. M. (2000). *Research guide to the records of MALDEF Mexican American Legal Defense and Education Fund (1968–1983).* Retrieved January 14, 2008, from http://library.stanford.edu/depts/spc/guides/m673.html

Olivas, M. (2005). *Plyler v. Doe,* the education of undocumented children, and the polity. In D. Martin & P. Schuck (Eds.), *Immigration stories.* New York: Foundation Press.

Reyes, A. H. (2008, in press). The right to an education for homeless students: The children of Katrina and immigration. *The Bilingual Review/La Revista Bilingue.* Arizona State University.

Legal Citations

Edgewood Independent School District v. Kirby, 917 S.W.2d 717 (Tex. 1989).

League of United Latin American Citizens v. Perry, 126 U.S. 2594 (2006).

Plyler v. Doe, 457 U.S. 202 (1982).

San Antonio Independent School District v. Rodriguez, 411 U.S. 1 (1973).

Meyer v. Nebraska

Meyer v. Nebraska (full title *Meyer v. State of Nebraska*) (1923) was the first of three Supreme Court cases, the other two being *Pierce v. Society of Sisters of the Holy Names of Jesus and Mary* (1925) and *Wisconsin v. Yoder* (1972), that shaped the right of parents, under the Fourteenth Amendment Liberty Clause, to direct the education of their children. In its first application of the Fourteenth Amendment's Liberty Clause to education, the Court ruled in *Meyer* that the state exceeded its power in an unreasonable law dictating both to a teacher and to students' parents the language that must be used in instruction.

Facts of the Case

Meyer involved the constitutionality of a post–World War I statute that the legislature of Nebraska enacted prohibiting instruction in any language other than English to any student who had not passed the eighth grade. This prohibition applied to all private, denominational, parochial, and public schools in the state. Any teacher who violated this statute could be charged with a misdemeanor and, if convicted, fined from $25 to $100 and confined in the county jail for up to 30 days.

Meyer, a teacher in a Nebraska parochial school, was charged and convicted under the statute for teaching reading in the German language to a 10-year-old student who had not yet completed the eighth grade. The Supreme Court of Nebraska upheld Meyer's conviction, determining that the statute under which he was convicted was a valid exercise of state police power. The court affirmed as reasonable the statute's purpose of requiring that "the English language should become the mother tongue of all children reared in this state." By seeking to prevent foreigners who had taken residence in this country from rearing and educating their children in the language of their native land, the court said, the state was trying to prevent the harmful effect that children taught in their native language might be inculcated in "ideas and sentiments foreign to the best interests of this country" (pp. 397–398).

The Court's Ruling

The U.S. Supreme Court granted certiorari and reversed Meyer's criminal conviction. In effect, the Court found two separate but related liberty clause claims, that of Meyer to practice his occupation of teaching and that of the parents to engage Meyer as the teacher for their children. While the Court recognized that a state's police power includes the physical, mental, and moral improvement of its citizens, it observed that protection under the U.S. Constitution extends to those who speak other languages as well as to those born with English as their native tongue. Although the Court acknowledged that the State of Nebraska framed its concern for a homogeneous people by a post–World War I aversion "toward every character of truculent adversaries" (p. 402), it nonetheless held that the state's chosen statutory means to accomplish its purpose, infringing on the Liberty

Clause rights of the teacher and the parents, exceeded its police power.

The Supreme Court later cited *Meyer* as a precedent in *Pierce v. Society of Sisters of the Holy Names of Jesus and Mary* and *Wisconsin v. Yoder* for its recognition of the Liberty Clause right of parents to direct their children's education. However, the Court also quoted *Meyer* for its statement regarding the Tenth Amendment's implied power of states to regulate education. In *Meyer,* the Court expressed the view in dictum that

> the power of the state to compel attendance at some school and to make reasonable regulations for all schools, including a requirement that they shall give instructions in English, is not questioned. Nor has challenge been made of the state's power to prescribe a curriculum for institutions which it supports. (p. 402)

In post–*Wisconsin v. Yoder* litigation, states sought to impose the same curricular and teacher qualification regulations on nonpublic schools that applied to their public school counterparts, thereby compelling state and federal courts to consider whether state regulations that satisfied the *Meyer* reasonableness standard could counter parent and private school liberty and free exercise claims. The results of the litigation varied, with some courts thinking that the reasonableness standard was sufficient to offset parental and school constitutional claims, while others added that states needed to demonstrate a higher compelling interest against these claims. By the end of the 20th century, though, most states had resolved the conflict by exempting nonpublic schools from many of the more onerous regulations at issue.

Ralph D. Mawdsley

See also Fourteenth Amendment; Nonpublic schools; Parental Rights; *Pierce v. Society of Sisters of the Holy Names of Jesus and Mary; Wisconsin v. Yoder*

Further Readings

Mawdsley, R. (2003). The changing face of parents' rights. *Brigham Young University Education and Law Journal, 165.*

Mawdsley, R. (2006). *Legal problems of religious and private schools.* Dayton: OH: Education Law Association.

Legal Citations

Meyer v. State of Nebraska, 187 N.W. 100 (Neb. 1922), 262 U.S. 390 (1923).

Pierce v. Society of Sisters of the Holy Names of Jesus and Mary, 268 U.S. 510 (1925).

Wisconsin v. Yoder, 406 U.S. 205 (1972).

Meyer v. Nebraska (Excerpts)

In Meyer v. Nebraska, *the Supreme Court invalidated a law against teaching a foreign language to students who had not yet reached the ninth grade on the grounds that it limited the rights of modern language teachers to teach, students to learn, and parents to direct the education of their children.*

Supreme Court of the United States.

MEYER

v.

STATE OF NEBRASKA.

262 U.S. 390

Argued Feb. 23, 1923.

Decided June 4, 1923.

Mr. Justice McREYNOLDS delivered the opinion of the Court.

Plaintiff in error was tried and convicted in the district court for Hamilton county, Nebraska, under an information which charged that on May 25, 1920, while an instructor in Zion Parochial School he unlawfully taught the subject of reading in the German language to Raymond Parpart, a child of 10 years, who had not attained and successfully passed the eighth grade. The information is based upon 'An act relating to the teaching of foreign languages in the state of Nebraska,' approved April 9, 1919. . . .

The Supreme Court of the state affirmed the judgment of conviction. It declared the offense charged and established was 'the direct and intentional teaching of the German language as a distinct subject to a child who had not passed the eighth grade,' in the parochial school maintained by Zion Evangelical Lutheran Congregation, a collection of Biblical stories being used therefore. And it held that the statute forbidding this did not conflict with the Fourteenth Amendment, but was a valid exercise of the police power. The following excerpts from the opinion sufficiently indicate the reasons advanced to support the conclusion: 'The salutary purpose of the statute is clear. The Legislature had seen the baneful effects of permitting foreigners, who had taken residence in this country, to rear and educate their children in the language of their native land. The result of that condition was found to be inimical to our own safety. To allow the children of foreigners, who had emigrated here, to be taught from early childhood the language of the country of their parents was to rear them with that language as their mother tongue. It was to educate them so that they must always think in that language, and, as a consequence, naturally inculcate in them the ideas and sentiments foreign to the best interests of this country. The statute, therefore, was intended not only to require that the education of all children be conducted in the English language, but that, until they had grown into that language and until it had become a part of them, they should not in the schools be taught any other language. The obvious purpose of this statute was that the English language should be and become the mother tongue of all children reared in this state. The enactment of such a statute comes reasonably within the police power of the state.

. . . .

The problem for our determination is whether the statute as construed and applied unreasonably infringes the liberty guaranteed to the plaintiff in error by the Fourteenth Amendment: 'No state . . . shall deprive any person of life, liberty or property without due process of law.'

While this court has not attempted to define with exactness the liberty thus guaranteed, the term has received much consideration and some of the included things have been definitely stated. Without doubt, it denotes not merely freedom from bodily restraint but also the right of the individual to contract, to engage in any of the common occupations of life, to acquire useful knowledge, to marry, establish a home and bring up children, to worship God according to the dictates of his own conscience, and generally to enjoy those privileges long recognized at common law as essential to the orderly pursuit of happiness by free men. The established

doctrine is that this liberty may not be interfered with, under the guise of protecting the public interest, by legislative action which is arbitrary or without reasonable relation to some purpose within the competency of the state to effect. Determination by the Legislature of what constitutes proper exercise of police power is not final or conclusive but is subject to supervision by the courts.

The American people have always regarded education and acquisition of knowledge as matters of supreme importance which should be diligently promoted. The Ordinance of 1787 declares: 'Religion, morality and knowledge being necessary to good government and the happiness of mankind, schools and the means of education shall forever be encouraged.'

Corresponding to the right of control, it is the natural duty of the parent to give his children education suitable to their station in life; and nearly all the states, including Nebraska, enforce this obligation by compulsory laws.

Practically, education of the young is only possible in schools conducted by especially qualified persons who devote themselves thereto. The calling always has been regarded as useful and honorable, essential, indeed, to the public welfare. Mere knowledge of the German language cannot reasonably be regarded as harmful. Heretofore it has been commonly looked upon as helpful and desirable. Plaintiff in error taught this language in school as part of his occupation. His right thus to teach and the right of parents to engage him so to instruct their children, we think, are within the liberty of the amendment.

The challenged statute forbids the teaching in school of any subject except in English; also the teaching of any other language until the pupil has attained and successfully passed the eighth grade, which is not usually accomplished before the age of twelve. The Supreme Court of the state has held that 'the so-called ancient or dead languages' are not 'within the spirit or the purpose of the act.' Latin, Greek, Hebrew are not proscribed; but German, French, Spanish, Italian, and every other alien speech are within the ban. Evidently the Legislature has attempted materially to interfere with the calling of modern language teachers, with the opportunities of pupils to acquire knowledge, and with the power of parents to control the education of their own.

It is said the purpose of the legislation was to promote civic development by inhibiting training and education of the immature in foreign tongues and ideals before they could learn English and acquire American ideals, and 'that the English language should be and become the mother tongue of all children reared in this state.' It is also affirmed that the foreign born population is very large, that certain communities commonly use foreign words, follow foreign leaders, move in a foreign atmosphere, and that the children are thereby hindered from becoming citizens of the most useful type and the public safety is imperiled.

That the state may do much, go very far, indeed, in order to improve the quality of its citizens, physically, mentally and morally, is clear; but the individual has certain fundamental rights which must be respected. The protection of the Constitution extends to all, to those who speak other languages as well as to those born with English on the tongue. Perhaps it would be highly advantageous if all had ready understanding of our ordinary speech, but this cannot be coerced by methods which conflict with the Constitution—a desirable end cannot be promoted by prohibited means.

. . . .

The desire of the Legislature to foster a homogeneous people with American ideals prepared readily to understand current discussions of civic matters is easy to appreciate. Unfortunate experiences during the late war and aversion toward every character of truculent adversaries were certainly enough to quicken that aspiration. But the means adopted, we think, exceed the limitations upon the power of the state and conflict with rights assured to plaintiff in error. The interference is plain enough and no adequate reason therefor in time of peace and domestic tranquility has been shown.

The power of the state to compel attendance at some school and to make reasonable regulations for all schools, including a requirement that they shall give instructions in English, is not questioned. Nor has challenge been made of the state's power to prescribe a curriculum for institutions which it supports. Those matters are not within the present controversy. Our concern is with the prohibition approved by the Supreme Court. *Adams v. Tanner* pointed out that mere abuse incident to an occupation ordinarily useful is not enough to justify its abolition, although regulation may be entirely proper. No emergency has arisen which renders knowledge by a child of some language other than English so clearly harmful as to justify its inhibition with the consequent infringement of rights long freely enjoyed. We are constrained to conclude that the statute as applied is arbitrary and without reasonable relation to any end within the competency of the state.

As the statute undertakes to interfere only with teaching which involves a modern language, leaving complete freedom as to other matters, there seems no adequate foundation for the suggestion that the purpose was to protect the child's health by limiting his mental activities. It is well known that proficiency in a foreign language seldom comes to one not instructed at an early age, and experience shows that this is not injurious to the health, morals or understanding of the ordinary child.

The judgment of the court below must be reversed and the cause remanded for further proceedings not inconsistent with this opinion.

Reversed.

Citation: *Meyer v. State of Nebraska*, 187 N.W. 100 (Neb. 1922), 262 U.S. 390 (1923).

MILLIKEN V. BRADLEY

At issue in *Milliken v. Bradley, I, II* (1974, 1977) was the implementation of school desegregation plans for the city of Detroit. The significance of the U.S. Supreme Court's rulings in *Milliken I* and *II* was that the plans involved a school system that was seeking to remedy an educational system that operated under de jure, as opposed to de facto, segregation, the usual condition in northern cities.

Background

School desegregation has been the subject of judicial scrutiny for over a century. The challenge of maintaining a diverse student body within each school building is complicated by various legal, social, political, and educational contexts. In *Brown v. Board of Education of Topeka* (1954), the Court revisited the previously held separate-but-equal doctrine, finding that the separation of children by race was a deliberate violation of the Fourteenth Amendment to the U.S. Constitution. While *Brown* abolished laws requiring or permitting segregated schools, it did not address de facto segregation until almost 20 years later in *Keyes v. School District No. 1, Denver, Colorado* (1973). Moreover, school desegregation was not uniformly implemented following the decision. Attempts to implement the promises of *Brown* created controversy in educational circles.

In light of *Brown*, two decades of civil rights legislation and judicial opinions ensued in an attempt to desegregate schools. The expansion of desegregation rights ended with the Supreme Court's decision in *Milliken I*. In *Milliken I*, the school board in Detroit sought to remedy official acts of racial discrimination that were committed by both local officials and the state. The local board's violations included the improper use of attendance zones, racially based transportation of school children, and improper use of grade structures. Michigan, through various agencies, acted directly to maintain the pattern of segregation in the Detroit schools. As a means of remedy, the board in Detroit sought to integrate students in the largely minority city schools with those in the surrounding metropolitan suburban schools by utilizing an interdistrict city-suburban desegregation remedy.

The Milliken I Ruling

In *Milliken I*, the first major defeat for proponents of desegregation, the Supreme Court ruled that surrounding suburban districts could not be ordered to help desegregate the city's schools unless plaintiffs could prove that the suburban systems were involved in illegally segregating city schools in the first place. The Court reasoned that it was improper to impose a multidistrict remedy for an individual board's de jure segregation in the absence of a finding that the other systems included in the interdistrict desegregation plan either failed to operate unitary school systems or committed acts that affected segregation within the other districts.

Reversing in favor of the suburban school systems in *Milliken I*, the Supreme Court determined that a federal trial court and the Sixth Circuit erred in upholding the desegregation plan insofar as there was no evidence that district boundary lines were established with the purpose of fostering racial segregation. The Court established that the plaintiffs failed to prove that the State of Michigan acted with a specific intent to segregate or that these actions caused the segregation before the judiciary could have applied interdistrict remedies such as busing. The Court added that it was troubled by the fact that the neighboring suburban school boards were not afforded any meaningful opportunities to be included in the plan to present evidence or to be heard on the suitability of the multidistrict remedy or on the constitutional violations that may have been imposed on them as a result of the plan. The Court concluded that because there was no interdistrict violation, there could be no interdistrict remedy.

Justice Thurgood Marshall's dissent in *Milliken I* admonished the Court for perpetuating the very action that Brown sought to remedy. In this way, he lamented the prospect of White flight coupled with the rapidly increasing percentage of students of color in the Detroit system that would ensue as a result of the Court's decision.

Many subsequent Supreme Court cases have invoked *Milliken I*, including *Parents Involved in Community Schools v. Seattle School District No. 1* (2007), wherein a plurality rejected a race conscious admissions plan. The Court continuously reaffirms *Milliken I*'s judgment that racial imbalances alone are not unconstitutional in and of themselves even in metropolitan areas where desegregation cannot be achieved within existing school district boundaries. At the same time, the Court continues to stress the underlying premise presented in *Milliken I*: that local school boards, rather than the judiciary, are better suited to understand their own communities and have a better knowledge of what in practice will best meet the educational needs of their students. *Milliken I* ultimately has blocked lower courts from accepting interdistrict desegregation remedy plans absent a showing of intentional segregation practices.

The *Milliken II* Ruling

On remand from *Milliken I,* the trial court immediately ordered the Detroit school board to resubmit a desegregation plan that was limited to the Detroit school system. Along with proposing a student reassignment strategy that would have eliminated racially identifiable schools, the new plan included 13 remedial programs, called educational components, in the areas of reading, teacher in-service training, testing, and counseling. According to its revised plan, all costs for these additional programs were to be shared between the board in Detroit and the State of Michigan. However, the state filed objections to the board's plan, contending that the remedy should be limited to student reassignments for the purpose of achieving desegregation. State officials argued that the educational components were excessive.

In a measure of vindication following *Milliken I,* in *Milliken II,* the Supreme Court affirmed the orders of the trial court and Sixth Circuit that directed the State of Michigan to fund the additional educational programs that were designed to remedy the negative educational effects of imposed segregation. The Court observed that insofar as student reassignments did not automatically remedy the impact of prior educational isolation, public officials had to deal with the consequences of segregation through various measures.

In *Milliken II,* the Court advanced three holdings. First, the justices were of the opinion that the lower court appropriately approved the remedial educational plan. Second, the Court pointed out that consistent with the Eleventh Amendment, the State of Michigan had to pay one half of the costs of implementing the educational components of its order. Third, the Court was satisfied that the earlier judicial orders to remedy the segregative student assignments did not violate the Tenth Amendment.

Rachel Pereira

See also *Brown v. Board of Education of Topeka; Brown v. Board of Education of Topeka* and Equal Educational Opportunities; Civil Rights Movement; Dual and Unitary Systems; Federalism and the Tenth Amendment; Segregation, De Facto; Segregation, De Jure; White Flight

Further Readings

Orfield, G., & Eaton, S. (1996). *Dismantling desegregation: The quiet reversal of* Brown v. Board of Education. New York: New Press.

Legal Citations

Brown v. Board of Education of Topeka I, 347 U.S. 483 (1954).
Brown v. Board of Education of Topeka II, 349 U.S. 294 (1955).
Green v. County School Board of New Kent County, 391 U.S. 430 (1968).
Keyes v. School District No. 1, Denver, Colorado, 433 U.S. 267 (1977).
Milliken v. Bradley I, 418 U.S. 717 (1974).
Milliken v. Bradley II, 433 U.S. 267 (1977).
Parents Involved in Community Schools v. Seattle School District No. 1, 127 S. Ct. 2738 (2007).
Plessy v. Ferguson, 163 U.S. 537 (1896).

MILLS V. BOARD OF EDUCATION OF THE DISTRICT OF COLUMBIA

Mills v. Board of Education of District of Columbia (1972) was one of two important federal trial court rulings that helped to lay the foundation that eventually led to the passage of Section 504 of the Rehabilitation Act of 1973 and the Education for All Handicapped Children Act (EAHCA), now the Individuals with Disabilities Education Act (IDEA), laws that changed the face of American education. Prior to 1975 and the enactment of these laws, many schools did not offer special education for students with disabilities. As such, millions of students were denied appropriate services or excluded from public education entirely. The other case was *Pennsylvania Association of Retarded Children v. Commonwealth of Pennsylvania* (1971, 1972).

Facts of the Case

Mills was a class action suit that was brought on behalf of seven children and other similarly situated students who resided in the District of Columbia. The students in the plaintiff class had been identified as having behavioral problems or being mentally retarded, emotionally disturbed, and/or hyperactive. All of the students had been excluded from school or denied educational services that would have addressed the needs that arose from their identified disabilities. The parents and guardians of the students successfully filed suit, arguing that the failure of the school board in the District of Columbia to provide them with a public school education constituted a denial of their right to an education.

The Court's Ruling

In a painstaking decision, the federal district court in the District of Columbia first made clear that the deprivation suffered by the children clearly violated their right to a public school education under the laws of the District of Columbia. Quoting liberally from *Brown v. Board of Education of Topeka* (1954), the court likened the treatment of the plaintiff students to the segregation outlawed by the Supreme Court in *Brown.*

The court reasoned that because the children would have been entitled under the school code in the District of Columbia to attend free public schools, each child had a right to such an education. The court explained that the school board's failure to meet its mandate could not be excused by its argument that there were insufficient funds available to pay for the services that the children needed. Instead, the court was of the opinion that the board's duty to educate the children had to outweigh its interest in preserving its resources.

The court added that if there were not enough funds available to provide all of the needed programming, then the board had to do its best to apportion the monies in such a way as to ensure that no child was denied the opportunity to benefit from a public school education. In sum, the court pointed out that the inadequacies present in the school system, whether caused by insufficient funding or poor administration, could not be allowed to impact more heavily on students with disabilities. To this end, the court ordered the board to adopt a detailed remedial plan in order to ensure that the children received their right to equal protection under the law.

The court-ordered comprehensive remedial plan included many elements that eventually made their way into the EAHCA/IDEA. Among these provisions, the court order included a provision mandating a free public education for each child with a disability, documentation delineating the individual special education services that would be necessary for each child who was identified as having a disability, the development of due process procedures when students faced suspensions or expulsions from school, the creation of procedures that granted parents the right to challenge the system if they disagreed with any aspect of the placement of their children, and a requirement that children suspected of having disabilities be identified and evaluated.

Julie F. Mead

See also Disabled Persons, Rights of; *Pennsylvania Association for Retarded Children v. Commonwealth of Pennsylvania;* Rehabilitation Act of 1973, Section 504

Legal Citations

Individuals with Disabilities Education Act, 20 U.S.C. §§ 1400 *et seq.*
Mills v. Board of Education of District of Columbia, 348 F. Supp. 866 (D.D.C. 1972).
Pennsylvania Association for Retarded Children v. Commonwealth of Pennsylvania, 334 F. Supp 1257 (E.D. Pa. 1971), 343 F. Supp. 279 (E.D. Pa. 1972)
Rehabilitation Act of 1973, Section 504, 29 U.S.C. § 794(a).

MINERSVILLE SCHOOL DISTRICT V. GOBITIS

At issue in *Minersville School District v. Gobitis* (1940) was the constitutionality of a mandatory flag salute ceremony in school. A local board of education required that both students and teachers participate in a daily flag salute ceremony that included the Pledge of Allegiance and extended hand to salute the American flag. Two children who were Jehovah's Witnesses refused to salute the national flag based on their religious beliefs and were expelled. Insofar as Pennsylvania law made school attendance compulsory, the parents placed their children in a private school. The father then filed suit on behalf of his children and himself challenging the flag salute on the ground that it infringed on their religious beliefs in violation of the Fourteenth Amendment. After a federal trial court ruled in favor of the plaintiffs, and the Third Circuit affirmed, the school board and various officials appealed.

On further review, the U.S. Supreme Court reversed in favor of the defendants. In reviewing the case, the Court identified the issue as whether the requirement of participating in the ceremony by children, who refused to do so because of their religious convictions, violated the Due Process Clause of the Fourteenth Amendment. Insofar as the Court viewed the school board's action as that of the legislature, the justices analyzed the legislature's constitutional authority to mandate the flag salute ceremony. The Court was of the opinion that individual liberties are not absolute and that the flag salute ceremony promoted national unity, which was the basis for national security. To this end, the Court determined that the legislature had the right to select appropriate means to accomplish this goal.

The Supreme Court thus found that the mandatory flag salute ceremony, with expulsion as the penalty for students who refused to participate, did not violate the Due Process Clause of the Fourteenth Amendment. Explaining that the ceremony was a reasonable exercise of legislative power, the Court urged judicial restraint in matters of education policy, which the justices thought was outside of the purview of their consideration. Insofar as it did not want to become the school board for the country, the Court pointed out, other remedial processes remained open to individuals who wished to change the policy and the law.

As the Supreme Court noted in its analysis, *Gobitis* represented an issue of reconciling conflicting claims about liberty and authority. Yet, the holding in *Gobitis* was short lived, because three years later, in *West Virginia State Board of Education v. Barnette* (1943), the Court reconsidered its opinion and reached a different result. In *Barnette*, the Court decided that the Free Speech Clause of the First Amendment and the Fourteenth Amendment prohibited the government from compelling the flag salute and the Pledge of Allegiance. In so ruling, the Court clearly rejected the due process reasonableness test of *Gobitis* and viewed the Free Speech Clause, applicable by the Fourteenth Amendment, as a direct limitation on legislative action.

Deborah Curry

See also **Elk Grove Unified School District v. Newdow;** Fourteenth Amendment

Legal Citations

Elk Grove Unified School District v. Newdow, 542 U.S. 1 (2004).
Minersville School District v. Gobitis, 310 U.S. 586 (1940).
Newdow v. U.S. Congress, 328 F.3d 466 (9th Cir.) (2002).
West Virginia State Board of Education v. Barnette, 319 U.S. 624 (1943).

Minimum Competency Testing

Student competency testing, although often controversial, has become the centerpiece of school reform legislation. Testing policies are widely supported by the general population and are used to raise academic standards. Conceptually, tests are designed to promote better teaching and learning, increase student motivation, increase graduation rates, lead to a more productive workforce, and instill greater confidence in the public schools system. However, the research regarding the effectiveness of competency testing is mixed.

Legal analysis of public school competency tests began with *Debra P. v. Turlington* (1984), a case involving a 1978 Florida statute requiring students to pass a functional literacy test prior to obtaining high school diplomas. Plaintiffs challenged the law, alleging a disproportionate impact on Black students. Initially, the Fifth Circuit upheld an injunction for the students, because the law violated Title VI of the Civil Rights Act of 1964 "by perpetuating past discrimination against black students who had attended segregated schools for the first four years of their education" (p. 1407).

On remand to a federal trial court, the Eleventh Circuit (since the Fifth Circuit was split, Florida was part of the new Eleventh Circuit) considered the legality of the test. The court held that the competency testing program was a valid measure of the instructional program and provided adequate notice for the students to pass the test. Additionally, the court ruled that there was no link between the disproportionate number of Black students failing the test and a history or prior discrimination. The Eleventh Circuit court acknowledged the state's right to deny diplomas to failing students.

In a more recent decision, the State Board of Education of Louisiana implemented a requirement that all public school students pass an exit examination prior to receiving high school diplomas. In *Rankins v. State Board of Education* (1994), five students who failed the test filed suit claiming that their equal protection rights were violated, because private school students were not held to the same requirement. The court upheld the testing requirement on the basis that it was rationally related to the state's interest of ensuring minimum competency for students who were awarded diplomas.

Although there is substantial evidence that competency testing has a disproportionate effect on children who are of limited English proficiency, minority students, and those with disabilities, the courts have not directed states to abandon their use of the tests for these students. For students with disabilities, the courts generally have supported the use of examinations as a criterion for graduation as long as there are accommodations and modifications available.

In *GI Forum v. Texas Education Agency* (2000), a federal trial court in Texas was of the opinion that although minority students performed significantly worse on a state competency examination than nonminority students, the former were rapidly closing the achievement gap as measured by the test. Consequently, the court found that because minority students were not disadvantaged, the examination did not violate their due process rights, because it was not unfair. In upholding the test, the court noted that the examination met the requirements of curricular validity by measuring what it purported to measure. In sum, the court ruled in favor of the state educational agency, permitting the use of the exit examination as a valid requirement for obtaining a diploma.

Some authors suggest that the use of minimum competency tests will bring about the resegregation of the public schools. The first argument proposes that children from historically low socioeconomic backgrounds, typically minority students, are unfairly tested alongside students from more affluent backgrounds. *Debra P.* and *G.I. Forum* appear to dismiss this argument. The second argument holds that these same students will be placed in special remedial classes, which will, in essence, resegregate student populations. This second argument is yet to be used as a challenge in court.

As the backbone of educational accountability and the subsequent teaching and curricular reforms, policymakers have become enamored with competency testing programs. Performance on competency tests often determines whether students are promoted from one grade level to another or are awarded high school diplomas. The courts tend to support the policy of competency testing as long as the system provides for validity (measures what it purports to measure) and reliability (consistently measures what it purports to measure) and the students have the opportunity to learn the material to be tested.

Mark Littleton

See also *Debra P. v. Turlington;* Graduation Requirements; Testing, High-Stakes

Further Readings

McCall, J. (1999). Now pinch hitting for educational reform: Delaware's minimum competency test and the diploma sanction. *The Journal of Law and Commerce, 18,* 373–395.

O'Neill, P. (2001). Special education and high stakes testing for high school graduation: An analysis of current law and policy. *Journal of Law and Education, 30,* 185–222.

Legal Citations

Debra P. v. Turlington, 474 F. Supp. 244 (M.D. Fla. 1979), *aff'd in part, vacated in part,* 644 F.2d 397 (5th Cir. 1981), *reh'g denied,* 654 F.2d 1079 (5th Cir. [Fla.] Sep 04, 1981), *on remand,* 564 F. Supp. 177 (M.D. Fla. 1983), *aff'd,* 730 F.2d 1405 (11th Cir. 1984).

G.I. Forum v. Texas Education Agency, 87 F. Supp.2d 667 (W.D. Tex. 2000).

Rankins v. State Board of Education, 637 So. 2d 548 (La. Ct. App. 1994), *write denied,* 635 So. 2d 250 (La. 2004), *cert. denied,* 513 U.S. 871 (1994).

Mississippi University for Women v. Hogan

At issue in *Mississippi University for Women v. Hogan* (1982) was whether a state-supported nursing program could deny admission to a male applicant based on his sex. The Supreme Court found the school's policy unconstitutional and used its decision to develop the standards that it continues to apply in sex discrimination cases.

Facts of the Case

The Mississippi University for Women (MUW), from its inception in 1884, had limited its enrollment to women. In the early 1970s, MUW started a four-year baccalaureate nursing program with its own faculty and admission process. Joe Hogan, a registered nurse without a baccalaureate degree, applied to the School of Nursing. Even though Hogan was otherwise qualified, officials denied him admission solely due to his sex.

Hogan filed a suit claiming that the MUW policy violated the Equal Protection Clause of the Fourteenth Amendment. The U.S. Supreme Court ultimately agreed with Hogan, ruling that the gender-based policy was not substantially related to the state's significant interest in providing educational opportunities.

The Court's Ruling

In *Mississippi University for Women*, the Supreme Court noted that insofar as MUW's policy discriminated on the basis of sex, it was subject to scrutiny under the Equal Protection Clause. Over the years, the Court developed three tests to determine whether state policies are unconstitutional. Strict scrutiny, applied in cases involving fundamental rights such as those protected under the federal Constitution for suspect classes such as those composed of members of a certain race, is the most difficult test for a state to overcome, because it requires a compelling governmental interest that is narrowly tailored. Rational basis, on the other hand, requires a state only to demonstrate the presence of a rational relationship to a legitimate state interest; it is usually easy for states to meet this burden. A third test, intermediate scrutiny, is discussed below.

As the dispute made its way to court, a federal trial court in *Mississippi University for Women* applied the rational basis test in upholding the female-only admission policy. However, the Supreme Court reasoned that the proper test was not rational basis, but rather, the so-called intermediate scrutiny test. Intermediate scrutiny requires that a state show that a gender-based classification is substantially related to an important government objective. By using the intermediate test, the Court recognized there might be limited circumstances that would allow a state to treat men and women differently. The Court was of the opinion that the judiciary will attempt to look at gender-based classifications without resorting to stereotypes about the proper roles for men and women in society.

Utilizing the intermediate scrutiny test, the Court determined that the admission policy at MUW was unconstitutional. First, the Court found that the Equal Protection Clause prohibits any discrimination on the basis of sex, whether manifested in unequal treatment of men or women. Thus, to the Court, the fact Hogan was male was inconsequential. Second, the Court explained that a defending institution has the burden of demonstrating an "exceedingly persuasive justification" for the discrimination. The Court rejected Mississippi's argument that it was justified in admitting only women to compensate for discrimination against women. In rejecting this claim, the Court determined that this was not a persuasive justification, because women were not being discriminated against in the nursing profession, and the policy, in fact, perpetuated the stereotype that nursing was "women's work."

Third, the Court indicated that an institution must prove that the actions serve "important governmental objectives" and that the actions are "substantially related to the achievement of the goal." The Court observed that the record showed that males were allowed to attend and audit nursing classes but not allowed to take course work for credit. This fact, according to the Court, undermined MUW's argument because there was a lack of evidence that the presence of men in the classroom negatively impacted women.

In a more recent case, *U.S. v. Virginia* (1996), the Supreme Court considered whether a state military, all-male school unconstitutionally discriminated against women. Using the intermediate scrutiny test and reasoning similar to the analysis it applied in *Mississippi University for Women*, the Court declared the male-only admission policy violated the Equal Protection Clause.

Mississippi University for Women, along with more recent Court cases regarding male-only military schools, provides insight on gender discrimination. Even so, it is important to keep in mind that Title IX, the primary vehicle for combating gender-based discrimination, explicitly limits what types of educational institutions are allowed to have single-sex admission policies. Private undergraduate programs are generally exempt from Title IX's prohibition of single-sex admission policies as are religious institutions if they obtain waivers. For most institutions, Title IX provides more guidance regarding discrimination based on sex and gender equity.

Karen Miksch

See also Civil Rights Act of 1964; Equal Protection Analysis; Title IX and Sexual Harassment; *United States v. Virginia*

Legal Citations

Mississippi University for Women v. Hogan, 458 U.S. 718 (1982).

Title IX of the Educational Amendments of 1972, 20 U.S.C. § 1681.

United States v. Virginia, 518 U.S. 515 (1996).

MISSOURI V. JENKINS

Long-running litigation involving the Kansas City, Missouri, School District (KCMSD) made its way to the U.S. Supreme Court on three occasions. In 1989, the Court decided that the school board could be responsible for attorney fees. In 1990, the Court affirmed that the federal judiciary could require the board to levy property taxes that were sufficient to fund a desegregation remedy. However, in 1995, the Court decreed that lower federal courts exceeded their discretion in mandating a costly desegregation remedy that required the state to pay for salary increases for almost all school personnel and quality education programs.

The First Round

In 1977, the KCMSD, its school board, and the children of two school board members sued the state, surrounding suburban school systems, and various federal agencies, alleging that the defendants created and continued a system of racially segregated schools in the Kansas City area. A federal trial court realigned the parties, making the KCMSD a defendant, finding that the state and KCMSD were liable for operating a segregated school system. The plaintiffs had sought an order affecting the entire metropolitan area. However, the court limited its orders to the area within the borders of KCMSD while dismissing the surrounding school systems and federal agencies from the litigation.

In its first remedial order in 1985, a federal trial court directed officials to reduce class sizes and to expand expensive programs, such as full-day kindergarten, summer school, early childhood offerings, and tutoring programs to increase educational opportunities for all students in the KCMSD. In addition, the court ordered cash grants for schools and a return of all schools to an AAA rating, the highest state accreditation standard. These improvements cost over $220 million.

When the case first arrived before the Supreme Court, the justices held that the Eleventh Amendment did not prohibit the award of attorney fees and that they could include payments for the work of paralegals, clerks, and recent law school graduates (*Missouri v. Jenkins I,* 1989).

The Second Round

In another aspect of the case, in 1986, a federal trial court embarked on a plan to retain and attract nonminority students back to the KCMSD by creating world-class facilities and converting its secondary schools and half of its elementary schools into magnet schools with specialized programs. The court-ordered improvements in school facilities eventually cost over $540 million. The court noted that the substantial expenditures financed air-conditioned high schools with 15 computers in every classroom, a planetarium, radio and television studios with an editing and animation lab, a model United Nations wired to allow language translation, an art gallery, movie editing and screening rooms, vocational facilities, swimming pools, and many other facilities exceeding those available in other school districts.

A year later, in 1987, the trial court ordered the state to fund increased salaries for KCMSD personnel at a cost of over $200 million per year. In 1990, the Supreme Court approved the method used in paying for the expensive improvements in the KCMSD educational system in upholding an order that required the board to increase a school levy to pay for the costs of desegregation (*Missouri v. Jenkins II,* 1990).

The Third Round

The Supreme Court agreed to hear arguments in this case for a third time when the state contended that the trial court's order to fund salary increases for KCMSD employees and to continue to pay for remedial quality education programs exceeded its desegregation remedial authority. The Eighth Circuit affirmed the trial court's order, observing that the funding increases were necessary for making the schools attractive for the purposes of desegregation and to reverse "White flight" to the suburbs. Further, the Eighth Circuit affirmed the rejection of the state's request that the KCMSD be awarded partial unitary status, under *Freeman v. Pitts* (1992), with respect to the high-quality education programs. The importance of this aspect of the case is that it would have released the state from its obligations to fund the programs.

On further review, a closely divided Supreme Court, in a 5-to-4 judgment, reversed in favor of the state (*Missouri v. Jenkins, III*). In its analysis, the Supreme Court reviewed and reconstructed the methodology for measuring the remedial authority of federal trial courts in desegregation actions. For example, the Court pointed out that in *Swann v. Charlotte-Mecklenburg Board of Education* (1971), it recognized the power of federal trial courts to fashion remedies for segregation while cautioning against their attempting to achieve purposes beyond the scope of the wrongs or purposes that lay outside the power of school officials.

At the same time, the Supreme Court grounded its rationale in *Milliken v. Bradley I,* wherein it rejected a trial court's order calling for an interdistrict remedy to eliminate segregation of Detroit's schools as beyond its remedial power, because the nature of the harm was intradistrict. The Court recognized that in *Milliken I* it also rejected the notion that having schools with a majority of minority students was a means of measuring whether they were desegregated,

instead asserting that such an inquiry should begin with a measure of the proportions of minority students in individual schools as compared with the proportions of the races in the school district as a whole.

Further, the Court explained that in *Milliken v. Bradley II* (1977), it had addressed the limits of federal trial courts in the exercise of their remedial authority in desegregation actions. Moreover, it is also worth noting that in *Freeman v. Pitts* (1992), the Court provided another test to guide federal trial courts in ordering a partial withdrawal from federal oversight in desegregation actions.

Continuing on with its analysis, the Supreme Court viewed the trial court's order for salary supplements and expensive programs in KCMSD as an attempt to right an intradistrict wrong, the vestiges of prior de jure segregation within KCMSD, with an interdistrict remedy. Consequently, the Court reasoned that the orders approving the salary increases and requiring the state to continue funding the expensive educational programs were beyond the trial court's authority. The justices concluded by directing the federal trial court to use the precedent provided by *Freeman v. Pitts* (1992), namely that it could relinquish its control over a desegregation plan incrementally once it was satisfied that officials made a good faith commitment to comply with its order, in determining when to terminate judicial supervision.

David L. Dagley

See also *Freeman v. Pitts; Milliken v. Bradley; Swann v. Charlotte-Mecklenburg Board of Education;* Segregation, De Jure; White Flight

Legal Citations

Freeman v. Pitts, 503 U.S. 467 (1992), *on remand,* 979 F.2d 1472 (11th Cir. 1992), *on remand,* 942 F. Supp. 1449 (N.D. Ga. 1996), *aff'd,* 118 F.3d 727 (11th Cir. 1997).
Milliken v. Bradley I, 418 U.S. 717 (1974).
Milliken v. Bradley II, 433 U.S. 267 (1977).
Missouri v. Jenkins I, 491 U.S. 274 (1989).
Missouri v. Jenkins II, 495 U.S. 33 (1990), *subsequent appeal, Jenkins v. Missouri,* 949 F.2d 1052 (8th Cir. 1991).
Missouri v. Jenkins III, 515 U.S. 70 (1995); *appeal after remand, Jenkins v. Missouri,* 103 F.3d 731 (8th Cir. 1997).
Swann v. Charlotte-Mecklenburg Board of Education, 402 U.S. 1 (1971).

MITCHELL V. HELMS

Mitchell v. Helms (2000) stands out as the case in which the U.S. Supreme Court held that a federal program that loaned instructional materials and equipment to schools, including those that were religiously affiliated, was permissible under the Establishment Clause of the First Amendment of the U.S. Constitution. The program, known as Chapter 2 of the Education Consolidation and Improvement Act of 1981 (Chapter 2), provided a mechanism for local educational agencies, usually public school boards, to use federal monies to purchase secular, neutral, and nonideological materials and equipment and lend them to nonpublic schools. The amount of federal funds spent on the schools was based on the number of children enrolled in each school.

Facts of the Case

At issue in *Mitchell* was implementation of Chapter 2 in Jefferson Parish, Louisiana. During an average year in Jefferson Parish, about 30% of the federal Chapter 2 monies were allocated for nonpublic schools. Officials at the local educational agency (LEA), a public entity, used the funds to purchase library and media materials and instructional equipment, such as books; computers; computer software; slide, movie, and overhead projectors; maps; globes; and films that were then lent to the private schools. The nonpublic schools were selected for participation based on the applications they submitted to the LEA. The vast majority of the nonpublic schools that benefited from the program were religiously affiliated.

After a federal trial court upheld the constitutionality of Chapter 2, the Fifth Circuit reversed in favor of its opponents. On further review, a plurality of the Supreme Court upheld the statute as constitutional.

The Court's Ruling

In its analysis, the four-justice plurality in *Mitchell* focused on the effects prong of the *Lemon v. Kurtzman* (1971) test, the long-time standard in disputes over the parameters of permissible state aid to religiously affiliated schools and their students, as modified

by *Agostini v. Felton* (1997). The justices specifically considered whether the government assistance was neutral toward religion.

As the plurality explained, a court must answer two fundamental questions in evaluating whether governmental assistance is permissible under the Establishment Clause. The first question that the justices posed was whether the aid was offered to a broad range of groups or persons without regard to religion and, if so, whether it reached private institutions only as a result of genuine, independent private choices, so that it did not result in governmental indoctrination. The second question that the plurality identified was whether the criteria for allocating the aid were neutral and secular, so that they did not define recipients by reference to religion and thereby create financial incentives to undertake religious indoctrination.

The plurality in *Mitchell* found that Chapter 2 was constitutionally permissible for two reasons. First, the justices agreed that the program was constitutional, because all public and nonpublic schools were eligible to participate in it, while the amount of aid provided to individual schools was determined by the number of students enrolled in them. The plurality considered this to be factor that was controlled by the independent choices of parents and students, not state actors, such that any resulting religious indoctrination could not have been attributed to the government. Second, the plurality decided that the program was acceptable because it used neutral, secular eligibility criteria that neither favored nor disfavored religion. The plurality observed that this did not create a financial incentive to undertake religious indoctrination, because the aid was offered to a broad array of both public and private schools without regard to their religious affiliations.

Mitchell is significant for four reasons. First, it broadened the scope of permissible aid to religiously affiliated nonpublic schools by allowing governmental entities to purchase and loan instructional materials and equipment to those schools. Second, the plurality expressly reversed those parts of *Meek v. Pittenger* (1975) and *Wolman v. Walter* (1977) that were contrary to its opinion on the types of instructional materials and equipment that could be loaned to religiously affiliated nonpublic schools. However, because the *Mitchell* decision was made by a plurality, its impact in this regard is limited.

Third, *Mitchell* moved the Supreme Court closer to a formal neutrality test in light of the plurality's reliance on neutrality. This trend continued in *Zelman v. Simmons-Harris* (2002), wherein the Court applied the formal neutrality test to uphold a voucher program for poor students in Cleveland, Ohio. Finally, *Mitchell* rejected some factors that were significant in deciding earlier Establishment Clause cases. In particular, the justices noted that nonpublic schools could receive aid even if they were pervasively sectarian, thereby rejecting the distinction between direct and indirect aid under which direct aid to religious schools was prohibited but indirect aid was permitted.

Regina R. Umpstead

See also *Agostini v. Felton;* Establishment Clause; *Lemon v. Kurtzman; Meek v. Pittenger; Wolman v. Walter*

Legal Citations

Agostini v. Felton, 521 U.S. 203 (1997).
Chapter 2 of the Education Consolidation and Improvement Act of 1981, 20 U.S.C. §§ 7301 *et seq.*
Lemon v. Kurtzman, 403 U.S. 602 (1971).
Meek v. Pittenger, 421 U.S. 349 (1975).
Mitchell v. Helms, 530 U.S. 793 (2000) *reh'g denied,* 530 U.S. 1296 (2000), *on remand sub nom. Helms v. Picard,* 229 F.3d 467 (5th Cir. 2000).
Wolman v. Walter, 433 U.S. 229 (1977).
Zelman v. Simmons-Harris, 536 U.S. 639 (2002).

MONROE V. BOARD OF COMMISSIONERS

Monroe v. Board of Commissioners (1968) involved the adequacy of the city of Jackson, Tennessee's, plan to desegregate its public schools in the wake of *Brown v. Board of Education of Topeka. Monroe* is another one of the cases in which the Supreme Court reviewed the efforts of school boards, finding that it developed and administered a plan that allowed it to remain segregated. The Court remanded *Monroe* for modifications to create a unitary school system.

Facts of the Case

A state law from 1954 required racially segregated schools in Tennessee. The city had eight elementary schools, three junior high schools, and two senior high schools. Five elementary schools, two junior high schools, and one senior high school were for Whites. After *Brown,* the state adopted a pupil placement law. Basically, the law allowed current students to stay put and gave local school boards the authority to approve pupil placement and transfer requests. Under this plan, no White students enrolled in African American schools, and only seven African American students applied for enrollment in the White schools.

In 1962, the Sixth Circuit ruled that the placement plan was inadequate when it came to dismantling a segregated school system. After the plaintiffs filed action in the district court in 1963, a plan with court-ordered modifications was adopted. Elementary students living within attendance zones were automatically assigned to schools in zones that had geographic or neutral boundaries; however, the plan also included a free transfer provision. Citing evidence that the African American schools had remained one-race schools and that only 118 African American students attended White schools, the court held that the plan had been administered in a racially discriminatory manner.

The board also filed its plan for desegregating the junior high schools. In 1964, all three junior high schools retained their traditional racial identities. The faculties of the schools were also segregated. Despite parental protests that the board had gerrymandered school attendance zones, the district court ruled for the board. The court further held that a feeder system recommended by expert witnesses did not have to be adopted. The court of appeals affirmed the decision but remanded for further proceedings on the issue of faculty desegregation.

The Court's Ruling

The Supreme Court granted certiorari and rendered its decision on the same day as the decision in *Green v. County School Board of New Kent County.* Reviewing the evidence and the holding in *Green,* the Supreme

Court concluded that the Jackson schools had remained one-race schools. After three years, Merry Junior High School was still a one-race school, for example. White students who had been assigned to Merry Junior High School transferred elsewhere. There were only seven African American students in the mainly White Tigrett Junior High School. The only exception was the Jackson School, where there were a substantial number of African American students. The same pattern was maintained in the elementary schools in the district.

The free transfer plan had not allowed the board to meet its affirmative duty to create a unitary school system "in which racial discrimination would be eliminated root and branch," the Supreme Court ruled. Until the district court intervened, the board had administered the plan in a discriminatory manner, the court said, and this resulted in a lengthy delay in the desegregation of the schools. Furthermore, the court asserted that no plan can have racial segregation as its consequence. The Court made no bones about the fact that the board had administered a plan that allowed it to remain comfortable and unchanged with regard to racial segregation.

The Court stopped short of saying that a board could never adopt a free choice plan. The key issue is whether the plan furthers the goal of achieving a unitary school system. The Supreme Court reversed the court of appeals with regard to its affirmation of the plan for the junior high schools. The case was remanded for proceedings consistent with the Court's decision in *Green.*

J. Patrick Mahon

See also *Brown v. Board of Education of Topeka* and Equal Educational Opportunities; Civil Rights Movement; Fourteenth Amendment

Legal Citations

Brown v. Board of Education of Topeka I, 347 U.S. 483 (1954).
Brown v. Board of Education of Topeka II, 349 U.S. 294 (1955).
Green v. County School Board of New Kent County, 391 U.S. 430 (1968).
Monroe v. Board of Commissioners, 391 U.S. 450 (1968).

MORSE V. FREDERICK

Morse v. Frederick (2007) is the most recent of the U.S. Supreme Court's four cases on the free speech rights of K–12 students. In *Morse,* the Court upheld the authority of educators to discipline a student who displayed a banner at a school event that promoted illegal drug use.

Facts of the Case

The dispute in *Morse* arose when a principal suspended a high school student who, with friends, displayed a 14-foot banner reading "BONG HiTS [sic] 4 JESUS" as they watched the winter Olympics torch relay pass through Juneau, Alaska. The principal had allowed students and staff, who supervised the activity, to leave class to watch the relay as an approved social event. Although the student had not made it to school that day due to snowy weather, he positioned himself on a sidewalk across from the school. On seeing the banner, the principal destroyed it and suspended the student, because she thought that the sign advocated illegal drug use by smoking marijuana.

The federal trial court in Alaska rejected the student's request for an injunction and damages in agreeing that the principal did not violate his First Amendment right to free speech. The Ninth Circuit reversed in favor of the student on the speech claim, adding that the principal was not entitled to qualified immunity from personal liability for destroying the banner.

The Court's Ruling

On further review, the Supreme Court, in an opinion by Chief Justice Roberts, reversed in favor of the principal and board. Chief Justice Roberts began his analysis by noting that the Court agreed to hear an appeal on "whether [the student] had a First Amendment right to wield his banner and, if so, whether that right was so clearly established that the principal may be liable for damages" (p. 2624). Consequently, he indicated that because the Court rejected the student's claim that he had such an established right, it was unnecessary to address the second question.

Roberts noted his reliance on the Supreme Court's precedent in its three other student speech cases, *Tinker v. Des Moines Independent Community School District* (1969), *Bethel School District No. 403 v. Fraser* (1986), and *Hazelwood School District v. Kuhlmeier* (1988). Beginning with *Tinker,* Roberts conceded that while students have rights in schools that are not equal to those of adults, they must be considered in light of the special circumstances in schools. To this end, he observed that educators may limit student speech that they think encourages illegal drug use.

Chief Justice Roberts next rejected the student's allegation that the admittedly cryptic banner was not school speech, because the display occurred during the day at a school-approved and supervised event. In finding that the principal had the power to act as she did, Roberts clarified that under *Tinker,* the free speech rights of students must be examined in light of the special characteristics of schools. Turning to *Fraser,* Roberts interpreted it as meaning both that student rights are not equal to those of adults and that *Tinker* was neither absolute nor the only justification on which officials can limit student speech. In differentiating *Fraser* from *Hazelwood,* because the banner could not reasonably have been viewed as having the approval of school officials, Roberts rejected the former's "plainly offensive" standard, because it gave educators too much discretion. Roberts thus concluded that the principal did not violate the student's right to free speech, because she disciplined him based on her legitimate concern of preventing him from promoting illegal drug use.

In his concurrence, Justice Thomas maintained that because the First Amendment does not confer any defense for the free speech rights of students, *Tinker* has no basis in the Constitution. Justice Alito, joined by Justice Kennedy, concurred because he agreed with the Court's wanting to restrict speech advocating illegal drug use, but he would not have expanded the ban to political or social issues. In his partial concurrence and partial dissent, which also joined the judgment of the Court, Justice Breyer would have limited the holding to the extent that the student's damages claim against the principal was barred by qualified immunity. Justice Stevens's dissent argued that the student's nonsensical banner was protected speech that neither violated a permissible school rule nor advocated conduct that was either illegal or harmful. He also agreed with the Court that the principal should not have been personally liable for destroying the banner.

Charles J. Russo

See also Bethel School District No. 403 v. Fraser; Free Speech and Expression Rights of Students; Hazelwood School District v. Kuhlmeier; Tinker v. Des Moines Independent Community School District

Legal Citations

Bethel School District No. 403 v. Fraser, 478 U.S. 675 (1986).
Hazelwood School District v. Kuhlmeier, 484 U.S. 260, 273 (1988).
Morse v. Frederick, 127 S. Ct. 2618 (2007).
Tinker v. Des Moines Independent Community School District, 393 U.S. 503 (1969).

Morse v. Frederick (Excerpts)

In Morse v. Frederick, the Supreme Court's most recent case on student free speech, the Justices upheld the right of educational officials to discipline a student for displaying a pro-drug message at a school-related activity.

Supreme Court of the United States

Deborah MORSE et al., Petitioners,

v.

Joseph FREDERICK.

127 S. Ct. 2618

Argued March 19, 2007.

Decided June 25, 2007.

Chief Justice ROBERTS delivered the opinion of the Court.

At a school-sanctioned and school-supervised event, a high school principal saw some of her students unfurl a large banner conveying a message she reasonably regarded as promoting illegal drug use. Consistent with established school policy prohibiting such messages at school events, the principal directed the students to take down the banner. One student—among those who had brought the banner to the event—refused to do so. The principal confiscated the banner and later suspended the student. The Ninth Circuit held that the principal's actions violated the First Amendment, and that the student could sue the principal for damages.

Our cases make clear that students do not "shed their constitutional rights to freedom of speech or expression at the schoolhouse gate." At the same time, we have held that "the constitutional rights of students in public school are not automatically coextensive with the rights of adults in other settings," and that the rights of students "must be 'applied in light of the special characteristics of the school environment.'" Consistent with these principles, we hold that schools may take steps to safeguard those entrusted to their care from speech that can reasonably be regarded as encouraging illegal drug use. We conclude that the school officials in this case did not violate the First Amendment by confiscating the pro-drug banner and suspending the student responsible for it.

I

On January 24, 2002, the Olympic Torch Relay passed through Juneau, Alaska, on its way to the winter games in Salt Lake City, Utah. The torchbearers were to proceed along a street in front of Juneau-Douglas High School (JDHS) while school was in session. Petitioner Deborah Morse, the school principal, decided to permit staff and students to participate in the Torch Relay as an approved social event or class trip. Students were allowed to leave class to observe the relay from either side of the street. Teachers and administrative officials monitored the students' actions.

Respondent Joseph Frederick, a JDHS senior, was late to school that day. When he arrived, he joined his friends (all but one of whom were JDHS students) across the street from the school to watch the event. Not all the students waited patiently. Some became rambunctious, throwing plastic cola bottles and snowballs and

scuffling with their classmates. As the torchbearers and camera crews passed by, Frederick and his friends unfurled a 14-foot banner bearing the phrase: "BONG HiTS 4 JESUS." The large banner was easily readable by the students on the other side of the street.

Principal Morse immediately crossed the street and demanded that the banner be taken down. Everyone but Frederick complied. Morse confiscated the banner and told Frederick to report to her office, where she suspended him for 10 days. Morse later explained that she told Frederick to take the banner down because she thought it encouraged illegal drug use, in violation of established school policy. Juneau School Board Policy No. 5520 states: "The Board specifically prohibits any assembly or public expression that . . . advocates the use of substances that are illegal to minors. . . ." In addition, Juneau School Board Policy No. 5850 subjects "[p]upils who participate in approved social events and class trips" to the same student conduct rules that apply during the regular school program.

Frederick administratively appealed his suspension, but the Juneau School District Superintendent upheld it, limiting it to time served (8 days). In a memorandum setting forth his reasons, the superintendent determined that Frederick had displayed his banner "in the midst of his fellow students, during school hours, at a school-sanctioned activity." He further explained that Frederick "was not disciplined because the principal of the school 'disagreed' with his message, but because his speech appeared to advocate the use of illegal drugs."

. . . .

Relying on our decision in [*Bethel School District No. 403 v. Fraser*], the superintendent concluded that the principal's actions were permissible because Frederick's banner was "speech or action that intrudes upon the work of the schools." The Juneau School District Board of Education upheld the suspension.

Frederick then filed suit under 42 U.S.C. § 1983, alleging that the school board and Morse had violated his First Amendment rights. He sought declaratory and injunctive relief, unspecified compensatory damages, punitive damages, and attorney's fees. The District Court granted summary judgment for the school board and Morse, ruling that they were entitled to qualified immunity and that they had not infringed Frederick's First

Amendment rights. The court found that Morse reasonably interpreted the banner as promoting illegal drug use—a message that "directly contravened the Board's policies relating to drug abuse prevention." Under the circumstances, the court held that "Morse had the authority, if not the obligation, to stop such messages at a school-sanctioned activity."

The Ninth Circuit reversed. Deciding that Frederick acted during a "school-authorized activit[y]," and "proceed[ing] on the basis that the banner expressed a positive sentiment about marijuana use," the court nonetheless found a violation of Frederick's First Amendment rights because the school punished Frederick without demonstrating that his speech gave rise to a "risk of substantial disruption." The court further concluded that Frederick's right to display his banner was so "clearly established" that a reasonable principal in Morse's position would have understood that her actions were unconstitutional, and that Morse was therefore not entitled to qualified immunity.

We granted certiorari on two questions: whether Frederick had a First Amendment right to wield his banner, and, if so, whether that right was so clearly established that the principal may be held liable for damages. We resolve the first question against Frederick, and therefore have no occasion to reach the second.

II

At the outset, we reject Frederick's argument that this is not a school speech case—as has every other authority to address the question. The event occurred during normal school hours. It was sanctioned by Principal Morse "as an approved social event or class trip" and the school district's rules expressly provide that pupils in "approved social events and class trips are subject to district rules for student conduct." Teachers and administrators were interspersed among the students and charged with supervising them. The high school band and cheerleaders performed. Frederick, standing among other JDHS students across the street from the school, directed his banner toward the school, making it plainly visible to most students. Under these circumstances, we agree with the superintendent that Frederick cannot "stand in the midst of his fellow students, during school hours, at a school-sanctioned activity and claim he is not at school." There is some uncertainty at the outer boundaries as to when courts should apply school-speech precedents, but not on these facts.

III

The message on Frederick's banner is cryptic. It is no doubt offensive to some, perhaps amusing to others. To still others, it probably means nothing at all. Frederick himself claimed "that the words were just nonsense meant to attract television cameras." But Principal Morse thought the banner would be interpreted by those viewing it as promoting illegal drug use, and that interpretation is plainly a reasonable one.

As Morse later explained in a declaration, when she saw the sign, she thought that "the reference to a 'bong hit' would be widely understood by high school students and others as referring to smoking marijuana." She further believed that "display of the banner would be construed by students, District personnel, parents and others witnessing the display of the banner, as advocating or promoting illegal drug use"—in violation of school policy.

We agree with Morse. At least two interpretations of the words on the banner demonstrate that the sign advocated the use of illegal drugs. First, the phrase could be interpreted as an imperative: "[Take] bong hits . . ."—a message equivalent, as Morse explained in her declaration, to "smoke marijuana" or "use an illegal drug." Alternatively, the phrase could be viewed as celebrating drug use—"bong hits [are a good thing]," or "[we take] bong hits"—and we discern no meaningful distinction between celebrating illegal drug use in the midst of fellow students and outright advocacy or promotion.

The pro-drug interpretation of the banner gains further plausibility given the paucity of alternative meanings the banner might bear. The best Frederick can come up with is that the banner is "meaningless and funny." The dissent similarly refers to the sign's message as "curious," "ambiguous," "nonsense," "ridiculous," "obscure," "silly," "quixotic," and "stupid." Gibberish is surely a possible interpretation of the words on the banner, but it is not the only one, and dismissing the banner as meaningless ignores its undeniable reference to illegal drugs.

The dissent mentions Frederick's "credible and uncontradicted explanation for the message—he just wanted to get on television." But that is a description of Frederick's *motive* for displaying the banner; it is not an interpretation of what the banner says. The *way* Frederick was going to fulfill his ambition of appearing on television was by unfurling a pro-drug banner at a school event, in the presence of teachers and fellow students.

Elsewhere in its opinion, the dissent emphasizes the importance of political speech and the need to foster "national debate about a serious issue," as if to suggest that the banner is political speech. But not even Frederick argues that the banner conveys any sort of political or religious message. Contrary to the dissent's suggestion, this is plainly not a case about political debate over the criminalization of drug use or possession.

IV

The question thus becomes whether a principal may, consistent with the First Amendment, restrict student speech at a school event, when that speech is reasonably viewed as promoting illegal drug use. We hold that she may.

In *Tinker*, this Court made clear that "First Amendment rights, applied in light of the special characteristics of the school environment, are available to teachers and students." *Tinker* involved a group of high school students who decided to wear black armbands to protest the Vietnam War. School officials learned of the plan and then adopted a policy prohibiting students from wearing armbands. When several students nonetheless wore armbands to school, they were suspended. The students sued, claiming that their First Amendment rights had been violated, and this Court agreed.

Tinker held that student expression may not be suppressed unless school officials reasonably conclude that it will "materially and substantially disrupt the work and discipline of the school." The essential facts of *Tinker* are quite stark, implicating concerns at the heart of the First Amendment. The students sought to engage in political speech, using the armbands to express their "disapproval of the Vietnam hostilities and their advocacy of a truce, to make their views known, and, by their example, to influence others to adopt them." Political speech, of course, is "at the core of what the First Amendment is designed to protect." The only interest the Court discerned underlying the school's actions was the "mere desire to avoid the discomfort and unpleasantness that always accompany an unpopular viewpoint," or "an urgent wish to avoid the controversy which might result from the expression." That interest was not enough to justify banning "a silent, passive expression of opinion, unaccompanied by any disorder or disturbance."

This Court's next student speech case was *Fraser*. Matthew Fraser was suspended for delivering a speech before a high school assembly in which he employed what this Court called "an elaborate, graphic, and explicit sexual metaphor." Analyzing the case under *Tinker*, the District Court and Court of Appeals found no disruption, and therefore no basis for disciplining Fraser. This Court reversed, holding that the "School District acted entirely within its permissible authority in imposing sanctions upon Fraser in response to his offensively lewd and indecent speech."

The mode of analysis employed in *Fraser* is not entirely clear. The Court was plainly attuned to the content of Fraser's speech, citing the "marked distinction between the political 'message' of the armbands in *Tinker* and the sexual content of [Fraser's] speech." But the Court also reasoned that school boards have the authority to determine "what manner of speech in the classroom or in school assembly is inappropriate."

We need not resolve this debate to decide this case. For present purposes, it is enough to distill from *Fraser* two basic principles. First, *Fraser's* holding demonstrates that "the constitutional rights of students in public school are not automatically coextensive with the rights of adults in other settings." Had Fraser delivered the same speech in a public forum outside the school context, it would have been protected. In school, however, Fraser's First Amendment rights were circumscribed "in light of the special characteristics of the school environment." Second, *Fraser* established that the mode of analysis set forth in *Tinker* is not absolute. Whatever approach *Fraser* employed, it certainly did not conduct the "substantial disruption" analysis prescribed by *Tinker*.

Our most recent student speech case, [*Hazelwood School District v.*] *Kuhlmeier*, concerned "expressive activities that students, parents, and members of the public might reasonably perceive to bear the imprimatur of the school." Staff members of a high school newspaper sued their school when it chose not to publish two of their articles. The Court of Appeals analyzed the case under *Tinker*, ruling in favor of the students because it found no evidence of material disruption to classwork or school discipline. This Court reversed, holding that "educators do not offend the First Amendment by exercising editorial control over the style and content of student speech in school-sponsored expressive activities so long as their actions are reasonably related to legitimate pedagogical concerns."

Kuhlmeier does not control this case because no one would reasonably believe that Frederick's banner bore the school's imprimatur. The case is nevertheless instructive because it confirms both principles cited above. *Kuhlmeier* acknowledged that schools may regulate some speech "even though the government could not censor similar speech outside the school." And, like *Fraser*, it confirms that the rule of *Tinker* is not the only basis for restricting student speech.

Drawing on the principles applied in our student speech cases, we have held in the Fourth Amendment context that "while children assuredly do not 'shed their constitutional rights ... at the schoolhouse gate,' ... the nature of those rights is what is appropriate for children in school." In particular, "the school setting requires some easing of the restrictions to which searches by public authorities are ordinarily subject."

Even more to the point, these cases also recognize that deterring drug use by schoolchildren is an "important—indeed, perhaps compelling" interest. Drug abuse can cause severe and permanent damage to the health and well-being of young people: "School years are the time when the physical, psychological, and addictive effects of drugs are most severe. Maturing nervous systems are more critically impaired by intoxicants than mature ones are; childhood losses in learning are lifelong and profound; children grow chemically dependent more quickly than adults, and their record of recovery is depressingly poor. And of course the effects of a drug-infested school are visited not just upon the users, but upon the entire student body and faculty, as the educational process is disrupted."

Just five years ago, we wrote: "The drug abuse problem among our Nation's youth has hardly abated since *Vernonia* was decided in 1995. In fact, evidence suggests that it has only grown worse."

The problem remains serious today. About half of American 12th graders have used an illicit drug, as have more than a third of 10th graders and about one-fifth of 8th graders. Nearly one in four 12th graders has used an illicit drug in the past month. Some 25% of high schoolers say that they have been offered, sold, or given an illegal drug on school property within the past year.

Congress has declared that part of a school's job is educating students about the dangers of illegal drug use. It has provided billions of dollars to support state and local drug-prevention programs, and required that schools receiving federal funds under the Safe and Drug-Free Schools and Communities Act of 1994 certify that their drug prevention programs "convey a clear and consistent message that ... the illegal use of drugs [is] wrong and harmful."

Thousands of school boards throughout the country—including JDHS—have adopted policies aimed at effectuating this message. Those school boards know that peer pressure is perhaps "the single most important factor leading schoolchildren to take drugs," and that students are more likely to use drugs when the norms in school appear to tolerate such behavior. Student speech celebrating illegal drug use at a school event, in the presence of school administrators and teachers, thus poses a particular challenge for school officials working to protect those entrusted to their care from the dangers of drug abuse.

The "special characteristics of the school environment," *Tinker*, and the governmental interest in stopping student drug abuse—reflected in the policies of Congress and myriad school boards, including JDHS—allow schools to restrict student expression that they reasonably regard as promoting illegal drug use. *Tinker* warned that schools may not prohibit student speech because of "undifferentiated fear or apprehension of disturbance" or "a mere desire to avoid the discomfort and unpleasantness that always accompany an unpopular viewpoint." The danger here is far more serious and palpable. The particular concern to prevent student drug abuse at issue here, embodied in established school policy, extends well beyond an abstract desire to avoid controversy.

Petitioners urge us to adopt the broader rule that Frederick's speech is proscribable because it is plainly "offensive" as that term is used in *Fraser*. We think this stretches *Fraser* too far; that case should not be read to encompass any speech that could fit under some definition of "offensive." After all, much political and religious speech might be perceived as offensive to some. The concern here is not that Frederick's speech was offensive, but that it was reasonably viewed as promoting illegal drug use.

Although accusing this decision of doing "serious violence to the First Amendment" by authorizing "viewpoint discrimination," the dissent concludes that "it might well be appropriate to tolerate some targeted viewpoint discrimination in this unique setting." Nor do we understand the dissent to take the position that schools are required to tolerate student advocacy of illegal drug use at school events, even if that advocacy falls short of inviting "imminent" lawless action. And even the dissent recognizes that the issues here are close enough that the principal should not be held liable in damages, but should instead enjoy qualified immunity for her actions. Stripped of rhetorical flourishes, then, the debate between the dissent and this opinion is less about constitutional first principles than about whether Frederick's banner constitutes promotion of illegal drug use. We have explained our view that it does. The dissent's

contrary view on that relatively narrow question hardly justifies sounding the First Amendment bugle.

. . . .

School principals have a difficult job, and a vitally important one. When Frederick suddenly and unexpectedly unfurled his banner, Morse had to decide to act—or not act—on the spot. It was reasonable for her to conclude that the banner promoted illegal drug use—in violation of established school policy—and that failing to act would send a powerful message to the students in her charge, including Frederick, about how serious the school was about the dangers of illegal drug use. The First Amendment does not require schools to tolerate at school events student expression that contributes to those dangers.

The judgment of the United States Court of Appeals for the Ninth Circuit is reversed, and the case is remanded for further proceedings consistent with this opinion.

It is so ordered.

Citation: *Morse v. Frederick*, 127 S. Ct. 2618 (2007).

MT. HEALTHY CITY BOARD OF EDUCATION V. DOYLE

At issue in *Mt. Healthy City Board of Education v. Doyle* (1977) was whether a school board could defend itself in a First Amendment retaliation claim by proving that it would have made the same employment decision in the absence of a teacher's allegedly protected free speech activity.

Facts of the Case

The dispute arose when a nontenured Ohio high school teacher, Doyle, sent a local radio station a copy of his principal's memo about a school dress code and included his own opinions. Doyle was employed under a series of one- and two-year teaching contracts between 1966 and 1971. Elected president of the teachers association in 1970, Doyle sought to expand

direct negotiations between the association and the school board. During the same year, Doyle engaged in an argument with another teacher who slapped him, resulting in their both being suspended for a day. Shortly thereafter, several teachers staged a walkout to protest the suspensions.

On other occasions, Doyle became involved in an argument with school cafeteria employees over the amount of spaghetti he was served. In a disciplinary report, the board noted that Doyle referred to students as "sons of bitches" (p. 573) and made an obscene gesture to two girls after they failed to obey commands he gave in his capacity as cafeteria supervisor.

The board said that Doyle conducted himself in a nonprofessional manner on several occasions, leading to its recommendation that his contract not be renewed. Doyle later apologized to the principal for contacting the radio station without discussing the policy with administrators. When he asked for reasons for the nonrenewal of his contract, board officials told

Doyle that he demonstrated a lack of tact in handling professional matters; used obscene gestures to correct students in the cafeteria, resulting in their discomfort; and notified the local radio station about the board's suggestions of an appropriate dress code for professional staff.

In response to the board's action, Doyle filed suit, alleging that it violated his First Amendment protected free speech rights. A federal trial court in Ohio, affirmed by the Sixth Circuit, was of the opinion that Doyle's telephone call to the radio station was protected First Amendment speech and that it played a substantial part in the nonrenewal of his contract. The court awarded Doyle $5,158 in back pay and reinstatement, even though he had accepted another job in a different school system paying $2,000 less.

The Court's Ruling

On appeal to the Supreme Court, in addition to the free speech claims, the school board raised the issue of immunity from suits under the Eleventh Amendment to the U.S. Constitution. The Court ruled the board was not entitled to the protection of sovereign immunity, because it is a political subdivision, not an arm of the state. The Court explained that while local school boards are subject to some guidance from the state board of education and receive state funds, they have extensive power to issue bonds and to levy taxes within specified restrictions of state law.

Turning to the issue of free speech, the Court pointed out that in *Board of Regents v. Roth* (1972), it ruled that while a nontenured employee may be dismissed without cause, if issues of constitutionally protected free speech play major roles in the termination of their contracts, they may have grounds for reinstatement. The Court observed that Doyle's behavior patterns played a major role in the dispute, because he offended other teachers and students.

The Court also acknowledged that in *Pickering v. Board of Education of Township High School District 205, Will County* (1968), it maintained that the question of free speech issues involves finding a balance between the interests of public school teachers as citizens in commenting on matters of public concern and the interest of the state qua school boards as employers

in promoting the efficiency of the public service they provide through their employees.

In its analysis, the Court determined that there were other factors in decisions to grant tenure to or rehire a borderline or marginal teacher such as Doyle, along with the First Amendment claims. The Court thus remanded the dispute for a consideration of whether factors other than the First Amendment issue would have led the board not to renew Doyle's contract.

On remand, the Sixth Circuit (*Doyle,* 1982) affirmed that the board demonstrated by a preponderance of the evidence that it would not have renewed Doyle's contract even if he had not contacted the radio station.

James Van Patten

See also *Board of Regents v. Roth; Connick v. Myers;* Eleventh Amendment; *Pickering v. Board of Education of Township High School District 205, Will County;* Teacher Rights

Legal Citations

Board of Regents v. Roth, 408 U.S. 564 (1972).
Mt. Healthy City Board of Education v. Doyle, 429 U.S. 274 (1977), *on remand, Doyle v. Mt. Healthy City School District Board of Education,* 670 F.2d 59 (6th Cir. 1982).
Mt. Healthy City Board of Education v. Doyle, 429 U.S. 274 (1977).
Pickering v. Board of Education of Township High School District 205, Will County, 391 U.S. 563 (1968).

MUELLER V. ALLEN

Mueller v. Allen (1983) involved a challenge to the State of Minnesota's allowance of tuition deductions for specified educational expenses, filed under the Establishment Clause, which prohibits government making laws "respecting an establishment of religion." The Supreme Court's landmark decision in *Mueller* to let the state law stand provided an important precedent for other cases involving state support for religious schools.

Facts of the Case

The Minnesota statute allowed all state taxpayers, in computing their state income taxes, to deduct expenses incurred in providing "tuition, textbooks, and transportation" for their children attending public or nonpublic elementary or secondary schools. Insofar as the statute permitted the deductions to be used for children attending sectarian schools, state taxpayers challenged the constitutionality of the statute both facially and in its application.

The federal trial court granted the state's motion for summary judgment, holding that the statute was neutral on its face and in its application and did not have a primary effect of either advancing or inhibiting religion. The Eighth Circuit affirmed.

The Court's Ruling

The Supreme Court granted certiorari and upheld the Eighth Circuit, relying on the three-part *Lemon v. Kurtzman* (1971) test. Regarding the first part of test, that of *secular purpose,* the Court observed that the tax deduction had the secular purpose of ensuring that the state's citizenry was well educated as well as of assuring the continued financial health of private schools, both sectarian and nonsectarian. More broadly, the Court noted that "a state's decision to defray the cost of educational expenses incurred by parents—regardless of the type of schools their children attend—evidences a purpose that is both secular and understandable" (p. 395).

Concerning the second, or *effects* test, the Court decided that the deduction did not have the primary effect of advancing the sectarian aims of nonpublic schools, because it was only one of many deductions—such as those for medical expenses and charitable contributions—available under the Minnesota tax laws. In addition, the Court noted that the deduction was available "for educational expenses incurred by *all* parents, whether their children attend public schools or private sectarian or nonsectarian private schools" (p. 397, emphasis in original). The Court distinguished *Mueller* from its earlier decision in *Committee for Public Education & Religious Liberty v. Nyquist* (1973), which had invalidated a tax deduction only for students in nonpublic schools, by observing that no state imprimatur of religious schools could exist where "aid to parochial schools is available only as a result of decisions of individual parents," in this

case to enroll students in either public or nonpublic schools (p. 399).

The Court explained that the state deduction statute was facially neutral in ignoring the plaintiffs' claim that "96% of the children in private schools in 1978–1979 attended religiously-affiliated institutions," in effect pointedly declaring that "the fact that private persons fail in a particular year to claim the tax relief to which they are entitled—under a facially neutral statute—should be of little importance in determining the constitutionality of the statute permitting such relief" (p. 401).

Finally, the Court refused to find a violation of the third part of the *Lemon* test, excessive entanglement. The Court found that evaluating whether textbooks qualified for tax deductions was not significantly different from the loaning of secular textbooks to religious schools, a process that the Court had upheld 35 years earlier in *Board of Education v. Allen* (1968).

Mueller was a landmark judgment, because it was the first Supreme Court education case to invoke neutrality as a way to block the *Lemon* "effects" test. In effect, *Mueller* allowed state and federal government to frame statutes neutral in their design without having to be unduly concerned about the numerical impact of the statutes. Eventually, *Mueller* was to have a significant impact on the Supreme Court's upholding the provision of special education services on site in religious schools (*Zobrest,* 1993), the provision of on-site Title I services at religious schools (*Agostini,* 1997), and the loaning of instructional materials and supplies (*Mitchell,* 2000) to religious schools.

In the broadest understanding of *Mueller,* though, the case stands for more than just facial neutrality; the *Mueller* Court acknowledged "the positive contributions of sectarian schools" (p.400). In so doing the Court rejected the "[risk] of deep political division along religious lines" (p. 400) that had formed part of the Supreme Court's "political divisiveness" rationale in *Lemon* (p. 622), used 12 years earlier to invalidate a variety of forms of governmental support for students and the religiously affiliated nonpublic schools that they attended.

Ralph D. Mawdsley

See also Agostini v. Felton; Board of Education v. Allen; Committee for Public Education & Religious Liberty v. Nyquist; Lemon v. Kurtzman; Mitchell v. Helms; State Aid and the Establishment Clause; Zobrest v. Catalina Foothills School District

Legal Citations

Agostini v. Felton, 521 U.S. 203 (1997).

Board of Education of Central School District No. 1 v. Allen, 392 U.S. 236 (1968).

Committee for Public Education & Religious Liberty v. Nyquist, 413 U.S. 756 (1973).

Lemon v. Kurtzman, 403 U.S. 602 (1971).

Mitchell v. Helms, 530 U.S. 793 (2000) *reh'g denied,* 530 U.S. 1296 (2000), *on remand sub nom. Helms v. Picard*, 229 F.3d 467 (5th Cir. 2000).

Mueller v. Allen, 463 U.S. 388 (1983).

Zobrest v. Catalina Foothills School District, 509 U.S. 1 (1993).

NABOZNY V. PODLESNY

At issue in *Nabozny v. Podlesny* (1996) was whether a student who was gay could proceed with a claim that school officials in Wisconsin violated his rights to equal protection and due process in light of their failure to protect him from harassment and harm by peers on account of his sexual orientation. The Seventh Circuit ruled that the student presented an actionable claim for violations of his right to equal protection but not due process.

Facts of the Case

Jamie Nabozny sued his school board in federal trial court under Title IX of the Education Amendments of 1972. Nabozny was a gay student who was subjected to such severe harassment and physical abuse that he left school before he graduated. Prior to *Nabozny,* queer (lesbian, gay, bisexual, transgendered, transsexual, and/or intersexual) students had little legal recourse in federal court to challenge the abuse they received in public school settings.

The record reflected the fact that beginning in seventh grade, the plaintiff was routinely and continually harassed, beaten, and called "fag" and "faggot." He was spat on, punched, urinated on, and even subjected to a mock rape where 20 students watched and even laughed but did not come to his aid. All of this harassment and bullying happened on school grounds, and almost all of this abuse was at the hands of fellow students. When the student's parents tried to intervene with school administrators after the mock rape, they were informed that if their son was going to act like a queer, then they should have expected that he would be subjected to this type of harassment.

In many instances, teachers and administrators witnessed the student being abused but failed to intervene. In fact, one teacher called the plaintiff a "fag," and a high school assistant principal told him he deserved to be abused because he was gay. During his sophomore year, the student was so savagely beaten and kicked in one attack that he needed extensive abdominal surgery to repair the damage. The constant abuse also led the student to attempt suicide twice. By eleventh grade, the student had dropped out of school, and administrators recommended that he should attend school somewhere else.

The student's subsequent successful suit in federal court against his middle school principal and the school board was the first such federal action in the United States. On further review of a grant of summary judgment in favor of school officials, the Seventh Circuit partially reversed in favor of the student.

The Court's Ruling

In its analysis, the Seventh Circuit found that school officials violated the student's Title IX right to be free of gender-based violence and to equal protection. However, the court affirmed the denial of the student's due process claim. As part of its judgment, the court pointed out that the board had antibullying policies in place and enforced them if the victims of harassment were female, but not male. To this end, the court awarded the student $900,000 in damages, a striking judgment against the board, especially because it added that the school officials were not entitled to qualified immunity with respect to equal protection claims because of their failure to protect him. Clearly, *Nabozny* sent a loud message that officials in public schools could be liable for serious financial damages if they failed to protect the homosexual students within their walls.

Catherine A. Lugg

See also Equal Protection Analysis; Sexual Harassment, Peer-to-Peer; Title IX and Sexual Harassment

Further readings

Broz, A. N. (1998). *Nabozny v. Podlesny:* A teenager's struggle to end anti-gay violence in public schools. *Northwestern University Law Review, 92,* 750–778.

Reese, S. (1997). The law and gay-bashing in schools. *Education Digest, 62*(9), 46–49.

Legal Citations

Nabozny v. Podlesny, 92 F.3d 446 (7th Cir. 1996).

NATIONAL ASSOCIATION FOR THE ADVANCEMENT OF COLORED PEOPLE (NAACP)

The National Association for the Advancement of Colored People (NAACP), founded in 1909, is the oldest and the largest civil rights organization in the United States. The NAACP seeks to ensure the political, educational, social, and economic equality of minority group citizens in the United States. The NAACP uses nonviolence and relies on the press, the petition, the ballot, and the courts to achieve its objectives. This entry looks at the history of the organization and its litigation efforts.

Historical Background

The NAACP, a membership organization with 2,200 local chapters in all 50 states and the District of Columbia, has approximately 500,000 members. Local chapters are managed by a national board of directors located in Baltimore, Maryland. In 1940, the NAACP established a new independent organization to pursue legal actions through the courts via its legal arm, the NAACP Legal Defense Fund (LDF). Thurgood Marshall became its first director and chief legal counsel. The LDF, a nonmembership organization, is located in New York City. When the name *NAACP* is mentioned, it refers to both organizations, the NAACP and the NAACP Legal Defense Fund.

In addition to making its stance on public issues known in its publication, *The Crisis,* the NAACP sponsors two important events annually. The first is its annual convention, which typically is addressed by the U.S. president; the second is the annual NAACP Image Awards ceremony that takes place in Hollywood, California.

The NAACP was patterned after the Niagara Movement, a group with an all Black membership that was founded by W. E. B. DuBois, a Black scholar from Atlanta University. The charter members of the NAACP included 53 Whites and 7 African Americans. The NAACP's first officers included five Whites and one Black, W. E. B. DuBois, who was elected director of publicity and research and editor of *The Crisis.*

Education Litigation

Prior to *Brown v. Board of Education of Topeka* (1954), the NAACP had set the stage for an attack on the U.S. Supreme Court's ruling in *Plessy v. Ferguson* (1896). In *Plessy,* the Court upheld the notion that states could satisfy the Equal Protection Clause of the Fourteenth Amendment by providing "separate but equal" public facilities for Black and White citizens. The NAACP first focused on higher education, based on the belief that it would be easier to prove inequality between Black and White graduate higher education programs.

The pre-*Brown* cases that the NAACP won, such as *Sweatt v. Painter* (1950) and *McLaurin v. Oklahoma State Regents for Higher Education* (1950), wherein the Supreme Court struck down inter- and intrainstitution segregation, respectively, in higher education, led Thurgood Marshall to believe that the Court would uphold the rights of Blacks to attend desegregated K–12 public schools. In fact, the NAACP's strategy originated in 1930 when Nathan Margold devised a plan to eliminate school segregation.

The NAACP's years of planning achieved success in *Brown I* (1954). In *Brown I,* the Court reasoned that because separate educational facilities were inherently unequal, they violated the Equal Protection Clause. A year later, in *Brown II* (1955), the justices set a schedule for the lower courts to implement *Brown I* with "all deliberate speed." Yet, 10 years after *Brown I,* only a small percentage of the Black students in the 11 Southern states attended desegregated public schools.

Other Efforts

In addition to legal action to achieve equality between the races, the NAACP sought other means to advance the cause of equal justice for all Americans. The NAACP led marches and demonstrations and lobbied for a better life for African Americans. In addition, the NAACP produced research on issues such as lynching, Jim Crow laws, and discrimination in employment, educational institutions, and the armed forces. The NAACP also encouraged and continues to encourage voter registration and grassroots protests of injustice.

The modern NAACP is not as popular today as in the past when it won many important legal cases before the Supreme Court. Part of this may stem from the fact that insofar as the NAACP is a nonprofit organization, it is barred from direct political involvement. This limitation is necessary, however, because, following *Brown,* the NAACP needed more funds and manpower to help to ensure that the more than 2,500 individual school systems that had been segregated achieved unitary status. In addition, the NAACP needed funds to litigate local cases of police brutality, employment discrimination, and voting rights. What happened in Alabama is a good example of how the NAACP became involved. The leaders of the Montgomery bus boycott were all members of the local NAACP, as several held office in the local chapter when they decided to organize the bus boycott. The Alabama group also won six race-related cases before the Supreme Court, beginning with the bus boycott. Similar local and state organizations were established across the country to handle similar situations.

The NAACP and LDF continue to conduct research on race-related political and legal issues, making the results available to local civil rights organizations.

Frank Brown

See also Brown v. Board of Education of Topeka; Brown v. Board of Education of Topeka *and Equal Educational Opportunities;* McLaurin v. Oklahoma State Regents for Higher Education; Sweatt v. Painter

Further Readings

Davis, M. D., & Clark, H. R. (1994). *Thurgood Marshall: Warrior at the bar, rebel on the bench.* New York: Citadel Press.

Flemming, A. S. (1974). Milliken v. Bradley: *The implications for metropolitan desegregation: Conference before the United States Commission on Civil Rights.* Washington, DC: U.S. Commission on Civil Rights.

Flemming, A. S. (1976). *Fulfilling the letter and spirit of the law: Desegregation of the nation's public schools.* Washington, DC: U.S. Commission on Civil Rights.

Gray, F. D. (2002). *Bus ride to justice.* Montgomery, AL: NewSouth Books.

Legal Citations

Brown v. Board of Education of Topeka I, 347 U.S. 483 (1954).
Brown v. Board of Education of Topeka II, 349 U.S. 294 (1955).
McLaurin v. Oklahoma State Regents for Higher Education, 339 U.S. 637 (1950).
Sweatt v. Painter, 339 U.S. 629 (1950).

NATIONAL COLLEGIATE ATHLETIC ASSOCIATION (NCAA)

The National Collegiate Athletic Association (NCAA) is a voluntary association of approximately 1,200 institutions, organizations, and individuals committed to the administration and regulation of intercollegiate athletics. The history of the NCAA spans a little over one century. While the NCAA is neither the first nor the only intercollegiate athletic association, it is the largest collegiate athletic association in the world and arguably the most influential. This entry looks at the organization and key issues it faces.

Background

According to the organization's Web site, multiple injuries and deaths related to the use of the "flying wedge" formation in college football spurred the organization's formation in 1905. That year, President Theodore Roosevelt summoned college athletic leaders to two separate White House conferences on the reform of collegiate athletics, specifically football. Later in 1905, Henry MacCracken, chancellor of New York University, convened a meeting of 13 institutions to initiate changes in the rules governing college football. At a subsequent meeting in New York on December 28, the Intercollegiate Athletic Association of the United States (IAAUS) was founded with 62 members. Four years later in 1910, the IAAUS took its present name.

In 1973, the NCAA's membership was separated into three legislative divisions: divisions I, II, and III. In 1978, Division I members voted to create subdivisions I-A and I-AA in the sport of football. The NCAA began administering women's athletics programs in 1980. A year later, at its historic 75th convention, the organization adopted an extensive governance plan to include women's athletics programs, services, and representation. The delegates expanded the women's championships program with the addition of 19 events.

The basic underlying distinctions between Division I, II, and III schools are the number of sports that member institution must offer and the levels of athletic scholarship awards. For example, Division I schools are the leaders in collegiate athletic programs, with larger budgets, more elaborate facilities, and significantly more athletic scholarships than the other two divisions. Division II schools tend to include smaller public universities and many private institutions. Athletic scholarships are offered in most sponsored sports at most institutions, but there are more stringent limits as to the numbers offered in any one sport than at the Division I level. For example, Division II schools may give up to 36 football scholarships (whereas Division I-A, the highest level, is allowed 85 football scholarships). Division III schools range in size from less than 500 to over 10,000 students. Division III schools compete in athletics as

a non–revenue-making, extracurricular activity for students; for this reason, they may not offer athletic scholarships but only academic and need-based financial aid to their student-athletes.

Similar to the separate legislative divisions, the NCAA also offers four categories of membership, each with different requirements, voting rights, and dues payments. These categories are active membership, conference membership, affiliated membership, and corresponding membership. Of the four, active membership schools are eligible to compete in NCAA championships in their respective divisions and have a single vote on NCAA legislation.

Key Policies

The NCAA has played a significant role in shaping collegiate athletics since its inception, providing leadership on issues ranging from athletic recruitment and eligibility to drug testing, sports wagering, and student-athlete reinstatement. Three recent policies provide evidence of the organization's influence and of the authority of the NCAA. These policies focus on issues of gender, student-athlete academic performance, and diversity.

Gender and Title IX

Congress approved Title IX of The Educational Amendments of 1972, and President Richard M. Nixon signed the statute into law, on June 23, 1972. On July 21, 1975, Congress reviewed and approved Title IX regulations. Title IX requires educational institutions to maintain policies, practices, and programs that do not discriminate against anyone based on sex. Under this law, males and females are expected to receive fair and equal treatment in all arenas of public schooling: recruitment, admissions, educational programs and activities, course offerings and access, scholarships, sexual harassment, and athletics. In the area of athletics, compliance with Title IX is evaluated on three issues: athletic financial assistance, accommodation of athletic interests and abilities, and other program areas.

When the regulations were adopted, high schools and colleges were given three years, and elementary schools one year, to comply. On February 17, 1976, the NCAA challenged the legality of Title IX. In 1978, the Department of Health, Education and Welfare issued a formal policy on Title IX and intercollegiate athletics for notice and comment. July 21, 1978, was the deadline for all high schools and colleges to have policies and practices in place that complied with Title IX athletic requirements.

Academic Reform

In April, 2004, the NCAA Division I Management Council approved the academic reform package. This program, commonly referred to as the incentives/disincentives program, is designed to punish institutions and teams that fail to demonstrate commitment toward the academic progress, retention, and graduation of student-athletes. This program forces institutions to submit annual documentation demonstrating compliance with a minimum academic progress rate, which will be determined after the collection of data during the academic year. The program includes measurements that account for variances in institutional mission, sport, culture, and gender while holding institutions accountable for their academic progress. Institutions or teams that excel academically are recognized, while those failing to meet established minimums are penalized through a loss of athletic scholarships and eligibility to play in sanctioned NCAA postseason venues such as bowl games and national championships.

Indian Mascots

In 2005, the NCAA Executive Committee issued guidelines for the use of Native American mascots at championship events. According to the NCAA Web site, "The presidents and chancellors who serve on the NCAA Executive Committee adopted a new policy prohibiting NCAA colleges and universities from displaying hostile and abusive racial/ethnic/national-origin mascots, nicknames, or imagery at any of the 88 NCAA championships." The decision was based on the articulated core values of the NCAA Constitution pertaining to cultural diversity, ethical sportsmanship, and nondiscrimination. The NCAA's final policy change,

effective August 1, 2008, prohibits colleges and universities that display American Indian references on their mascots, cheerleaders, dance teams, and band uniforms from displaying them at any championship event.

George J. Petersen

See also Title IX and Athletics

Further Readings

Green, G. A., Uryasz, F. D., Petr, T. A., & Bray, C. D. (2001). NCAA study of substance use and abuse habits of college student-athletes. *Clinical Journal of Sport Medicine, 11*(1), 51–56.

Grimes, P. W., & Chressanthis, G. A. (1994). Alumni contributions to academics: The role of intercollegiate sports and NCAA sanctions. *American Journal of Economics and Sociology, 53*(1), 27–40.

Fleisher, A. A., Goff, B. L., & Tollison, R. D. (1992). *The National Collegiate Athletic Association: A study in cartel behavior.* Chicago, IL: University of Chicago Press.

National Collegiate Athletic Association. (n.d.) Retrieved February 26, 2007, from http://www.ncaa.org/wps/myportal

Sadker, D., & Sadker, M. (2007). *What is Title IX?* Retrieved from http://www.american.edu/sadker/titleix.htm

Washington, M. (2004). Field approaches to institutional change: The evolution of the National Collegiate Athletic Association 1906–1995. *Organizational Studies, 25*(3), 393–414.

Legal Citations

Title IX of the Educational Amendments of 1972, 20 U.S.C. § 1681.

NATIONAL DEFENSE EDUCATION ACT

The National Defense Education Act of 1958 (NDEA), enacted by the 85th Congress as Public Law 85–864 on September 2, 1958, was the principal federal support program for public education in the 1950s. This legislation, like federal policy at the time, was based on the belief that because education at all levels was directly linked with military research, it was an essential component of cold war strategies. The law provided federal funds in targeted areas. This entry summarizes the law's historical background, its content, and its impact.

Historical Background

With the start of the cold war at the end of World War II, members of scientific organizations were concerned with the lack of science, engineering, and mathematics majors in American universities. Insofar as these individuals placed the blame for this dearth of students in the technical fields directly on the public schools, they issued a call for a greater federal role in education. Even so, in light of the fact that education is a responsibility of states under the Tenth Amendment, the states and local school boards were reluctant to give up their control over education.

The national situation began to change when, on October 4, 1957, the Soviet Union launched *Sputnik I,* prompting fears that the United States was losing the cold war. Using the bully pulpit, President Eisenhower warned that national security was at risk. In speeches, he stated that in just 40 years the Soviet Union had gone from a nation of peasants to one that was technologically advanced. Eisenhower credited this transformation to the Soviet educational system, which was highly adept at identifying and educating talented students. To this end, Eisenhower stressed that the United States needed to gain superiority in military power, technological advancement, and research. Moreover, he pointed out that making such a transformation would require specialized education. According to Eisenhower, the improvement of the educational system was imperative to national defense, quelling many of the objections to federal intervention from those who supported local control of education.

What the Law Said

Perhaps the greatest fear that critics of federal intervention, who were also proponents of local control, raised was the imposition of a national curriculum. Title I of NDEA quelled this fear, because it prohibited federal control over curriculum, administration, and personnel.

Title II of the NDEA provided low-interest federal loans for college students. As an added incentive, the loan program included funds for students who demonstrated superior capacity for mathematics, science, engineering, and modern foreign languages. The purpose of this Title was to ensure an adequate flow of qualified graduates. Title III of the NDEA provided federal funds for staff development of teachers in mathematics, science, and modern languages. This was to ensure that students in public schools were adequately prepared to take on rigorous courses of study in these areas at the university level.

Title IV provided funds for graduate fellowships. This was premised on the need to ensure an adequate number of college faculties in mathematics, science, engineering, and modern languages. In order to ensure that promising students were identified, Title V provided funds for testing and counseling in public schools. It also allocated funds for guidance training institutes for secondary school guidance counselors. The role of the guidance counselor changed as a consequence of Title V insofar as it placed an emphasis on identifying and counseling talented students into curricular areas that were important to national defense. At the same time, there was a subsequent reduction in their role in caring for students with personality problems.

Title VI of the NDEA provided funds for language institutes as well as language centers and research, because there was a growing concern that the Soviet Union was surpassing the United States in world influence due to an American lack of knowledge about many areas of the world. Title VI also allocated funds for studies of history, anthropology, political science, economics, geography, and geology, to ensure satisfactory teaching in these areas.

In sum, the purpose of NDEA was for the federal government to assist states in shoring up weaker areas of education. In furtherance of this effort, the NDEA also provided grant funds for collecting statistical data in the assessment of science, math, and language education. These data were also to be reported to the Office of Education.

The Law's Impact

At its heart, the NDEA offered categorical aid to local school boards, funds that were allocated for specific programs, materials, and curricula. In this way, the federal government was able to impose significant control on schools. This strategy would be used again in the authorizations of the Elementary and Secondary Education Act, now reauthorized as the No Child Left Behind Act.

Another significant legacy of NDEA was the federal government's reliance on the views of members of the scientific community over those of education professionals in its development. This not only eroded the power of national education groups, such as the National Education Association, but also allowed the federal government greater control over educational priorities and practices. Finally, in light of the NDEA, because education was linked to the interests of both national security and economic prosperity, its main focus was perceived as being designed to support these interests.

Patricia A. L. Ehrensal

See also Federalism and the Tenth Amendment; No Child Left Behind Act

Legal Citations

National Defense Education Act of 1958, P.L. 85–864.

NATIONAL LABOR RELATIONS ACT

The National Labor Relations Act was passed during the Great Depression in an effort to define employer practices that would be considered unfair, thus protecting workers and in particular their right to organize and bargain collectively. What some consider to be the *Magna Carta* of American Labor, the law changed the workplace environment and led to a series of other laws that added restraints on workers and expanded existing laws to cover public employees. This entry describes the law and its impact.

The Law and Its Context

The Great Depression had settled across the country bringing with it anxiety, loss, and fear. The economic hard times produced uncertainty, resulting in a quest for security. There were more workers than jobs, and workers that had jobs sought to protect them. Strikes, lockouts, and violence marred labor relations. Employers punished, interrogated, blacklisted, and fired workers who joined unions. Workers and union leaders shut down factories and businesses. News stories regularly reported the clash of workers, intent on organizing, with employers and their private security forces, often backed by the police, equally intent on breaking the union. In 1933 and 1934, the nation was rocked by large-scale work stoppages, citywide strikes, and the occupation of factories as workers sought to organize.

Against this backdrop of deepening labor unrest and growing militant organizing, Senator Robert F. Wagner, a Democrat from New York, submitted a bill in 1933 titled the National Labor Relations Act (NLRA). Secretary of Labor Frances Perkins backed the NLRA. The NLRA became known as the Wagner Act when, on July 5, 1935, Congress enacted it. President Roosevelt signed the act, but he did not take part in its development. The NLRA was designed to diminish labor disputes by protecting the rights of employees to organize and bargain collectively with the employer. Further, the NLRA sought to safeguard "commerce from injury, impairment, or interruption, and promote the flow of commerce by removing certain recognized sources of industrial strife and unrest."

The NLRA protects workers who seek to form and join unions through self-organizing efforts, with the goal of selecting a representative of their choice. According to the NLRA, employers must meet with the exclusive representatives of their employees to bargain in good faith over wages, benefits, and terms and conditions of employment. The NLRA, in essence, altered the unilateral decision-making power that employers enjoyed, replacing it with bilateral negotiations over issues that were subject to bargaining. Under the NLRA, workers gained the full right of freedom of association and with it the protection to seek mutual aid and protection. In addition, the NLRA prohibited management from interfering with or restraining employees from exercising their right to organize and bargain; it also prohibited management from dominating or influencing a labor union.

The NLRA created the National Labor Relations Board (NLRB), a quasi-judicial body, to administer its provisions. The NLRB conducts elections for exclusive representatives, determining who is in the unit through a process of evaluating which employees have a "community of interest" in their positions, and investigates charges of unfair labor practices in violation of its provisions. The NLRB can also issue "cease and desist" orders against unfair labor practices. While the NLRB has no enforcement mechanism of its own, it can seek enforcement of its orders in the U.S. Court of Appeals. Similarly, parties to disputes that come before the NLRB may seek relief through the courts. The NLRB currently consists of five members and its general counsel selected by the president of the United States subject to approval by the Senate. Thirty-three regional directors assist the board.

Impact and Evolution

Prior to the passage of the NLRA, only about 10% of the private sector workforce was organized. After the NLRA was enacted, there was a dramatic surge in union membership, including both men and women. Industries such as automakers, manufacturing, steel, and rubber saw a significant increase in union membership. As their membership increased, so did the political clout of unions. Strikes over union recognition were reduced as the union movement's fight for recognition moved from the economic arena, characterized by such concerted actions as strikes, lockouts, and strife, to the political arena, in which the rights of employees were resolved through a quasi-judicial process.

The NLRA faced a legal challenge, but the Supreme Court upheld its constitutionality in *National Labor Relations Board v. Jones & Laughlin Steel Corporation* in 1937. While the NLRA survived this legal challenge, it changed 10 years later. The legislation responded to employers' and labor opponents' concern that the NLRA had gone too far in giving power to unions. Some asserted that the unions were corrupt and riddled with Communists.

In 1947, at the start of the cold war, Congress enacted the Labor-Management Relations Act, commonly known as the Taft-Hartley Act. A Republican-controlled Congress passed the act over the veto of President Truman. Opponents of the bill dubbed it the "slave labor bill," arguing that it would usher in an era of industrial slavery.

The NLRA envisioned a restraint only on management's action. There were no union activities that could be considered unfair labor practices. Taft-Hartley leveled the playing field by adding prohibitions on labor while retaining the prohibitions on management. Taft-Hartley classified such union acts as secondary boycotts; sympathy strikes, which anti-union groups called "blackmail strikes"; and closed shops as unfair labor practices. Another course correction of Taft-Hartley was a move toward individualistic rights and a diminishment of group rights. For example, the Taft-Hartley bill outlawed closed shops and protected employees from coercive and discriminatory acts committed by the union. The act also compelled union officials to take an oath that they were not Communists.

The NLRA and the Taft-Hartley Act both pertain to the private sector. Neither extended the rights granted to private employees to government workers. However, starting in 1962, with President John F. Kennedy's Executive Order 10988, public sector bargaining took root. The resulting public sector collective bargaining laws were largely grafts from the NLRA and the Taft-Hartley Act. This wholesale importation of law developed for the private-sector, largely industrial, union workplace has had and still has wide-reaching ramifications for states, local school boards, and teachers in public schools.

Todd A. DeMitchell

See also Agency Shop; Arbitration; Closed Shop; Collective Bargaining; Impasse in Bargaining; *National Labor Relations Board v. Catholic Bishop of Chicago;* Unions

Further Readings

Baum, E. B. (2005). NLRB refuses to harm "academic freedom" at universities by permitting graduate student assistants to unionize. *Mercer Law Review, 56,* 793–803.

DeMitchell, T. A., & Cobb, C. (2006). Teachers: Their union and their profession. A tangled relationship. *Education Law Reporter, 212,* 1–20.

Gould, W. B. (2000). *Labored relations: Law, politics, and the NLRB: A memoir.* Cambridge: MIT Press.

Legal Citations

National Labor Relations Act, 29 U.S.C. §§ 151 *et seq.* (1947), includes Taft-Hartley revision.

National Labor Relations Board v. Jones & Laughlin Steel Corporation, 301 U.S. 1 (1937).

NATIONAL LABOR RELATIONS BOARD V. CATHOLIC BISHOP OF CHICAGO

In *National Labor Relations Board v. Catholic Bishop of Chicago* (1979), the only case on the legal issue of unions in Roman Catholic schools, a closely divided U.S. Supreme Court affirmed an earlier ruling from the Seventh Circuit that the National Labor Relations Board (NLRB) lacked jurisdiction to mandate collective bargaining between teachers and their secondary school employers. The dispute in *Catholic Bishop* mirrored, in many respects, developments in the then-recent growth of unions in public education.

The controversy arose after the seemingly bright future of labor relations in Roman Catholic schools received an unexpected boost in 1975, when the NLRB asserted its jurisdiction over union organizing activities in two Catholic secondary schools, one in the Archdiocese of Chicago, Illinois, and the other in the Diocese of Fort Wayne–South Bend, Indiana. Yet, despite an order from the NLRB that the boards and the leadership in the schools recognize, and meet, with the bargaining representatives selected by their teachers, officials refused to comply with the directive. Instead, school officials appealed to the Seventh Circuit, which held that the NLRB improperly exercised its discretion in light of the religious nature of the schools and that related First Amendment considerations precluded it from asserting its jurisdiction. When the NLRB sought further review, the U.S. Supreme Court agreed to hear an appeal.

On March 24, 1979, the U.S. Supreme Court, in a 5-to-4 judgment that was destined to become a landmark in the history of teacher organizations and labor relations in Roman Catholic schools, affirmed that the NLRB lacked the authority to mandate collective bargaining between teachers and their religious employers. In its analysis, the Court framed two issues for consideration. The first question was whether Congress intended to grant the NLRB jurisdiction over teachers in religiously affiliated nonpublic schools. The second issue asked that if Congress had intended to confer such authority on the NLRB, whether its doing so would have violated the constitutionally sensitive First Amendment Religion Clause questions by engaging in impermissible and excessive governmental entanglement with the religious missions and day to-day-activities of the schools.

Sidestepping the thorny First Amendment Religion Clause issues, the Court relied on long-established precedent that it should not interpret an act of Congress as violating the Constitution if any other possible interpretation of a law remains available. Based on a review of the legislative history of the National Labor Relations Act (NLRA), the Court answered the initial question by pointing out that Congress did not display a clear and affirmative intent to extend the NLRB's jurisdiction to Roman Catholic and other religiously affiliated nonpublic schools. Accordingly, the Court found it unnecessary to resolve what would have been highly contentious First Amendment Religion Clause issues.

This case's impact on labor relations in Roman Catholic and, by extension, other religiously affiliated nonpublic schools is legally significant in two important ways. First, the Court's opinion created a void, leaving educators in religious schools without legal recourse to neutral third-party decision makers who could resolve labor disputes where governing bodies and/or educational officials refused to consent to the jurisdiction of appropriate agencies designed to protect the employment rights of teachers. Second, although the Court challenged leaders in Roman Catholic schools, in particular, the largest group of religiously affiliated nonpublic schools in the United States, to devise an alternative plan to provide some form of representations for their teachers in disputes about labor relations, those leaders failed to act and have yet to do so.

Charles J. Russo

See also Collective Bargaining; First Amendment; Nonpublic schools; Unions

Further Readings

Russo, C. J. (1990). *NLRB v. Catholic Bishop of Chicago:* Collective bargaining in Roman Catholic secondary schools ten years later. *West's Education Law Reporter, 57*(4), 1113–1121.

Legal Citations

NLRB v. Catholic Bishop of Chicago, 440 U.S. 490 (1979).

NATIONAL LEAGUE OF CITIES V. USERY

National League of Cities v. Usery (1976) is an important case in the long debate over the division of powers between the U.S. government and the governments of the individual states. Although the U.S. Supreme Court's ruling in *Usery,* favoring state powers, was overruled just a few years later, the decision is often cited as one of the first to signal the new era of states' rights that has existed since the last quarter of the 20th century. This movement toward states' rights reached a high water mark under the Rehnquist Court and in a particular decision, *United States v. Lopez* (1995), where the Court ruled that federal rules limiting gun possession in school zones did not relate closely enough to commerce to be justified under the Commerce Clause. This entry discusses *Usery* and its impact.

Usery concerned amendments to the Fair Labor Standards Act (FLSA), which set out minimum wage and maximum hour provisions for state employees. Traditionally, the states have controlled their own employees without federal intervention over wages and hours. Thus, the states, along with the National League of Cities and the National Governors Association, challenged the new provisions adopted by Congress as unconstitutional.

The central issue in *Usery* was to weigh the Commerce Power given to the federal government in Article I of the Constitution against the essential sovereignty the states retained: specifically, whether the ability of states to determine the wages and hours of state employees was essential to their independence,

to the degree that federal involvement would undermine their very existence.

The case has implications for education, because the latter is traditionally a function of the states. Thus, when controversies between the power of the federal government and the sovereignty of the states arise, these decisions directly impact the possible control over education that the federal government may seek to wrest from the states.

Ultimately, the majority of the Supreme Court concluded that the FLSA's minimum wage and maximum hour requirements for public employees were unconstitutional. The law's provisions undermined traditional practices of the states and would imperil their independent identities and existence, the court said. Although the Tenth Amendment was not specifically used as a justification for the decision, the court found that is was more than a truism and contained some limits on Congress's power to act against interests reserved for the states. Such functions as building and maintaining hospitals, fire and police departments, and schools were clearly and traditionally within the purview of the states, the Court ruled. Thus, the interests inherent in traditional governmental functions of the states were found to override the federal authority granted to Congress in the Commerce Clause.

The *Usery* decision lasted only eight years before being explicitly overruled in *Garcia v. San Antonio Metropolitan Transit Authority* (1985). In that case, the Supreme Court found that the "traditional governmental functions" rule was too unwieldy to serve any practical purpose. It was extremely difficult to identify what governmental functions were traditionally allotted to the states, even though some such functions, including education, were found to be state functions by the court in *Usery.* Further, the Court found that the Tenth Amendment had little practical meaning and did not limit the Commerce Clause, because the political process is sufficient to ensure states' rights.

In the recent cases discussed in this entry, including the overruled *Usery,* the Supreme Court has indicated there are limitations to the reach of the Commerce Clause of Article I of the Constitution. Thus, while the General Welfare Clause of Article I has allowed for substantial federal involvement in education under its spending powers, the application of the Commerce Clause to education has been very limited, partly as a result of these cases.

Justin M. Bathon

See also Federalism and the Tenth Amendment; *United States v. Lopez*

Further Readings

Delon, F. G., & Van Zandt, M. A. (1985). The pendulum continues to swing: *Garcia v. San Antonio Metropolitan Transit Authority. West's Education Law Reporter, 26,* 1–11.

Legal Citations

Garcia v. San Antonio Metropolitan Transit Authority, 469 U.S. 528 (1985).
National League of Cities v. Usery, 426 U.S. 833 (1976).
United States. v. Lopez, 514 U.S. 549 (1995).

National Treasury Employees Union v. Von Raab

National Treasury Employees Union v. Von Raab (1989), along with its companion case of *Skinner v. Railway Labor Executives' Association* (1989), stands out for the proposition that under some circumstances, public employers may be able to require staff members to submit to suspicionless drug testing. Although Von Raab was not set in a school context, it raises interesting implications for employees of public school systems.

Facts of the Case

In Von Raab, employees of the U.S. Customs Service and their union filed suit on behalf of employees who were preparing to apply for "covered" positions. The suit challenged the Customs Service's urinalysis drug testing program, alleging that it violated, among other things, their Fourth Amendment rights, because it called for suspicionless drug searches.

It is worth noting that the Customs Service, whose function is to monitor and seize illegal drugs being smuggled or otherwise brought into the United States, began a drug testing program for employees who wished to apply for transfers or promotions to positions having more responsibilities, namely covered positions. The program mandated that if applicants sought to work in the areas of direct involvement with drug interdiction, possession and/or use of firearms, or classified materials, then they had to have been tested for five illegal drugs. Among other things, the program required that applicants be notified that their selection was contingent on successful completion of drug screening; it set forth procedures for collection and analysis of the requisite samples and procedures designed both to ensure against adulteration or substitution of specimens and to limit the intrusion on employee privacy. In addition, the program provided that test results were not to be turned over to any other agencies, including criminal prosecutors, without the employees' written consent. Passing the urinalysis tests was the final determinant for promotion to these covered positions. Employees who failed the urinalysis tests without plausible explanations were subject to dismissal from the Customs Service.

A federal trial court in Louisiana rejected the government's motion to dismiss. Instead, the court called for the testing to stop, because it found that the suspicionless nature of the program violated the employees' expectations of privacy. However, the Fifth Circuit reversed in favor of the Customs Service on the basis that although the urinalysis drug testing program was a search within the meaning of the Fourth Amendment, it was reasonable because of its limited scope. The court also justified the search in light of the mission of the Customs Service and the government's strong interest in detecting drug use among employees in covered positions.

The Court's Ruling

At the outset of its analysis in *Von Raab*, the Supreme Court noted that the program had to satisfy the Fourth Amendment's reasonableness requirement. The *Von Raab* Court created a three-pronged test for determining reasonableness. First, the Court noted that it was necessary to evaluate whether a search provides the basis for a special need that goes beyond the regular need for law enforcement. Here the Court acknowledged that because the program was designed to deter drug use among selected Customs agents, and not to meet the ordinary needs of criminal prosecution, it presented a special need that justified departing from the usual warrant and probable cause requirements. Second, the Court indicated that it had to decide whether it was necessary to obtain a warrant for the search or if there was any level of suspicion that was needed to balance the individual privacy rights against the governmental interest in context. Third, the Court pointed out that it had to establish whether the intrusion was reasonable and would obtain the desired information. As such, the Court eliminated any subjectivity as a measure for reasonableness, instead establishing a balancing test as long as the positive characteristics justifying its application were present.

Insofar as the Supreme Court was unable to address the reasonableness of testing for agents who handled classified materials, it remanded for further proceedings to clarify the scope of employees subject to testing. *Von Raab*'s significance lies in the fact that the Supreme Court abolished the need for suspicion as a prerequisite for justifying the search from the beginning as was the original standard.

Marilyn J. Bartlett

See also Drug Testing of Teachers; *O'Connor v. Ortega*

Legal Citations

National Treasury Employees Union v. Von Raab, 489 U.S. 656 (1989).
O'Connor v. Ortega, 480 U.S. 709 (1987).
Skinner v. Railway Labor Executives' Association, 489 U.S. 602 (1989).

NEGLIGENCE

Educators, including teachers and school administrators, are often concerned about the extent of their legal liability for injuries sustained by children who are under their direct supervision as students. When educators are sued for injuries to children, it is under the broad rubric of the tort of negligence. Torts are civil wrongs that occur when persons suffer harms or losses as a direct consequence of the improper conduct of others.

One type of tort, intentional torts, such as assault, battery, and defamation, are expressly characterized as the intent to do harm to others. For example, while assault is the threat of an unwanted touch, battery is the actual unwanted intentional contact with another person, such as striking a child while in the act of imposing corporal punishment.

By far, the most common tort occurring in schools is negligence. Negligence occurs when accidents take place resulting in injuries to others because one failed to act reasonably. In determining liability for negligence, courts and others such as insurance companies must assess whether the persons alleged to have been responsible acted as reasonable and prudent persons would have acted under the same or similar circumstances.

In order to present valid causes of action for negligence, plaintiffs, the parties filing suit, must prove the four legal elements of this tort: duty of care (along with the related notion of foreseeability), breach of duty, actual injury or loss, and cause, meaning that the defendant was the proximate cause of the resulting injury. To escape full or partial liability, defendants must assert all or parts of the three defenses: immunity, comparative or contributory negligence, and assumption of risk. This entry describes these legal elements and defenses in the education context.

Causes of Action

In school settings, educators have a duty of care to act as "reasonable and prudent" persons under the circumstances toward others, particularly students, with whom they have either common-law or statutory relationships. In other words, teachers must adequately supervise their students in order to satisfy their legal responsibility of duty of care. However, the degree of this supervision depends on a multitude of factors, including the ages of the students as well as the nature of their activities. For instance, courts impose higher duties of care on educators in potentially dangerous classroom settings such as a chemistry laboratory when compared to traditional classroom environments. Moreover, courts have consistently ruled that educators owe higher duties of care to younger students or those who have diminished mental capacities and lesser duties of care to older students and those who are not disabled.

Under their responsibility of duty of care, educators have a legal duty to anticipate reasonably foreseeable injuries or risks to students and take reasonably proactive steps to protect students from harm. Educators can be liable only for those negligent acts that were reasonably foreseeable or those acts of which they were aware.

In terms of the second element of negligence, breach of duty, there are generally two legal conditions that are taken into account in assessing whether educators breached their duty of care. The first addresses how educators performed their duties. Teachers can breach their duty in one of two ways: either by nonfeasance, or not acting when there is a duty to do so (such as not breaking up a fight), or by misfeasance, acting incorrectly under the circumstances (such as using too much force in breaking up a fight).

When evaluating whether individuals met the second element under breach, the appropriate standard of care, the courts have adopted the legal standard of reasonableness, also referred to as "the reasonably prudent person" standard. Increasingly, courts are moving toward the adoption of a standard for educators that requires them to provide a level of care based on factors such as age, training, education, and experience. Put another way, under the reasonable educator standard, courts ordinarily expect teachers and other school staff to provide a higher duty of care than the "reasonable persons" who are not educators but less than the degree of care that "reasonable parents" might perform.

The third element of negligence is the proof of actual loss or injury. In order for injured parties to prevail in negligence suits and receive compensation, they must prove that their injuries were the direct result of negligent acts of others. Courts may award three kinds of damages to injured parties in negligence suits. The most common award in a negligence suit is compensatory damages that compensate injured parties for their actual losses, including medical expenses, lost salary, and court-related costs. Even so, in most negligence actions, attorneys work on the basis of contingency fee arrangements, meaning that they are not paid unless they prevail in court for their clients or are able to procure so-called out-of-court settlements.

Nominal damages refer to small, symbolic awards that courts grant where injured parties were wronged but were unable to prove they suffered any legal damages. Punitive damages, which courts rarely award, are designed to compensate injured parties when there is evidence of reckless disregard of the safety or constitutional rights of injured persons.

The final element of negligence, proximate cause, indicates that a causal connection must exist between educators' conduct and the resulting injuries for legally valid claims of negligence to prevail. Courts consistently agree that negligent liability may be mitigated if the defense can prove that the cause of the injury was the result of an intervening act, for example, if a child ignored orders not to run out of a school yard to chase a ball and was injured on being struck by a car.

Legal Defenses

In negligence suits, the legal burden of proof is usually on the injured persons, or plaintiffs, to prove that the defendants were negligent. Despite instances where the injured parties have successfully established that the four elements of negligence were present, the three defenses are available in negligence suits. In the educational environment, these legal defenses recognize that while school officials have a legal duty of care to protect students, they cannot be legally responsible for all unintentional harms that occur within school settings.

Immunity is the defense that school boards and their employees may use in negligence actions. The immunity defense is premised on the notion that because public school boards are agents of the state, they should not be liable for corporate activity unless the state legislature has specifically ruled otherwise.

A second pair of defenses, contributory and comparative negligence, are based on the premise that injured parties played an integral part in contributing toward their injuries. Contributory and comparative negligence defenses, which not only sound very much alike but also apply in an almost equal number of jurisdictions, produce very different results. Under contributory negligence, parties whose actions led to the cause of their injuries are unable to recover for the harm that they suffered. Yet, insofar as this approach has led to inequitable results, a growing number of states have adopted comparative negligence, which allows courts to direct juries to apportion fault between the parties. As such, the recoveries that injured parties make may be reduced by the degree to which they played a part in causing their own injuries.

According to the third, and final, defense, assumption of risk, if injured parties understood and appreciated the risks associated with their activities and resulting injuries, their recoveries may be limited or eliminated. Such a limitation is based on the degree to which their conduct contributed to their accident as well as on whether they exposed themselves to a known or appreciated risk of harm. In school environments, the assumption of risk defense is most often applied in negligence suits involving students who are injured while participating in sports-related activities.

Kevin P. Brady

See also Assault and Battery, Civil; Attorney Fees; Immunity

Further Readings

Dodd, V. J. (2003). *Practical education law for the twenty-first century.* Durham, NC: Carolina Academic Press.

Russo, C. J. (2004). *Reutter's the law of public education* (5th ed.). New York: Foundation Press.

Vacca, R. S., & Bosher, W. C. (2003). *Law and education: Contemporary issues and court decisions* (6th ed.). Charlottesville, VA: LexisNexis.

New Jersey v. T. L. O.

The U.S. Supreme Court's decision in *New Jersey v. T. L. O.* (1985) was a landmark opinion concerning the Fourth Amendment rights of students, protecting them from unreasonable searches and seizures while in schools. In *T. L. O.*, the Court ruled that when carrying out searches or other disciplinary procedures, school officials act as agents of the state, that students do have a legitimate expectation of privacy but that it must be balanced against the needs of educators to maintain order and safety, and that the "reasonable suspicion" standard applies when school officials choose to search students.

Facts of the Case

At issue in *T. L. O.* was a vice principal's search of a student's purse for cigarettes while investigating a smoking violation. Uncovering cigarettes in the student's purse, the vice principal also discovered rolling papers. Suspecting drug use by T. L. O., the vice principal continued his search of the purse, discovering a small amount of marijuana, a pipe, plastic bags, a substantial quantity of money in one-dollar bills, a list containing the names of students who owed T. L. O. money, and two letters implicating her in marijuana dealing.

T. L. O. was turned over to the police and confessed that she had been dealing drugs. On the basis of the confession and the evidence seized by the vice principal, the state brought delinquency charges against T. L. O. Seeking to suppress the evidence found in her purse, T. L. O. contended that the vice principal violated her Fourth Amendment rights.

A juvenile court in New Jersey, finding that the search was reasonable, adjudicated T. L. O. delinquent. An appellate court affirmed as to the Fourth Amendment, but remanded on other grounds. The Supreme Court of New Jersey reversed and ordered the suppression of the evidence found in T. L. O.'s purse on the basis that the search was unreasonable.

The Court's Ruling

The case was appealed to the U.S. Supreme Court, which reversed the order of the Supreme Court of New Jersey. At issue before the Court was whether the Fourth Amendment restricted the actions of public school officials in school settings. The Court ruled that when conducting searches and disciplinary actions, school officials act as agents of the state and therefore are restricted by the Fourth Amendment. Additionally, the Court explained that while students have a legitimate expectation of privacy while in school, this needs to be balanced with school officials' need to maintain safety and order. Therefore, the Court decided that the school setting requires some easing of the restrictions usually applied to searches by public authorities. The Court pointed out that the warrant requirement was unsuited to schools, as it would have overly impeded the disciplinary procedures needed in that situation.

The Court was of the opinion that the school setting required some modification of the level of suspicion of illicit activity needed to justify a search. The Court noted that school officials only need "reasonable suspicion" to conduct a search of a student, a standard that is much lower than the "probable cause" requirement that applies to the police. The Court was of the opinion that a search is justified at its inception when there is reasonable basis for suspecting that a search will produce evidence that a student has or is violating either the law or school rules. The Court added that a search is reasonable in its scope as long as the intrusiveness of the search is justified given the object of the search and is not excessively intrusive in light of the age and sex of the child. The Court hoped that this standard would at once facilitate school officials' need to maintain order and safety and not intrude on students' expectation of privacy.

T. L. O. was a narrow judgment that left three questions unresolved, because they were not at issue. The first unanswered question dealt with the need for individualized suspicion when applying the reasonable suspicion standard. In this case, because T. L. O. was accused of smoking, and there was individualized suspicion, the Court found it unnecessary to address whether the reasonableness standard applied to cases without individualized suspicion. The second unresolved issue was whether the reasonableness standard applies in more intrusive searches, such as strip searches. Insofar as it did not think that the search of T. L. O.'s purse was intrusive, the Court did not have to resolve this issue. Third, because only school officials took part in the search, the Court did not consider whether the reasonableness standard applied to searches conducted by nonschool officials such as the police.

Other Justices Speak

In his concurrence, Justice Lewis F. Powell, Jr., emphasized that the nature of the institution favors the use of the reasonable suspicion standard in school settings. For Powell, schools are different from other public institutions, because their mission is the educating and training of young people. Powell acknowledged that such activity takes place in an environment where students and teachers daily spend many hours in close

association, which gives rise to a unique relationship between the students and school officials. Owing to the unique relationships and the state's compelling interest in the activities that occur within school, Powell determined that students have a lesser expectation of privacy. In addition, Powell believed that the Fourth Amendment did not restrict school officials in their relationships with students to the extent that it does law enforcement agents in their dealings with criminals.

Justice Harry Blackmun's concurrence emphasized the need for the reasonableness standard in making three points. First, he acknowledged that the disciplinary problems posed by the increase in the presence of drugs and weapons in schools require immediate responses. Second, Blackmun indicated that school officials are not trained in the complexities of probable cause. Third, he wrote that requiring school officials to rely on probable cause would have severely disrupted the educational process.

In dissenting in part, Justice William Brennan argued that full-scale searches, including those of students by school officials, unaccompanied by probable cause violated the Fourth Amendment. Based on the close association of school officials and students in the schoolhouse and the "untechnical" nature of determining probable cause, he asserted that searches in schools should have been based on probable cause. Brennan posited that the establishment of the lesser "reasonableness" standard was not only unnecessary but improper.

Justice John Paul Stevens's dissent claimed that one needs to distinguish between minor and serious offenses in evaluating the reasonableness of a school search. Additionally, he contended that the reasonable suspicion standard taught children the wrong lesson about the nature and power of the government.

Patricia A. L. Ehrensal

See also *Board of Education of Independent School District No. 92 of Pottawatomie County v. Earls;* Drugs, Dog Searches for; Juvenile Courts; Locker Searches; Strip Searches; *Vernonia School District 47J v. Acton*

Legal Citations

Board of Education of Independent School District No. 92 of Pottawatomie County v. Earls, 536 U.S. 822 (2002), *on remand,* 300 F.3d 1222 (10th Cir. 2002)
New Jersey v. T. L. O., 469 U.S. 325 (1985).

New Jersey v. T. L. O. (Excerpts)

New Jersey v. T. L. O. *is noteworthy as the first case wherein the Supreme Court addressed the Fourth Amendment rights of students in school settings.*

Supreme Court of the United States
NEW JERSEY
v.
T. L. O.
469 U.S. 325
Argued March 28, 1984.
Reargued Oct. 2, 1984.
Decided Jan. 15, 1985.

Justice WHITE delivered the opinion of the Court.

We granted certiorari in this case to examine the appropriateness of the exclusionary rule as a remedy for searches carried out in violation of the Fourth Amendment by public school authorities. Our consideration of the proper application of the Fourth Amendment to the public schools, however, has led us to conclude that the search that gave rise to the case now before us did not violate the Fourth Amendment. Accordingly, we here address only the questions of the proper standard for assessing the legality of searches conducted by public school officials and the application of that standard to the facts of this case.

I

On March 7, 1980, a teacher at Piscataway High School in Middlesex County, N.J., discovered two girls smoking in a lavatory. One of the two girls was the respondent T. L. O., who at that time was a 14-year-old high school freshman. Because smoking in the lavatory was a violation of a school rule, the teacher took the two girls to the Principal's office, where they met with Assistant Vice Principal Theodore Choplick. In response to questioning by Mr. Choplick, T. L. O.'s companion admitted that she had violated the rule. T. L. O., however, denied that she had been smoking in the lavatory and claimed that she did not smoke at all.

Mr. Choplick asked T. L. O. to come into his private office and demanded to see her purse. Opening the purse, he found a pack of cigarettes, which he removed from the purse and held before T. L. O. as he accused her of having lied to him. As he reached into the purse for the cigarettes, Mr. Choplick also noticed a package of cigarette rolling papers. In his experience, possession of rolling papers by high school students was closely associated with the use of marihuana. Suspecting that a closer examination of the purse might yield further evidence of drug use, Mr. Choplick proceeded to search the purse thoroughly. The search revealed a small amount of marihuana, a pipe, a number of empty plastic bags, a substantial quantity of money in one-dollar bills, an index card that appeared to be a list of students who owed T. L. O. money, and two letters that implicated T. L. O. in marihuana dealing.

Mr. Choplick notified T. L. O.'s mother and the police, and turned the evidence of drug dealing over to the police. At the request of the police, T. L. O.'s mother took her daughter to police headquarters, where T. L. O. confessed that she had been selling marihuana at the high school. On the basis of the confession and the evidence seized by Mr. Choplick, the State brought delinquency charges against T. L. O. in the Juvenile and Domestic Relations Court of Middlesex County. Contending that Mr. Choplick's search of her purse violated the Fourth Amendment, T. L. O. moved to suppress the evidence found in her purse as well as her confession, which, she argued, was tainted by the allegedly unlawful search. The Juvenile Court denied the motion to suppress. Although the court concluded that the Fourth Amendment did apply to searches carried out by school officials, it held that "a school official may properly conduct a search of a student's person if the official has a reasonable suspicion that a crime has been or is in the process of being committed, *or* reasonable cause to believe that the search is necessary to maintain school discipline or enforce school policies."

Applying this standard, the court concluded that the search conducted by Mr. Choplick was a reasonable one. The initial decision to open the purse was justified by Mr. Choplick's well-founded suspicion that T. L. O. had violated the rule forbidding smoking in the lavatory. Once the purse was open, evidence of marihuana violations was in plain view, and Mr. Choplick was entitled to conduct a thorough search to determine the nature and extent of T. L. O.'s drug-related activities. Having denied the motion to suppress, the court on March 23, 1981, found T. L. O. to be a delinquent and on January 8, 1982, sentenced her to a year's probation.

On appeal from the final judgment of the Juvenile Court, a divided Appellate Division affirmed the trial court's finding that there had been no Fourth Amendment violation, but vacated the adjudication of delinquency and remanded for a determination whether T. L. O. had knowingly and voluntarily waived her Fifth Amendment rights before confessing. T. L. O. appealed the Fourth Amendment ruling, and the Supreme Court of New Jersey reversed the judgment of the Appellate Division and ordered the suppression of the evidence found in T. L. O.'s purse. . . .

    . . . .

We granted the State of New Jersey's petition for certiorari. Although the State had argued in the Supreme Court of New Jersey that the search of T. L. O.'s purse did not violate the Fourth Amendment, the petition for certiorari raised only the question whether the exclusionary rule should operate to bar consideration in juvenile delinquency proceedings of evidence unlawfully seized by a school official without the involvement of law enforcement officers. When this case was first argued last Term, the State conceded for the purpose of argument that the standard devised by the New Jersey Supreme Court for determining the legality of school searches was appropriate and that the court had correctly applied that standard; the State contended only that the remedial purposes of the exclusionary rule were not well served by applying it to searches conducted by public authorities not primarily engaged in law enforcement.

Although we originally granted certiorari to decide the issue of the appropriate remedy in juvenile court proceedings for unlawful school searches, our doubts regarding the wisdom of deciding that question in isolation from the broader question of what limits, if any, the Fourth Amendment places on the activities of school authorities prompted us to order reargument on that question. Having heard argument on the legality of the search of T. L. O.'s purse, we are satisfied that the search did not violate the Fourth Amendment.

II

In determining whether the search at issue in this case violated the Fourth Amendment, we are faced initially with the question whether that Amendment's prohibition on unreasonable searches and seizures applies to searches conducted by public school officials. We hold that it does.

It is now beyond dispute that "the Federal Constitution, by virtue of the Fourteenth Amendment, prohibits unreasonable searches and seizures by state officers." Equally indisputable is the proposition that the Fourteenth Amendment protects the rights of students against encroachment by public school officials: "The Fourteenth Amendment, as now applied to the States, protects the citizen against the State itself and all of its creatures—Boards of Education not excepted. These have, of course, important, delicate, and highly discretionary functions, but none that they may not perform within the limits of the Bill of Rights. That they are educating the young for citizenship is reason for scrupulous protection of Constitutional freedoms of the individual, if we are not to strangle the free mind at its source and teach youth to discount important principles of our government as mere platitudes."

These two propositions—that the Fourth Amendment applies to the States through the Fourteenth Amendment, and that the actions of public school officials are subject to the limits placed on state action by the Fourteenth Amendment—might appear sufficient to answer the suggestion that the Fourth Amendment does not proscribe unreasonable searches by school officials. On reargument, however, the State of New Jersey has argued that the history of the Fourth Amendment indicates that the Amendment was intended to regulate only searches and seizures carried out by law enforcement officers; accordingly, although public school officials are concededly state agents for purposes of the Fourteenth Amendment, the Fourth Amendment creates no rights enforceable against them.

It may well be true that the evil toward which the Fourth Amendment was primarily directed was the resurrection of the pre-Revolutionary practice of using general warrants or "writs of assistance" to authorize searches for contraband by officers of the Crown. But this Court has never limited the Amendment's prohibition on unreasonable searches and seizures to operations conducted by the police. Rather, the Court has long spoken of the Fourth Amendment's strictures as restraints imposed upon "governmental action"—that is, "upon the activities of sovereign authority." Accordingly, we have held the Fourth Amendment applicable to the activities of civil as well as criminal authorities: building inspectors, Occupational Safety and Health Act inspectors, and even firemen entering privately owned premises to battle a fire are all subject to the restraints imposed by the Fourth Amendment. As we observed in *Camara v. Municipal Court*, "[t]he basic purpose of this Amendment, as recognized in countless decisions of this Court, is to safeguard the privacy and security of individuals against arbitrary invasions by governmental officials." Because the individual's interest in privacy and personal security "suffers whether the government's motivation is to investigate violations of criminal laws or breaches of other statutory or regulatory standards," it would be "anomalous to say that the individual and his private property are fully protected by the Fourth Amendment only when the individual is suspected of criminal behavior."

Notwithstanding the general applicability of the Fourth Amendment to the activities of civil authorities, a few courts have concluded that school officials are exempt from the dictates of the Fourth Amendment by virtue of the special nature of their authority over schoolchildren. Teachers and school administrators, it is said, act *in loco parentis* in their dealings with students: their authority is that of the parent, not the State, and is therefore not subject to the limits of the Fourth Amendment.

Such reasoning is in tension with contemporary reality and the teachings of this Court. We have held school officials subject to the commands of the First Amendment and the Due Process Clause of the Fourteenth Amendment. If school authorities are state actors for purposes of the constitutional guarantees of freedom of expression and due process, it is difficult to understand why they should be deemed to be exercising parental rather than public authority when conducting searches of their students. More generally, the Court has recognized that "the concept of parental delegation" as a source of school authority is not entirely "consonant with compulsory education laws." Today's public school officials do not merely exercise authority voluntarily conferred on them by individual parents; rather, they act in furtherance of publicly mandated educational and disciplinary policies. . . . In carrying out searches and other disciplinary functions pursuant to such policies, school officials act as representatives of the State, not merely as surrogates for the parents, and they cannot claim the parents' immunity from the strictures of the Fourth Amendment.

III

To hold that the Fourth Amendment applies to searches conducted by school authorities is only to begin the inquiry into the standards governing such searches. Although the underlying command of the Fourth Amendment is always that searches and seizures be reasonable, what is reasonable depends on the context within which a search takes place. The determination of the standard of reasonableness governing any specific class of searches requires "balancing the need to search against the invasion which the search entails." On one side of the balance are arrayed the individual's legitimate expectations of privacy and personal security; on the other, the government's need for effective methods to deal with breaches of public order.

We have recognized that even a limited search of the person is a substantial invasion of privacy. We have also recognized that searches of closed items of personal luggage are intrusions on protected privacy interests, for "the Fourth Amendment provides protection to the owner of every container that conceals its contents from plain view." A search of a child's person or of a closed purse or other bag carried on her person, no less than a similar search carried out on an adult, is undoubtedly a severe violation of subjective expectations of privacy.

Of course, the Fourth Amendment does not protect subjective expectations of privacy that are unreasonable or otherwise "illegitimate." To receive the protection of the Fourth Amendment, an expectation of privacy must be one that society is "prepared to recognize as legitimate." . . .

Although this Court may take notice of the difficulty of maintaining discipline in the public schools today, the situation is not so dire that students in the schools may claim no legitimate expectations of privacy. We have recently recognized that the need to maintain order in a prison is such that prisoners retain no legitimate expectations of privacy in their cells, but it goes almost without saying that "[t]he prisoner and the schoolchild stand in wholly different circumstances, separated by the harsh facts of criminal conviction and incarceration." We are not yet ready to hold that the schools and the prisons need be equated for purposes of the Fourth Amendment.

Nor does the State's suggestion that children have no legitimate need to bring personal property into the schools seem well anchored in reality. Students at a minimum must bring to school not only the supplies needed for their studies, but also keys, money, and the necessaries of personal hygiene and grooming. In addition, students may carry on their persons or in purses or wallets such nondisruptive yet highly personal items as photographs, letters, and diaries. Finally, students may have perfectly legitimate reasons to carry with them articles of property needed in connection with extracurricular or recreational activities. In short, schoolchildren may find it necessary to carry with them a variety of legitimate, noncontraband items, and there is no reason to conclude that they have necessarily waived all rights to privacy in such items merely by bringing them onto school grounds.

Against the child's interest in privacy must be set the substantial interest of teachers and administrators in maintaining discipline in the classroom and on school grounds. Maintaining order in the classroom has never been easy, but in recent years, school disorder has often taken particularly ugly forms: drug use and violent crime in the schools have become major social problems. Even in schools that have been spared the most severe disciplinary problems, the preservation of order and a proper educational environment requires close supervision of schoolchildren, as well as the enforcement of rules against conduct that would be perfectly permissible if undertaken by an adult. "Events calling for discipline are frequent occurrences and sometimes require immediate, effective action." Accordingly, we have recognized that maintaining security and order in the schools requires a certain degree of flexibility in school disciplinary procedures, and we have respected the value of preserving the informality of the student-teacher relationship.

How, then, should we strike the balance between the schoolchild's legitimate expectations of privacy and the school's equally legitimate need to maintain an environment in which learning can take place? It is evident that the school setting requires some easing of the restrictions to which searches by public authorities are ordinarily subject. The warrant requirement, in particular, is unsuited to the school environment: requiring a teacher to obtain a warrant before searching a child suspected of an infraction of school rules (or of the criminal law) would unduly interfere with the maintenance of the swift and informal disciplinary procedures needed in the schools. Just as we have in other cases dispensed with the warrant requirement when "the burden of obtaining a warrant is likely to frustrate the governmental purpose behind the search," we hold today that school officials need not obtain a warrant before searching a student who is under their authority.

The school setting also requires some modification of the level of suspicion of illicit activity needed to justify a search. Ordinarily, a search—even one that may permissibly be carried out without a warrant—must be based upon "probable cause" to believe that a violation of the law has occurred. However, "probable cause" is not an irreducible requirement of a valid search. The fundamental command of the Fourth Amendment is that searches and seizures be reasonable, and although "both the concept of probable cause and the requirement of a warrant bear on the reasonableness of a search, ... in certain limited circumstances neither is required." Thus, we have in a number of cases recognized the legality of searches and seizures based on suspicions that, although "reasonable," do not rise to the level of probable cause. Where a careful balancing of governmental and private interests suggests that the public interest is best served by a Fourth Amendment standard of reasonableness that stops short of probable cause, we have not hesitated to adopt such a standard.

We join the majority of courts that have examined this issue in concluding that the accommodation of the privacy interests of schoolchildren with the substantial need of teachers and administrators for freedom to maintain order in the schools does not require strict adherence to the requirement that searches be based on probable cause to believe that the subject of the search has violated or is violating the law. Rather, the legality of a search of a student should depend simply on the reasonableness, under all the circumstances, of the search. Determining the reasonableness of any search involves a twofold inquiry: first, one must consider "whether the ... action was justified at its inception;" second, one must determine whether the search as actually conducted "was reasonably related in scope to the circumstances which justified the interference in the first place." Under ordinary circumstances, a search of a student by a teacher or other school official will be "justified at its inception" when there are reasonable grounds for suspecting that the search will turn up evidence that the student has violated or is violating either the law or the rules of the school. Such a search will be permissible in its scope when the measures adopted are reasonably related to the objectives of the search and not excessively intrusive in light of the age and sex of the student and the nature of the infraction.

This standard will, we trust, neither unduly burden the efforts of school authorities to maintain order in their schools nor authorize unrestrained intrusions upon the privacy of schoolchildren. By focusing attention on the question of reasonableness, the standard will spare teachers and school administrators the necessity of schooling themselves in the niceties of probable cause and permit them to regulate their conduct according to the dictates of reason and common sense. At the same time, the reasonableness standard should ensure that the interests of students will be invaded no more than is necessary to achieve the legitimate end of preserving order in the schools.

IV

There remains the question of the legality of the search in this case. We recognize that the "reasonable grounds" standard applied by the New Jersey Supreme Court in its consideration of this question is not substantially different from the standard that we have adopted today. Nonetheless, we believe that the New Jersey court's application of that standard to strike down the search of T. L. O's purse reflects a somewhat crabbed notion of reasonableness. Our review of the facts surrounding the search leads us to conclude that the search was in no sense unreasonable for Fourth Amendment purposes.

The incident that gave rise to this case actually involved two separate searches, with the first—the search for cigarettes—providing the suspicion that gave rise to the second—the search for marihuana. Although it is the fruits of the second search that are at issue here, the validity of the search for marihuana must depend on the reasonableness of the initial search for cigarettes, as there would have been no reason to suspect that T. L. O. possessed marihuana had the first search not taken place. Accordingly, it is to the search for cigarettes that we first turn our attention.

The New Jersey Supreme Court pointed to two grounds for its holding that the search for cigarettes was unreasonable. First, the court observed that possession of cigarettes was not in itself illegal or a violation of school rules. Because the contents of T. L. O's purse would therefore have "no direct bearing on the infraction" of which she was accused (smoking in a lavatory where smoking was prohibited), there was no reason to search her purse. Second, even assuming that a search of T. L. O's purse might under some circumstances be reasonable in light of the accusation made against T. L. O., the New Jersey court concluded that Mr. Choplick in this particular case had no reasonable grounds to suspect that T. L. O. had cigarettes in her purse. At best, according to the court, Mr. Choplick had "a good hunch."

Both these conclusions are implausible. T. L. O. had been accused of smoking, and had denied the accusation in the strongest possible terms when she stated that she did not smoke at all. Surely it cannot be said that under these circumstances, T. L. O's possession of cigarettes would be irrelevant to the charges against her or to her response to those charges. T. L. O's possession of cigarettes, once it was discovered, would both corroborate the report that she had been smoking and undermine the credibility of her defense to the charge of smoking. To be sure, the discovery of the cigarettes would not prove that T. L. O. had been smoking in the lavatory; nor would it, strictly speaking, necessarily be inconsistent with her claim that she did not smoke at all. But it is universally

recognized that evidence, to be relevant to an inquiry, need not conclusively prove the ultimate fact in issue, but only have "any tendency to make the existence of any fact that is of consequence to the determination of the action more probable or less probable than it would be without the evidence." The relevance of T. L. O's possession of cigarettes to the question whether she had been smoking and to the credibility of her denial that she smoked supplied the necessary "nexus" between the item searched for and the infraction under investigation. Thus, if Mr. Choplick in fact had a reasonable suspicion that T. L. O. had cigarettes in her purse, the search was justified despite the fact that the cigarettes, if found, would constitute "mere evidence" of a violation.

Of course, the New Jersey Supreme Court also held that Mr. Choplick had no reasonable suspicion that the purse would contain cigarettes. This conclusion is puzzling. A teacher had reported that T. L. O. was smoking in the lavatory. Certainly this report gave Mr. Choplick reason to suspect that T. L. O. was carrying cigarettes with her; and if she did have cigarettes, her purse was the obvious place in which to find them. Mr. Choplick's suspicion that there were cigarettes in the purse was not an "inchoate and unparticularized suspicion or 'hunch'"; rather, it was the sort of "common-sense conclusio[n] about human behavior" upon which "practical people"—including government officials—are entitled to rely. Of course, even if the teacher's report were true, T. L. O. *might* not have had a pack of cigarettes with her; she might have borrowed a cigarette from someone else or have been sharing a cigarette with another student. But the requirement of reasonable suspicion is not a requirement of absolute certainty: "sufficient probability, not certainty, is the touchstone of reasonableness under the Fourth Amendment. . . ." Because the hypothesis that T. L. O. was carrying cigarettes in her purse was itself not unreasonable, it is irrelevant that other hypotheses were also consistent with the teacher's accusation. Accordingly, it cannot be said that Mr. Choplick acted unreasonably when he examined T. L. O's purse to see if it contained cigarettes.

Our conclusion that Mr. Choplick's decision to open T. L. O's purse was reasonable brings us to the question of the further search for marihuana once the pack of cigarettes was located. The suspicion upon which the search for marihuana was founded was provided when Mr. Choplick observed a package of rolling papers in the purse as he removed the pack of cigarettes. Although T. L. O. does not dispute the reasonableness of Mr. Choplick's belief that the rolling papers indicated the presence of marihuana, she does contend that the scope of the search Mr. Choplick conducted exceeded permissible bounds when he seized and read certain letters that implicated T. L. O. in drug dealing. This argument, too, is unpersuasive. The discovery of the rolling papers concededly gave rise to a reasonable suspicion that T. L. O. was carrying marihuana as well as cigarettes in her purse. This suspicion justified further exploration of T. L. O.'s purse, which turned up more evidence of drug-related activities: a pipe, a number of plastic bags of the type commonly used to store marihuana, a small quantity of marihuana, and a fairly substantial amount of money. Under these circumstances, it was not unreasonable to extend the search to a separate zippered compartment of the purse; and when a search of that compartment revealed an index card containing a list of "people who owe me money" as well as two letters, the inference that T. L. O. was involved in marihuana trafficking was substantial enough to justify Mr. Choplick in examining the letters to determine whether they contained any further evidence. In short, we cannot conclude that the search for marihuana was unreasonable in any respect.

Because the search resulting in the discovery of the evidence of marihuana dealing by T. L. O. was reasonable, the New Jersey Supreme Court's decision to exclude that evidence from T. L. O.'s juvenile delinquency proceedings on Fourth Amendment grounds was erroneous. Accordingly, the judgment of the Supreme Court of New Jersey is
Reversed.

Citation: *New Jersey v. T. L. O.*, 469 U.S. 325 (1985).

New York v. Cathedral Academy

As the U.S. Supreme Court underwent change in the latter part of the 20th century, the balance in its membership impacted the way that it resolved cases in many areas, not the least of which included the parameters of acceptable state aid to religiously affiliated nonpublic schools. The conflict that this transformation engendered was evident in *New York v. Cathedral Academy* (1977), a dispute over a statute that officials at religiously affiliated nonpublic schools relied on in good faith as a means of recovering payments for performing state-mandated sectarian services such as record keeping and testing. The Court stuck the statute down as unconstitutional.

Facts of the Case

The dispute in *Cathedral Academy* arose over a state statute that was enacted to provide an equitable remedy for religiously affiliated nonpublic schools. The statute was enacted in response to the Supreme Court's having struck down an earlier version of the law in *Committee for Public Education and Religious Liberty v. Levitt* (1973). Officials at a religiously affiliated nonpublic school unsuccessfully filed suit, seeking to obtain reimbursements under a statute that paid schools for the costs of specified state-mandated record keeping and testing services. On further review of a judgment of the Court of Appeals of New York in favor of the school, the Supreme Court reversed in declaring the statute unconstitutional.

At the heart of its analysis, the Supreme Court was of the opinion that the new statute violated the First Amendment, because it failed the *Lemon v. Kurtzman* (1971) test to the extent that it would necessarily have had the primary effect of aiding religion or would have resulted in excessive state involvement in religious affairs.

The Court's Ruling

In another aspect of its rationale, the Supreme Court rejected the notion that the revised statute was acceptable under *Lemon v. Kurtzman II* (*Lemon II*, 1973), wherein the justices were satisfied that school officials could accept good faith reimbursements based on a law's viability. The Court indicated that even though it might have been willing to tolerate some constitutional infirmities if other equitable considerations were present, this was simply not the situation in *Cathedral Academy*. Instead, because the revised statute was designed to reimburse the religious schools, the Court was convinced that it amounted to a new and independently significant infringement of constitutional rights such that the religious school could have relied on prior law only by spending its own funds for nonmandated, and perhaps sectarian, activities that it might otherwise have been unable to afford.

Chief Justice Burger, joined by Justice Rehnquist, dissented on the basis that insofar as he believed that the dispute was controlled by *Lemon II*, he would have affirmed the judgment of the Court of Appeals of New York. Further, Justice White dissented in light of his assertion that "the Court continues to misconstrue the First Amendment in a manner that discriminates against religion and is contrary to the fundamental educational needs of the country" (pp. 134–135).

As a kind of postscript, it is worth noting that the situation that *Cathedral Academy* created in denying reimbursements to religiously affiliated nonpublic schools existed until 1980. At that time, the Supreme Court upheld another revision of the statute in *Committee for Public Education and Religious Liberty v. Regan* (1980), concluding that it passed constitutional muster under the *Lemon* test, because it included adequate safeguards to ensure that the reimbursements would not be spent for religious purposes.

James P. Wilson

See also *Committee for Public Education and Religious Liberty v. Regan; Lemon v. Kurtzman;* State Aid and the Establishment Clause

Legal Citations

Committee for Public Education and Religious Liberty v. Regan, 444 U.S. 646 (1980).
Lemon v. Kurtzman, 403 U.S. 602 (1971), 411 U.S. 192 (1973).
Levitt v. Committee for Public Education, 413 U.S. 472 (1973).
New York v. Cathedral Academy, 434 U.S. 125 (1977).

NO CHILD LEFT BEHIND ACT

Perhaps the most controversial of all federal education statutes is the No Child Left Behind Act (NCLB). Not long after taking office in 2001, President George W. Bush indicated that he would make the proposed NCLB Act the cornerstone of his administration's educational policy. About a year later, on January 8, 2002, Bush signed the NCLB into law. This entry describes the law's background and contents.

Background

The NCLB was actually enacted as part of the reauthorization of the Elementary and Secondary Education Act (ESEA), the most expansive federal education statute in history. The ESEA was initially enacted in 1965 during the height of the civil rights movement, and its later re-authorizations made federal funds available to provide support for states based on whether they complied with its provisions and those of the Civil Rights Act of 1964. At the same time, the ESEA was the first federal statute to provide large-scale support for education, both public and nonpublic.

Using its far-reaching provisions, the NCLB's congressional authors hoped to create a framework to improve the performance of America's elementary and secondary schools. Key elements included in the NCLB are intended to make school systems accountable for student achievement, especially by imposing standards for adequate yearly progress for students and districts; to require school systems to rely on teaching methods that are research based and that have been proven effective; to improve academic achievement among students who are economically disadvantaged; to assist in preparing, training, and recruiting highly qualified teachers; and to make better choices available for parents through innovative educational programs where local school boards are unresponsive to their needs.

The ESEA/NCLB, which was reauthorized as the almost 400-page Strengthening and Improvement of Elementary and Secondary Schools Act, is divided into nine subchapters. The remainder of this entry briefly reviews the contents of the NCLB's subchapters.

What the Law Says

Subchapter I, Improving the Academic Achievement of the Disadvantaged, perhaps the best known part of the ESEA, requires local educational agencies, typically local school boards that receive federal financial assistance, to improve academic achievement among students who are economically disadvantaged. The NCLB's various parts are designed to provide basic programmatic requirements such as remedial instruction for specifically identified children from poor families, grants in order to help them to improve the reading skills, education for migratory children, and prevention and intervention programs for children and youth who are neglected, delinquent, or at risk. The Supreme Court's 1997 decision in *Agostini v. Felton,* which removed earlier barriers, now permits the on-site delivery of Title I services to students who attend religiously affiliated nonpublic schools.

Subchapter II, Preparing, Training, and Recruiting High Quality Teachers and Principals, contains some of the NCLB's most controversial and far-reaching provisions. The major sections in this part of the law address a teacher and principal training and recruiting fund; mathematics and science partnerships; innovations for enhancing teacher quality; and programs for enhancing education through technology.

Subchapter III, Language Instruction for Limited English Proficient and Immigrant Students, requires school officials to provide improved language instruction for the children who are in need of such programs.

Subchapter IV, 21st Century Schools, concerns safe and drug-free schools and communities while also focusing on 21st century learning centers.

Subchapter V, Promoting Informed Parental Choice and Innovative Programs, covers innovative programs, public charter schools, assistance for magnet schools, and funds for improving education. Among the initiatives identified under the funding provisions in this part of the NCLB are programs for partnerships in character education; students who are gifted and talented; foreign language assistance; physical education; and excellence in economic education; it also provides grants to improve the mental health of children and to combat domestic violence. These programs are intended to make better choices available to parents by creating innovative educational programs, especially if local school boards are unresponsive to their needs and those of their children.

Subchapter VI, Flexibility and Accountability, addresses improving academic achievement, rural education initiatives, and general provisions.

Subchapter VII, Indian, Native Hawaiian, and Alaska Native Education, supports the educational efforts of states, local school boards, and postsecondary educational institutions that serve the target populations.

Subchapter VIII, Impact Aid, offers financial aid to local school boards experiencing substantial and continuing financial burdens due to the acquisition of real property by the federal government. This part of the NCLB is supposed to provide education for children who live, and whose parents are employed, on federal property, and for those whose parents are in the military and live in low-rent housing. In addition, this part of the act covers students who are part of heavy concentrations of children whose parents are federal employees but do not reside on federal property; experience sudden and substantial increases or decreases in enrollments due to military realignments; and/or need special help with capital expenditures for construction projects.

Subchapter IX, General Provisions, largely contains operational details with regard to the NCLB's implementation, such as definitions, flexibility in the use of administrative and other funds, program coordination, waivers, uniform provisions that include participation by students and teachers in nonpublic schools, complaint processes for participating nonpublic schools, and evaluation procedures.

Insofar as controversy rages on about the future of the NCLB, it remains to be seen what changes Congress may make in its provisions. It is probably safe to assume that the basic elements of the ESEA/NCLB, such as programs designed to help children from economically deprived families as well as those who belong to specifically targeted groups, will survive. However, it remains to be seen whether the act's controversial features that include mandatory adequate yearly progress and requirements for highly qualified teachers will remain in the reauthorized version of the law.

Charles J. Russo

See also Adequate Yearly Progress; *Agostini v. Felton;* Civil Rights Act of 1964

Further Readings

Daniel, P. T. K. (2006). No Child Left Behind: The balm of Gilead has arrived in American education. *Education Law Reporter, 206*(3), 791–814.

Osborne A. G., & Russo, C. J. (1997). The ghoul is dead, long live the ghoul: *Agostini v. Felton* and the delivery of Title I services in nonpublic schools. *Education Law Reporter, 119,* 781–797.

Legal Citations

Agostini v. Felton, 521 U.S. 203 (1997).
No Child Left Behind Act, 20 U.S.C. §§ 6301 *et seq.*

NONPUBLIC SCHOOLS

At the beginning of the republic, there were no public schools as they are known today. All children were schooled either in private venues or at home. However, fairly early in the 19th century, publicly supported schools became common. While they were indeed public schools, religion with a Protestant flavor was much in evidence. In response, in the late 19th century, Roman Catholics developed their own schools where their children could be educated in settings conducive to their religious convictions. Eventually, Lutherans, Seventh Day Adventists, and congregations of other faith traditions followed suit. In addition, a variety of private and proprietary schools sprang up around the country. Today, it is estimated that 10% to 12% of children in the U.S. attend nonpublic schools. Some of the principal legal issues faced by nonpublic schools are discussed in this entry.

At the most basic level, the legal right of nonpublic schools to exist was tested when Oregon enacted a law requiring all children there to attend public schools. The Supreme Court ruled the state law unconstitutional in *Pierce v. Society of Sisters of the Holy Names of Jesus and Mary* (1925) in upholding the right of parents to direct the education of their children. The Court also upheld the right of the state "reasonably to regulate all schools," including nonpublic schools, in matters dealing with health and safety.

Reasonable Regulation

What is a reasonable regulation of nonpublic schools has been well tested in the courts. Regulations frequently come in the form of compulsory school attendance laws, in which states mandate that all children of set ages attend either public or nonpublic schools. Most prominent is the requirement for teachers to have state teaching certificates. Courts consistently upheld teacher certification requirements for nonpublic schools as well as other regulations such as mandatory registration with the state education agency.

Administrators in religiously affiliated nonpublic schools are typically nervous about governmental attempts to regulate their operations, particularly worrying that such outside control might interfere with the religious aspects of their schools' missions. The courts recognize the dual role nonpublic schools play in having both religious and secular goals. Moreover, while the courts give religious schools much latitude in their operations, they acknowledge the state's compelling interest in the proper education of all children who reside within the state.

The Supreme Court of Nebraska upheld rigid, comprehensive regulations in *State of Nebraska v. Faith Baptist Church of Louisville* (1981). The regulations, which included a requirement for state-certified teachers, were, in the eyes of the court, "minimal in nature" and necessary for the state to carry out its compelling interest. Further, the Court took a dim view of the claim by the church that such regulations interfered with its religious freedom. The case generated so much negative publicity that the legislature enacted an exemption for parents whose "sincerely held religious beliefs" would have been violated by compliance with the regulations.

There are limits to the regulations state government may impose on nonpublic schools. The Supreme Court of Ohio, in *State of Ohio v. Whisner* (1976), struck down that state's minimum standards in finding that they went beyond the reasonable regulations that nonpublic schools may be required to meet. The regulations, which were so intrusive as to blur the distinction between public and nonpublic schools, would have interfered with the teaching of religion in religiously affiliated schools. The courts seem to have struck a balance between protecting the legitimate interest of the government to ensure an educated population and the interest of nonpublic schools in maintaining some degree of freedom from overly restrictive regulation by government. Insofar as education is a state concern under the American federal system of government, regulations affecting nonpublic schools vary from one jurisdiction to the next.

Finances and Contracts

As to government financial aid for nonpublic schools of a religious nature, the courts have forbidden direct aid because it violates the First Amendment's prohibition of the "establishment of religion." In *Lemon v. Kurtzman* (1971), the Supreme Court laid out a three-part test to evaluate whether or not impermissible establishment has occurred. To be acceptable, first, aid must have a secular purpose; second, it must have a principle or primary effect that neither advances nor inhibits religion; and, third, it must not foster an excessive entanglement between government and religion. Aid that is directed primarily toward children, such as transportation or the loan of textbooks, is usually considered permissible, while financial aid more directly benefiting school operations is usually unacceptable.

More recently, vouchers were subjected to judicial scrutiny. Vouchers allow parents to enroll their children in approved schools, including those that are nonpublic schools, at public expense. In *Zelman v. Simmons-Harris,* (2002) the Supreme Court upheld the Ohio voucher plan, even though it involved the state in making direct payments to religious schools, because the plan was broad based and not directed just to religious schools. While some supporters of nonpublic schools hope that *Zelman* will open the door to additional government financial support, others point to the narrowness of the Ohio program and suggest that a significant flow of government aid to religious schools is far in the future, if ever.

When parents enroll their children in nonpublic schools, they enter into contractual relationships. Because public schools are an integral part of state government, students are protected by the Constitution from unreasonable restrictions on their behavior. Students in public schools must be afforded due process when subject to major disciplinary procedures. This is not so in nonpublic schools. In *Bright v. Isenbarger* (1970), a federal trial court in Indiana ruled that because a nonpublic school was not involved in state action, it was not required to give due process to students prior to their expulsion from the school. Other courts have followed suit by requiring nonpublic schools to provide only fundamental fairness in disciplinary matters.

The contractual relationship between nonpublic schools and their students is guided by school bulletins and/or handbooks. Thus, school officials would be wise to spell out in clear terms just what services they will supply and what students may expect. The financial arrangements for payment of tuition and fees must also be clearly stated. In many cases, schools reserve the right to decline release of student records such as transcripts if the student's account is not paid in full. State laws vary on the legality of such an action.

Like their relationships with students, relationships between nonpublic schools and their employees are contractual. Accordingly, it is important for the provisions of the employment contract to be clearly stated in writing. In some cases, religiously affiliated schools have viewed teaching more as a ministry than a job and have not provided a written employment contract. If there is a dispute between schools and teachers, schools may be at the mercy of the court system to interpret what, by implication, is the contractual arrangement between the two parties.

Other Issues

Some disputes have arisen regarding the imposition of religious requirements for teachers in religiously affiliated schools. The courts have been reluctant to be involved in such disputes involving church doctrine, following the Supreme Court's refusal to do so in the nonschool case of *Serbian Eastern Orthodox Diocese v. Milivojevich* (1976). However, courts are not shy about interpreting the provisions of civil contracts or the application of civil law to employment issues in religious schools. An Ohio case provides a good example. In *Basinger v. Pilarczyk* (1997), two teachers were dismissed for being married in violation of church standards; the court refused to intervene. Yet, the court did address the teachers' age discrimination claim, remanding that part of the dispute for further consideration.

Nonpublic schools face legal concerns in the matter of tort liability and especially in relation to negligence, the failure to exercise a duty to care for another that results in injury or loss. Schools, including nonpublic schools, have a heightened duty to care for the children under their control. School personnel must make every effort to foresee situations that might cause harm to a child and create an environment free of such conditions. This duty falls into three major categories: maintenance of facilities and equipment, proper instruction regarding the nature of activities or conditions that might cause harm, and proper supervision. The amount of supervision necessary depends on the age and maturity of children and the nature and condition of the activity. Young children or activities that might have inherent safety concerns require more supervision by adults than more mature children or activities that are more passive.

While this entry touched on the most common areas of law affecting nonpublic schools, there are other matters that are not discussed yet should be considered. Among these are the legal organization and incorporation of schools, ownership of property, zoning ordinances, building codes and health regulations, fire and safety regulations, and governing board liability; all of these matters must be considered by those who operate nonpublic schools. In addition, one must be constantly aware that laws vary from one state to the next. Thus, the old saw applies to nonpublic schools when it comes to matters of the law: eternal vigilance is the price of liberty.

Lyndon G. Furst

See also *Lemon v. Kurtzman; Pierce v. Society of Sisters of the Holy Names of Jesus and Mary;* State Aid and the Establishment Clause; Vouchers; *Zelman v. Simmons-Harris*

Further Readings

Mawdsley, R. D. (2006). *Legal problems of religious and private schools* (5th ed.). Dayton, OH: Education Law Association.

Legal Citations

Basinger v. Pilarczyk, 707 N.E.2d 1149 (Ohio Ct. App. 1997).
Bright v. Isenbarger, 314 F. Supp. 1382 (N.D. Ind. 1970).
Lemon v. Kurtzman, 403 U.S. 602 (1971).
Pierce v. Society of Sisters of the Holy Names of Jesus and Mary, 268 U.S. 510 (1925).
Serbian Eastern Orthodox Diocese v. Milivojevich, 426 U.S. 696 (1976).

State of Nebraska v. Faith Baptist Church of Louisville, 207 Neb. 802; 301 N.W.2d 571 (Neb. 1981).
State of Ohio v. Whisner, 351 N.E.2d 750 (Ohio 1976).
Zelman v. Simmons-Harris, 536 U.S. 639 (2002).

NORTHCROSS V. BOARD OF EDUCATION OF THE MEMPHIS CITY SCHOOLS

At issue in the final iteration of the long-running dispute in *Northcross v. Board of Education of the Memphis City Schools* (1979) was whether a federal trial court could award attorney fees and costs in a school desegregation case. More specifically, after the U.S. Supreme Court directed the school board to operate a unitary system in 1970, litigation continued. The dispute in this final round of litigation in *Northcross* involved an appeal to the Sixth Circuit over two fee awards at the end of the long, convoluted history of a hotly contested school desegregation case.

Facts of the Case

Northcross was originally filed in 1960, but a federal trial court in Tennessee dismissed the action. The Sixth Circuit reinstated the claim and remanded for development of a desegregation plan. Once the school board adopted a limited plan in 1963, the Sixth Circuit again reversed, rebuffing it as inadequate. In 1966, the trial court tentatively approved a modified plan, bringing about a lull in the litigation. When the plaintiffs objected to some aspects of the plan, the trial court denied their motion for an injunction. Nevertheless, the court put the school board on notice that some aspects of the plan were in need of further study and that pending results, it might order additional relief. In 1970, the Supreme Court ruled that because the board had failed to operate a unitary schools system, the court had to do so.

In April 1974, the plaintiffs unsuccessfully petitioned the Supreme Court seeking a review of the Sixth Circuit's approval of what was termed "Plan Z," the board's proposed desegregation plan. Following this denial, *Northcross* entered another lull with an effective desegregation plan finally in place. Soon after, the plaintiffs filed their application for attorney fees and costs. This first application was initially based on the Emergency School Aid Act, which became effective July 1, 1972. Five years later, the federal trial court entered its final order, partially granting the plaintiffs' request. Dissatisfied, the plaintiffs sought further review of the partial award.

In the meantime, the school board sought substantial modification of Plan Z, which would have undermined the progress of desegregation. At the end of a five-day trial in 1977, the court largely rejected the board's proposals. In 1978, the trial court awarded attorney fees to the plaintiffs to cover the services that had been rendered to them in connection with the 1977 hearing, but again, it only partially granted their request for fees and costs. Therefore, the plaintiffs sought further review, because they regarded the second award as inadequate. The related appeals stemming from questions of the two fee awards were consolidated insofar as they raised the same issues.

The Court's Ruling

In a closer examination of both the statute and its legislative history, the Sixth Circuit thought that the Civil Rights Attorney's Fees Awards Act of 1976 provided a clear indication of Congressional intent. To this end, the appellate panel reviewed the trial court's 1977 and 1978 fee awards, deciding that as long as there was an active controversy at the time the act became effective, it applied to authorize fees for the entire case unless special circumstances existed that would have made an award manifestly unjust. Insofar as the Sixth Circuit, unlike the trial court, could not uncover any substantial differences between the purposes of that Civil Rights

Attorney's Fees Awards Act and the Emergency School Aid Act, it reasoned that the former was clearly applicable to both fee awards, because *Northcross* was pending when the statutes became law.

The Sixth Circuit next discussed "special circumstances" that would have been necessary to defeat a statutory fee award and did not find the awards unjust. The court noted that the plaintiffs in school desegregation cases were "private attorneys general" operating at a tremendous disadvantage to the defendants in terms of finances and resources. The court added that desegregation cases were a matter of "great national concern" as opposed to mere differences between individuals. Moreover, in an attorney fee issue, the court was of the opinion that a change in the law has no effect on any party's right that has matured or become unconditional. The court thus pointed out that no additional obligation was being imposed on the defendants, because they may ultimately have been required to pay fees anyway, and the new statute simply created an additional source.

Hence, the panel indicated that it had been improper for the trial court to have reduced the compensation because the plaintiffs did not prevail on "parts of issues." In concluding, the court observed that the plaintiffs' attorneys were also entitled to be compensated for time spent litigating the issue of whether they could recover their fees.

Mark A. Gooden

See also Attorney Fees; Dual and Unitary Systems

Legal Citations

Northcross v. Board of Education of the Memphis City Schools, 397 U.S. 232 (1970), 611 F.2d 624 (1979), *cert.*, 447 U.S. 911 (1980).

O'CONNOR, SANDRA DAY (1930–)

Sandra Day O'Connor was sworn in as a member of the U.S. Supreme Court on September 25, 1981. She was the first female associate justice of the Supreme Court, and she served from 1981 to 2006. Justice O'Connor distinguished herself on the Supreme Court as an articulate voice. As part of the federalism movement, she approached each dispute on a case-by-case basis. O'Connor's opinions were conservative during the years of the Burger Court. However, she was later regarded as occupying the ideological center, often serving as the Court's swing vote.

Early Years

O'Connor was born on March 26, 1930, in El Paso, Texas, the daughter of Harry A. Day and Ad Mae Wilkey Day. In 1952, she married John Jay O'Connor III; they have three sons, Scott, Brian, and Jay. She graduated from high school at 16 and received her BA in Economics at Stanford University in 1950, graduating magna cum laude.

O'Connor continued at Stanford Law School, serving as the editor of the *Stanford Law Review* and a member of Order of the Coif, a legal honorary society. She received her LLB in 1952, graduating third in her class, which also included William Rehnquist, future chief justice of the Supreme Court, as valedictorian.

The road for a woman in the judiciary or in politics was not easy at this time in the history of the United States. Despite her accomplishments, O'Connor was unable to gain employment as a lawyer; one firm offered her a position as a legal secretary. She therefore turned to public service, taking a position as deputy county attorney of San Mateo County, California (1952–1953), and working as an attorney for the Quartermaster Market Center in Frankfurt, Germany, from 1954 to 1957. O'Connor was able to practice law from 1958 to 1960 in Phoenix, Arizona, and served as the assistant attorney general of Arizona from 1965 to 1969.

In 1969, O'Connor's path moved to politics when she was appointed to the Arizona State Senate and reelected to two additional terms. In 1973, she became the first woman to serve as a state senate majority leader in any state. Prior to her appointment to the Supreme Court, O'Connor was elected judge of the Maricopa County Superior Court in Phoenix, Arizona, serving from 1975 to 1979. She was then appointed to the Arizona Court of Appeals and served from 1979 to 1981.

Court Record

O'Connor was nominated to the Supreme Court by President Ronald Reagan on July 7, 1981, and was confirmed by the U.S. Senate (99–0) on September 22 of that year. She replaced Justice Potter Stewart, who retired after 23 years on the Court.

In education, Justice O'Connor wrote for a 5-to-4 majority in *Agostini v. Felton* (1997), an important case in Establishment Clause law upholding the provision of publicly funded educational programs designed to benefit students attending religion-affiliated schools. She advocated the adoption and application of the "endorsement test" in Establishment Clause cases, explaining that public school decisions involving religion should be judged on their intent to endorse and whether they conveyed a message of endorsement or whether school officials sent "a message to nonadherents that they are outsiders, not full members of the political community" (*Lynch v. Donnelly,* 1984, p. 688). Justice O'Connor also advocated the application of the endorsement test in a concurring opinion in *Elk Grove Unified School District v. Newdow* (2004), wherein the Court rejected a claim to the inclusion of the words "under God" in the Pledge of Allegiance on the basis that the plaintiff lacked standing.

Perhaps the most noteworthy education law opinions late in Justice O'Connor's career were those in *Gratz v. Bollinger* (2003) and *Grutter v. Bollinger* (2003), the University of Michigan affirmative action cases. In *Grutter,* the Court upheld an admissions policy for the law school, but in *Gratz,* it struck down the admissions policy for the university's College of Literature, Science, and the Arts. Justice O'Connor was the only justice in the majority in both cases.

In 1988, Justice O'Connor was successfully treated for breast cancer. As a result, there was public speculation for the following 17 years that she might retire. On July 1, 2005, O'Connor announced her retirement. In her letter to President George W. Bush, she stated that her retirement would take effect on the confirmation of her successor.

O'Connor hoped that her replacement to the Court might be a woman. However, President Bush nominated D.C. Circuit Judge John G. Roberts, Jr. In an address to the Ninth Circuit conference, O'Connor criticized the media for sensationalizing the Senate Judiciary Committee hearings, while declaring that President Reagan had made historic strides in opening the doors for women.

On October 3, 2005, Chief Justice Rehnquist died. Two days later, President Bush withdrew his nomination of Roberts for O'Connor's seat and appointed him to fill the office of the chief justice of the Supreme Court. The president then nominated White House Counsel Harriet Miers to the seat, and on October 27, he accepted her request to withdraw her nomination. On October 31, 2005, Third Circuit Court Judge Samuel A. Alito, Jr., was nominated to replace O'Connor. Justice Alito was confirmed and sworn in on January 31, 2006.

Deborah E. Stine

See also Affirmative Action; *Agostini v. Felton;* Burger Court; *Gratz v. Bollinger; Grutter v. Bollinger;* Rehnquist Court; Roberts Court; U. S. Supreme Court Cases in Education

Further Readings

Baum, L. (2006). *Judges and their audiences: A perspective on judicial behavior.* Princeton, NJ: Princeton University Press.

Goldinger, C. (Ed.). (1990). *The Supreme Court at work.* Washington, DC: Congressional Quarterly.

Lazarus, E. (1999). *Closed chambers: The rise, fall, and future of the modern Supreme Court.* New York: Penguin Books.

O'Connor, S. D. (2003). *The majesty of the law: Reflections of a Supreme Court justice.* New York: Random House.

Legal Citations

Agostini v. Felton, 521 U.S. 203 (1997).

Elk Grove Unified School District v. Newdow, 542 U.S. 1 (2004).

Gratz v. Bollinger, 529 U.S. 244 (2003).

Grutter v. Bollinger, 529 U.S. 306 (2003).

Lynch v. Donnelly, 465 U.S. 668 (1984).

O'CONNOR V. ORTEGA

The Fourth Amendment to the U.S. Constitution protects citizens against unreasonable searches and seizures of their persons, houses, papers, and effects. However, this protection limits governmental searches and seizures only—citizens are not guaranteed protection from unreasonable searches and seizures conducted by private citizens or organizations. The central issue in *O'Connor v. Ortega* (1987) was whether officials at a public hospital violated a doctor's Fourth Amendment rights. The Supreme Court held that public employees have reasonable expectations of privacy in their offices and that their employers must meet strict criteria to conduct legal searches of these areas.

Facts of the Case

O'Connor involved a doctor employed at a state hospital who trained physicians in its psychiatric residency program. After being accused of misconduct, including acquiring a computer by coercing residents to contribute funds, sexually harassing female employees, and taking inappropriate disciplinary action against a resident, the doctor was placed on administrative leave while hospital officials investigated the allegations. As part of the hospital's investigation, officials searched the doctor's office, seizing items belonging to the hospital, which was an arm of the state as a public institution, as well as personal items belonging to the doctor. As a result of the investigation, hospital officials terminated the doctor's employment.

The doctor alleged that the search of his office was unreasonable in that the search violated the protections afforded him under the Fourth Amendment. The doctor thus brought suit against his former employer, the hospital, and various officials. A federal trial court in California, in granting the hospital's motion for summary judgment, found that the search was proper because officials there needed to secure the state's property contained within the doctor's office. However, the Ninth Circuit reversed in favor of the doctor, ruling that since he had a reasonable expectation of privacy in his office, the search by hospital officials violated his Fourth Amendment rights.

The Court's Ruling

On further appeal by the hospital, the U.S. Supreme Court, in turn, reversed and remanded the dispute. The Court agreed with the Ninth Circuit to the extent that public employees have, and are entitled to, reasonable expectations of privacy in their individual offices, desks, and files; the Court also concurred that public employees are covered by the Fourth Amendment's protection against unreasonable searches and seizures.

However, the Court disagreed insofar as it was of the opinion that since the record did not reveal the extent to which hospital officials may have had work-related reasons to enter the doctor's office, the Ninth Circuit should have remanded the matter to the trial court for further consideration. Even so, a majority of the Court agreed with the Ninth Circuit that the doctor had a reasonable expectation of privacy in his office. Further, regardless of any expectation of privacy in the office itself, the Court pointed out that the undisputed evidence supported the finding that the doctor had a reasonable expectation of privacy at least in his desk and file cabinets.

While recognizing the protection from unreasonable searches and seizures afforded for public employees, the Court noted that public employers may conduct reasonable searches if officials satisfy two conditions. First, the Court explained that there must be reasonable grounds to believe that a search will reveal evidence that a public employee has engaged in work-related misconduct. Second, the Court maintained that the search methods adopted must be reasonably related to the objectives of the search and not excessively intrusive in light of the nature of the alleged misconduct of the employee. The Court concluded that public employers must also produce evidence to demonstrate compliance with this two-prong test.

Although *O'Connor* arose in a hospital rather than a school setting, the Supreme Court's holding could arguably support the notion that school staff, by virtue of being public employees, have the protections against unreasonable searches and seizures afforded by the Fourth Amendment. Specifically, school employees are protected by the Fourth Amendment if they can demonstrate that they have reasonable expectations of privacy in their individual office, desk, handbag, purse, briefcase, and other personal items brought onto school grounds and are not accused of having engaged in work-related misconduct. The specific facts of how the work areas of school employees are regulated would be determinative as to whether they could be said to have had a reasonable expectation of privacy. At the same time, school employees would likely have no reasonable expectation of privacy in desks, filing cabinets, storage areas, or lockers that are shared with other employees.

Carolyn L. Carlson

See also *National Treasury Employees Union v. Von Raab; New Jersey v. T. L. O.; Skinner v. Railway Labor Executives' Association*

Further Readings

Roberts, N., & Fossey, R. (2004). Searches and seizures in the school workplace: Where does the teacher stand? *Education Law Reporter, 192,* 1–14.

Legal Citations

O'Connor v. Ortega, 480 U.S. 709 (1987).

OHIO CIVIL RIGHTS COMMISSION V. DAYTON CHRISTIAN SCHOOLS

Ohio Civil Rights Commission v. Dayton Christian Schools (1986) raised important questions about the issue of sexual discrimination by a religiously affiliated nonpublic school against one of its female teachers. The school board required its employees to subscribe to a specified set of religious beliefs. In addition to these beliefs, the board expected all employees to acknowledge, as a contractual requirement, that they would present any grievances to their immediate supervisors and agree to abide by its final decision, rather than pursue a judicial remedy.

Facts of the Case

The dispute in *Dayton Christian* arose after a teacher at the school notified her supervisor that she was pregnant and she was informed that her contract would not be renewed due to the board's religious belief that mothers should stay home with their preschool-aged children. The teacher then contacted an attorney, who threatened the school with litigation under state and federal sex discrimination laws. In response, school officials rescinded the original decision not to renew the teacher's contract on the grounds that she did not receive adequate

notice of their position concerning a mother's duty to stay home with her young children. Even so, officials terminated the teacher's employment for violating the school's dispute resolution procedures.

On being dismissed, the teacher filed a complaint with the Ohio Civil Rights Commission alleging that the original nonrenewal of her contract violated state statutes regarding unlawful sex discrimination. While the commission was conducting administrative procedures involving the sex discrimination complaint against the school, officials went to federal court seeking an injunction against the state investigation, arguing that it infringed on their freedom of religion under the First Amendment to the U.S. Constitution since they were acting pursuant to deeply held religious beliefs. The commission, on the other hand, responded that the court should abstain from exercising its jurisdiction under the federal abstention doctrine and simply permit it to do its job. The trial court refused the request to grant an injunction and, finding that the commission's proposed action would not have violated the First Amendment, dismissed the case. On appeal, the Sixth Circuit reversed in favor of the school. The court explained that such an exercise of jurisdiction would have violated both the Free Exercise Clause and the Establishment Clause of the First Amendment.

The Court's Ruling

On further review, the U.S. Supreme Court reversed and remanded based on *Younger v. Harris* (1971) and its progeny. More specifically, the Court decided that the trial court should have abstained from asserting any jurisdiction in the dispute. In *Younger,* the Court identified "comity" for its action, meaning that one court should defer jurisdiction to another, such as a federal court deferring to state courts. In cases where multiple jurisdictions may be represented, the justices pointed out that courts are advised to use comity except in very unusual situations, such as when an injunction is necessary to prevent great and immediate irreparable injury. In *Younger,* the trial court did, in fact, issue an injunction barring a criminal prosecution in the state court. As such, in *Dayton Christian,* the Court was of the opinion that since the school's constitutional claim should have been resolved on its merits, the Ohio Civil Rights Commission did not violate the First Amendment by merely investigating the circumstances of the nonrenewal of the teacher's contract to determine whether the reason school officials acted was solely religion based.

On remand, the Sixth Circuit vacated its earlier judgment as directed by the Supreme Court and remanded the dispute to the trial court, with instructions to dismiss the action based on abstention.

Dayton Christian is noteworthy in light of its implications with regard to judicial remedies when religious entities are involved, especially in jurisdictions such as Ohio, where state law authorized the Ohio Civil Rights Commission to investigate complaints of the type filed by the teacher and does not contain exemptions for religion-based entities. In rendering its judgment, the Supreme Court weighed the need for the states to achieve their goal of ending discrimination against the rights of schools to maintain religion-based policies. The justices thus concluded that insofar as prohibiting sexual discrimination is an important state interest, school officials in *Dayton Christian* should have had their day in court to raise the appropriate constitutional issues as to whether their actions were permissible.

Michael J. Jernigan

See also First Amendment; Due Process Rights: Teacher Dismissal; Teacher Rights

Further Readings

Mawdsley, R. D. (2006). *Legal problems of religious and private schools* (5th ed.). Dayton, OH: Education Law Association.

Legal Citations

Ohio Civil Rights Commission v. Dayton Christian Schools, 477 U.S. 619 (1986), *on remand*, 802 F.2d 457 (6th Cir. 1986).
Younger v. Harris, 401 U.S. 37 (1971).

ONCALE V. SUNDOWNER OFFSHORE SERVICES

At issue in *Oncale v. Sundowner Offshore Services* (1998) was whether an employer could be liable for same-sex sexual harassment. Even though *Oncale* was not set in a school context, the U.S. Supreme Court's holding that such a claim is actionable should be instructive for all educators.

Facts of the Case

Joseph Oncale worked for Sundowner Offshore Services as a roustabout on a Chevron Oil Company oil platform in the Gulf of Mexico, as one member of an eight-man crew. Two other members of the crew were supervisors. During the time Oncale worked on the platform, the two supervisors and another employee repeatedly subjected him to sex-related, humiliating actions in front of the rest of the crew. The supervisors also physically assaulted him in a sexual way, and one of the supervisors threatened to rape Oncale, who then complained to higher supervisors. Even so, the second-level supervisors did nothing to change the situation.

Oncale complained to a safety compliance clerk that the two supervisors picked on him, too; the clerk then called Oncale a name connected with homosexuality. Oncale eventually quit his job but asked that his employment record show that he left due to verbal abuse and sexual harassment. In his deposition, Oncale said that he feared that if he did not leave his job, he would have been raped or forced to engage in sexual relations.

Oncale subsequently unsuccessfully sued his employer, alleging that he was subjected to employment discrimination because of his sex. A federal trial court in Louisiana, in granting the employer's motion for summary judgment, maintained that a male employee cannot sustain a cause of action under Title VII for sexual harassment by male coworkers. On appeal, the Fifth Circuit affirmed in favor of the employer.

The Court's Ruling

On further review, at issue before the Supreme Court was whether workplace sexual harassment can violate Title VII of the Civil Rights Act when the harasser and the harassed are of the same sex. In a unanimous decision penned by Justice Scalia, the Court reversed in favor of the plaintiff, ruling that sex discrimination consisting of same-sex sexual harassment is actionable under Title VII. Justice Thomas filed a one-sentence concurrence, in which he specified that a "plaintiff must plead and ultimately prove Title VII's statutory requirement that there be discrimination because of . . . sex" (*Oncale*, p. 83).

In its analysis, the Supreme Court observed that Title VII protects both men and women. To this end, the Court pointed out that in a previous case, *Castaneda v. Partida* (1977), set in the context of racial discrimination, it never accepted the view that a member of one definable group would not discriminate against other members of the same group. The Court noted that the judiciary has generally had little trouble in recognizing the application of Title VII to same-sex harassment involving a tangible work benefit such as quid pro quo sex harassment. At the same time, the Court acknowledged a perplexing array of legal standards in the lower courts when it came to hostile work environment sexual harassment. The Court explained that some lower courts viewed sexual harassment in the workplace as always actionable, regardless of the characteristics of the harasser and the harassed, while others believed that same-sex claims were never possible under Title VII. The Court indicated that a third group of courts took the position that a same-sex Title VII claim is actionable if the harasser is homosexual and motivated by sexual desire. In *Oncale*, the Court settled the issue that Title VII protects individuals from same-sex discrimination on the basis of sex and that it makes no difference as to a harasser's sex, sexual orientation, or motivation.

As part of its rationale, the Supreme Court denied that Title VII creates a general civility code for the workplace. Rather, the Court was of the opinion that Title VII does not address the different ways that men and women customarily interact with each other and with members of their own sex. Instead, the Court pointed out that the proscription against sexual harassment prohibits behavior that is objectively severe or pervasive enough to change an employee's conditions of employment; it does not reach to what the Court called "ordinary socializing in the workplace—such as male-on-male horseplay or inter-sexual flirtation" (*Oncale*, p. 81). The Court stressed that the objective severity of harassment should take into account

the perspective of a reasonable person in the victim's position, considering all the circumstances. Consequently, the Court reasoned that the context of the behavior should help courts and juries resolve whether they are looking at teasing and horseplay, as opposed to conduct a reasonable person would find severely hostile or abusive wherever in the workplace individuals find themselves, including educational institutions.

David L. Dagley

See also *Burlington Industries v. Ellerth; Faragher v. City of Boca Raton;* Hostile Work Environment; *Meritor Savings Bank v. Vinson;* Sexual Harassment, Quid Pro Quo; Sexual Harassment, Same-Sex; Sexual Orientation; Teacher Rights; Title VII

Further Readings

Achampong, F. (1999). The evolution of same-sex sexual harassment law: A critical examination of the latest development in workplace sexual harassment litigation. *St. John's Law Review, 73,* 701–745.

Diefenbach, C. (2007). Same-sex sexual harassment after *Oncale:* Meeting the "because of . . . sex" requirement. *Berkeley Journal of Gender, Law, and Justice, 22,* 42–94.

Kirshenbaum, A. M. (2005). "Because of . . . sex": Rethinking the protections afforded under Title VII in the post-*Oncale* world. *Albany Law Review, 69,* 139–177.

Legal Citations

Castaneda v. Partida, 430 U.S. 482 (1977).
Oncale v. Sundowner Offshore Services, 523 U.S. 75 (1998).

OPEN MEETINGS LAWS

Throughout the United States, a variety of state statutes mandate that meetings of the governing bodies of public entities be open to the public. In some states, such as Vermont, the legal basis for open meetings of public entities derives from the state constitution. Being public entities, the governing bodies of public schools, public colleges, and public universities generally must comply with states' open meetings laws. For example, meetings of the board of education of a local school district and meetings of the governing board of a public community college district must be open to the public, and, in addition, the public school or college district must comply with a variety of rules that are applicable to board meetings. This entry discusses what such laws require.

The primary underlying public policy of open meetings laws is to require governmental entities, including public educational institutions, to conduct their business in a transparent manner, exposed to public scrutiny and open to public participation, particularly because the expenditure of public funds is involved.

Many of the open meetings statutes set forth an express statement of public policy. For example, in enacting New York's Open Meetings Law, the legislature declared,

> It is essential to the maintenance of a democratic society that the public business be performed in an open and public manner and that the citizens of this state be fully aware of and able to observe the performance of public officials and attend and listen to the deliberations and decisions that go into making of public policy.

In light of these strong public policies, many states also have express statutory provisions declaring that the open meetings laws are to be strictly interpreted in favor of openness.

What Is Required

Under open meetings laws, it generally is unlawful to have private or "secret" meetings; for school boards, it is also unlawful to have public meetings without providing proper notice to the public. Distinctions are often made as to what constitutes a "meeting" for purposes of being encompassed within the open meetings laws. Under California's Ralph M. Brown Act, for example, a "meeting" means "any congregation of a majority of the members of a [board] at the same time and place to hear, discuss, or deliberate upon any item that is within the subject matter jurisdiction of the [institution]." Statutes often carve out exceptions to allow a majority of board members to attend conferences,

meetings of other public entities, community meetings, or ceremonies without complying with the open meetings laws.

Circumventing open meetings laws by convening "serial meetings" or by developing what is known as a "collective concurrence" by having an intermediary essentially poll the majority of board members on a particular issue would constitute a violation of open meetings laws. In other words, violations occur if board votes are somehow achieved outside the context of public meetings, even if a majority of a board is not actually meeting together in a secret fashion.

There are exceptions, however, when boards are permitted to meet privately, not in view of the public, in certain situations where they may convene in "closed" or "executive" session. These topics typically include the following: The board meets with its legal counsel to discuss, for example, pending or threatened litigation; the board meets with its labor negotiators to discuss strategies for dealing with an employee union; the board meets with its real property negotiators to discuss how much money the board might offer for a parcel of realty; meetings to discuss a security threat or to deal with employee appointment, discipline, or performance evaluation may also be closed. In these situations, a balance has been reached between the public's right to know about the business of the public entity, on one hand, and the privacy rights of public employees, the attorney-client privilege, the bargaining power of the public entity, or public safety, on the other.

Open meetings laws usually apply not only to boards themselves but also to many of their committees. In addition, within the context of higher education, certain constituent groups, such as student government and faculty senates, may also be required to comply with open meetings laws. Moreover, those newly elected to boards who have not yet taken office are generally covered by open meetings laws.

In addition to the right to attend board meetings, states' open meetings laws usually permit members of the public to make an audiotape or videotape of board meetings, to have items placed on the agenda, and to comment at meetings. It is allowable and customary for a board to place time restrictions (e.g., 3 minutes per person) on public comment at a board meeting.

Agenda Issues

The agenda for board meetings typically must be publicly posted during a specified period of time, such as 72 hours in advance of the meeting. If there is an urgent situation or emergency, the agenda can be amended after the posting deadline. There may be different requirements for special meetings, as opposed to regular meetings.

There often are specific guidelines as to the language of the agendas of board meetings, both in terms of content and in terms of amount of detail required. There may be even-more-specific agenda requirements for items to be considered in closed sessions. The wording of agendas is important because it frames the issues for meetings and it generally is unlawful for boards to consider or take actions on any matters not appearing on their agendas.

Violations of open meetings laws can be associated with criminal penalties in addition to various civil remedies. In this regard, a violation of open meetings laws could result in action taken by the board to be invalidated, and if the requisite criminal intent is involved, there could be a criminal prosecution against the offending board members.

Jack P. Lipton

See also Open Records Laws; School Board Policy; School Boards

Further Readings

Schwing, A. T., & Taylor, C. (2000). *Open meeting laws* (2nd ed.). Anchorage, Alaska: Fathom.

Legal Citations

Open Meetings Law, N.Y. Pub. Off., Article 7, §§ 100 *et seq.*
Ralph M. Brown Act, Cal. Gov't Code §§ 54950 *et seq.*
Vermont Constitution, Chapter 1, Article 6.

Open Records Laws

Everywhere in the United States, there are statutory schemes mandating that the records and documents generated by public entities be made available to the public. In some states, like California, the legal basis for open public records derives from the state constitution. Accordingly, the governing bodies of public schools, public colleges, and public universities typically must comply with states' open records laws. Indeed, generally speaking, records of public schools and public colleges must be made available for public inspection upon request. States' open records laws are analogous to the federal Freedom of Information Act.

The primary underlying public policy of the open records laws is to encourage open government and to discourage governmental secrecy. Many of the states' open records statutes set forth express statements of public policy. For example, New York, in enacting that state's Freedom of Information Law, declared "that government is the public's business and that the public, individually and collectively and represented by a free press, should have access to the records of government." In light of these strong public policies, many states have express statutory provisions declaring that the open records laws are to be strictly interpreted in favor of public disclosure.

Tricky questions often arise as to whether a particular document must be made available to the public upon request. Under Montana law, for instance, a clear dichotomy is expressly established between "public" documents and "private" documents, but the more difficult questions typically concern not whether a particular document is "public," but rather, presuming that it is a public document, whether the document is somehow exempt from public disclosure.

In this regard, public documents that typically are exempt from disclosure include employee personnel files, such as the personnel files of public school teachers or public university professors; public school employees' medical records; certain documents pertaining to pending claims or litigation; documents that are privileged, such as under the attorney-client privilege; test questions and scoring keys; library circulation records; and student records. Litigation sometimes arises when there are disputes as to whether particular documents were properly withheld by a public school or public university.

Open records laws often set forth procedures regarding how public records are to be requested by the public and how and when a public entity must respond to the requests. Also, there often are provisions not only for inspection of public records but also for obtaining photocopies of the records upon payment of fees. Schools or institutions of higher learning usually have a certain time frame in which officials must respond to requests by indicating their willingness to comply or by asserting one or more applicable exemptions.

Requests for public records generally must be reasonably clear and specific. Even so, underscoring the legal emphasis on public disclosure in some states, such as California, school or institutions of higher learning are legally required to assist members of the public in formulating their requests if they are having difficulty in doing so.

Considering that public documents are now often stored in electronic formats, open records laws now typically specify that electronically stored data are considered public documents that must be made available to the public unless otherwise exempt. Sometimes the school or college may produce the documents to the public in electronic format, rather than in paper format.

When schools or institutions of higher learning make documents available to the public that may be exempt from disclosure, the disclosure could constitute a waiver of the applicable exemption.

Jack P. Lipton

See also Open Meetings Laws; School Board Policy; School Boards

Legal Citations

California Constitution, Article 1, § 3.
California Public Records Act, Cal. Gov't Code §§ 6250 *et seq.*
Freedom of Information Act, 5 U.S.C. § 552.
New York Freedom of Information Law, N.Y. Pub. Off., Article 76 §§ 84 *et seq.*

OPEN SHOP

The term *open shop* refers to a business or organization wherein employees are not required to become union members as a precondition of employment. An open shop can be distinguished from a *closed shop,* which refers to a business or organization wherein union membership is a precondition of employment. Historically, an open shop was a slogan adopted by American employees during the early 20th century as a means of attempting to drive unions out of the construction industry. Under the National Labor Relations Act (NLRA), open shops are deemed legal labor practices in the United States.

The passage of the Taft-Hartley Labor Act in 1947 officially declared closed shops illegal throughout the United States. The Taft-Hartley Labor Act specifically gave states the legal authority to create "right-to-work" laws while granting federal courts jurisdiction over the enforcement of collective bargaining agreements between employers and employees. In 1959, Wisconsin became the first state to legislate collective bargaining by public sector employees, including public school teachers. More than 30 states presently have legislation allowing public school teachers the right to unionize or collectively negotiate with school board authorities. At present, only a few states, most notably North Carolina, Texas, Utah, and Virginia, expressly prohibit teachers from collective bargaining with school district authorities.

In states with "right-to-work" laws, open shops are primarily viewed as the legal norm. Employers may not legally fire employees who fail or refuse to pay union dues. In states with open shops or right-to-work laws, since union membership is not required for jobs, employees can choose whether they want to be union members even if their employers are unionized. Currently, 22 states, mostly in the South (Alabama, Arizona, Arkansas, Florida, Georgia, Idaho, Iowa, Kansas, Louisiana, Mississippi, Nebraska, Nevada, North Carolina, North Dakota, Oklahoma, South Carolina, South Dakota, Tennessee, Texas, Utah, Virginia, and Wyoming), are deemed right-to-work states.

Proponents of open-shop or right-to-work laws argue that employees should be given the right to choose whether they wish to join unions. Moreover, open-shop advocates contend that it is wrong for unions to be legally able to force employees to either join unions or pay union dues or fair-share/agency fees as a condition of employment. Nationwide, 28 states permit unions to collect mandatory agency fees from their public employees, and 22 states disallow this practice.

In 1977, the U.S. Supreme Court dealt with the first of four cases involving the legal issue of agency shop fees as it applies to public sector unions' use of nonunion member fees for political purposes. In *Abood v. Detroit Board of Education* (1977), the Court held that the First Amendment explicitly prohibits public sector unions from using nonmembers' agency fees for ideological purposes not related to the union's collective bargaining duties and responsibilities.

The Court, in *Chicago Teachers Union, Local No. 1 v. Hudson* (1986), subsequently imposed the procedural requirement that public sector unions must inform nonmembers in open shops how much of their agency fees go to noncollective bargaining purposes and offer these nonmembers a refund in that amount. To be in compliance with the law, many public sector unions send what is commonly referred to as "Hudson" packets to all their nonmembers, informing them of their legal right to refuse the use of agency fees for noncollective-bargaining-related expenditures.

In the third case, *Lehnert v. Ferris Faculty Association* (1991), which was set in higher education, the Supreme Court clarified what union expenses are chargeable to dissenting nonmembers in open shops. The Court explained that nonunion members could be charged a pro rata share of costs associated with activities of state and national union affiliates even if they did not directly benefit their bargaining units.

Most recently, in *Davenport v. Washington Education Association* (2007), a unanimous Supreme Court placed further restrictions on the ability of unions to spend the fair-share fees of nonmembers in open shops. The Court held that "it does not violate the First Amendment for a State to require that its public-sector [teacher] unions receive affirmative authorization from a nonmember before spending that nonmember's agency fees for election-related purposes" (p. 2383). In sum, then, while unions can charge some fees in open shops, the Court has continued to narrow the purposes for which labor organizations can use these funds.

Kevin P. Brady

See also *Abood v. Detroit Board of Education;* Agency Shop; Closed Shop; Collective Bargaining; Contracts; *Davenport v. Washington Education Association;* Unions

Further Readings

Brady, K. P. (2006). Bargaining. In C. J. Russo (Ed.), *The yearbook of education law: 2006* (pp. 101–110). Dayton, OH: Education Law Association.

DeMitchell, T. A., & Cobb, C. D. (2006). Teachers: Their union and their profession: A tangled relationship. *West's Education Law Reporter, 212,* 1–18.

Kerchner, C., & Koppich, J. (1993). *A union of professionals: Labor relations and educational reform.* New York: Teachers College Press.

Legal Citations

Abood v. Detroit Board of Education, 431 U.S. 209 (1977).

Chicago Teachers Union, Local No. 1 v. Hudson, 475 U.S. 292 (1986), *on remand*, 922 F.2d 1306 (7th Cir. 1991), *cert. denied*, 501 U.S. 1230 (1991).

Davenport v. Washington Education Association, 127 S. Ct. 2372 (2007).

Lehnert v. Ferris Faculty Association, 500 U.S. 507 (1991).

National Labor Relations Act, 29 U.S.C. § 157.

OWASSO INDEPENDENT SCHOOL DISTRICT NO. 1011 V. FALVO

In *Owasso Independent School District No. 1011 v. Falvo* (2002), the Supreme Court considered whether peer-graded materials are education records under the Family Educational Rights and Privacy Act (FERPA). The Supreme Court held that peer-graded materials are not considered education records under FERPA and thus peer grading does not violate the act.

It is unusual for the Supreme Court to accept a case such as *Owasso,* which questioned the legality of a teaching strategy, especially a commonplace practice such as peer grading, which has been prevalent in schools for years. However, *Owasso* is known today as one of the few Supreme Court cases providing schools with practical guidance about how the language of FERPA should be interpreted.

Facts of the Case

Under FERPA, federally funded schools must protect students' privacy. Specifically, FERPA mandates that schools cannot release students' education records without parental consent. Kristja Falvo, a parent of three children, alleged that the Owasso Independent School District was in violation of FERPA by allowing the practice of peer grading to occur in her children's classrooms. Ms. Falvo claimed that her children were embarrassed when their classmates scored their papers, tests, or assignments and when the teacher asked the children to call out the grades for the teacher to record.

Prior to the Supreme Court's decision, the federal trial court in Oklahoma decided that peer-graded assignments are not education records; however, the Tenth Circuit reversed. The Tenth Circuit found that Ms. Falvo could sue for damages under Title 42 of the U.S. Code § 1983, in order to enforce FERPA, and that peer grading violated FERPA because the peer-graded assignments were educational records that should not have been released without parental permission.

The Court's Ruling

The Supreme Court unanimously reversed the Tenth Circuit's holding. The Court analyzed the language of FERPA, which defines "education records" as "records, files, documents, and other materials" that contain student information and "are maintained by an educational agency or institution or by a person acting for such agency or institution" (20 U.S.C. § 1232g(a)(4)(A)). The Court reasoned that the term *maintain* implies that the student work is kept over a period of time and is stored in a filing cabinet or some type of permanent database. Yet during peer grading, neither the student grading the assignment nor the teacher receiving the score maintains the peer-graded work within this meaning of the act. In addition, the phrase "a person acting for" was interpreted to mean employees of the school, such as teachers and administrators, not students.

The Court also maintained that it would not have been good policy to define peer-graded papers as education records. If peer grading were found to be in violation of FERPA, teachers across the country would be burdened with extra work. For instance,

requiring teachers to grade every homework paper or classroom assignment would mean that teachers would be left with less time to teach new material. It is doubtful that Congress intended FERPA to change the customary practices of schools or desired that the federal government intervene in traditional state functions, the Court said.

Justice Scalia offered a concurring opinion, in which he agreed with the Court's judgment that student-graded papers are not education records; however, he disagreed that education records are limited only to those that are maintained in some type of main storage area.

The Supreme Court left two questions unanswered in *Owasso*: whether the peer-graded scores, once turned in to the teacher and placed in his or her grade book (electronic or hard copy), would be considered an education record and whether a private party such as Ms. Falvo could bring a case under § 1983 to enforce FERPA. The question of whether a teacher's grade book is considered an education record remains unanswered; however, soon after *Owasso* was decided, the Supreme Court held in *Gonzaga University v. Doe* (2002) that a private party cannot bring an individual cause of action under § 1983 to enforce FERPA. Therefore, Ms. Falvo could not have brought her case before the court using the same grounds today. Nevertheless, *Owasso* continues to be an important education law decision because of its clarification of some of the ambiguous language of FERPA and its ultimate deference to the time-honored educational practice of peer grading.

Janet R. Rumple

See also Family Educational Rights and Privacy Act; Privacy Rights of Students

Legal Citations

Family Educational Rights and Privacy Act, 20 U.S.C. § 1232g (2002).
Gonzaga University v. Doe, 536 U.S. 273 (2002).
Owasso Independent School District No. 1011 v. Falvo, 534 U.S. 426 (2002).

PARENS PATRIAE

Parens patriae can be translated as "the father of the country." This concept generally means that a government has the authority, as a sovereign over its citizens, to act in a protective manner. The term is often applied in disputes over the well-being of children and people with disabilities. The doctrine of parens patriae consists of a set of interests that the government, such as the state, has in the well-being of its populace.

The State's Interest

The concept of parens patriae was adopted from English precedent and is the origin of the state's power to preserve and protect the health, patriotism, morality, efficiency, industry, and integrity of its citizens. As a result, the state, as parent to all its citizens, has the inherent prerogative to provide for the welfare of both the commonwealth and individuals and to protect those individuals who are not legally competent to act on their own behalf.

In relationship to education, the state, in its role of parens patriae, can act to serve and protect the well-being of children and the parental interests in having children educated. The parens patriae concept gives states standing to sue on behalf of these citizens to protect what courts deem a quasi-sovereign interest, defined by the U.S. Supreme Court as those interests that the state has in the well-being of its populace. In order to act in its capacity as parens patriae, state officials must articulate an interest apart from those of private parties, usually one that the state could address through its sovereign law-making powers. The state has a quasi-sovereign interest in the health and well-being, both physical and economic, of its residents in general, and thus can act to protect children and people who are incompetent, helpless, or infirm and require protection.

In applying the concept of parens patriae to schools, states often assert their authority to enforce minimum educational and welfare requirements for the benefit of their citizenry. It is well accepted that education is a benefit to the society; education supports state goals, such as the continuity of having an enlightened electorate, an educated populace, and an educated workforce.

Legally, because education is viewed as a benefit to the entire society, state legislatures have the power to tax citizens for support of public schools. The early theorists examined this notion and asserted that education was a public obligation that must be nurtured to develop the entire civic intelligence and to better govern through an enlightened republic. In other words, because the state, as parens patriae, has an interest in enforcing minimum education and welfare requirements, it also has the force and power to use taxation to fund schooling.

A final tenet of the parens patriae authority of the state within the context of schooling is its right to compel all parents to provide their children with a minimum secular education. This includes compulsory education as a basis for fostering basic educational requirements. State legal authority to require school attendance is found in the common-law doctrine of parens patriae. The authority for requiring compulsory attendance is the state's ability, through the exercise of the police power of the legislature, to establish reasonable laws as it may judge are necessary for the good of the state and its inhabitants.

State Versus Parents

Under some circumstances, the state's parens patriae authority collides with parental rights. In *Pierce v. Society of Sisters of the Holy Names of Jesus and Mary* (1925), the Supreme Court ruled that parents have a liberty interest under the Fourteenth Amendment to control the upbringing of their children, including the right to direct the content of their education. In *Pierce,* the issue was whether a state's compulsory education law requiring all children to attend only public schools violated the Fourteenth Amendment rights of parents to determine the upbringing of their children.

The Court reasoned that states have the power to regulate reasonably all schools and to inspect, supervise, and examine them, their teachers, and pupils. States may require that all children of proper age attend some school, that teachers be of good moral character and patriotic disposition, that students be taught subjects essential to good citizenship, and that nothing be taught that is manifestly inimical to the public welfare. However, in *Pierce,* the Court found that the State of Oregon violated the parents' constitutional liberty interests when it unreasonably interfered with their liberty to direct the upbringing and education of children under their control by prohibiting parents from meeting state compulsory attendance requirements by sending their offspring to nonpublic schools as an alternative to public schools.

The power of parents may also be limited by states' parens patriae authority when it appears that parental decisions will jeopardize the health or safety of children. Historically, courts have held that the family itself is not beyond regulation on behalf of the public interest. Acting to guard the general interest in a child's well-being, the state, as parens patriae, may restrict a parent's control by requiring school attendance, regulating or prohibiting the child's labor, and in many other ways.

In *Wisconsin v. Yoder* (1972), the Supreme Court rejected the applicability of parens patriae to compulsory attendance but upheld the general principle that the state has the authority to regulate education. The Court decided that when the state's compulsory school attendance law, under its power to extend the benefit of secondary education to children, conflicts with parents' religious beliefs protected under the First Amendment of the Constitution, the parents' rights prevail. Yet, in other cases, the general welfare is always the concern of the state and gives the state authority to exercise the parens patriae doctrine.

The state's invocation of the doctrine of parens patriae in matters of education has arisen when parents did not assist or support children in obtaining an education or where children sought financial assistance from parents for education as a necessity, along with food, lodging, clothing, and medical care. There have also been cases where the state's parens patriae authority has been invoked to support parents who were unable to control their own children or where children became a nuisance to the public.

Protecting Children

The parens patriae authority of the state extends to protecting children from parental abuse or neglect. Courts have stated that it is the unquestioned right and imperative duty of government, in its character of parens patriae, to protect and provide for the comfort and well-being of its citizens who by reason of infancy are unable to take care of themselves. Thus, under this doctrine, a child has a right to be protected from abuse of his or her parents. Under the umbrella of their authority as parens patriae, states have traditionally intervened between parents and children when the parents have been found to be legally unfit. In each case, the state's action must be supported by a compelling or a rational state interest where the rights of either the child or parent are restricted.

The state's authority as parens patriae has been exercised in other areas related to children. In some circumstances, acting as parens patriae, the state has regulated and sometimes severed the parent-child relationship through divorce, neglect, or child abuse statutes. States have used the doctrine of parens patriae to regulate compulsory medical care over the objection of parents, if they are found legally neglectful by not providing medical care for their children.

More recently, states have exercised their parens patriae authority in regulating both public and nonpublic schools. Today, many states have legislated minimum state requirements for private schools under the parens patriae doctrine. These requirements often include prescribed courses, personnel requirements, and specific curricula as well as outcome measures such as requiring students in nonpublic schools to participate in statewide testing programs.

Vivian Hopp Gordon

See also Fourteenth Amendment; Parental Rights; *Pierce v. Society of Sisters of the Holy Names of Jesus and Mary;* Statute; *Wisconsin v. Yoder*

Legal Citations

Alfred L. Snapp and Sons, Inc., et al. v. Puerto Rico ex rel. Barez, Secretary of Labor and Human Resources, 458 U.S. 592 (1982).
Pierce v. Society of Sisters of the Holy Names of Jesus and Mary, 268 U.S. 510 (1925).
Prince v. Massachusetts, 321 U.S. 158 (1944).
Wisconsin v. Yoder, 406 U.S. 205 (1972).

PARENTAL RIGHTS

The right of parents to make educational decisions for their children has evolved since the earliest reported state law cases in the last quarter of the 19th century. As state governments became more involved in regulating education, conflicts between parents and public officials led to litigation. Most recently, the rights of students themselves are being recognized. This entry summarizes the development of parental rights as evidenced in judicial decisions.

Natural Law

The earliest cases involved the application of state common law to requests by parents to make educational decisions on behalf of their children. The origin of this common law is not clear, but presumably it devolved from the notion that the responsibilities of parents to maintain, protect, and educate their children were undergirded by "principles of natural law and affection laid on [parents] by Nature itself, [and] by [the parents'] own proper act of bringing [children] into the world" (*School Board District No. 18, Garvin County v. Thompson,* 1909, p. 579).

State courts eventually applied this natural law to parental requests regarding the education of their children pursuant to states' implied authority under the Tenth Amendment to control education. The result in many state cases was a broad protection of parent educational choices for their children, either because the parental choices were assumed to be in the children's best interests or because the choices were not considered to be disruptive to the school setting (*State of Nebraska ex rel. Kelly v. Ferguson,* 1914; *Trustees of School v. People ex rel. Van Allen,* 1877; *State ex rel. Sheibley v. School District No. 1 of Dixon County,* 1891).

However, parents were not always successful in imposing their choices upon schools. In some cases, courts, in rejecting parental choices, relied on the authority of both state legislatures and school boards to set course requirements and on a fear that citizens should not be able to nullify reasonable school board requirements or state legislation (*Sewell v. Board of Education of Defiance Union School, Ohio,* 1876).

The success of parents in advancing the common-law claims to control the education of their children not only varied among the states but represented an agrarian society, where both the authority of local school boards and parents were significant forces. With the end of World War I, state legislatures became more active in education by enacting compulsory attendance laws. The shift to statewide legislation had a diluting effect on the common-law authority of parents. While parental authority was a prominent force when balanced against the authority of local school boards, it was not as significant when balanced against state-legislated rules.

State Regulation

At the end of World War I, the state legislatures of Nebraska and Oregon enacted statutes that required the teaching of all courses in English (Nebraska) and attendance by all students at public schools (Oregon). The challenge to these two statutes resulted in two important U.S. Supreme Court decisions, *Meyer v. Nebraska* (1923) and *Pierce v. Society of Sisters of the Holy Names of Jesus and Mary* (1925), which created a constitutional right of parents pursuant to the Liberty Clause of the Fourteenth Amendment to make educational decisions for their children.

In both *Meyer* and *Pierce,* the Supreme Court considered that prohibiting the teaching of a subject in German in a religious school (*Meyer*) and prohibiting students from attending nonpublic schools (*Pierce*) "unreasonably interfere[d] with the liberty or parents and guardians to direct the upbringing and education of their children" (*Pierce,* p. 534). Even though the Supreme Court invalidated the state statutes in *Meyer* and *Pierce,* the Court was careful to note that "the power of the state to compel attendance at some school and to make reasonable regulations for all schools . . . is not questioned" (*Meyer,* p. 402).

Forty-seven years later, the Supreme Court, in *Wisconsin v. Yoder* (1972), addressed a challenge to the state of Wisconsin's charge of truancy against two Amish fathers who refused to keep their children enrolled in a school until the children reached the age of 16. At stake was the authority of the state to enforce its compulsory attendance statute requiring attendance at school until age 16 versus Amish religious beliefs that opposed the enrollment of their children in a public school past the completion of eighth grade, where such attendance could cause a significant number of children to leave the Amish community.

In supporting the Amish parents' claim that they were exempt from the compulsory attendance requirement because of their religious beliefs, which were grounded in a 300-year-old, cohesive, religious-based, Amish community, the Court relied on the Liberty Clause used in *Meyer* and *Pierce,* as well as the Free Exercise of Religion Clause of the First Amendment. The Court reasoned that, when a free exercise claim was raised, government was required to demonstrate a compelling interest before if could overcome parents' religious beliefs, something the state of Wisconsin was unable to do in this case, because the children's

eighth- grade education satisfied the state's interests in a literate and productive citizenry.

Unlike *Meyer* and *Pierce,* though, *Yoder* did not invalidate the state's compulsory attendance statute. Rather, because it struck down only the statute's application to the Amish, the question for post-*Yoder* courts was the extent to which state compulsory attendance laws would not apply to parents whose religious beliefs did not share the community values of the Amish. Generally, the success of these other religious challenges varied among the states and devolved into the reasonableness of the state regulations (see *State of Nebraska v. Faith Baptist Church of Louisville,* 1981) or into whether the *Yoder* exemption should apply to other religious belief systems (see *Fellowship Baptist Church v. Benton,* 1987).

Recent Developments

In 1990, the Supreme Court, in *Employment Division, Department of Human Resources of Oregon v. Smith,* eliminated the Free Exercise Clause as a defense against state action that was neutral and generally applicable. *Smith* has gone a long way toward reducing the effectiveness of parental invocation of religious-based claims pursuant to *Yoder* for purposes of exemption from state regulation.

A more substantial challenge to parental rights is embedded in the emergence of student rights in the aftermath of *Tinker v. Des Moines Independent Community School District* (1969), where the ongoing question has been the extent to which the rights of parents to make decisions for their children can be undercut by the rights of students themselves. Justice Douglas, in his dissenting opinion in *Yoder,* had observed that, while parents

> normally speak for the entire family . . . , it is the student's judgment, not the parents', that is essential if we are to give full meaning to what we have said about the Bill of Rights and of the right of students to be the masters of their own destiny. (pp. 244–245)

Congress has continued to accord rights to parents, such as access to student records in the Family

Educational Rights and Privacy Act (FERPA, 1974) and the right to negotiate an individualized education plan (IEP) for their children under the Individuals with Disabilities Education Act (IDEA, 1975). Nonetheless, courts have taken a small step toward separating student and parent rights by acknowledging that students may have legal claims against schools separate from their parents (see *Circle Schools v. Pappert,* 2004). To date, though, no court has discounted all parent interests in the education of their children.

Ralph D. Mawdsley

See also *Employment Division, Department of Human Resources of Oregon v. Smith;* Family Educational Rights and Privacy Act; *Meyer v. Nebraska; Pierce v. Society of Sisters of the Holy Names of Jesus and Mary; Tinker v. Des Moines Independent Community School District; Wisconsin v. Yoder*

Further Reading

Mawdsley, R. (2006). *Legal problems of religious and private schools* (5th ed.). Dayton, OH: Education Law Association.

Legal Citations

Circle Schools v. Pappert, 381 F.3d 172 (3d Cir. 2004).

Employment Division, Department of Human Resources of Oregon v. Smith, 494 U.S. 872 (1990).

Family Educational Rights and Privacy Act, 20 U.S.C. § 1232g (2002).

Fellowship Baptist Church v. Benton, 815 F.2d 485 (8th Cir. 1987).

Individuals with Disabilities Education Act, 20 U.S.C. §§ 1400 *et seq.*

Meyer v. Nebraska, 187 N.W. 100 (1922), 262 U.S. 390 (1923).

Pierce v. Society of Sisters of the Holy Names of Jesus and Mary, 268 U.S. 510 (1925).

School Board District No. 18, Garvin County v. Thompson, 103 P. 578 (Okla. 1909).

Sewell v. Board of Education of Defiance Union School, 29 Ohio 89 (Ohio 1876).

State of Nebraska ex rel. Kelly v. Ferguson, 144 N.W. 1039 (Neb. 1914).

State of Nebraska ex rel. Sheibley v. School District No. 1 of Dixon County, 48 N.W. 393 N.W. 393 (Neb. 1891).

State of Nebraska v. Faith Baptist Church of Louisville, 301 N.W.2d 571 (Neb. 1981).

Tinker v. Des Moines Independent Community School District, 393 U.S. 503 (1969).

Trustees of School v. People ex rel. Van Allen, 87 Ill. 303 (Ill. 1877).

Wisconsin v. Yoder, 406 U.S. 205 (1972).

PARENTS INVOLVED IN COMMUNITY SCHOOLS V. SEATTLE SCHOOL DISTRICT NO. 1

Parents Involved in Community Schools v. Seattle School District No. 1 (*PICS,* 2005, 2007), which was combined with *Meredith v. Jefferson County Public Schools* (2007), stands out as the U.S. Supreme Court's most recent case addressing the constitutionality of race-conscious admissions plans. The Court struck down both plans in *PICS* in a plurality opinion in a consolidated appeal.

Facts of the Case

The disputes arose when two school systems, one in Seattle, Washington, the other in Louisville, Kentucky, voluntarily adopted race-conscious student assignment plans as both a remedial measure to address de facto segregation and, concomitantly, to achieve the educational goal of a diverse student body that would be reflective of the racial make-up of the entire school district community. Both plans evolved from many years of prior attempts to desegregate and also to address the issue of "White flight." Yet, Seattle never operated under a desegregation order, and Louisville had been released from judicial oversight. The objective of the plans was to promote the pedagogical and social benefits flowing from diversity in an increasingly pluralistic society and global marketplace.

At the completion of an en banc rehearing, the Ninth Circuit upheld the constitutionality of the Seattle plan (*PICS,* 2005). During the same year, the Sixth Circuit upheld the constitutionality of the plan from Louisville (*McFarland*).

On further review, the Supreme Court, in a plurality judgment, invalidated both plans. Writing for a Court plurality, Chief Justice John Roberts explained the consolidated plans were unconstitutional insofar as neither was implemented to address the ongoing vestiges of intentional discrimination and that both plans were based on what the Court considered the inappropriate consideration of race. Chief Justice Roberts further indicated that diversity was not a compelling governmental interest in K–12 education, a position that the majority of the Court rejected and with which Justice Kennedy disagreed in a concurring opinion.

The Court's Ruling

In his analysis, the chief justice observed that the school boards did not meet their heavy burden of demonstrating that the interest they sought to achieve justified the highly suspect means of discriminating among individual students based on race by relying on racial classifications in making school assignments, because "racial classifications are simply too pernicious to permit any but the most exact connection between justification and classification" (*PICS,* p. 2752, citing *Johnson v. California,* 2005, pp. 505–506). Accordingly, Roberts determined that school boards need to demonstrate that their use of such classifications was sufficiently narrowly tailored to achieve a compelling governmental interest. He conceded that remedying the effects of past intentional discrimination is a compelling interest under the strict scrutiny test. Even so, Roberts pointed out that such an interest was not involved in *PICS,* because the Seattle schools were never segregated by law nor subject to court-ordered desegregation, and the desegregation decree that covered *Louisville* had been dissolved.

At the same time, Chief Justice Roberts remarked that the *PICS* cases were not governed by the rule in *Grutter v. Bollinger* (2003) in which the Court ruled that, for the purposes of strict scrutiny, the government had a compelling interest in ensuring the diversity of student bodies in the context of higher education. Roberts added that the classification was appropriate in *Grutter,* because it was not focused on race alone but encompassed all factors that might have contributed to student body diversity. To this end, he posited that in the two cases that were consolidated in *PICS,* race-conscious admissions plans were unacceptable, because race was not considered as part of a broader

effort to achieve diversity, and its use was utterly determinative of where particular students were assigned.

In sum, *PICS* can be read as standing for four points. First, the use of racial classification is injurious and detrimental, not just when it is used to subordinate or stigmatize groups. Second, with very rare exceptions, racial classifications may be used only to reverse institutions' prior, state-sanctioned segregation; voluntary improvements are inapposite. Third, governmental interest in diversity with respect to education encompasses a broad array of interests and, as of *PICS,* is limited to higher education. Fourth, the judicial doctrine of strict scrutiny is to be used to address all uses of race, and there is no invidious/benign continuum on this issue.

In his concurrence, Justice Kennedy agreed that because the *PICS* plans were not narrowly tailored to advance a compelling governmental interest, the plans did not survive strict scrutiny. However, he wrote separately in light of his belief that the chief justice went too far in proscribing the use of race in instances where it might be appropriate. He was of the opinion that "diversity . . . is a compelling educational goal a school district may pursue . . . without treating each student in a different fashion solely on the basis of a systematic, individual typing by race" (*PICS,* 2007, p. 2792). Kennedy further proposed that diversity may be infused in student assignment plans based on the following:

> School boards may pursue the goal of bringing together students of diverse backgrounds and races through other means, including strategic site selection of new schools; drawing attendance zones with general recognition of the demographics of neighborhoods; allocating resources for special programs; recruiting students and faculty in a targeted fashion; and tracking enrollments, performance, and other statistics by race. (p. 2792)

Justice Kennedy's concurrence can be understood as representing four propositions. First, school boards do have a compelling interest in diversity. Second, school officials may construct assignment plans where students are "considered for a whole range of talents with race as a . . . consideration" (p. 2794). Third, the classifications used in *PICS* are subject to strict scrutiny and may be used only after more narrow approaches have been tried and have not succeeded. Fourth, he suggested that the uses of race that have no adverse affect do not require strict scrutiny.

Justice Thomas also filed a concurrence in which he expressed his full agreement with the plurality. He penned a separate opinion to detail his disagreements with Justice Breyer's dissent.

Justice Breyer's dissenting opinion, which was joined by Justices Stevens, Souter, and Ginsburg, lamented the Supreme Court's breaking with its own well-established precedent in ensuring equal educational opportunities for students.

Justice Stevens's dissent essentially chided the plurality for ignoring history and misunderstanding the use of race in making school assignments.

PICS has generated intense interest among educators and legal scholars alike. While it is currently too early to evaluate what the overall reaction to *PICS* will be, the alternatives before school officials are to reduce race-conscious efforts substantially in student assignment plans based on Justice Roberts's plurality analysis or to develop more all-inclusive and expansive policies under the criteria established under Justice Kennedy's concurrence.

Philip T. K. Daniel

See also *Brown v. Board of Education of Topeka* and Equal
    Educational Opportunities; Equal Protection Analysis;
    Grutter v. Bollinger; White Flight

Legal Citations

Grutter v. Bollinger, 539 U.S. 306 (2003).

Johnson v. California, 543 U.S. 499 (2005).

McFarland v. Jefferson County Public Schools, 416 F.3d 513
    (6th Cir. 2005).

*Parents Involved in Community Schools v. Seattle School
    District No. 1*, 426 F.3d 1162 (9th Cir. 2005), 127 S. Ct.
    2738 (2007).

Parents Involved in Community Schools v. Seattle School District No. 1 (Excerpts)

In a plurality in Parents Involved in Community Schools v. Seattle School District No. 1, *the Supreme Court struck down a race-conscious admissions plan. The Court ruled that school officials failed not only to demonstrate that the use of racial classifications in their student assignment plans was necessary to achieve their stated goal of racial diversity but also that they failed to consider alternative approaches adequately.*

Supreme Court of the United States

PARENTS INVOLVED IN COMMUNITY SCHOOLS, Petitioner,

v.

SEATTLE SCHOOL DISTRICT NO. I et al.

127 S. Ct. 2738

Argued Dec. 4, 2006.

Decided June 28, 2007.

Chief Justice ROBERTS announced the judgment of the Court, and delivered the opinion of the Court with respect to Parts I, II, III-A, and III-C, and an opinion with respect to Parts III-B and IV, in which Justices SCALIA, THOMAS, and ALITO join.

The school districts in these cases voluntarily adopted student assignment plans that rely upon race to determine which public schools certain children may attend. The Seattle school district classifies children as white or nonwhite; the Jefferson County school district as black or "other." In Seattle, this racial classification is used to allocate slots in oversubscribed high schools. In Jefferson County, it is used to make certain elementary school assignments and to rule on transfer requests. In each case, the school district relies upon an individual student's race in assigning that student to a particular school, so that the racial balance at the school falls within a predetermined range based on the racial composition of the school district as a whole. Parents of students denied assignment to particular schools under these plans solely because of their race brought suit, contending that allocating children to different public schools on the basis of race violated the Fourteenth Amendment guarantee of equal protection. The Courts of Appeals below upheld the plans. We granted certiorari, and now reverse.

I

Both cases present the same underlying legal question—whether a public school that had not operated legally segregated schools or has been found to be unitary may choose to classify students by race and rely upon that classification in making school assignments. Although we examine the plans under the same legal framework, the specifics of the two plans, and the circumstances surrounding their adoption, are in some respects quite different.

A

Seattle School District No. 1 operates 10 regular public high schools. In 1998, it adopted the plan at issue in this case for assigning students to these schools. The plan allows incoming ninth graders to choose from among any of the district's high schools, ranking however many schools they wish in order of preference.

Some schools are more popular than others. If too many students list the same school as their first choice, the district employs a series of "tiebreakers" to determine who will fill the open slots at the oversubscribed school. The first tiebreaker selects for admission students who have a sibling currently enrolled in the chosen school. The next tiebreaker depends upon the racial composition of the particular school and the race of the individual student. In the district's public schools approximately 41 percent of enrolled students are white; the remaining 59 percent, comprising all other racial groups, are classified by Seattle for assignment purposes as nonwhite. If an oversubscribed school is not within 10 percentage points of the district's overall white/nonwhite racial balance, it is what the district calls "integration positive," and the district employs a tiebreaker that selects for assignment students whose race "will serve to bring the school into balance." If it is still necessary to select students for the school after using the racial tiebreaker, the next tiebreaker is the geographic proximity of the school to the student's residence.

Seattle has never operated segregated schools—legally separate schools for students of different races—nor has it ever been subject to court-ordered desegregation. It nonetheless employs the racial tiebreaker in an attempt to address the effects of racially identifiable housing patterns on school assignments. Most white students live in the northern part of Seattle, most students of other racial backgrounds in the southern part. Four of Seattle's high schools are located in the north—Ballard, Nathan Hale, Ingraham, and Roosevelt—and five in the south—Rainier Beach, Cleveland, West Seattle, Chief Sealth, and Franklin. One school—Garfield—is more or less in the center of Seattle. . . .

For the 2000–2001 school year, five of these schools were oversubscribed—Ballard, Nathan Hale, Roosevelt, Garfield, and Franklin—so much so that 82 percent of incoming ninth graders ranked one of these schools as their first choice. Three of the oversubscribed schools were "integration positive" because the school's white enrollment the previous school year was greater than 51 percent—Ballard, Nathan Hale, and Roosevelt. Thus, more nonwhite students (107, 27, and 82, respectively) who selected one of these three schools as a top choice received placement at the school than would have been the case had race not been considered, and proximity been the next tiebreaker. Franklin was "integration positive" because its nonwhite enrollment the previous school year was greater than 69 percent; 89 more white students were assigned to Franklin by operation of the racial tiebreaker in the 2000–2001 school year than otherwise would have been. Garfield was the only oversubscribed school whose composition during the 1999–2000 school year was within the racial guidelines, although in previous years Garfield's enrollment had been predominantly nonwhite, and the racial tiebreaker had been used to give preference to white students.

Petitioner Parents Involved in Community Schools (Parents Involved) is a nonprofit corporation comprising the parents of children who have been or may be denied assignment to their chosen high school in the district because of their race. The concerns of Parents Involved are illustrated by Jill Kurfirst, who sought to enroll her ninth-grade son, Andy Meeks, in Ballard High School's special Biotechnology Career Academy. Andy suffered from attention deficit hyperactivity disorder and dyslexia, but had made good progress with hands-on instruction, and his mother and middle school teachers thought that the smaller biotechnology program held the most promise for his continued success. Andy was accepted into this selective program but, because of the racial tiebreaker, was denied assignment to Ballard High School. Parents Involved commenced this suit in the Western District of Washington. . . .

The District Court granted summary judgment to the school district, finding that state law did not bar the district's use of the racial tiebreaker and that the plan survived strict scrutiny on the federal constitutional claim because it was narrowly tailored to serve a compelling government interest. The Ninth Circuit initially reversed based on its interpretation of the Washington Civil Rights Act (*Parents Involved II*) and enjoined the district's use of the integration tiebreaker, *id.*, at 1257. Upon realizing that the litigation would not be resolved in time for assignment decisions for the 2002–2003 school year, the Ninth Circuit withdrew its opinion (*Parents Involved III*), vacated the injunction, and . . . certified the state-law question to the Washington Supreme Court (*Parents Involved IV*).

The Washington Supreme Court determined that the State Civil Rights Act bars only preferential treatment programs "where race or gender is used by government to select a less qualified applicant over a more qualified applicant," and not "[p]rograms which are racially neutral, such as the [district's] open choice plan." *Parents Involved in Community Schools v. Seattle School Dist., No. 1* (*Parents Involved V*). The state court returned the case to the Ninth Circuit for further proceedings.

A panel of the Ninth Circuit then again reversed the District Court, this time ruling on the federal constitutional question, *Parents Involved VI* . The panel determined that while achieving racial diversity and avoiding racial isolation are compelling government interests Seattle's use of the racial tiebreaker was not narrowly tailored to achieve these interests. The Ninth Circuit granted rehearing en banc and overruled the panel decision, affirming the District Court's determination that Seattle's plan was narrowly tailored to serve a compelling government interest, *Parents Involved VII.* We granted certiorari.

B

Jefferson County Public Schools operates the public school system in metropolitan Louisville, Kentucky. In 1973 a federal court found that Jefferson County had maintained a segregated school system, [the Supreme Court] vacated and remanded, reinstated with modifications, and in 1975 the District Court entered a desegregation decree. Jefferson County operated under this decree until 2000, when the District Court dissolved the decree after finding that the district had achieved unitary status by eliminating "[t]o the greatest extent practicable" the vestiges of its prior policy of segregation.

In 2001, after the decree had been dissolved, Jefferson County adopted the voluntary student assignment plan at issue in this case. Approximately 34 percent of the district's 97,000 students are black; most of the remaining 66 percent are white. The plan requires all nonmagnet schools to maintain a minimum black enrollment of 15 percent, and a maximum black enrollment of 50 percent.

At the elementary school level, based on his or her address, each student is designated a "resides" school to which students within a specific geographic area are assigned; elementary resides schools are "grouped into clusters in order to facilitate integration." The district assigns students to nonmagnet schools in one of two ways: Parents of kindergartners, first-graders, and students new to the district may submit an application indicating a first and second choice among the schools within their cluster; students who do not submit such an application are assigned within the cluster by the district. "Decisions to assign students to schools within each cluster are based on available space within the schools and the racial guidelines in the District's current student assignment plan." If a school has reached the "extremes of the racial guidelines," a student whose race would contribute to the school's racial imbalance will not be assigned there. After assignment, students at all grade levels are permitted to apply to transfer between nonmagnet schools in the district. Transfers may be requested for any number of reasons, and may be denied because of lack of available space or on the basis of the racial guidelines.

When petitioner Crystal Meredith moved into the school district in August 2002, she sought to enroll her son, Joshua McDonald, in kindergarten for the 2002–2003 school year. His resides school was only a mile from his new home, but it had no available space— assignments had been made in May, and the class was full. Jefferson County assigned Joshua to another elementary school in his cluster, Young Elementary. This school was 10 miles from home, and Meredith sought to transfer Joshua to a school in a different cluster, Bloom Elementary, which—like his resides school—was only a mile from home. Space was available at Bloom, and intercluster transfers are allowed, but Joshua's transfer was nonetheless denied because, in the words of Jefferson County, "[t]he transfer would have an adverse effect on desegregation compliance" of Young.

Meredith brought suit in the Western District of Kentucky, alleging violations of the Equal Protection Clause of the Fourteenth Amendment. The District Court found that Jefferson County had asserted a compelling interest in maintaining racially diverse schools, and that the assignment plan was (in all relevant respects) narrowly tailored to serve that compelling interest. The Sixth Circuit affirmed in a *per curiam* opinion relying upon the reasoning of the District Court, concluding that a written opinion "would serve no useful purpose." We granted certiorari.

II

As a threshold matter, we must assure ourselves of our jurisdiction. . . .

III

A

It is well established that when the government distributes burdens or benefits on the basis of individual racial classifications, that action is reviewed under strict scrutiny. As the Court recently reaffirmed, "racial classifications are simply too pernicious to permit any but the most exact connection between justification and classification." In order to satisfy this searching standard of review, the school districts must demonstrate that the use of individual racial classifications in the assignment plans here under review is "narrowly tailored" to achieve a "compelling" government interest.

Without attempting in these cases to set forth all the interests a school district might assert, it suffices to note that our prior cases, in evaluating the use of racial classifications in the school context, have recognized two interests that qualify as compelling. The first is the compelling interest of remedying the effects of past intentional discrimination. Yet the Seattle public schools have not shown that they were ever segregated by law, and were not subject to court-ordered desegregation decrees. The Jefferson County public schools were previously segregated by law and were subject to a desegregation decree entered in 1975. In 2000, the District Court that entered that decree dissolved it. . . .

. . . .

The second government interest we have recognized as compelling for purposes of strict scrutiny is the interest in diversity in higher education upheld in *Grutter*. The specific interest found compelling in *Grutter* was student body diversity "in the context of higher education." The diversity interest was not focused on race alone but encompassed "all factors that may contribute to student body diversity." . . .

. . . .

The entire gist of the analysis in *Grutter* was that the admissions program at issue there focused on each applicant as an individual, and not simply as a member of a particular racial group. The classification of applicants by race upheld in *Grutter* was only as part of a "highly individualized, holistic review." As the Court explained, "[t]he importance of this individualized consideration in the context of a race-conscious admissions program is paramount." The point of the narrow tailoring analysis in which the *Grutter* Court engaged was to ensure that the use of racial classifications was indeed part of a broader assessment of diversity, and not simply an effort to achieve racial balance, which the Court explained would be "patently unconstitutional."

In the present cases, by contrast, race is not considered as part of a broader effort to achieve "exposure to widely diverse people, cultures, ideas, and viewpoints"; race, for some students, is determinative standing alone. The districts argue that other factors, such as student preferences, affect assignment decisions under their plans, but under each plan when race comes into play, it is decisive by itself. It is not simply one factor weighed with others in reaching a decision, as in *Grutter*; it is *the* factor. Like the University of Michigan undergraduate plan struck down in *Gratz*, the plans here "do not provide for a meaningful individualized review of applicants" but instead rely on racial classifications in a "nonindividualized, mechanical" way.

Even when it comes to race, the plans here employ only a limited notion of diversity, viewing race exclusively in white/nonwhite terms in Seattle and black/"other" terms in Jefferson County. The Seattle "Board Statement Reaffirming Diversity Rationale" speaks of the "inherent educational value" in "[p]roviding students the opportunity to attend schools with diverse student enrollment." But under the Seattle plan, a school with 50 percent Asian-American students and 50 percent white students but no African-American, Native-American, or Latino students would qualify as balanced, while a school with 30 percent Asian-American, 25 percent African-American, 25 percent Latino, and 20 percent white students would not. It is hard to understand how a plan that could allow these results can be viewed as being concerned with achieving enrollment that is "broadly diverse."

Prior to *Grutter*, the courts of appeals rejected as unconstitutional attempts to implement race-based assignment plans—such as the plans at issue here—in primary and secondary schools. After *Grutter*, however, the two Courts of Appeals in these cases, and one other, found that race-based assignments were permissible at the elementary and secondary level, largely in reliance on that case.

In upholding the admissions plan in *Grutter*, though, this Court relied upon considerations unique to institutions of higher education, noting that in light of "the expansive freedoms of speech and thought associated with the university environment, universities occupy a special niche in our constitutional tradition." The Court explained that "[c]ontext matters" in applying strict scrutiny, and repeatedly noted that it was addressing the use of race "in the context of higher education." The

Court in *Grutter* expressly articulated key limitations on its holding—defining a specific type of broad-based diversity and noting the unique context of higher education—but these limitations were largely disregarded by the lower courts in extending *Grutter* to uphold race-based assignments in elementary and secondary schools. The present cases are not governed by *Grutter*.

B

Perhaps recognizing that reliance on *Grutter* cannot sustain their plans, both school districts assert additional interests, distinct from the interest upheld in *Grutter*, to justify their race-based assignments. In briefing and argument before this Court, Seattle contends that its use of race helps to reduce racial concentration in schools and to ensure that racially concentrated housing patterns do not prevent nonwhite students from having access to the most desirable schools. Jefferson County has articulated a similar goal, phrasing its interest in terms of educating its students "in a racially integrated environment." Each school district argues that educational and broader socialization benefits flow from a racially diverse learning environment, and each contends that because the diversity they seek is racial diversity—not the broader diversity at issue in *Grutter*—it makes sense to promote that interest directly by relying on race alone.

The parties and their *amici* dispute whether racial diversity in schools in fact has a marked impact on test scores and other objective yardsticks or achieves intangible socialization benefits. The debate is not one we need to resolve, however, because it is clear that the racial classifications employed by the districts are not narrowly tailored to the goal of achieving the educational and social benefits asserted to flow from racial diversity. In design and operation, the plans are directed only to racial balance, pure and simple, an objective this Court has repeatedly condemned as illegitimate.

The plans are tied to each district's specific racial demographics, rather than to any pedagogic concept of the level of diversity needed to obtain the asserted educational benefits. In Seattle, the district seeks white enrollment of between 31 and 51 percent (within 10 percent of "the district white average" of 41 percent), and nonwhite enrollment of between 49 and 69 percent (within 10 percent of "the district minority average" of 59 percent). In Jefferson County, by contrast, the district seeks black enrollment of no less than 15 or more than 50 percent, a range designed to be

"equally above and below Black student enrollment systemwide," based on the objective of achieving at "all schools . . . an African-American enrollment equivalent to the average district-wide African-American enrollment" of 34 percent. In Seattle, then, the benefits of racial diversity require enrollment of at least 31 percent white students; in Jefferson County, at least 50 percent. There must be at least 15 percent nonwhite students under Jefferson County's plan; in Seattle, more than three times that figure. This comparison makes clear that the racial demographics in each district-whatever they happen to be—drive the required "diversity" numbers. The plans here are not tailored to achieving a degree of diversity necessary to realize the asserted educational benefits; instead the plans are tailored, in the words of Seattle's Manager of Enrollment Planning, Technical Support, and Demographics, to "the goal established by the school board of attaining a level of diversity within the schools that approximates the district's overall demographics."

The districts offer no evidence that the level of racial diversity necessary to achieve the asserted educational benefits happens to coincide with the racial demographics of the respective school districts—or rather the white/nonwhite or black/"other" balance of the districts, since that is the only diversity addressed by the plans. . . .

In fact, in each case the extreme measure of relying on race in assignments is unnecessary to achieve the stated goals, even as defined by the districts. . . .

In *Grutter*, the number of minority students the school sought to admit was an undefined "meaningful number" necessary to achieve a genuinely diverse student body. Although the matter was the subject of disagreement on the Court, the majority concluded that the law school did not count back from its applicant pool to arrive at the "meaningful number" it regarded as necessary to diversify its student body. Here the racial balance the districts seek is a defined range set solely by reference to the demographics of the respective school districts.

This working backward to achieve a particular type of racial balance, rather than working forward from some demonstration of the level of diversity that provides the purported benefits, is a fatal flaw under our existing precedent. We have many times over reaffirmed that "[r]acial balance is not to be achieved for its own sake." *Grutter* itself reiterated that "outright racial balancing" is "patently unconstitutional."

Accepting racial balancing as a compelling state interest would justify the imposition of racial proportionality throughout American society, contrary to our repeated recognition that "[a]t the heart of the Constitution's guarantee of equal protection lies the simple command that the Government must treat citizens as individuals, not as simply components of a racial, religious, sexual or national class." Allowing racial balancing as a compelling end in itself would "effectively assur[e] that race will always be relevant in American life, and that the 'ultimate goal' of 'eliminating entirely from governmental decisionmaking such irrelevant factors as a human being's race' will never be achieved." An interest "linked to nothing other than proportional representation of various races . . . would support indefinite use of racial classifications, employed first to obtain the appropriate mixture of racial views and then to ensure that the [program] continues to reflect that mixture."

The validity of our concern that racial balancing has "no logical stopping point" is demonstrated here by the degree to which the districts tie their racial guidelines to their demographics. As the districts' demographics shift, so too will their definition of racial diversity.

. . . .

The principle that racial balancing is not permitted is one of substance, not semantics. Racial balancing is not transformed from "patently unconstitutional" to a compelling state interest simply by relabeling it "racial diversity." While the school districts use various verbal formulations to describe the interest they seek to promote—racial diversity, avoidance of racial isolation, racial integration—they offer no definition of the interest that suggests it differs from racial balance.

. . . .

C

The districts assert, as they must, that the way in which they have employed individual racial classifications is necessary to achieve their stated ends. The minimal effect these classifications have on student assignments, however, suggests that other means would be effective.

. . . .

While we do not suggest that *greater* use of race would be preferable, the minimal impact of the districts' racial classifications on school enrollment casts doubt on the necessity of using racial classifications. In *Grutter,* the consideration of race was viewed as indispensable in more than tripling minority representation at the law school—from 4 to 14.5 percent. Here the most Jefferson County itself claims is that "because the guidelines provide a firm definition of the Board's goal of racially

integrated schools, they 'provide administrators with the authority to facilitate, negotiate and collaborate with principals and staff to maintain schools within the 15–50% range.' " Classifying and assigning schoolchildren according to a binary conception of race is an extreme approach in light of our precedents and our Nation's history of using race in public schools, and requires more than such an amorphous end to justify it.

The districts have also failed to show that they considered methods other than explicit racial classifications to achieve their stated goals. Narrow tailoring requires "serious, good faith consideration of workable race-neutral alternatives," and yet in Seattle several alternative assignment plans—many of which would not have used express racial classifications—were rejected with little or no consideration. Jefferson County has failed to present any evidence that it considered alternatives, even though the district already claims that its goals are achieved primarily through means other than the racial classifications.

IV

Justice BREYER's dissent takes a different approach to these cases, one that fails to ground the result it would reach in law. Instead, it selectively relies on inapplicable precedent and even dicta while dismissing contrary holdings, alters and misapplies our well-established legal framework for assessing equal protection challenges to express racial classifications, and greatly exaggerates the consequences of today's decision.

To begin with, Justice BREYER seeks to justify the plans at issue under our precedents recognizing the compelling interest in remedying past intentional discrimination. Not even the school districts go this far, and for good reason. The distinction between segregation by state action and racial imbalance caused by other factors has been central to our jurisprudence in this area for generations. The dissent elides this distinction between *de jure* and *de facto* segregation, casually intimates that Seattle's school attendance patterns reflect illegal segregation and fails to credit the judicial determination—under the most rigorous standard—that Jefferson County had eliminated the vestiges of prior segregation. The dissent thus alters in fundamental ways not only the facts presented here but the established law.

Justice BREYER's reliance on *McDaniel v. Barresi,* highlights how far removed the discussion in the dissent is from the question actually presented in these cases. *McDaniel* concerned a Georgia school system that had been segregated by law. There was no doubt that the county had operated a "dual school system," and no one questions that the obligation to disestablish a school system segregated by law can include race-conscious remedies—whether or not a court had issued an order to that effect. The present cases are before us, however, because the Seattle school district was never segregated by law, and the Jefferson County district has been found to be unitary, having eliminated the vestiges of its prior dual status. The justification for race-conscious remedies in *McDaniel* is therefore not applicable here. . . .

Justice BREYER's dissent next relies heavily on dicta from *Swann v. Charlotte-Mecklenburg Bd. of Ed.*—far more heavily than the school districts themselves. The dissent acknowledges that the two-sentence discussion in *Swann* was pure dicta, *post*, at 2811–2812, but nonetheless asserts that it demonstrates a "basic principle of constitutional law" that provides "authoritative legal guidance." Initially, as the Court explained just last Term, "we are not bound to follow our dicta in a prior case in which the point now at issue was not fully debated." That is particularly true given that, when *Swann* was decided, this Court had not yet confirmed that strict scrutiny applies to racial classifications like those before us. There is nothing "technical" or "theoretical," *post*, at 2816, about our approach to such dicta.

Justice BREYER would not only put such extraordinary weight on admitted dicta, but relies on the statement for something it does not remotely say. *Swann* addresses only a possible state objective; it says nothing of the permissible *means*—race conscious or otherwise—that a school district might employ to achieve that objective. The reason for this omission is clear enough, since the case did not involve any voluntary means adopted by a school district. The dissent's characterization of *Swann* as recognizing that "the Equal Protection Clause permits local school boards to use race-conscious criteria to achieve positive race-related goals" is—at best—a dubious inference. Even if the dicta from *Swann* were entitled to the weight the dissent would give it, and no dicta is, it not only did not address the question presented in *Swann*, it also does not address the question presented in these cases—whether the school districts' use of racial classifications to achieve their stated goals is permissible.

. . . .

Justice BREYER's dissent also asserts that these cases are controlled by *Grutter*, claiming that the existence of a compelling interest in these cases "follows *a fortiori*" from *Grutter* and accusing us of tacitly overruling that case. The dissent overreads *Grutter*, however, in suggesting that it renders pure racial balancing a constitutionally

compelling interest; *Grutter* itself recognized that using race simply to achieve racial balance would be "patently unconstitutional." The Court was exceedingly careful in describing the interest furthered in *Grutter* as "not an interest in simple ethnic diversity" but rather a "far broader array of qualifications and characteristics" in which race was but a single element. We take the *Grutter* Court at its word. We simply do not understand how Justice BREYER can maintain that classifying every schoolchild as black or white, and using that classification as a determinative factor in assigning children to achieve pure racial balance, can be regarded as "less burdensome, and hence more narrowly tailored" than the consideration of race in *Grutter* when the Court in *Grutter* stated that "[t]he importance of . . . individualized consideration" in the program was "paramount," and consideration of race was one factor in a "highly individualized, holistic review." Certainly if the constitutionality of the stark use of race in these cases were as established as the dissent would have it, there would have been no need for the extensive analysis undertaken in *Grutter*. In light of the foregoing, Justice BREYER's appeal to *stare decisis* rings particularly hollow.

At the same time it relies on inapplicable desegregation cases, misstatements of admitted dicta, and other noncontrolling pronouncements, Justice BREYER's dissent candidly dismisses the significance of this Court's repeated *holdings* that all racial classifications must be reviewed under strict scrutiny, arguing that a different standard of review should be applied because the districts use race for beneficent rather than malicious purposes.

This Court has recently reiterated, however, that "all racial classifications [imposed by government] . . . must be analyzed by a reviewing court under strict scrutiny." Justice BREYER nonetheless relies on the good intentions and motives of the school districts, stating that he has found "no case that . . . repudiated this constitutional asymmetry between that which seeks to exclude and that which seeks to include members of minority races." We have found many. Our cases clearly reject the argument that motives affect the strict scrutiny analysis.

This argument that different rules should govern racial classifications designed to include rather than exclude is not new; it has been repeatedly pressed in the past and has been repeatedly rejected.

The reasons for rejecting a motives test for racial classifications are clear enough. "The Court's emphasis on 'benign racial classifications' suggests confidence in its ability to distinguish good from harmful governmental uses of racial criteria. History should teach greater humility. . . . '[B]enign' carries with it no independent meaning, but reflects only acceptance of the current generation's conclusion that a politically acceptable burden, imposed on particular citizens on the basis of race, is reasonable." . . .

Justice BREYER speaks of bringing "the races" together (putting aside the purely black-and-white nature of the plans), as the justification for excluding individuals on the basis of their race). Again, this approach to racial classifications is fundamentally at odds with our precedent, which makes clear that the Equal Protection Clause "protect[s] *persons, not groups.*" This fundamental principle goes back, in this context, to *Brown* itself. For the dissent, in contrast, " 'individualized scrutiny' is simply beside the point."

Justice BREYER's position comes down to a familiar claim: The end justifies the means. He admits that "there is a cost in applying 'a state-mandated racial label,'" but he is confident that the cost is worth paying. Our established strict scrutiny test for racial classifications, however, insists on "detailed examination, both as to ends and as to means." Simply because the school districts may seek a worthy goal does not mean they are free to discriminate on the basis of race to achieve it, or that their racial classifications should be subject to less exacting scrutiny.

Despite his argument that these cases should be evaluated under a "standard of review that is not 'strict' in the traditional sense of that word," Justice BREYER still purports to apply strict scrutiny to these cases. It is evident, however, that Justice BREYER's brand of narrow tailoring is quite unlike anything found in our precedents. Without any detailed discussion of the operation of the plans, the students who are affected, or the districts' failure to consider race-neutral alternatives, the dissent concludes that the districts have shown that these racial classifications are necessary to achieve the districts' stated goals. This conclusion is divorced from any evaluation of the actual impact of the plans at issue in these cases—other than to note that the plans "often have no effect." Instead, the dissent suggests that some combination of the development of these plans over time, the difficulty of the endeavor, and the good faith of the districts suffices to demonstrate that these stark and controlling racial classifications are constitutional. The Constitution and our precedents require more.

In keeping with his view that strict scrutiny should not apply, Justice BREYER repeatedly urges deference to local school boards on these issues. Such deference "is fundamentally at odds with our equal protection jurisprudence. We put the burden on state actors to demonstrate that their race-based policies are justified."

Justice BREYER's dissent ends on an unjustified note of alarm. It predicts that today's decision "threaten[s]" the validity of "[h]undreds of state and federal statutes and regulations." But the examples the dissent mentions—for example, a provision of the No Child Left Behind Act that requires States to set measurable objectives to track the achievement of students from major racial and ethnic groups—have nothing to do with the pertinent issues in these cases.

Justice BREYER also suggests that other means for achieving greater racial diversity in schools are necessarily unconstitutional if the racial classifications at issue in these cases cannot survive strict scrutiny. These other means—*e.g.,* where to construct new schools, how to allocate resources among schools, and which academic offerings to provide to attract students to certain schools—implicate different considerations than the explicit racial classifications at issue in these cases, and we express no opinion on their validity—not even in dicta. Rather, we employ the familiar and well-established analytic approach of strict scrutiny to evaluate the plans at issue today, an approach that in no way warrants the dissent's cataclysmic concerns. Under that approach, the school districts have not carried their burden of showing that the ends they seek justify the particular extreme means they have chosen—classifying individual students on the basis of their race and discriminating among them on that basis.

. . . .

If the need for the racial classifications embraced by the school districts is unclear, even on the districts' own terms, the costs are undeniable. "[D]istinctions between citizens solely because of their ancestry are by their very nature odious to a free people whose institutions are founded upon the doctrine of equality." Government action dividing us by race is inherently suspect because such classifications promote "notions of racial inferiority and lead to a politics of racial hostility," "reinforce the belief, held by too many for too much of our history, that individuals should be judged by the color of their skin" and "endorse race-based reasoning and the conception of a Nation divided into racial blocs, thus contributing to an escalation of racial hostility and conflict." As the Court explained in *Rice v. Cayetano,* "[o]ne of the principal reasons race is treated as a forbidden classification is that it demeans the dignity and worth of a person to be judged by ancestry instead of by his or her own merit and essential qualities."

All this is true enough in the contexts in which these statements were made—government contracting, voting districts, allocation of broadcast licenses, and electing state officers—but when it comes to using race to assign children to schools, history will be heard. In *Brown v. Board of Education* (*Brown I*), we held that segregation deprived black children of equal educational opportunities regardless of whether school facilities and other tangible factors were equal, because government classification and separation on grounds of race themselves denoted inferiority. It was not the inequality of the facilities but the fact of legally separating children on the basis of race on which the Court relied to find a constitutional violation in 1954. The next term, we accordingly stated that "full compliance" with *Brown I* required school districts "to achieve a system of determining admission to the public schools on a nonracial basis."

The parties and their *amici* debate which side is more faithful to the heritage of *Brown*, but the position of the plaintiffs in *Brown* was spelled out in their brief and could not have been clearer: "[T]he Fourteenth Amendment prevents states from according differential treatment to American children on the basis of their color or race." What do the racial classifications at issue here do, if not accord differential treatment on the basis of race? As counsel who appeared before this Court for the plaintiffs in *Brown* put it: "We have one fundamental contention which we will seek to develop in the course of this argument, and that contention is that no State has any authority under the equal-protection clause of the Fourteenth Amendment to use race as a factor in affording educational opportunities among its citizens." There is no ambiguity in that statement. And it was that position that prevailed in this Court, which emphasized in its remedial opinion that what was "[a]t stake is the personal interest of the plaintiffs in admission to public schools as soon as practicable on a nondiscriminatory basis," and what was required was "determining admission to the public schools on a nonracial basis." What do the racial classifications do in these cases, if not determine admission to a public school on a racial basis?

Before *Brown*, schoolchildren were told where they could and could not go to school based on the color of their skin. The school districts in these cases have not carried the heavy burden of demonstrating that we should allow this once again—even for very different reasons. For schools that never segregated on the basis of race, such as Seattle, or that have removed the vestiges of past segregation, such as Jefferson County, the way "to achieve a system of determining admission to the public schools on a nonracial basis" is to stop assigning students on a racial basis. The way to stop discrimination on the basis of race is to stop discriminating on the basis of race.

The judgments of the Courts of Appeals for the Sixth and Ninth Circuits are reversed, and the cases are remanded for further proceedings.

It is so ordered.

Citation: *Parents Involved in Community Schools v. Seattle School District No. 1*, 426 F.3d 1162 (9th Cir. 2005), 127 S. Ct. 2738 (2007).

PARENT TEACHER ASSOCIATIONS/ORGANIZATIONS

Organizations that connect parents with the schools their children attend provide a vital link with teachers and other personnel who have a shared interest in their children. Through these groups, parents get a voice in the daily activities of schools and their administration. In turn, parents become valuable allies for teachers, educational leaders, and their schools, serving a variety of functions, among them classroom volunteers, community contacts, political allies, and fundraisers. Those groups that call themselves Parent Teacher Associations (PTAs) have a long shared history and a network of local, regional, and national organizations. Parent teacher organizations (PTOs) are more informal and localized groups, but they have the same composition and goals. This entry looks at both kinds of parent and teacher linkages.

PTAs and PTOs

In 1897, Alice McLellan Birney and Phoebe Apperson Hearst founded an organization whose challenge was to better the lives of children. Originally known as the National Congress of Mothers, it later became the National Parent Teacher Association (PTA). The creation of the organization occurred when social activism was unacceptable, and women did not possess the right to vote. The founders believed it was time for mothers across this country to help eliminate the threats endangering children. The national PTA has a long history of support to students and their communities. The national PTA's history of hard work advocating for children includes the creation of kindergarten classes, child labor laws, a public health system, and mandatory immunizations.

Parent-teacher groups provide educators with participants from the surrounding community. Although membership is voluntary and typically requires a small monetary membership fee, the ability to generate support for school initiatives is invaluable to educators. Another area of importance is the ability of these groups to generate funds to support the school or district. These funds do not have the same legal implications that state, federal, or local monies provided to schools and districts have. Ethical considerations are the primary principles that drive the appropriate use of these funds by educators.

The PTA is an organization composed of parents, teachers, and administrators, and it may also include community representatives, working together to promote student achievement and success. The PTA has several levels of organization. The basic level begins at the local school or school district PTA, followed by the state PTA, and finally the national PTA. All organizations using the PTA acronym are affiliated with the state and national PTAs. Membership in the PTA is open to anyone. If individuals join local PTAs, they are also made members of the state and national PTAs. Individuals are free to join as many local or state PTAs as they desire.

Those parent teacher organizations not affiliated with the state or national PTAs are referred to generically as PTOs, which are individual organizations usually affiliated with only one school or school district.

Functions of PTAs and PTOs

The two different types (PTA and PTO) function on a daily basis in very similar ways. Both are advocates for children and pursue remedies that will enable all school-aged children the opportunity to learn in a safe environment. Both organizations operate under bylaws. The PTO usually is created and agrees to operate based on local requirements. The PTA also creates bylaws at the local level, but it must also comply with state and national bylaws.

PTAs and PTOs also serve as fundraising organizations to improve the school environment. PTA and PTO members are volunteers interested in supporting their school and helping to improve the school, which will help students. There is a multitude of areas in which members help the school on a daily basis. Members volunteer in classrooms, assist on playgrounds, help in libraries, and act as chaperones on field trips or at school functions such as dances. Members provide schools with support as adults supervising student activities when an inadequate number of teachers are available. This support is provided as volunteer work, which saves the school district money. These examples are just a few of the many ways PTAs and PTOs help the school or district to improve the learning environment.

PTAs and PTOs function as civic organizations whose goal is to improve local schools and districts. Parent and teacher involvement are key for community understanding of the vision and mission of the school and district. Open communication among administrators, the board of education, school/district staff, and parent-teacher groups adds immeasurably to the success of the school's and district's goals. An active parent-teacher group can become a powerful advocate for the school/district in the community.

Besides the civic aspects of these two types of organizations, there is another function that is political. PTOs influence local politics, because most members are eligible to vote in local elections. These include elections for school board members, city officials, county representatives, state representatives, and national representatives. Because a PTO has no national affiliation, and each is independent of all others, the ability to generate political pressure at the state and national levels is limited. PTAs, on the other hand, have state and national affiliations that provide a broad base of political influence. The national PTA can lobby for legislation that affects all states, while the state PTAs can lobby for state legislation affecting schools and school districts. Local PTAs can influence politics in a fashion similar to that of local PTOs, but they also have the advantage of state and national recognition and presence to advocate for changes at all levels.

PTAs and PTOs provide educators with an avenue for two-way communication with their surrounding communities. This can prove to be an essential element for schools and districts when changes are needed to improve student performance or in response to state or federal agency mandated legislation. The PTAs and PTOs can be used as sounding boards or resources for ideas to meet new legislative demands. Community support is essential to the success of a school or district. PTAs and PTOs provide a useful mechanism to garner that support from within communities.

Michael J. Jernigan

See also Kindergarten, Right to Attend; Parental Rights

Further Readings

National Parent Teacher Association. (n.d.). http://www
.pta.org

National Parent Teacher Association. (1997). *The PTA story: A century of commitment to children.* Chicago: Author.

National Parent Teacher Association. (2000). *Building successful partnerships: A guide for developing parent and family involvement programs.* Bloomington, IN: National Educational Service.

National Parent Teacher Association. (2004). *National standards for parent/family involvement programs.* Chicago: Author.

What is the difference in PTA and PTO? (n.d.). Retrieved February 19, 2007, from http://beginnersguide
.com/secondary-education/parentteacher-associations-and-organizations/what-is-the-difference-in-pta-and-pto.php

PASADENA CITY BOARD OF EDUCATION V. SPANGLER

At issue in *Pasadena City Board of Education v. Spangler* (1976) was the validity of a court order that would have required a school board to engage in the annual rearrangement of school attendance zones in order to ensure a specified racial mix of students in schools. In *Spangler,* by finding that it was unnecessary for a board to make such an arrangement, the Court continued its retreat from support for efforts to desegregate schools.

Facts of the Case

Spangler began in 1968, when students and their parents sought to enjoin the alleged unconstitutional segregation of the high schools in Pasadena, California. A federal trial court held that the school board's educational policies violated the Fourteenth Amendment. In addition, the court ordered the board to adopt a plan for desegregating the schools by the 1970–1971 school year. The court indicated that the plan had to be designed to assure that there would be no school with a majority enrollment of minority students. Subsequently, the court approved the plan.

In 1974, the school board sought to modify the 1970 order by filing a motion to eliminate the "no majority of a minority" requirement insofar as it was ambiguous. In addition, the board wanted to dissolve the injunction and terminate the court's jurisdiction over the plan. However, the only year in which the board was in total compliance with the desegregation plan was in its first year of operation. The trial court denied the board's motion because of its failure to comply with the plan, because a number of schools did not meet the "no majority of a minority" requirement. The court explained that no majority of any minority requirement was a continual inflexible requirement that was to be applied each year even though subsequent changes in the racial mix of the schools may have been caused by other factors outside of the school's responsibility. When the board appealed, the Ninth Circuit upheld the desegregation plan.

The Court's Ruling

On further review, the Supreme Court vacated and remanded *Spangler* in favor of the board for further proceedings. The justices held that the plan established a racially neutral system of student assignment and that the trial court exceeded its authority in enforcing the order that required annual readjustment of attendance zones so that a majority of minority students would not be in any school. As part of its analysis, the justices were of the opinion that the trial court erred in interpreting *Swann v. Charlotte-Mecklenburg Board of Education* (1971) as seemingly creating a constitutional right to a specified degree of racial balance or mixing in schools. The Court thus relied on *Swann* in maintaining that there are limits beyond which courts may not go in dismantling dual school systems. According to the Court, absent a constitutional violation, there was no basis for a court to order assignments on a racial basis.

At the same time, the Supreme Court ruled that the plan that the trial court approved did achieve the objective of creating a system of assignments to public schools on a nonracial basis. The Court also reviewed the trial court's record that rejected the school board's argument that the changes in the racial mix of schools were due to White flight. To this end, the Court found that shifts in racial demographics were due to people randomly moving in and out of the area, not to any actions of the school board. This led the Court to stress that once the board met its affirmative duty to desegregate and once racial discrimination was eliminated, there was no need to make year-to-year adjustments. Rounding out its analysis, the Court remanded for further proceedings to determine whether the school board had achieved a unitary system with respect to all aspects of the desegregation plan.

Spangler is notable because it was the first desegregation case to arise in California, which, unlike the South, did not have a history of dual systems of education. In pointing out that once a school system achieves unitary status it is no longer obligated to adjust boundaries, the Supreme Court signaled its continued retreat from strong enforcement of desegregation. The Court concluded that because officials must achieve a racial balance in the schools only once, the obligation to desegregate may be terminated when they have met this goal.

Deborah Curry

See also *Brown v. Board of Education of Topeka;* Fourteenth Amendment; Segregation, De Facto; *Swann v. Charlotte-Mecklenburg Board of Education*

Further Readings

Deavins, N. (1984). School desegregation law in the 1980's: The court's abandonment of *Brown v. Board of Education*. *William & Mary Law Review, 26,* 7–43.

Hunter, R. C., & Donahoo, S. (2004). The implementation of *Brown* in achieving unitary status. *Education and Urban Society, 36,* 342–354.

Russo, C. J., Harris, J. J., III, & Sandridge, R. F. (1994). *Brown v. Board of Education* at 40: A legal history of equal educational opportunities in American public education. *Journal of Negro Education, 63*(3), 297–309.

Legal Citations

Pasadena City Board of Education v. Spangler, 427 U.S. 424 (1976).

Swann v. Charlotte-Mecklenburg Board of Education, 402 U.S. 1 (1971).

Pennsylvania Association for Retarded Children v. Commonwealth of Pennsylvania

Two cases, *Mills v. Board of Education of District of Columbia* (1972) and *Pennsylvania Association for Retarded Children v. Commonwealth of Pennsylvania* (*PARC,* 1971, 1972), were major elements in helping to lay the foundation for the 1975 enactment of the Education for All Handicapped Children Act, now known as the Individuals with Disabilities Education Act (IDEA). Prior to that time, millions of students with disabilities were either excluded from public education totally or were admitted but did not receive appropriate services. While only heard at the federal trial court level, the decisions in *Mills* and *PARC* are truly landmark cases in the evolution of federal special education law.

Facts of the Case

PARC was a class action suit filed on behalf of 13 children with cognitive disabilities, each residing in a different Pennsylvania school system. At the time, Pennsylvania had a statute in effect that specifically allowed school boards to exclude any children that school psychologists deemed to be either "uneducable" or "untrainable" under the terminology used to identify children with disabilities. These exclusions could have occurred when the parents sought to enroll their children in schools or at some time after admittance, whenever school psychologists determined the students failed to meet acceptable educational criteria.

Any child so designated became the responsibility of the Department of Welfare, even though that agency did not provide any educational services. The plaintiffs filed suit, arguing that this practice violated the students' rights under both the Due Process and Equal Protection clauses of the Fourteenth Amendment.

The Court's Ruling

The federal trial court that heard the claim found merit in both of the plaintiffs' arguments. As to the Due Process claim, the court ruled that children could not be denied their right to an education without some sort of process. One aspect that the court pointed out as particularly troubling was the stigmatizing effect of the Pennsylvania statute. To this end, the court cited empirical studies that demonstrated the negative effects of the label and documented that 25% of the students were erroneously labeled, while another large group had questionable diagnoses.

Turning to the Equal Protection allegation, the court reasoned that there were "serious doubts" as to the rational basis to support the exclusion of this broad class of children from the educational benefits provided by the commonwealth. The court was of the opinion that the plaintiffs had presented a colorable claim under the Equal Protection Clause.

As a result of the court's analysis in *PARC*, it approved a detailed consent agreement between the parties. The consent agreement outlined remedies that, in essence, required Pennsylvania and its school systems to create means to identify children with disabilities in the commonwealth, a system of special education services to meet their educational needs, and a way for parents to participate in decision making and have any disputes with school districts settled by an impartial third party. *PARC* stands out as significant insofar as numerous provisions in today's IDEA can trace their origins to the settlement agreement that the parties reached in their consent decrees.

Julie F. Mead

See also Disabled Persons, Rights of; Equal Protection Analysis; Fourteenth Amendment; *Mills v. Board of Education of the District of Columbia*

Further Readings

Huefner, D. S. (2006). *Getting comfortable with special education law: A framework for working with children with disabilities* (2nd ed.). Norwood, MA: Christopher-Gordon.

Legal Citations

Mills v. Board of Education of District of Columbia, 348 F. Supp. 866 (D.D.C. 1972).
Pennsylvania Association for Retarded Children v. Commonwealth of Pennsylvania, 334 F. Supp. 1257 (E.D. Pa. 1971), 343 F. Supp. 279 (E.D. Pa. 1972).

PERRY EDUCATION ASSOCIATION V. PERRY LOCAL EDUCATORS' ASSOCIATION

After an election in which the Perry Education Association (PEA) was selected as the bargaining agent for public school teachers in Perry Township, Indiana, the school board denied the rival union and election loser, the Perry Local Educators' Association (PLEA), access to the district's mail system. PLEA argued that this action violated the organization's rights under the First Amendment and the Equal Protection Clause of the Fourteenth Amendment. Ultimately, the U.S. Supreme Court held that the union did not have such a right.

Facts of the Case

In 1977, public school teachers in the Metropolitan School District of Perry Township, Indiana, elected the PEA as their exclusive representative for bargaining with their local school board. Prior to the election, the teachers were represented by PEA or by a rival union, PLEA, and both unions used the school mailboxes and interschool mail system to communicate with their respective members. However, after the election, the PLEA had no official status with the teachers or the school board. Consequently, the 1978 collective bargaining agreement with the board provided that the PEA, but no other union, would have access to the interschool mail system.

After its exclusion from school mail facilities, PLEA and two of its members filed suit in a federal trial court, contending that the PEA's exclusive access violated their constitutional rights, because the mail facilities had been opened to the YMCA, Cub Scouts, other civic organizations, and parochial schools in the past. Therefore, the PLEA argued that because the mail facilities had become a limited public forum for expression, the school board could not arbitrarily exclude it from participation.

The trial court denied the PLEA's claim in granting motions for summary judgment on behalf of the PEA and board. According to the court, the mail system was not a public forum merely because it had accommodated outside groups periodically or because PLEA had equal access prior to PEA's certification as the sole bargaining agent for the teachers. PLEA appealed, and the Seventh Circuit reversed in its favor. The court held that once the board opened its mail system to PEA but denied access to PLEA, it violated both the First and Fourteenth Amendments.

The Court's Ruling

On further review, the U.S. Supreme Court ruled that the school board could deny PLEA access to its mail facilities. In the first place, the Court explained that the board had the authority to decide how its facilities would be used, and by whom, in accomplishing school objectives. The Court was of the opinion that because the mail facilities were not a limited public forum, the board could deny access to any and all outside groups if it chose to do so.

The Court pointed out that because the PLEA was no longer authorized to represent teachers in the district, it had no official relationship with teachers or the board. Therefore, the Court maintained that the PLEA could not claim that access to the mail system was necessary for it to carry out legal and contractual responsibilities to its membership or the school board. Insofar as the exclusive access policy applied only to use of the mail system, the Court reasoned, the PLEA was not prevented from using other school facilities to communicate with teachers. For example, the Court noted that the PLEA could post notices on bulletin boards, conduct meetings on school property after regular school hours, and with approval of the building principals, make announcements on the public address system.

Moreover, the Court acknowledged that, of course, the PLEA could always communicate with teachers by telephone, U.S. mail, or word of mouth.

The Court also observed that the exclusive access extended to the PEA was consistent with the board's interest in reserving school property for its intended purpose. More specifically, the Court recognized that the use of the mail system enabled the PEA to carry out its legal obligations in representing classroom teachers. Under Indiana law, the Court reasoned that the PLEA was guaranteed equal access to all modes of communication when a union representation election was in progress. Therefore, the Court decided that it would have equal opportunity to inform potential members about its aims and services prior to elections. In the meantime, the Court interpreted the board's exclusion of the defeated PLEA was a reasonable means of ensuring labor peace within the district. To the Court, the board's excluding the PLEA significantly reduced the possibility that the Metropolitan School District would become "a battlefield for inter-union squabbles."

In sum, the Supreme Court ruled that PEA's exclusive access to school mail facilities was permissible and essential. Under law, the Court determined that the PEA was responsible for negotiating and administering a collective bargaining agreement and representing classroom teachers in settling disputes and processing grievances. To this end, the Court conceded that having access to the mail system made it easier for PEA officials to carry out those difficult tasks efficiently and effectively, thereby advancing an important state function. Consequently, the Court concluded that the preferential access granted to PEA did not violate the constitutional rights of PLEA.

Robert C. Cloud

See also *Abood v. Detroit Board of Education;* Collective Bargaining; Equal Protection Analysis; Fourteenth Amendment; School Boards; Unions

Legal Citations

Abood v. Detroit Board of Education, 431 U.S. 209 (1977).
Healy v. James, 408 U.S. 169 (1972).
Perry Education Association v. Perry Local Educators' Association, 460 U.S. 37 (1983).

Police Department of Chicago v. Mosley, 408 U.S. 92 (1972).

San Antonio School District v. Rodriguez, 411 U.S. 1 (1973).

United States Postal Service v. Council of Greenburgh, 453 U.S. 114 (1981).

PERRY V. SINDERMANN

At issue in *Perry v. Sindermann* (1972) was whether a college faculty member's lack of a contractual or tenure right to re-employment, taken alone, defeats his claim that the nonrenewal of his contract violated the First and Fourteenth Amendments. The U.S Supreme Court held in *Perry* that it did not. Although a government employer may choose not to renew a contract for any number of reasons, it may not deny a contract extension to a faculty member on a basis that infringes on his constitutional rights, particularly the rights to freedom of speech and association, the court ruled.

Tenured faculty members in colleges and universities, in a manner similar to their colleagues in elementary and secondary schools, have property interests in continued employment, and they are entitled to due process prior to termination. Nontenured faculty members usually receive one-year contracts that, if renewable, must be renewed every year. Additionally, unless employer policy or state law hold otherwise, faculty members working under such contracts are not entitled to due process if their contracts are not extended, because they have no property interests in continued employment. However, due process may be required if nontenured faculty members can demonstrate that they had a liberty interest in employment and that the nonrenewal of their contracts was based on constitutionally impermissible reasons.

Facts of the Case

Robert Sindermann, a nontenured teacher at Odessa (Texas) Junior College (OJC) and the respondent in this case, served in four different public institutions in Texas over 10 years, the last 4 at OJC. During the 1968–1969 academic year, Sindermann served as president of the Texas Junior College Teachers Association (TJCTA) and was frequently in Austin, the state capital, representing the association before the Texas legislature. On more than one occasion, he disagreed publicly with policies of the OJC Board of Regents. At the time, OJC had no formal faculty tenure system. All faculty members, including Sindermann, received one-year contracts, even though the following statement had been in the faculty handbook for many years:

> Teacher Tenure: Odessa College has no tenure system. The Administration of the College wishes the faculty member to feel that he has *permanent tenure* as long as his teaching services are satisfactory and as long as he displays a cooperative attitude toward his coworkers and his superiors, and as long as he is happy in his work. (*emphasis added*)

In May 1969, the OJC Board of Regents voted not to renew Sindermann's contract for the 1969–1970 academic year. The board released a statement alleging insubordination by Sindermann, but he was not given a hearing to respond to the charge. Sindermann filed suit in a federal trial court in Texas, contending that his contract was not renewed because of his public criticism of the OJC board and that he was entitled to a hearing. Sindermann argued that the board's action violated his First and Fourteenth Amendment rights. The board countered that Sindermann was not entitled to a hearing, because his contract had expired, and he had no property interest in continued employment. Subsequently, the trial court granted the board's motion for summary judgment, concluding that Sindermann had no expectancy of continued employment, because his contract had, in fact, expired.

The Fifth Circuit reversed in favor of Sindermann, maintaining that he might have been able to show an expectancy of continued employment if he had received a hearing. Petitioners appealed, and the Supreme Court granted certiorari.

The Court's Ruling

The Supreme Court announced its decision in *Perry v. Sindermann* on June 29, 1972. First, the Court could not determine whether Sindermann's speech was the sole reason for nonrenewal, and it did not find for either petitioners or respondent. Second, the Court decided that Sindermann had First Amendment rights regardless of his employment status. Therefore, as far as the Court was concerned, Sindermann's lack of tenure status was immaterial to his free speech claim. The Court agreed that it was impossible to determine whether Sindermann's free speech rights were violated without a hearing. Third, the Court concluded that Sindermann had a right to due process based on the de facto tenure system that was referenced (albeit unintentionally) in the faculty handbook statement. Finally, the Court reasoned that Sindermann had a right to prove the legitimacy of his free speech and due process claims in a hearing. Consequently, the Supreme Court affirmed the judgment of the Fifth Circuit and remanded the case back to the trial court for review.

Legal implications from the *Perry* decision include the following. First, a due process hearing is required on contract nonrenewal if a teacher whose contract is not renewed can demonstrate property or liberty interests. Second, both tenured and nontenured faculty may have due process rights within the terms of a contract. However, when term contracts expire, nontenured teachers have no due process rights, unless they can demonstrate an expectancy of continued employment. Third, a de facto tenure system can lead to an expectancy of continued employment. Consequently, contract terms and policies must be carefully written according to legal guidelines and reviewed regularly by college counsel. Fourth, because faculty members whose contracts are terminated often claim that their constitutional rights were violated, officials should conduct hearings to ensure that due process is extended to all faculty regardless of employment status.

Robert C. Cloud

See also Due Process; Fourteenth Amendment; School Board Policy; Teacher Rights; Tenure

Legal Citations

Board of Regents v. Roth, 408 U.S. 504 (1972).
Keyishian v. Board of Regents, 385 U.S. 589 (1967).
Pickering v. Board of Education of Township High School District 205, Will County, 391 U.S. 563 (1968).
Shelton v. Tucker, 364 U.S. 479 (1960).

PERSONNEL RECORDS

Organizations that employ individuals routinely create and need to maintain records concerning their employees. Some records are kept because the law requires that they be kept. Other records are maintained because of employment policy mandates.

Accurate personnel records provide the employer with information that it needs to make good decisions. Personnel records help management determine whether staff resources may be available to meet work requirements and how staff are doing in regard to organizational goals; they also provide a readily available record to assess levels of performance and productivity. Accurate personnel records also help to ensure that employees receive their correct pay and pension contributions as well as other benefits. They help to monitor and promote consistency in regard to employee development, including promotion, discipline, and discharge.

Some records are maintained because state and/or federal law require that they be so maintained. Employers must maintain records to document compliance with state and federal laws prohibiting employment discrimination, for example. Compliance with state and federal tax laws requires employers to maintain records for each employee documenting wages, hours, withholding, and deductions. Similar recordkeeping is important in documenting compliance with the Family and Medical Leave Act, the Fair Labor Standards Act, and similar employment regulations. Maintaining these records allows the employer to monitor compliance with regulatory requirements.

Other records are maintained as a matter of employment policy. Personnel records help employers implement and monitor personnel actions from time of hire to separation. Records concerning attendance, job evaluation, discipline, and professional development fall into these categories.

Many states have laws that regulate personnel files and/or personnel records. The laws generally guarantee access to personnel files by the employee and provide that the records are confidential; that is, they are not subject to review by unauthorized persons. Laws generally give an employee an opportunity to access his or her own personnel file on a periodic basis. An employee also generally has the right to authorize another person, like an attorney or union representative, to access the records. Many states provide an employee the opportunity to ask that personnel records be modified or removed if the employee believes that the record is not accurate. If the employer agrees with the employee, the record is modified or removed. If not, some states may allow an employee the opportunity to attach a written statement to the record in dispute.

Not all records maintained by an employer concerning its employees are open to inspection. Laws commonly exempt some records from disclosure. Common exemptions are letters of reference from when the employee was hired, information concerning criminal investigations, and other documents that the employer may be using for staff management purposes.

Most employers provide employees with a copy of the documents contained within their personnel files. For example, discipline or evaluation documents are commonly given to employees at the same time as they are put in a personnel file. Providing an employee with these types of documents avoids claims of surprise in the future and will provide an employee with a reasonable opportunity to improve performance.

Personnel records should be maintained as confidential. Records should be kept in a locked file, and access restricted pursuant to the requirements of law and/or policy. Medical records concerning an employee are frequently collected as part of the employer/employee relationship. Special guidelines may apply to such medical information. The Americans with Disabilities Act (ADA) offers strict rules for handling medical information obtained through postoffer medical examinations. Employers covered by the ADA are required to keep such records confidential and separate from other personnel records. Access to this information is restricted to human resource professionals and, in appropriate cases, the employee's supervisor, if needed for an accommodation due to a disability or as otherwise authorized by law.

The Health Insurance Portability and Accountability Act (HIPAA) also imposes confidentiality obligations on many employers who purchase group health plans. State laws may also have special provisions for exempting medical information.

Jon E. Anderson

See also Americans with Disabilities Act; Title VII

Legal Citations

Americans with Disabilities Act, 42 U.S.C. §§ 12101 *et seq.*

Health Insurance Portability and Accountability Act, codified in part at 29 U.S.C. §§ 1181 *et seq.*; 42 U.S.C. §§ 200gg (various); 42 U.S.C. §§ 1320d, 1320d 1–8; 26 U.S.C. §§ 9801 *et seq.*

Title VII of the Civil Rights Act of 1964, 42 U.S.C. §§ 2000 *et seq.*

PICKERING V. BOARD OF EDUCATION OF TOWNSHIP HIGH SCHOOL DISTRICT 205, WILL COUNTY

At issue in *Pickering v. Board of Education of Township High School District 205, Will County* (1968) was whether a school board's dismissal of a public school teacher for expressing his opinion about actions taken by the board and its administration violated his First Amendment rights to free speech. In *Pickering,* the U.S. Supreme Court ruled that "absent proof of false statements knowingly or recklessly made" (p. 574), a teacher's statements on public issues can't be used as grounds for dismissal in public schools. According to the Court, teachers are entitled to speak as citizens on matters of public interest, including controversial issues in their own school districts, and their comments on those issues may not be the reason for dismissals even when they are critical of school board officials.

Facts of the Case

The school board at Township High School District No. 205, Will County, Illinois, fired Marvin Pickering for sending a letter to the local newspaper that criticized its fiscal policies and actions of the superintendent. The letter included false statements allegedly damaging the reputations of school officials. Pursuant to Illinois law, the board granted Pickering a hearing at which he could challenge his dismissal.

At the hearing, officials asserted that his statements "would foment controversy, conflict, and dissension among teachers, administrators, board members, and residents in the district" (p. 570). Finding that Pickering's statements were detrimental to the efficient operation of the schools, the board decided that he should be dismissed. Subsequently, Illinois courts upheld Pickering's dismissal. In response to Pickering's appeal, the Supreme Court granted certiorari and heard his case on March 27, 1968.

The Court's Ruling

In reversing the orders of the state courts, the Supreme Court emphasized that speech relating to matters of public concern is constitutionally protected, holding that the fiscal and policy issues that Pickering raised were clearly of significant public interest. Further, the Court reasoned that because Pickering's comments did not jeopardize his relationships with immediate supervisors and coworkers, they were not likely to cause disharmony in the workplace. Insofar as Pickering did not work closely with the board and superintendent, the Court maintained that it was fallacious to argue that he could not have expressed a dissenting opinion about school operations out of personal loyalty to the system. To the Supreme Court, Pickering's statements were more likely to foster healthy debate on public matters than they were to "foment controversy, conflict, and dissension among [constituents] in the district" (p. 570).

The Supreme Court found no evidence that Pickering's letter damaged the reputations of officials or caused controversy and conflict in the schools as the board claimed. As a matter of fact, the Court pointed out that the record reflected that "Pickering's letter was greeted with apathy and disbelief by everyone except the Board and administration who were the main targets of the letter" (p. 570). While conceding that Pickering's letter did include several false statements, such as his accusation about excessive athletic spending, the Court noted that the school board could easily have rebutted his inaccurate remarks by publishing the facts available to them in school records. The Court acknowledged that Pickering had made erroneous statements but held that this did not interfere with his work as a teacher or cause disruption in the school.

The Court was of the view that whether true or false, Pickering's statements merited public attention. He spoke as a citizen on matters of public concern, namely school funding, the wise use of limited financial resources, and the competence of school officials. The Court recognized that Pickering's statements did not compromise his performance of assigned duties and did not disrupt the efficient operation of the schools or cause controversy in the community. To the contrary, the Court was convinced that Pickering's statements focused needed attention on matters of legitimate concern to the public. Consequently, the Court concluded that the school board had insufficient reason to limit his speech or fire him. As the Supreme Court wrote in summarizing its analysis,

> Free and open debate is vital to informed decision-making by the electorate. Teachers are, as a class, the members of a community most likely to have informed and definite opinions as to how funds allotted to the operation of the schools should be spent. Accordingly, it is essential that they be able to speak freely on such questions without fear of retaliatory dismissal. (pp. 571–572)

While endorsing Pickering's right to speak as a citizen on matters of public concern, the Court acknowledged the right of schools and other government employers to supervise employees properly and provide public services efficiently. As such, First Amendment jurisprudence since 1968 has sought a delicate balance between the free speech rights of public employees such as teachers and the interests of public employers such as school boards in efficient operations. In an effort to locate and maintain a delicate balance, the Supreme Court articulated its now famous *Pickering* balancing test:

> It cannot be gainsaid that the State has interests as an employer in regulating the speech of its employees that differ significantly from those it possesses in connection with regulation of the speech of the citizenry in general. The problem in any case is to arrive at a balance between the interests of the teacher, as a citizen, in commenting upon matters of public concern and the interests of the State, as an employer, in promoting the efficiency of the public services it performs through its employees. (p. 568)

In the years following *Pickering*, federal courts have sought a proper balance between the right of public employees to speak as citizens on public issues with the equally legitimate right of public employers to deliver services efficiently and effectively. Maintaining the balance is not easy, and the search continues.

Robert C. Cloud

See also *Connick v. Myers*; School Board Policy; Teacher Rights

Legal Citations

Connick v. Myers, 461 U.S. 138 (1983).
Garcetti v. Ceballos, 547 U.S. 410 (2006).
Keyishian v. Board of Regents, 385 U.S. 589 (1967).
Kinsey v. Salado Independent School District, 950 F.2d 988, 661 (5th Cir. 1992) *en banc, vacating* 916 F.2d 273 (5th Cir. 1990).
Pickering v. Board of Education of Township High School District 205, Will County, 391 U.S. 563 (1968).
Shelton v. Tucker, 364 U.S. 479 (1960).
Wieman v. Updegraff, 344 U.S. 183 (1952).

Pickering v. Board of Education of Township High School District 205, Will County (Excerpts)

In Pickering v. Board of Education of Township High School District 205, Will County, *the Supreme Court reasoned that public school teachers have the right to speak out on matters of public concern, even if it involved their school boards.*

Supreme Court of the United States

PICKERING

v.

BOARD OF EDUCATION OF TOWNSHIP HIGH SCHOOL DISTRICT 205, WILL COUNTY, ILLINOIS.

391 U.S. 563

Argued March 27, 1968.

Decided June 3, 1968.

Mr. Justice MARSHALL delivered the opinion of the Court.

Appellant Marvin L. Pickering, a teacher in Township High School District 205, Will County, Illinois, was dismissed from his position by the appellee Board of Education for sending a letter to a local newspaper in connection with a recently proposed tax increase that was critical of the way in which the Board and the district superintendent of schools had handled past proposals to raise new revenue for the schools. Appellant's dismissal resulted from a determination by the Board, after a full hearing, that the publication of the letter was 'detrimental to the efficient operation and administration of the schools of the district' and hence, under the relevant Illinois statute that 'interests of the schools require(d) (his dismissal).'

Appellant's claim that his writing of the letter was protected by the First and Fourteenth Amendments was rejected. Appellant then sought review of the Board's action in the Circuit Court of Will County, which affirmed his dismissal on the ground that the determination that appellant's letter was detrimental to the interests of the school system was supported by substantial evidence and that the interests of the schools overruled appellant's First Amendment rights. On appeal, the Supreme Court of Illinois, two Justices dissenting, affirmed the judgment of the Circuit Court. We noted probable jurisdiction of appellant's claim that the Illinois statute permitting his dismissal on the facts of this case was unconstitutional as applied under the First and Fourteenth Amendments. For the reasons detailed below we agree that appellant's rights to freedom of speech were violated and we reverse.

I

In February of 1961 the appellee Board of Education asked the voters of the school district to approve a bond issue to raise $4,875,000 to erect two new schools. The proposal was defeated. Then, in December of 1961, the Board submitted another bond proposal to the voters which called for the raising of $5,500,000 to build two new schools. This second proposal passed and the schools were built with the money raised by the bond sales. In May of 1964 a proposed increase in the tax rate to be used for educational purposes was submitted to the voters by the Board and was defeated. Finally, on September 19, 1964, a second proposal to increase the tax rate was submitted by the Board and was likewise defeated. It was in connection with this last proposal of the School Board that appellant wrote the letter to the editor (which we reproduce in an Appendix to this opinion) that resulted in his dismissal.

Prior to the vote on the second tax increase proposal a variety of articles attributed to the District 205 Teachers' Organization appeared in the local paper. These articles urged passage of the tax increase and stated that failure to pass the increase would result in a decline in the quality of education afforded children in the district's schools. A letter from the superintendent of schools making the same point was published in the paper two days before the election and submitted to the voters in mimeographed form the following day. It was in response to the foregoing material, together with the failure of the tax increase to pass, that appellant submitted the letter in question to the editor of the local paper.

The letter constituted, basically, an attack on the School Board's handling of the 1961 bond issue proposals and its subsequent allocation of financial resources between the schools' educational and athletic programs. It also charged the superintendent of schools with attempting to prevent teachers in the district from opposing or criticizing the proposed bond issue.

The Board dismissed Pickering for writing and publishing the letter. Pursuant to Illinois law, the Board was then required to hold a hearing on the dismissal. At the hearing the Board charged that numerous statements in the letter were false and that the publication of the statements unjustifiably impugned the 'motives, honesty, integrity, truthfulness, responsibility and competence' of both the Board and the school administration. The Board also charged that the false statements damaged the professional reputations of its members and of the school administrators, would be disruptive of faculty discipline, and would tend to foment 'controversy, conflict and dissension' among teachers, administrators, the Board of Education, and the residents of the district. Testimony was introduced from a variety of witnesses on the truth or falsity of the particular statements in the letter with which the Board took issue. The Board found the statements to be false as charged. No evidence was introduced at any point in the proceedings as to the effect of the publication of the letter on the community as a whole or on the administration of the school system in particular, and no specific findings along these lines were made.

The Illinois courts reviewed the proceedings solely to determine whether the Board's findings were supported by substantial evidence and whether, on the facts as found, the Board could reasonably conclude that appellant's publication of the letter was 'detrimental to the best interests of the schools.' Pickering's claim that his letter was protected by the First Amendment was rejected on the ground that his acceptance of a teaching position in the public schools obliged him to refrain from making statements about the operation of the schools 'which in the absence of such position he would have an undoubted right to engage in.' It is not altogether clear whether the Illinois Supreme Court held that the First Amendment had no applicability to appellant's dismissal for writing the letter in question or whether it determined that the particular statements made in the letter were not entitled to First Amendment protection.

In any event, it clearly rejected Pickering's claim that, on the facts of this case, he could not constitutionally be dismissed from his teaching position.

II

To the extent that the Illinois Supreme Court's opinion may be read to suggest that teachers may constitutionally be compelled to relinquish the First Amendment rights they would otherwise enjoy as citizens to comment on matters of public interest in connection with the operation of the public schools in which they work, it proceeds on a premise that has been unequivocally rejected in numerous prior decisions of this Court. '(T)he theory that public employment which may be denied altogether may be subjected to any conditions, regardless of how unreasonable, has been uniformly rejected.' At the same time it cannot be gainsaid that the State has interests as an employer in regulating the speech of its employees that differ significantly from those it possesses in connection with regulation of the speech of the citizenry in general. The problem in any case is to arrive at a balance between the interests of the teacher, as a citizen, in commenting upon matters of public concern and the interest of the State, as an employer, in promoting the efficiency of the public services it performs through its employees.

III

The Board contends that 'the teacher by virtue of his public employment has a duty of loyalty to support his superiors in attaining the generally accepted goals of education and that, if he must speak out publicly, he should do so factually and accurately, commensurate with his education and experience.' Appellant, on the other hand, argues that the test applicable to defamatory statements directed against public officials by persons having no occupational relationship with them, namely, that statements to be legally actionable must be made 'with knowledge that (they were)...false or with reckless disregard of whether (they were)...false or not.' *New York Times Co. v. Sullivan* should also be applied to public statements made by teachers. Because of the enormous variety of fact situations in which critical statements by teachers and other public employees may be thought by their superiors, against whom the statements are directed to furnish grounds for dismissal, we do not deem it either appropriate or feasible to attempt to lay down a general standard against which all such statements may be judged. However, in the course of evaluating the conflicting claims of First Amendment protection and the need for orderly school administration in the context of this case, we shall indicate some of the general lines along which an analysis of the controlling interests should run.

An examination of the statements in appellant's letter objected to by the Board reveals that they, like the letter as a whole, consist essentially of criticism of the Board's allocation of school funds between educational and athletic programs, and of both the Board's and the superintendent's methods of informing, or preventing the informing of, the district's taxpayers of the real reasons why additional tax revenues were being sought for the schools. The statements are in no way directed towards any person with whom appellant would normally be in contact in the course of his daily work as a teacher. Thus no question of maintaining either discipline by immediate superiors or harmony among coworkers is presented here. Appellant's employment relationships with the Board and, to a somewhat lesser extent, with the superintendent are not the kind of close working relationships for which it can persuasively be claimed that personal loyalty and confidence are necessary to their proper functioning. Accordingly, to the extent that the Board's position here can be taken to suggest that even comments on matters of public concern that are substantially correct, such as statements (1)-(4) of appellant's letter may furnish grounds for dismissal if they are sufficiently critical in tone, we unequivocally reject it.

We next consider the statements in appellant's letter which we agree to be false. The Board's original charges included allegations that the publication of the letter damaged the professional reputations of the Board and the superintendent and would foment controversy and conflict among the Board, teachers, administrators, and the residents of the district. However, no evidence to support these allegations was introduced at the hearing. So far as the record reveals, Pickering's letter was greeted by everyone but its main target, the Board, with massive apathy and total disbelief. The Board must, therefore, have decided, perhaps by analogy with the law of libel, that the statements were per se harmful to the operation of the schools.

However, the only way in which the Board could conclude, absent any evidence of the actual effect of the letter, that the statements contained therein were per se detrimental to the interest of the schools was to equate the Board members' own interests with that of the schools. Certainly an accusation that too much money is being spent on athletics by the administrators of the school system (which is precisely the import of that portion of appellant's letter containing the statements that we have found to be false) cannot reasonably be regarded as per se detrimental to the district's schools. Such an accusation reflects rather a difference of opinion between Pickering and the Board as to the preferable manner of operating the school system, a difference of opinion that clearly concerns an issue of general public interest.

In addition, the fact that particular illustrations of the Board's claimed undesirable emphasis on athletic programs are false would not normally have any necessary impact on the actual operation of the schools, beyond its tendency to anger the Board. For example, Pickering's letter was written after the defeat at the polls of the second proposed tax increase. It could, therefore, have had no effect on the ability of the school district to raise necessary revenue, since there was no showing that there was any proposal to increase taxes pending when the letter was written.

More importantly, the question whether a school system requires additional funds is a matter of legitimate public concern on which the judgment of the school administration, including the School Board, cannot, in a society that leaves such questions to popular vote, be taken as conclusive. On such a question free and open debate is vital to informed decision-making by the electorate.

Teachers are, as a class, the members of a community most likely to have informed and definite opinions as to how funds allotted to the operations of the schools should be spent. Accordingly, it is essential that they be able to speak out freely on such questions without fear of retaliatory dismissal.

In addition, the amounts expended on athletics which Pickering reported erroneously were matters of public record on which his position as a teacher in the district did not qualify him to speak with any greater authority than any other taxpayer. The Board could easily have rebutted appellant's errors by publishing the accurate figures itself, either via a letter to the same newspaper or otherwise. We are thus not presented with a situation in which a teacher has carelessly made false statements about matters so closely related to the day-to-day operations of the schools that any harmful impact on the public would be difficult to counter because of the teacher's presumed greater access to the real facts. Accordingly, we have no occasion to consider at this time whether under such circumstances a school board could reasonably require that a teacher make substantial efforts to verify the accuracy of his charges before publishing them.

What we do have before us is a case in which a teacher has made erroneous public statements upon issues then currently the subject of public attention, which are critical of his ultimate employer but which are neither shown nor can be presumed to have in any way either impeded the teacher's proper performance of his daily duties in the classroom or to have interfered with the regular operation of the schools generally. In these circumstances we conclude that the interest of the school administration in limiting teachers' opportunities to contribute to public debate is not significantly greater than its interest in limiting a similar contribution by any member of the general public.

IV

The public interest in having free and unhindered debate on matters of public importance—the core value of the Free Speech Clause of the First Amendment—is so great that it has been held that a State cannot authorize the recovery of damages by a public official for defamatory statements directed at him except when such statements are shown to have been made either with knowledge of their falsity or with reckless disregard for their truth or falsity. The same test has been applied to suits for invasion of privacy based on false statements where a 'matter of public interest' is involved. It is therefore perfectly clear that, were appellant a member of the general public, the State's power to afford the appellee Board of Education or its members any legal right to sue him for writing the letter at issue here would be limited by the requirement that the letter be judged by the standard laid down in *New York Times*.

This Court has also indicated, in more general terms, that statements by public officials on matters of public concern must be accorded First Amendment protection despite the fact that the statements are directed at their nominal superiors. In *Garrison* [*v. State of Louisiana*], the New York Times test was specifically applied to a case involving a criminal defamation conviction stemming from statements made by a district attorney about the judges before whom he regularly appeared.

While criminal sanctions and damage awards have a somewhat different impact on the exercise of the right to freedom of speech from dismissal from employment, it is apparent that the threat of dismissal from public employment is nonetheless a potent means of inhibiting speech. We have already noted our disinclination to make an across-the-board equation of dismissal from public employment for remarks critical of superiors with awarding damages in a libel suit by a public official for similar criticism. However, in a case such as the present one, in which the fact of employment is only tangentially and insubstantially involved in the subject matter of the public communication made by a teacher, we conclude that it is necessary to regard the teacher as the member of the general public he seeks to be.

In sum, we hold that, in a case such as this, absent proof of false statements knowingly or recklessly made by him, a teacher's exercise of his right to speak on issues of public importance may not furnish the basis for his dismissal from public employment. Since no such showing has been made in this case regarding appellant's letter, his dismissal for writing it cannot be upheld and the judgment of the Illinois Supreme Court must, accordingly, be reversed and the case remanded for further proceedings not inconsistent with this opinion. It is so ordered.

Judgment reversed and case remanded with directions.

Citation: *Pickering v. Board of Education of Township High School District 205, Will County*, 391 U.S. 563 (1968).

PIERCE V. SOCIETY OF SISTERS OF THE HOLY NAMES OF JESUS AND MARY

In *Pierce v. Society of Sisters of the Holy Names of Jesus and Mary* (1925), the Supreme Court upheld the right of parents to make educational decisions on behalf of their children, while acknowledging the states' right to regulate education, even in nonpublic schools. The decision remains one of the most prominent and frequently cited cases in the area of parental rights.

Facts of the Case

In 1922, the state of Oregon, as part of post–World War I nationalism, amended its compulsory attendance statute to require that "every parent, guardian, or other person having control or charge or custody of a child between 8 and 16 years to send him to a public school . . . between [the ages of] 8 and 16" (p. 529).

Two organizations operating private schools in Oregon, the Society of Sisters of the Holy Names of Jesus and Mary and the Hill Military Academy, challenged the constitutionality of the statute under the Fourteenth Amendment, alleging that the statute deprived them of property without due process of law. A three-judge federal district court entered judgment for the schools, enjoining the state from enforcing the statute and finding that "the right to conduct schools was property" and that the state's statute had not only taken the schools' property without due process but had also deprived parents of the right to "direct the education of children by selecting reputable teachers and places" (p. 534).

The Court's Ruling

On appeal, the Supreme Court affirmed that the Oregon statute "unreasonably interfere[d] with the liberty of parents and guardians to direct the upbringing and education of children" (p. 534). In addition, the Court held that the two schools, as Oregon corporations and property owners within the state, were entitled to "protection against arbitrary, unreasonable, and unlawful interference with their patrons and the consequent destruction of their business and property"

(p. 536). However, the Court circumspectly limited the reach of its decision to the abuse of state power. The Court declared language in dictum that has frequently been cited in cases involving state control of schools:

> No question is raised concerning the power of the state reasonably to regulate all schools, to inspect, supervise and examine them, their teachers and pupils; to require that all children of proper age attend some school, that teachers shall be of good moral character and patriotic disposition, that certain studies plainly essential to good citizenship must be taught, and that nothing be taught which is manifestly inimical to the public welfare. (p. 534)

Thus, the *Pierce* Court invalidated only state action that prevents parents from making an educational choice for their children; the Court did not prohibit states from exercising regulatory control over education, including nonpublic schools. In effect, the *Pierce* dictum simply acknowledged a basic principle of federalism, namely that because control over education is an implied state function under the Tenth Amendment to the Constitution, the Supreme Court may prohibit the abuse of state control, but it cannot prevent altogether a state from exercising its constitutional authority over education.

Pierce has been cited in a wide range of cases to protect the rights of parents to make decisions on behalf of their children. The Supreme Court relied on *Pierce* in *Wisconsin v. Yoder* (1972) in prohibiting the state of Wisconsin's application of its compulsory attendance statute in such a manner as to violate the religious beliefs of Amish parents that their children should be educated only through the eighth grade. More recently, the Supreme Court, in *Troxel v. Granville* (2000), used *Pierce* to invalidate an Oregon statute that provided a right of access by grandparents to visit their grandchildren, even when such access was opposed by a parent.

In an interesting federal circuit court of appeals case, *Barrett v. Steubenville City Schools* (2004), the Sixth Circuit expanded *Pierce* to employment, holding that a public school superintendent could not demand that a person remove his child from a religious school and place the child in public school before that person would be given a regular teaching position.

At the same time, federal courts have not been receptive to claims under *Pierce* that address the content of school curriculum. Thus, in *Mozert v. Hawkins* (1987), the Sixth Circuit rejected a parent claim under *Pierce* that her child be taught with a reading series different from the one used by other children, one that did not contain references the parent considered objectionable to her religious beliefs. In *Brown v. Hot, Sexy, and Safer Productions* (1995), the First Circuit refused to recognize some parents' claim under *Pierce* to object to the heavily sexual content of a school assembly that their children were required to attend.

More recently, in *Fields v. Palmdale School District* (2006), the Ninth Circuit rejected outright a parent's objection to a survey concerning students' sexual and religious beliefs, observing that

the *Pierce* due process right of parents to make decisions regarding their children's education does not entitle individual parents to enjoin school boards from providing information the boards determine to be appropriate in connection with the performance of their educational functions. (p. 1191)

Ralph D. Mawdsley

See also Nonpublic Schools; Parental Rights; *Wisconsin v. Yoder*

Legal Citations

Barrett v. Steubenville City Schools, 388 F.3d 967 (6th Cir. 2004).

Brown v. Hot, Sexy, and Safer Productions, 68 F.3d 525 (1st Cir. 1995) *cert. denied*, 516 U.S. 1159 (1996).

Fields v. Palmdale School District, 447 F.3d 1187 (9th Cir. 2006).

Mozert v. Hawkins County Board of Education, 827 F.2d 1058 (6th Cir. 1987).

Pierce v. Society of Sisters of the Holy Names of Jesus and Mary, 268 U.S. 510 (1925).

Troxel v. Granville, 530 U.S. 57 (2000).

Wisconsin v. Yoder, 406 U.S. 205 (1972).

Pierce v. Society of Sisters of the Holy Names of Jesus and Mary (Excerpts)

Pierce v. Society of Sisters of the Holy Names of Jesus and Mary stands out not only because the Supreme Court upheld the right of nonpublic schools, whether religiously affiliated or nonsectarian, to operate, but also because it recognized the critical role of parents in directing the upbringing of their children.

Supreme Court of the United States

PIERCE

v.

SOCIETY OF THE SISTERS OF THE HOLY NAMES OF JESUS AND MARY.

268 U.S. 510

Argued March 16 and 17, 1925.

Decided June 1, 1925.

Mr. Justice McREYNOLDS delivered the opinion of the Court.

These appeals are from decrees, based upon undenied allegations, which granted preliminary orders restraining appellants from threatening or attempting to enforce the Compulsory Education Act adopted November 7, 1922, under the initiative provision of her Constitution by the voters of Oregon. They present the same points of law; there are no controverted questions of fact. Rights said to be guaranteed by the federal Constitution were specially set up, and appropriate prayers asked for their protection.

The challenged act, effective September 1, 1926, requires every parent, guardian, or other person having control or charge or custody of a child between 8 and 16 years to send him 'to a public school for the period of time a public school shall be held during the current year' in the district where the child resides; and failure so to do is declared a misdemeanor. There are exemptions—not specially important here—for children who are not normal, or who have completed the eighth grade, or whose parents or private teachers reside at considerable distances from any public school, or who hold special permits from the county superintendent. The manifest purpose is to compel general attendance at public schools by normal children, between 8 and 16, who have not completed the eighth grade. And without doubt, enforcement of the statute would seriously impair, perhaps destroy, the profitable features of appellees' business and greatly diminish the value of their property.

Appellee the Society of Sisters is an Oregon corporation, organized in 1880, with power to care for orphans, educate and instruct the youth, establish and maintain academies or schools, and acquire necessary real and personal property. It has long devoted its property and effort to the secular and religious education and care of children, and has acquired the valuable good will of many parents and guardians. It conducts interdependent primary and high schools and junior colleges, and maintains orphanages for the custody and control of children between 8 and 16. In its primary schools many children between those ages are taught the subjects usually pursued in Oregon public schools during the first eight years. Systematic religious instruction and moral training according to the tenets of the Roman Catholic Church are also regularly provided. All courses of study, both temporal and religious, contemplate continuity of training under appellee's charge; the primary schools are essential to the system and the most profitable. It owns valuable buildings, especially constructed and equipped for school purposes. The business is remunerative—the annual income from primary schools exceeds $30,000— and the successful conduct of this requires long-time contracts with teachers and parents. The Compulsory Education Act of 1922 has already caused the withdrawal from its schools of children who would otherwise continue, and their income has steadily declined. The appellants, public officers, have proclaimed their purpose strictly to enforce the statute.

After setting out the above facts, the Society's bill alleges that the enactment conflicts with the right of parents to choose schools where their children will receive appropriate mental and religious training, the right of the child to influence the parents' choice of a school, the right of schools and teachers therein to engage in a useful business or profession, and is accordingly repugnant to the Constitution and void. And, further, that unless enforcement of lthe measure is enjoined the corporation's business and property will suffer irreparable injury.

Appellee Hill Military Academy is a private corporation organized in 1908 under the laws of Oregon, engaged in owning, operating, and conducting for profit an elementary, college preparatory, and military training school for boys between the ages of 5 and 21 years. The average attendance is 100, and the annual fees received for each student amount to some $800. The elementary department is divided into eight grades, as in the public schools; the college preparatory department has four grades, similar to those of the public high schools; the

courses of study conform to the requirements of the state board of education. Military instruction and training are also given, under the supervision of an army officer. It owns considerable real and personal property, some useful only for school purposes. The business and incident good will are very valuable. In order to conduct its affairs, long-time contracts must be made for supplies, equipment, teachers, and pupils. Appellants, law officers of the state and county, have publicly announced that the Act of November 7, 1922, is valid and have declared their intention to enforce it. By reason of the statute and threat of enforcement appellee's business is being destroyed and its property depreciated; parents and guardians are refusing to make contracts for the future instruction of their sons, and some are being withdrawn.

The Academy's bill states the foregoing facts and then alleges that the challenged act contravenes the corporation's rights guaranteed by the Fourteenth Amendment and that unless appellants are restrained from proclaiming its validity and threatening to enforce it irreparable injury will result. The prayer is for an appropriate injunction.

No answer was interposed in either cause, and after proper notices they were heard by three judges on motions for preliminary injunctions upon the specifically alleged facts. The court ruled that the Fourteenth Amendment guaranteed appellees against the deprivation of their property without due process of law consequent upon the unlawful interference by appellants with the free choice of patrons, present and prospective. It declared the right to conduct schools was property and that parents and guardians, as a part of their liberty, might direct the education of children by selecting reputable teachers and places. Also, that appellees' schools were not unfit or harmful to the public, and that enforcement of the challenged statute would unlawfully deprive them of patronage and thereby destroy appellees' business and property. Finally, that the threats to enforce the act would continue to cause irreparable injury; and the suits were not premature.

No question is raised concerning the power of the state reasonably to regulate all schools, to inspect, supervise and examine them, their teachers and pupils; to require that all children of proper age attend some school, that teachers shall be of good moral character and patriotic disposition, that certain studies plainly essential to good citizenship must be taught, and that nothing be taught which is manifestly inimical to the public welfare.

The inevitable practical result of enforcing the act under consideration would be destruction of appellees' primary schools, and perhaps all other private primary schools for normal children within the state of Oregon. Appellees are engaged in a kind of undertaking not inherently harmful, but long regarded as useful and meritorious. Certainly there is nothing in the present records to indicate that they have failed to discharge their obligations to patrons, students, or the state. And there are no peculiar circumstances or present emergencies which demand extraordinary measures relative to primary education.

Under the doctrine of *Meyer v. Nebraska*, we think it entirely plain that the Act of 1922 unreasonably interferes with the liberty of parents and guardians to direct the upbringing and education of children under their control. As often heretofore pointed out, rights guaranteed by the Constitution may not be abridged by legislation which has no reasonable relation to some purpose within the competency of the state. The fundamental theory of liberty upon which all governments in this Union repose excludes any general power of the state to standardize its children by forcing them to accept instruction from public teachers only. The child is not the mere creature of the state; those who nurture him and direct his destiny have the right, coupled with the high duty, to recognize and prepare him for additional obligations.

Appellees are corporations, and therefore, it is said, they cannot claim for themselves the liberty which the Fourteenth Amendment guarantees. Accepted in the proper sense, this is true. But they have business and property for which they claim protection. These are threatened with destruction through the unwarranted compulsion which appellants are exercising over present and prospective patrons of their schools. And this court has gone very far to protect against loss threatened by such action.

The courts of the state have not construed the act, and we must determine its meaning for ourselves. Evidently it was expected to have general application and cannot be construed as though merely intended to amend the charters of certain private corporations, as in *Berea College v. Kentucky*. No argument in favor of such view has been advanced.

Generally, it is entirely true, as urged by counsel, that no person in any business has such an interest in possible customers as to enable him to restrain exercise of proper power of the state upon the ground that he will be deprived of patronage. But the injunctions here sought are not against the exercise of any proper power. Appellees asked protection against arbitrary, unreasonable, and unlawful interference with their patrons and the consequent destruction of their business and property. Their interest is clear and immediate, within the rule approved in . . . many . . . cases where injunctions have issued to protect business enterprises against interference with the freedom of patrons or customers.

The suits were not premature. The injury to appellees was present and very real, not a mere possibility in the remote future. If no relief had been possible prior to the effective date of the act, the injury would have become irreparable. Prevention of impending injury by unlawful action is a well-recognized function of courts of equity.

The decrees below are *affirmed*.

Citation: *Pierce v. Society of Sisters of the Holy Names of Jesus and Mary*, 268 U.S. 510 (1925).

PLAGIARISM

Plagiarism means stealing words or ideas from someone else's work without giving that person appropriate credit in some form of documentation. This entry examines three issues related to plagiarism: what kind of information has to be documented, whether the plagiarism must be intentional, and whether the accused is entitled to due process.

The General Knowledge Defense

A person who is charged with plagiarism may raise the defense that material allegedly plagiarized is general knowledge. That defense was used by a university professor whose article about a poem caught the eye of a colleague, who thought parts of the article had been copied from an earlier book by another author. A committee reviewing the charge found several questionable similarities between book and article.

In the ensuing litigation, *Newman v. Burgin* (1991), the professor unsuccessfully claimed that the charge of plagiarism should be dismissed because "most of the common passages simply reflected general knowledge among scholars in the field and did not require attribution." (p. 958). She also noted that her article was the product of her research for a master's degree, completed 20 years earlier and approved by a noted scholar in the field who recommended the allegedly plagiarized book to her. Nevertheless, the committee found her to be at fault and barred her from participating on specified academic committees or holding administrative offices for five years. The faculty member appealed.

The First Circuit, in upholding the university's discipline of the faculty member, agreed that the similarity between the book used as the basis for the master's thesis and the content of the thesis itself was too close to make credible any defense of general knowledge. In *Newman,* the faculty member had three footnotes in the article referring to the book, but significant portions of the article had no footnote references, resulting in the conclusion by the university faculty investigating the alleged plagiarism that the faulty member's scholarship had been "negligent" and contained "an objective instance of plagiarism" (p. 959). *Newman* highlights an important feature of plagiarism, namely that unless limited by the code of conduct of an academic institution, a charge of plagiarism has no statute of limitations.

Newman also reveals another important issue in plagiarism as to whether a violation requires intent to plagiarize. The First Circuit in *Newman* observed that "one can plagiarize *through negligence or recklessness without intent to deceive*" (p. 962) (emphasis in original).

The Issue of Intent

The leading case illustrating the relationship between intent and plagiarism is *Napolitano v. Princeton University* (1982). A senior at Princeton University with a 3.7 (out of 4.0) grade point average submitted a paper for an elective Spanish literature course during her last semester. The professor charged the student with plagiarism, pursuant to the university's student handbook definition: "the deliberate use of any outside source without proper acknowledgement" (*Napolitano,* p. 281). A faculty-student committee on discipline found the student to have violated the definition. The committee recommended, and the university administration agreed, that the student's diploma would be withheld for one year.

The student filed a lawsuit alleging that her conduct had not satisfied the university's definition of plagiarism. She pointed out that she had cited the source six times in her paper and that the professor had

recommended the book and so should not have been surprised at her use of it. However, the state court of appeals, in affirming the university's discipline of the plaintiff student, applied an objective standard to find a mosaic of grammatical and syntactical student choices indicating that plagiarism had occurred. Some pieces of this mosaic were the following: (1) A few statements taken from the source had been put in quotation marks but not the rest; (2) the use of "it is evident," "it is important to note that," and "one can assume that" suggested that following comments were the student's, when in fact they were borrowed from the source; (3) the source's comments about passages in a Spanish novel were borrowed, but only the novel was cited and not the source; (4) verb tenses from the source were changed to the present tense for the sake of consistency; and (5) words were deleted from the source where their presence in the paper would seem to be technical or awkward (p. 276).

As *Napolitano* indicates, the intent to plagiarize is not a necessary element of the charge of plagiarism (unless specifically required as such in a code of conduct), and a charge can be supported by objective evidence, regardless of an accused person's alleged lack of intent to plagiarize. However, the good faith of a person charged with plagiarism will tend to demonstrate lack of intent to plagiarize, and, and that in turn may have an impact on the nature of the penalty.

Due Process Hearings

Persons charged with plagiarism in public educational institutions may be entitled to procedural due process rights. However, plagiarism is generally considered to be academic, as opposed to disciplinary, misconduct. The Supreme Court in the leading case of *Board of Curators of University of Missouri v. Horowitz* (1978) held that persons charged with academic misconduct were not entitled to the same "stringent procedural protection" as for disciplinary misconduct, even though the penalties for both can be similar. Nonetheless, state law or university handbook language can confer such rights.

For example, in *Hand v. Matchett* (1992), the Tenth Circuit upheld the authority of the board of regents for the University of New Mexico to establish and enforce procedures that could be used to revoke a student's PhD because his dissertation contained excerpts that had been plagiarized. The court declared that "the ability to revoke degrees obtained through fraudulent means is a necessary corollary to the Regents' power to confer those degrees" (pp. 794–795).

Yet, in New Mexico, final authority to confer degrees is vested in the Board of Regents, which therefore must have some involvement in degree revocation. In this case, although the process for degree revocation was upheld, the case was remanded and the degree revocation declared void "because the Board of Regents had not exercised final authority in the decision to revoke the alumnus' degree" (p. 795).

Ralph D. Mawdsley

See also Cheating

Further Readings

Mawdsley, R. (1994). *Academic misconduct: Cheating and plagiarism.* Dayton, OH: Education Law Association.

Weidenborner, S., & Caruso, D. (1982). *Writing research papers: A guide to the process.* New York: St. Martin's Press.

Winkler, A. C., & McCuen, J. R. (1985). *Writing the research paper.* (San Diego, CA: Harcourt Brace Jovanovich.

Legal Citations

Board of Curators of University of Missouri v. Horowitz, 435 U.S. 78 (1978).

Hand v. Matchett, 957 F.2d 791 (10th Cir.1992).

Napolitano v. Princeton University, 453 A.2d 263 (N.J. Super. Ct. App. 1982).

Newman v. Burgin, 930 F.2d 955 (1st Cir. 1991).

PLEDGE OF ALLEGIANCE

The Pledge of Allegiance is a brief recited statement of commitment to the United States. First developed at the end of the 19th century, the pledge has become a common feature of classroom activity in schools across the nation, sometimes required by state law. Almost from the beginning, parents challenged the fact that their children were required to participate in the recitation of the pledge. More recently, parents thought that schools should not be using a statement that includes the words "under God." This entry briefly summarizes the history of the pledge and the litigation that has followed it through more than a century.

Historical Background

In 1892, amidst a national desire to promote patriotism in the schools, the U.S. flag salute ceremony with the Pledge of Allegiance originated. In 1898, one day after the United States declared war on Spain, New York passed the first flag salute law. By 1940, 18 states had statutes with a provision for "some sort of teaching regarding the flag." The phrase "under God" was added by a congressional amendment in 1954. The historic role of religion in the political development of the nation was the reason given for this consideration.

The Pledge of Allegiance reads as follows:

> I pledge allegiance to the Flag of the United States of America and to the Republic for which it stands, one Nation under God, indivisible, with liberty and justice for all.

Classrooms throughout the nation responded by having students salute the flag in the morning, as a general response to the statute. Immediately, numbers of religious groups protested, with the Jehovah's Witnesses being the most prevalent, and litigation followed.

Early Litigation

In 1937, the Georgia Supreme Court, in *Leoles v. Landers*, declared that religious freedom had not been violated and that the salute was a patriotic exercise rather than a religious rite. In 1938, California's Supreme Court upheld the expulsion of students for refusing to salute the flag (*Gabrielli v. Knickerbocker*). The next year, New York's high court concluded that because the flag had nothing to do with religion, there were no religious freedoms being offended (*People ex rel. Fish v. Sandstrom*, 1939).

Multiple cases followed, echoing the national patriotic voice, and in 1940, the Supreme Court held that a Pennsylvania statute that required the flag salute and Pledge of Allegiance did not violate the freedom of religion guaranteed by the First Amendment

(*Minersville School District v. Gobitis*, 1940). The justices agreed that the Constitution required the states, as much as Congress, to respect the freedom of religion, but concluded that the state was not violating religious liberty by requiring the pledge of schoolchildren. In contrast, some state courts throughout the country concluded that the flag salute requirements violated their own constitutions.

The Jehovah's Witnesses and others next challenged the constitutionality of a revised regulation of a state board of education, which held that refusal to participate in saluting the flag could be treated as an act of insubordination with a resultant expulsion from school. The Jehovah's Witnesses argued that the pledge violated their rights to religious freedom. The U.S. Supreme Court, in *West Virginia State Board of Education v. Barnette* (1943), overruled *Gobitis*. The Court held that a state may require students to attend patriotic exercises based on American history and to teach unifying patriotic values, but that compulsory activities such as the flag salute were unconstitutional. In so doing, the Court reframed the case as one about free speech rather than the free exercise of religion. Students, according to this ruling could opt out and not participate in the flag salute.

In 1966, the supreme court of New Jersey faced the issue of whether Black Muslim children who refused to pledge allegiance to the flag on the grounds that the ceremony violated their religious beliefs could be excluded from public school (*Holden v. Board of Education,* 1966). School officials excluded the children, and the court, while not stating whether the refusal to salute the flag was religious or political, ordered their return to the schools. The court pointed out that the students stood quietly during the pledge and were not disruptive.

Schools and courts throughout the nation grappled with the issue and reasonably emphasized that as long as there was not a disruption, a student could choose to stand quietly, and in some cases leave the room, but could not be disciplined for choosing not to participate (*Banks v. Board of Public Instruction of Dade County,* 1971; *State of Maryland v. Lundquist,* 1971).

More recently, the Seventh Circuit court found that school officials could lead the pledge, including the words "under God," as long as students were free not

to participate (*Sherman v. Community Consolidated School District 21 of Wheeling Township,* 1993). According to the court, the use of the phrase in the context of the secular vow of allegiance was patriotic or ceremonial rather than religious.

A New Century of Conflict

In 2003, legislatures in Colorado, Minnesota, Texas, and Utah addressed the Pledge of Allegiance. Colorado required the daily recitation of the pledge in its public schools. Non-American citizens and those who objected to the recitation of the pledge on religious grounds were released from the obligation. Minnesota required all students in public schools to recite the pledge one or more times each week. Here, the local board could choose to waive the requirement, and students and teachers could also decline to participate. Texas required students to recite the pledge with the option of opting out on parental request, and Utah amended a statute, requiring daily recitation in elementary schools and weekly recitation in secondary schools.

The Ninth Circuit took on this controversy again in 2002, deciding that a school policy requiring the words "under God" violated the Establishment Clause. Michael Newdow, the parent initiating the case, did not seek to exempt his child from the flag salute but rather to bar the practice for children in all public schools as long as the words were present. The court maintained that the policy failed the purpose prong of the *Lemon* test (*Newdow v. U.S. Congress,* 2002). The case addressed two major questions. The first question asked whether the non-custodial father had standing to challenge the board policy that required teachers to lead willing students in reciting the Pledge of Allegiance. The second inquiry addressed whether the policy violated the Establishment Clause.

The Ninth Circuit determined that the father had a right to direct his daughter's religious education and that the school district's policy violated the Establishment Clause. This case was not only controversial but affected schools throughout the entire Ninth Circuit, putting many schools throughout this area on hold with respect to whether they would have students recite the pledge, and in general, confusing some of the schoolchildren. To further complicate the proceedings, the mother, sole legal guardian, filed a motion to dismiss this case, stating that it was not in the child's interest to become involved in this suit. The Ninth Circuit ruled in favor of *Newdow* on the basis that he retained the right to expose his child to his particular religious views. (He is an atheist.)

The Supreme Court reviewed the controversy under the watchful eyes of a nation divided in sentiments between church and state. Yet, the Court sidestepped the question of the constitutionality of the district's policy that required schoolchildren to recite the pledge. Instead, the Court was of the opinion that because the noncustodial father did not have standing to bring this suit to court, the earlier judgments had to be set aside (*Elk Grove Unified School District v. Newdow*, 2004). This issue had the potential of dividing the nation, and it will almost certainly come before the Supreme Court again. Thus, the constitutionality of the words "under God" in the pledge remain to be litigated at a future date.

In 2005, for example, the Fourth Circuit held that a Virginia state statute providing for daily, voluntary recitation of the pledge did not violate the Establishment Clause, as it was not a religious exercise, despite the existence of the words "under God" (*Myers v. Loudon County Public School*, 2005). The pledge battle also rages in California, as Newdow and other like-minded parents had the policy enjoined (*Newdow v. Congress of the United States*, 2005). Although it seems unlikely that the wording of the pledge will be changed, the law is clear that offended students may not be required to recite the pledge or be punished for declining to participate.

Deborah E. Stine

See also *Elk Grove Unified School District v. Newdow;* First Amendment; Prayer in Public Schools; U.S. Supreme Court Cases in Education; *West Virginia State Board of Education v. Barnette*

Further Readings

Feldman, N. (2005). *Divided by God: America's church-state problem—and what we should do about it.* New York: Farrar, Straus & Giroux.

Looney, S. (2004). *Education and the legal system: A guide to understanding the law.* Columbus, OH: Pearson Education.

Manwaring, D. R. (1962). *Render unto Caesar: The flag- salute controversy.* Chicago, IL: University of Chicago Press.

Legal Citations

Banks v. Board of Public Instruction of Dade County, 314 F. Supp. 285 (S.D. Fla.), *aff'd*, 450 F.2d 1103 (5th Cir. 1971).

Elk Grove Unified School District v. Newdow, 542 U.S. 1 (2004).

Gabrielli v. Knickerbocker, 82 P.2d 391 (1938).

Holden v. Board of Education, Elizabeth, 216 A.2d 387 (N.J. 1966).

Leoles v. Landers, 184 Ga. 580, 192 S.E. 218, *appeal dismissed*, 302 U.S. 656 (1937).

Minersville School District v. Gobitis, 310 U.S. 586 (1940).

Myers v. Loudon County Public Schools, 418 F.3d 395 (4th Cir. 2005).

Newdow v. Congress of the United States, 383 F. Supp.2d 1229 (E.D. Cal. 2005).

Newdow v. U.S. Congress, 328 F. 3d 466. (9th Cir. 2002).

People ex rel. Fish v. Sandstrom, 279 N.Y. 523 (N.Y. 1939).

Pledge of Allegiance, 4 U.S.C. § 4 (2006).

Sherman v. Community Consolidated School District of Wheeling Township, 508 U.S. 950 (1993).

State of Maryland v. Lundquist, 278 A.2d 263 (Md. 1971).

PLESSY V. FERGUSON

In *Plessy v. Ferguson* (1896), the best known of early segregation cases, the U.S. Supreme Court upheld the conviction of Homer Plessy, who was seven-eighths White and one-eighth Black, for attempting to sit in a public railway car reserved for Whites. In its analysis, the Court decided that distinctions based on race did not violate the Thirteenth or Fourteenth Amendments of the U.S. Constitution. By accepting the notion that "separate but equal" facilities met the requirements of the Constitution, the Court laid a firm legal basis for subsequent segregation, although the actual phrase "separate but equal" cannot be found in the Court's opinion. *Plessy* served as the foundation for sustaining the principle of racial segregation for over 50 years in maintaining that separate accommodations—including schools—did not deprive Blacks of equal rights if the accommodations were equal.

Leading up to *Plessy* were the civil rights cases of 1883, in which the Supreme Court ruled that the Fourteenth Amendment prohibited state governments from discriminating against individuals due solely to their race but did not restrict private organizations or individuals from doing so. As a result of the Court's holdings, privately owned railroads, hotels, theaters, and similar enterprises could legally practice segregation. In *Plessy*, the Court also validated state legislation that specifically discriminated against Blacks, in this case, a state law from Louisiana that required separate seating arrangements for the races on railroad cars.

Not long after *Plessy*, in *Cumming v. Board of Education of Richmond County* (1899), the Court went even further by refusing to strike down a state law from Georgia that permitted local school boards to establish separate schools for White children even though officials failed to provide comparable schools for Black students. The Court expressly extended the notion of separate but equal in education in *Gong Lum v. Rice* (1927), a case from Mississippi wherein it permitted officials to exclude a student of Chinese ancestry from a school for White children.

For several decades, a de jure segregated system of schools existed in the South resulting from *Plessy* and its progeny. At the same time, in seeking to comply with the "equal protection" requirement, several states allegedly created "separate but financially equal" education systems, also known as dual systems, one for Whites and another for Blacks. These policies barred minority students from attending the White schools.

Justice John M. Harlan wrote the dissenting opinion for *Plessy* in words that would be remarkably prophetic of early victories in the 1950s civil rights movements. Justice Harlan protested that states could not impose criminal penalties on citizens simply because they wished to use the public highways and common carriers. Harlan's pleas that the Constitution is color-blind fell on deaf ears. Ultimately, a series of suits that the National Association for the Advancement of Colored People filed in the 1950s successfully attacked the injustice of segregated schools, culminating in the Court's landmark decision in *Brown v. Board of Education of Topeka* (1954).

In *Brown*, the plaintiffs raised the issue of whether separation of children for public education created a suspect class of individuals, arguing that separate was inherently unequal. In *Brown* the Court agreed with the plaintiffs, thus for the first time identifying race as a suspect class and outlawing all governmental actions that had the impact of treating individuals differently according to their race.

In coming to grips with the constitutionality of the *Plessy* "separate but equal" doctrine, which it had long left intact, the Court concluded that the segregation of students in public schools solely on the basis of race, even though the physical facilities and other tangible factors may have been equal, deprived the children of the minority group of equal educational opportunities. Yet, for years, the ghost of *Plessy* lingered on as *Brown* served the beginning of the fight to end racial segregation in education based solely on race.

Gary W. Kinsey

See also *Brown v. Board of Education of Topeka; Brown v. Board of Education of Topeka* and Equal Educational Opportunities; Dual and Unitary Systems; Equal Protection Analysis; *Gong Lum v. Rice*; National Association for the Advancement of Colored People (NAACP); Segregation, De Facto; Segregation, De Jure

Further Reading

Woodward, C. V. (1974). *The strange career of Jim Crow* (3rd ed.). New York: Oxford University Press.

Legal Citations

Brown v. Board of Education of Topeka I, 347 U.S. 483 (1954).
Brown v. Board of Education of Topeka II, 349 U.S. 294 (1955).
Cumming v. Board of Education of Richmond County, 175 U.S. 528 (1899).
Gong Lum v. Rice, 275 U.S. 78 (1927).
Plessy v. Ferguson, 163 U.S. 537 (1896).

PLYLER V. DOE

In the 1982 case of *Plyler v. Doe*, the Supreme Court was asked to rule on the constitutionality of denying undocumented immigrants access to a free K–12 public education. A divided Court issued a 5-to-4 decision, including three concurring opinions and one dissenting opinion. The Court held that Texas education code § 21.031 violated the Equal Protection Clause of the Fourteenth Amendment when it denied schools funding for undocumented children. The opinion emphasized the critical importance of education in our society and the consequences of a complete denial of school access to undocumented immigrants.

Further, the Court stressed that states may not penalize undocumented students for the illegal actions of their parents. Technically, the Court applied rational-basis scrutiny, yet these factors appeared to generate a type of intermediate-level scrutiny, with the Court ultimately declaring that the state did not present a "substantial" state interest to deny undocumented immigrant children a free public education. *Plyler* is a complex case in which the Court straddled immigration law and education policy.

Facts of the Case

The statute in question was passed by the Texas legislature in 1975. It limited state education funding to children who could demonstrate legal residence in the United States. The state was required by law to withhold from local school districts funding for undocumented immigrants. Following two class action suits filed on behalf of—and decided in favor of—undocumented students, the state of Texas asked the U.S. Supreme Court to review the decision of the Fifth Circuit (*Doe v. Plyler*, 1980).

The Court's Ruling

The Supreme Court focused first on how to examine the case. Texas unsuccessfully argued that undocumented immigrants were not "persons" legally within the jurisdiction of the state and therefore did not merit the protections of the Fourteenth Amendment. Texas also argued, this time successfully, that undocumented immigrants are not members of a suspect class, because they voluntarily enter into marginalized group status. Therefore, Texas maintained that the Court did not have to apply strict scrutiny.

However, as noted, the Court did apply a type of intermediate scrutiny, based in part on the classification set forth by a particular statute, as established in *Craig v. Boren* (1976) and also based in part on the critical importance of education in U.S. society and the consequences of a complete denial of school access. *Plyler* is thus notable for this rare decision to expand the reasons for using intermediate scrutiny.

Although education is not a fundamental right, as established by the Court in *San Antonio Independent School District v. Rodriguez* (1973), Justice Brennan's majority opinion recognized that "neither is it [education] merely some governmental 'benefit' indistinguishable from other forms of social welfare legislation" (*Plyler*, p. 221). The Court viewed the critical role of education to be its integrative functions, its transmission of values, and its ability to provide opportunities in the United States. Justice Powell's concurring opinion stressed that if undocumented students are denied the benefits of a free public education, this would effectively create "a subclass of illiterate persons many of whom will remain in the State, adding to the problems and costs of both State and National Governments attendant upon unemployment, welfare, and crime" (*Plyler*, p. 241, Brennan, J., concurring). The Court also called attention to the unjust penalties that § 21.031 places on children due to their parents' illegal presence in the United States, something the children had no direct control over. The Court deemed such punishment to be illogical.

The dissenting opinion filed by Chief Justice Burger cautioned that the Court's majority overstepped its judicial boundaries, arguing that the Supreme Court was not an arena to set policy.

California's Proposition 187, approved by voters in November of 1994, also sought to deny undocumented immigrants access to social services, including public schooling and health care. The proposition required social service personnel to report all undocumented immigrants to state and federal officials. Relying on the Court's *Plyler* decision, other courts prevented key parts of this law from ever going into effect.

Nevertheless, *Plyler* leaves open three significant questions. First, the Court did not find that it is always unconstitutional for states to deny a free public education for undocumented immigrants. Instead, it requires that a state must prove that providing a free public education would compromise a substantial state interest. Second, the Court addressed a complete denial of education; a partial denial might yield a different legal outcome. Third, in distinguishing education "from other forms of social welfare legislation" (*Plyler*, p. 221), the Court suggested that it may not be unconstitutional to deny other forms of social welfare to undocumented immigrants.

Emily Wexler Love

See also Equal Educational Opportunity Act; Equal Protection Analysis; Fourteenth Amendment

Legal Citations

Craig v. Boren, 429 U.S. 190 (1976).
Doe v. Plyler, 628 F.2d 448 (5th Cir. 1980).
Plyler v. Doe, 457 U.S. 202 (1982).
San Antonio v. Rodriguez, 411 U.S. 1 (1973).

Plyler v. Doe (Excerpts)

In Plyler v. Doe *the Supreme Court ruled that, under the Equal Protection Clause, the right of children to attend school does not depend on the immigration status of their parents.*

Supreme Court of the United States

PLYLER

v.

DOE

457 US 202

Argued Dec. I, 1981.

Decided June 15, 1982.

Rehearings Denied Sept. 9, 1982.

See 458 U.S. II3I.

Justice BRENNAN delivered the opinion of the Court.

The question presented by these cases is whether, consistent with the Equal Protection Clause of the Fourteenth Amendment, Texas may deny to undocumented school-age children the free public education that it provides to children who are citizens of the United States or legally admitted aliens.

I

Since the late 19th century, the United States has restricted immigration into this country. Unsanctioned entry into the United States is a crime and those who have entered unlawfully are subject to deportation. But despite the existence of these legal restrictions, a substantial number of persons have succeeded in unlawfully entering the United States, and now live within various States, including the State of Texas.

In May 1975, the Texas Legislature revised its education laws to withhold from local school districts any state funds for the education of children who were not "legally admitted" into the United States. The 1975 revision also authorized local school districts to deny enrollment in their public schools to children not "legally admitted" to the country. These cases involve constitutional challenges to those provisions.

No. 80–1538

Plyler v. Doe

This is a class action, filed in the United States District Court for the Eastern District of Texas in September 1977, on behalf of certain school-age children of Mexican origin residing in Smith County, Tex., who could not establish that they had been legally admitted into the United States. The action complained of the exclusion of plaintiff children from the public schools of the Tyler Independent School District. The Superintendent and members of the Board of Trustees of the School District were named as defendants; the State of Texas intervened as a party-defendant. After certifying a class consisting of all undocumented school-age children of Mexican origin residing within the School District, the District Court preliminarily enjoined defendants from denying a free education to members of the plaintiff class. In December 1977, the court conducted an extensive hearing on plaintiffs' motion for permanent injunctive relief.

The District Court held that illegal aliens were entitled to the protection of the Equal Protection Clause of the Fourteenth Amendment, and that § 21.031 violated that Clause.... The District Court also concluded that the Texas statute violated the Supremacy Clause.

The Court of Appeals for the Fifth Circuit upheld the District Court's injunction. The Court of Appeals held that the District Court had erred in finding the Texas statute pre-empted by federal law. With respect to equal protection, however, the Court of Appeals affirmed in all essential respects the analysis of the District Court, concluding that § 21.031 was "constitutionally infirm regardless of whether it was tested using the mere rational basis standard or some more stringent test." We noted probable jurisdiction.

No. 80–1934

In re Alien Children Education Litigation

During 1978 and 1979, suits challenging the constitutionality of § 21.031 and various local practices undertaken on the authority of that provision were filed in the United States District Courts for the Southern, Western, and Northern Districts of Texas. Each suit named the State of Texas and the Texas Education Agency as defendants, along with local officials. In November 1979, the Judicial Panel on Multidistrict Litigation, on motion of the State, consolidated the claims against the state officials into a single action to be heard in the District Court for the Southern District of Texas. A hearing was conducted in February and March 1980. In July 1980, the court entered an opinion and order holding that § 21.031 violated the Equal Protection Clause of the Fourteenth Amendment. The court held that "the absolute deprivation of education should trigger strict judicial scrutiny, particularly when the absolute deprivation is the result of complete inability to pay for the desired benefit." The court determined that the State's concern for fiscal integrity was not a compelling state interest; that exclusion of these children had not been shown to be necessary to improve education within the State; and that the educational needs of the children statutorily excluded were not different from the needs of children not excluded. The court therefore concluded that § 21.031 was not carefully tailored to advance the asserted state interest in an acceptable manner. While appeal of the District Court's decision was pending, the Court of Appeals rendered its decision in No. 80–1538. Apparently on the strength of that opinion, the Court of Appeals, on February 23, 1981, summarily affirmed the decision of the Southern District.

We noted probable jurisdiction and consolidated this case with No. 80–1538 for briefing and argument.

II

The Fourteenth Amendment provides that "[n]o State shall ... deprive any person of life, liberty, or property, without due process of law; nor deny to any person within its jurisdiction the equal protection of the laws." Appellants argue at the outset that undocumented aliens, because of their immigration status, are not "persons within the jurisdiction" of the State of Texas, and that they therefore have no right to the equal protection of Texas law. We reject this argument. Whatever his status under the immigration laws, an alien is surely a "person" in any ordinary sense of that term. Aliens, even aliens whose presence in this country is unlawful, have long been recognized as "persons" guaranteed due process of law by the Fifth and Fourteenth Amendments. Indeed, we have clearly held that the Fifth Amendment protects aliens whose presence in this country is unlawful from invidious discrimination by the Federal Government.

Appellants seek to distinguish our prior cases, emphasizing that the Equal Protection Clause directs a State to afford its protection to persons within its jurisdiction while the Due Process Clauses of the Fifth and Fourteenth Amendments contain no such assertedly limiting phrase. In appellants' view, persons who have entered the United States illegally are not "within the jurisdiction" of a State even if they are present within a State's boundaries and subject to its laws. Neither our cases nor the logic of the Fourteenth Amendment supports that constricting construction of the phrase "within its jurisdiction." We have never suggested that the class of persons who might avail themselves of the equal protection guarantee is less than coextensive with that entitled to due process. To the contrary, we have recognized that both provisions were fashioned to protect an identical class of persons, and to reach every exercise of state authority.

"The Fourteenth Amendment to the Constitution is not confined to the protection of citizens. It says: 'Nor shall any state deprive any person of life, liberty, or property without due process of law; nor deny to any person within its jurisdiction the equal protection of the laws.' These provisions are universal in their application, to all persons within the territorial jurisdiction, without regard to any differences of race, of color, or of nationality; and the protection of the laws is a pledge of the protection of equal laws."

In concluding that "all persons within the territory of the United States," including aliens unlawfully present, may invoke the Fifth and Sixth Amendments to challenge actions of the Federal Government, we reasoned from the understanding that the Fourteenth Amendment was designed to afford its protection to all within the boundaries of a State. Our cases applying the Equal Protection Clause reflect the same territorial theme:

"Manifestly, the obligation of the State to give the protection of equal laws can be performed only where its laws operate, that is, within its own jurisdiction. It is there that the equality of legal right must be maintained. That obligation is imposed by the Constitution upon the States severally as governmental entities—each responsible for its own laws establishing the rights and duties of persons within its borders."

There is simply no support for appellants' suggestion that "due process" is somehow of greater stature than "equal protection" and therefore available to a larger class of persons. To the contrary, each aspect of the Fourteenth Amendment reflects an elementary limitation on state power. To permit a State to employ the phrase "within its jurisdiction" in order to identify subclasses of persons whom it would define as beyond its jurisdiction, thereby relieving itself of the obligation to assure that its laws are designed and applied equally to those persons, would undermine the principal purpose for which the Equal Protection Clause was incorporated in the Fourteenth Amendment. The Equal Protection Clause was intended to work nothing less than the abolition of all caste-based and invidious class-based legislation. That objective is fundamentally at odds with the power the State asserts here to classify persons subject to its laws as nonetheless excepted from its protection.

Although the congressional debate concerning § I of the Fourteenth Amendment was limited, that debate clearly confirms the understanding that the phrase "within its jurisdiction" was intended in a broad sense to offer the guarantee of equal protection to all within a State's boundaries, and to all upon whom the State would impose the obligations of its laws. Indeed, it appears from those debates that Congress, by using the phrase "person within its jurisdiction," sought expressly to ensure that the equal protection of the laws was provided to the alien population. . . .

. . . .

Use of the phrase "within its jurisdiction" thus does not detract from, but rather confirms, the understanding that the protection of the Fourteenth Amendment extends to anyone, citizen or stranger, who is subject to the laws of a State, and reaches into every corner of a State's territory. That a person's initial entry into a State, or into the United States, was unlawful, and that he may for that reason be expelled, cannot negate the simple fact of his presence within the State's territorial perimeter. Given such presence, he is subject to the full range of obligations imposed by the State's civil and criminal laws. And until he leaves the jurisdiction—either voluntarily, or involuntarily in accordance with the Constitution and laws of the United States—he is entitled to the equal protection of the laws that a State may choose to establish.

Our conclusion that the illegal aliens who are plaintiffs in these cases may claim the benefit of the Fourteenth Amendment's guarantee of equal protection only begins the inquiry. The more difficult question is whether the Equal Protection Clause has been violated by the refusal of the State of Texas to reimburse local school boards for the education of children who cannot demonstrate that their presence within the United States is lawful, or by the imposition by those school boards of the burden of tuition on those children. It is to this question that we now turn.

III

The Equal Protection Clause directs that "all persons similarly circumstanced shall be treated alike." But so too, "[t]he Constitution does not require things which are different in fact or opinion to be treated in law as though they were the same." The initial discretion to determine what is "different" and what is "the same" resides in the legislatures of the States. A legislature must have substantial latitude to establish classifications that roughly approximate the nature of the problem perceived, that accommodate competing concerns both public and private, and that account for limitations on the practical ability of the State to remedy every ill. In applying the Equal Protection Clause to most forms of state action, we thus seek only the assurance that the classification at issue bears some fair relationship to a legitimate public purpose.

But we would not be faithful to our obligations under the Fourteenth Amendment if we applied so deferential a standard to every classification. The Equal Protection Clause was intended as a restriction on state legislative action inconsistent with elemental constitutional premises. Thus we have treated as presumptively invidious those classifications that disadvantage a "suspect class," or that impinge upon the exercise of a "fundamental right." With respect to such classifications, it is appropriate to enforce the mandate of equal protection by requiring the State to demonstrate that its classification has been precisely tailored to serve a compelling governmental interest. In addition, we have recognized that certain forms of legislative classification, while not facially invidious, nonetheless give rise to recurring constitutional difficulties; in these limited circumstances we have sought the assurance that the classification reflects a reasoned judgment consistent with the ideal of equal protection by inquiring whether it may fairly be viewed as furthering a substantial interest of the State. We turn to a consideration of the standard appropriate for the evaluation of § 21.031.

A

Sheer incapability or lax enforcement of the laws barring entry into this country, coupled with the failure to establish an effective bar to the employment of undocumented aliens, has resulted in the creation of a substantial "shadow population" of illegal migrants—numbering in the millions—within our borders. This situation raises the specter of a permanent caste of undocumented resident aliens, encouraged by some to remain here as a source of cheap labor, but nevertheless denied the benefits that our society makes available to citizens and lawful residents. The existence of such an underclass presents most difficult problems for a Nation that prides itself on adherence to principles of equality under law.

The children who are plaintiffs in these cases are special members of this underclass. Persuasive arguments support the view that a State may withhold its beneficence from those whose very presence within the United States is the product of their own unlawful conduct. These arguments do not apply with the same force to classifications imposing disabilities on the minor children of such illegal entrants. At the least, those who elect to enter our territory by stealth and in violation of our law should be prepared to bear the consequences, including, but not limited to, deportation. But the children of those illegal entrants are not comparably situated. Their "parents have the ability to conform their conduct to societal norms," and presumably the ability to remove themselves from the State's jurisdiction; but the children who are plaintiffs in these cases "can affect neither their parents' conduct nor their own status." Even if the State found it expedient to control the conduct of adults by acting

against their children, legislation directing the onus of a parent's misconduct against his children does not comport with fundamental conceptions of justice.

. . . .

Of course, undocumented status is not irrelevant to any proper legislative goal. Nor is undocumented status an absolutely immutable characteristic since it is the product of conscious, indeed unlawful, action. But § 21.031 is directed against children, and imposes its discriminatory burden on the basis of a legal characteristic over which children can have little control. It is thus difficult to conceive of a rational justification for penalizing these children for their presence within the United States. Yet that appears to be precisely the effect of § 21.031.

Public education is not a "right" granted to individuals by the Constitution. But neither is it merely some governmental "benefit" indistinguishable from other forms of social welfare legislation. Both the importance of education in maintaining our basic institutions, and the lasting impact of its deprivation on the life of the child, mark the distinction. The "American people have always regarded education and [the] acquisition of knowledge as matters of supreme importance." We have recognized "the public schools as a most vital civic institution for the preservation of a democratic system of government" and as the primary vehicle for transmitting "the values on which our society rests." "[A]s . . . pointed out early in our history, . . . some degree of education is necessary to prepare citizens to participate effectively and intelligently in our open political system if we are to preserve freedom and independence." And these historic "perceptions of the public schools as inculcating fundamental values necessary to the maintenance of a democratic political system have been confirmed by the observations of social scientists." In addition, education provides the basic tools by which individuals might lead economically productive lives to the benefit of us all. In sum, education has a fundamental role in maintaining the fabric of our society. We cannot ignore the significant social costs borne by our Nation when select groups are denied the means to absorb the values and skills upon which our social order rests.

In addition to the pivotal role of education in sustaining our political and cultural heritage, denial of education to some isolated group of children poses an affront to one of the goals of the Equal Protection Clause: the abolition of governmental barriers presenting unreasonable obstacles to advancement on the basis of individual merit. Paradoxically, by depriving the children of any disfavored group of an education, we foreclose the means by which that group might raise the level of esteem in which it is held by the majority. But more directly, "education prepares individuals to be self-reliant and self-sufficient participants in society." Illiteracy is an enduring disability. The inability to read and write will handicap the individual deprived of a basic education each and every day of his life. The inestimable toll of that deprivation on the social economic, intellectual, and psychological well-being of the individual, and the obstacle it poses to individual achievement, make it most difficult to reconcile the cost or the principle of a status-based denial of basic education with the framework of equality embodied in the Equal Protection Clause. What we said 28 years ago in *Brown v. Board of Education*, still holds true: "Today, education is perhaps the most important function of state and local governments. . . ."

B

These well-settled principles allow us to determine the proper level of deference to be afforded § 21.031. Undocumented aliens cannot be treated as a suspect class because their presence in this country in violation of federal law is not a "constitutional irrelevancy." Nor is education a fundamental right; a State need not justify by compelling necessity every variation in the manner in which education is provided to its population. But more is involved in these cases than the abstract question whether § 21.031 discriminates against a suspect class, or whether education is a fundamental right. Section 21.031 imposes a lifetime hardship on a discrete class of children not accountable for their disabling status. The stigma of illiteracy will mark them for the rest of their lives. By denying these children a basic education, we deny them the ability to live within the structure of our civic institutions, and foreclose any realistic possibility that they will contribute in even the smallest way to the progress of our Nation. In determining the rationality of § 21.031, we may appropriately take into account its costs to the Nation and to the innocent children who are its victims. In light of these countervailing costs, the discrimination contained in § 21.031 can hardly be considered rational unless it furthers some substantial goal of the State.

IV

It is the State's principal argument, and apparently the view of the dissenting Justices, that the undocumented status of these children vel non establishes a sufficient

rational basis for denying them benefits that a State might choose to afford other residents. The State notes that while other aliens are admitted "on an equality of legal privileges with all citizens under non-discriminatory laws," the asserted right of these children to an education can claim no implicit congressional imprimatur. Indeed, in the State's view, Congress' apparent disapproval of the presence of these children within the United States, and the evasion of the federal regulatory program that is the mark of undocumented status, provides authority for its decision to impose upon them special disabilities. Faced with an equal protection challenge respecting the treatment of aliens, we agree that the courts must be attentive to congressional policy; the exercise of congressional power might well affect the State's prerogatives to afford differential treatment to a particular class of aliens. But we are unable to find in the congressional immigration scheme any statement of policy that might weigh significantly in arriving at an equal protection balance concerning the State's authority to deprive these children of an education.

The Constitution grants Congress the power to "establish an uniform Rule of Naturalization." Drawing upon this power, upon its plenary authority with respect to foreign relations and international commerce, and upon the inherent power of a sovereign to close its borders, Congress has developed a complex scheme governing admission to our Nation and status within our borders. The obvious need for delicate policy judgments has counseled the Judicial Branch to avoid intrusion into this field. But this traditional caution does not persuade us that unusual deference must be shown the classification embodied in § 21.031. The States enjoy no power with respect to the classification of aliens. This power is "committed to the political branches of the Federal Government." Although it is "a routine and normally legitimate part" of the business of the Federal Government to classify on the basis of alien status and to "take into account the character of the relationship between the alien and this country," only rarely are such matters relevant to legislation by a State.

. . . .

To be sure, like all persons who have entered the United States unlawfully, these children are subject to deportation. But there is no assurance that a child subject to deportation will ever be deported. An illegal entrant might be granted federal permission to continue to reside in this country, or even to become a citizen. In light of the discretionary federal power to grant relief from deportation, a State cannot realistically determine that any particular undocumented child will in fact be deported until after deportation proceedings have been completed. It would of course be most difficult for the State to justify a denial of education to a child enjoying an inchoate federal permission to remain.

We are reluctant to impute to Congress the intention to withhold from these children, for so long as they are present in this country through no fault of their own, access to a basic education. In other contexts, undocumented status, coupled with some articulable federal policy, might enhance state authority with respect to the treatment of undocumented aliens. But in the area of special constitutional sensitivity presented by these cases, and in the absence of any contrary indication fairly discernible in the present legislative record, we perceive no national policy that supports the State in denying these children an elementary education. The State may borrow the federal classification. But to justify its use as a criterion for its own discriminatory policy, the State must demonstrate that the classification is reasonably adapted to "the purposes for which the state desires to use it."

V

Appellants argue that the classification at issue furthers an interest in the "preservation of the state's limited resources for the education of its lawful residents." Of course, a concern for the preservation of resources standing alone can hardly justify the classification used in allocating those resources. The State must do more than justify its classification with a concise expression of an intention to discriminate. Apart from the asserted state prerogative to act against undocumented children solely on the basis of their undocumented status—an asserted prerogative that carries only minimal force in the circumstances of these cases—we discern three colorable state interests that might support § 21.031.

First, appellants appear to suggest that the State may seek to protect itself from an influx of illegal immigrants. While a State might have an interest in mitigating the potentially harsh economic effects of sudden shifts in population, § 21.031 hardly offers an effective method of dealing with an urgent demographic or economic problem. There is no evidence in the record suggesting that illegal entrants impose any significant burden on the State's economy. To the contrary, the available evidence suggests that illegal aliens underutilize public services, while contributing their labor to the local economy and tax money to the

state fisc. The dominant incentive for illegal entry into the State of Texas is the availability of employment; few if any illegal immigrants come to this country, or presumably to the State of Texas, in order to avail themselves of a free education. Thus, even making the doubtful assumption that the net impact of illegal aliens on the economy of the State is negative, we think it clear that "[c]harging tuition to undocumented children constitutes a ludicrously ineffectual attempt to stem the tide of illegal immigration," at least when compared with the alternative of prohibiting the employment of illegal aliens.

Second, while it is apparent that a State may "not... reduce expenditures for education by barring [some arbitrarily chosen class of] children from its schools," appellants suggest that undocumented children are appropriately singled out for exclusion because of the special burdens they impose on the State's ability to provide high-quality public education. But the record in no way supports the claim that exclusion of undocumented children is likely to improve the overall quality of education in the State. As the District Court in No. 80–1934 noted, the State failed to offer any "credible supporting evidence that a proportionately small diminution of the funds spent on each child [which might result from devoting some state funds to the education of the excluded group] will have a grave impact on the quality of education." And, after reviewing the State's school financing mechanism, the District Court in No. 80–1538 concluded that barring undocumented children from local schools would not necessarily improve the quality of education provided in those schools. Of course, even if improvement in the quality of education were a likely result of barring some number of children from the schools of the State, the State must support its selection of this group as the appropriate target for exclusion. In terms of educational cost and need, however, undocumented children are "basically indistinguishable" from legally resident alien children.

Finally, appellants suggest that undocumented children are appropriately singled out because their unlawful presence within the United States renders them less likely than other children to remain within the boundaries of the State, and to put their education to productive social or political use within the State. Even assuming that such an interest is legitimate, it is an interest that is most difficult to quantify. The State has no assurance that any child, citizen or not, will employ the education provided by the State within the confines of the State's borders. In any event, the record is clear that many of the undocumented children disabled by this classification will remain in this country indefinitely, and that some will become lawful residents or citizens of the United States. It is difficult to understand precisely what the State hopes to achieve by promoting the creation and perpetuation of a subclass of illiterates within our boundaries, surely adding to the problems and costs of unemployment, welfare, and crime. It is thus clear that whatever savings might be achieved by denying these children an education, they are wholly insubstantial in light of the costs involved to these children, the State, and the Nation.

VI

If the State is to deny a discrete group of innocent children the free public education that it offers to other children residing within its borders, that denial must be justified by a showing that it furthers some substantial state interest. No such showing was made here. Accordingly, the judgment of the Court of Appeals in each of these cases is

Affirmed.

Citation: *Plyler v. Doe,* 457 U.S. 202 (1982).

POLITICAL ACTIVITIES AND SPEECH OF TEACHERS

The First Amendment rights of teachers and other school employees—whether they can speak out on various topics and freely associate with the political party of their choice—have been the subject of several Supreme Court cases. In general, the Court has protected speech that is related to issues of community interest but not to internal office operations; it has found that political affiliation may be the basis of hiring and firing for policy-making employees but not for others. This entry briefly summarizes those cases.

Free Speech

In the context of examining the political rights of teachers and other public school employees, it is worth noting that the U.S. Supreme Court first constructed a test for deciding under what circumstances public employers, including school boards, could dismiss employees for speaking out on matters of public concern in *Pickering v Board of Education of Township High School District 205, Will County* (1968). In *Pickering,* the Court held that

> the problem in any case is to arrive at a balance between the interests of the [employee], as a citizen, in commenting on matters of public concern and the interest of the State, as an employer in promoting the efficiency of the public services it performs through its employees. (p. 568)

In *Pickering,* the board unsuccessfully sought to discharge a teacher for sending a letter to the editor of a local newspaper that criticized its handling of a bond issue and its allocation of financial resources between a school's educational and athletic programs. While the Court recognized that protecting the interest of the state was important, it believed the application of a balancing test between the teacher's interests as a citizen and the board "in promoting the efficiency of the public services it performs" (p. 568) was at stake.

The *Pickering* Court identified several considerations in evaluating the extent of the efficiency of public service, including whether speech directly impaired the supervisory ability of employers, whether the speech adversely affected the organizational climate, whether the employee's relationship with the board was so close as to suggest a breach of confidence, whether the employee's performance at the job suffered, and whether the speech had an adverse effect on school operations. In applying these tests, the Court concluded that the board violated the teacher's rights.

Refining the Decision

The Supreme Court again reviewed the free speech rights of teachers in *Mt. Healthy City Board of Education v. Doyle* (1977). In *Doyle,* the Court examined the impact of including a constitutionally protected right as a factor in not renewing the contract of a nontenured teacher who had a record of being difficult in school. The teacher claimed that the board dismissed him because he called into a radio talk show and criticized a memo from his principal dealing with a faculty dress code.

In remanding for further consideration, the Court decided that where a teacher shows that protected conduct about a school matter was a substantial or motivating factor in the nonrenewal of an employment contract, the school or board must be given the opportunity to prove that it would have done the same even absent the protected conduct. On remand, the court accepted the board's assertion that it would not have renewed the teacher's contract regardless of whether he placed the call to the radio talk show (*Doyle v. Mt. Healthy City School District Board of Education,* 1982).

In *Givhan v. Western Line Consolidated School District* (1979), the Court indicated that *Pickering* applies to teachers who express themselves during private conversations with supervisors. When school officials chose not to renew the contract of a nontenured teacher, she was told that this was partly in response for her allegedly making petty and unreasonable demands on the principal and addressing him in an inappropriate manner. In refusing to reinstate the teacher, the justices explained that the lower court erred in declaring that school officials were justified in not renewing her contract, suggesting that under *Doyle,* they may have had sufficient cause on other grounds that would have required further proceedings. The Court thought that under *Pickering,* the judiciary has to consider working relationships of personnel along with the contents of communications in evaluating whether private communications are beyond the scope of First Amendment protection.

A Two-Part Test

The Supreme Court's next case involving the speech of public employees was *Connick v. Myers* (1983). In *Connick,* the Court distinguished the case at bar from *Pickering,* pointing out that *Pickering* applied to situations when employee speech is a matter of public concern. In *Connick,* an assistant district attorney distributed a questionnaire to fellow employees regarding the internal workings of the office. Insofar as only one question was considered to be of public concern, it alone seemed to be protected by *Pickering.* Even after

the Court analyzed the one question under *Pickering,* it ruled that the employer did not violate the First Amendment rights of the discharged employee. In the process, the Court created a new two-part *Pickering-Connick* test. Under this test, only if employee speech is a matter of public concern will courts go to step two and evaluate whether that right is outweighed by employers' rights to run efficient organizations.

Courts applied the two-part analysis for over 20 years, until *Garcetti v. Ceballos* (2006). In *Garcetti,* the Supreme Court simplified its interpretation, making it more difficult for employees to enjoy their First Amendment rights. At issue was whether public employees were free to speak on matters pertaining to their official capacity. The Court wrote that insofar as employees talk about topics related to their jobs and are not speaking on matters of public concern, they give up their First Amendment protection with regard to being disciplined.

Political Affiliation

Pursuant to the legal reasoning from the freedom of speech cases, it is possible to evaluate claims dealing with political affiliations. In these cases, the Supreme Court considered whether employees could be discharged from public service due to their political associations.

Politics and Efficiency

In *Elrod v. Burns* (1976), a plurality maintained that dismissing employees due to political affiliations would violate the First Amendment. In this case, the Court applied heightened scrutiny, declaring that

> if conditioning the retention of public employment on the employee's support of the in-party is to survive constitutional challenge, it must further some vital government end by a means that is least restrictive of freedom of belief and association in achieving that end, and the benefit gained must outweigh the loss of constitutionally protected rights. (p. 363)

The plurality rejected the state's asserted justification for discharging employees based on the need to maintain the organization's efficient operation.

The plurality in *Elrod* disagreed with the board in considering whether or not an organization becomes less efficient because employees are of a different political persuasion than their employers. Even when employees are politically associated with opposing views, the court found that mere political association is not enough reason to assume they would behave badly; the court added that firing employees because they belong to another political party as a means to make other workers better was not the least restrictive way of accomplishing the goal of efficiency. The plurality also examined the state's proffered need for political loyalty, rejecting the notion that partisan loyalty might guarantee that politically motivated policies could best be accomplished by employees who are similarly affiliated. The plurality interpreted this as suggesting that discharging employees along partisan lines might be justifiable under the reasoning that organizational efficiency and the pursuit of political goals would be enhanced by identical party affiliation. In so doing, the plurality made a major distinction between employees who are in policy-making positions and those who are not in such roles. The plurality decided that employees in policy-making positions may be dismissed if they are affiliated with oppositional parties, but those who are not may not be dismissed. Herein is the difference between *Pickering- Connick* and *Elrod*. The plurality required a lower court to apply the balancing test of *Pickering-Connick* for each case, while *Elrod* merely asks whether employees were in policy-making positions when making statements.

Politics and Policy

In 1980, the Supreme Court again revised the standard for addressing when one's political affiliation is cause for employee discharge. In *Branti v. Finkel* (1980), the Court observed that "the ultimate inquiry is . . . whether the hiring authority can demonstrate that party affiliation is an appropriate requirement for the effective performance of the public office involved" (p 518).

Finally, in *Rutan v. Republican Party of Illinois* (1990), the Supreme Court broadened *Elrod* and *Branti* to include all internal employment decisions such as promotions and transfers based on political

affiliation. In fact, *Rutan* actually broadened the protection of *Elrod* as the Court drew a bright line distinction between basic freedom of speech and patronage cases by looking to the freedoms that each protects. In sum, when dealing with employees in policy-making positions, school boards should have greater leeway when dismissing employees who are in policy-making roles as opposed to being classroom teachers.

Marilyn J. Bartlett

See also *Connick v. Myers; Givhan v. Western Line Consolidated School District; Mt. Healthy City Board of Education v. Doyle; Pickering v. Board of Education of Township High School District 205, Will County;* Teacher Rights

Legal Citations

Branti v. Finkel, 445 U.S. 507 (1980).
Connick v. Myers, 461 U.S. 138 (1983).
Elrod v. Burns, 427 U.S. 347 (1976).
Garcetti v. Ceballos, 547 U.S. 410 (2006).
Givhan v. Western Line Consolidated School District, 439 U.S. 410 (1979).
Mt. Healthy City Board of Education v. Doyle, 429 U.S. 274 (1977), *on remand, Doyle v. Mt. Healthy City School District Board of Education*, 670 F.2d 59 (6th Cir.1982).
Pickering v. Board of Education of Township High School 205, Will County, 391 U.S. 563 (1968).
Rutan v. Republican Party of Illinois, 497 U.S. 62 (1990).

PRAYER IN PUBLIC SCHOOLS

Until the 1950s, prayer was routinely offered in public schools across the nation and generally supported by the courts. This reflected the quest for religious freedom that was part of American history and the religious, mostly Protestant, influences that were common from colonial times to the mid-20th century. Beginning in the 1960s, however, the U.S. Supreme Court issued a series of decisions related to prayer and other religion-oriented activities in schools, setting tests for what is constitutionally permissible, as discussed in this entry.

Early Rulings

More than half the states have, at some point, allowed or required prayer and/or Bible reading in public school classrooms. This was considered to be part of the exercise of freedom of religion, and proponents of religious exercises, mostly prayer and Bible reading, generally argued in defense of the practices as voluntary and traditional. In the 1960s, prayer and Bible reading faced legal challenges. Since the 1960s, there has been a continual battle between church and state, in the form of public schools, over the right of freedom of expression to address prayer in the schools since that time.

Many significant court cases have reflected the will of individuals, areas of the country, and the nation itself. In 1962, in *Engle v. Vitale*, the U.S. Supreme Court resolved its first case involving school prayer, finding that a prayer composed by the New York State Board of Regents was unconstitutional. The dispute arose after a local school board adopted this prayer as part of a policy, requiring it to be recited in class and allowing students to be exempted from this recitation.

Subsequent litigation defined religious exercises as clearly unconstitutional. A year after *Engel,* in the companion cases of *Abington Township School District v. Schempp* and *Murray v. Curlett* (1963), the Supreme Court struck down prayer and Bible reading, creating the first two parts of the tripartite *Lemon v. Kurtzman* (1971) test in deciding that these practices were invalid, because they lacked a secular purpose and they advanced religion.

The *Lemon* Test

The legal battle between religion and the public school sector raged on in the Supreme Court's landmark 1971 decision in *Lemon v. Kurtzman*. While the constitutionality of government aid to religious schools was at issue in *Lemon,* rather than prayer, the Court developed a standard that continues to be applied in questions of the right to prayer in the schools as well as when dealing with state aid to religiously affiliated nonpublic schools. According to the Court, any time that religion and government intersect, first, the statute must have "a secular legislative purpose"; second, its primary effect must neither advance nor inhibit religion; finally, the statute must not foster "an excessive government entanglement with religion" (p. 615). Laws or policies that fail any one of the three parts of the *Lemon* test are invalid.

The Supreme Court turned to the issue of a period of silence in schools in *Wallace v. Jaffree* (1985). At issue were three statutes from Alabama. The Court found that the first, which allowed a period of silence for meditation, was constitutional. Conversely, the Court struck down the second law that authorized teachers to lead willing students in a prayer to "Almighty God . . . the Creator and Supreme Judge of the world" (p. 40). The Court also invalidated a statute that authorized a period "for meditation or voluntary prayer" (p. 57) on the basis that the inclusion of the words, "or voluntary prayer," was made for the specific unconstitutional purpose of returning prayer in public classrooms.

Classroom times for silence for student meditation are constitutional if they are neutrally conducted and if the laws and policies authorizing such times are neutrally written. Applying *Lemon,* the Eleventh Circuit, in *Bown v. Gwinnett County School District* (1997), refused to find an Establishment Clause violation in a law from Georgia that required a moment for silent reflection in all public school classrooms at the beginning of the school day. Similarly, the Fourth Circuit upheld a law from Virginia that provided for a daily observance of one minute of silence in all classrooms, so that students could meditate, pray, or engage in other silent activity (*Brown v. Gilmore,* 2001).

Coercion and Access

The *Lemon* test continues to be applied. Even so, the Supreme Court adopted the coercion test in *Lee v. Weisman* (1992) to evaluate whether individuals were compelled to participate in prayer at graduation ceremonies. In *Lee,* the Court clarified that school-sponsored prayer was unconstitutional. *Lee* arose when a middle school principal invited members of the clergy to give an invocation and benediction at the school's graduation ceremony. Following *Lee,* the lower federal courts remained divided over the question of student-sponsored prayer at graduation.

Eight years later, in *Santa Fe Independent School District v. Doe* (2000), the Supreme Court addressed a school board's policy of permitting student-led, student-initiated prayer at football games. In ruling that the policy violated the Establishment Clause, the Court specified that its purpose and effect were to endorse religion. However, *Santa Fe* did not end this debate. In *Adler v. Duval County School Board* (2001), a high school senior, whom the graduating class elected, was allowed to deliver a message of his own choosing at graduation. These cases demonstrate the controversial and fact-specific nature of the litigation. In *Adler,* the Eleventh Circuit decided that student-initiated prayer was acceptable, because it was part of the entire process of planning the graduation. Yet, in a case from Texas (*Ward v. Santa Fe Independent School District,* 2002), a federal trial court struck down a policy that encouraged students to read religious messages at public events as violating the Establishment Clause.

Additional issues emerged with respect to prayer in schools. In 1984, Congress enacted the Equal Access Act, which allows noncurricular prayer and Bible study clubs to gather during noninstructional time in public secondary schools that receive federal assistance. In *Board of Education of Westside Community Schools v. Mergens* (1999), the Supreme Court upheld the Equal Access Act, reasoning that most high school students could recognize that allowing a religious club to meet in a high school was not the same as a school's endorsing religion.

Recent Issues

Congress has become involved in the status of school prayer in the No Child Left Behind Act (NCLB). The NCLB requires that schools that receive federal funds must certify that they have no policies that either deny or prevent participation in constitutionally protected prayer in schools.

More and more there has been an expression on the part of students to pray before and after school activities. Students may read Bibles or other religious materials, pray, or engage other consenting students in religious instruction during noninstructional time such as passing periods, recess, and lunch. While

school officials may impose rules to guarantee order and student rights, they may not prohibit lawful activities that are religiously based. School officials have generally been cautioned not to encourage, discourage, or participate in these activities. Even though the federal Department of Education has supported greater accommodation of religion than in the 1970s and 1980s, courts continue to render controversial decisions in this area. In light of these rulings, the courts are likely to treat challenges to prayer in schools on case-by-case bases.

Deborah E. Stine

See also *Abington Township School District v. Schempp* and *Murray v. Curlett; Board of Education of Westside Community Schools v. Mergens; Engel v. Vitale;* Equal Access Act; *Lee v. Weisman; Lemon v. Kurtzman;* No Child Left Behind Act; Religious Activities in Public Schools; *Santa Fe Independent School District v. Doe*

Legal Citations

Abington Township School District v. Schempp and *Murray v. Curlett,* 374 U.S. 203 (1963).
Bown v. Gwinnett County School District, 112 F.3d 1464 (11th Cir. 1997).
Brown v. Gilmore, 258 F.3d 265 (4th Cir. 2001).
Engel v. Vitale, 370 U.S. 421 (1962).
Equal Access Act, 20 U.S.C. §§ 4071 *et seq.*
Lee v. Weisman, 505 U.S. 577 (1992).
Lemon v. Kurtzman, 403 U.S. 602 (1971).
No Child Left Behind Act, 20 U.S.C. §§ 6301 *et seq.*
Santa Fe Independent School District v. Doe, 530 U.S. 290 (2000).
Wallace v. Jaffree, 472 U.S. 38 (1985).
Ward v. Santa Fe Independent School District, 393 F. 3d 599 (5th Cir. 2004).

PRECEDENT

Precedent refers to the use of previous court decisions in resolving current judicial questions. Precedent is thus, in some ways, a historical recollection of the development of legal matters or conflicts. Under the common-law concept of precedent, decisions that have been rendered on issues should be exemplars or guides for later cases when similar issue arises. By applying precedent, lower courts are essentially bound by the judgments of higher courts. While precedent is a practice and not a law, its use is binding in judicial decisions. This entry looks at types of precedent, conditions for overruling precedents, and practical application.

Types of Precedent

Precedent can fall into one of two categories: binding or persuasive. Binding precedent is set by higher courts and must be established in their legal reasoning; it is also known as its *ratio decidendi,* literally, "the reason for a decision." Binding precedent refers back to the doctrine of stare decisis, in which lower courts are bound by the decisions of higher courts. The doctrine of *stare decisis,* "to stand by that which is decided," requires adherence to precedent. When courts render their judgments, their doing so dictates future interpretations of a similar dispute unless an even higher court establishes a different outcome, thereby setting new precedent. When higher courts rule, lower courts are bound by their orders in future cases.

Persuasive precedent refers to precedent that is not mandatory or binding. For example, in cases involving circumstances that have not yet been addressed, typically referred to as cases of first impression, courts may rely on persuasive precedent by applying decisions from courts in other jurisdictions. In cases of first impression, there is no mandatory precedent for courts to apply. If earlier judgments dealt with similar circumstances, then courts may rely on persuasive precedent.

Courts can also consider customs and traditions in making their decisions in the absence of binding precedent. In addition, persuasive precedent is created by decisions of courts of the same level, particularly appellate panels. As such, courts should take such judgments into consideration but are not obligated to reach the same outcomes. If higher courts apply persuasive precedent is their opinions, it can become binding.

Insofar as precedent has such far-reaching implications for future cases, courts seek to set it as narrowly as possible. To this end, courts typically rule with great specificity, such that when they use rationales as

binding or persuasive precedents, other courts can understand the circumstances under which the precedents were set.

Overturning Precedent

In rare cases, a higher court may overturn precedent. When this happens, courts usually try to distinguish the new rulings from the precedent, again making the scope of their decisions as specific as possible so that different circumstances allow for distinct decisions. For example, in *Brown v. Board of Education of Topeka* (1954), the Supreme Court distinguished its holding from *Plessy v. Ferguson* (1896), which dealt with public railway accommodations, in noting that its judgment applied to public education, because only schooling was at issue. Of course, Brown opened the door to the end of "separate but equal" throughout American society.

When courts overrule precedent, they consider issues including the age of the precedent, the degree to which the public in general or members of a private sector rely on this precedent, and the precedent's harmony and fit with other related laws. In fact, the Supreme Court has explained its reasons for overruling precedents:

> When convinced of former error, this Court has never felt constrained to follow precedent. In constitutional questions, where correction depends upon amendment, and not upon legislative action, this Court throughout its history has freely exercised its power to reexamine the basis of its constitutional decisions. (*Smith v. Allwright,* p. 665)

In adhering to the legal doctrine of *stare decisis* and following precedent, courts typically reverse rulings most often and/or easily in cases involving constitutional issues, particularly those involving due process rights.

How Precedent Is Used

For practical purposes, and due to the sheer volume of judicial decisions that are handed down each year, courts can almost always find previous decisions to support their judgments. Accordingly, precedents are used to validate, rationalize, or substantiate the conclusion that courts make in addition to actually helping direct or channel opinions.

Case law also greatly impacts the notion of *stare decisis,* meaning that precedent impacts judicial decisions based on a number of criteria, including the degree of similarity between the issues being resolved. In addition, courts consider the time and location of the precedent, such as whether it was set in the same jurisdiction and therefore binding. In this way, courts ask about how long ago a precedent was set and what new rules or circumstances may have arisen in the interim. When ruling, courts first consider whether there is a binding precedent, such as from the U.S. Supreme Court, before looking to more localized cases in the same jurisdiction. After that, courts may give some weight to decisions from lower courts, to disputes on matters that are slightly different, or to cases that are out of date, such as where a new law has been enacted since the precedent was set.

The wisdom behind strict adherence to judicial precedent is debated. Supporters maintain that adherence to precedent allows decisions to be predictable and free from chaos. In essence, proponents assert that because persons should be reasonably sure of the outcome of cases if the facts and issues are similar to those of earlier disputes, then precedent is valuable. On the other hand, critics counter that following the doctrine of precedent and stare decisis may perpetuate judgments such as Plessy v. Ferguson that were not good or sound in the first place.

Similarly, a precedent that was questionable when first established can be used in further decisions, each with slightly different interpretations, to the point that it results in judgments that are grossly incorrect. Insofar as the U.S. Constitution does not require following precedent, opponents argue that ensuring that the Constitution is upheld correctly is more important than ensuring that previous decisions are followed with exactness.

Regardless of which side of the equation one falls on, it is clear that precedent is a useful tool in analyzing judicial trends. Moreover, precedent can be meaningful for predicting future outcomes of cases.

Stacey L. Edmonson

See also Common Law; Rule of Law; Stare Decisis

Further Readings

Best, A., & Barnes, D. (2007). *Basic tort law: Cases, statutes, and problems* (2nd ed.). New York: Aspen Press.
Precedent. (2007). Available from http://www.lectlaw.com

Legal Citations

Brown v. Board of Education of Topeka I, 347 U.S. 483 (1954).
Brown v. Board of Education of Topeka II, 349 U.S. 294 (1955).
Plessy v. Ferguson, 163 U.S. 537 (1896).
Smith v. Allwright, 321 U.S. 649 (1994).

PREVENTATIVE LAW

The most effective approach for handling legal challenges is to prevent them from occurring in the first place. However, in recent years, school boards have had to allocate a much higher proportion of their overall budgets for legal fees. Unfortunately, as American educational systems become more complex, and the number of laws that schools operate under increases, the amount of litigation also increases. This is particularly true in the field of special education, where the amount of litigation has increased at a greater rate than in any other school-related sphere. At the same time, the amount of litigation in the myriad other areas that fall under the umbrella of education law continues to increase. In addition to their own legal expenses, school boards may be responsible for reimbursing parents for their legal expenses when parents are the prevailing parties in litigation.

School officials, aware of the need to evade unnecessary litigation, have developed an interest in the field of preventative law. Utilizing the principles of preventative law, school personnel try to eliminate legal conflicts before they can surface, thus putting school boards in favorable positions should litigation occur down the road. In order to be most successful, educational officials need to apply preventative law principles on a daily basis by looking for permanent solutions to the situations that give rise to conflict in school settings. By and large, it is much less expensive to find lasting solutions by enacting proactive policies and procedures than to engage in what amounts to reactive or after-the-fact defenses in long-drawn-out litigation.

A prerequisite to any formal program of preventative law is for school officials, including administrators, teachers, aides, and other support personnel, to be knowledgeable about the legal requirements of their respective roles. School personnel can gain basic knowledge of education law by taking courses offered by local schools of education. In fact, almost all school administrator preparation programs include at least one course in legal issues. Even so, because the law is constantly evolving, it can be a big challenge for school officials to be diligent in their efforts to remain current. New cases that can alter the status of the law are decided daily. Thus, school officials must take positive steps to stay knowledgeable about changes in the legal landscape.

Fortunately, numerous sources of information exist about issues and developments in education law. First, there is a plethora of texts and monographs on the market today dealing with both general issues and specific topics within the field of school law. One professional organization, the Education Law Association (ELA), headquartered at the University of Dayton, in Dayton, Ohio, is devoted to disseminating current information on education law. ELA publishes *The Yearbook of Education Law,* which includes chapters on various topics such as school governance, employee issues, sports, student issues, bargaining, students with disabilities, and torts. ELA also publishes a quarterly newsletter, *ELA Notes,* that includes practical articles, and a monthly reporter, the *School Law Reporter,* as well as monographs that provide up-to-date information on school law.

Many education journals frequently contain articles on legal issues, especially those involving issues relevant to the journal's subscribers. Professional organizations such as the Council for Exceptional Children, the National School Boards Association, the National Association of Elementary School Principals, and the Association of School Business Officials generally include sessions at their annual conferences that address legal issues. In addition, the schools of education in many colleges and universities offer courses on school law that can serve as excellent resources for educators. Workshops on education law should be part of every school system's professional development program. In providing such ongoing professional development for staff, school administrators should consider having the board's attorneys join in the presentations so that they can provide up-to-date legal perspectives.

One of the best ways to steer clear of litigation is always to be equipped for such a possibility. School board officials can reduce their risk of litigation by making sure that all employees understand the law as it applies to their respective positions and know and follow proper procedures. Employees who are familiar with their legal obligations and responsibilities are less likely to make serious errors. In this respect, the need for constant in-service training on legal requirements cannot be overemphasized.

Conflicts are inevitable, and when they do arise, it does not necessarily mean that litigation will follow. Many disagreements can, and should, be resolved through more communication between the parties involved. Parents, school officials, and other stakeholders can smooth over misunderstandings and reach compromises. Further, the parties to disagreements can also engage in less confrontational forms of dispute resolution such as arbitration or mediation to solve their disagreements.

Allan G. Osborne, Jr.

See also Arbitration; Mediation

Further Reading

Zirkel, P. A., & D'Angelo, A. (2002). Special education case law: An empirical trends analysis. *Education Law Reporter, 161,* 731–753.

PRIVACY RIGHTS OF STUDENTS

The Fourth Amendment to the U.S. Constitution, enacted as part of the Bill of Rights in 1791, guarantees all persons the freedom from unreasonable searches and seizures. Specifically, this amendment states that "the right of the people to be secure in their persons, houses, papers, and effects, against unreasonable searches and seizures, shall not be violated, and no Warrants shall issue, but upon probable cause, supported by Oath or affirmation, and particularly describing the place to be searched, and the persons or things to be seized." This protection requires close examination in one very important context, that of students in public schools; this entry provides a brief survey.

Basic but Limited Rights

The right to privacy is neither explicitly guaranteed nor mentioned in the U.S. Constitution. In addition, students who are enrolled in public schools have even more limited privacy rights than does the average adult citizen. Insofar as school officials are responsible for students when serving in loco parentis, or in the place of the parent, any privacy rights that children might have in educational settings are considered in relation to the overall safety and well-being of others in school environments as a whole. In other words, the duty and ability of school officials to provide a safe and secure learning environment typically outweighs individual students' rights to privacy.

The Supreme Court enunciated perhaps the greatest impact on students' rights to privacy in schools in *New Jersey v. T. L. O.* in 1985. *T. L. O.* involved a high school student who had marijuana in her purse, which was discovered when an assistant principal was actually looking only for cigarettes. In *T .L. O.,* the Court for the first time recognized that the rights of students are protected by the Fourth Amendment. Even so, the Court ruled that this protection is limited in scope by a school's need and the responsibility of educators to maintain safe and orderly learning environments.

In *T. L. O,* the Court exempted school officials from the requirements of probable cause and a warrant (which law enforcement officials must have) for conducting searches of students or their effects. Instead, the Court maintained that school employees are held to the standard of reasonable suspicion in order to justify a search. This means that school officials have to have reasonable cause, based on totality of the circumstances, to suspect that students have broken or are breaking school rules or the law at the inception of searches. In

addition, the Court explained that searches must be reasonable in scope depending on the age and sex of students as well as the severity of the alleged offenses. The *T. L. O.* standard applies to all individualized searches of student effects, including their purses, backpacks, desks, pockets, and other such places.

Some Specific Instances

School lockers may also be subject to search without violating the rights of students. Most courts have agreed that school lockers are indeed school property and thus subject to search at any time. It is well settled that students are issued lockers for their own use, but that the lockers are owned by schools and jointly controlled by both schools and students. As such, students' expectations of privacy of items in their lockers is lower than average. Still, "ownership" of lockers should be mentioned explicitly in local board policies in order to avoid conflict.

Likewise, drug dogs that are trained to sniff drugs in school lockers and other areas of school premises constitute individual searches. Courts have reached mixed results over whether the use of drug dogs violates the Fourth Amendment rights of students. However, when it comes to more intrusive actions such as strip searches, the majority of courts have generally agreed that school officials will have violated the privacy rights of students.

Another primary issue is random, suspicionless drug testing. The Supreme Court seemingly answered this question in *Board of Education of Independent School District No. 92 of Pottawatomie County v. Earls* (2002), wherein it upheld a random suspicionless drug testing policy that was directed at all students involved in extracurricular activities but was only applied to those who participated in interscholastic sports. *Earls* allowed for much more liberal testing of students with much more lenient circumstances than previously. The precedent was established in *Vernonia School District 47J v. Acton* (1995), where the student drug testing was upheld but was done so with specific characteristics, including student athletes' decreased expectations of privacy, the relative unobtrusiveness of the search procedures, and the seriousness of the need met by this search.

While students do have some rights to privacy in school settings, they are greatly diminished in light of the duty of educational officials to maintain safe and orderly learning environments. As case law demonstrates with situations involving searches of student effects (whether by persons or dogs) and drug testing, student privacy goes only as far as safety allows; courts are not as understanding when it comes to strip searches. Finally, the courts have gone so far as to rule that even random suspicionless drug testing, if conducted with the intent of establishing safety precautions for students in extracurricular activities, does not violate the Fourth Amendment.

Stacey L. Edmonson

See also *Board of Education of Independent School District No. 92 of Pottawatomie County v. Earls;* Drugs, Dog Searches for; Drug Testing of Students; Locker Searches; *New Jersey v. T. L. O.*; Strip Searches; *Vernonia School District 47J v. Acton*

Further Readings

Edmonson, S. L. (2002). Student drug testing in Texas: What every principal should know. *Texas Study of Secondary Education, 12*(1), 17–19.

Edmonson, S. L. (2003). The balance between student drug testing and Fourth Amendment rights in response to *Board of Education v. Earls. Education and the Law, 14*(4), 265–274.

Walsh, J., Kemerer, F., & Maniotis, L. (2005). *The educator's guide to Texas school law.* Austin: University of Texas Press.

Legal Citations

Board of Education of Independent School District No. 92 of Pottawatomie County v. Earls, 536 U.S. 822 (2002), *on remand,* 300 F.3d 1222 (10th Cir. 2002).

New Jersey v. T. L. O., 469 U.S. 325 (1985).

Vernonia School District 47J v. Acton, 515 U.S. 646 (1995).

PRIVACY RIGHTS OF TEACHERS

It is commonly believed that teachers, especially in public schools, enjoy a measure of privacy in their personal lives. The freedoms that teachers have on the job regarding what and how they may teach, what they may do and say, what organizations they may join, even what they may wear are under scrutiny and face growing challenges. Within the context of privacy rights, teachers may exercise personal choices, ranging from living with a person of the opposite sex to other lifestyle choices. The constitutional rights considered among the most basic for all include freedom of expression, religion, and association and freedom from discrimination.

Recent years have seen a movement toward reemphasizing teachers' responsibilities as moral exemplars in and out of school. Many parents have demanded that school officials reinforce traditional values among students, and school district policies generally require that teachers serve as positive role models. Based in part on such requirements, the supreme court of Colorado upheld the dismissal of a tenured teacher for immorality, because she violated board policy by drinking beer with students while acting in her official capacity as cheerleader sponsor (*Blaine v. Moffat County School District RE No. 1,* 1988). This case represents one of many that stand for the proposition that teacher misbehavior outside the school that reduces teachers' capacity to serve as positive role models can justify reprimands or dismissals as long as procedural and substantive due process rights are not violated. Against this backdrop, the interpretation of teachers' constitutional rights—such as freedom of expression, freedom to express religious views inside or outside of the classroom, and freedom of association—continues to evolve.

Speech and Religion

Teachers have the freedom and knowledge to educate America's youth. Yet, this freedom comes with significant responsibilities and some restrictions because of the potential impact on impressionable children. Consequently, what teachers may or should say is often scrutinized. The U.S. Supreme Court, in the landmark case *Pickering v. Board of Education of Township High School District 205, Will County* (1968), explained that teachers maintain some rights of expression as long as they are commenting on matters of public concern. In this case, the Court noted that there should be a balance between the interests of the teacher, as a citizen, in commenting upon matters of public concern, and the interest of the state.

In *Pickering,* the Supreme Court held that the teacher had the right to express his views on a matter of legitimate public concern and that his criticism of school policy was not adequate grounds for dismissal. At the same time, if a teacher's comments are sarcastic, unprofessional, insulting, or based on private disagreements, many cases support the notion that the teacher may be disciplined or even dismissed. Like all determinations on the limits of speech, the comments of teachers are subject to time, place, and manner restrictions. In litigation related to teacher rights and responsibilities, the courts typically examine the consequences and the context of teachers' actions or words and factor them into an equation balancing the public interests of school boards against the private rights of teachers.

On another matter, just like any citizen, teachers have the right to practice their religion outside of the normal hours of employment. However, this cannot include proselytizing or indoctrinating students in schools, a ban that may also include efforts to present a religious viewpoint outside of class. The rationale is that a teacher's position of authority could lead students to assume that the teacher's view is endorsed by the school. Therefore, teachers may not subject others, especially their students, to expressions of their religious beliefs or ideologies. With respect to religion, they must remain neutral in their relationship with students. In one such case, for example, the federal trial court in Connecticut ruled that a teacher could not wear a T-shirt with a religious message on it because of the impact that it might have on her students (*Downing v. West Haven Board of Education,* 2001).

Association and Behavior

Teachers may associate with whomever they wish as long as their associations do not involve illegal activity and their behavior does not render them unfit to perform their teaching functions effectively. While some teachers may be prohibited from some political activity because of federal and local regulations, they are not generally penalized for their political activity or association. Teachers may feel the indirect retribution of an administration unhappy with that activity. It is important to note that teachers enjoy a constitutional right to associate, to run for a political office, and to join unions, although this last right is limited in some states.

Teachers must exhibit prudent professional behavior and ensure that their participation in political or external organizations does not interfere with their classroom duties or disrupt the operations of their school systems. In one such case, the Second Circuit upheld the dismissal of a tenured teacher due to his membership in an organization that identified its primary goal as seeking to bring about a change in the attitudes and laws governing sexual activity between men and boys while advocating the abolition of laws governing the age of consent for such activities (*Melzer v. Board of Education of City School District of City of New York,* 2003, 2004). The court ruled that the orderly operation of a high school outweighed the teacher's interest in commenting on matters of public concern through his membership in the group and that the school board was not retaliating against him due to his belonging to the organization.

In exercising preferences in areas such as dress, grooming, and lifestyle choices, teachers must be mindful of the professional nature of their positions and the impact that their appearance and behavior may have on their students. The right of school boards to penalize teachers for private conduct rests on their ability to demonstrate that such conduct impaired their effectiveness in classrooms.

When teachers have demonstrated a consistent and effective record of teaching, have an effective and professional relationship with students, and are respected in their communities, it is unlikely that school officials will succeed in such serious action as dismissal or revoking their certificates. Even so, school officials may act if the private conduct of teachers becomes publicized to the point that it impairs their reputation and relationships with parents and students, thus rendering them ineffective in executing their duties. Teacher rights to privacy should be respected to the extent that teachers are not engaging in criminal acts that violate the trust of the community or render teachers ineffective in performing their professional duties. Teachers are entitled to constitutional rights, as are other citizens, and these rights must be protected.

Doris G. Johnson

See also Collective Bargaining; Due Process Rights: Teacher Dismissal; *Pickering v. Board of Education of Township High School District 205, Will County;* Political Activities and Speech of Teachers; Teacher Rights

Further Readings

Ornstein, A. C., & Levine, D. U. (2006). *Foundations of education.* New York: Houghton Mifflin.

Legal Citations

Blaine v. Moffat County School District RE No. 1, 748 P.2d 1280 (Colo.1988).

Downing v. West Haven Board of Education, 162 F.Supp.2d 19 (D. Conn.2001).

Melzer v. Board of Education of City School District of City of New York, 336 F.3d 185, 198 (2d Cir.2003), *cert. denied,* 540 U.S. 1183 (2004).

Pickering v. Board of Education of Township High School District 205, Will County, 391 U.S. 563 (1968).

RANEY V. BOARD OF EDUCATION

At issue in *Raney v. Board of Education* (1968) was the adequacy of a freedom-of-choice plan in terms of its compliance with the mandate of *Brown v. Board of Education of Topeka II* (1955). The U.S. Supreme Court, ruling on three related cases on the same day, found that the plan was not adequate to ensure the required unitary school system.

Facts of the Case

In *Brown II,* the U.S. Supreme Court ordered school boards in segregated school systems to transition to racial nondiscriminatory unitary systems. *Raney* involved a freedom-of-choice plan that a local board in Arkansas adopted in 1965. Prior to that time, the board operated a state-imposed segregated school system in a town where there was no residential segregation. The African American elementary and high schools were called the "Field Schools," and the White elementary and high schools were identified as the "Gould Schools."

As part of the freedom-of-choice plan, the board required students to select between the two sets of schools. Students who did not make a choice were assigned to the schools they previously attended. About 85 African American students attended the Gould Schools; no White students sought attendance at the Field Schools. In short, both the Gould Schools and

Field Schools continued to preserve their racially identifiable characteristics as segregated schools, as they had been prior to the freedom-of-choice plans. The African American students unsuccessfully filed suit when they were denied admission at the Gould Schools because the enrollment of children for the 5th, 10th, and 11th grades exceeded the number of places available. The Eighth Circuit affirmed the dismissal of the suit.

The Court's Ruling

On further review in *Raney,* one of three desegregation cases that it handed own on the same day, the Supreme Court unanimously reversed and remanded in favor of the African American students. In examining the adequacy of the plan under *Brown II,* the Court relied heavily on *Green v. County School Board of New Kent County* (1968), the second of the three cases that it decided the same day as *Raney* and one that involved a similar freedom-of-choice plan. The Court used its extensive review of *Green* in striking down the freedom of choice in *Raney* insofar as *Brown* directed school boards to develop realistic plans that had promise of dismantling desegregated systems immediately and turning them in unitary systems.

In both *Raney* and *Green,* the Supreme Court found that rather than dismantling the segregated school systems, the boards perpetuated dual systems. According to the *Raney* Court, the freedom-of-choice plan burdened students and parents with the responsibility that *Brown II* clearly mandated should have been the affirmative duty of school boards. In both *Raney* and *Green,* the Court reasoned that the plans were inadequate to move the segregated dual systems to unitary nonracial systems. *Green* also provided what became known as the "*Green* factors," which continue to be widely applied in evaluating overall effectiveness of desegregation plans and whether dual systems have achieved unitary status. These factors address the composition of a student body, faculty, staff, transportation, extracurricular activities, and facilities.

The *Raney* Court thus reversed and remanded for further proceedings that would include the issue of the location of a new high school. At the same time, the justices made it clear that the trial court's rejection of the complaint was an inappropriate exercise of its discretion. To this end, the justices concluded that the trial court should have maintained jurisdiction over the dispute in order to ensure that the board adopted constitutional plans and achieved the goal of a nonracial system. As Justice Douglas noted in his concurring opinion in *Jones v. Alfred H. Mayer Company* (1968) and as reflected in *Raney,* the Court was tiring of the contrivances states had invented to ignore the command of *Brown I.*

In the third case completing the trilogy with *Raney* and *Green, Monroe v. Board of Commissioners* (1968), the Supreme Court struck down another freedom-of-choice plan. In *Monroe,* the Court was of the opinion that a free transfer plan from Tennessee was inadequate for the same reasons as in *Raney* and *Green.* In *Raney, Green,* and *Monroe,* the Court did not declare that freedom-of-choice plans were per se unconstitutional. Rather, the Court examined the facts in each dispute in noting that the plans at issue did not pass constitutional muster.

Deborah Curry

See also *Brown v. Board of Education of Topeka; Brown v. Board of Education of Topeka* and Equal Educational Opportunities; Dual and Unitary Systems; *Green v. County School Board of New Kent County*

Further Readings

Hunter, R. C., & Donahoo, S. (2004). The implementation of *Brown* in achieving unitary status. *Education and Urban Society, 36,* 342–354.

Russo, C. J., Harris, J. J., III, & Sandridge, R. F. (1994). *Brown v. Board of Education* at 40: A legal history of equal educational opportunities in American public education. *Journal of Negro Education, 63,* 297–309.

Legal Citations

Brown v. Board of Education of Topeka I, 347 US 483 (1954).
Brown v. Board of Education of Topeka II, 349 U.S. 294 (1955).
Green v. County School Board of New Kent County, 391 U.S. 430 (1968).
Jones v. Alfred H. Mayer Company, 392 U.S. 409 (1968).
Monroe v. Board of Commissioners of the City of Jackson, 391 U.S. 450 (1968).
Raney v. Board of Education, 391 U.S. 443 (1968).

REDUCTION IN FORCE

Almost all states have statutes directly addressing the abolition of teaching or other jobs in schools without fault on the part of individual employees, a practice commonly referred to as *reduction in force* (RIF). The grounds for RIF, the order in which employees are released or can "bump" others from their jobs, and call-back rights are matters of state law subject to modifications by school board policies and operative collective bargaining agreements. Unless school boards modify their RIF policies pursuant to the agreements in effect with their employees, state statutes control.

State laws typically permit RIFs due to declines in student enrollments, financial exigencies, elimination of jobs or programs, and board discretion. While courts ordinarily defer to the discretion of school boards on the need for RIFs, if challenged, school officials must demonstrate that their use of RIFs complied with state laws, board policies, or collective bargaining contracts. In addition, courts expect RIF policies to include descriptions of the criteria that boards used in selecting employees to be dismissed, who made the judgments, and how the criteria were weighed in implementing RIFs.

Once school boards decide upon a RIF, they must establish the order of release. Insofar as RIFs are ordinarily based on seniority, courts typically treat this as a rational, but not exclusive, factor in selecting employees for RIFs. Courts thus often interpret tenure statutes broadly as including seniority rights within the category of probationary employees, so that those with more time on the job have greater rights compared with those employees with fewer years of service. Courts have also upheld board policies to rely on criteria such as race and gender as well as academic subject matter in high-demand areas, including science and mathematics, when implementing RIFs, as long as the boards can demonstrate justifiable bases for acting, thereby granting protected individuals additional years of seniority in order to help them to preserve their jobs.

The courts place the burden of proving that positions are unnecessary on school officials. In evaluating seniority, absent modifications based on board polices or collective bargaining agreements, the first criterion is number of years of full-time service in school systems. Beyond that, the methods that boards rely on must be reasonable and not prohibited by either state or federal law, such as dismissing individuals in protected categories, such as race or gender.

By way of illustration, a controversial legal case involving RIF, race, and seniority was days away from oral argument at the U.S. Supreme Court when the parties reached a settlement agreement, thereby ending the litigation. At issue was a dispute from New Jersey wherein a school board mistakenly believed that its affirmative action program required it to terminate the contract of a White rather than an African American teacher, due solely to race. The board dismissed the White woman, even though the two had virtually identical credentials. The Third Circuit affirmed that since the board's RIF plan, which was adopted to promote racial diversity rather than remedy discrimination or its past effects in the district, violated the rights of nonminorities, it was unconstitutional (*Taxman v. Board of Education of the Township of Piscataway,* 1996, 1997a, 1997b).

When tenured staff members lose their jobs as part of RIFs, nontenured employees usually cannot be retained, nor may boards grant them the status of tenured staff. In other words, current employees who are about to have their jobs eliminated as part of RIFs are entitled to "bump" less-senior staff members. "Bumping" makes it possible for employees with more seniority and at least the same credentials to retain the

jobs for which they were certificated, even if those positions are occupied by equally qualified staff members with less seniority.

Individuals who lose their jobs in RIFs must assure school officials that their credentials or certifications for other positions are valid when it is time for bumping. Courts generally agree that since being eligible for certification is not the same as having certification, those who lack certificates in areas where RIFs may occur do not have the legal right to bump others. Moreover, courts rule that bumping rights apply only to staff members who are qualified for their jobs, not those who seek to have new positions created within their school systems in an attempt to retain their employment.

Subject to board policies and collective bargaining agreements, RIF statutes usually stipulate that the jobs of certificated employees who have been released cannot be filled until they have first been offered their jobs back. State law, board policies, and bargaining contracts may even specify how much seniority individuals retain while on preferred eligibility or callback lists. Moreover, these laws, policies, and bargaining contracts may also specify how long former employees remain on preferred eligibility lists, typically for periods of 2 or 3 years, time frames that can be extended by bargaining agreements. Under preferred eligibility provisions, employees are usually called back to work in the order of seniority, such that the first to be released from their jobs are the first to be called back.

Charles J. Russo

See also Collective Bargaining; Contracts; Tenure; Unions

Further Readings

Hartmeister, F., & Russo, C. J. (1999). "Taxing" the system when selecting teachers for reduction-in-force. *West's Education Law Reporter, 130,* 989–1008.

Legal Citations

Taxman v. Board of Education of the Township of Piscataway, 91 F.3d 1547 (3d Cir. 1996), *cert. granted,* 521 U.S. 1117 (1997a), *cert. dismissed,* 522 U.S. 1010 (1997b).

REGENTS OF THE UNIVERSITY OF CALIFORNIA V. BAKKE

In *Regents of the University of California v. Bakke* (1978), the question before the U.S. Supreme Court was whether a medical school admissions policy that allowed for a separate process for minority applicants was constitutional. The unusual split decision endorsed diversity as a compelling government interest but set limitations on how race could be used in admissions to ensure a diverse student body, with a lasting impact on race-conscious education policy.

Facts of the Case

Alan Bakke, a White male, applied to the University of California at Davis medical school in 1973 and 1974 but was denied admission both times. Bakke then filed suit against the university, alleging so-called reverse discrimination. Bakke also contended that the admissions process discriminated against him on the basis of his race, violating his rights under both the Equal Protection Clause of the Fourteenth Amendment and Title VI of the 1964 Civil Rights Act.

University officials relied on an admissions process that separated Whites from minority students during deliberations, reserving 16 spots in a class of 100 specifically for minority applicants. In addition, the minority applicants were considered in the majority pool. Applicants to the medical school were required to have a minimum college grade point average (GPA) of 2.5. Five reviewers assessed each applicant's Medical College Admissions Test (MCAT) score, GPA, letters of recommendation, extracurricular activities, and other biographical data and assigned each factor a "benchmark" score of 0 to 100. These benchmark scores were added up so that each applicant received a final application score between 0 and 500.

Applicants who indicated their minority status (Black, Chicano, Asian, or American Indian, as determined by the university) on their applications went through a separate review process. Minority applicants were not required to meet the minimum 2.5 GPA, but their applications did undergo the same "benchmark" scoring system as nonminority applicants. The 16 spots reserved in this process were insulated from competition with the outside applicant pool. Bakke's attorney maintained that his scores were substantially higher than those of students who were admitted through the affirmative action process.

After the Supreme Court of California vitiated the admissions policy, the university sought further review.

The Court's Ruling

The Supreme Court struck down the university's policy on the basis of equal protection because of its quota nature, shielding minority applicants from competition with a larger applicant pool. Even so, Justice Powell's key concurring opinion effectively approved the use of race in college admissions in order to promote a diverse student body.

In its analysis, the Supreme Court ruled that in order to be acceptable, governmental programs that rely on suspect classifications such as race must pass *strict scrutiny analysis,* meaning that they must serve a compelling governmental purpose and must be narrowly tailored to suit that purpose. The medical school argued that its program passed strict scrutiny for four reasons: to help to reduce the historic deficit of minority groups in medical schools and professions, to counter the effects of societal discrimination, to increase the number of physicians serving in underserved areas, and to achieve the educational benefits that flow from a diverse student body. The Court considered each of these reasons.

Four justices signed on to an opinion upholding the university's policy based on the second rationale, to remedy societal discrimination. Four other justices signed on to an opinion that rejected all rationales and that struck down the policy as unconstitutional. Justice Powell, the ninth justice, filed an opinion that concurred with the latter four justices, striking down the policy. However, in so doing, Powell's concurrance endorsed the fourth, or diversity, rationale. According to Powell, an affirmative action policy in university admissions would be narrowly tailored to achieve this diversity interest if it met two conditions. First, he noted that he would uphold a policy if there were no racial quotas involved and all students were evaluated under common standards by a common admissions committee.

Second, Powell thought that race could be used only as a "plus" factor, on a par with other diversity factors designed to yield a heterogeneous student body. Interpreting the disputed policy at issue as a quota, Powell was of the view that it was unconstitutional.

Insofar as the Court was split 4-4-1, Justice Powell's concurring opinion is generally perceived as setting forth the relevant law that colleges and universities were required to follow. Yet the split decision in *Bakke,* coupled with subsequent Supreme Court decisions striking down affirmation action programs in hiring, promotion, and contracting (*Wygant v. Jackson Board of Education,* 1986; *Richmond v. J. A. Croson Company,* 1989; *Adarand Constructors, Inc. v. Pena,* 1995), resulted in confusion as to whether Justice Powell's judgment was still binding.

For example, in *Hopwood v. Texas* (1996), the Fifth Circuit ruled in favor of four White plaintiffs who sued the University of Texas Law School alleging that the university's affirmative action policy was discriminatory on equal protection grounds. This court concluded that Powell's *Bakke* opinion was not binding law. Other lower courts reached similar conclusions.

The uncertainty over *Bakke* continued until 2003, when a majority of the Court effectively adopted Powell's opinion in *Grutter v. Bollinger.* In upholding the affirmative action policy of the University of Michigan Law School, the Court held that the attainment of a diverse student body was, in fact, a compelling governmental interest and that the policy was sufficiently narrowly tailored to withstand judicial scrutiny. In a companion case, *Gratz v. Bollinger* (2003), involving undergraduates at the same university, the Court agreed that diversity was a compelling governmental interest, but it was not convinced that the policy was sufficiently narrowly tailored.

Lauren P. Saenz

See also Affirmative Action; Equal Protection Analaysis; Fourteenth Amendment; *Gratz v. Bollinger; Grutter v. Bollinger; Wygant v. Jackson Board of Education*

Legal Citations

Adarand Constructors, Inc. v. Pena, 515 U.S. 200 (1995).
Gratz v. Bollinger, 539 U.S. 244 (2003).
Grutter v. Bollinger, 539 U.S. 306 (2003).
Hopwood v. Texas, 78 F.3d 932 (5th Cir. 1996).
Regents of the University of California v. Bakke, 438 U.S. 265 (1978).
Richmond v. J. A. Croson Company, 488 U.S. 469 (1989).
Wygant v. Jackson Board of Education, 476 U.S. 267 (1986).

REGULATION

Although education is primarily an issue reserved for state and local control, federal involvement in the form of funding, legislative enactments, and subsequent regulations has dramatically increased. Thus, numerous regulations have emerged from federal departments and agencies such as the U.S. Department of Education and the Office for Civil Rights. These regulations provide guidance to state and local educational agencies regarding educators' responsibilities and students' rights. For example, the rights of students with disabilities are protected under the Individuals with Disabilities in Education Act (IDEA) and are further explained in the IDEA regulations, which are issued by the Department of Education. Likewise, the educational rights of English language learners (ELLs) are protected by Title VI of the Civil Rights Act of 1964 and are enforced through regulations issued by the Office for Civil Rights. The legal background of regulations and how they are created are discussed in this entry.

Legal Context

Governmental powers are vested by the U.S. Constitution in three separate branches: the executive, legislative, and judicial. Following a strict concept of separation of powers, each of these three governmental branches has the power and responsibility to act according to constitutional guidelines. The legislative branch has the primary power to make laws and to provide for the necessary policies and procedures to enact the laws. Regulations typically emerge as a direct result of this exercise of lawmaking power by the legislative branch.

Federal or state legislatures may delegate rulemaking authority and regulatory powers to specific agencies or departments in the executive branch of government. These governmental agencies or departments may then fulfill these delegated powers and responsibilities by issuing, or promulgating, regulations. During the 1930s, a surge of New Deal legislation emerged from Congress that began to delegate greater authority for issuing detailed regulations to various federal departments and agencies.

Regulations are issued by governmental agencies in order to accomplish the specific purposes of federal, state, or local statutes. In other words, governmental agencies are granted the authority and responsibility to promulgate reasonable rules and regulations in furtherance of the delegated legislative powers. While governmental agencies may be granted specific authority to carry out the terms of a given law, this authority is subject to various limitations upon such regulatory functions.

These limitations include, for example, a limit upon the regulatory authority of governmental agencies based upon constitutional rules and legal standards. Another limitation upon the regulatory authority is the mandate requiring that regulations conform to or not exceed the delegated powers inherent in the originating statute. Finally, governmental agencies are expected to adopt regulations in order to provide a mechanism for understanding, interpreting, enforcing, and overseeing the legislative purpose of a given statute or law.

How Regulations Are Made

Regulations typically emerge following consultation with the various individuals, industries, and institutions that will be affected by the regulations. In fulfillment of these expectations, governmental agencies publish a proposed regulation and then offer a period of time during which interested and affected parties are given an opportunity to comment on the proposed regulation. Federal agencies mush adhere to the Administrative Procedure Act, which mandates the publication of proposed and final regulations or rules in the *Federal Register* following the provision of notice and the opportunity for interested persons to share their views via written or oral presentation.

At the federal level, the proposed regulation appears in the *Federal Register,* which is published 5 days a week, while at the state level, the commentary

process varies widely and may depend heavily upon which state agency is proposing the regulation. During and following the public commentary period, a proposed regulation may be altered significantly. The final regulation, however, is expected to provide practical guidance to affected individuals and to the public agency responsible for implementing the originating statute. Final regulations issued by federal agencies are published in the Code of Federal Regulations and are arranged by subject. Regulations affecting education can be found primarily in Title 34 (Education) of the Code of Federal Regulations.

Even though the definition of regulation is typically broad, this term does not encompass all agency pronouncements. First, courts have determined that federal regulations have the full force and effect of law only when they have been adopted by governmental agencies for the purpose enforcing acts of Congress. Second, courts have repeatedly held that regulations must be filed and published in order to be effective as a matter of law. In theory, however, regulations do not have the effect of law because they are not the work of legislatures. Yet given the practice of judicial review of administrative action, regulations are typically a significant factor influencing the outcome of cases in which regulatory activity is involved.

Legislative efforts to reauthorize existing federal statutes and to adopt new laws are likely to continue. With the passage of the Elementary and Secondary Education Act of 1965 (ESEA), currently reauthorized as the No Child Left Behind Act of 2001, the legislative and executive branches of government have demonstrated a heightened interest in state and local educational issues. As a result of this interest, federal departments and agencies have issued and continue to issue regulations that directly impact state and local educational agencies.

Susan C. Bon

See also English as a Second Language; No Child Left Behind Act

Legal Citations

Elementary and Secondary Education Act of 1965, 20 U.S.C. §§ 6301 *et seq.*
Title VI of the Civil Rights Act of 1964, 42 U.S.C. § 2000d.

Rehabilitation Act of 1973, Section 504

Section 504 of the Rehabilitation Act of 1973 was the first civil rights law explicitly ensuring the rights of individuals with disabilities to employment and services. Section 504 specifically prohibits discrimination against individuals with disabilities in programs receiving federal funds. The provisions of Section 504 are similar to those in Titles VI and VII of the Civil Rights Act of 1964, which forbid employment discrimination on the basis of race, color, religion, sex, or national origin in programs that receive federal financial assistance. Individuals who have physical or mental impairments that substantially limit one or more major life activities, have a record of such impairments, or are regarded as having impairments are covered by Section 504 (29 U.S.C. § 706(7)(b)). Major life activities are "functions such as caring for oneself, performing manual tasks, walking, seeing, hearing, speaking, breathing, learning, and working" (28 C.F.R. § 41.31). Specifically, Section 504 states as follows:

> No otherwise qualified individual with a disability in the United States . . . shall, solely by reason of her or his disability, be excluded from the participation in, be denied the benefits of, or be subjected to discrimination under any program or activity receiving Federal financial assistance or under any program or activity conducted by any Executive agency or by the United States Postal Service. (29 U.S.C. § 794(a))

U.S. Supreme Court decisions have indicated that individuals are "otherwise qualified" under the terms of Section 504 if they are capable of meeting all of a program's requirements despite their disabilities (*School Board of Nassau County v. Arline*, 1987; *Southeastern Community College v. Davis*, 1979). Thus, to be "otherwise qualified," individuals with disabilities must be able to participate in programs or activities despite impairments as long as they can do so with reasonable accommodations. If individuals are otherwise qualified, recipients of federal funds are required to make reasonable accommodations that will allow them to participate in programs or activities, unless doing so would create undue hardships on the programs (34 C.F.R. § 104.12(a)). Reasonable accommodations may require adaptations to allow access, such as the construction of a wheelchair ramp, but do not require program officials to eliminate essential prerequisites to participation or to lower their standards. In the educational context, Section 504 applies to employees; students; and others, such as parents, who may access schools and their programs.

Application to Employees

To maintain discrimination claims under Section 504, employees with disabilities must show that they were treated differently than other employees or that an adverse employment decision was made because of their disabilities. Employees with disabilities will not be successful in their discrimination claims if they do not have the skills to perform the job in question, even when provided with accommodations, or if their alleged disabilities are not covered by Section 504. Further, courts do not uphold discrimination claims when school boards can show that officials made adverse employment decisions for nondiscriminatory, or legitimate business, reasons.

Persons with disabilities are "otherwise qualified" if they can perform all essential requirements of the position in question despite their impairments. Accordingly, individuals who cannot perform essential functions of the position, even with reasonable accommodations, are not otherwise qualified. For example, in the school context, failure to meet teacher certification requirements could disqualify individuals, even if the failures were allegedly due to disabilities. In one case, a teacher from Virginia, who claimed to be learning disabled but had not passed the communications section of the National Teachers Examination after several attempts, was not deemed to be otherwise qualified for teacher certification (*Pandazides v. Virginia Board of Education*, 1991). The court wrote that the skills measured by the communications part of the examination were necessary for competent performance as a classroom teacher. Section 504 also does not protect misconduct, even when it can be attributed to a disability.

Employers need to provide reasonable accommodations so that otherwise-qualified employees with disabilities can work and compete with other employees who do not have disabilities. Accommodations may include adjustments to an employee's schedule, minor changes in the employee's job responsibilities, or changes in the physical work environment. Even so, school boards are not required to furnish accommodation if doing so would place an undue burden on the board. For the most part, it is the school board's responsibility to show that requested accommodations would create an undue financial or administrative burden.

School boards are also not required to make accommodations that would fundamentally alter the nature of the position. However, board officials could be required to reassign employees with disabilities to other vacant positions that involve tasks that the employees are able to carry out. Even so, reassignment is not required when no other positions are available for which the employees are qualified. In addition, boards are not required to create new positions or accommodate employees with disabilities by eliminating essential aspects of their current positions.

Application to Students and Others

Section 504 offers protection against discrimination to students who have disabilities but are not eligible for special education. For example, students with infectious diseases, such as HIV/AIDS, cannot be discriminated against or excluded from schools under Section 504 unless there is a high risk of transmission of their diseases. A federal trial court in Illinois decided that a student who had been diagnosed with AIDS was entitled to the protection of Section 504 because he was regarded as having a physical impairment that substantially interfered with his life activities (*Doe v. Dolton Elementary School District No. 148,* 1988). He could not be excluded from school because there was no significant risk that he would transmit AIDS in the classroom setting. Students with physical challenges are also protected. One court has even required a school to allow a student to be accompanied by a service dog (*Sullivan v. Vallejo City Unified School District,* 1990).

In making accommodations for students, school personnel must provide aid, benefits, and/or services that are comparable to those available to children who do not have impairments. Thus, students with disabilities must receive comparable materials, teacher quality, length of school term, and daily hours of instruction. In addition, programs for students with disabilities should not be separate from those available to students who

are not impaired unless such segregation is necessary to provide needed services. When programs are offered separately, facilities must, of course, be comparable (34 C.F.R. § 104.34(c)).

School boards are also required to provide reasonable accommodations to others who may access a school's facilities or programs. For example, parents who have disabilities may need accommodations so they can participate in activities essential to their children's educations. For example, a federal trial court in New York required a school board to provide a sign language interpreter so that parents who were hearing impaired could take part in school-initiated conferences related to the academic and disciplinary aspects of their child's educational program (*Rothschild v. Grottenthaler,* 1989). On the other hand, school boards would not be required to provide accommodations for other school functions in which parental participation is not necessary, such as school plays or even graduation ceremonies.

Allan G. Osborne, Jr.

See also Civil Rights Act of 1964; *School Board of Nassau County v. Arline; Southeastern Community College v. Davis*

Legal Citations

Doe v. Dolton Elementary School District No. 148, 694 F. Supp. 440 (N.D. Ill. 1988).
Pandazides v. Virginia Board of Education, 946 F.2d 345 (4th Cir. 1991).
Rehabilitation Act of 1973, Section 504, 29 U.S.C. § 794(a).
Rothschild v. Grottenthaler, 725 F. Supp. 776 (S.D.N.Y. 1989), *aff'd in part, vacated and remanded in part,* 907 F.2d 286 (2d Cir. 1990).
School Board of Nassau County v. Arline, 480 U.S. 273 (1987).
Southeastern Community College v. Davis, 442 U.S. 397 (1979).
Sullivan v. Vallejo City Unified School District, 731 F. Supp. 947 (E.D. Cal. 1990).

REHNQUIST, WILLIAM H. (1924–2005)

During his long career on the U.S. Supreme Court, William Rehnquist went from an associate justice with conservative views on a predominantly liberal

Court where his role was primarily that of dissenter, to a powerful chief justice who in areas such as affirmative action, states' rights, and First Amendment freedom of religion helped turn the Court in a new direction. Insofar as the Court has now accepted a majority of Justice Rehnquist's formerly minority views, his impact has been especially significant in the field of education law.

Early Years

William H. Rehnquist was born on October 1, 1924, in Milwaukee, Wisconsin, where his political ideology was molded at an early age. He grew up in a predominantly Republican suburban community to staunch conservative parents who disliked President Franklin Roosevelt and opposed most of his New Deal programs. In high school, Rehnquist excelled academically and was awarded a scholarship to a small, liberal arts school, Kenyon College. He dropped out after one quarter and joined the Army Air Corps, serving as a weather observer in North Africa during World War II.

After the war, Rehnquist enrolled at Stanford University, where he earned a bachelor's and a master's degree in political science and was elected to Phi Beta Kappa. He then received a second master's degree in government from Harvard University. Rehnquist returned to Stanford to attend law school. He was an outstanding student and graduated first in his class. At Stanford, he was a classmate and friend of Sandra Day O'Connor, with whom he would later serve on the Supreme Court.

Rehnquist was selected to serve as a clerk for Supreme Court Justice Robert H. Jackson. During his clerkship, Rehnquist often disagreed with his fellow clerks, many of whom he believed to be far too liberal in their political views. As a clerk, he drafted a memo to Justice Jackson arguing the position that the doctrine of "separate but equal" should not be overturned.

Following his clerkship, Rehnquist married and moved to Phoenix, Arizona, where he practiced law and became an active member of the Republican Party. He was an outspoken opponent of school busing, and according to critics at his Senate confirmation hearing, he participated in a scheme to make it more difficult for African Americans to register and vote. Through participation in Arizona politics, Rehnquist became friends with Richard Kleindienst. When Kleindienst was appointed deputy attorney general by President Richard Nixon, he helped Rehnquist secure a post as assistant attorney general in the Justice Department Office of Legal Counsel.

On the Bench

At the Justice Department, Rehnquist vigorously defended the Nixon administration's programs of surveillance and wiretapping of civil rights and anti–Vietnam War protestors. He also was involved in the process of screening potential nominees for federal judgeships. In 1971, when justices John Harlan II and Hugo Black retired from the Supreme Court, Rehnquist was high on the list of possible replacements. President Nixon barely knew Rehnquist, but administration insiders highly recommended him because of his strong conservatism, loyalty, and intellect. Rehnquist was nominated to fill the seat held by Harlan, and despite his lack of judicial experience and what opponents considered to be radically conservative views, his appointment was approved by the Senate by a vote of 68 to 26.

In January 1972, Rehnquist and Lewis Powell, who was nominated to fill Justice Black's post, took their seats on the Supreme Court. Powell went on to be a judicial moderate, but Rehnquist staked out his position as the Court's most conservative member. In his first few years on the Court, he frequently cast the sole dissenting vote and was dubbed by some observers as the "Lone Ranger."

Over the years, as the membership of the Court changed, Rehnquist began to exert more influence. A turning point in his career was in the case of *National League of Cities v. Usery* (1976), where writing for the majority, Rehnquist ruled that provisions of the Fair Labor Standards Act applying federal wage and hour regulations to state employees violated the reserve powers of the states under the Tenth Amendment. Although *Usery* was subsequently overturned, Rehnquist's restricted interpretation of congressional power under the Commerce Clause of Article I § 8 and expansive view of state power under the Tenth Amendment resurfaced. In *United States v. Lopez* (1995), he wrote the majority opinion maintaining that Congress exceeded its authority to regulate interstate commerce when it passed the Gun-Free School Zones Act.

In 1987, when Chief Justice Warren Burger retired from the Court, President Ronald Reagan nominated Justice Rehnquist as his replacement. The Senate confirmation hearings on Rehnquist's nomination were, at times, acrimonious. Senator Edward Kennedy led the opposition, attacking Rehnquist's voting record on the Court as too extreme to be chief justice. Critics reintroduced the memo that Rehnquist wrote while clerking for Justice Jackson criticizing racial desegregation, along with the allegations that he harassed Black voters as a young lawyer in Phoenix. Rehnquist unapologetically defended his conservative record, and the charges of racial bias proved too tenuous. The Senate approved his nomination by a vote of 65 to 33. Rehnquist thus became only the third chief justice in United States history to be elevated from associate justice to chief.

Supreme Court Record

As chief justice, Rehnquist proved to be more flexible and less of an ideologue than his critics feared. He was more collegial and less austere than his predecessor, Warren Burger, and earned the respect of liberals, such as Justice William Brennan, who despite their ideological differences praised Rehnquist for his leadership style and effectiveness as a manager.

Race and Schools

Throughout his career, Justice Rehnquist gave a narrow construction to the Fourteenth Amendment Equal Protection Clause. He opposed affirmative action and joined the majority of the Supreme Court in *City of Richmond v. J. A. Croson Company* (1989), holding that the city's minority set-aside plan for the construction industry unlawfully discriminated against White contractors and that strict scrutiny should be the proper standard to apply in cases of reverse discrimination. More recently as chief justice, Rehnquist authored the Court's opinion in *Gratz v. Bollinger* (2003), striking down as unconstitutional the University of Michigan's undergraduate admissions system of awarding extra points to racial minorities. He dissented in the companion case of *Grutter v. Bollinger* (2003), wherein the Court allowed racial diversity to be considered as a factor in admission to law school at the University of Michigan.

In school desegregation cases, Rehnquist made it easier for formerly segregated schools systems to be released from supervision by federal courts. In *Dowell v. Board of Education of Oklahoma City Public Schools* (1991), he wrote the opinion of the Court noting that desegregation orders were not meant to operate in perpetuity, finding that in cases in which previously unlawfully segregated school systems had resegregated as the result of private residential housing patterns, federal trial courts should inquire as to whether the school boards complied in good faith with desegregation decrees and whether the vestiges of past discrimination had been eliminated to the extent practicable.

In *Missouri v. Jenkins* (1995), Rehnquist wrote for the majority in pointing out that the lower federal courts exceeded their authority by ordering salary increases for staff and funding for quality education programs for the district because student achievement was at or below national norms. Rehnquist reasoned that improved achievement on test scores was not required for the state to achieve unitary status. Since these factors were not the result of segregation, he did not think that they should have figured into the remedial calculus.

Gender Issues

Justice Rehnquist was reluctant to extend the constitutional guarantees of equal protection in gender discrimination cases. He dissented in *Craig v. Boren* (1976), wherein the Supreme Court invalidated a statute from Oklahoma requiring males to be 21 to purchase 3.2 beer but allowing females to purchase it at the age of 18. Rehnquist argued that traffic safety statistics provided a rational basis for the state legislation; he also questioned the basis for the Court's adoption of a new "midlevel" test as a standard of review in gender discrimination cases.

As chief justice, Rehnquist occasionally modified his views to build consensus, as exemplified by his vote in *United States v. Virginia* (1996) rejecting the state-funded Virginia Military Institute's policy of admitting male cadets only. Also, in cases involving statutory interpretation of laws enacted by Congress, he was more supportive of claims of gender discrimination. Writing for the Court in *Meritor Savings Bank v. Vinson* (1986), Rehnquist ruled that in the case in which a bank employee was subjected to repeated demands for sex and other forms of inappropriate sexual conduct by her supervisor, she stated a "hostile environment" claim under Title VII, even if she did not suffer an economic detriment.

Religious Freedom

One of the areas in which Justice Rehnquist brought about jurisprudential change was in First Amendment religion cases. An accommodationist, he believed that for years, the Supreme Court had erred in adhering to a policy of strict separation between church and state. In his dissenting opinion in *Wallace v. Jaffree* (1985), wherein the Court invalidated Alabama's moment of prayer or silent meditation statue, Rehnquist asserted that since its landmark ruling in *Everson v. Board of Education of Ewing Township* (1947), the Court had overly relied on Thomas Jefferson's metaphor of a "Wall of Separation" of church from state, incorrectly interpreting the "original intent" of the founders regarding what constituted an "establishment of religion." In Rehnquist's view, the First Amendment prohibited government creation of an "established church," or preference for one religion over another, but did not prevent government assistance to religion in general or favoring religion over nonreligion.

One of Rehnquist's first major victories in Establishment Clause jurisprudence was in *Mueller v. Allen* (1983). Writing for the Court, he upheld a statute from Minnesota that provided income tax reimbursements to parents for expenses incurred for tuition, texts, and transportation in sending their children to nonpublic or public schools. His philosophy, that government assistance to religious schools was constitutionally permissible if it only indirectly benefited religion or was the result of individual private choices, became the accepted view of a majority of the Court.

In *Zobrest v. Catalina Foothills School District* (1993), Rehnquist authored the opinion of the Court, acknowledging that government providing a sign language interpreter for a deaf student attending a religious school did not violate the Establishment Clause.

Perhaps the ultimate triumph for Rehnquist's philosophy came in the case of *Zelman v. Simmons-Harris* (2002), wherein he authored the Court's opinion upholding the constitutionality of a school voucher program from Cleveland, rejecting the argument that allowing public funds to directly fund religious schools violated the First Amendment.

Rehnquist also took an accommodationist position on issues regarding religious activities in public schools and access of religious groups to public facilities. He voted to uphold the constitutionality of granting equal access to public school facilities to noncurricular religious student organizations and by community church groups. In *Rosenberger v. Rector and Visitors of University of Virginia* (1995), Rehnquist joined the Court in agreeing that denying university student activity funds to support the printing of a Christian organization's newsletter violated freedom of speech.

Justice Rehnquist dissented in *Stone v. Graham* (1980), wherein the Supreme Court invalidated the posting of the Ten Commandments in public school classrooms. More recently, in the case of *Van Orden v. Perry* (2005), he authored the opinion of the Court upholding the public display of the Ten Commandments on Texas statehouse grounds as merely one of numerous monuments honoring the nation's and states' historical traditions. He dissented in the companion case, *McCreary County, Kentucky v. American Civil Liberties Union of Kentucky* (2005), wherein the Court invalidated the posting of the Ten Commandments at a county court house. Rehnquist also dissented in disputes over whether to allow prayer at public school graduation ceremonies (*Lee v. Weisman*, 1992) and at public-school-sponsored football games (*Santa Fe Independent School District v. Doe*, 2000).

In First Amendment free-exercise cases, Rehnquist often declined to support the rights of religious minorities. He joined the majority in *Employment Division, Department of Human Resources of Oregon v. Smith* (1990), denying an exemption to Native Americans to use peyote in religious ceremonies when a state law prohibiting its use was neutral on its face and of general applicability. However, as in his rulings in gender discrimination cases, he was more likely to find violations of religious freedom if the claims were based on federal statutes. For example, in a dispute involving granting school leave to fulfill a teacher's religious obligations, *Ansonia Board of Education v. Philbrook* (1986), Rehnquist authored the Court's opinion interpreting Title VII as requiring employers to make reasonable accommodations to meet the religious needs of their staff.

Student Issues

In students' right cases, Rehnquist generally sided with school officials. He voted to uphold random drug testing of student athletes and participants in extracurricular activities in *Vernonia School District 47J v. Acton* (1995) and *Board of Education of Independent School District No. 92 of Pottawatomie County v. Earls* (2002). He also supported restrictions on student speech that was vulgar but not obscene and speech that was part of school-sponsored expressive activities in *Bethel School District No. 403 v. Fraser* (1986).

One of the most important opinions written by Justice Rehnquist, though not directly a school law case but one that has had tremendous impact on education law, was *DeShaney v. Winnebago Department of Social Services* (1989). In finding that employees of a state family services agency owed no constitutional duty to a minor to protect him from injury while in the custody of an abusive father, the Court established the principle that the state has no constitutional obligation to protect its citizens from assaults by fellow citizens. Other courts have relied on this precedent in ruling that school boards have as a general rule no constitutional duty to protect students from harm by other students.

Teacher Issues

In the area of employment law, Justice Rehnquist's rulings made it more difficult for teachers and administrators to assert their First and Fourteenth Amendment rights to freedom of speech and protection of procedural due process. In *Mt. Healthy City School District Board of Education v. Doyle* (1977), Rehnquist wrote the majority opinion of the Court establishing the standard of review for "mixed-motive" cases involving termination of employment or nonrenewal of contracts. In cases in which protected conduct, such as the exercise of freedom of speech, is shown to be a substantial or motivating factor in the school board's decision, the Court pointed out that school boards must be given the opportunity to demonstrate that they would have reached the same employment decision in the absence of the protected conduct.

Justice Rehnquist had a mixed record in cases dealing with the law of special education. In the first Supreme Court case interpreting the meaning of a "free appropriate public education," *Board of Education of Hendrick Hudson Central School District v. Rowley* (1982), Rehnquist authored the opinion of the Court giving the phrase a limited interpretation. Rejecting the plaintiff's contention that federal special education law mandated the school board provide a student who was deaf with a sign language interpreter, Rehnquist decided that the law did not require such children to receive special services sufficient to maximize the child's education to a level commensurate with those of peers who were not disabled. Instead, he explained that a program must only confer "some educational benefit" on students. On the other hand, in *Burlington School Committee v. Department of Education, Commonwealth of Massachusetts* (1985), Rehnquist wrote the Court's opinion asserting that parents who disagree with the placement of their children may enroll them in private schools and recover the costs of tuition if they can show that school officials failed to provide appropriate placements and their chosen nonpublic school placements were appropriate.

Legacy

In his last years on the Court, Rehnquist's health began to suffer. In October 2004, it was publicly announced that he was diagnosed with thyroid cancer. In the next few months, his condition deteriorated, and although he still participated in some decisions, he missed most oral arguments. Rumors circulated about his impending retirement, especially after the resignation of his colleague Sandra Day O'Connor. On September 3, 2005, Rehnquist died, just short of his 81st birthday.

During his tenure on the Supreme Court, Chief Justice Rehnquist had a major impact on the field of education law. He was an incrementalist, not a revolutionary. While liberals criticize many of his opinions as overly restrictive as to the civil rights of minorities, students, and teachers, the Rehnquist Court did not completely roll back precedents established by the Warren and Burger courts. For example, school-sponsored prayer is still prohibited, and race may be considered as a factor in school admissions. Even though the powers of Congress under the Commerce Clause have been restricted, the authority of the federal government to regulate education is still great.

Even so, significant changes in education law have occurred. School boards may not engage in de jure segregation, but it is easier for them to be released from federal court supervision. The constitutional standard in "reverse discrimination" cases has been heightened, whereas the standard in free exercise cases has been lowered. Student free speech is still protected, but major exceptions have emerged. State aid to religiously affiliated nonpublic schools is more acceptable, and access by religious organizations to public institutions is more readily granted. Chief Justice Rehnquist brought about conservative change, but he did not usher in a whole new conservative era.

Michael Yates

See also Burger Court; Free Appropriate Public Education; Rehnquist Court; Segregation, De Facto; Segregation, De Jure; Tuition Tax Credits; U.S. Supreme Court Cases in Education; Vouchers; Warren Court

Further Readings

Hudson, D. (2006). *The Rehnquist Court: Understanding its impact and legacy.* Westport, CT: Praeger.

Tushnet, M. (2005). *A court divided: the Rehnquist Court and the future of constitutional law.* New York: Norton.

Legal Citations

Ansonia Board of Education v. Philbrook, 479 U.S. 60 (1986).

Bethel School District No. 403 v. Fraser, 478 U.S. 675 (1986).

Board of Education of Hendrick Hudson Central School District v. Rowley, 458 U.S. 176 (1982).

Board of Education of Independent School District No. 92 of Pottawatomie County v. Earls, 536 U.S. 822 (2002), *on remand*, 300 F.3d 1222 (10th Cir. 2002).

Burlington School Committee v. Department of Education, Commonwealth of Massachusetts, 471 U.S. 359 (1985).

City of Richmond v. J. A. Croson Company, 488 U.S. 469 (1989).

Craig v. Boren, 429 U.S. 190 (1976).

DeShaney v. Winnebago Department of Social Services, 489 U.S. 189 (1989).

Dowell v. Board of Education of Oklahoma City Public Schools, 498 U.S. 237 (1991), *on remand*, 778 F. Supp. 1144 (W.D. Okla. 1991), *aff'd*, 8 F.3d 1501 (10th Cir. 1993).

Employment Division, Department of Human Resources of Oregon v. Smith, 494 U.S. 872 (1990).

Everson v. Board of Education of Ewing Township, 330 U.S. 1 (1947), *reh'g denied*, 338 U.S. 855 (1947).

Gratz v. Bollinger, 539 U.S. 244 (2003).

Grutter v. Bollinger, 539 U.S. 306 (2003).

Lee v. Weisman, 505 U.S. 577 (1992).

McCreary County, Kentucky v. American Civil Liberties Union of Kentucky, 545 U.S. 844 (2005).

Meritor Savings Bank v. Vinson, 477 U.S. 57 (1986).

Missouri v. Jenkins, 515 U.S. 70 (1995).

Mueller v. Allen, 463 U.S. 388 (1983).

Mt. Healthy City School District Board of Education v. Doyle, 429 U.S. 274 (1977), *on remand*, *Doyle v. Mt. Healthy City School District Board of Education*, 670 F.2d 59 (6th Cir. 1982).

National League of Cities v. Usery, 426 U.S. 833 (1976).

Rosenberger v. Rector and Visitors of University of Virginia, 515 U.S. 819 (1995).

Santa Fe Independent School District v. Doe, 530 U.S. 290 (2000).

Stone v. Graham, 449 U.S. 39 (1980), *reh'g denied*, 449 U.S. 1104 (1981), *on remand*, 612 S.W.2d 133 (Ky. 1981).

United States v. Lopez, 514 U.S. 549 (1995).

United States v. Virginia, 518 U.S. 515 (1996).

Van Orden v. Perry, 545 U.S. 677 (2005).

Vernonia School District 47J v. Acton, 515 U.S. 646 (1995), *on remand*, 66 F.3d 217 (9th Cir. 1995).

Wallace v. Jaffree, 472 U.S. 38 (1985).

Zelman v. Simmons-Harris, 536 U.S. 639 (2002).

Zobrest v. Catalina Foothills School District, 509 U.S. 1 (1993).

REHNQUIST COURT

The term *Rehnquist Court* refers to the period from October 1986 to June 2005, when William H. Rehnquist served as chief justice. During this period, the U.S. Supreme Court was sharply divided along liberal and conservative lines. Between October 1986 and October 1991, the Court arguably had a liberal majority. From October 1991 until June 2005, the Court arguably had a conservative majority. However, during both of these eras, there were numerous circumstances in which one or more justices switched sides and rendered liberal or conservative opinions. Insofar as the Court was sharply divided and some justices had a tendency to "swing," it was difficult for the Court to reach clear and logical decisions. Thus, the Rehnquist Court's jurisprudence, particularly during its last 5 years, could be characterized as embodying "split the difference" jurisprudence.

Legacy on Federalism

Despite the ambiguity of the Rehnquist Court's decisions, it did leave a significant legacy in one area, federalism. Prior to the Rehnquist Court, the principles of federalism, which is more appropriately called "dual sovereignty," were largely useless as a limitation on the powers of the national government. Change began to emerge with *Gregory v. Ashcroft* (1991), wherein the Court held that the states could impose mandatory retirement on state judges. A year later, in *New York v. United States* (1992), the Court ruled that Congress could not compel the states to enact specific legislation. Similarly, in *Printz v. United States* (1997), the Court found that Congress could not compel state officials to enforce federal law.

Beginning with *Seminole Tribe of Florida v. Florida* (1996) and extending through a series of other cases, the Court limited the power of Congress to abrogate the states' sovereign immunity, a development that is particularly important to states' litigation strategies. However, the more significant federalism cases were those that limited the power of Congress over interstate commerce, *United States v. Lopez* (1995) and *United States v. Morrison* (2000), and those that limit the power of Congress to enforce the Fourteenth Amendment, *City of Boerne v. Flores* (1997) and *Morrison.*

Legacy on Education

The Rehnquist Court's legacy for education law is also significant. As with its jurisprudence in other areas, the Supreme Court largely "split the difference" in cases involving education law.

On Race

First, the Court pursued a "split the difference" approach to race. Most obviously in the University of Michigan racial preference cases, *Grutter v. Bollinger* (2003) and *Gratz v. Bollinger* (2003), the Court, respectively, upheld the law school admissions system, which utilized race as one factor among many, but invalidated the undergraduate admissions system, which assigned a specific number of points based on race.

In doing so, the Court noted that the achievement of the educational benefits of a broadly defined diversity was a compelling governmental interest that might justify the use of race. At the same time, the Court emphasized that a system in which race was the determining factor was not narrowly tailored. The practical effect of these cases is that they have adopted the diversity rationale that Justice Powell presented in *Regents of the University of California v. Bakke* (1978). Yet the cases also impose significant limitations on how institutions may use race.

In like fashion, the Rehnquist Court steered a middle course with respect to desegregation. Although the Court did not end court-ordered busing, it did substantially limit the power of the lower courts to use it as a remedy. *Dowell v. Board of Education of Oklahoma City Public Schools* (1991) significantly narrowed the definition of a unitary school system, thereby making it substantially easier for boards to end federal court supervision. In *Freeman v. Pitts* (1992), the Court pointed out that there was no duty to remedy a racial imbalance that was caused by residential housing patterns rather than intentional discrimination by the school board; the Court added that districts can be declared unitary incrementally. Subsequently, in *Missouri v. Jenkins* (1995), the Court placed limits on the ability of trial courts to order broad remedies.

On Religion

Second, the Rehnquist Court followed a "split the difference" approach in religion cases involving education. On one hand, the Court upheld actions in which the government favored religion, at least indirectly. In *Zelman v. Simmons-Harris* (2002), the Court reasoned that Ohio could implement a school choice program wherein parents choose to send their children to religiously affiliated nonpublic schools at public expense. The Court's rationale here was similar to *Zobrest v. Catalina Foothills School District* (1993), wherein the justices decided that a student in a religious school was entitled to receive special education services at public expense. *Board of Education of Westside Community Schools v. Mergens* (1990), *Rosenberger v. Rector and Visitors of the University of Virginia* (1995), and *Good News Club v. Milford Central School* (2001) all agreed that student religious clubs must be treated the same as nonreligious clubs. Moreover, *Lamb's Chapel v. Center Moriches Union Free School District* (1993) ensured that outside religious groups had the same rights of access to school facilities as outside nonreligious groups.

On the other hand, the Rehnquist Court invalidated assistance to religion or religious expression. In *Lee v. Weisman* (1990), the Court rejected prayers by nonstudents at graduation ceremonies, while in *Santa Fe Independent School District v. Doe* (2000), it struck down the practice of prayer at the beginning of high school football games. Previously, in *Board of Education of Kiryas Joel Village School District v. Grumet* (1994), the Court had invalidated a school district that was drawn to benefit only a small religious sect.

On Sexual Harassment

Third, the Rehnquist Court displayed its "split the difference" rationale in school sexual harassment cases. After *Franklin v. Gwinnett County Public Schools* (1992) established that school boards were liable for damages for Title IX violations, *Gebser v. Lago Vista Independent School District* (1998) pointed out that boards could be liable when their employees sexually harassed students. Even so, the Court limited liability to those situations in which school officials actually knew of the misconduct and responded with deliberate indifference. As such, the Court charged a middle course between absolute liability (the position of the plaintiff) and no liability whatsoever (the position of the school

board). In *Davis v. Monroe County Board of Education* (1999), the Court essentially extended *Gebser* to sexual harassment in situations involving student-on-student harassment.

On Special Education

Fourth, the Rehnquist Court's special education decisions reflect an expansion of the rights of the disabled. *Honig v. Doe* (1988) established that school boards could not unilaterally expel or impose lengthy suspensions on students with disabilities if their misbehaviors were manifestations of their disabilities. In *Cedar Rapids Community School District v. Garret F.* (1999), the Court was of the opinion that school boards can be required to provide related services, such as the full-time care of nurses, for qualified students with disabilities. Previously, in *School Board of Nassau County, Florida v. Arline* (1987), the Court had required school board officials to accommodate the needs of teachers with disabilities.

On Student Rights

Finally, although the Rehnquist Court refused to overturn the student rights that the justices recognized, starting in *Tinker v. Des Moines Independent Community School District* (1968) and *New Jersey v. T. L. O* (1985), it did impose significant limitations on those rights. In *Bethel School District No. 403 v. Fraser* (1986), the Court upheld the authority of school officials to discipline a student for a vulgar but not obscene speech that he delivered as part of school-sponsored expressive activities. Further, in *Hazelwood School District v. Kuhlmeier* (1988), the Court indicated that since student expression in school-sponsored publications was not absolute, it was subject to control by school officials whose actions were reasonably related to legitimate pedagogical concerns. Moreover, in *Vernonia School District No. 47J v. Acton* (1995), the Court held that student athletes could be subjected to random drug tests. The Court extended this holding in *Board of Education of Independent School District No. 92 of Pottawatomie County v. Earls* (2002).

William E. Thro

See also Burger Court; Federalism and the Tenth Amendment; Rehnquist, William H.; U.S. Supreme Court Cases in Education; Warren Court

Further Readings

Meers, E. B., & Thro, W. E. (2004). *Race conscious admissions and financial aid after the University of Michigan decisions.* Washington, DC: National Association of College and University Attorneys.

Thro, W. E. (2005). No direct consideration of race: The lessons of the University of Michigan decisions. *West's Education Law Reporter, 196,* 755–764.

Wilkinson, J. H., III. (2006). The Rehnquist Court at twilight: The lures and perils of split-the-difference jurisprudence. *Stanford Law Review, 58,* 1969–1996.

Legal Citations

Bethel School District No. 403 v. Fraser, 478 U.S. 675 (1986).

Board of Education of Independent School District No. 92 of Pottawatomie County v. Earls, 536 U.S. 822 (2002), *on remand*, 300 F.3d 1222 (10th Cir. 2002).

Board of Education of Kiryas Joel Village School District v. Grumet, 512 U.S. 687 (1994).

Board of Education of Westside Community Schools v. Mergens, 496 U.S. 226 (1990).

Cedar Rapids Community School District v. Garret F., 526 U.S. 66 (1999).

City of Boerne v. Flores, 521 U.S. 507 (1997).

Davis v. Monroe County Board of Education, 526 U.S. 629 (1999).

Dowell v. Board of Education of Oklahoma City Public Schools, 498 U.S. 237 (1991), *on remand*, 778 F. Supp. 1144 (W.D. Okla. 1991), *aff'd*, 8 F.3d 1501 (10th Cir. 1993).

Franklin v. Gwinnett County Public Schools, 503 U.S. 60 (1992).

Freeman v. Pitts, 503 U.S. 467 (1992).

Gebser v. Lago Vista Independent School District, 524 U.S. 274 (1998).

Good News Club v. Milford Central School, 533 U.S. 98 (2001).

Gratz v. Bollinger, 539 U.S. 244 (2003).

Gregory v. Ashcroft, 501 U.S. 452 (1991).

Grutter v. Bollinger, 539 U.S. 306 (2003).

Hazelwood School District v. Kuhlmeier, 484 U.S. 260 (1988).

Honig v. Doe, 484 U.S. 305 (1988).

Lamb's Chapel v. Center Moriches Union Free School District, 508 U.S. 384 (1993).

Lee v. Weisman, 505 U.S. 577 (1990).

Missouri v. Jenkins, 515 U.S. 70 (1995).

New Jersey v. T. L. O., 469 U.S. 325 (1985).

New York v. United States, 505 U.S. 144 (1992).

Printz v. United States, 521 U.S. 98 (1997).

Regents of the University of California v. Bakke, 438 U.S. 265 (1978).

Rosenberger v. Rector and Visitors of University of Virginia, 515 U.S. 819 (1995).

Santa Fe Independent School District v. Doe, 530 U.S. 290 (2000).

School Board of Nassau County, Florida v. Arline, 480 U.S. 273 (1987).

Seminole Tribe of Florida v. Florida, 517 U.S. 44 (1996).

Tinker v. Des Moines Independent Community School District, 393 U.S. 503 (1968).

United States v. Lopez, 514 U.S. 549 (1995).

United States v. Morrison, 529 598 U.S. (2000).

Vernonia School District No. 47J v. Acton, 515 U.S. 646 (1995).

Zelman v. Simmons-Harris, 536 U.S. 639 (2002).

Zobrest v. Catalina Foothills School District, 509 U.S. 1 (1993).

RELATED SERVICES

The Individuals with Disabilities Education Act (IDEA) requires states to provide related, or supportive, services through local school boards to students with disabilities to the extent that such children may need these services to benefit from their special education programs. In its definition of *related services,* the IDEA specifically lists developmental, supportive, and corrective services such as transportation, speech-language pathology, audiology, interpreting services, psychological services, physical therapy, occupational therapy, recreation (including therapeutic recreation), social work services, school nurse services, counseling services (including rehabilitation counseling), orientation and mobility services, and medical services (for diagnostic or evaluative purposes only) (20 U.S.C. § 1401(26)).

Since this list is not exhaustive, however, other unlisted services may be considered to be related services if they help students with disabilities to benefit from special education. Thus, services such as artistic and cultural program or art, music, and dance therapy could be related services under the appropriate circumstances. Related services may be provided by persons of varying professional backgrounds with a variety of occupational titles. The only limit placed on what school officials must provide as related services is that medical services are exempted unless they are specifically for diagnostic or evaluative purposes. The 2004 IDEA amendments clarified that related services do not include a medical device that is surgically implanted or the replacement of such a device.

Related services must be provided only to students who are receiving special education services. By definition, children have a disability under the IDEA only when they require special education services. Accordingly, there is no requirement to provide related services to students who are not receiving special education. On the other hand, inasmuch as many related services could qualify as accommodations under Section 504 of the Rehabilitation Act of 1973, it is not uncommon for school boards to provide these to students who are qualified to receive assistance under Section 504 but do not qualify for special education services under the IDEA. This entry looks at court rulings on two related services.

Health Services

One of the more controversial aspects of the IDEA's related services mandate, in part due to their cost, involves the extent to which school health services must be furnished. In one of its early special education cases, the U.S. Supreme Court in *Irving Independent School District v. Tatro* (1984) ruled that catheterization was a required related service. In this case, because the student could not voluntarily empty her bladder due to spina bifida, she had to be catheterized every 3 to 4 hours. The Court emphasized that services, such as catheterization, that allow a student to remain in class during the school day are no less related to the effort to educate than services that allow the student to reach, enter, or exit the school. Inasmuch as the catheterization procedure could be performed by a school nurse or trained health aide, the Court was convinced that Congress did not intend to exclude these services as medical services.

Tatro indicates that services that may be provided by school nurses, health aides, or even trained laypersons fall within the IDEA's mandated related-services provision. However, many students with disabilities have fragile medical conditions that require the presence of full-time nurses. A decade and a half after *Tatro,* in its second case dealing with the IDEA's related-services provision, the U.S. Supreme Court ruled in *Cedar Rapids Community School District v. Garret F.* (1999) that a school board was required to provide full-time nursing services for a student who was quadriplegic. The Court commented that although continuous services may be more costly and may require additional school personnel, this alone does not make them more medical. Stressing that cost was not a factor in the definition of related services, the Court insisted that even costly related services must be provided to help guarantee that students with significant medical needs are integrated into the public schools.

Transportation

In *Tatro,* the Supreme Court acknowledged that school health services may sometimes need to be provided for a student to be physically present in the classroom. It almost goes without saying that a student cannot benefit from educational programs if the student cannot get to school. Thus, school boards must provide special transportation arrangements for students who are unable to access standard transportation provisions. The term *transportation,* as used in the IDEA's regulations, encompasses travel to and from school, between schools, and around school buildings. Moreover, school boards must provide students with disabilities with specialized equipment, such as adapted buses, lifts, and ramps, if needed for transportation.

In an early case, the First Circuit maintained that transportation may encompass moving a student from a building to a vehicle (*Hurry v. Jones,* 1983, 1984). In this case, the student challenged the denial of his request for assistance in getting from his house to a school bus. When the student could not get to the vehicle without assistance, his father brought him to school for a time. When the father was unable to bring his son to school, the student was unable to attend classes. The situation was finally resolved, but the First Circuit awarded the parents compensation for their efforts in transporting him to school after insisting that transportation clearly was the responsibility of the school board.

In a similar situation, the federal trial court for the District of Columbia ordered the school board to provide an aide to convey a student from his apartment to the school bus (*District of Columbia v. Ramirez*, 2005). Even so, door-to-door transportation is required only when a student cannot get to school without such assistance (*Malehorn v. Hill City School District*, 1997).

Allan G. Osborne, Jr.

See also *Cedar Rapids Community School District v. Garret F.; Compensatory Services; Disabled Persons, Rights of; Irving Independent School District v. Tatro*

Legal Citations

Cedar Rapids Community School District v. Garret F., 526 U.S. 66 (1999).

District of Columbia v. Ramirez, 377 F. Supp.2d 63 (D.D.C. 2005).

Hurry v. Jones, 560 F. Supp. 500 (D.R.I. 1983), *aff'd in part, rev'd in part*, 734 F.2d 879 (1st Cir. 1984).

Individuals with Disabilities Education Act, 20 U.S.C. §§ 1400 *et seq.*

Irving Independent School District v. Tatro, 468 U.S. 883 (1984).

Malehorn v. Hill City School District, 987 F. Supp.2d 772 (D.S.D. 1997).

RELEASED TIME

School boards and state officials have attempted to devise plans to allow for the delivery of religious instructions to public school students during the academic day. According to the Rutherford Institute, 19 states have enacted statutes that allow released-time instruction off campus during the school day. This entry looks at case law related to this practice.

Supreme Court Cases

The Supreme Court of the United States first dealt with religious instruction in public schools in 1948, in *Illinois ex rel. McCollum v. Board of Education*. At issue was a board program that allowed religious instruction during the public school day. Under the program, Protestant, Catholic, and Jewish members of the community entered the schools to provide 30 minutes of religious instruction per week to lower-level students. Upper-level students received 45 minutes of instruction.

In addition, school officials kept attendance records on the students who attended the religious instruction classes with parental permission. Insofar as the program used school buildings and facilities and officials cooperated closely with the released-time program, the Supreme Court struck it down on the basis that the state's compulsory attendance law abetted the religious instruction. More specifically, the Court spoke of the need for the complete separation of church and state.

Fours years later, the Supreme Court addressed released time directly in *Zorach v. Clauson* (1952). In *Zorach*, the City of New York released students for religious instruction during the school day as long as their parents gave their permission. The religious school reported attendance to public school officials on a weekly basis. Unlike *McCollum*, the instruction was not conducted in public school classrooms, and no public funds were used to support the program. The Court found that this program did not amount to the establishment of religion because it accommodated the religious wishes of the parents. Since *Zorach*, courts have reached mixed results in cases involving released-time programs.

Other Rulings

The Supreme Court of Washington (*Perry v. School District No. 81, Spokane*, 1959) struck down a released-time program on the basis of the state constitution. The court was of the opinion that the program was unconstitutional because it allowed public funds to be used for religious purposes and public educational officials made announcements about it in school to captive student audiences.

In a case with a twist, a federal trial court in Virginia granted a temporary restraining order that essentially stopped a released-time program from operating (*Doe v. Shenandoah County School Board*, 1990). The court maintained that the program was unacceptable because its sponsors parked the school buses they owned and used for the instruction, which looked like the public school's buses, on or close to school premises and sought to enter the schools to solicit student participants.

On the other hand, the Fourth Circuit previously upheld a released-time program in Virginia (*Smith v. Smith*, 1975). In applying the tripartite *Lemon v. Kurtzman* (1971) test, the traditional standard in matters involving religion and public education, the court ruled that the program had the secular purpose of accommodating parental wishes, did not advance or inhibit religion, and did not create excessive entanglement because the involvement of school officials was minimal and passive.

In like fashion, the Tenth Circuit largely upheld a released-time program in Utah (*Lanner v. Wimmer,* 1981). The court was satisfied that although the program did not constitute a per se violation of the Establishment Clause, some aspects of it were unconstitutional. The court specified that the program had the secular purpose of accommodating parental wishes for such instruction and was not concerned with the fact that public school officials prepared and distributed standard attendance forms to the released-time programs. However, the court declared that there were entanglement problems with having the students return the attendance forms in their schools, along with requiring educators in the public schools to evaluate what content was religious and what was secular in order to grant academic credit.

Most recently, the Second Circuit upheld a released-time program from New York in *Pierce ex rel. Pierce v. Sullivan West Central School District* (2004). The court affirmed that the program was constitutional insofar as it did not use public funds or on-site religious instruction and was voluntary and that school officials did not apply any coercion or pressure on students to participate

J. Patrick Mahon

See also *Illinois ex rel. McCollum v. Board of Education; Lemon v. Kurtzman;* Religious Activities in Public Schools; *Zorach v. Clauson*

Further Readings

The Rutherford Institute. (n.d.). *Released-time programs.* Retrieved December 5, 2006, from http://www.rutherford .org/resources/briefs/B26-ReleaseTime.pdf

Legal Citations

Doe v. Shenandoah County School Board, 737 F. Supp. 913 (W.D. Va. 1990).

Illinois ex rel. McCollum v. Board of Education, 333 U.S. 203 (1948).

Lanner v. Wimmer, 662 F.2d 1349 (10th Cir. 1981).

Lemon v. Kurtzman, 403 U.S. 602 (1971).

Perry v. School District No. 81, Spokane, 344 P.2d 1036 (Wash. 1959).

Pierce ex rel. Pierce v. Sullivan West Central School District, 379 F.3d 56 (2d Cir. 2004).

Smith v. Smith, 523 F.2d 121 (4th Cir. 1975).

Zorach v. Clauson, 343 U.S. 306 (1952).

RELIGIOUS ACTIVITIES IN PUBLIC SCHOOLS

Over the past four decades, the U.S. Supreme Court has regularly addressed disputes governing religious activities in public schools. Although school prayer is the issue that has received the most attention, the Court's decisions in this area have also considered the allowable sources, methods, places, times, and content for the distribution of religious materials, as well as the permissible content of classroom assignments. Other cases have examined the development of school policies on the distribution of materials dealing with evolution and materials with religious content submitted by members of the larger community. This entry reviews the main cases in these areas and considers the responses that schools can make as a result of the Court's judgments.

Supreme Court Rulings on Prayer in Public Schools

In three separate opinions spanning 32 years, the Supreme Court struck down efforts by school boards to incorporate prayer into their schools or school events, in *Engel v. Vitale* (1962), *Lee v. Weisman* (1992), and *Santa Fe Independent School District v. Doe* (2000). Beyond that, the Court has addressed issues such as student-sponsored prayer clubs in school and access to school facilities by non-school groups (*Lamb's Chapel v. Center Moriches Union Free School District*, 1993; *Good News Club v. Milford Central Schools*, 2001), and such curricular issues as evolution (*Edwards v. Aguillard,* 1987; *Epperson v. State of Arkansas,* 1968). Lower federal courts have dealt with an array of similar issues. In light of the contentious relationship between prayer and religious activity in public schools, this entry examines the wide range of issues that have given rise to litigation over the past half century.

Decisions on Prayer in Schools

Engel v. Vitale

In *Engel,* the Supreme Court invalidated a directive of the Board of Education of Union Free School District No. 9, New Hyde Park, New York, to a principal that the following voluntary prayer to be said aloud by each class in the presence of a teacher at the beginning of the school day: "Almighty God, we acknowledge our dependence upon Thee, and we beg Thy blessings upon us, our parents, our teachers and our Country" (*Engel,* p. 422). The Court observed that "neither the fact that the prayer may be denominationally neutral nor the fact that its observance on the part of the students is voluntary can serve to free it from the limitations of the Establishment Clause" (p. 430).

Lee v. Weisman

Thirty years later, in *Lee v. Weisman,* the Supreme Court addressed prayer at a middle school graduation that students were not required to attend. Invoking but not relying on the Establishment Clause principles from the *Lemon v. Kurtzman* (1971) test, the Court struck down a long-standing school practice of permitting a member of the clergy to deliver an invocation and benediction at school district graduations. The Court found that the middle school principal's involvement in the prayer was the same "as if a state statute decreed that the prayers must occur" (*Lee,* p. 587). The principal determined that prayer would be delivered at the graduation, the principal selected the clergy member to conduct the prayers, and the principal submitted to that person a set of guidelines for preparing a non-sectarian prayer. Although attendance at graduation was voluntary, the Court was of the opinion that since graduations are life-changing, family-celebratory events that are likely to be well attended, such prayer

carried "a particular risk of indirect coercion" and "a reasonable perception" that a "dissenter of high school age . . . is being forced by the State to pray in a manner her conscience will not allow" (p. 593).

Santa Fe Independent School District v. Doe

Eight years after *Lee,* in *Santa Fe Independent School District v. Doe* (2000), the Court invalidated a student-initiated and student-led prayer prior to high school football games in Texas. Invoking the coercion test from *Lee,* the Court in *Santa Fe* declared the school-authorized prayer was impermissibly coercive to cheerleaders, football players, and band members, for whom attendance prior to the start of the game was not voluntary. The Court broadly ruled that the policy violated the Establishment Clause insofar as the prayer took place on government property at a government-sponsored, school-related event and expressed the purpose of a school district policy encouraging selection of a religious message. The Court added that the policy was unacceptable because it was perceived as public expression of majority views delivered with the school board's approval.

Distribution of Religious Materials in Public Schools

Navigation of the shifting sands between what is prohibited by the Establishment Clause and what is required under the Free Speech Clause has not always been an easy journey for public school districts. Although the Supreme Court has recognized that public school endorsement of religion and religious messages is prohibited under the Establishment Clause, it has conceded that public school enablement of private speech is protected by the Free Speech Clause in the First Amendment. Distribution of materials in schools is an access issue and presents a variety of factual patterns involving the source of distribution, such as students or community organizations; the method of distribution, whether by hand or over school intercoms; the place of distribution, such as in classrooms or hallways; the time of distribution, whether during noninstructional or instructional time; and the content of distributed information as proselytizing or nonproselytizing.

Sources of Materials: Community Organizations and Students

The Supreme Court's decisions in *Lamb's Chapel* and *Good News Club* determined that community organizations had a right of access to public school facilities during nonschool hours as long as other non-religious groups were permitted to meet. However, neither *Lamb's Chapel* nor *Good News* addressed whether these organizations have a free speech right to distribute their information during school time. Over 30 years ago, in *Tinker v. Des Moines Independent Community School District* (1969), the Supreme Court ruled that students in public schools had private free speech expression rights in public schools. Yet similar to community organizations, *Tinker* did not consider the extent to which private speech included religious expression. In 1984, Congress gave students an added advantage under the Equal Access Act (EAA), which prohibited school districts with limited open forums from discriminating on the basis of "religious, political, philosophical, or other speech content" (EAA, 20 U.S.C. § 4071(a)). The result of the EAA is that while both community organizations and students have limited rights regarding access to public schools, the rights are not necessarily the same for both groups.

Methods of Distribution

The communication of religious information has been challenged involving a number of different forms of distribution. In *Child Fellowship of Maryland v. Montgomery County Public Schools* (2006), the Fourth Circuit held that an elementary school engaged in viewpoint discrimination when it refused to include Good News Club flyers as part of its "take-home flyer forum." The forum permitted governmental and non-profit organizations to submit their materials to the school, where they were placed in student packets to be collected by the students at the end of the school day and taken home to their parents. The Fourth Circuit reversed an earlier order that refused to grant the club's request for an injunction, while rejecting the board's rationale that it could refuse the club's nonproselytizing

flyers because its after-school meetings were proselytizing. In addition, the Fourth Circuit pointed out that including the nonproselytizing religious flyers in the take-home folders did not violate the Establishment Clause. In its analysis, the court relied on the position established in *Board of Education of Westside Community Schools v. Mergens* (1990). In *Mergens,* the Supreme Court noted that right of access under the EAA could include "access to the school newspaper, bulletin boards, the public address system, and the annual Club Fair" (p. 247). Consistent with *Mergens,* in *Prince v. Jacoby* (2002), the Ninth Circuit indicated that the EAA required a school board to provide a religious club equal access to its public address system in order to publicize its activities.

In *Child Evangelism Fellowship of New Jersey v. Stafford Township School District* (2004), the Third Circuit maintained that like other community groups, a Good News Club was entitled to distribute promotional material in elementary schools at back-to-school nights and to post materials on a school bulletin board. Insofar as school officials had no part in writing, paying for, producing, or approving the materials, the court explained that they constituted private speech and that educators could not regulate their content under the theory that they were part of the school's "pedagogical concerns" under *Hazelwood School District v. Kuhlmeier* (1988).

In *Rusk v. Clearview Local Schools* (2004), the Sixth Circuit reached a similar result to *Montgomery County* regarding the Establishment Clause and distribution of Good News Club flyers. The notable difference between *Montgomery County/Stafford* and *Rusk* is that Clearview Local Schools wanted to include the Good News Club flyers in student folders. As a result, the Sixth Circuit in *Rusk* court saw no need to address whether distribution was required under the Free Speech Clause.

A federal trial court in *Westfield High School L. I. F. E. Club v. City of Westfield* (2003) suggested the outer limits of free speech for students in elementary schools. In *Westfield,* the court pointed out that an elementary student could distribute candy canes with proselytizing religious messages as part of "private, school-tolerated speech" (p. 114). The result of this litigation suggests that student rights under free speech to distribute religious materials may be somewhat more extensive than for community organizations. The effect of enactment of the EAA by Congress has been to extend student rights of distribution of religious material to noninstructional time.

Places of Distribution

Courts have distinguished between classrooms and other locations within schools in terms of free speech rights. Generally, classrooms are reserved for curriculum-related information and are not accessible for distribution of materials by either students or community organizations (*Walz v. Egg Harbor Township Board of Education,* 2003). Distribution of materials in nonclassroom areas, such as hallways, depends on whether school officials created a limited public forum (*Hills v. Scottsdale Unified School District,* 2003) and whether the distribution is considered disruptive under *Tinker* (*Westfield,* p. 105). While school officials can engage in government speech without including other viewpoints, they may be subject to viewpoint discrimination analysis under free speech as long as they choose to permit views other than religious ones (*Hansen v. Ann Arbor Public Schools,* 2003).

Time of Distribution

Any right by students or community organizations to distribute materials applies to noninstructional time. The concept of noninstructional time owes its clearest definition to the EAA, which for schools that created limited open forums limit meeting times for student groups only to noninstructional time (EAA, 20 U.S.C. § 4071(b)). What constitutes "noninstructional time" under the EAA differs, with the Third Circuit holding in *Donovan v. Punxsutawney Area School Board* (2003) that an activity period during which noncurriculum-related clubs were permitted to meet was noninstructional even though attendance was taken. On the other hand, in *Prince v. Jacoby* (2002), the Ninth Circuit ruled that a meeting time at which attendance was taken could not be noninstructional under EAA, but could be a limited public forum under free speech. As such, the court decided that a religious

club could meet during a student/staff period because officials created a limited public forum in permitting other student groups to gather. Further, in *Ceniceros v. Board of Trustees* (1997), the Ninth Circuit interpreted noninstructional time under the EAA as applying to lunchtime.

Community organizations in such cases as *Montgomery County, Rusk,* and *Hills* have designated noninstructional time for purposes of distributing curriculum-related and noncurriculum-related materials as that time at the end of the instructional day but prior to dismissal. In all three cases (*Montgomery County, Rusk,* and *Hills*), the material included flyers or brochures for religious organizations. Similar to the reasoning in *Prince,* the courts in *Montgomery County* and *Hills* agreed that the end of the school day fell within free speech protection, even though still subject to compulsory attendance, since officials created a limited public forum by permitting distribution of nonreligious, noncurriculum-related materials.

Content of Materials

No court to date has protected the distribution of the proselytizing materials of community organizations. *Montgomery County* and *Rusk* upheld distribution of nonproselytizing materials, a result not dissimilar to high school graduation cases in which school officials required student religious messages to be nonproselytizing and nondenominational (*American Civil Liberties Union of New Jersey v. Black Horse Pike Regional Board of Education,* 1995). Courts have not been as restrictive for student distribution and have permitted distribution of materials with religious messages outside classrooms during noninstructional time, such as in hallways or at lunch, where educators created limited public forums for distribution of materials by other students, as in *Walz* and *Westfield.*

Constructing School-District Policies on Distribution of Religious Materials

School boards and educators must be aware that their policies will be reviewed under free speech. As such, public school boards have too often created policies or practices that do not treat religious materials the same way they treat nonreligious materials. As a result, courts tend to look with disfavor on policies that permit distribution of nonreligious materials but exclude those that are religious.

As reflected in the litigation on this contentious topic, past habits of treating religious access issues differently than access by other groups have been hard to break. School boards that seek to exclude only religious messages will find such practices challenged today. In *Montgomery County,* subsequent to the Fourth Circuit's decision requiring distribution of a religious community organization's flyers in student end-of-the-day packets, the school board voted to limit classroom distribution of materials to parent-teacher associations, government agencies, student groups, day care centers, nonprofit sports leagues, and the school system. The board claimed that this new policy was necessary to keep out proselytizing material. On appeal, the Fourth Circuit again maintained that this policy violated the free expression rights of Child Evangelism Fellowship (*Montgomery County,* 2006). Such methodical efforts to exclude all religious distribution could have an effect on other community organizations, such as the Scouts or 4-H Clubs, that could likewise be directly affected by a prohibition as well. Chief Justice Rehnquist in *Santa Fe Independent School District v. Doe* (2000) questioned whether such efforts to exclude religious influences "bristle with hostility to all things religious in public life" (*Santa Fe,* p. 318).

Evolution and the Public School Curriculum

The teaching of evolution in public schools has become a lightning rod in some states and school districts, galvanizing public opinion as to the appropriate approach to take in instructing students about the origin of life. Opposition to evolution has taken a number of forms, from imposing limitations on the instructional content about evolution to requiring that alternative theories be presented.

In the past several decades, a number of technical articles and books have challenged the creative power of Darwin's mutation/selection process (e.g., *Of Pandas and People: The Central Question of Biological Origins,* by Percival Davis and Dean H. Kenyon). Some

instructional content limitations included requiring that science teachers teach evolution as a theory only and inserting into science books written disclaimers emphasizing the theoretical nature of evolution. A more limited restriction on instruction has not restricted the teaching of evolution, but has permitted parents to remove their children from the portions of courses in which evolution is presented. The most persistent pressure has been to require alternative theories of origins of life when evolution is taught. Past debate centered on the teaching of creation science, and that theory still has its advocates, but the current popular alternative to evolution is "intelligent design" or, as it has been expressed in some cases, "divine design" (e.g., *The Design Inference: Eliminating Chance Through Small Probabilities,* by William Dembski). "Design theory" holds that intelligent causes rather than undirected natural causes best explain many features of living systems. During recent years, design theorists have developed both a general theory of design detection and many specific empirical arguments to support their views. (e.g., the article "Teaching the Origins Controversy: Science, or Religion, or Speech," by David DeWolf, Stephen Meyer, and Mark DeForest).

Supreme Court Guidelines on Teaching Evolution

The Supreme Court has twice entered the arena of state restrictions on the teaching of evolution. In *Epperson v. State of Arkansas* (1968), the Court invalidated two Arkansas statutes that prohibited and criminalized "the teaching in its public schools and universities of the theory that man evolved from other species of life" (p. 98). The Supreme Court of Arkansas, in a two-sentence opinion, had upheld the constitutionality of the statutes, declaring that "statutes pertaining to teaching of theory of evolution [are] constitutional exercise of state's powers to specify curriculum in public schools" (*Epperson,* p. 322). The Supreme Court reversed the state supreme court, finding a violation of the Establishment Clause because there can be no doubt that Arkansas sought to prevent teachers from discussing the theory of evolution insofar as it is contrary to the belief of some that the book of Genesis must be the exclusive source of doctrine as to the origin of man. In its analysis, the Supreme Court was unable to uncover any suggestion that Arkansas law may have been justified by considerations of state policy other than the religious views of some of its citizens.

It is worth noting in *Epperson* that, because the Court ruled that there was an Establishment Clause violation, it chose not to address the constitutional Liberty Clause rights of teachers and students "to engage in any of the common occupations of life and to acquire useful knowledge" (p. 107). Thus, it was left for the future as to whether a state's curricular choice regarding the teaching of evolution while not violating the Establishment Clause nonetheless might violate the Fourteenth Amendment's Due Process Clause as explicated by the Supreme Court in *Meyer v. Nebraska* (1923).

In a second decision 19 years later, *Edwards v. Aguillard* (1987), the Supreme Court struck down a Louisiana balanced-treatment statute that required that creation science be taught if evolution was taught in public schools. Even though, unlike *Epperson,* the Louisiana statute did not prohibit the teaching of evolution, the Court still determined that it facially violated the Establishment Clause. The Court in *Edwards* rejected the state's claim that "the purpose of the Act [was] to protect a legitimate secular interest, namely, academic freedom" (p. 581), observing that, instead,

> It is equally clear that requiring schools to teach creation science with evolution does not advance academic freedom. The act does not grant teachers a flexibility that they did not already possess to supplant the present science curriculum with the presentation of theories, besides evolution, about the origin of life. (p. 587)

The *Edwards* Court did not explicitly address whether public school teachers have academic freedom to teach differing theories of origins. Instead, the Court simply responded to the state's claim, namely, that if pursuance of academic freedom was its purpose, it failed to achieve that purpose because the statute had "a distinctly different purpose of discrediting evolution by counterbalancing its teaching at every turn with the teaching of creationism" (*Edwards,* p. 589). In sum, the Court concluded that the statute violated the Establishment Clause because it "require[d] either the banishment of the theory of evolution from public

school classrooms or the presentation of a religious viewpoint that rejects evolution in its entirety" (p. 596).

Against this Supreme Court less-than-clear backdrop, lower federal courts, state boards of education, and local school boards have been expected to determine how much constitutional latitude exists in teaching origins of life. Much of the debate regarding evolution has focused on creation science and the federal district court decision, *McLean v. Arkansas Board of Education* (1982), in which the Court maintained that a state statute requiring a balanced teaching of evolution and scientific creationism violated the Establishment Clause. More recently, a federal trial court invalidated an attempt by a local school board to include a statement to students that intelligent design is an alternative to evolution (*Kitzmiller v. Dover Area School District,* 2005). Yet even if religious-based alternative theories of origin were to escape Establishment Clause scrutiny, that clause is by nature permissive and not mandatory. As such, eluding an Establishment Clause proscription does not ensure a right to present alternative theories of origins as a matter of free speech.

The Supreme Court's opinions in *Lamb's Chapel* declared religious speech to be a fully protected subset of First-Amendment-protected speech. Even so, that protection has not readily extended into the classroom, in large part because of the Court's earlier ruling in *Hazelwood* (1988). In *Hazelwood,* the Court upheld a reasonableness standard for administrative control over curriculum. As a result, lower courts have sustained school board requirements that classroom teachers follow their curricular guidelines, even if it means instruction only in the naturalistic approach to evolution. Courts have been willing to accord constitutional protection to teachers for out-of-classroom remarks that affect instructional services being provided students. Still, courts are reluctant to grant free speech protection to teacher comments in classrooms, especially when those remarks might be associated with religious views about evolution.

Classroom Assignments and Student Religious Speech

Classrooms traditionally are nonpublic forums, meaning that limitations on speech are established by a reasonableness standard, as opposed to the strict scrutiny standard associated with speech in public or limited public forums. Until recently, the Sixth Circuit's opinion in Settle v. Dickson County School Board (1995) was a fairly accurate representation of the law of student expressive rights in the classroom. In Settle, the court upheld a teacher's rejection of a ninth-grade student's assignment to research and write on a topic that was "interesting, researchable and decent" and that required four sources (p. 153). When the teacher denied the student's request to write a biography of Jesus Christ, the teacher indicated that "deal[ing] with personal religious beliefs . . . is just not an appropriate thing to do in a public school" and that "the law says that we are not to deal with religious issues in the classroom, and that the only sources . . . documenting the life of Jesus Christ derive from one source, the Bible" (p. 154). Even though the teacher's reasoning was both legally and factually inaccurate, the court affirmed a grant of summary judgment in favor of the board, observing that "so long as the teacher violates no positive law or school policy, the teacher has broad authority to base her grades for students on her view of the merits of the students' work" (p. 155).

Referencing Hazelwood, in which the Supreme Court permitted school officials' exercise of "editorial control over the style and context of student speech in school-sponsored activities [school newspaper] so long as their actions are reasonably related to legitimate pedagogical concerns" (p. 273), the Sixth Circuit in Settle explained that "student speech may be even more circumscribed [in the classroom] than in the school newspaper or other open forum" (p. 155). The Court in Settle further noted in dictum as follows:

> So long as the teacher limits speech or grades speech in the classroom in the name of learning and not as a pretext for punishing the student for her race, gender, economic class, religion or political persuasion, the federal courts should not interfere. (p. 155)

Settle suggests that students have few, if any, protected rights associated with classroom assignments. Even so, one needs to consider whether Lamb's Chapel has changed that status for students. In Lamb's Chapel, the Supreme Court ruled that public school officials cannot prohibit religious viewpoints on subject matter as long as secular viewpoints have been permitted. While Lamb's Chapel did not involve a classroom, two post–Lamb's Chapel federal appellate cases, Peck v. Baldwinsville Central School District (2005) and C. H. v. Oliva (2000), suggest that the same reasoning could apply there as well.

Legal principles can be applied only to the facts before courts. As such, an understanding of the facts that generated particular principles is useful. Insofar as the protection of the free expressive rights of students in classrooms is an emerging concept with few relevant cases and since the impact of such rights on the operation of schools could be significant, an examination of the facts of Peck and C. H. is important.

Analysis of Peck

In Peck, the Second Circuit addressed a display of a kindergarten student's poster prepared as "an assignment in which students in the class were instructed to create a poster showing what they had learned about the environment [during a 2-month environmental unit]" (p. 617). To assist in preparing the posters, part of a larger end-of-school-year environmental program, the teacher sent two notes home to parents, the first informing them that "the children may use pictures or words, drawn or cut out of magazines or computer drawn by the children depicting ways to save our environment, i.e., pictures of the earth, water, recycling, trash trees, etc. This should be done by the student with your assistance" (p. 621). The second note notified parents that the posters would "be hung up at the [environmental] program. Ideas should involve ways to save our earth and it should be the child's work. Pictures drawn, cut out of magazines, or computer drawn are all great ideas" (p. 621).

The teacher, supported by the principal and superintendent, rejected the student's first poster submission replete with religious images because "she [the teacher] legally didn't think she could hang the poster for religious reasons, and because the poster didn't demonstrate Antonio's learning of the environmental lessons" (Peck, p. 622). The student's second poster depicted, on its left side, the same robed, praying figure pictured in the first poster. It also showed, in the center, a church with a cross. To the right of the church were pictures of people picking up trash and placing it in a recycling can; children holding hands encircling the globe; and clouds, trees, a squirrel, and grass.

The teacher and principal chose to display the second poster, with the "kneeling figure folded under," but when actually displayed, "both the kneeling figure and half of the church [were] folded under" (*Peck*, pp. 622, 623). Both the teacher and principal deposed that the kneeling figure had no relationship to the assignment and that the work conceptually was not that of the student. While the principal testified that he "did not object to [the poster] solely on its religious content," neither the principal nor the teacher had "asked [the student] to explain the relevance to the environmental unit of the images on either of his posters" (p. 623).

A federal trial court responded to the boy's mother's Free Speech and Establishment Clause claims by granting the school board's motion for summary judgment. In reversing the summary judgment motion and remanding for trial on the free speech claim, the Second Circuit noted that although the school was a nonpublic forum with respect to the creation and display of the posters as part of a curricular assignment, this did not end the free speech analysis. The court recognized that while *Hazelwood* requires only a reasonable relationship between a school's curricular actions and its pedagogical interests, the school still cannot engage in viewpoint discrimination. Thus, even as to "school-sponsored student speech," the court interpreted *Hazelwood* as meaning that "a manifestly viewpoint discriminatory restriction on school-sponsored speech is, prima facie, unconstitutional, even if reasonably related to legitimate pedagogical interests" (*Peck*, p. 633). Further, the appellate court affirmed dismissal of the establishment clause claim because of no evidence "demonstrat[ing] hostility toward religion" (p. 634). On remand, the trial court had to determine whether the school officials acted pursuant to a viewpoint-neutral reason in the display of the poster, such as the fact that it did not meet the requirements of the course or that not displaying the full poster was necessary so as not to violate the Establishment Clause.

Analysis of C. H.

The Third Circuit in *C. H.* dealt with a set of facts similar to *Peck*. A kindergarten student responded to

a teacher's assignment near Thanksgiving Day "to make posters depicting what they [the students] were 'thankful for'" by producing a poster "indicating that he was thankful for Jesus" (*C. H.*, p. 201). The poster was placed on the wall of a hallway, was removed the following day, when the teacher was absent from school, by unknown school employees "because of the poster's religious theme," and was replaced by the teacher on her return but "at a less prominent location at the end of said hallway" (p. 201).

C. H.'s mother sued, alleging a free speech violation for both the removal and the less prominent display of the poster. In a case resolved on the pleadings, the federal trial court found that since the school and the classroom were nonpublic forums, pursuant to *Hazelwood*, educators could impose content-based restrictions on speech that it needed only to be reasonable in light of the purpose served by the forum and viewpoint neutral. The Third Circuit, in an evenly divided en banc judgment, affirmed with a vigorous dissent by then-judge and now Supreme Court Associate Justice Samuel Alito. Given his new prominence on the Supreme Court, his comments regarding the interface of *Hazelwood* and free speech, and the possibility that a case raising a set of facts similar to *Peck* or *C. H.* may reach the Court, a brief examination of his reasoning is useful. In addressing the merits of plaintiff's claim in *C. H.*, Justice Alito held as follows:

> Public school students have the right to express religious views in class discussion or in assigned work, provided that their expression falls within the scope of the discussion or the assignment and provided that the school's restriction on expression does not satisfy strict scrutiny. (p. 210)

According to Alito, this standard of strict scrutiny would have applied even in a nonpublic forum. Insofar as the subject of the student's poster in *C. H.* fell within the assignment, namely, something that the student was thankful for, removal and then less favorable placement constituted impermissible viewpoint discrimination unless school officials "[could] show that allowing [the student's] poster to be displayed with his classmates' on a non-discriminatory basis" would have "materially disrupt[ed] classwork or involve[d] substantial disorder or invasion of the rights of other [students]" (*C. H.,* p. 212). School officials made no such showing in their pleadings. In addition, the board had no compelling interest under the Establishment Clause because "the Establishment Clause is not violated when the government treats religious speech and other speech equally and a reasonable observer would not view the government practice as endorsing religion" (p. 212). Even had any danger existed that someone might have reasonably interpreted the display of the student's poster as seeking to constitute "an effort by the school to endorse Christianity or religion, the school could have posted a sign explaining that the children themselves had decided what to draw" (p. 213).

The Second Circuit's decision in *Peck* and Justice Alito's dissent in *C. H.* raised the bar in terms of viewpoint discrimination in public schools. The notion that teachers and school boards may be liable for expressive speech in student assignments may be alarming when one considers the number of assignments that elementary teachers make in the course of a school year. Clearly, not all assignments raise expressive issues, but some probably will.

Practical Suggestions for Public School Teachers

1. Teachers have the authority to specify both the subjects that students may discuss and that their assignments be limited to material covered in class. Thus, if teachers ask students to solve problems in mathematics or to write essays on great American poets, they clearly do not have a right to speak or write about the Bible instead.

2. Teachers can prohibit students from expressing religious viewpoints in their assignments but must also exclude secular viewpoints. The difficulty in excluding religious content is that teachers may find themselves mired in factual dilemmas as to the treatment of secular topics. While teachers can prohibit students from offering their personal opinions as part of written assignments, they need to be aware that student expression can occur, as in *C. H.* and *Peck,* through symbols. Prohibiting religious content up front can be problematic if doing so is later used to demonstrate viewpoint discrimination.

3. Teachers can limit student work to the material taught in class, while asking students to explain the relevance of their assignments to course content.

Thus, in *Peck,* the teacher and principal prolonged a controversy that should not have had to be remanded by failing to ask the student how the robed figure and church related to course content. Of course, the teachers would have to demonstrate their experience of, or at least commitment to, making the same inquiry regarding nonreligious content.

4. Teachers may enforce viewpoint-neutral rules on matters such as the length of oral presentations or written assignments. If papers are limited to 20 pages, educators may insist that all students, including any who wish to express religious viewpoints, adhere to that rule.

5. Teachers can to some extent change assignments if they consider students' religious viewpoints offensive. Absent proof of disruption under *Tinker,* religious viewpoints that teachers consider personally offensive are not a basis for differential treatment. However, teachers can treat all student submissions in the same way. In other words, if the teacher and principal in *Peck* thought that the religious symbols were offensive, they could have changed the directions on the assignment and refused to post any student displays. Whatever public relations problems that such an approach may create, it avoids a problem with viewpoint discrimination.

6. If teachers and/or principals are concerned about the public's response to religious viewpoints on displayed student work, they can post signs stating that the work represents the viewpoints and interpretation of the students, not the school.

Solicitations of Community Expression on Public School Premises

When school board officials invite members of the public to present personal messages to be displayed on school premises, they thereby invite legal scrutiny on the criteria for message content and the steps that they will take to enforce their standards. Not surprisingly, litigation has arisen over whether individuals can place religious messages on tiles or bricks that are located on the grounds of public schools.

Opposing Religious Content

The most prominent of the cases is *Fleming v. Jefferson County School District* (2002), in which the school board decided to reopen Columbine High

School, in Colorado, in the fall of 1999 following the shooting of 12 students and one teacher that April. To assist the community healing process, the school board invited a group of persons, including family members of the victims, to paint 4″ x 4″ tiles that would be displayed in the high school halls. In the directions they distributed, school officials indicated that "religious symbols" were not permitted. When officials refused to display titles with religious messages painted by one of the parents of a victim, such as "Jesus Christ is Lord," they unsuccessfully sued, alleging violations of their right to free speech.

On further review, the Tenth Circuit upheld the school board's ban on religious messages, finding that the tile painting and display constituted school-sponsored speech within a nonpublic forum for purposes of free speech. Relying extensively on *Hazelwood,* the court determined that the board's extending the painting of tiles to community members had not affected the nature of the forum or its pedagogical interest in "disassociating itself from speech inconsistent with its educational mission" (*Fleming,* p. 931). When a school board's own speech is at stake, the court maintained that "viewpoint neutrality is neither necessary nor appropriate, as the school is . . . responsible for determining the content of education it provides" (p. 927).

Supporting Religious Content

In contrast, two federal trial courts, *Seidman v. Paradise Valley Unified School District* (2004) and *Demmon v. Loudon County Public Schools* (2004), rejected the Tenth Circuit's analysis and the claims of school officials who refused to allow religious messages on tiles and bricks. In *Seidman,* officials at an elementary school encouraged parents to purchase 4" × 8" tiles on which to "immortalize their child or family" with no limitation on religious content. After officials rejected parent inscriptions such as "God Bless Haley" because they were concerned about separation of church and state, the parents successfully sued the school board. A federal trial court held that the parents' messages clearly fit within the criteria of "love, praise, encouragement, and recognition of students" (*Seidman,* pp. 1110–1111) and that no reasonable person would have thought that the school was sponsoring religion.

In fact, the court concluded that the rejection of the religious message constituted viewpoint discrimination in violation of the parents' rights to free speech. Another federal trial court in *Demmon* reached a similar result regarding the sale of bricks for a path near the entrance to a high school. Parents wished to place a Latin cross on their brick. After officials withdrew the cross as an acceptable symbol, the court ruled in favor of the parents in rejecting the school's claim that the bricks were school sponsored and that controlling their content amounted to a valid pedagogical interest under *Hazelwood.* As in *Seidman,* the *Demmon* court determined that school officials engaged in impermissible viewpoint discrimination.

Options for School Districts

Encouraging members of the community to submit messages for display on school premises can be fraught with problems. School officials basically have three options available:

Option 1: Permit no personal expression and limit comments to prepared words, for example, "John/Mary Doe, 2007."

Option 2: Permit no religious expression but face the possibility of lawsuits for viewpoint discrimination.

Option 3: Prohibit only those messages that disrupt or threaten to disrupt a school's educational function, thereby facially eliminating whether the content of a message is religious.

Ralph D. Mawdsley

See also *Board of Education of Westside Community Schools v. Mergens; Edwards v. Aguillard; Engel v. Vitale; Epperson v. State of Arkansas; Good News Club v. Milford Central School; Hazelwood School District v. Kuhlmeier; Lamb's Chapel v. Center Moriches Union Free School District; Lee v. Weisman; Lemon v. Kurtzman, Santa Fe Independent School District v. Doe; Tinker v. Des Moines Independent Community School District*

Further Readings

Davis, P., & Kenyon, D. H. (1993). *Of pandas and people: The central question of biological origins* (2nd ed.). Dallas, TX: Haughton.

Dembski, W. (1998). *The design inference: Eliminating chance through small probabilities.* New York: Cambridge University Press.

DeWolf, D., Meyer, S., & DeForest, M. (2000). Teaching the origins controversy: Science, or religion, or speech? *Utah Law Review, 39,* 59–66.

Mawdsley, R. D., & Russo, C. J. (1996). Religious expression and teacher control of the classroom: A new battleground for free speech. *West's Education Law Reporter, 107,* 1–14.

Legal Citations

American Civil Liberties Union of New Jersey v. Black Horse Pike Regional Board of Education, 84 F.3d 1471 (3d Cir. 1995).

Board of Education of Westside Community Schools v. Mergens, 496 U.S. 226 (1990).

Ceniceros v. Board of Trustees, 106 F.3d 878 (9th Cir. 1997).

C. H. v. Oliva, 226 F.3d 198 (3d Cir. 2000).

Child Evangelism Fellowship of Maryland, Inc. v. Montgomery County Public Schools, 457 F.3d 376 (4th Cir. 2006).

Child Evangelism Fellowship of New Jersey v. Stafford Township School District, 386 F.3d 514 (3d Cir. 2004).

Demmon v. Loudon County Public Schools, 342 F. Supp. 2d 474 (E.D. Va. 2004).

Donovan v. Punxsutawney Area School Board, 336 F.3d 211 (3d Cir. 2003).

Edwards v. Aguillard, 482 U.S. 578 (1987).

Engel v. Vitale, 370 U.S. 421 (1962).

Epperson v. State of Arkansas, 393 U.S. 97 (1968).

Equal Access Act, 20 U.S.C. §§ 4071 *et seq.*

Fleming v. Jefferson County School District, 298 F.3d 918 (10th Cir. 2002).

Good News Club v. Milford Central Schools, 533 U.S. 98 (2001).

Hansen v. Ann Arbor Public Schools, 293 F. Supp.2d 780 (E.D. Mich. 2003).

Hazelwood School District v. Kuhlmeier, 484 U.S. 260 (1988).

Hills v. Scottsdale Unified School District, 329 F.3d 1044 (9th Cir. 2003).

Kitzmiller v. Dover Area School District, 400 F. Supp.2d 707 (M.D. Pa. 2005).

Lamb's Chapel v. Center Moriches Union Free School District, 508 U.S. 384 (1993).

Lee v. Weisman, 505 U.S. 577 (1992).

Lemon v. Kurtzman, 403 U.S. 602 (1971).

McLean v. Arkansas Board of Education, 529 F. Supp. 1255 (E.D. Ark. 1982).

Meyer v. Nebraska, 187 N.W. 100 (1922), 262 U.S. 390 (1923).

Peck v. Baldwinsville Central School District, 426 F.3d 617 (2d Cir. 2005).

Prince v. Jacoby, 303 F.3d 1074 (9th Cir. 2002).

Rusk v. Clearview Local Schools, 379 F.3d 418 (4th Cir. 2004).

Santa Fe Independent School District v. Doe, 530 U.S. 290 (2000).

Seidman v. Paradise Valley Unified School District, 327 F. Supp. 2d 1098 (D. Ariz. 2004).

Settle v. Dickson County School Board, 532 F.3d 152 (6th Cir. 1995).

State of Arkansas v. Epperson, 416 S.W.2d 322 (Ark. 1967).

Tinker v. Des Moines Independent Community School District, 393 U.S. 503 (1969).

Walz v. Egg Harbor Township Board of Education, 342 F.3d 271 (3d Cir. 2003).

Westfield High School L. I. F. E. Club v. City of Westfield, 249 F. Supp. 2d 98 (D. Mass. 2003).

RELIGIOUS FREEDOM RESTORATION ACT

The Religious Freedom Restoration Act (RFRA), in its original and amended versions, represents Congress's side of an exchange with the U.S. Supreme Court on the issue of state interference with individual religious practice. The RFRA was an attempt to ameliorate a ruling of the Court that came down on the side of the state in such conflicts. This entry summarizes that dialogue.

The Original Law and Response

Congress enacted the RFRA in 1993 in response to the Supreme Court's decision in *Employment Division, Department of Human Resources v. Smith* (1990). In that case, the Court held that people could no longer seek exemption from neutral, generally applicable laws on the grounds that those laws violated their First Amendment rights. Congress pointed out that "laws 'neutral' toward religion may burden religious exercise as surely as laws intended to interfere with religious exercise" (RFRA, § 2000bb(a)(2)).

In enacting the RFRA, Congress identified two purposes: restoration "of the compelling interest test as set forth in *Sherbert v. Verner* (1963) and *Wisconsin v. Yoder*" (1972); and provision of "a claim or defense to persons whose religious exercise is substantially burdened by government" (RFRA, § 2000bb(b)).

Congress allowed government to substantially burden a person's exercise of religion only if it demonstrated that the burden was "(1) in furtherance of a compelling governmental interest; and (2) [was] the least restrictive means of furthering that compelling governmental interest" (RFRA, § 2000bb-1(b)). The RFRA specifically directs that the statute not be applied to alleged violations of the Establishment Clause, declaring that "granting government funding, benefits, or exemptions, to the extent permissible under the Establishment Clause, shall not constitute a violation of this chapter" (RFRA, § 2000bb-4)).

In *City of Boerne v. Flores* (1997), the Supreme Court struck down the RFRA as applied to a city zoning ordinance in Texas as interfering with the constitutional relationship between federal and state governments. In invalidating RFRA as applied to states, the Court observed that the law's impact on the states, in terms of both a heavy litigation burden and restrictions on its traditional regulatory power, "far exceed[s] any pattern or practice of unconstitutional conduct under the Free Exercise Clause as interpreted in [*Employment Division*]" (*City of Boerne,* p. 534).

While the Court acknowledged that Congress has authority under Section 5 of the Fourteenth Amendment to legislate rights protected under the Fourteenth Amendment, it added that Congress may not do so in a manner that "pervasively prohibits constitutional state action in an effort to remedy or to prevent unconstitutional state action" (*City of Boerne,* p. 533).

The Revised Law and Response

In response to *City of Boerne,* Congress amended the RFRA in 2000 by limiting the application of the RFRA enacted in 1997 to only the federal government (RFRA, § 2000bb-2(1)). Congress also added a new statute, Religious Land Use and Institutionalized Persons Act (RLUIPA), which although not technically an amendment to RFRA, immediately follows RFRA in the federal code and applies the same principles of RFRA to local, state, and federal governments. RLUIPA prohibits any government from imposing or implementing a land use regulation that treats a religious assembly or institution any differently from nonreligious ones or from discriminating against a religious assembly or institution (RLUIPA, § 2000cc(b)).

RLUIPA, unlike RFRA, is grounded in Congress's spending power and prohibits government at any level from "impos[ing] a substantial burden on the religious exercise of a person . . . in a program or activity that receives Federal financial assistance" (RLUIPA, § 2000cc(1) and (2)). In addition, RLUIPA prohibits a substantial burden on religious exercise that affects interstate commerce (RLUIPA, § 2000cc(2)(b)). RLUIPA imposes on all levels of government the same "compelling government interest" and "least restrictive means" tests required under RFRA (20 U.S.C. § 2000cc(a)(1)).

Following Congress's 2000 amendment to RFRA, the Supreme Court has not addressed another challenge to the statute. However, in *Hankins v. Lyght* (2006), the Second Circuit upheld the constitutionality of the statute against a separation-of-powers claim that Congress had imposed greater protection from federal actors and statutes than was required by the Supreme Court. The Second Circuit pointed out that "Congress can provide more individual liberties in the federal realm than the Constitution requires without violating vital separation of powers principles" (p. 107).

Hankins is an interesting case because although the Second Circuit remanded the case to a federal district court for trial, the appellate panel indicated that RFRA could serve as a church's defense against a former bishop's Age Discrimination Employment Act (ADEA) claim that he had been compelled by the church to retire at age 70; this was a somewhat extraordinary position, since the RFRA protects against federal, not individual, actions. In a more recent case involving the federal government and a more contemporary issue, the District of Columbia Circuit in *Holy Land Foundation for Relief and Development v. Ashcroft* (2003) found no violation of RFRA in the Department of the Treasury's designation of the Holy Land Foundation for Relief and Development as a Specially Designated Global Terrorist.

In another case involving the federal government, in *O'Bryan v. Bureau of Prisons* (2003), the Seventh Circuit decided that since the RFRA applied to Bureau of Prison personnel, it governed a federal prison inmate's action challenging the bureau's rule against "casting of spells/curses" that effectively prohibited the inmate from practicing his Wiccan religion. *O'Bryan* is a useful case because it clarified the Supreme Court's decision in *City of Boerne.* The Seventh Circuit noted in *O'Bryan* that the Supreme Court in *City of Boerne* had not declared the RFRA to have violated any substantive constitutional right. Rather, the RFRA "permit[ted] Congress to determine how the national government will conduct its own affairs" but offered no "source of authority to apply the RFRA to state and local governments" (*O'Bryan,* p. 401), including public schools.

Ralph D. Mawdsley

See also *City of Bourne v. Flores; Wisconsin v. Yoder*

Legal Citations

Age Discrimination Employment Act, 29 U.S.C. § 621.
City of Boerne v. Flores, 521 U.S. 507 (1997).
Employment Division, Department of Human Resources v. Smith, 494 U.S. 872 (1990).
Hankins v. Lyght, 441 F.3d 96 (2d Cir. 2006).
Holy Land Foundation for Relief and Development v. Ashcroft, 333 F.3d 156 (D.C. Cir. 2003).
O'Bryan v. Bureau of Prisons, 349 F.3d 399 (7th Cir. 2003).
Religious Freedom Restoration Act, 42 U.S.C. §§ 2000bb *et seq.*
Religious Land Use and Institutionalized Persons Act, 42 U.S.C. §§ 2000cc *et seq.*
Sherbert v. Verner, 374 U.S. 398 (1963).
Wisconsin v. Yoder, 406 U.S. 205 (1972).

REMEDIES, EQUITABLE VERSUS LEGAL

Remedies represent the manner in which parties may determine their legal rights and/or assert enforcement of those rights to recover for harm, loss, injury, or deterioration. In most cases, remedies also evaluate the appropriate relief for parties that exercise their legal rights. Insofar as remedies are intended to correct or compensate for wrongdoing from one party to another, multiple forms of remedies are available.

A significant distinction among types of remedies available to parties resides between *remedies at law*

and *remedies in equity.* Historically, the distinction between remedies at law and in equity arose because monetary damages were at times inappropriate methods to judicial relief of a matter. Consequently, special courts were created to address matters that could not have been resolved through monetary awards. Today, the distinctions between remedies at law and remedies in equity typically occur in two ways: the form of the remedy and the right to a jury. This entry describes both kinds of remedies, with examples from education.

Remedies at Law

Although cases at law and in equity are now typically heard by the same courts, the remedies available for each are distinct. Remedies at law typically assert some monetary value for damages sustained or restitution, such as repayment for property. For example, when a contractor fails to fulfill material portions of its contract with a school board, absent a valid legal excuse, the system, as an injured party, may seek redress by collecting money damages sustained from the contractor's failure to comply with the material terms of their agreement. A remedy of this type acknowledges the board's legal rights and for this illustration awards money damages. Of course, a board can also seek the equitable form of relief known as *specific performance,* discussed below.

Damages as legal remedies are the financial awards for the harm, loss, injury, or detriment from one party to another. However, various forms of legal damages exist; common forms of damages issued in education law cases are compensatory, nominal, liquidated, statutory, and punitive. Depending on the right violated and the severity, courts can award one or more type of damages.

Compensatory damages, sometimes simply referred to as *actual damages,* represent an amount to compensate the injured party for value of the harm, loss, injury, or detriment caused by the other party. The purpose of compensatory damages is to place the injured party in the original position before the occurrence.

Liquidated damages represent a predetermined value of loss from a violation of a party's rights. Typically, liquidated damages apply to contract breaches, and the terms of their contracts spell out good-faith estimates of actual damages when one party fails to properly execute a contract.

Statutory damages outline the parameters for the calculation of damages. In some states, when teachers resign without providing proper notice, statutory provisions permit their school boards to deduct ordinary and necessary expenses associated with finding replacements. Similarly, some statutes, particularly antitrust and fraud legislation, contain provisions of treble damage awards, permitting plaintiffs to seek three times their actual damage awards.

Punitive damages represent awards above and beyond compensatory or nominal damages. The purpose of punitive damages is to punish parties for their willful, malicious, reckless, or fraudulent conduct and deter repetition of the act by the wrongdoer as well as others.

Remedies in Equity

In contrast, remedies in equity compel parties to act or refrain from acting. Remedies in equity are awarded when monetary damages or other remedies at law are insufficient or inadequate means of relief. Perhaps the best-known example of equitable relief occurred as a result of *Brown v. Board of Education of Topeka* (1954), wherein the Supreme Court ruled that segregation based on race was unconstitutional, thereby opening the door to a plethora of litigation designed to implement integration.

In addition, courts are capable of and do not violate maxims of fairness by ordering equitable relief along with legal damages. For instance, if a school board receives government construction funding and the funding is conditioned for a special purpose, the government entity may compel the contractor to complete the terms of the contract as another form of equitable remedy known as *specific performance*. Here, specific performance would require a board to use the building under terms of the agreement unless there is a legal excuse to void the conditions, such as a tornado having swept the building or the expressed purpose does not exist.

Typically, coercive remedies occur in one of two forms, as either injunctive relief (or a restraining order) or relief through specific performance. An injunction

is a court-mandated prohibition of some act, and it applies to both criminal and civil cases. Generally, the party requesting the injunction must demonstrate likelihood of winning the case on its merits, threat of irreparable injury absent the injunction, and injury outweighing the threatened harm of an injunction; also, its issuance must not run counter to the public's interest. For example, a school may host a program that parents truly believe violates the Establishment Clause of the First Amendment. In such an instance, if parents can show that the four components to an injunction are met, a court may issue a preliminary injunction to restrain the school from continuing that program.

A special variation of an injunction applies to the special education context. Under the Individuals with Disabilities Education Act (IDEA), a *stay-put injunction* is essentially a preliminary injunction, which may be asserted pending the case outcome (20 U.S.C. § 1415(j)). A stay-put injunction permits a party to keep the child in the current setting until the case is decided.

Relief through specific performance is a contractual remedy when monetary damages by itself cannot fulfill the obligations of the parties. When plaintiffs successfully obtain specific performance, courts direct the other parties to perform the material terms of their contracts.

Second, the role of judges and juries may differ depending on the remedies that a plaintiff seeks. Based on the Seventh Amendment, remedies at law in federal cases generally provide a right to a jury trial. Although the Seventh Amendment does not apply to state courts, cases with remedies at law frequently afford jury trial options. Remedies in equity are decided by judges. Insofar as equitable relief grants courts powers to control the acts of others and the judicial administration required to follow up on these remedies can be burdensome, the law considers coercive remedies as extraordinary relief. Put another way, equitable remedies are exercised only upon showing that they are required to avoid, mitigate, or address wrongful acts.

Jeffrey C. Sun

See also *Brown v. Board of Education of Topeka; Brown v. Board of Education of Topeka* and Equal Educational Opportunities

Further Readings

Fisher, J. M. (2006). *Understanding remedies* (2nd ed.). Newark, NJ: LexisNexis.

Holtzoff, A. (1943). Equitable and legal rights and remedies under the new federal procedure. *California Law Review, 31*(2), 127–144.

Legal Citations

Brown v. Board of Education of Topeka I, 347 U.S. 483 (1954).

Brown v. Board of Education of Topeka II, 349 U.S. 294 (1955).

Individuals with Disabilities Education Act, 20 U.S.C. §§ 1400 *et seq.*

RENDELL-BAKER V. KOHN

In *Rendell-Baker v. Kohn* (1982), the U.S. Supreme Court decided that actions of administrators in discharging teachers at a private school that provided mandatory services to maladjusted students did not rise to the level of a "state action," regardless of the amount of state (or more properly "commonwealth," since Massachusetts is not a state) and federal funding the school received. In a companion case that did not arise in a school setting, *Blum v. Yaretsky* (1982), the Court similarly ruled that when hospital staff transferred patients from one level of care to another, lower level, there was no state action involved. In both cases, since the alleged wrongdoings did not rise to the level of state actions, the Court found that the aggrieved parties were not afforded the due process protections of the Fourteenth Amendment.

Facts of the Case

The dispute in *Kohn* arose after a teacher was fired because she supported a student's petition to the board that requested that students be given more responsibility on the student-staff council concerning hiring decisions. Insofar as the school's director was opposed to students having a greater say on the committee, she had dismissed the platintiff becauss the teacher supported the petition.

On being dismissed, the teacher unsuccessfully filed suit under 42 U.S.C. §1983 (Section 1983) in the federal trial court in Massachusetts. The court rejected the claim on the basis that the plaintiff failed to present a cause of action involving the state that would allow it to exercise jurisdiction under Section 1983, which allows citizens to seek redress if their constitutional rights have been violated by state actions such as legislation or regulation. When the plaintiff appealed to the First Circuit, her case was consolidated with five other teachers who were similarly dismissed because they had in some way opposed the administration as to the school's learning environment and lack of free speech rights for students. The First Circuit largely affirmed, noting that the plaintiff failed to present a claim of state action under Section 1983.

The Court's Ruling

On further review, the Supreme Court affirmed that since school officials had not acted under color of state law in discharging the teachers, the latter failed to present a Section 1983 claim. In its rationale, the Court performed three levels of analyses in ruling out any possibility of state action being present. First, the Court considered the nature of the relationship between the private facility and the state, namely, whether a "symbiotic relationship," a "nexus," and/or "public function" existed. Insofar as the Court could not uncover any symbiotic relationship between the school and the state, it focused on the "nexus" and "public function" analyses.

When considering the "nexus" relationship, the Court examined two elements separately: the existence of state funding and the requirement that the facility follow state and federal regulations. The Court was of the opinion that since there was no such nexus present, there could be no state action to bring the dispute under the aegis of Section 1983. In addition, the Court pointed out that even though the school received public funding, there was no nexus between the funds and the actions of the officials in discharging the teachers. Insofar as Massachusetts officials did not coerce the school to release the employees, the Court was sastified that the mere receipt of public funding did not implicate state action. In other words, the Court explained that funding was not synonymous with state control.

Turning to the school's complying with state and federal regulations, the Supreme Court determined that even though public officials regulated the educational programs to a great extent, especially in private schools that received special education funding, that alone was insufficient to suggest that commonwealth officials were involved in discharging the teachers. As such, the Court again reasoned that there were no grounds on which to base a Section 1983 claim.

In a final issue, the Supreme Court did acknowledge that the special education mandate in Massachusetts was a public function. Even so, in evaluating whether the fact that the school provided special education services brought the issue to the level of coming exclusively under the province of the commonwealth, the Court handily rejected the teachers' arguments. The Court contended that to the extent that the school was not basically any different from a variety of private corporations whose businesses depended largely on governmental contracts and that this did not turn the actions of its adminsitrators into state action, the teachers failed to present a claim under Section 1983.

Marilyn J. Bartlett

See also Civil Rights Act of 1871 (Section 1983); Due Process Rights: Teacher Dismissal; Fourteenth Amendment; Nonpublic Schools; Teacher Rights

Legal Citations

Blum v. Yaretsky, 457 U.S. 991 (1982).
Rendell-Baker v. Kohn, 457 U.S. 830 (1982).

RESPONSE TO INTERVENTION (RTI)

Response to intervention (RTI) is an alternative assessment approach used in identifying students with specific learning disabilities (SLD). The 2004 revision of the Individuals with Disabilities Education Act (IDEA) authorized RTI as a permissible method for identifying SLD students. The IDEA allows states, through local educational agencies or school boards, to use scientific, research-based interventions in determining which students are eligible for SLD services, rather than relying on a severe discrepancy between intellectual ability and achievement.

The RTI approach is typically a multitiered, systematic method of providing research-based interventions to students with reading difficulties and carefully monitoring their progress in order to evaluate the need for future educational services. RTI is not mandated, but provides an additional method for state educational agencies to use in assessing students who have special educational needs.

RTI, as part of IDEA, was authorized by Congress and signed into law by President George W. Bush in December 2004. The changes in IDEA, which led to the addition of RTI as a method for improving the identification of SLD students, were largely based on influential reports from the President's Commission on Excellence in Special Education and other experts in special education. The commission reported that reliance on the typical evaluation process, made up of academic achievements, behavioral functioning, and intelligence, is expensive and burdensome to an educational agency that already has limited resources in terms of staff and finances. The commission's findings suggested that allowing for RTI-based assessments would provide better outcomes to students by implementing intervention-based assessments sooner and alleviate the resource drain on educational agencies.

RTI was developed in response to the growing need to develop an assessment tool, which provides early educational assistance to students with learning difficulties and accurately places students within appropriate special education programs. One goal of RTI is to reduce the number of students identified with SLD and unnecessarily placed in special education programs. The use of RTI may also improve the accuracy of identifying students whose academic difficulties arise from improper instruction rather than problems related to intellectual ability. The use of RTI allows for students to receive interventions earlier than they would have otherwise obtained them had they been referred to special education services using traditional evaluation methods. In addition, RTI allows for educators to receive individualized data on students' response, which can be used in providing specialized services targeted directly to the particularized needs of individual children.

States may no longer require the use of the severe discrepancy model in identifying SLD students. Instead, states must allow the use of scientific, research-based interventions in considering eligibility of SLD services. Prior to the 2004 revisions, state educational agencies were mandated to assess students for SLD using a model based on discrepancy between IQ and ability, sometimes referred to as the "IQ discrepancy" or "severe discrepancy" model. With the IDEA revisions, state educational agencies may not require the use of the severe discrepancy model in evaluating students and must permit local agencies to use RTI to assess student educational needs.

Specific documentation is required when officials at educational agencies use RTI as a method of determining SLD eligibility. The federal regulations require that documentation include, along with additional criteria, the type of strategies used and the student-centered data that were collected, documentation of parental notification, and strategies for increasing learning rates in students. Each member of student evaluation teams must individually certify concurrence with the findings. RTI student response data should be collected at reasonable intervals. In making final SLD recommendations, agency officials should compare the results of RTI to state standards for grade- and age-level learning.

Many experts hope that the use of RTI will show greater educational benefit in SLD students as well as an increased efficiency in the use of special education resources. Results from the use of RTI will assist educational agencies in further strategizing methods for improving outcomes.

Aimee N. Gravelle

See also Disabled Persons, Rights of; Free Appropriate Public Education; Individualized Education Program (IEP)

Further Readings

President's Commission on Excellence in Special Education.(2002). *Final Report to the President, President's Commission on Excellence in Special Education.* Retrieved from http://www.ed.gov/inits/commissionsboards/whspecialeducation/reports/index.html

Legal Citations

Code of Federal Regulations, "Specific Learning Disabilities," 34 CFR §§ 300.307 *et seq.*
Individuals with Disabilities Education Act, 20 U.S.C. §§ 1400 *et seq.*

Rights of Students and School Personnel With HIV/AIDS

Following the growth of HIV/AIDS in the general population since it was first classified as a separate disease in 1981 in the United States, litigation ensued concerning the rights of students and educators who suffer from this pernicious illness. All but one of the suits directly addressing the rights of individuals with HIV/AIDS in regular school settings involved students; the final case dealt with a teacher.

Medical evidence is clear that students with HIV/AIDS do not pose significant health risks to peers. Even so, parents have had to resort to litigation to protect the rights of their children who were infected with HIV/AIDS to attend school, primarily under Section 504 of the Rehabilitation Act of 1973 (Section 504, 2006). Parents also filed suit under the Individuals with Disabilities Education Act (IDEA) (2005) and the Americans with Disabilities Act (ADA, 2005).

The earliest and perhaps best-known case involving a child with AIDS concerned Ryan White, a student in Indiana with hemophilia who contracted the disease through a blood transfusion. A state court, in refusing to interpret a statute on the rights of students with communicable diseases as prohibiting him from attending school, ordered Ryan to be admitted to a regular classroom (*Bogart v. White,* 1986).

Students with AIDS have successfully challenged state and local policies that would have limited their ability to attend school. A trial court in New York overturned a board policy that would have automatically excluded students with AIDS from school, subject to individual reviews (*District 27 Community School Board v. Board of Education of New York,* 1986). The court explained that a blanket exclusion would have violated Section 504 since the children were otherwise qualified to attend public schools. Even though a similar dispute from New Jersey was rendered moot when school officials admitted students who suffered from AIDS and related illnesses, the state's high court decided that the policy guidelines, which provided adequate due process protection for individuals and the public at large, were valid as modified (*Board of Education of Plainfield v. Cooperman*, 1987).

Two cases from Illinois rejected attempts by school systems to exclude children with AIDS for failing to exhaust administrative remedies under the IDEA. Both courts rebuffed the arguments on the ground that insofar as the parents filed suit pursuant to Section 504, they were not bound by the IDEA's exhaustion of remedies doctrine (*Doe v. Belleville Public School District No. 118*, 1987; *Robertson v. Granite City Community Unit School District No. 9*, 1988). Further, in a case filed pursuant to the IDEA, a federal trial court in Oklahoma rejected an attempt by officials who sought to bar an HIV-positive, hemophiliac child with an emotional disorder from school under a state law on contagious diseases. The court found that since the child had an identifiable mental disability under the IDEA, he was entitled to its protections (*Parents of Child, Code No. 870901W v. Coker*, 1987).

Three courts refused to allow schools officials to place children with AIDS on homebound placements in order to remove them from general school populations. Courts in Florida (*Ray v. School Dist. of De Soto County*, 1987), California (*Phipps v. Saddleback Valley Unified School District*, 1988), and Illinois (*Doe v. Dolton Elementary School District No. 148*, 1988) agreed that such actions violated the rights of the students for a variety of reasons.

Two cases examined issues in which students may have presented risks of harm to others. In California, a federal trial court permitted a kindergarten-aged child with AIDS who bit a classmate to attend school since there were "no reported cases of the transmission of the AIDS virus in a school setting" and the "overwhelming weight of medical evidence [was] that the AIDS virus is not transmitted by human bites, even bites that break the skin" (*Thomas v. Atascadero Unified School District*, 1987, p. 380). The court also found that the child was otherwise qualified to attend regular kindergarten under Section 504 insofar as there was no evidence that he

posed a significant risk to others. A lengthy dispute from Florida reached a similar outcome in which a federal trial court, on remand from the Eleventh Circuit (*Martinez v. School Board of Hillsborough County, Florida*, 1988, 1989), directed educators to admit a "trainable mentally handicapped" kindergarten child with AIDS who was incontinent, often had blood in her saliva, and sucked her fingers in class, in light of the low overall risk of her transmitting AIDS.

The only case that was not resolved in favor of a child with AIDS, albeit as a nonschool case under the ADA, arose in Virginia. The Fourth Circuit affirmed that the proprietor of a private karate school, whose parents had not disclosed their son's condition in advance, was not required to admit the child to a group class because his condition posed a direct threat to the health and safety of others (*Montalvo v. Radcliffe*, 1999).

The only case involving the rights of a teacher with AIDS was litigated in California. A teacher successfully challenged his being reassigned to an administrative position by relying on Section 504. In ordering the teacher's reinstatement, the Ninth Circuit held that absent adequate medical evidence that he would pass the disease on to his students or coworkers, there was no reason to ban him from work (*Chalk v. United States District Court, Central District of California*, 1988).

In a case that did not address the merits of the claims of a teacher who was HIV positive, the federal trial court in Puerto Rico dismissed the case he filed under the ADA alleging that his contract was not renewed due to his illness (*Velez Cajigas v. Order of St. Benedict*, 2000). The court held that school officials relied on legitimate nondiscriminatory grounds that the teacher was often late for work and was unable to control his students.

In sum, while reported litigation involving students and teachers with HIV/AIDS has lessened dramatically, it is clear that those affected by this dreadful disease cannot legally be excluded from school or work based on medical conditions associated with their conditions.

Charles J. Russo

See also Americans with Disabilities Act; Inclusion; Least Restrictive Environment; Rehabilitation Act of 1973, Section 504; Zero Reject

Further Readings

Russo, C. J. (2005). HIV/AIDS inclusion and the law in American public schools. In N. Harris & P. Meredith (Eds.), *Children, education and health* (pp. 167–181). Hampshire, UK: Ashgate.

Legal Citations

Americans with Disabilities Act, 42 U.S.C. §§ 12101 *et seq.*

Board of Education of Plainfield v. Cooperman, 523 A.2d 655 (N.J. 1987).

Bogart v. White, No. 86–144 (Clinton Cir. Ct. Apr. 10, 1986).

Chalk v. United States District Court, Central District of California, 840 F.2d 701 (9th Cir. 1988).

District 27 Community School Board v. Board of Education of New York, 502 N.Y.S.2d 325 (N.Y. Sup. Ct. 1986).

Doe v. Belleville Public School District No. 118, 672 F. Supp. 342 (S.D. Ill. 1987).

Doe v. Dolton Elementary School District No. 148, 694 F. Supp. 440 (N.D. Ill. 1988).

Individuals with Disabilities Education Act, 20 U.S.C. §§ 1400 *et seq.*

Martinez v. School Board of Hillsborough County, Florida, 861 F.2d 1502 (11th Cir. 1988), *on remand*, 711 F. Supp. 1066 (M.D. Fla. 1989).

Montalvo v. Radcliffe, 167 F.3d 873 (4th Cir. 1999).

Parents of Child, Code No. 870901W v. Coker, 676 F. Supp. 1072 (E.D. Okla. 1987).

Phipps v. Saddleback Valley Unified School District, 251 Cal. Rptr. 720 (Cal. Ct. App. 1988).

Ray v. School District of De Soto County, 666 F. Supp. 1524, 1535 (M.D. Fla. 1987).

Rehabilitation Act of 1973, Section 504, 29 U.S.C. § 794(a) (2006).

Robertson v. Granite City Community Unit School District No. 9, 684 F. Supp. 1002 (S.D. Ill. 1988).

Thomas v. Atascadero Unified School District, 662 F. Supp. 376 (C.D. Cal. 1987).

Velez Cajigas v. Order of St. Benedict, 115 F. Supp. 246 (D. Puerto Rico 2000).

RIGHT-TO-WORK LAWS

Right-to-work laws prohibit making union membership a condition of employment. Although federal law allows states to pass such laws, fewer than half have done so, and a national law is being considered. This entry describes these laws, relevant U.S. Supreme Court rulings, and arguments offered by supporters and opponents of such legislation.

Background

The National Labor Relations Act as amended in 1947 allows states to enact right-to-work laws. The U.S. Department of Labor records show that at least 23 states have enacted right-to-work laws and state constitutional amendments: Alabama, Arizona, Arkansas, Florida, Georgia, Idaho, Indiana, Iowa, Kansas, Louisiana, Mississippi, Nebraska, Nevada, North Carolina, North Dakota, Oklahoma, South Carolina, South Dakota, Tennessee, Texas, Utah, Virginia, and Wyoming. The federal government is currently working on the National Right to Work Act, which would extend the right to refuse union membership to all states. Other states have not formally enacted such laws, but some of these have state codes or other legal language in state laws that identify and control union activities.

Right-to-work state statutes vary greatly in language, though all contain basic commonalities in the provision stating that union membership cannot be made a condition of employment; it is best for educators to consult with the attorneys for their school boards for specific requirements of their states of residence. Principally, the National Right to Work Act would repeal other federal labor laws that allowed dismissal of employees for failure to pay union dues or loss of union membership. Right to work is an important area of law, given the current growth in the number of teachers' unions and associations being formed.

Right to work specifically addresses the *closed shop*. In closed shops, employers are permitted to hire only union members to fill open positions. Right-to-work laws ban closed shops and require *fair share*, also known as *agency shops*, or *open shops*. Further, right-to-work laws afford employees the opportunity to withdraw from union membership at any time without fear of the loss of their jobs. Another provision required by the right-to-work law is fair and equal representation of employees regardless of membership status.

In contrast to closed shops, open shops do not limit employees hired to fill positions. The middle ground is fair share or agency shops. These require nonmembers to pay a fair share (agency fee) of the dues associated with negotiating salaries and benefits. The fair share or agency fee amount must be disclosed by the union when requested by an employee prior to payment. Unions must identify the portion of their dues used solely for the purpose of negotiating salary and benefits.

The Supreme Court ruled that the fair share or agency fee cannot be used for activities not related to negotiations of salaries and benefits (*Chicago Teachers Union Local No. 1 v. Hudson,* 1986). The Court found that the formula used by the union to calculate the fee was constitutionally inadequate. In *Lehnert v. Ferris Faculty Association* (1991), the Court clarified expenses that are chargeable to nonunion members as part of the fair share or agency fee. The Court most recently decided that it does not violate the First Amendment to require teacher unions to receive affirmative authorization from nonmembers before spending their agency shop fees for election related purposes (*Davenport v. Washington Education Association,* 2007).

Pros and Cons

Supporters of right-to-work laws argue that employees should be able to freely choose whether to join or not join the union. Proponents also invoke the First Amendment right to freedom of association, which allows employees the choice of membership or nonmembership. Finally, this group believes that right-to-work laws increase competition in the marketplace and thus contribute to economic growth. A commonly cited factor in an employee's decision not to join a union is the use of union dues to support causes that are contrary to the employee's political beliefs.

Labor leaders oppose right-to-work laws because they feel nonmembers are "free riders" who share in the benefit of union negotiations without contributing toward the outcomes. Opponents of right-to-work laws argue that the laws weaken the union and therefore contribute to lower wages and safety concerns. Further, union members see right-to-work laws as a threat to their very existence. Given a choice between membership or nonmembership in unions without repercussions, some employees choose not to join labor organizations. This choice is seen as weakening the union's membership while requiring the union to

expend resources in representing nonmembers fairly and equally in any work-related grievances or disputes.

Looking Ahead

As the House of Representatives and the Senate consider the National Right to Work Act, some states have passed laws or constitutional amendments identifying right-to-work language. Although the National Right to Work Act is in committee and has not become law, states are free (under the Taft-Hartley Act) to enact their own right-to-work laws or identify specific requirements in state codes regarding collective bargaining, unions, and other conditions of employment.

Educators must be aware of state collective bargaining and/or right-to-work laws prior to engaging in negotiations with the representative(s) of teachers or support staff. Failure of administrators to know what state laws or codes identify as legally negotiable items and management rights (nonnegotiable) will not be a defense when they try to recover items reserved as management rights.

Michael J. Jernigan

See also *Abood v. Detroit Board of Education; Chicago Teachers Union, Local No. 1 v. Hudson; Davenport v. Washington Education Association;* First Amendment; Teacher Rights; Unions

Further Readings

Russo, C. J. (2002). Right-to-work and fair share agreements: A delicate balance. *School Business Affairs, 68*(4), 12–15.

U.S. Department of Labor. (2007). *State right-to-work laws and constitutional amendments.* Retrieved January 5, 2007, from http://www.dol.gov/esa/programs/whd/state/righttoworkpf.htm

Legal Citations

Abood v. Detroit Board of Education, 431 U.S. 209 (1977).

Chicago Teachers Union Local No. 1 v. Hudson, 475 U.S. 292 (1986), *on remand,* 922 F.2d 1306 (7th Cir. 1991), *cert. denied,* 501 U.S. 1230 (1991).

Davenport v. Washington Education Association, 127 S. Ct. 2372 (2007).

Lehnert v. Ferris Faculty Association, 500 U.S. 507 (1991).

National Right-to-Work Act, S. 270, H.R. 500 (2007). Available from http://www.govtrack.us

ROBERTS, JOHN G., JR. (1955–)

John G. Roberts, Jr., became the 17th chief justice of the United States on September 29, 2005, and currently serves in that post. Prior to becoming chief justice, Roberts served as a judge on the U.S. Court of Appeals for the District of Columbia Circuit from June 2, 2003, to September 29, 2005.

Early Years

Chief Justice Roberts was born on January 27, 1955, in Buffalo, New York. He was raised in a small town in Indiana and attended a Roman Catholic boarding high school in LaPorte, Indiana. Roberts earned his undergraduate degree summa cum laude, with a degree in history and a Phi Beta Kappa key from Harvard College in 1976. In 1979, he earned his law degree magna cum laude from Harvard Law School, where he was managing editor of the *Harvard Law Review.*

Roberts began his legal career as a law clerk to Judge Henry Friendly of the Second Circuit in 1979 to 1980 and to Associate Justice William Rehnquist in 1980 to 1981. At the conclusion of his Supreme Court clerkship, he served as special assistant to the attorney general of the United States (1981 to 1982) and as associate counsel to the president of the United States (1982 to 1986). Roberts then entered private practice as an appellate attorney with the Washington law firm of Hogan & Hartson but returned to government service in 1989 as principal deputy solicitor general of the United States (1989 to 1993). In 1992, President George H. W. Bush nominated him to be a judge on the District of Columbia Circuit. However, after Bush lost the 1992 election, Roberts's nomination expired.

Having missed an opportunity to serve on the federal bench, Roberts returned to private practice at Hogan & Hartson. Having argued 17 cases before the Supreme Court while serving in the solicitor general's office, Roberts already had a reputation as an outstanding appellate advocate. In arguing 22 additional cases between 1993 and 2003, he established a reputation as one of the best Supreme Court advocates of his generation.

On the Bench

In 2001, President George W. Bush nominated Roberts for a second time for a seat on the District of Columbia Circuit, but the Democratic majority in the Senate refused to act on his nomination. When the Republican Party won a Senate majority in 2002, the president again nominated him. He was confirmed shortly thereafter.

After Associate Justice Sandra Day O'Connor announced her retirement from the Court in the summer of 2005, the president nominated Roberts to replace her. When Chief Justice Rehnquist died in early September 2005, the president withdrew his nomination of Roberts for associate justice and nominated him for chief justice.

Roberts, a Roman Catholic, is married to Jane Marie Sullivan Roberts and has two adopted children.

William E. Thro

See also Roberts Court

Further Readings

Greenburg, J. C. (2007). *Supreme conflict: The struggle for the Supreme Court.* New York: Penguin.

ROBERTS COURT

The phrase *Roberts Court* refers to the era during which John G. Roberts, Jr., has served as chief justice of the U.S. Supreme Court. The Roberts Court began with the October 2005 term and continues to the present day.

Following the completion of the October 2004 term, Justice Sandra Day O'Connor announced her retirement. At that time, President George W. Bush nominated Judge John Roberts to take her place. However, before Roberts's confirmation hearings could begin, Chief Justice William H. Rehnquist died. The president then withdrew Roberts's nomination for Justice O'Connor's seat and nominated Roberts for chief justice. Justice O'Connor remained on the Court until January 2006, when she was replaced by Justice Samuel Alito.

While the short tenure of the Roberts Court makes it difficult to draw decisive conclusions regarding its general direction and ultimate place in history, it has rendered significant decisions in cases involving education law. The remainder of this entry discusses these cases and closes with brief reflections.

Record on Education

In *Parents Involved for Community Schools v. Seattle School District* (2007), a plurality of the Supreme Court in an opinion written by Chief Justice Roberts agreed that "a public school that had not operated legally segregated schools or has been found to be unitary" (p. 2746) may not "choose to classify students by race and rely upon that classification in making school assignments" (p. 2746). Significantly, the Court indicated that the achievement of diversity was a compelling governmental interest only in the higher-education context. Effectively, *Parents Involved* precludes school boards from using race in the assignment of individual students. As a practical matter, *Parents Involved* makes it extraordinarily difficult for urban school systems to maintain racially balanced schools.

Two days prior to ruling in *Parents Involved,* in *Morse v. Frederick* (2007) in another opinion by Chief Justice Roberts, the Court held "that schools may take steps to safeguard those entrusted to their care from speech that can reasonably be regarded as encouraging illegal drug use" (p. 2622). Even though *Morse* leaves many questions unanswered regarding the exact scope of student free-expression rights, it does provide clarity on speech that encourages illegal drug use.

In *Zuni Public Schools Dist. No. 89 v. Department of Education* (2007), the Supreme Court upheld the U.S. Department of Education standards for the distribution of federal impact aid monies. Specifically, the Court found that the secretary could consider the population of individual school systems in determining whether states had programs in place that equalized expenditures among their districts.

Winkelman ex rel. Winkelman v. Parma City School District (2007) was the third of a trilogy of Supreme Court cases addressing special education. In *Winkelman,* the Court was of the opinion that the parents of a student with disabilities have rights under the Individuals with Disabilities Education Act (IDEA)

that were separate and distinct from the rights of their child. As such, the Court decided that since the parents have their own personal rights, they can bring pro se actions challenging the decisions of school officials in determining appropriate placements for their children. *Winkelman* seems to expand the scope of IDEA litigation.

A year earlier, in *Arlington Central School District Board of Education v. Murphy* (2006), the Supreme Court reasoned that the IDEA, which was enacted pursuant to congressional authority under the Spending Clause in Article I of the U.S. Constitution, did not impose conditions on states unless they were set out unambiguously in the statutory text. The Court's interpretation meant that states could not be required to reimburse parents for the cost of expert witnesses and other fees, the issue at bar, absent a clear congressional intent to do so. Accordingly, *Murphy* makes it more difficult for litigants to advocate expansive interpretations of the IDEA. Moreover, because *Murphy* applies to all Spending Clause statutes, it has significant ramifications of Title IX, Title VI, and Section 504 claims that remain to be seen.

In *Schaffer ex rel. Schaffer v. Weast* (2005), the Supreme Court noted that when parents and school board officials cannot agree on the contents of a child's individualized education program (IEP), the party challenging the IEP bears the burden of proof in the absence of a state statute to the contrary. The Court observed that since a board-proposed IEP constitutes the status quo, the party challenging the status quo must bear the burden of proof.

The Supreme Court's major case involving higher education during the Roberts term was *Rumsfeld v. Forum for Academic and Institutional Rights* (2006). In *Rumsfeld,* a judgment that came after years of legal wrangling surrounding the question of military recruitment on college and university campuses, the Court said that the Solomon Amendment is constitutional. At issue in *Rumsfeld* was the fact that many institutions of higher learning sought to exclude military recruiters from their campuses because they thought that the federal law concerning homosexuality in the military and the resultant sexual orientation discrimination was offensive to their institutional values.

Directions

Insofar as the Solomon Amendment was enacted to override those exclusions by mandating that educational institutions afford military recruiters the same access provided to other recruiters or lose specified federal funds, the Court maintained that its mandate was consistent with the First Amendment. According to the *Rumsfeld* Court, the Solomon Amendment did not violate institutional freedoms of speech or association.

Clearly, two terms are not enough time in which to render clear conclusions about the direction of the Roberts Court. Yet in light of a collection of cases that demonstrate clarity and judicial humility, it appears that the Supreme Court may be heading into a period within which the justices apply judicial restraint rather than activism. While it is still too early to tell what direction the justices will ultimately adopt collectively, it is evident that under the discretion of Chief Justice John Roberts, the Supreme Court will continue to have a major impact on education law and American life in general.

William E. Thro

See also *Arlington Central School District Board of Education v. Murphy; Morse v. Fredrick; Parents Involved in Community Schools v. Seattle School District No. 1; Schaffer ex rel. Schaffer v. Weast; Winkelman ex rel. Winkelman v. Parma City School District*

Further Readings

Thro, W. E. (2007). The Roberts Court at dawn: Clarity, humility, and the future of education law. *West's Education Law Reporter, 222,* 491–514.

Legal Citations

Arlington Central School District Board of Education v. Murphy, 548 U.S. 291 (2006).

Morse v. Fredrick, 127 S. Ct. 2618 (2007).

Parents Involved in Community Schools v. Seattle School District, 127 S. Ct. 2738 (2007).

Rumsfeld v. Forum for Academic and Institutional Rights, 547 U.S. 126 (2006).

Schaffer ex rel. Schaffer v. Weast, 546 U.S. 49 (2005).

Winkelman ex rel. Winkelman v. Parma City School District, 127 S. Ct. 1994 (2007).

Zuni Public Schools Dist. No. 89 v. Department of Education, 127 S. Ct. 1534 (2007).

ROBERTS V. CITY OF BOSTON

At issue in *Roberts v. City of Boston* (1849) was whether Sarah C. Roberts was unlawfully excluded from public school instruction under an 1845 Massachusetts statute that allowed any child to recover damages based on such exclusion. *Roberts* is noteworthy because it stands out as the first recorded opinion in the United States to address, and essentially uphold, the concept of "separate but equal."

Facts of the Case

At the time of the Roberts's suit, the city of Boston was divided into 21 nonterritorial primary school districts. While the city supported and provided instruction to each of the district's several primary schools, two of the primary schools were for the exclusive education of Black students. White students could attend any of the schools and were not required to attend the school that was geographically closest to their homes.

The primary school committee was responsible for overseeing primary school admissions. Pursuant to the committee's regulations, students could not be admitted without tickets of admission from district committee members, every committee member should have accepted all appropriately qualified applicants, and students should have been admitted to the schools geographically closest to the their homes. Black citizens of Boston requested that the primary school committee eliminate schools exclusively for Black children. However, the committee decided that separate schools were legal, just, and best suited to provide education to Black students.

In 1847, Sarah C. Roberts was a 5-year-old Black child whose father properly applied for admission to a school near the family's home. The nearest all-Black student school was Belknap, located 2,100 feet from Sarah's home; other schools were closer. The committee denied Sarah's application to attend a closer school because she was Black and there were two schools exclusively for Black children. Sarah appealed this decision to the primary school committee for the district and then the general primary school committee but was denied admission by both.

After Sarah's father was notified that she could attend Belknap, he refused to send her there. In February 1848, Sarah went to the primary school geographically closest to her home, approximately 900 feet away. Sarah did not have a ticket of admission or other permission to attend the all-White school, and she was removed by the teacher. Sarah's father then unsuccessfully filed suit for her to attend the school closer to her home.

The Court's Ruling

On further review, the Supreme Judicial Court of Massachusetts affirmed that the Roberts family did not have a claim. In its opinion, the court discussed constitutional and legal rights in Massachusetts, where commonwealth law directed that each town should raise money for schools and divide itself into districts. The court pointed out that the law did not require specific organization, qualifications of admission, quantity of schools, or age of entry. Instead, the court noted that legislature granted these decision-making powers to the individual school committees. The court added that the superintendent had the authority to determine the methods for distribution and classification of students to individual schools based on the proficiency and welfare of individual children. The court explained that there were conditions under which different populations of students should be taught separately from others, such as on the basis of age, gender, or poverty.

The court next declared that the committee had acted within its authority in deciding that separate schools were good for both Black and White students. According to the court, the committee should have continued to use its reason and judgment when regulating school assignments. The court further thought that integrating Black and White students might have increased prejudice and discrimination. Even so, the question before the court was not the legality of separate primary schools, but whether students could be prevented from attending the schools closest to their homes. The court was of the opinion that Sarah was not unlawfully excluded from public school, because she had access to a school that was capable of providing equally qualified instruction as the other primary

schools; that the committee had the authority to determine school assignments; and that officials acted under this authority when they required Black students to attend one of two schools. The court thus concluded that the requirement that Sarah travel further to school was not unreasonable or illegal and did not amount to unlawful exclusion from a public school, and her action was properly dismissed below.

Suzann VanNasdale

See also *Brown v. Board of Education of Topeka; Gong Lum v. Rice; Plessy v. Ferguson*

Legal Citations

Brown v. Board of Education of Topeka I, 347 U.S. 483 (1954).
Brown v. Board of Education of Topeka II, 349 U.S. 294 (1955).
Gong Lum v. Rice, 275 U.S. 78 (1927).
Plessy v. Ferguson, 163 U.S. 537 (1896).
Roberts v. City of Boston, 59 Mass. 198 (1849).

ROBINSON V. CAHILL

Robinson v. Cahill (1973) is the name of the initial dispute in the long-running school finance litigation from New Jersey. *Robinson* stands out not only because it lasted so long but also because it exemplifies the kind of analysis that arises in disputes over funding for public education.

The Initial Ruling

After the U.S. Supreme Court refused to intervene in *Robinson* (1975) for the first time, the Supreme Court of New Jersey found that the state's system of school finance violated the state's education clause pertaining to the provision of a thorough and efficient system of education. According to the court, the "thorough and efficient" clause gave the state the ultimate responsibility to ensure that students receive a thorough and efficient education. Further, the Court ruled that a funding system that is reliant on local taxes was not thorough and efficient.

In *Robinson,* the Supreme Court of New Jersey examined two questions: whether the state or local boards had the principal responsibility for funding schools and whether urban taxpayers, who faced higher tax rates than those in other municipalities, had a right to equal taxation. At the outset of its analysis, the court cited the "thorough and efficient clause" in the state constitution: "The Legislature shall provide for the maintenance and support of a thorough and efficient system of free public schools for the instruction of all the children in the State between the ages of five and eighteen years" (*Robinson,* p. 716, citing New Jersey Constitution, Article VIII, Section IV, 1).

The court explained that in seeking to provide funding for public schools, the state's financing system relied heavily on local property taxes. Under this formula, the court commented that there was a wide disparity in the amount of money spent per pupil, depending on a child's district of residence, with the result that in some systems with low property wealth and high taxes, the schools were underfunded. As part of its analysis, the court acknowledged that the school funding was provided from three sources: local taxes, which provided about 67% of the total; state aid, which accounted for about 28%; and federal aid for the last 5%. As such, the court specified that the state aid did not substantially equalize the dollar amount spent per pupil.

At the same, the plaintiffs claimed that due to the financing disparity, the state offered a "thorough" education to some but not all students, as the system discriminated against property owners who were taxed at different rates for the same underlying purpose. The plaintiffs further alleged that since the language in the state constitution imposed an obligation on the state to fund public education, any tax imposed to fund education should be a "state" tax that should have been applied uniformly across the state as a whole. The court rejected this argument, responding that state functions could be delegated to the local level and funded by local taxes. If the state chose to fund education at the state level, then the court would be satisfied that property taxes would be uniformly imposed across all property in the state. Conversely, the court posited that, as was the situation in New Jersey, since the state chose to assign responsibility to the local government, all property in any given municipality should have been taxed equally.

Continuing its analysis, the state high court observed that the trial court thought that the state constitution's language required equal taxation among all school systems and that the state had the duty to raise funds by imposing levies on all taxpayers equally. The court also rejected the idea that the constitution required equal treatment of all taxpayers in all jurisdictions. Noting that other essential services, such as police and fire protection, come out of the same tax base as the one that funds education, the court judged that it was inevitable that local per-pupil expenditures would vary, as each locality would be willing or able to pay different amounts. In fact, the court added that such funding discrepancies existed in these other essential state services.

The court recognized the importance of schooling but was unwilling to categorize education as a fundamental right under the state constitution's equal protection clause. While remarking that public education is vital, the court found that other needs, such as food and lodging, were more appropriately entitled to equal protection status. To this end, the court pointed out that police and fire protection, along with water and other public health services, are essential needs that are provided by local funding and that the dollar amounts vary by jurisdiction. The court did decide that insofar as the funding system was unconstitutional because of its impact on education, it ordered the state to provide enough funding to the poorest districts in order to ensure that children received a thorough and efficient education.

A Second Round

Following the court's 1975 opinion in *Robinson,* the U.S. Supreme Court again refused to intervene in *Robinson.* Legislators in New Jersey then struggled to develop a constitutionally permissible funding system. Although the legislators did enact a new system in the Public School Education Act of 1976 (PSEA), controversy would soon return.

The successor suit to *Robinson, Abbott by Abbott v. Burke* (1990), was initially filed in 1981, as students in urban school districts claimed that the new funding system still did not satisfy the thorough and efficient clause. Following a long and complicated procedural history, in *Abbott* (1990), the Supreme Court of New Jersey determined that the PSEA was constitutional on its face but that, as applied, it failed to meet the requirements of the thorough and efficient clause.

In its judgment, the court maintained that since the PSEA failed poorer districts, the state had to provide aid to the poorest systems, identified as "special needs" districts, in an amount that would equal their per-pupil spending for those in locations with the highest socioeconomic levels. The court observed that the "special needs" districts could not be forced to rely solely on their local tax availability and that the state was responsible for providing sufficient resources to these districts. According to the court, while the PSEA did not require equal expenditures, there was a minimum amount that all school systems should be entitled to receive. If the local tax base could not offer the needed amount, then the court expected the state to provide the rest. In this way, the court forced the state to allocate significantly more money to urban schools with the realization that they would need more resources than their tax base would, or could, provide.

The *Abbott* court noted that providing a thorough and efficient education involved much more than simply giving schools money to operate. The court concluded that since money can make a difference if it is used effectively, because it provides all children with a chance to succeed, the state was obligated to abide by its constitution in making a thorough and efficient education available to all children. Insofar as controversy lingered on, the Supreme Court of New Jersey had to clarify its order. As such, the court subsequently addressed issues surrounding the credentials of non-certified preschool teachers who would serve children in the state's poorest districts (*Abbot,* 2004a, 2004b).

Megan L. Rehberg

See also *San Antonio Independent School District v. Rodriguez;* School Finance Litigation; Thorough and Efficient Systems of Education

Legal Citations

Abbott by Abbott v. Burke, 575 A.2d 359 (N.J. 1990), 643 A.2d 575 (N.J. 1994); 693 A.2d 417 (N.J. 1997); *appeal after remand,* 710 A.2d 450 (N.J. 1998); *opinion clarified,* 751 A.2d 1032 (N.J. 2000); 748 A.2d 82 (N.J. 2000); *order clarified,* 790 A.2d 842 (N.J. 2002), *modified in part,* 852 A.2d 185 (N.J. 2004a), *modified,* 857 A.2d 173 (N.J. 2004b).

Robinson v. Cahill, 303 A.2d 273 (N.J. 1973), *cert. denied,* 414 U.S. 976 (1973); 339 A.2d 193 (N.J. 1975), *republished,* 351 A.2d 713 (N.J. 1975), *cert. denied sub nom. Klein v. Robinson,* 423 U.S. 913 (1975).

San Antonio Independent School District v. Rodriguez, 411 U.S. 1 (1973).

ROBINSON V. JACKSONVILLE SHIPYARDS

At issue in *Robinson v. Jacksonville Shipyards* (1991) was whether a court could apply the "reasonable woman" standard in a Title VII case involving sexual harassment in the workplace. In finding that the employer in *Jacksonville Shipyards* allowed for the creation of a sexually hostile work environment, a federal trial court in Florida decided that the female employee's Title VII claim was actionable. Although *Jacksonville Shipyards* was not set in an educational context, it is informative for educators concerning issues in sexual harassment.

Facts of the Case

The dispute in *Jacksonville Shipyards* arose when a female employee complained to company executives and supervisors that male coworkers created a sexually hostile work environment by displaying inappropriate pictures of women and making derogatory comments about her and other women. After the plaintiff made multiple attempts to resolve the hostile environment within the company, the woman filed suit in a federal trial court alleging that officials perpetuated a sexually hostile work environment.

During the company's defense presentation, the court viewed the testimony of its two expert witnesses as not useful to the specifics of the dispute. As such, the court gave this testimony little credence. The company also tried to explain how officials attempted to reduce the hostile environment by marking off areas of the shops as "men only" and encouraging the men to post the pictures of nude or partially nude women only in the designated areas. Further, officials indicated that they encouraged the men to ask female employees to leave areas when they were going to tell off-color jokes and/or stories.

At the same time, testimony revealed that company policy never permitted the posting of pictures of nude or partially dressed men and that even though it did not allow magazines and newspapers on the job site, employees admitted there were pornographic material strewn about the shops and offices. Moreover, officials had to concede that the woman was told that since she chose the company's work environment and the men had constitutional rights to post the pictures, she would essentially have to tolerate their behavior.

The plaintiff's two expert witnesses testified that the ongoing presence of the demeaning pictures of women created conditions for sexual stereotyping that encouraged male workers and supervisors to view the female workers in terms of their sexuality rather that as able-bodied coworkers. The witnesses pointed out that with this form of stereotyping, members of the majority group, namely, the males, minimized the concerns of the women, who were in the minority, with the result that the women were frequently perceived as the problem. Further, the testimony stated that members of the minority group frequently combated the hostile environment by denying the impact of the event and blocking it out, avoiding the workplace by taking sick leave, telling harassers to stop, engaging in joking or other banter in the workplace in order to defuse the situation, and threatening to make or actually making informal or formal complaints.

The Court's Ruling

For the Title VII claim of sexual discrimination to proceed, the court noted that the plaintiff had to prove that she was a member of a protected class, that the sexual harassment was unwelcome, that it was based on her sex, that it affected her employment, that the employer knew or should have known of it, and that she neither solicited nor incited the offending behaviors. Insofar as the court was satisfied that the plaintiff met these tests, it permitted the case to proceed.

The court conceded that in situations in which inappropriate sexual slurs and behaviors are isolated,

company officials may not be able to curb all such misbehaviors. However, as in the case at bar, wherein officials were aware that the actions were frequent and severe enough that they should have intervened and that a reasonable woman would have been offended by the behavior that the plaintiff had been subjected to, the company was liable for the creation of a hostile environment. The court thus granted the plaintiff's request for injunctive relief while requiring the company to institute the sexual harassment plan that she proposed. However, since the plaintiff was unable to document the specific and/or exact number of days she missed work due to stress resulting from the hostile environment, the judge was unable to calculate a financial award due her and so awarded her $1 in nominal damages.

Brenda R. Kallio

See also Hostile Work Environment; *Meritor Savings Bank v. Vinson;* Sexual Harassment; Title VII

Legal Citations

Meritor Savings Bank v. Vinson, 477 U.S. 57 (1986).
Robinson v. Jacksonville Shipyards, 760 F. Supp. 1486 (M.D. Fla. 1991).

ROGERS V. PAUL

In *Rogers v. Paul* (1965), the U.S. Supreme Court essentially overturned the gradual "one grade per year" desegregation plan that it had permitted in an earlier case from Arkansas, *Cooper v. Aaron* (1958). In *Rogers,* the Court rejected a school board's clear attempt to exclude students from a broader curriculum based solely on race. In looking at the passage of time since *Brown v. Board of Education of Topeka* (1954), the Court also demonstrated its impatience with the school board's unacceptably slow movement to converting the system to unitary status.

Facts of the Case

At issue in *Rogers* was the constitutionality of a "grade-per-year" desegregation plan. The plan that a local board in Arkansas adopted in 1957 called for desegregating its school system one grade per year. Yet the 10th through 12th grades were still segregated. Moreover, African American students in the segregated schools were not allowed to take courses that were available only at the high school for White students.

After the African American students and their parents filed a class action suit against the board, they unsuccessfully challenged the fact that the plan did not grant them access to equal educational opportunities. The Eighth Circuit affirmed that the plan was properly set in place. On further review in Rogers, a unanimous Supreme Court, in a brief per curiam opinion, vacated and remanded in favor of the plaintiffs.

The Court's Ruling

In its analysis, the Supreme Court held that the assignment of students to the African American high school on the basis of their race was constitutionally impermissible pursuant to the precedent that it set in *Brown v. Board of Education of Topeka* (1954). To this end, the Court was of the opinion that the African American students were entitled to relief in the form of being able to transfer out of their high schools immediately so they could avail themselves of the more extensive curriculum at the high school for Whites.

At the same time, the Supreme Court stressed that delays in desegregating the school system were no longer tolerable. The Court noted that more than 10 years had passed since its order calling for the desegregation of public schools. The Court also found that petitioners had standing to challenge the constitutionality of the allocation of faculty on a racial basis, as a separate issue, due to the impact that this could have on the potential denial of equal educational opportunities. However, insofar as this issue was not at bar, the Court vacated and remanded for further consideration on this point.

Deborah Curry

See also *Brown v. Board of Education of Topeka; Brown v. Board of Education of Topeka* and Equal Educational Opportunities; *Cooper v. Aaron;* Dual and Unitary Systems

Future Readings

Hunter, R. C., & Donahoo, S. (2004). The implementation of *Brown* in achieving unitary status. *Education and Urban Society, 36,* 342–354.

Russo, C. J., Harris, J. J., III, & Sandridge, R. F. (1994). *Brown v. Board of Education* at 40: A legal history of equal educational opportunities in American public education. *Journal of Negro Education, 63,* 297–309.

Legal Citations

Brown v. Board of Education of Topeka I, 347 U.S. 483 (1954).
Brown v. Board of Education of Topeka II, 349 U.S. 294 (1955).
Cooper v. Aaron, 358 U.S. 1 (1958).
Rogers v. Paul, 382 U.S. 198 (1965).

ROSE V. COUNCIL FOR BETTER EDUCATION

Rose v. Council for Better Education (1989) was a major school-funding case based on adequacy arguments inspired by the language of state constitutions. In *Rose,* the Supreme Court of Kentucky interpreted the commonwealth's constitutional provision as mandating its general assembly to "provide an efficient system of common schools throughout the state." The court held that the general assembly fell far short of its duty by failing to enact laws to provide an "efficient" education. In a sweeping opinion, *Rose* struck down not just the commonwealth's education finance system, but the entire educational bureaucracy in Kentucky. In other words, the court essentially invalidated the entire system and ordered the legislature to start over. The result, the Kentucky Educational Reform Act, has been a sweeping overhaul of public education in Kentucky.

Finance Litigation

To place *Rose* in context, school-finance litigation is categorized by the different legal theories that drive the arguments. The first wave of school-finance litigation, beginning in the late 1960s, relied on the Equal Protection Clause of the federal, and then state, constitutions. Basically, plaintiffs challenged the disparities in per-pupil expenditures and argued that by relying on local property taxes, states created funding systems for public education in which the differences in educational opportunities were vast, unfair, and unlawful on account of disparities in district wealth. The plaintiffs in these cases claimed that education was a fundamental right; as such, funding systems that classified resource allocation on the basis of individual districts' property tax base required strict judicial scrutiny. In *San Antonio Independent School District v. Rodriguez* (1973), the U.S. Supreme Court rejected a federal equal protection argument and ultimately found that education was not a fundamental right guaranteed by the U.S. Constitution.

Following *Rodriguez,* school-finance litigation focused on state constitutions. The first state-level cases, *McInnis v. Shapiro* (1968) and *Burruss v. Wilkerson* (1970), mirrored the *Rodriguez* arguments. When the courts asked for a standard measuring educational need, no such standard existed and the courts found the cases nonjusticiable. Rejecting the precedents set by *McInnis* and *Burruss,* the Supreme Court of California, in *Serrano v. Priest I* (1971), found that education was a fundamental right. As a result, the court found that California's school-finance system violated the Equal Protection Clauses of both the U.S. and California constitutions, a position that the Supreme Court repudiated, as applied to the federal constitution in *San Antonio.* On further review, in *Serrano v. Priest II* (1976, 1977), the Supreme Court of California affirmed its earlier ruling that education is a fundamental right based on the state constitution.

The ensuing second wave of school funding litigation shifted away from equal protection arguments in the federal Constitution and focused on the education clauses that exist in every state constitution, in some cases combining the two. Plaintiffs in these cases argued that education was a fundamental right determined by the education clause and in some instances unequal funding levels violated the Equal Protection Clause. Litigants were not very successful in making equity arguments. However, in Arkansas, *Dupree v. Alma School District* (1983) found that the school-finance system was unconstitutional on both grounds. The court required the Arkansas legislature to create a new funding system.

The *Rose* Case

With the evolution of standards-based education in the 1980s and more recently the No Child Left Behind Act of 2001, a third wave of litigation based on adequacy arguments developed. *Rose* is recognized as one of the first cases in the third wave. The logic of adequacy suits is as follows: States have expectations, or standards, for school districts, schools, and students; assessments are given to measure success in meeting these expectations; there are ramifications for those who do not meet the standards; and, therefore, states should provide an adequate amount of funding and resources so that the standards can be met. Interestingly, when *Rose* was argued, Kentucky did not already have a set of educational standards. Rather, in a very scathing opinion, the court interpreted the commonwealth's education clause and then required the legislature to "re-create" the entire educational system almost from the ground up.

In 2003, plaintiffs in Kentucky filed a complaint alleging that the per-pupil foundation level, created as a result of the findings in *Rose,* had not increased as quickly as inflation and the cost of education. While this case is as yet unreported and unlitigated on the merits, it may be the beginning of a fourth wave of litigation. Certainly, as the landscape of school-finance litigation has shifted from equality of funding to quality of education, legal theory has also changed from broad equal protection provisions to narrow education clauses. These changes have been accompanied by some sweeping education reforms. The question that remains is whether an emerging fourth wave of school-finance litigation is emerging and, if so, what this may mean for adequacy cases like *Rose.*

Jennifer Silverstein

See also *San Antonio Independent School District v. Rodriguez;* School Finance Litigation; *Serrano v. Priest*

Legal Citations

Burruss v. Wilkerson, 310 F. Supp. 572 (W.D. Va. 1969), aff'd, 397 U.S. 44 (1970).
Dupree v. Alma School District, 651 S.W.2d 90 (Ark. 1983).
McInnis v. Shaprio, 293 F. Supp. 327 (N.D. Ill. 1968).
Rose v. Council for Better Education, 790 S.W.2d 186 (1989).

San Antonio Independent School District v. Rodriguez, 411 U.S. 1 (1973).
Serrano v. Priest I, 487 P.2d 1241 (Cal. 1971).
Serrano v. Priest II, 557 P.2d 929 (Cal. 1976), *cert. denied*, 432 U.S. 907 (1977).

RULE OF LAW

The phrase *rule of law* describes a legal system in which universally applicable laws are established publicly according to regularly established procedures. The rule of law in the Anglo-American common law tradition is based on the principles of constitutionality, equality before the law, and separation of powers. A system based on the rule of law is designed to prevent the arbitrary exercise of political power either for the personal benefit of the rulers or to the personal detriment of the rulers' opponents. In the Western tradition, the concept of a rule of law began with the Romans. In contrast to the Greek democracies, where the majority could rewrite the law to suit its whims, the Romans placed limits on the power of their government to change the law.

Equality before the law means that all people, including those who exercise governmental authority, are subject to the same laws. The rule of law is usually not characterized by laws that apply only to certain individuals or groups. As such, the Fourteenth Amendment to the U.S. Constitution forbids states from denying equal protection of the laws to persons within their jurisdiction; the Fifth Amendment's Equal Protection Clause applies to the federal government.

Under the Fourteenth Amendment, if government action is based on a suspect classification such as race, courts apply strict scrutiny to the law. Pursuant to strict scrutiny analysis, there is usually little or no presumption in favor of governmental actions; this often results in courts striking governmental actions as unconstitutional. The goal of such analysis is to prevent the government, popularly elected by the majority, from passing laws that disadvantage minority groups. Accordingly, the principle of equal protection serves to uphold the rule of law by ensuring that the government applies the same rules to all.

At the same time, the rule of law depends on regular, clearly established legal procedures. In criminal proceedings, for example, appropriate procedures provide assurance that the accused will be treated fairly. Much of the Bill of Rights is designed to prevent the arbitrary exercise of power against the people and thereby to preserve the rule of law. The Fourth, Fifth, Sixth, Seventh, and Eighth Amendments all concern the rights of criminal suspects and defendants as well as civil litigants. The Fourth Amendment's requirement of probable cause for issuing warrants, along with the Fifth Amendment's requirement of a grand jury indictment for serious crimes, together reflect a concern with preventing the government from arresting people and charging them with crimes without ever having to demonstrate the validity of the charges to impartial arbiters. By requiring government officials acting on behalf of the state to observe the same procedures no matter who is the subject of the actions, the due process requirements of the Fifth and Fourteenth Amendments ensure that the state acts equitably and fairly.

The Massachusetts Constitution, I Article XXX, drafted by John Adams, mandated a strict separation of powers in order to preserve "a government of laws and not of men." To this end, the American system maintained and expanded on the common-law tradition of an independent judiciary. The independence and impartiality of judges is crucial to any system in which the rule of law is observed, in order to prevent legislators or the executive branch from unduly influencing the judicial process. The danger in such situations is not only that too much power might be concentrated in the hands of a single person or group of individuals but also that the judiciary would lose its position as an independent arbiter that can prevent a popular majority from oppressing an unpopular minority. Federal judges enjoy lifetime appointments both in order to insulate them from the popular pressures faced by elected legislators and to protect them from electoral retaliation for unpopular verdicts.

In common-law systems, the rule of law is closely connected to the concepts of judicial precedent and stare decisis. Courts defer to earlier rulings in order to minimize the danger that each new judgment might be based solely on the whims of judges who hear cases. Insofar as judges in most American jurisdictions are not directly answerable to the voters for their performances, a strong tradition of judicial precedent is necessary to constrain judges from rendering capricious decisions. Such deference further serves to minimize the possible interference from the legislative and executive branches, since judges tend to rely on other courts for guidance on the interpretation of the law rather than looking to the other branches of government. Adherence to precedent therefore prevents the arbitrary exercise of judicial power, while making legal outcomes more predictable.

The ability to foresee the outcome of legal proceedings makes it possible for citizens to act within the limits set by the law. The U.S. Constitution, for example, forbids ex post facto laws, in which crimes are defined only after their commission. Unless people have a fair idea of the rules by which their actions will be judged, they cannot voluntarily avoid breaking the law. Thus, the rule of law could be said to help encourage lawful behavior. Moreover, the rule of law reduces the inefficiency that results when resources are directed toward activities in good faith, only to have the government, through its officials, step in unexpectedly to halt those activities.

James Mawdsley

See also Bill of Rights; Civil Law; Civil Rights Movement; Common Law; Due Process; Equal Protection Analysis; Fourteenth Amendment; Precedent; Stare Decisis

Further Readings

Bellamy, R. (Ed.). (2005). *The rule of law and the separation of powers.* Burlington, VT: Dartmouth.

Cantor, N. F. (1997). *Imagining the law.* New York: HarperCollins.

Dicey, A. V. (1889). *Introduction to the study of the law of the Constitution.* New York: Macmillan.

Hayek, F. A. (1944). *The road to serfdom.* Chicago: University of Chicago Press.

Runyon v. McCrary

Runyon v. McCrary (1976) stands out because it was the first time the U.S. Supreme Court was asked to determine whether private schools were subject to Section 1981 of the Civil Rights Act of 1866 and therefore prohibited from discriminating on the basis of race. The Court answered in the affirmative.

Facts of the Case

Section 1981 provides all persons with an equal right to enter into and enforce contracts and prohibits racial discrimination in contract formation. While Section 1981 expressly disallowed any discriminatory practices derived from public state action, the implicit question in *Runyon* was whether the authority of Congress extended to prevent racial discrimination of a private nature.

Runyon originated in the 1960s, when public school systems in southeastern United States were subjected to sweeping federal court desegregation decrees opening formerly White schools to Black children. In an effort to circumvent the Supreme Court's ruling in *Brown v. Board of Education of Topeka* (1954, 1955), a number of states closed all or portions of their public school systems and offered support for students to attend private, segregated academies. In *Griffin v. School Board of Prince Edward County* (1963), the Supreme Court ruled that the Commonwealth of Virginia's closing of the entire Prince Edward County school system violated the Equal Protection Clause of the Fourteenth Amendment, and it ordered the schools reopened. Even so, the Court's order did not, and could not, compel the return of White students to the public schools from which they had fled to avoid desegregation. It was in this time period and social context that *Runyon* arose.

In *Runyon,* African American students attempted to establish contractual relationships with two private schools but were denied educational services based on their race. Neither private school ever enrolled a Black student in any of its programs. The African American families that sought admittance for their children were informed that the schools were not integrated and were subsequently denied admittance. Through their parents, the two Black students sued the schools, alleging that their policies of excluding non-Whites violated Section 1981.

The Court's Ruling

On further review of judgments in favor of the students from a federal trial court in Virginia and the Fourth Circuit, the Supreme Court affirmed that the schools violated Section 1981. In its analysis, a unanimous Court applied Section 1981 to the facts and found that the policies of the private schools that denied admittance to qualified Black students based solely on race violated Section 1981, despite the lack of state action typically required to enforce the Fourteenth Amendment's Equal Protection Clause.

Based on the legislative history of Section 1981, the *Runyon* Court reasoned that Section 1981 extended to purely private acts of racial discrimination. Further, the Court was of the opinion that the educational services of the private schools were widely advertised and offered to the general public in a contractual capacity in which educational benefits for qualified students could be exchanged for payment rendered to the facility. As such, the Court pointed out that the general offers of educational services constituted potential commercial contracts, and, as such, the private schools could not refuse to contract with otherwise qualified African American students. In 1991, Congress confirmed the application of Section 1981 to private schools by codifying the prohibition against intentional racial discrimination in private contracting set forth in *Runyon* in Section 1981(c).

In deciding affirmatively that Section 1981 applied to private, commercially operated schools, the Supreme Court further explained that such statutory application did not interfere with the constitutionally protected First Amendment right of free association or the Liberty Clause involving the parental right to direct the education of a child. While the Court conceded that parents have a constitutional right to select educational institutions for their children that espouse certain beliefs even if those beliefs are unconstitutional, the constitution does not protect these institutions if they are engaged in invidious discrimination. Moreover, the Court indicated that the application of Section 1981 to private schools did not circumvent the right of parents to direct the education of their children, nor did it mandate the values and standards to be taught by private schools. The Court thus concluded that the private institutions' and parental Liberty Clause arguments were unpersuasive.

Runyon represents the first foray of Section 1981 into the private sphere of racial discrimination that is divorced from state action. Prior to *Runyon,* invidious racial discrimination in contracting within the private school sector was left largely unregulated and unsanctioned. This expanded scope of antidiscriminatory regulation with respect to contract formation was one of the Court's initial methods of circumscribing private schools' exclusionary enrollment practices based on race. Although the Court has upheld the federal government's denial of tax-exempt status to private schools that discriminate in admissions (*Coit v. Green,* 1971), *Runyon* is particularly significant because it makes the segregation of private schools unlawful, prohibiting them from proffering admission to Whites while denying such opportunities to prospective non-White students.

Aimee R. Vergon

See also *Brown v. Board of Education of Topeka; Brown v. Board of Education* and Equal Educational Opportunities; Equal Protection Analysis; Fourteenth Amendment; Parental Rights

Legal Citations

Brown v. Board of Education of Topeka I, 347 U.S. 483 (1954).
Brown v. Board of Education of Topeka II, 349 U.S. 294 (1955).
Green v. Connally, 330 F. Supp. 1150, *aff'd sub nom. Coit v. Green,* 404 U.S. 991 (1971).
Griffin v. School Board of Prince Edward County, 377 U.S. 218 (1963).
Runyon v. McCrary, 427 U.S. 160 (1976).

RURAL EDUCATION

Many legal and policy issues face rural public schools. These challenges are also somewhat related to the issues facing urban schools, including poverty, increasing populations of English language learners (ELLs) and newcomers, and political isolation. However, others are specific to rural schools, including a shortage of resources, funding inequities, and changing demographics, as described in this entry.

Definition Issues

First, the term *rural,* which is monolithic neither as a taxonomical classification nor as a political economy, encompasses many political ecologies and arenas within one classification. The issues facing rural schools in states with high percentages of private ownership of lands and with an evenly dispersed population in southeastern or midwestern states may be very different from those facing western states.

In the West, a high percentage of land is publicly owned, effectively taking it off the tax rolls. Also, there may be a higher geographical isolation for rural schools and communities in the West based on geography, hydrology, the scarcity of arable soils and water resources, and geologic barriers, such as mountain ranges, deserts, and canyons. Rural schools in communities where populations are "bedroom communities," that is, "rural" communities within reasonable driving or commuting distances of larger metropolitan areas available for employment and purchasing, may be very different from rural small communities that are principal county seats as well as employment and merchant centers for other more rural and isolated communities and dispersed populations.

Until the mid-1960s or earlier, many political scientists suggested that rural areas had disproportionately great political power and political representation because of the U.S. system of regional representation. As rural populations declined, with many people migrating to urban settings, rural districts tended to keep the same number of elected representatives. In the early 1960s, many urban legislative districts had over 1,000 times the number of residents as did equally represented rural districts.

In the recent past, then, the majority of the U.S. population lived in either rural or urban settings. However, this has changed drastically, and the majority of the U.S. population currently lives in suburban settings, neither rural nor urban. This has had a great impact on the law and policy of rural political representation as well as the funding of rural schools and, parenthetically, the policies affecting strictly urban schools and school systems.

Comparative Disadvantage

Regardless of whether it is intended, many federal and state laws and programs tend to advantage suburban/urban over rural schools. For example, the No Child Left Behind Act (NCLB) (2002) provides some key rights to students in failing schools. These rights include, at different levels of school failure or non-compliance with provisions for "adequate yearly progress," having highly qualified teachers; the right to have private tutors; and, ultimately, the right to attend another public or private school.

In many rural communities, no such tutoring or alternate school resources exist. Moreover, rural public schools and districts often do not have high enough populations of teacher candidates and students in schools to allow all teachers to be "highly qualified" under the NCLB's mandates. It is very common, often essential, that teachers in rural schools teach several different subjects, subjects in which they may not have undergraduate majors or teaching certificates. Yet insofar as such schools and systems must employ teachers who are able to teach a number of subjects and levels, rural schools will continually be noncompliant because they will lack an appropriate percentage of "highly qualified" teachers as defined by NCLB.

Finance Issues

Funding inequities plague rural schools vis-à-vis state and federal laws coupled with funding formulas and policies. Often, equalization of funding pressures that are, in and of themselves, useful for other salutary purposes may in some areas have the unintended consequence of harming rural schools. In some regions, there have been many rural school "consolidations," with the attendant closing of small rural schools to achieve greater "efficiencies" of scale. Even so, in such calculations, the impact on rural communities, their identities, and child development are not always easily measured in cost-benefit analyses. In other regions, especially in dispersed and remote western counties and areas, there are few or no schools close enough to consolidate with, and the expense of operating small schools in geographically dispersed areas may be higher than the costs associated with operating suburban schools, including transportation costs and "inefficiently" small class sizes.

Another legal and policy issue confronting rural communities and their schools is the high percentage of federal lands and otherwise reserved lands in many rural counties and school districts. This is especially a western-state issue, because states in this region all have high percentages of federal ownership. The General Services Administration reports, for example, that Arizona is 48% federal land, Utah 57%, Alaska 69%, and Nevada 85%, with all western states having very high percentages of federal ownership. This removes such land from tax rolls. When one includes state-owned lands, situations arise such as in Arizona, in which 48% of the land is federally owned and after removing state and other public types of land ownership, only 18% of the state is privately owned, and thus potentially subject to property taxes. In addition, federal law providing for in lieu payments to school districts for federally reserved land that is not taxed for the benefit of public schools is specifically limited to land reserved before 1938, before almost all the federal parks, forests, and reservation lands were reserved.

While federal land ownership is a significant burden on states, it can be especially burdensome on individual rural school districts and counties within western states. For example, Teton Country in Wyoming is 96% federally owned, and Emery County in Utah is 80%. Even though some statutes return limited amounts of money to such counties through mechanisms such as forest reserve payments, in some western states, these payments often flow to urban and suburban schools that are contiguous to forest land, while truly isolated rural schools with less sources of funding than these urban and suburban schools have been apportioned a smaller amount within the same state.

Further, funding formulas established in dispersed western states often are set up with parameters that advantage urban schools. Even the landing taxes imposed on airliners landing in municipal airports have been sought in one western state, Utah. To the extent that all of those monies went to the urban school districts that are contiguous to the state's principal airport, rural educators sought a statute taxing airliners a percentage as a "flyover" tax. Although the statute was appropriately declared unconstitutional, it highlights another of many inequities in funding that accrue to the benefit of urban and mostly suburban schools, while harming rural schools.

Demographic Challenges

Of course, these funding challenges have coincided with lower birthrates and continuing exodus from many rural school districts. At the same time, rural counties and schools, which may already be experiencing mixed success at meeting the needs of Native American and low-income students, are experiencing a great influx of ELLs. Many rural school districts in the West and the South have gone from almost no ELLs in 1985 to 35% to 40% ELLs or more. This has been a mixed blessing. Many commentators and researchers in rural issues have noted that rural communities' schools and their educators have been generally welcoming of this population of predominantly Latino ELLs.

The influx of students has helped sustain school districts experiencing a decline in enrollments or population. However, these school districts do not always have the capacity in terms of teacher training and community organizations to meet such students' additional learning needs, while often being disadvantaged in funding compared with many suburban and urban districts. Certainly, there are many issues yet to be addressed in meeting the educational needs of rural students from diverse language, cultural, and ethnic communities, while dealing with dwindling resources and lack of sufficient advocacy on national and state levels on behalf of rural populations.

Scott Ellis Ferrin

See also Adequate Yearly Progress; Bilingual Education; English as a Second Language; Highly Qualified Teachers; Limited English Proficiency

Further Readings

Collins, T. (1999). *Attracting and retaining teachers in rural areas.* Charleston, WV: ERIC Clearinghouse on Rural Education and Small Schools. (ERIC Document Reproduction Service No. ED438152)

Education Commission of the States. (n.d.). *Rural overview.* Retrieved from http://www.ecs.org/html/IssueSection.asp? issueid=100&s=Overview

General Accounting Office. (1996, March). *Report to congressional requesters: Land ownership: information on the acreage, management and use of federal and other lands.* Available from http://www.gao.gov/archive/1996 /rc96040.pdf

Gibbs, R., Swain, P. L., & Teixeira, R. A. (Eds.). (1998). *Rural education and training in the new economy: The myth of the rural skills gap.* Ames: Iowa State University Press.

Rural School and Community Trust. (2000, November). North Dakota losing both students and teachers. *Rural Policy Matters, 2*(11). Retrieved from http://www.ruraledu.org/rpm/rpm211b.htm

Rural School and Community Trust. (1999. November). Rural teacher shortages. *Rural Policy Matters, 1*(9). Retrieved from http://www.ruraledu.org/rpm/rpm109e.htm

Legal Citations

No Child Left Behind Act, 20 U.S.C. §§ 6301 *et seq.* (2002).

S

SAN ANTONIO INDEPENDENT SCHOOL DISTRICT V. RODRIGUEZ

San Antonio Independent School District v. Rodriguez (1973) stands out as the only case in which the U.S. Supreme Court addressed the issue of school finance. In *Rodriguez,* the Court upheld Texas's school funding system, which relied on local taxes, finding that it was not unconstitutional under the Equal Protection Clause of the Fourteenth Amendment. In so doing, the Court held that education was not a fundamental right and was not afforded explicit protection under the U.S. Constitution. In addition, the Court essentially repudiated *Serrano v. Priest I* (1971) wherein the Supreme Court of California had decided that education was so protected by the federal constitution. In *Serrano II* (1975), the Supreme Court of California asserted that education was a fundamental right under the state constitution.

Facts of the Case

In *Rodriguez,* parents in several school districts filed suit against state school officials, claiming that Texas's method of funding schools was unconstitutional under the Equal Protection Clause of the Fourteenth Amendment. The record revealed that the system in Texas, under which boards relied on local property taxes to supplement state funds, resulted in substantial disparities in per-pupil funding. This disparity in funding was attributed chiefly to the difference in the amount of money raised through property taxes in each district.

A federal trial court, entering a judgment in favor of the parents, was of the opinion that because the system discriminated on the basis of wealth, it was unconstitutional under the Equal Protection Clause. The court agreed with the parents' argument that because wealth was a so-called suspect class, and education was a fundamental interest, the funding system was subject to the strict scrutiny test under equal protection analysis. This test requires governmental entities to demonstrate the need for a compelling state interest in order to justify their actions. The court was not even satisfied that the state proved that it had a reasonable basis for its system.

The Court's Ruling

On further review, the Supreme Court reversed in favor of the State of Texas. In an opinion authored by Justice Powell, the Court reasoned that education was not a fundamental right, so the strict scrutiny test did not apply. Moreover, he indicated that there was no showing that the funding system discriminated against any discernable category of "poor" people. Recognizing that some families resided in districts with financial disadvantages, Powell rejected the notion that poorer districts met the criterion of being a suspect class.

In his analysis, Justice Powell explained that the system did not deny any child the opportunity to obtain an education, and there was no showing that it denied any child an adequate education. At the same time, he pointed out that the system had a rational relationship to furthering a legitimate state purpose, namely funding public education, because the judiciary traditionally defers to state legislatures in areas of education policy and local taxation. Powell also noted that even though the financing system in Texas was imperfect, it was not the product of purposeful discrimination, and it assured a basic education for every child while encouraging local control of schools through taxation.

Justice Powell next determined that strict scrutiny was an inappropriate test in *Rodriguez*. To this end, he observed that strict scrutiny was the appropriate test when state action resulted in suspect classifications of people or hampered their ability to exercise their constitutionally protected rights. Insofar as the Court refused to identify education as a fundamental right under the U.S. Constitution, Powell held that the test was inappropriate in *Rodriguez*. In light of the particularly sensitive and delicate topics of local taxation, educational policy, fiscal planning, and federalism, Powell maintained that the Texas system should have been scrutinized with principles that were cognizant of the state's efforts in creating it while respecting the rights that are reserved to the states under the Tenth Amendment to the federal Constitution.

According to Justice Powell, the traditional standard of review required only that the funding system in Texas bore some rational relationship to a legitimate state purpose. Because he identified the dispute as a direct attack on the way Texas chose to fund its schools, he posited that interfering with its decision-making authority would have been an intrusion in an area that traditionally was left for the state legislatures. Powell remarked that the justices were neither well versed in nor familiar with the local problems of raising revenue to fund schools, nor did they have the specialized knowledge to make proper decisions about educational policy in Texas. Insofar as the state legislature and local school boards would have been better equipped and more knowledgeable to handle these problems, he decided that the authority to make financing decisions was properly left to state officials.

Rounding out his opinion, Justice Powell took a close look at the Texas system, acknowledging that it provided an adequate minimum education for children. He noted that the system provided enough funds to assure that there was one teacher for every 25 students, all necessary administrative personnel, transportation, and textbooks. While Texas provided the minimum in state funds, Powell found that none of the local school boards was content to rely solely on those funds. Even though this approach created a funding disparity, because some districts had higher property values and more revenue for use in local schools, because the state of Texas provided the necessary minimum amount to ensure that every child received a free public school education, Powell concluded that there was no violation of the Equal Protection Clause in *Rodriguez*.

Justice Stewart concurred on the basis that the funding system in Texas did not create classes of persons that would have been recognized and protected under the Equal Protection Clause. He added that even if the classes did exist, they were not the type that the Equal Protection Clause was intended to protect.

Justice Brennan, joined in dissent by Justices White and Marshall, asserted that education was a fundamental right, because it was inextricably linked to the right to vote and the free speech rights protected by the First Amendment. He therefore was of the view that any classification affecting education should have been subjected to strict scrutiny.

Justice White, along with Justice Douglas and Justice Brennan, also dissented on the ground that the parents constituted a class that should have been offered protection under the Equal Protection Clause.

Megan L. Rehberg

See also Equal Protection Analysis; Federal Role in Education; Federalism and the Tenth Amendment; Fourteenth Amendment; School Finance Litigation; Thorough and Efficient Systems of Education

Legal Citations

San Antonio Independent School District v. Rodriguez, 411 U.S. 1 (1973).
Serrano v. Priest, 96 Cal. Rptr. 601 (Cal. 1971), 135 Cal. Rptr. 345 (Cal. 1976) *cert. denied*, 432 U.S. 907 (1977).

San Antonio Independent School District v. Rodriguez (Excerpts)

In San Antonio Independent School District v. Rodriguez, *its only case involving school finance, the Supreme Court ruled that education is not a fundamental right under the United States Constitution.*

Supreme Court of the United States

SAN ANTONIO INDEPENDENT SCHOOL DISTRICT

v.

RODRIGUEZ

411 US 1

Argued Oct. 12, 1972.

Decided March 21, 1973.

Rehearing Denied April 23, 1973

See 411 U.S. 959.

Mr. Justice POWELL delivered the opinion of the Court.

This suit attacking the Texas system of financing public education was initiated by Mexican-American parents whose children attend the elementary and secondary schools in the Edgewood Independent School District, an urban school district in San Antonio, Texas. They brought a class action on behalf of schoolchildren throughout the State who are members of minority groups or who are poor and reside in school districts having a low property tax base. Named as defendants were the State Board of Education, the Commissioner of Education, the State Attorney General, and the Bexar County (San Antonio) Board of Trustees. The complaint was filed in the summer of 1968 and a three-judge court was impaneled in January 1969. In December 1971 the panel rendered its judgment in a per curiam opinion holding the Texas school finance system unconstitutional under the Equal Protection Clause of the Fourteenth Amendment. The State appealed, and we noted probable jurisdiction to consider the far-reaching constitutional questions presented. For the reasons stated in this opinion, we reverse the decision of the District Court.

I

The first Texas State Constitution, promulgated upon Texas' entry into the Union in 1845, provided for the establishment of a system of free schools. [The Supreme Court then reviewed this history]....

Until recent times, Texas was a predominantly rural State and its population and property wealth were spread relatively evenly across the State. Sizable differences in the value of assessable property between local school districts became increasingly evident as the State became more industrialized and as rural-to-urban population shifts became more pronounced. The location of commercial and industrial property began to play a significant role in determining the amount of tax resources available to each school district. These growing disparities in population and taxable property between districts were responsible in part for increasingly notable differences in levels of local expenditure for education.

In due time it became apparent to those concerned with financing public education that contributions from the Available School Fund were not sufficient to ameliorate these disparities. Prior to 1939, the Available School Fund contributed money to every school district at a rate of $17.50 per school-age child. Although the amount was increased several times in the early 1940's, the Fund was providing only $46 per student by 1945.

Recognizing the need for increased state funding to help offset disparities in local spending and to meet Texas' changing educational requirements, the state legislature in the late 1940's undertook a thorough evaluation of public education with an eye toward major reform. In 1947, an 18-member committee, composed of educators and legislators, was appointed to explore alternative systems in other States and to propose a funding scheme that would guarantee a minimum or basic educational offering to each child and that would help overcome interdistrict disparities in taxable resources. The Committee's efforts led to the passage of the Gilmer-Aikin bills, named for the Committee's co-chairmen, establishing the Texas Minimum Foundation School Program. Today, this Program accounts for approximately half of the total educational expenditures in Texas.

. . . .

The design of this complex system was twofold. First, it was an attempt to assure that the Foundation Program would have an equalizing influence on expenditure levels between school districts by placing the heaviest burden on the school districts most capable of paying. Second, the Program's architects sought to establish a Local Fund Assignment that would force every school district to contribute to the education of its children but that would not by itself exhaust any district's resources. Today every school district does impose a property tax from which it derives locally expendable funds in excess of the amount necessary to satisfy its Local Fund Assignment under the Foundation Program.

In the years since this program went into operation in 1949, expenditures for education—from state as well as local sources—have increased steadily. Between 1949 and 1967, expenditures increased approximately 500%. In the last decade alone the total public school budget rose from $750 million to $2.1 billion and these increases have been reflected in consistently rising per pupil expenditures throughout the State....

The school district in which appellees reside, the Edgewood Independent School District, has been compared throughout this litigation with the Alamo Heights Independent School District. This comparison between the least and most affluent districts in the San Antonio area serves to illustrate the manner in which the dual system of finance operates and to indicate the extent to which substantial disparities exist despite the State's impressive progress in recent years. Edgewood is one of seven public school districts in the metropolitan area. Approximately 22,000 students are enrolled in its 25 elementary and secondary schools. The district is ... situated in the core-city sector of San Antonio in a residential neighborhood that has little commercial or industrial property. The residents are predominantly of Mexican-American descent: approximately 90% of the student population is Mexican-American and over 6% is Negro. The average assessed property value per pupil is $5,960—the lowest in the metropolitan area—and the median family income ($4,686) is also the lowest. At an equalized tax rate of $1.05 per $100 of assessed property—the highest in the metropolitan area—the district contributed $26 to the education of each child for the 1967–1968 school year above its Local Fund Assignment for the Minimum Foundation Program. The Foundation Program contributed $222 per pupil for a state—local total of $248. Federal funds added another $108 for a total of $356 per pupil.

. . . .

. . . . substantial interdistrict disparities in school expenditures found by the District Court to prevail in San Antonio and in varying degrees throughout the State still exist. And it was these disparities, largely attributable to differences in the amounts of money collected through local property taxation, that led the District Court to conclude that Texas' dual system of public school financing violated the Equal Protection Clause. The District Court held that the Texas system discriminates on the basis of wealth in the manner in which education is provided for its people. Finding that wealth is a 'suspect' classification and that education is a 'fundamental' interest, the District Court held that the Texas system could be sustained only if the State could show that it was premised upon some compelling state interest. On this issue the court concluded that '(n)ot only are defendants unable to demonstrate compelling state interests ... they fail even to establish a reasonable basis for these classifications.'

. . . .

. . . . We must decide, first, whether the Texas system of financing public education operates to the disadvantage of some suspect class or impinges upon a fundamental right explicitly or implicitly protected by the Constitution, thereby requiring strict judicial scrutiny. If so, the judgment of the District Court should be affirmed. If not, the Texas scheme must still be examined to determine whether it rationally furthers some legitimate, articulated state purpose and therefore does not constitute an invidious discrimination in violation of the Equal Protection Clause of the Fourteenth Amendment.

II

The District Court's opinion does not reflect the novelty and complexity of the constitutional questions posed by appellees' challenge to Texas' system of school financing. In concluding that strict judicial scrutiny was required, that court relied on decisions dealing with the rights of indigents to equal treatment in the criminal trial and appellate processes, and on cases disapproving wealth restrictions on the right to vote. Those cases, the District Court concluded, established wealth as a suspect classification. Finding that the local property tax system discriminated on the basis of wealth, it regarded those precedents as controlling. It then reasoned, based on decisions of this Court affirming the undeniable importance of education, that there is a fundamental right to education and that, absent some compelling state justification, the Texas system could not stand.

We are unable to agree that this case, which in significant aspects is sui generis, may be so neatly fitted into the conventional mosaic of constitutional analysis under the Equal Protection Clause. Indeed, for the several reasons that follow, we find neither the suspect—classification not the fundamental—interest analysis persuasive.

A

The wealth discrimination discovered by the District Court in this case, and by several other courts that have recently struck down school-financing laws in other States, is quite unlike any of the forms of wealth discrimination heretofore reviewed by this Court. Rather than focusing on the unique features of the alleged discrimination, the courts in these cases have virtually assumed their findings of a suspect classification through a simplistic process of analysis: since, under the traditional systems of financing public schools, some poorer people receive less expensive educations than other more affluent people, these systems discriminate on the basis of wealth. This approach largely ignores the hard threshold questions, including whether it makes a difference for purposes of consideration under the Constitution that the class of disadvantaged 'poor' cannot be identified or defined in customary equal protection terms, and whether the relative—rather than absolute—nature of the asserted deprivation is of significant consequence. Before a State's laws and the justifications for the classifications they create are subjected to strict judicial scrutiny, we think these threshold considerations must be analyzed more closely than they were in the court below.

The case comes to us with no definitive description of the classifying facts or delineation of the disfavored class. . . .

The precedents of this Court provide the proper starting point. The individuals, or groups of individuals, who constituted the class discriminated against in our prior cases shared two distinguishing characteristics: because of their impecunity they were completely unable to pay for some desired benefit, and as a consequence, they sustained an absolute deprivation of a meaningful opportunity to enjoy that benefit. . . .

. . . .

Only appellees' first possible basis for describing the class disadvantaged by the Texas school-financing system—discrimination against a class of defineably 'poor' persons—might arguably meet the criteria established in these prior cases. Even a cursory examination, however, demonstrates that neither of the two distinguishing characteristics of wealth classifications can be found here. First, in support of their charge that the system discriminates against the 'poor,' appellees have made no effort to demonstrate that it operates to the peculiar disadvantage of any class fairly definable as indigent, or as composed of persons whose incomes are beneath any designated poverty level. Indeed, there is reason to believe that the poorest families are not necessarily clustered in the poorest property districts. A recent and exhaustive study of school districts in Connecticut concluded that '(i)t is clearly incorrect . . . to contend that the 'poor' live in 'poor' districts. . . .

Second, neither appellees nor the District Court addressed the fact that, unlike each of the foregoing cases, lack of personal resources has not occasioned an absolute deprivation of the desired benefit. The argument here is not that the children in districts having relatively low assessable property values are receiving no public education; rather, it is that they are receiving a poorer quality education than that available to children in districts having more assessable wealth. Apart from the unsettled and disputed question whether the quality of education may be determined by the amount of money expended for it, a sufficient answer to appellees' argument is that, at least where wealth is involved, the Equal Protection Clause does not require absolute equality or precisely equal advantages. . . .

For these two reasons—the absence of any evidence that the financing system discriminates against any definable category of 'poor' people or that it results in the absolute deprivation of education—the disadvantaged class is not susceptible of identification in traditional terms.

As suggested above, appellees and the District Court may have embraced a second or third approach, the second of which might be characterized as a theory of relative or comparative discrimination based on family income. Appellees sought to prove that a direct correlation exists between the wealth of families within each district and the expenditures therein for education. That is, along a continuum, the poorer the family the lower the dollar amount of education received by the family's children.

. . . .

This brings us, then, to the third way in which the classification scheme might be defined—district wealth discrimination. Since the only correlation indicated by the evidence is between district property wealth and expenditures, it may be argued that discrimination might be found without regard to the individual income characteristics of district residents. Assuming a perfect correlation between district property wealth and expenditures from top to bottom, the disadvantaged class might be viewed as encompassing every child in every district except the district that has the most assessable wealth and spends the most on education. . . .

. . . .

We thus conclude that the Texas system does not operate to the peculiar disadvantage of any suspect class. But in recognition of the fact that this Court has never heretofore held that wealth discrimination alone provides an adequate basis for invoking strict scrutiny, appellees have not relied solely on this contention. They also assert that the State's system impermissibly interferes with the exercise of a 'fundamental' right and that accordingly the prior decisions of this Court require the application of the strict standard of judicial review. It is this question—whether education is a fundamental right, in the sense that it is among the rights and liberties protected by the Constitution—which has so consumed the attention of courts and commentators in recent years.

B

In _Brown v. Board of Education,_ a unanimous Court recognized that 'education is perhaps the most important function of state and local governments.' . . .

. . . .

Nothing this Court holds today in any way detracts from our historic dedication to public education. We are in complete agreement with the conclusion of the three-judge panel below that 'the grave significance of education both to the individual and to our society' cannot be doubted. But the importance of a service performed by the State does not determine whether it must be regarded as fundamental for purposes of examination under the Equal Protection Clause. . . .

'The Court today does not 'pick out particular human activities, characterize them as 'fundamental,' and give them added protection. . . .' To the contrary, the Court simply recognizes, as it must, an established constitutional right, and gives to that right no less protection than the Constitution itself demands.'

. . . .

Education, of course, is not among the rights afforded explicit protection under our Federal Constitution. Nor do we find any basis for saying it is implicitly so protected. As we have said, the undisputed importance of education will not alone cause this Court to depart from the usual standard for reviewing a State's social and economic legislation. It is appellees' contention, however, that

education is distinguishable from other services and benefits provided by the State because it bears a peculiarly close relationship to other rights and liberties accorded protection under the Constitution. Specifically, they insist that education is itself a fundamental personal right because it is essential to the effective exercise of First Amendment freedoms and to intelligent utilization of the right to vote. In asserting a nexus between speech and education, appellees urge that the right to speak is meaningless unless the speaker is capable of articulating his thoughts intelligently and persuasively. The 'marketplace of ideas' is an empty forum for those lacking basic communicative tools. Likewise, they argue that the corollary right to receive information becomes little more than a hollow privilege when the recipient has not been taught to read, assimilate, and utilize available knowledge.

. . . .

Even if it were conceded that some identifiable quantum of education is a constitutionally protected prerequisite to the meaningful exercise of either right, we have no indication that the present levels of educational expenditures in Texas provide an education that falls short. Whatever merit appellees' argument might have if a State's financing system occasioned an absolute denial of educational opportunities to any of its children, that argument provides no basis for finding an interference with fundamental rights where only relative differences in spending levels are involved and where—as is true in the present case—no charge fairly could be made that the system fails to provide each child with an opportunity to acquire the basic minimal skills necessary for the enjoyment of the rights of speech and of full participation in the political process.

. . . .

We have carefully considered each of the arguments supportive of the District Court's finding that education is a fundamental right or liberty and have found those arguments unpersuasive. In one further respect we find this a particularly inappropriate case in which to subject state action to strict judicial scrutiny. The present case, in another basic sense, is significantly different from any of the cases in which the Court has applied strict scrutiny to state or federal legislation touching upon constitutionally protected rights. Each of our prior cases involved legislation which 'deprived,' 'infringed,' or 'interfered' with the free exercise of some such fundamental personal right or liberty. A critical distinction between those cases and the one now before us lies in what Texas is endeavoring to do with respect to education. . . .

IV

In light of the considerable attention that has focused on the District Court opinion in this case and on its California predecessor [in *Serrano v. Priest*], a cautionary postscript seems appropriate. It cannot be questioned that the constitutional judgment reached by the District Court and approved by our dissenting Brothers today would occasion in Texas and elsewhere an unprecedented upheaval in public education. Some commentators have concluded that, whatever the contours of the alternative financing programs that might be devised and approved, the result could not avoid being a beneficial one. But, just as there is nothing simple about the constitutional issues involved in these cases, there is nothing simple or certain about predicting the consequences of massive change in the financing and control of public education. Those who have devoted the most thoughtful attention to the practical ramifications of these cases have found no clear or dependable answers and their scholarship reflects no such unqualified confidence in the desirability of completely uprooting the existing system.

The complexity of these problems is demonstrated by the lack of consensus with respect to whether it may be said with any assurance that the poor, the racial minorities, or the children in over-burdened core-city school districts would be benefited by abrogation of traditional modes of financing education. Unless there is to be a substantial increase in state expenditures on education across the board—an event the likelihood of which is open to considerable question—these groups stand to realize gains in terms of increased per-pupil expenditures only if they reside in districts that presently spend at relatively low levels, i.e., in those districts that would benefit from the redistribution of existing resources. Yet, recent studies have indicated that the poorest families are not invariably clustered in the most impecunious school districts. Nor does it now appear that there is any more than a random chance that racial minorities are concentrated in property-poor districts. . . .

These practical considerations, of course, play no role in the adjudication of the constitutional issues presented here. But they serve to highlight the wisdom of the traditional limitations on this Court's function. The consideration and initiation of fundamental reforms with respect to state taxation and education are matters reserved for the legislative processes of the various States, and we do no violence to the values of federalism and separation of powers by staying our hand. We hardly need add that this Court's action today is not to be viewed as placing its judicial imprimatur on the status quo. The need is apparent for reform in tax systems which may well have relied too long and too heavily on the local property tax. And certainly innovative thinking as to public education, its methods, and its funding is necessary to assure both a higher level of quality and greater uniformity of opportunity. These matters merit the continued attention of the scholars who already have contributed much by their challenges. But the ultimate solutions must come from the lawmakers and from the democratic pressures of those who elect them.

Reversed.

Citation: *San Antonio Independent School District v. Rodriguez*, 411 U.S. 1 (1973).

Santa Fe Independent School District v. Doe

In *Santa Fe Independent School District v. Doe* (2000), its most recent case on the topic of school prayer as this encyclopedia heads to press, the U.S. Supreme Court held that the policy of a school board in a Texas district that allowed students to deliver a nonsectarian, nonproselytizing "invocation and/or message" (i.e., prayer) before varsity high school football games violated the Establishment Clause of the First Amendment. In this landmark case regarding the legality of school prayer, the board contended that control of the pregame message was left to students who also chose the speaker and the content of the message by a majority vote. (Initially, the student who led the prayer, also noted in the policy as an "invocation," was the chaplain of the student council.) However, the Court found that the policy in effect coerced students who chose to attend a high school football game into listening to a school-sponsored religious message. While the board argued that the message that was permitted by the district's policy allowed "private speech," the Court ruled that

the delivery of such a message—over the school's public address system, by a speaker representing the student body, under the supervision of school faculty, and pursuant to a school policy that explicitly and implicitly encourages public prayer—is not properly characterized as "private" speech. (p. 310)

The policy at issue specifically permitted a pregame prayer, student-led and student-initiated, prior to high school football games. In a decidedly narrow ruling, the Supreme Court maintained that such a policy violates the Establishment Clause, noting that unlike a graduation ceremony, football games were not occasions that needed to be "solemnized" by prayer, even prayer described as merely a pregame message led by a student who was selected by a majority of the student body.

In its analysis, the Supreme Court specifically rejected the board's claim that the pregame messages were actually private student speech protected by the First Amendment's Free Speech and Free Exercise clauses. According to the Court, not only did the school board allow the prayer to take place, officials had created a policy outlining how this prayer at a school-sponsored event, on school property, was to take place. In fact, the Court determined that the policy actually encouraged and invited a religious prayer and that students interpreted the policy in just such a manner. Thus, the Court was of the opinion that the policy would only lead to student messages that were, rather than private speech, actually religious speech directly sponsored and endorsed by a governmental agency.

The board also argued that because the football games were completely voluntary, there was no issue of mandatory attendance or coercion of students to attend and be subjected to the prayer. The Supreme Court observed that many students are obligated to attend football games, even to earn credit in classes such as athletics, band, and other extracurricular activities. Still, the Court indicated that students who did choose to attend the football games, regardless of whether they were mandatory, would have been subject to board-sponsored prayer.

In applying the *Lemon* test to this policy, the Supreme Court noted that the district's policy did not have a secular legislative purpose; in fact, the only purpose the Court found for this policy was to endorse student-led prayer. Although the decision was split

6-to-3, the Court concluded that even when the policy was amended to allow only nonsectarian, nonproselytizing prayer, it still violated the Establishment Clause of the First Amendment.

Stacy L. Edmonson

See also First Amendment; *Lemon v. Kurtzman;* Prayer in Public Schools; Religious Activities in Public Schools

Further Reading

Thompson, D., & Edmonson, S. (2002). Policy alternatives for student pre-activity and graduation messages in light of *Santa Fe v. Doe. West's Education Law Reporter, 163*(2), 541–550.

Legal Citations

Santa Fe Independent School District v. Doe, 530 U.S. 290 (2000).

SCALIA, ANTONIN (1936–)

President Ronald Reagan nominated Antonin Scalia to serve on the U.S. Supreme Court in 1986. After his appointment was affirmed unanimously in the U.S. Senate, he officially took his oath on September 26, 1986. At his Senate Judiciary Committee confirmation hearing, he stated that his only agenda was to be a good judge.

Early Years

Antonin Scalia was born on March 11, 1936, in Trenton, New Jersey, the sole child of S. Eugene and Catherine Scalia. His father came to the United States from Sicily and was a professor of Romance languages. His mother, who was also of Italian heritage, was a teacher. Justice Scalia was the first justice of Italian American heritage and is a purveyor of the American dream.

Scalia attended a military prep school, St. Francis Xavier, and Georgetown University, where he graduated first in his class in 1957. He went to Harvard Law School, serving as notes editor of the *Harvard Law*

Review and graduating magna cum laude in 1960. While at Harvard, Scalia met and married Maureen McCarthy, an English major at Radcliffe College; they have nine children.

After graduating from law school, Scalia worked at a law firm and taught at the University of Virginia Law School. He began his career in government service as general counsel for the U.S. Office of Telecommunications Policy during the administration of President Nixon and served in President Ford's Department of Justice as assistant attorney general in charge of the Office of Legal Counsel. Additionally, he worked as a resident scholar at the American Enterprise Institute while also teaching at the Georgetown University Law Center and the University of Chicago Law School.

In 1982, President Reagan appointed Scalia to the U.S. Court of Appeals for the District of Columbia Circuit.

Supreme Court Record

In his time on the Supreme Court, Scalia has been defined through his debates and opinions as a textualist, or one who begins with the legal text of the Constitution, and an originalist as one who seeks the original meaning of a text in his interpretations and understanding of the role of the Supreme Court. He has often argued that specific parts of statutes did not fit the intent of the federal Constitution. To this end, Scalia has a talent for putting complex arguments about fundamental principles in easy-to-understand terms. His opinions and concurrences, along with his often strident dissents, span topics including free speech, separation of powers, race, abortion, the death penalty, religious freedom, and gender equity.

Scalia has declared his "original meaning" or textual stance consistently, indicating that it is a judge's duty to apply the textual language of the Constitution or a statute when it is clear and to apply the appropriate legal precedents when it is not. Given this position, he believes that insofar as laws say what they mean and mean what they say, judges should focus on their texts. Moreover, Scalia has maintained that judges should determine whether a text provides support for the individual rights or governmental authority in question. If the text provides the support, then he would argue that a claim is valid. Conversely, Scalia is of the view that if a text does not support a claim, then it should be struck down as invalid.

Justice Scalia has added that the American people, not the justices, can alter the U.S. Constitution through the amendment process to meet the needs of a changing society. He has continually emphasized that justices need to interpret the Constitution as it is written and enforce general and clear rules. From Scalia's perspective, the American people will receive consistent and equal treatment if courts apply this principle and will not be subjected to the whims of preference or changes in popular opinions. In over 600 rulings, Scalia's majority, concurring, and dissenting opinions reflect this belief, a system that entails looking at what a text says while examining how it might fit into social or practical contexts.

Prior to Justice Scalia's appointment to the Court, the justices would often begin with the text, but then move to its legislative history. Today, the justices consult legislative history less frequently. While Scalia's constitutional opinions are full of text and tradition, his positions have not always prevailed, especially in areas dealing with religion such as prayer at public school graduation ceremonies (*Lee v. Weisman,* 1992) or the posting of the Ten Commandments in public places (*American Civil Liberties Union v. McCreary County, Kentucky,* 2005).

Because Justice Scalia is in good health and already has more than 20 years of service on the Supreme Court, his tenure may well span at least three decades as a justice.

Deborah E. Stine

See also Lee v. Weisman; Rehnquist Court; Roberts Court; U.S. Supreme Court Cases in Education

Further Readings

Eastland, T. (2006). The good judge: Antonin Scalia's two decades on the Supreme Court. *The Weekly Standard, 12*(09). Retrieved January 23, 2008, from http://www .weeklystandard.com/Content/Public/Articles/000/000/ 012/905supsw.asp

Lazarus, E. (1999). *Closed chambers: The rise, fall and future of the modern Supreme Court.* New York: Penguin Books.

Ring, K. A. (Ed.). (2004). *Scalia dissents: Writings of the Supreme Court's wittiest, most outspoken justice.* Washington, DC: Regnery.

Rossum, R. A. (2006). *Antonin Scalia's jurisprudence: Text and tradition.* Lawrence: University Press of Kansas.

Legal Citations

American Civil Liberties Union v. McCreary County, Kentucky, 545 U.S. 844 (2005).

Lee v. Weisman, 505 U.S. 577 (1992).

SCHAFFER EX REL. SCHAFFER V. WEAST

In *Schaffer ex rel. Schaffer v. Weast* (2005), the U.S. Supreme Court declared that the party challenging an individualized education program (IEP) bears the burden of proof at an administrative due process hearing under the Individuals with Disabilities Education Act (IDEA). Because it is generally the parents of students with disabilities who bring IEP challenges, *Schaffer* effectively placed the burden of proof on parents in most situations. This entry summarizes the case and the court ruling.

Facts of the Case

The original dispute in *Schaffer* concerned the appropriate program for a student with learning disabilities, language disabilities, and other health impairments who attended a private school. In spite of small classes, the student was not successful, and his parents contacted the public school district seeking special education services. The school board determined that the student was eligible for services and proposed an IEP, but the parents rejected the proposed IEP and requested a due process hearing. At the same time, the parents enrolled their son in a private school for students with disabilities.

Following a hearing, an administrative law judge (ALJ) concluded that the school board offered the student a free appropriate public education (FAPE). In reaching that decision, the ALJ determined that the parents bore the burden of proof in establishing that the proposed IEP was inadequate. The parents appealed, and the federal district court in Maryland remanded to the ALJ, holding that the burden of proof should be placed on the board in any administrative hearing regarding an initial IEP (*Brian S. v. Vance*, 2000).

On remand, the ALJ reversed, concluding that the proposed IEP would not have provided the student with an appropriate education. In the meantime, the school board appealed the district court's ruling to the Fourth Circuit, which vacated the trial court's order and remanded with directions to consider the case on its merits (*Schaffer v. Vance*, 2001). On remand, the trial court again held that the school board bore the burden of proof at the administrative level. The court also decided that the board failed to offer the child a FAPE (*Schaffer v. Vance*, 2002).

Following another appeal, the Fourth Circuit reversed and placed the burden of proof back on the parents (*Weast v. Schaffer*, 2004). The court maintained that a school board should not have the burden of proof in an IEP challenge just because it has the statutory obligation to propose an appropriate educational program for a child. Further, the court did not see that the school board had an unfair information or resource advantage that would compel the court to reassign the burden of proof to the school board when the parents initiate the proceedings. Basically, the Fourth Circuit could not find any reason to depart from the general rule that a party initiating a proceeding bears the burden of proof.

The Court's Ruling

In a 6-to-2 decision, with newly appointed Chief Justice Roberts abstaining, the Supreme Court affirmed. Writing for the majority, Justice O'Connor, in her last education-related case on the Court, agreed with the Fourth Circuit that the ordinary default rule is that plaintiffs bear the risk of failing to prove their claims. Noting that assigning the burden of persuasion to school boards might encourage educators to put more resources into preparing IEPs and presenting evidence, she wrote that the IDEA is silent about whether marginal dollars should be allocated to litigation and administrative expenditures or to educational services.

Further, O'Connor reasoned that the IDEA relies heavily on the expertise of school officials to meet its goals. School officials have a natural advantage in information and expertise, but O'Connor thought that Congress addressed this when it required school boards to safeguard the procedural rights of parents and to share information with them. Thus, in her view, the IDEA ensures parents access to an expert who can evaluate all the materials that the school must make available and who can give an independent opinion. O'Connor added that parents are not left to challenge school boards without realistic opportunities to access the necessary evidence or without an expert with the firepower to match the opposition.

Justice Ginsburg filed a dissenting opinion. Basically, Justice Ginsburg pointed out that policy considerations, convenience, and fairness called for assigning the burden of proof to the school board in this case, because the IDEA is atypical in that it casts an affirmative beneficiary-specific obligation on providers of public education. Noting that school boards are charged with the responsibility to offer an IEP to each disabled child, Ginsburg was of the opinion that the proponent of the IEP is properly called upon to demonstrate its adequacy.

Allan G. Osborne, Jr.

See also Disabled Persons, Rights of; Due Process Hearing, Free Appropriate Public Education; Individualized Education Program (IEP)

Further Readings

Osborne, A. G., & Russo, C. J. (2005). The burden of proof in special education hearings: Schaffer v. Weast. *Education Law Reporter, 200,* 1–12.

Russo, C. J., & Osborne, A. G. (2006). The Supreme Court clarifies the burden of proof in special education due process hearings: *Schaffer ex rel. Schaffer v. Weast. Education Law Reporter, 208,* 705–717.

Legal Citations

Brian S. v. Vance, 86 F. Supp.2d 538 (D. Md. 2000).

Individuals with Disabilities Education Act, 20 U.S.C. §§ 1400 *et seq.*

Schaffer v. Vance, 2 Fed. Appx. 232 (4th Cir. 2001); 240 F. Supp. 2d 396 (D. Md. 2002).

Schaffer ex rel. Schaffer v. Weast, 546 U.S. 49 (2005).

Weast v. Schaffer, 377 F.3d 449 (4th Cir. 2004).

SCHOOL-BASED DECISION MAKING

The record of American public education is characterized by sporadic alterations between centralization and decentralization of influence and control. In times of greater centralized authority, large managerial structures such as state and local boards of education maintain control over educational decision making and management. When the trend swings toward decentralization, much of this power shifts to smaller managerial units such as smaller schools and an array of school councils.

During the last 20 years or so, educational systems in the United States have been evolving from largely centralized to more decentralized structures. In fact, virtually all jurisdictions have laws in place that either mandate or permit decentralization, whether at the state (or commonwealth) level as in Kentucky or on a district level as in Chicago. While this trend goes by many names, it is often referred to as school-based decision making (SBDM), site-based management, or participatory decision making. This entry looks at the practice and its history.

Historical Background

There are about 16,000 school districts in the United States, down from over 100,000 at the start of the 1900s. Most of the early districts, which consisted of one school in rural areas, were small, locally operated organizations that spawned favoritism, nepotism, and deception. These characteristics led to the call for reform, consolidation, and centrally controlled schools. This trend continued through the 1960s, when critics began to call on boards to be responsive to the needs of local communities.

The pendulum began to swing the other way, and considerable decentralization did occur in levels of authority. For instance, starting in the 1960s, in many locations, building-level administrators and faculty were granted increased autonomy and responsibility as site councils developed. At this time, decision making at school sites increased, and roles began to change.

During the 1970s and 1980s, there was something of a power shift back to the centralized model as states and the federal governments attempted to bring about top-down educational reform through legislation. The problem, now widely recognized, was that highly centralized educational organizations simply do not engender the desired outcomes, because they can easily become bogged down with trivia. The result was, and is, inertia, pessimism, inefficiency, cynicism, and long delays for making decisions of any kind, even on the smallest of matters. An equally significant concern was the repeated failure of centralized bureaucratic organizations to inspire the prerequisite attitudes and behaviors in school personnel for bringing about educational improvements.

Looking at the Practice

Early attempts to decentralize control over public schools in locations such as New York City in the 1960s were aimed at moving authority from large, central units to smaller, site-based boards. This innovation was an attempt to replace one form of bureaucracy with another, moving decision making closer to the level where decisions would be implemented. However, proponents believe that SBDM is considerably more that a new name for an old and recurring phenomenon. Supporters of this approach maintain that unlike previous approaches to decentralizing education, SBDM invokes fundamental changes. As one author points out, past forms of governance transferred control from large to small units, while SBDM changes entire district organizations by restructuring most roles in school systems.

The implementation of SBDM is typically accompanied by organizational and managerial questions. Among the key issues are defining what it means to be site based, how roles change for school personnel, and what the obstacles are to implementing and sustaining this approach, as well as considering whether research supports the move to this model of school governance.

The current rationale for decentralized schooling, and particularly SBDM, has developed both in recognition of the foregoing issues and in response to research findings about more promising arrangements for improving educational outcomes in students. This research concludes that because schools are the primary units of change, those who work directly with children should have the most informed and credible opinions as to what educational arrangements are most beneficial to their students. This approach acknowledges that because significant and lasting improvements take considerable time, educators at the local level, often acting in conjunction with parents and community members, are in the best position to sustain improvement efforts over time.

At the same time, an approach that supports decentralization notes that school administrators are key figures in school improvement. It also acknowledges that significant change is brought about by staff and community participation in project planning and implementation. Further, SBDM supports the professionalization of teaching, which can lead to more desirable student outcomes while keeping the focus of schooling where it belongs—on academic achievement.

What Happens in Schools

Many changes occur when school systems elect to implement SBDM in some or all of their schools. According to the growing body of implementation research, the major impact of setting SBDM in place is that the roles of all educational stakeholders— superintendents, other central office personnel, board members, principals, teachers, and students—are profoundly affected by the shift. Additionally, SBDM and joint decision-making strategies directly challenge the multifaceted and well-entrenched patterns of instructional and individual behavior that remain untouched by most reforms

It is almost impossible to make radical changes in the roles of school-level personnel without modifying traditional district administrative roles. Many writers have presented specific findings about these changes. Experience in districts that have adopted SBDM demonstrates that strong support from superintendents is absolutely necessary for its proper implementation; virtually all who study SBDM concur with this perspective. To this end, superintendents should be the ones to communicate to their communities what SBDM is and why it is desirable in order to foster shared understanding and support. Along with change for superintendents, under SBDM, the role of central office personnel shifts from a primary focus on giving directives and monitoring compliance to serving as resources for and facilitators of school-level change efforts.

Under site-based management, the role of the principal is most subject to change. This transformation is sometimes expressed as changing the principal's role from that of building manager to that of educational leader. Instead of simply enforcing policies made elsewhere, SBDM principals work collegially with personnel, including parents, by sharing power collaboratively. In SBDM schools, principals typically move closer to the educational process, serving as instructional leaders who climb higher in the organization's chain of command due to the increased authority and accountability that shifts into their hands.

Prior to the advent of SBDM, teachers have often been cut off from participating in decision making and meaningful contact with one another. Another benefit of SBDM is that it tends to augment teacher participation in educational decision making, often to a considerable extent, typically giving teachers a renewed sense of dedication.

Parents and community representatives have generally been unaware of and detached from educational decision making and school operations. In an attempt to gain their participation, many SBDM statutes and policies, especially in Kentucky and Chicago, not only make use of increased parent/community input but also provide training to help these individuals become more capable participants in the process. Students have traditionally been isolated from operational and policy decisions. Under SBDM, students, particularly older ones, often have influence in these areas by giving advice and input.

A final group that has not yet been identified in the SBDM process is school boards. Although some board members feared that SBDM would usurp their power, they still have the duty to provide general direction for their districts by establishing goals and policy statements, allocating resources, and monitoring progress. Clear messages of support from boards for SBDM can lend credibility and foster positive community attitudes toward the process. In fact, the role of boards does not change as dramatically as that of some other stakeholders, but their support remains vital in implementing SBDM.

Challenges

Some of the literature on SBDM focuses on difficulties that schools and boards have had with the process. Some of these difficulties involve implementation, others arise in connection with the operation of SBDM structures, and yet others concern the failure of many initiatives to bring about the academic results desired by educators and other stakeholders. One difficulty that emerges is that many schools pilot-testing SBDM tend to undertake too many projects and procedural changes during their first year or two of operation rather than focus on the primary concern for fostering student achievement through curricular innovation. The research on SBDM makes it abundantly clear that its full institutionalization can take a long time, as long as five years or more.

SBDM councils, the bodies concerned with planning and decision making in most statutes, often have extensive responsibilities, including making recommendations for replacing personnel who leave schools. Typical problems that SDBM groups face in starting up include lack of knowledge of school operations, of group process skills, and of the law, as well as a lack of clarity about their roles. Another obstacle that frequently hampers SBDM efforts is lack of adequate financial resources. This may take the form of insufficient released time for planning and/or insufficient resources to implement plans once they are made. SBDM groups also have a tendency to fail to focus on instructional programs and student outcomes.

Research clearly establishes that teachers' desire to participate in decision making centers on their schools' technical core, its curriculum, and its instructional program. Unfortunately, absent clear legislative mandates in SBDM statutes, school boards are often unwilling to delegate real decision-making authority to SBDM groups in these areas. Such an approach may not sit well with principals, but it is almost universally frustrating to teachers. For one thing, teachers resent being excluded from decision making in areas about which they know a great deal. Just as distressing, teachers often discover that they are expected to use time and energy that they would ordinarily have spent on activities related to their teaching responsibilities for decision making in areas they would just as soon leave to administrators. In addition, the research reveals that increased board flexibility and selective waiving of these constraints is associated with more successful SBDM efforts.

The frequent failure of SBDM efforts to address schools' programs of instruction is related to another and perhaps more critical challenge. This difficulty involves the tendency of those implementing SBDM to forget that it is not an end in itself, but rather a means to improving student performance through bringing about positive changes in the quality of schooling.

The ultimate goal of SBDM is to improve student learning. Even so, the data are thin relative to finding direct links between student performance and the implementation of SBDM in schools. In some settings, student scores on state and national tests have improved slightly, while in others, they have declined slightly. However, in most SBDM schools, it has made little difference.

States have considerable power to help SBDM arrangements to succeed through providing their practitioners with real support. These states have done so by encouraging or mandating school boards to utilize SBDM as a means for improving student performance and overall educational conditions. Moreover, state officials can assist by making it clear to superintendents and central office staff that schools require considerable authority and flexibility in order to be able to engender real improvements under SBDM. Successful states have also provided professional development opportunities, research-based information, and on-site assistance to help in the implementation of SBDM.

C. Daniel Raisch

See also Charter Schools; School Boards; School Choice

Further Readings

Conley, S. C., & Bacharach, S. B. (1990). From school-site management to participatory school-site management. *Phi Delta Kappan, 71*(7), 539–544.

Cromwell, S. (2005). Site-based management: Boon or boondoggle? Available from http://www.educationworld .com

David, J. L. (1989). Synthesis of research on school based management. *Educational Leadership, 46*(8), 45–53.

Odden, A. R. (1995). *Critical issue: Transferring decision making to local schools: Site-based management.* North Central Regional Education Laboratory. Retrieved January 18, 2008, from http://www.ncrel.org/sdrs/areas/ issues/envrnmnt/go/go100.htm

White, P. A. (1989). An overview of school-based management: What does the research say? *NASSP Bulletin, 73*(518), 1–8.

SCHOOL BOARD OF NASSAU COUNTY V. ARLINE

School Board of Nassau County v. Arline (1987) centered on the difficult dilemma that occurs when the rights of individuals with disabilities must be balanced against the authority of officials in school systems to take action to protect the health and well-being of others. At issue in *Arline* was whether Section 504 of the Rehabilitation Act of 1973 applied to persons with communicable diseases and if so, what should be done in evaluating whether such individuals could be reasonably accommodated. According to Section 504, "No otherwise qualified handicapped individual . . . shall, solely by reason of his handicap, be excluded from the participation in, be denied the benefits of, or be subjected to discrimination under any program or activity receiving Federal financial assistance." In *Arline,* the U.S. Supreme Court held that Section 504 applied to a teacher who had tuberculosis and wished to remain at her job.

Facts of the Case

Gene Arline, who taught elementary school in Nassau County, Florida, had recurring lapses of tuberculosis. After a third bout with the disease, school board officials terminated her employment; the teacher filed suit, claiming that because her dismissal constituted discrimination on the basis of a "handicap," it was prohibited under Section 504. Moreover, the teacher claimed that she was "otherwise qualified" for her job but excluded because of her disability.

When a federal trial court in Florida ruled that the teacher did not have a disability as defined by Section 504, it entered a judgment in favor of the school board. However, after the Eleventh Circuit reversed in favor of the teacher, the board appealed.

The Court's Ruling

On further review, a seven-member majority of the Supreme Court affirmed in favor of the teacher. As an initial matter, in writing for the Court, Justice Brennan was of the opinion that persons with contagious diseases that substantially affected a major life activity such as work enjoyed protection as persons with disabilities under Section 504. Therefore, he rejected the school board's assertion that its decision based on contagiousness proved that its action was not made on the basis of a disability.

Justice Brennan next adopted a four-part test taken from the amicus curiae brief filed by the American Medical Association to evaluate whether persons with contagious diseases could be considered "otherwise qualified" under Section 504. The test requires the consideration of

> (a) the nature of the risk (how the disease is transmitted), (b) the duration of the risk (how long is the carrier infectious), (c) the severity of the risk (what is the potential harm to third parties), and (d) the probabilities the disease will be transmitted and will cause varying degrees of harm. (p. 288, citing brief at p. 19)

Finding that the lower courts had neither made findings of fact on these issues nor had they engaged in an analysis related to each factor, Justice Brennan remanded the dispute for further consideration consistent with the test articulated in his order.

Chief Justice Rehnquist's dissent was joined by Justice Scalia. These justices essentially agreed with the school board that persons who were contagious were not disabled within the meaning of Section 504.

The *Arline* test has subsequently been used to consider whether accommodations could be made for persons with other contagious diseases, including Acquired Immune Deficiency Syndrome (AIDS), and for children who were HIV-positive as in another case from Florida, *Martinez v. School Board of Hillsborough County* (1988).

Julie F. Mead

See also Americans with Disabilities Act; Disabled Persons, Rights of; Rehabilitation Act of 1973, Section 504; *Southeastern Community College v. Davis*

Further Readings

Fitzpatrick, R. B., & Benaroya E. A. (1992). Americans with Disabilities Act and AIDS. *Labor Lawyer, 8,* 249–268.
Colker, R. (2002). The death of Section 504. *University of Michigan Journal of Law Reform, 35,* 219–234.

Legal Citations

Martinez v. School Board of Hillsborough County, 861 F.2d 1502 (11th Cir. 1988).
Rehabilitation Act of 1973, Section 504, 29 U.S.C. § 794(a).
School Board of Nassau County v. Arline, 480 U.S. 273 (1987).

SCHOOL BOARD POLICY

School board policy provides a legal and administrative framework governing a board's procedures, decisions, and actions. Policy at the school district level addresses both direct and indirect functions of schooling. Policies adopted by local school boards ordinarily control student academic achievement levels, curricula, instruction, and grading as well as student enrollment, attendance, discipline, and disciplinary removal procedures. Matters involving board election procedures, board meeting protocols, and board decision-making processes are also codified in board policies. In addition, policies control board fiscal activities such as payroll, purchasing, facilities, and transportation as well as personnel matters relating to contracts, employee evaluation, and dismissal. This entry describes some relevant court rulings and current issues.

Insofar as the U.S. Constitution makes no mention of public education as a right, it is historically regarded as a matter of state and local control. Education is typically a provision embedded within state constitutions, from which power is delegated to state legislatures and other state educational bodies. With the exception of Hawaii, which consists of a single district, a considerable degree of school governance is accorded by the state legislature to local educational officials. Further, state statutes defer most issues governing responsibilities, which to varying degrees involve executive, legislative, and judicial tasks, to local educational units, which in turn formulate a broad range of policies to suit the needs of their respective districts. At the same time, it must be noted that while school boards serve and act locally, they are considered state agencies. As such, school board policy making is circumscribed by state statutes.

Court Rulings

Case law is instructive with regard to the policy-making power of school boards. Case law suggests that school boards encounter particular difficulties when executing implied or discretionary policy-making powers or those powers not delineated by state law. In *McGilvra v. Seattle School District No. 1* (1921), the Supreme Court of Washington ruled that a school board's financial support and maintenance of a medical care facility for students was unlawful, because it exceeded the limitations of state law. Unlike playgrounds and gymnasiums, the court expressed that "rendering medical, surgical, and dental services" was "foreign to the powers to be exercised by a school district or its officers . . ." (p. 14).

In like fashion, the Supreme Court of Pennsylvania, in *Barth v. Philadelphia School District* (1958), decided that because school boards were not "constitutional bodies" (p. 561), they were not entitled to "the wide basic powers, functions and duties of Municipal Government" (p. 564). In this dispute, a local board was party to an agreement with the city of Philadelphia in financially supporting a program to curb juvenile delinquency. The court invalidated the program on the basis that it related marginally if at all to the statutory support of essential educational functions.

More recent cases reflect a more accommodating judicial stance toward implied policy-making power, part of which may be due to changes in social conditions and government. For example, in *Clark v. Jefferson County Board of Education* (1982), the Supreme Court of Alabama upheld a school board's power to support the operation of day care centers. Stressing the importance of the community education aspect, the school district was persuasive in demonstrating that such an effort was "in the best interest of the public schools in Alabama" (p. 27).

Past and present, the discretionary powers of school boards in policy matters continue to be challenged in areas such as curriculum and materials (e.g., *Board of Education, Island Trees Union Free School District No. 26 v. Pico,* 1982; *Mozert v. Hawkins County Public Schools,* 1987), bilingual education (e.g., *Lau v. Nichols,* 1974), graduation requirements (e.g., *Debra P. v. Turlington,* 1984), and student attendance, assignment, and classification (*Plyler v. Doe,* 1982; *Parents Involved in Community Schools v. Seattle School District No. 1,* 2007), to name a few.

Current Issues

There is also much debate as to whether those serving on school boards have sufficient policy-making ability. With heightened productivity expectations, stakes for school boards have increased. Mayoral takeovers or the threats thereof and greater federal and state inspection of local governance, such as with regard to curricula, underscore the need for effective leadership at the board level. Even so, it appears that policy-making capacities of board members are complex and multifaceted.

Yet, some depict school boards as entities lacking sufficient "bureaucratic intelligence" to micromanage policy development in technical form. To this end, maintaining legitimacy as a governing body is of vital interest to board members who place secondary importance on the interests of the community. Further, school boards rationally and irrationally govern in ways that shield them from criticism and disruption.

The arrival of the No Child Left Behind Act (2002) has forced local school boards to focus greater attention on standards, teacher quality, and performance data, among other items. Moreover, school boards are called on to utilize funds more efficiently. It seems that without question, accountability and fiscal efficiency are two of the most critical issues facing board members today. All the same, little is known about the effect that overconcentration on these issues by school boards bears on their attention to other policy domains, particularly student speech and expression. While demands intensify for board members to acquire an increasingly technical expertise of educational issues such as examining test data, little is known about the extent to which school boards intervene in academic and legal policy development.

To be sure, public interest in school boards has gradually faded over time. Even though school boards remain revered symbols in local politics, they have generally failed to capture a high level of public interest and attention. Some believe that the apathy is partly due to the adversarial, nondeliberative democratic nature of school boards. Others suggest that the geographical placement and the size of the school district predict the level of board participation and responsiveness. Research also suggests that typical urban school governance is less community oriented, less responsive, and more bureaucratic in terms of control over curriculum, personnel, and finance than its rural counterpart. Greater interest on the whole might be attained through tinkering with elements such as consolidating school board elections with larger general elections. This might generate more participation in elections for public school boards, even as governance remains largely unmonitored by the public despite the considerable power that local boards wield.

Mario S. Torres, Jr.

See also Authority Theory; Bureaucracy; Federalism and the Tenth Amendment; School Boards

Legal Citations

Barth v. Philadelphia School District, 132 A.2d 909 (Pa. 1958).
Board of Education, Island Trees Union Free School District No. 26 v. Pico, 4555 U.S. 903 (1982).
Clark v. Jefferson County Board of Education, 410 So. 2d 23 (Ala. 1982).
Debra P. v. Turlington, 730 F.2d 1405 (11th Cir. 1984).
Lau v. Nichols, 483 F.2d 791 (9th Cir. 1973); 414 U.S. 563 (1974).
McGilvra v. Seattle School District No. 1, 194 P. 817 (Wash. 1921).
Mozert v. Hawkins County Public Schools, 827 F.2d 1058 (6th Cir. 1987).
No Child Left Behind Act, 20 U.S.C. §§ 6301 *et seq.* (2002).
Parents Involved in Community Schools v. Seattle School District No. 1, 127 S. Ct. 2738 (2007).
Plyler v. Doe, 458 U.S. 1131 (1982).

School Boards

The almost 16,000 school boards in the United States, which trace their origins to colonial America, are an integral part of a complex system of school governance. State legislatures created local school boards to carry out the state function of providing public education by executing and administering statutes and policies. School boards, then, are state agencies. Therefore, even though board members are elected locally, they are, in fact, state officials. Further, school board functions and authority are delineated in state statutes, as described in this entry.

What They Do

As educational agencies, school boards have three functions: legislative, executive, and quasi-judicial. The legislative function includes the authority to make rules and regulations for the effective operation of school systems. School boards may also levy taxes for the funding of the educational enterprises over which they have authority.

School board executive functions fall into two categories. The first type of power that boards exercise is discretionary, the larger portion of their administrative authority. Discretionary functions are actions that entail a board's judgment, such as hiring personnel, entering into contracts with vendors, or deciding whether to offer course electives or extracurricular activities for students. Boards also exercise ministerial functions, tasks that are carried out by administrators and do not require judgment. School boards may delegate ministerial but not discretionary functions.

The quasi-judicial function of school boards deals with the authority to make decisions that involve individuals. These include disciplinary hearings for both students and employees. Determinations in these decisions are binding. School boards must ensure that subjects of hearings receive fairness and due process.

Membership and Meetings

School board members are public officers, indicating that they have a delegation of sovereign power of the state. Put another way, board members have powers and duties conferred by their state legislatures which they must carry out independently and without the control of superior powers. Most school board members are elected, although a small number of boards, often in large cities, are actually appointed. Whether elected or appointed, school board membership is a public office, and each member takes an oath of office.

School boards can act only as a body. This means that the only formal power that school boards or individual members have is to cast their votes on items at formal board meetings. Members have no authority to act individually, separate from their entire boards. Even so, individual board members have the informal ability to influence the actions of the board as well as school staff.

All official board transactions and business, including voting, must take place during regular school board meetings or at special meetings convened for a certain purpose. Any actions or decisions that occur outside of formal meetings are invalid. Moreover, a basic rule is that such meetings must take place within the geographical boundaries of the district that members represent. Additionally, unless specified in legislation, individual school boards choose the procedure by which to conduct their meetings. While courts have been lenient concerning meeting procedures, boards must comply with open meetings and open or public record laws.

As a means of making them more open and accessible to the public, school board meetings must comply with state "sunshine laws." The criteria for evaluating whether meetings satisfy these laws include the following:

- whether the matters under discussion were crucial to policy decisions
- whether there was a quorum of the board present
- whether those in opposition were absent
- whether the intentions of those present were to obscure the action taken
- the nature and planning of the meeting
- the length of the meeting
- the opportunity and venue for private discussion, and
- the effect of private or closed meetings on the decisions that the boards made.

With variations from one jurisdiction to another, boards are allowed to meet in executive sessions to discuss issues of personnel or court proceedings.

In general, the business of school boards is a matter of public record. However, what actually constitutes a meeting is often controversial. For example, it is unclear whether a social gathering where a quorum of board members is present is business that is subject to open meetings as a matter of public record. For all boards—not just school boards—courts must weigh the extent of the public interest involved when deciding the public nature of meetings and records of meetings. The criteria used to make such a determination include whether the board performed governmental functions at the meeting, the level of governmental funding used to support the meeting, the extent and involvement of governmental regulation in the meeting, and whether the board that was meeting was related to the government.

Effectiveness

There are a wide range of opinions concerning the efficacy of local school boards as educational policy-making bodies. Many critics of boards argue that they have outlived their usefulness. Other detractors claim that because boards tend to be dominated by White middle-class and mostly male members, they do not adequately represent the stakeholders. Still other critics maintain that boards perpetuate inequality in educational funding. Many educators assert that because such issues as globalization and school choice, along with the multifaceted issues facing urban schools particularly, have rendered education too complex, policy should not be set by lay people at the local level. Additionally, critics argue that given the increased federal role in education, especially under the Individuals with Disabilities Education Act and the No Child Left Behind Act, local school boards have become obsolete.

On the other hand, proponents of local school boards argue that they are an essential component in public school governance. Some of these advocates believe that boards are needed to implement federal and state policies. Additionally, supporters view boards as being vital for the representation of the local context to state level policy makers. Others assert that, insofar as education is a public good, local boards are necessary and important for the representation of entire communities. These supporters express the view that because the purpose of public education is to prepare citizens, entire communities have an interest in their operations.

Proponents add that without school boards, many members of local communities would not have accessible means of expressing their concerns. Consequently, supporters fear that school governance would be reduced to issues of parental consumer rights. This, school board advocates argue, would undermine the purpose of public education in a democratic society.

In sum, while local school boards have a long-standing tradition in the educational system, the debate on whether they continue to serve a useful purpose is far from being resolved.

Patricia A. L. Ehrensal

See also Open Meetings Laws; Open Records Laws

Further Readings

Conley, D. T. (2003). *Who governs our schools? Changing roles and responsibilities.* New York: Teachers College Press.

Mathews, D. (2006). *Reclaiming public education by reclaiming our democracy.* Dayton, OH: Kettering Foundation Press.

SCHOOL CHOICE

School choice refers to programs wherein parents select the schools that their children will attend at public expense, regardless of where they choose to reside. Although some scholars trace its roots to the 1770s and Adam Smith, Thomas Paine, and John Stuart, most name Milton Friedman as the father of modern school choice. This entry looks at how school choice was used to foster desegregation and how it was refashioned in a context of quality education; it also briefly discusses related court decisions.

Choice and Desegregation

In his book, *Capitalism and Freedom* (1962), Friedman asserted that public education should not be defined so much by the operation of a system of schools as by a method of public funding that would allow parents to obtain the education that they deem suitable for their children.

He proposed that parents be given vouchers for each child's education, which could be redeemed at any public or nonpublic school. According to Friedman, competition would then drive the provision of education, as good schools would thrive while poor schools would eventually close for lack of clientele. He maintained that such a system would be both more efficient and more effective than the traditional system of public education. However, this proposal never really captured widespread public attention or support until much later.

During the 1970s, proponents of desegregation began to utilize school choice initiatives as a means of promoting voluntary integration within public school systems. Educators developed so-called magnet schools, which used innovative and distinctive programming in order to attract students to enroll in schools outside of their traditional, often racially homogeneous, attendance areas. For example, schools were developed that focused on the arts, mathematics and science, vocational training, or particular philosophies or methodologies of teaching. Under such plans, parents petitioned school officials in the hope of having their children admitted to magnet programs. Magnet schools have been supported by federal grants and required by federal trial court desegregation orders.

States and school boards also encouraged integration by crafting open enrollment programs. In some instances, boards created intradistrict transfer plans that, with or without employing magnet schools, allowed parents to choose from among their schools, using this approach rather than residence to decide where children would attend school. Likewise, states created interdistrict voluntary integration programs around large urban areas that provided financial incentives to suburban schools to accept transfer students from urban districts and vice versa.

Choice and Educational Quality

The late 1980s witnessed the rebirth of Friedman's voucher proposal and the reapplication of free market principles to public education. This time, two of the most vocal and perhaps influential heralds were John Chubb and Terry Moe from the Brookings Institute of Washington, D.C. The reemergence of school choice as a viable approach to public school reform also signaled a shift in the rationale for its support. Prior to this time, racial and ethnic equity had been the driving force behind the choice plans in operation. However, this incarnation of choice focused heavily on considerations of excellence. The 1983 report by the National Commission on Excellence in Education, *A Nation at Risk,* posited that the current system of public education was critically failing and in need of immediate infusions of reform and restructuring if American students were to achieve their potential and the United States was to maintain (or regain) its status as the world's economic, political, technological, and intellectual leader.

In response to this call for school reform, a number of forms of school choice evolved along with magnet and open enrollment plans. First, some states expanded interdistrict open enrollment programs to allow transfers between public school districts statewide. Currently, at least 41 states have adopted some sort of interdistrict open enrollment policy. Second, at least 40 states have created charter school programs.

Charter schools are public schools created by virtue of a charter or contract with authorizing agencies, usually school boards, although authorizers vary from state to state. Charter schools are relieved from compliance with some state regulation in exchange for agreeing to be bound by performance contracts. While charter schools are creations of state statutes and are largely governed by state law, federal grant funds exist to support the development of innovative charter schools.

Finally, some states, such as Wisconsin, Ohio, Florida, and Utah, have created voucher programs that allow students to attend nonpublic schools with full or partial public financial support. For example, in both Milwaukee and Cleveland, low-income students may elect to attend participating nonpublic schools in addition to public schools.

In addition to state and local efforts, a federal effort was made when Congress included a school choice provision in the No Child Left Behind Act (NCLB) (2002). Under NCLB, all schools must demonstrate that they are making adequate yearly progress (AYP) toward having all of their students demonstrate proficiency on state assessments of reading, mathematics,

and science achievement. If schools fail to make AYP for 2 consecutive years, parents must be informed of the option of transferring their children to other schools that meet their AYP goals. As Congress works to reauthorize NCLB, these school choice provisions are likely to be debated once more. In other words, Congress will have to decide whether to retain, expand, modify, or eliminate the requirement for school choice currently set forth in NCLB.

Choice in the Courts

Ever since its inception, school choice has generated strong disagreement about its wisdom and effectiveness as an educational policy. In addition to extensive policy debate on the advantages and disadvantages to school choice as a whole or in one of its forms, considerable litigation has ensued to challenge various iterations of choice. Numerous issues have been litigated and range from challenges under education clauses of state constitutions to core principles of the U.S. Constitution. While the space allotted here does not allow for a full explication of all the issues raised, two lines of cases are most prominent.

First, opponents have challenged voucher programs that allow religiously affiliated nonpublic schools to participate as violating the Establishment Clause of the First Amendment to the Constitution. That litigation culminated in the Supreme Court's 5-to-4 decision in *Zelman v. Simmons-Harris* (2002). In *Zelman,* the Court ruled that the program from Cleveland did not violate the Establishment Clause, because it was enacted to further a legitimate secular purpose, the recipients of the vouchers were not defined by religious criteria, and parents had a genuine choice from among a variety of publicly funded options, both secular and religious, at which to spend their vouchers.

Most recently, the Supreme Court considered the propriety of two voluntary integration programs that considered students' race during the admissions process. Challengers alleged that conditioning admission to schools in the Seattle and Louisville intradistrict choice programs violated the Equal Protection Clause of the Fourteenth Amendment. The Supreme Court agreed, striking down both plans in *Parents*

Involved in Community Schools v. Seattle School District No. 1 (PICS, 2007). While *PICS* was decided by a plurality, five justices agreed that the Seattle and Louisville choice programs under scrutiny were not narrowly tailored to a compelling state interest. Of the five justices voting to overturn the plans, only Justice Kennedy pointed out that consideration of racial diversity in public elementary and secondary schools could be compelling. The four other members who ruled that the plans were unconstitutional reasoned that race could only properly be considered if necessary to remedy past discriminatory behavior. The effect of this precedent on currently operating forms of school choice across the country is just beginning to be explored.

While *Zelman* and *PICS* settled the questions presented by the cases, they did not resolve all legal issues associated with school choice. Further, neither did the Supreme Court's pronouncements quell the policy debates surrounding school choice. Accordingly, both legal and policy disagreements around school choice are likely to continue. Given its current prevalence, it is likely that school choice, whether interdistrict open enrollment, intradistrict open enrollment, magnet schools, charter schools, or vouchers, will remain part of the public educational landscape for years to come.

Julie F. Mead

See also Charter Schools; Equal Protection Analysis; Fourteenth Amendment; No Child Left Behind Act; *Parents Involved in Community Schools v. Seattle School District No. 1;* State Aid and the Establishment Clause; Vouchers; *Zelman v. Simmons-Harris*

Further Readings

Chubb, J., & Moe, T. (1990). *Politics, markets, and America's schools.* Washington, DC: The Brookings Institute.

Friedman, M. (1962). *Capitalism and freedom.* Chicago: University of Chicago Press.

Green, P. C., & Mead, J. F. (2004). *Charter schools and the law: Establishing new legal relationships.* Norwood, MA: Christopher-Gordon.

Witte, J. F. (2000). *The market approach to education: An analysis of America's first voucher program.* Princeton, NJ: Princeton University Press.

Legal Citations

Parents Involved in Community Schools v. Seattle School District No. 1, 127 S. Ct. 2738 (2007).

Zelman v. Simmons-Harris, 536 U.S. 639 (2002).

SCHOOL COMMITTEE OF THE TOWN OF BURLINGTON V. DEPARTMENT OF EDUCATION

School Committee of the Town of Burlington v. Department of Education (1985) involved a dispute over the rights of parents under the Education for All Handicapped Children Act (EAHCA), now the Individuals with Disabilities Education Act (IDEA). At issue was whether parents could be reimbursed for unilaterally placing their child in private school after they disagreed with the individualized education program (IEP) that school officials designed for their son.

Facts of the Case

The IDEA provides procedural safeguards to ensure that qualified students with disabilities receive a free appropriate public education (FAPE) in the least restrictive environment. Among these procedures are the parents' right to participate in the creation of IEPs for their children and to challenge proposed IEPs if they disagree with any of their content. In addition, the IDEA gives courts the authority to grant whatever relief they determine is appropriate.

The child in *Burlington* was a student with disabilities who attended a public school. Insofar as the child was not attending a school that could adequately meet his needs, his parents requested a new IEP for him, but they did not agree with the new IEP that school officials proposed. As such, they sought review consistent with the IDEA's provisions.

In the meantime, the parents enrolled their son in a commonwealth-approved private school for special education students at their own expense. Following a series of hearings, a hearing officer was of the view that the private school was the most appropriate placement for the child. Consequently, the Bureau of Special Education Appeals (BSEA) directed town officials to pay the child's tuition at the school and to reimburse his parents for the expenses that they had already incurred.

When town officials ignored the BSEA's order, commonwealth officials threatened to freeze all of their special education funds unless they complied with the directive that they pay for the child's education. During this time, the child remained at his private school. Eventually, town officials agreed to pay for one school year but not a subsequent one. After a four-day trial, the federal trial court ordered the parents to reimburse the town for placement and transportation expenses for the last two years of their son's placement. Not surprisingly, the parents appealed.

In the appeals process, the First Circuit remanded twice, eventually holding that the parents' reliance on the BSEA order allowed them to be reimbursed for the tuition that they paid for their son's education. The Supreme Court then agreed to hear an appeal.

The Court's Ruling

Writing for a unanimous Supreme Court, Justice Rehnquist explored whether the language of the IDEA, which granted the judiciary the authority to award the relief that judges deemed appropriate, included reimbursement for tuition at private schools if they thought that this would be a proper placement. Interpreting the IDEA as authorizing such reimbursement, and finding that "relief" was not specified further, Rehnquist noted that the courts had broad discretionary power. While the language in the act focused primarily on providing education for students with disabilities, Rehnquist pointed out that the IDEA provided for placements in private schools at public expense if necessary. In so doing, he determined that if a private school can be considered a proper placement, then in order for relief to be appropriate, school officials would have to create IEPs to permit children to attend the private schools and reimburse their parents retroactively. While town officials claimed that reimbursement should have been seen as damages, Rehnquist disagreed. Rather, he indicated that reimbursing parents was only paying what the town would, or should, have spent in the first place had officials initially developed a proper IEP.

Town officials also argued that the parents waived their right to be reimbursed because they chose to move their son to a private school unilaterally. The town officials adopted this stance based on language in the IDEA that requires children to remain in their then current educational placements while IEP contests are pending. In rejecting the town's position, Justice Rehnquist observed that the parents had not changed their son's placement, because before the parents moved him to the private school, commonwealth educational officials and they had agreed that he should attend a new school. If anything, Rehnquist specified that the parents reviewed their son's IEP, disagreed with it, and chose to enroll him in the private school. As a result, Rehnquist considered the private school to be his placement during the IEP appeals proceedings.

Justice Rehnquist also examined the BSEA's decision that called for the child being placed in the private school. To this end, he recognized that the IDEA allows changes of placements if officials in the state (commonwealth, here) or local educational agencies agree with such modifications. Insofar as he considered the BSEA's order to be an agreement with regard to the child's placement, Justice Rehnquist was satisfied that the parents had not violated the IDEA.

Rounding out his opinion, Justice Rehnquist reasoned that the parental change of their son's educational setting did not constitute a waiver of reimbursement. As such, he examined the IDEA's purpose, which was to grant students with disabilities a FAPE. In an effort to avoid construing the act in such a way that forced parents to choose between an inappropriate education and a free one, Rehnquist concluded that the parents should have been reimbursed, because the Supreme Court ultimately decided that the private school was the child's appropriate placement. However, Rehnquist clarified that if parents unilaterally choose to place their children in private schools that are not required or appropriate based on their IEPs, they do so at their own financial risk if courts later disagree that this would have been their appropriate placements. Put another way, if parents unilaterally place their children in schools that courts find inappropriate, then they will not be reimbursed for their expenses.

Eight years later, in *Florence County School District Four v. Carter* (1993), the Court was of the opinion that parents could be reimbursed for tuition expenses for their children even if the schools that they selected were not state approved, as long as they were otherwise appropriate.

Megan L. Rehberg

See also Disabled Persons, Rights of; Free Appropriate Public Education; Individualized Education Program (IEP); Least Restrictive Environment; Tuition Reimbursement

Legal Citations

Florence County School District Four v. Carter, 510 U.S. 7 (1993).
Individuals with Disabilities Education Act, 20 U.S.C. §§ 1400 *et seq.*
School Committee of the Town of Burlington v. Department of Education, 471 U.S. 359 (1985).

SCHOOL FINANCE LITIGATION

The availability of funds to support schools varies from district to district in most states, and the amount of money has a clear link with the quality of education provided. Often, districts with modest finances are also home to low-income students from underrepresented minorities. Thus, school finance has become associated with issues of equity, and it is often a target of parties seeking more equitable education for children. This entry looks at the background and some important legal cases in this area.

Background

Education is not a fundamental right under the U.S. Constitution. Instead, because, pursuant to the Tenth Amendment, it is governed by state law, every state constitution has a provision mandating, at a minimum, that the state provide a system of free public schools. Thus, in America, free public education is a constitutional value. Although free public education for all is a constitutional value, America's public schools remain unequal and often fail to provide students with

the education they need. Moreover, because the failure of public schools is more frequent and better documented in cities than in suburbs or rural areas, the consequences are felt most among minority students, who are more likely to be urban dwellers. Many, perhaps most, of these inequalities are the direct result of significant financial disparities among the public schools. While local school boards receive funds from both federal and state sources, all local districts, except those in Hawai'i (which is a single district) and Michigan raise much of the money necessary for operations through a percentage tax, with the rate set by the local residents, on the value of the real property in the district. Due to differences in rates and in the value of real property, this system results in vast disparities. As a result, some districts have trouble providing even the basics, while others are able to offer educational luxuries. While the states' legislatures and executives have adopted various mechanisms to correct this financial inequality, the disparities remain.

Given the obvious conflict between the constitutional value of free public education for all and the funding disparities created by the states' school finance systems, it is not surprising that the courts have been asked to intervene and vindicate the constitutional value of free public education for all by declaring that the current system of financing the schools is unconstitutional. Indeed, over the last four decades, the supreme court of virtually every state has wrestled with the question of whether the state's school financing system is constitutional.

School finance suits have taken two forms. First, there are "equity suits," where the plaintiffs assert that all children are entitled to have the same amount of money spent on their education and/or that children are entitled to equal educational opportunities. In effect, the plaintiffs believe that more money means a better education, and have little or no tolerance for any differences among districts in expenditures and/or opportunities. In an equity suit, the plaintiffs assert that education is a fundamental right and that any disparities in funding violate that right. The equity approach tended to be the dominant legal theory during the 1970s and 1980s.

Second, there are "quality suits" in which the plaintiffs argue that all children are entitled to an education of at least a certain quality, and that more money is necessary to bring the worst school districts up to the minimum level mandated by the state constitution. The emphasis is on differences in the quality of education delivered rather than on the resources available to the districts. The systems are struck down by the courts not because some boards have more money than others do, but because the quality of education in some schools, not necessarily the poorest in financial terms, is inadequate. In quality suits, the plaintiffs assert that the state constitution establishes a particular standard of quality and that the schools named in their suits do not measure up to that standard. The plaintiffs assume that the reason for this failure is inadequate funds. While many cases have equity suit arguments, the quality suit is the dominant strategy of the 1990s and early 21st century.

Historical Sequence

The history of school finance litigation consists of three waves. During the first wave, which lasted from the late 1960s until Supreme Court's decision in *San Antonio Independent School District v. Rodriguez,* this litigation relied on the federal Equal Protection Clause. Essentially, the plaintiffs asserted that all children were entitled to have the same amount of money spent on their education and/or that children were entitled to equal educational opportunities; that is, they brought equity suits. In effect, the plaintiffs believed that more money meant a better education, and they had little or no tolerance for any differences among students in expenditures and/or opportunities. In order to prevail under this equity theory, the plaintiffs had to persuade the court that education was a fundamental right, or that wealth was a suspect class, or that the finance system was irrational.

Similarly, during the second wave, which lasted from the New Jersey Supreme Court's 1973 ruling in *Robinson v. Cahill* until early 1989, the emphasis continued to be on equity suits. However, because *Rodriguez* had foreclosed the use of the federal constitution, the plaintiffs were forced to rely on state constitutional provisions. Although the plaintiffs were able to prevail in Arkansas, California, Connecticut, New Jersey, Washington, West Virginia, and Wyoming, the overwhelming majority of the cases resulted in victories for the state. In contrast, the third wave, which began

with plaintiffs' victories in suits in Montana, Kentucky, and Texas in 1989 and continues to the present, has been fundamentally different. Unlike the first and second waves, the third wave emphasizes quality of education rather than equality of funds, uses the narrow education clauses rather than the broad equal protection provisions, and seeks sweeping reform and/or continued court supervision of school districts. This represents the future of school finance reform litigation.

William E. Thro

See also *Robinson v. Cahill; Rose v. Council for Better Education; San Antonio Independent School District v. Rodriguez; Serrano v. Priest;* Thorough and Efficient Systems of Education

Further Readings

Coons, J., Clune, W., & Sugarman, S. (1970). *Private wealth and public education.* Cambridge, MA: Belknap Press.

Dayton, J. (2001). *Serrano* and its progeny: An analysis of thirty years of school finance litigation. *Education Law Reporter, 157,* 447, 457–458.

Johnson, A. (1979). State court intervention in school finance reform. *Cleveland State Law Review, 28*(3), 325–372.

Kozol, J. (1991). *Savage inequalities: Children in America's schools.* New York: Crown.

Levin, B. (1977). Current trends in school finance reform litigation: A commentary. *Duke Law Journal, 1977*(6), 1099–1138.

Murray, C. (1984). *Losing ground: American social policy, 1950–1980.* New York: Basic Books.

Thro, W. E. (1989). Note, To render them safe: The analysis of state constitutional provisions in public school finance reform litigation. *Virginia Law Review, 75,* 1639–1679.

Thro, W. E. (1990). The third wave: The implications of the Montana, Kentucky, and Texas decisions for the future of public school finance reform litigation. *Journal of Law & Education, 19,* 219–250.

Thro, W. E. (1993). The role of language of the state education clauses in school finance litigation. *Education Law Reporter, 79,* 19–31.

Thro, W. E. (1994). Judicial analysis during the third wave of school finance litigation: The Massachusetts decision as a model. *Boston College Law Review, 35,* 597–617.

Thro, W. E. (1998). A new approach to state constitutional analysis in school finance litigation. *Journal of Law & Politics, 14,* 525–540.

Thro, W. E. (2005). The school finance paradox: How the constitutional values of decentralization and judicial restraint inhibit the achievement of quality education. *Education Law Reporter, 197,* 477–487.

Wood, R. C., & Thompson, D. C. (1996). *Educational finance law: Constitutional challenges to state aid plans—an analysis of strategies.* Dayton, OH: Education Law Association.

Legal Citations

Robinson v. Cahill, 303 A.2d 273 (N.J. 1973).

San Antonio Independent School District v. Rodriguez, 411 U.S. 1 (1973).

SCOPES MONKEY TRIAL

Called the "world's most famous court trial" at the time, the case of *State of Tennessee v. John Thomas Scopes* (1925) concerned a young biology teacher who taught that man had descended from a lower order of animals rather than having been divinely created as described in the Bible.

The Scopes trial occurred as a result of legislation advocated by John Washington Butler, a Primitive Baptist and former farmer and schoolteacher who had learned that evolution was being taught in the public schools of Tennessee. As a member of the Tennessee legislature, Butler succeeded in passing a law that made it unlawful to teach evolution in the public schools. The Butler Act, as it came to be called, was also being promoted by William Jennings Bryan, former U.S. secretary of state and a three-time candidate for president, as an antidote to Darwin's theory of evolution, a notion that he regarded as heresy.

The Butler Act was immediately challenged by the American Civil Liberties Union (ACLU), which was searching for a test case. The selection of Dayton, Tennessee, as the site for the testing of the anti-evolution law occurred as a result of opposition to the Butler Act by a small group of Dayton men who enlisted the help of the local science teacher, John Thomas Scopes. F. E. Robinson, owner of the local drug store and chairman of the school board, got things going when he called the newspaper in Chattanooga to report the arrest of a teacher who had taught evolution.

William Jennings Bryan volunteered to represent Tennessee in its prosecution of young Scopes. This brought Clarence Darrow and Dudley Field Malone, a New York barrister, into the fray as volunteers for the defense. At first, the ACLU did not want Darrow on its team, believing that the 68-year-old former attorney was too controversial and not technically as skilled a lawyer as they believed the case required. However, young Scopes insisted that the Darrow/ Malone team was just the tandem he believed was necessary in the ugly legal brawl he knew would ensue in his hometown. The Scopes defense team was anchored by Darrow and Malone and joined by Arthur Garfield Hays, another New York attorney; W. O. Thompson, Darrow's law partner from Chicago; and John Randolph Neal, a former Tennessee judge and dean of the law school at the University of Tennessee.

From the beginning, the Scopes "monkey" trial was more than a simple test of an anti-evolution law. Rather, as Darrow later said near the end of the trial, it was contested for the purpose of preventing bigots and ignoramuses from controlling education in the United States. It was bitterly fought before a partisan crowd of what H. L. Mencken of the *Baltimore Sun* described as "yokels," a derogatory term for unsophisticated country folk who made up the town and the jury, one member of which was illiterate.

The Scopes defense team set up a dense battery of prominent scientists regarding the efficacy of the theory of evolution. However, the prosecution succeeded in overcoming this plan by showing that the trial was not about the theory of evolution, but rather was a simple question of whether Scopes had violated the Butler Act. After Judge John T. Raulston ruled that expert testimony on evolution was inadmissible, many considered the trial to be over and began to leave town. What then occurred propelled the Scopes trial into infamy. The defense team called William Jennings Bryan to the stand as an expert on the Bible. While his prosecutorial colleagues strenuously objected, Bryan succumbed to the lure of being a defender of the faith before the cross-examination skills of his legal nemesis Clarence Darrow, whose agnosticism was widely known. What then ensued was a clash of legal titans in a set piece battle that has subsequently become the verbiage of Broadway plays and Hollywood celluloid. Darrow walked, weaved, and sucker-punched Bryan through the Biblical story of Jonah and the whale, the fable of Joshua making the sun stand still, the unnamed wife of Cain, and into the length of a day in the act of creation set forth in Genesis. In an acerbic courtroom fight in which both exchanged clenched fists at one another, Darrow showed plainly that in the face of textual ambiguity, a reader of the Bible had to interpret what was written, because a literal interpretation was not consistent with what was generally accepted as scientific fact, even by Christian literalists such as Bryan. While Bryan was not shown to be a complete idiot and was initially skillful in his rejoinders to Darrow, he was publicly humiliated and exposed as naïve and irrational.

Bryan knew he had made a major miscue. Even when Judge Raulston threw out his entire testimony, he was not satisfied, because he wanted the world to know that he had worked to protect the word of God against the greatest atheist or agnostic in the United States. He never got his chance, however, as Darrow pushed for the jury to find young Scopes guilty so that the case could be appealed to the Tennessee Supreme Court. Under Tennessee law, such a request prevented the defense from offering a closing statement and thus deprived Bryan of the opportunity to present a final appeal. Darrow's public relations coup was then complete. Scopes was brought before the jury, which convicted him of violating the Butler Act. Judge Raulston imposed a fine of $100. After the trial, Bryan traveled about Tennessee trying to find a suitable forum to redeem himself, but after having a heavy noon-day meal, he died in his sleep.

The ACLU appealed the decision of the lower court, and once again, there was acrimony over the continuing presence of Clarence Darrow as the case went to the Tennessee Supreme Court. This time the argument was engineered to avoid favoring Darrow, who was not a good lawyer in appellate cases. But Darrow doggedly stuck to his guns and argued the case with Arthur Garfield Hays in Nashville. The high court reversed the Scopes decision on a technicality: Scopes's fine should have been determined by the jury rather than by Judge Raulston. It was not until 1967 that the Butler Act was repealed in Tennessee. A year later, an anti-evolution law in Arkansas was declared unconstitutional by the U.S. Supreme Court.

The legacy of the Scopes monkey trial lies largely today in the public imagination and in the court of public opinion. It was the first time that science and faith came face to face in the courtroom and were personified by two protagonists who were larger than life. The irony is that John Thomas Scopes never testified on his own behalf. Darrow was afraid that the jury would discover that Scopes had never taught biology. Once the trial began, Scopes himself was a bystander to the larger issues being argued.

Fenwick W. English

See also Darrow, Clarence S.; Religious Activities in Public Schools

Further Readings

Darrow, C. (1932). *The story of my life.* New York: Grossett & Dunlap.

Tierney, K. (1979). *Darrow: A biography.* New York: Thomas Y. Crowell.

Weinberg, A., & Weinberg, L. (1980). *Clarence Darrow: A sentimental rebel.* New York: G. P. Putnam's Sons.

Legal Citations

Scopes v. State, 289 S.W. 363 (Tenn. 1927).

SECTION 504

See REHABILITATION ACT OF 1973, SECTION 504

SEGREGATION, DE FACTO

De facto racial segregation is the result of the actions of private individuals or societal forces rather than governmental action, law, or policy. De facto segregation can be distinguished from de jure segregation, a condition that is caused by governmental actions or law. De facto segregation is typically the result of housing patterns, population movements, and economic conditions that are often reinforced by governmental policies that are not aimed at creating segregation but have a segregative effect. For example, most American metropolitan areas have large single central-city school districts that serve primarily minority students; these systems are usually surrounded by suburban school districts that serve mostly White students. This entry looks at the history of de facto segregation and discusses key Supreme Court rulings.

Background

Documentation reveals that schools in many parts of the North were substantially segregated in the years leading up to 1954 and in the decades following *Brown v. Board of Education of Topeka* (1954). To be sure, most of this segregation was de facto, rather than de jure, and was aided by the small size of many school districts. The small size of many of these districts had the effect of guaranteeing that residential segregation would be translated into school segregation as long as boards could not be required to move students across jurisdictional lines.

In some states outside of the South, segregation carried the imprimatur of official policy. Perhaps the best, or more properly worst, example among the cases identified in this entry was Kansas, home to *Brown*. However, more frequently, high degrees of segregation, falling short of complete separation of the races, were maintained in more than a few Northern school districts, owing to housing patterns. Fueled by racial discrimination among homeowners, real estate brokers, and banks, residential de facto segregation was bolstered by government action and inaction.

In its most active mode, governmentally enforced residential segregation existed through legislation, such as the ordinance in Stockton, California, that required all Chinese to live south of Main Street. One of the most prominent tools for maintaining residential segregation, a California innovation of the 1890s that was used widely until shortly after World War II, was the restrictive covenant, the insertion into deeds of the promise not to sell a property to Blacks or members of other specified groups. More extreme was the practice of some suburban communities to exclude Blacks altogether. Combined with the selective location of public housing projects and the largely unchecked discrimination in the housing market, many large and midsize urban areas of the North became highly segregated under de facto conditions. Detroit's inner city epitomized de facto segregation;

as late as 1970, this city had 14 suburban communities with populations of 36,000 or more, none of which had more than 50 Black residents.

Court Rulings

The U.S. Supreme Court first used the term *de facto segregation* in *Swann v. Charlotte-Mecklenburg Board of Education* (1971). Three years later, the Court addressed its first case of de facto segregation in *Keyes v. School District No. 1, Denver, Colorado* (1973), a case that addressed the rights of students of Mexican ancestry. In *Keyes,* the Court held that even though the schools were not segregated by law or the state constitution, the board's actions led to the creation of a core of inner-city schools for minority students that were inferior to those educating children in predominately White schools in the rest of the city. *Keyes* is often discussed as a case of de jure segregation, even though it primarily focused on de facto segregation. Based on its finding that the board's action created a case of intentional discrimination, the Court concluded that school officials had to prove that they had not deliberately created schools that were segregated.

The Supreme Court's distinction in *Keyes* between de facto and de jure segregation has been questioned at the top of the nation's legal system. Justice Lewis Powell concurred with Justice William Douglas in *Keyes* (1973), noting that the difference between de facto and de jure segregation is a distinction without a difference. Douglas argued that many governmental actions, such as restrictive covenants and the actions of urban development agencies, led to so-called de facto segregation. The Court's allowing the legal distinction between de jure and de facto segregation to stand has severely limited the ability of minority students to sue for more integrated public schools under the Fourteenth Amendment of the federal Constitution.

A year later, in *Milliken v. Bradley I* (1974), the Supreme Court was of the opinion that the judiciary could not demand an interdistrict remedy to segregation that did not result from explicit governmental actions even though its effect was de jure. Two years later, in *Washington v. Davis* (1976), the Court went a step further, albeit not set in a school context because it involved the selection of police officers, deciding that de jure segregation was unconstitutional only if it was the result of a racially discriminatory governmental purpose. Further, in *Crawford v. Board of Education of the City of Los Angeles* (1982), the Court upheld an amendment to the state constitution of California that prohibited state officials from mandating busing to eliminate de facto segregation.

In sum, it can be argued that given enough resources, one could prove that because de jure segregation existed in many urban school systems and no longer does, the courts have had a measure of success dealing with this problem. However, when segregation has been labeled as de facto, because it involves the amorphous concept of governmental action or inaction coupled with larger societal trends, the cost of litigating such disputes means that the courts and educational officials continue to wrestle with ways of eliminating de facto segregation in schools.

Paul Green

See also *Brown v. Board of Education of Topeka; Crawford v. Board of Education of the City of Los Angeles;* Dual and Unitary Systems; *Keyes v. School District No. 1, Denver, Colorado;* Segregation, De Jure; *Swann v. Charlotte-Mecklenburg Board of Education*

Further Readings

Armor, D. J. (1995). *Forced justice: School desegregation and the law.* New York: Oxford University Press

Hall, K. L. (1992). *The Oxford companion to the Supreme Court of the United States.* New York: Oxford University Press.

Legal Citations

Crawford v. Board of Education of the City of Los Angeles, 458 U.S. 527 (1982).

Keyes v. School District No. 1, Denver, Colorado, 413 U.S. 189 (1973).

Milliken v. Bradley I, 418 U.S. 717 (1974).

Milliken v. Bradley II, 433 U.S. 267 (1977).

Swann v. Charlotte-Mecklenburg Board of Education, 402 U.S. 1 (1971).

Washington v. Davis, 426 U.S. 229 (1976).

SEGREGATION, DE JURE

De jure segregation is racial segregation that is caused by governmental actions or law. De jure school segregation can be distinguished from de facto school segregation on the basis that the latter results from the private actions of individuals or societal forces rather than the state. This entry looks at the legal history of de jure segregation.

Court-Supported Segregation

In *Plessy v. Ferguson* (1896), its first case directly on this point, the U.S. Supreme Court upheld de jure segregation as long as facilities for Whites and Blacks were "separate but equal." Three years later, the Court extended de jure segregation that was not equal in *Cumming v. County Board of Education of Richmond County* (1899), wherein the justices allowed a school board to close a Black high school while maintaining high schools for Whites. The Court explicitly applied "separate but equal" to K–12 education in *Gong Lum v. Rice* (1927) when it concluded that school officials could deny a child of Chinese extraction access to a school for Whites. De jure segregation was the rule in the South during the Jim Crow era, not only in schools but in all areas of life.

The Supreme Court began to change its course with regard to de jure segregation in *Missouri ex rel. Gaines v. Canada* (1938). In *Gaines,* the Court ruled that because graduate and professional schools for Blacks could not be both separate and equal, both Blacks and Whites had to be admitted to the same programs. Even so, de jure segregation continued in elementary and secondary schools in the South and six border states as merely one part of a vast and elaborate superstructure that was the segregated South. Subsequently, the success that the NAACP and its Legal Defense Fund had in *Sweatt v. Painter* (1950) and *McLaurin v. Oklahoma State Regents for Higher Education* (1950), wherein the justices struck down inter- and intrainstitution segregation, respectively, in higher education, led Thurgood Marshall and others in the organizations he worked with to believe that the Court would uphold the rights of Blacks to attend desegregated K–12 public schools.

The Impact of *Brown*

In 1954, the Supreme Court's landmark judgment in *Brown v. Board of Education of Topeka,* in striking down segregation in public schools based on race, declared "that in the field of public education the doctrine of 'separate but equal' has no place. Separate educational facilities are inherently unequal" (p. 495). A year later, in a follow-up case, *Brown II,* the justices directed lower federal courts to proceed in dismantling segregated, or dual, school systems "with all deliberate speed" (p. 301).

Yet, a decade after *Brown,* only a small fraction of schools in border states and the South had complied with the Court's order, signaling that the battle to end segregated schools would rage on for years. As evidence of ongoing disputes with regard to school segregation, the Department of Justice's fiscal year 2008 performance budget for its Civil Rights Division shows that about 308 school systems continue to operate under desegregation orders nationwide (p. 22).

In light of the struggle to implement desegregation remedies, whether in de jure or de facto settings, some, including Supreme Court Justice Lewis Powell, questioned the distinction between de jure and de facto school segregation. In light of Justice Powell's concern, one view is that given enough resources, plaintiffs or the government can prove that de jure segregation exists in almost any school. A second view is that insofar as the function of schooling in American society requires all groups to be taught together under the common school theory, segregation based on race for whatever reason, whatever the cause, is unconstitutional. Further, the distinction between de jure segregation, which was practiced almost exclusively in the South, and de facto segregation, which was found in the North, has led to different standards in the two regions of the nation, an untenable and unwise outcome.

Contemporary Segregation

David Armor, in *Forced Justice,* maintained that de jure segregation must meet two criteria. First, he was of the opinion that de jure segregation must have both the intent to discriminate and an effect that leads to significant segregation; an example is the segregation enforced by the Jim Crow laws that existed in the American South. Second, he asserted that because the standards by which segregative intent are determined are unclear, they should be clarified. For example, he pointed out that lower courts had adopted a foreseeable effects standard, according to which school boards that adopted courses of action that were obviously going to increase segregation should have been liable for intentional segregation. Such a standard reduces the distinction between de jure and de facto segregation.

Today, identifying the vestiges of de jure segregation is becoming an increasingly difficult task, as the Supreme Court recognized in such cases as *Milliken v. Bradley II* (1977) and *Dowell v. Board of Education of Oklahoma City Public Schools* (1991). This difficulty arises because school boards have, by now, for the most part, eliminated the racial disparities that were most readily traceable to de jure segregation, such as the assignment of students to separate schools based on race. Although racial disparities certainly still exist, the courts have acknowledged that not all instances of racial disparity result from segregation, because "segregation is the conscious, deliberate act of separating people by race" (*Hampton v. Jefferson County Board of Education,* 2000, p. 371). The courts have refused to interpret apartness as unconstitutional.

It cannot be doubted that school boards have eliminated most of the overt racial disparities that were most readily traceable to de jure segregation. Still, this issue can become complicated when elementary or secondary schools use race as a factor in admitting students to particularly desirable programs. Absent either the compelling governmental interest in remedying past de jure segregation or an assignment system narrowly tailored to achieving such a remedy, a plurality of the Supreme Court, in *Parents Involved in Community Schools v. Seattle School District No. 1* (2007), ruled that such race-conscious systems, in both Seattle, Washington, and Louisville, Kentucky, were unconstitutional.

In other words, evaluating whether disparities such as scores on standardized tests are vestiges of de jure segregation is more difficult, because the relationship between present disparities and those that existed under the prior system of segregation is less clear. While the cause of a present racial disparity might be a prior system of de jure segregation, it might also be social or economic factors over which school board officials have no control, thereby making it all the more difficult to ensure equal educational opportunities for all children.

Paul Green

See also *Brown v. Board of Education of Topeka; Brown v. Board of Education of Topeka* and Equal Educational Opportunities; *Cumming v. Board of Education of Richmond County;* Dual and Unitary Systems; *Gong Lum v. Rice; McLaurin v. Oklahoma State Regents for Higher Education; Milliken v. Bradley; Parents Involved in Community Schools v. Seattle School District No. 1; Plessy v. Ferguson; Roberts v. City of Boston; Sweatt v. Painter*

Further Readings

Armor, D. J. (1995). *Forced justice: School desegregation and the law.* New York: Oxford University Press.

Bickel, A. M. (1973). Untangling the busing snarl. In N. Mills, *The great school bus controversy* (pp. 27–44). New York: Teachers College Press.

Clotfelter, C. T. (2004). *After Brown: The rise and retreat of school desegregation.* Princeton, NJ: Princeton University Press.

Hall, K. L. (1992). *The Oxford companion to the Supreme Court of the United States.* New York: Oxford University Press.

United States Department of Justice. (n.d.). *FY 2008 performance budget: Civil Rights Division* [Congressional Budget Submission]. Available from http://www.usdoj.gov/jmd/2008justification/pdf/18_crt.pdf

Legal Citations

Brown v. Board of Education of Topeka I, 347 U.S. 483 (1954).

Brown v. Board of Education of Topeka II, 349 U.S. 294 (1955).

Cumming v. County Board of Education, 175 U.S. 528 (1899).

Dowell v. Board of Education of Oklahoma City Public Schools, 498 U.S. 237 (1991), *on remand,* 778 F. Supp. 1144 (W.D. Okla. 1991), *aff'd,* 8 F.3d 1501 (10th Cir. 1993).

Gong Lum v. Rice, 275 U.S. 78 (1927).

Hampton v. Jefferson County Board of Education, 102 F. Supp. 2d. 358 (W.D. Ky. 2000).

McLaurin v. Oklahoma State Regents for Higher Education, 339 U.S. 637 (1950).

Milliken v. Bradley II, 433 U.S. 267 (1977).

Missouri ex rel. Gaines v. Canada, 305 U.S. 337 (1938).

Parents Involved in Community Schools v. Seattle School District No. 1, 127 S. Ct. 2738 (2007).

Plessy v. Ferguson, 163 U.S. 537 (1896).

Roberts v. City of Boston, 59 Mass. 198, 5 Cush. 198 (1850).

Sweatt v. Painter, 339 U.S. 629 (1950).

SERRANO V. PRIEST

The 1971 case of *Serrano v. Priest*—known commonly as *Serrano I*—marked the first major decision in a state supreme court that struck down a state educational funding system as unconstitutional. In *Serrano I,* the Supreme Court of California ruled that the state's school funding system violated the equal protection clause of the Fourteenth Amendment to the U.S. Constitution. In a footnote, the court mentioned that the state's funding practices also violated the California state constitution's equal protection clause.

In *Serrano I,* the Supreme Court of California acknowledged that the state's public school general fund financing structure resulted in large variations in per-pupil expenditures and depended largely on a school district's property tax base. The court explained that these kinds of tax-base disparities resulted in inequalities in actual educational expenditures per pupil, because districts with higher property values could generate more funding with lower tax rates. The court added that the state aid mechanisms in place at the time were inadequate to offset the large disparities. A year later, in 1972, the California legislature enacted Senate Bill 90, which established a formula to begin leveling school district incomes based on the average daily attendance revenue limits, the amount of funds that public schools receive to pay for the operations.

The Supreme Court of California based *Serrano I* on two main constitutional findings: First, education in the public schools is a fundamental interest or right; and second, a school district's wealth, namely, its real-property tax base, is a suspect classification. In making this second determination, the court was of the opinion that wealth was a suspect classification, declaring that the school "funding scheme invidiously discriminated against the poor because it made the quality of a child's education a function of the wealth of his parents and neighbors" (p. 1244). The court invoked strict-scrutiny review and rejected the state's compelling governmental interest argument for tying per-pupil education expenditures to the assessed value of a district's realty and that the current system was necessary to maintain local control.

However, the court's interpretation of wealth as a suspect classification under the federal Constitution did not hold for long. Two years later, the U.S. Supreme Court's opinion in *San Antonio Independent School District v. Rodriguez* (1973), its only case ever on school finance, reasoned that the Equal Protection Clause of the U.S. Constitution does not extend to schools. *Rodriguez* effectively precluded litigants from using the federal Equal Protection Clause as a vehicle for school finance reform.

In the 1976 case of *Serrano v. Priest* (known as *Serrano II*), the Supreme Court of California returned to its earlier, brief mention of the state constitution's Equal Protection Clause. The court essentially rendered the same judgment as it had five years earlier, but its sole authority now was the California constitution. According to *Serrano II,* the finance reform legislation passed in response to *Serrano I* was insufficient. The court clearly established education as a fundamental right under the state constitution. The court maintained that the state's property tax–based school-finance system violated the state's Equal Protection Clause, because it did not withstand the strict scrutiny that is given to the denial of a fundamental right. The court indicated that property tax rates and per-pupil expenditures should be equalized, charging the legislature with the task of leveling revenue such that, by 1980, the difference in revenue limits per pupil would be less than $100. This figure, called the "*Serrano* band," included a built-in inflation factor that increased the size of the band to $300 by the year 2000.

Rather than level school funding up to the amount spent in high-wealth districts, though, the legislature ultimately equalized school funding down to the level spent by the low-wealth districts. Proposition 13, passed by state voters in 1978, limited property tax rates to 1% of the cash value of real property subject to taxation, and it had the effect of severely limiting the growth in spending for public schools. In 1986, *Serrano V* responded to concerns about this limited

spending growth. Yet, an appellate court scrutinized the equality of the funding structure, concluding that the legislature had not violated the state constitution's Equal Protection Clause. Although the initial opinion was superseded and transferred for further review, there have been no additional judgments in *Serrano.* In sum, *Serrano I* and its progeny stand out as the beginning of an era that led to about one-half of the states reforming their systems of funding public education.

Sara E. Rabin

See also Equal Protection Analysis; *San Antonio Independent School District v. Rodriguez;* School Finance Litigation; Thorough and Efficient Systems of Education

Legal Citations

San Antonio Independent School District v. Rodriguez, 411 U.S. 1 (1973).
Serrano v. Priest, 487 P.2d 1241 (Cal. 1971) (*Serrano I*); 557 P.2d 929 (Cal. 1976) *cert. denied*, 432 U.S. 907 (1977) (*Serrano II*); *Serrano v. Priest*, 200 Cal. App.3d 897 (Cal. Ct. App. 1986), *review granted, opinion superseded*, 723 P.2d 1248 (Cal. 1986), *cause transferred*, 763 P.2d 852 (Cal. 1988) (*Serrano V*).

SEXUAL HARASSMENT

School-based sexual harassment can be defined as a form of sex discrimination that involves unwelcome or unwanted conduct of a sexual or sexist nature that directly interferes with the rights of victims to receive equal educational opportunities. Discrimination based on sexual harassment occurs in a variety of ways, including sexual propositions, lewd comments or jokes, unwanted use of pornographic materials, or inappropriate touching. This entry provides an overview of school-based sexual harassment, focusing in turn on some of its more common expressions and related case law.

Definitions

School-based sexual harassment can take place between students, between teachers and students, or between other educational staff persons and students. Sex discrimination in the public school environment is expressly prohibited by the Equal Protection Clause of the Fourteenth Amendment, Title VII of the Equal Rights Act of 1964, and by Title IX of the Education Amendments of 1972 as well as state- and local-level human rights acts. Students are protected by Title IX, while employees are covered by Title VII. Sexual harassment can be classified under a variety of different legal claims, including gender harassment, unwanted sexual attention, or sexual coercion.

School-based sexual harassment is a serious and growing problem and is found in classrooms throughout the country. For instance, a 1993 national survey conducted by the American Association of University Women (AAUW), titled "Hostile Hallways: The AAUW Survey on Sexual Harassment in America's Schools," reported that 83% of the girls and 60% of the boys surveyed reported experiencing unwanted sexual attention in the school environment. Reported instances of school-based sexual harassment or abuse appear to be on the rise.

Historically, sexual harassment and abuse charges against school boards and their employees were often dismissed. However, the impact of recent research and scholarship demonstrating sexual harassment's detrimental impact on the educational environment through increased student absenteeism, lower achievement, increased dropout rates for victims of sexual harassment, and other negative results has drawn the attention of the courts to the discriminatory impact of school-based sexual harassment. According to statistics, the majority of reported school-based sexual harassment cases occur among students, often referred to as peer-to-peer sexual harassment. In a report by the National Coalition for Women and Girls in Education, 90% of the students who reported sexual harassment were harassed by other students. Researchers assert that the most common reason for sexual harassment of students by other students is related to the need to assert power.

The courts typically refer to the U.S. Equal Employment Opportunity Commission (EEOC) for legal guidance relating to sexual harassment issues originating in the workplace. Beginning in 1988, the EEOC has published a document annually, *Policy Guidance on Current Issues of Sexual Harassment,* outlining behavior that legally qualifies as sexual harassment. Specifically, the EEOC guidelines indicate that sexual harassment is a form of sexual discrimination that is illegal under Title VII of the 1964 Civil Rights Act. Title VII provides that employees have the right to work in an environment free from discrimination based on intimidation, insult, or ridicule. Pursuant to EEOC guidelines, two distinct forms of sexual harassment have evolved: quid pro quo and hostile work environment.

The first category of sexual harassment is referred to as a quid pro quo claim. Quid pro quo is a Latin maxim that translates to mean "this for that." A quid pro quo sexual harassment claim in the educational environment takes place when a person in an authority position, such as a teacher, demands sexual favors in exchange for a certain benefit, such as grades. The most common quid pro quo sexual harassment claim in school-based settings occurs when teachers threaten to lower students' grades or refuse to write letters of recommendation if students fail to accept sexual advances or requests. An incident of quid pro quo sexual harassment need only occur once to legally qualify as a valid sexual harassment claim. The deprivation of educationally related benefits, namely interpreting the teaching process, allow a victim of quid pro quo sexual harassment an opportunity to ask a court for monetary relief.

Hostile work environment is often described as the most prevalent as well as misunderstood sexual harassment claim. Hostile work environment sexual harassment claims are defined as unwelcome sexual behavior that creates intimidating or offensive environments. The concept of hostile work environment is confusing, because what some employees might see as harmless jokes or teasing, victims consider blatantly offensive sexual harassment.

An important legal distinction between quid pro quo and hostile work environment sexual harassment claims is that victims of hostile work environment sexual harassment do not need to suffer tangible economic losses, such as reductions in wages or tangible benefits, in order to satisfy a successful sexual harassment claim. However, unlike quid pro quo sexual harassment claims that only require a single event to constitute a violation, hostile work environment claims require consistent and multiple patterns of behavior to constitute a violation. For a hostile work environment sexual harassment claim to be successful, the behavior must be considered "sufficiently pervasive and severe."

Insofar as the remainder of this essay addresses sexual harassment involving students, the discussion focuses on Title IX.

The Legal Significance of Title IX

Title IX of the Education Amendments of 1972 is a federal law that expressly prohibits discrimination based on sex. According to the language of Title IX, "No person in the United States shall, on the basis of sex, be excluded from participation in, be denied the benefits of, or be subjected to discrimination under any education program or activity receiving Federal financial assistance."

Prior to 1992, victims of successful sexual harassment claims could not receive monetary damages as a legal remedy from the courts. Instead, victims who successfully filed sexual harassment claims could only request that federal funding be removed from the organizations where individuals accused of sexual harassment were employed.

In a landmark and unanimous decision, the U.S. Supreme Court in *Franklin v. Gwinnett County Public Schools* (1992) expanded the legal scope of Title IX to include sexual harassment specifically in school settings. *Franklin* is legally significant, because it brought the nation's attention to the extensive problem of sexual harassment in schools. *Franklin* also established the right of student victims of sexual harassment to sue for compensatory, or monetary, damages under Title IX. As a direct result of the legal precedent established in *Franklin,* a major legal factor now considered in determining whether school officials are liable for sexual harassment under Title IX is whether educators have actual knowledge of alleged sexual harassment.

The facts surrounding *Franklin* involved a female high school student and a male teacher who were engaged in coercive sexual intercourse three times on school grounds. When the 15-year old female student initially reported the sexual activity to school administrators, the student was discouraged from informing others of the incident, including her parents, police, or her boyfriend. Officials told the student that the male teacher involved in the incident would be removed from the school. He agreed to resign, and the school agreed to drop all legal charges against him. In reversing previous legal judgments in favor of the local school board, the Supreme Court decided in favor of the student and provided compensatory damages.

Including *Franklin,* the Supreme Court has resolved three sexual harassment cases involving students in elementary through secondary school settings. Unquestionably, this level of judicial activity by the nation's highest court reveals that the issue of sexual harassment in schools is a matter of national concern. In addition to *Franklin,* the Court decided two additional and significant school-based sexual harassment cases in *Gebser v. Lago Vista Independent School District* (1998) and *Davis v. Monroe County Board of Education* (1999).

A 2004 study conducted by the U.S. Department of Education indicated that approximately 10% of public school students who reported being sexually harassed revealed that the sexual harassment was initiated by a teacher or another school staff member. The Court in *Gebser* developed the present legal standard for a legally actionable claim of sexual harassment of a student by a teacher under Title IX. In *Gebser,* the Supreme Court was of the opinion that student victims of sexual harassment may not recover monetary damages unless school officials who have the authority to institute corrective measures have actual knowledge of and are deliberately indifferent to teachers' misconduct. In *Gebser,* a mother and her daughter sued a local school board after the student was involved in a sexual relationship with a male teacher at her school. A police officer had discovered the student and teacher having sexual intercourse in a car. The ninth-grade student, who was involved in a sexual relationship with her teacher for over a year, never told her mother or a school official. When the local school board found out, unlike the board in *Franklin,* the board promptly dismissed the teacher, and he was ultimately criminally prosecuted for having sex with a minor. The Court concluded that local school officials were not liable under Title IX for the acts of the teacher against the student.

In 1999, in *Davis,* the Supreme Court reasoned that schools that are recipients of federal financial assistance could be liable for peer or student-to-student sexual harassment if the sexual harassment was sufficiently severe and school officials treated the allegations of harassment with deliberate indifference. Additionally, the Court referred to instances where, if school officials had actual knowledge of sexual harassment that was "severe, pervasive, and objectively offensive," they could be held liable.

Davis involved a fifth-grade female student who was subjected to continuous sexual harassment by a male classmate. The female's parents filed suit under Title IX. More specifically, during the duration of the school year, the male engaged in sexually inappropriate behavior toward the female student, including verbal requests for sexual favors and numerous attempts to touch the female student's breasts and genital area. At the end of the school year, the female student's father found that his daughter had written suicide notes based on the sexual harassment she was subjected to by the male. Even though the male's behavior had been reported to the teacher by the student's parents, the teacher failed to assign the student a different desk away form the boy.

In *Davis,* the Supreme Court pointed out that students do have private rights of action to initiate Title IX legal actions asserting peer sexual harassment against public school boards that are recipients of federal funds. *Davis* developed a two-part legal test to evaluate whether sexual harassment existed. The first part of the test asks whether school boards or their officials acted with deliberate indifference to known acts of sexual harassment. The second part of the test considers whether the sexual harassment was so severe, pervasive, and objectively offensive that it effectively barred the victim's access to educational opportunity or benefit. Following *Davis,* students and school officials are better informed regarding the legal boundaries concerning the rights and responsibilities of school-based sexual harassment. Even so, litigation continues at a brisk pace over this contentious topic.

Harassment Based on Sexual Orientation

More recently, legal developments in the area of school-based sexual harassment have taken place to prevent the sexual abuse and harassment of students based solely on their sexual orientation. Statistics reveal that lesbian, gay, bisexual, and transgendered students, commonly referred to as LGBT students, are sexually harassed and bullied significantly more than other members of the overall student population in U.S. middle and secondary schools. Moreover, national surveys reveal that LGBT students are at a statistically greater risk of dropping out of school or considering suicide due to sexual harassment than are other students. For example, the 2001 National School Climate Survey reported that approximately 83% of LGBT students reported that they were sexually harassed at school due to their sexual orientation, and 70% of LGBT students reported feeling unsafe at school. Unclear school- and district-level antidiscrimination policies, school officials' relative inaction toward student sexual harassment incidents based on sexual orientation, and inadequate or nonexistent training of school staff pertaining to issues unique to LGBT students are among the primary reasons schools are often perceived as unsafe environments for students who are sexually harassed based on their sexual orientation.

Two federal-level court decisions, *Nabozny v. Podlesny* (1996) and *Flores v. Morgan Hill Unified School District* (2003) have affirmatively found that school officials have a legal obligation under both the Fourteenth Amendment's Equal Protection Clause and Title IX to protect students from discrimination and sexual harassment based on their sexual orientation. In *Nabozny,* the Seventh Circuit ruled that a public high school student, who was repeatedly physically and verbally harassed throughout middle and high school because he was gay, could sue his school board for violating his right to equal protection. *Nabozny* was a groundbreaking case, because it represented the first time an American court rendered both a public school board and individual school employees monetarily liable for failing to protect a student who was gay from discrimination.

In *Flores,* the Ninth Circuit, in denying a school board's motion for summary judgment that essentially would have dismissed the claim, maintained that officials who failed to take formal action based on the consistent discrimination and sexual harassment of six former middle and high school students violated the Equal Protection Clause of the Fourteenth Amendment. As a result of *Flores,* the school board agreed that teachers, school officials, and staff would receive annual training in the recognition and prevention of sexual harassment based on sexual orientation.

A major legal implication of both *Nabozny* and *Flores* is that local school officials must take proactive steps to prevent sexual harassment of and discrimination against students based on a their sexual orientation. The failure of school officials to do so could potentially result not only in violating students' equal protection and Title IX rights but also in having to pay costly monetary damages.

Harassment in Cyberspace

The sexual harassment of students is no longer confined solely to classrooms. For example, while the Internet has been embraced, especially by young people, as a socialization tool, it is increasingly being used to sexually harass and denigrate students. For example, a 2005 survey of 1,500 teenagers using the Internet reported that 32% of male respondents and 36% of female respondents had experienced cyberbullying to some degree. Cyberbullying has been defined as the use of communication technologies, such as e-mail, cell phone and pager text messages, instant messaging, and defamatory personal Web sites to facilitate deliberate, repeated, and hostile behavior by an individual or group toward another.

A recent case in the federal trial court in Idaho, *Drews v. Joint School District* (2006), illustrates the potential for sexual harassment harm associated with cyberbullying and cyberharassment. Although the court did not have to address the merits of the underlying claim, because the dispute arose in connection with the use (and abuse) of the Internet, it can be seen as a precautionary tale when dealing with the emerging issue of cyberharassment.

The dispute in *Drews* involved a high school student with peer relationship issues. After her mother took a joke snapshot of the student kissing a female friend, other "friends" posted the photo on the Internet and spread rumors that she was a lesbian. Students called the student names, avoided her, and would not undress for basketball games when she was in the locker room. The student purportedly quit the basketball team and opted to be homeschooled for her science class. Insofar as the student and her parents alleged that school officials acted with deliberate indifference to her being harassed, they filed suit, alleging violations of her Title IX rights, her civil rights, and her privacy rights under the Family Educational Rights and Privacy Act (FERPA), as well as other state and constitutional claims. When the board moved for reconsideration before the court, a different set of facts emerged. It turns out that the student did not quit the basketball team because of the peer harassment and that she actually preferred her homeschooled science class to her former in-school instruction. After the facts were revealed, the court granted the board's motion for summary judgment and dismissed the remaining Title IX claims, because the student failed to sustain her burden of proof that she was subject to sexual harassment.

Insofar as cyberbullying occurs in a multitude of electronic forums, including e-mail, Web sites, online forums, chat rooms, blogs, instant messaging, and voice or text sent to cell phones, it is extremely difficult for school officials to monitor and control this behavior or the sexual harassment of other students through Internet-based communications. Unlike traditional sexual harassment and bullying, where the offenders are known, those using the Internet to sexually harass other students are often anonymous. Additionally, those who sexually harass others online can instigate harmful attacks 24 hours a day at any location with Internet access.

Recommendations for Policies

While the Supreme Court has deemed that school officials are liable under Title IX for failing to protect students that are sexually harassed, there are some proactive policy measures that schools can adopt to avoid liability. These policies should include the following items. First, local school boards must develop comprehensive and clearly written antidiscrimination policies expressly prohibiting sexual harassment and apply those policies to all involved stakeholders in the schools, including students, teachers, school staff, and parents. Second, board sexual harassment policies must be aligned with other relevant policies, including codes of conduct, personnel guidelines, and student handbooks. Third, school-based sexual harassment polices should include all forms of sexual harassment. For example, sexual harassment policies must not only prohibit "traditional" sexual harassment but must also explicitly prohibit sexual harassment based on sexual orientation. Fourth, school-based sexual harassment policies must explicitly include conditions regarding how to specifically address and resolve sexual harassment claims in a timely manner. Fifth, school-based sexual harassment policies must be reviewed annually to ensure legal compliance with the latest developments in federal and state law.

Kevin P. Brady

See also *Davis v. Monroe County Board of Education;* Equal Protection Analysis; *Franklin v. Gwinnett County Public Schools; Gebser v. Lago Vista Independent School District;* Hostile Work Environment; *Nabozny v. Podlesny;* Sexual Harassment, Peer-to-Peer; Sexual Harassment, Quid Pro Quo; Sexual Harassment, Same-Sex; Sexual Harassment of Students by Teachers; Sexual Orientation

Further Readings

American Association of University Women (AAUW). (1993). *Hostile hallways: The AAUW survey on sexual harassment in America's schools.* Washington, DC: Author.

Brady, K. P. (2004). Local school officials' legal duty to prevent anti-gay student harassment: The impact of *Nabozny* and *Flores. West's Education Law Reporter, 187,* 383–387.

Russo, C. J., Mawdsley, R. D., & Ilg, T. J. (2003). Guidelines for addressing sexual harassment in educational institutions. *West's Education Law Reporter, 182,* 15–20.

Shoop, R. J., & Edwards, D. L. (1994). *How to stop sexual harassment in our schools: A handbook and curriculum guide for administrators and teachers.* Boston, MA: Allyn and Bacon.

Stein, N. (1999). *Classrooms and courtrooms: Facing sexual harassment in K–12 schools.* New York: Teachers College Press.

Legal Citations

Davis v. Monroe County Board of Education, 526 U.S. 629 (1999).

Drews v. Joint School District, 2006 WL 851118 (Mar. 29, 2006 D. Idaho).

Flores v. Morgan Hill Unified School District, 324 F.3d 1130 (9th Cir. 2003).

Franklin v. Gwinnett County Public Schools, 503 U.S. 60 (1992).

Gebser v. Lago Vista Independent School District, 524 U.S. 274 (1998).

Nabozny v. Podlesny, 92 F.3d 446 (7th Cir. 1996).

SEXUAL HARASSMENT, PEER-TO-PEER

Complaints from students regarding sexual harassment from peers are not only common but are on the increase. What was once treated as innocent teasing or behavior that was typically described as "boys will be boys" is now often viewed as offensive, provocative conduct unacceptable at school. These acts of harassment occur on school grounds, at extracurricular events, and on school buses. The increase in reported peer-to-peer sexual harassment may be due to a combination of the increased awareness of sexuality by students, societal acceptance of reporting sexually inappropriate behavior, and an increase in sexually aggressive acts by students.

Much of the peer-to-peer sexual harassment involves bullying types of behavior. Females are often the victims of sexual bullying in the forms of inappropriate or suggestive comments, graphic graffiti in school halls or bathroom walls, and overt acts of touching or groping. Moreover, there appears to be a rapid increase of same-sex sexual harassment. Insofar as society has become more tolerant and accepting of students who are openly gay or lesbian, school officials have witnessed increases in bullying, hate, and sexually harassing behaviors directed at these students. There is evidence that, left unchecked, sexually harassing behaviors, regardless of the sexual orientations or genders of the students involved, will continue.

Sexually harassing behavior has also invaded elementary schools. Students as young as five years old have engaged in verbal and physical abuse of a sexual nature. Although newsworthy sex-related incidents, such as an innocent kiss leading to extreme discipline, have gained wide media attention, far too common aggressive sexual acts by preteens have been disregarded as childish naiveté.

In light of judicial developments, school boards may be held liable for peer-to-peer sexual harassment pursuant to Title IX of the Educational Amendments of 1972. In *Davis v. Monroe County Board of Education* (1999), a female student complained about sexually harassing behavior from a fellow male student. The parents, on behalf of their fifth-grade daughter, sued the school board under Title IX for failure to stop the classmate's sexually harassing behavior. After a federal trial court in Georgia and the Eleventh Circuit rejected the claims, the Supreme Court reversed in favor of the student and her parents and remanded for further consideration in light of analysis. In its only case involving peer-to-peer sexual harassment, the Court ruled that while school boards that receive federal financial assistance may not be liable for the conduct of the students, they may be accountable when school officials fail to prevent inappropriate student conduct. More specifically, the Court determined that school boards

> are properly held liable in damages only when they are deliberately indifferent to sexual harassment, of which they have actual knowledge, that is so severe, pervasive, and objectively offensive that it can be said to deprive the victims of access to the educational opportunities or benefits provided by the school. (p. 650)

At the same time, the Court added that a board can be liable for damages when officials have "substantial control over both the harasser and the context in which the known harassment occurs" (p. 646).

The Office for Civil Rights (OCR) provides guidance to school systems to help prevent acts of sexual harassment and to address incidents of harassment. First, the OCR (2001) guidelines direct school boards to develop policies addressing sexual harassment. Polices should include a definition of sexual harassment, an explanation of the penalties for engaging in harassing conduct, an outline of the grievance procedures, contact information for those who receive complaints, and an expressed commitment to keep complaints confidential. Further, school officials are advised to be prompt in the investigation of complaints of sexual harassment and to avoid ignoring the plight of the alleged victim. In order to assist with the complaint process, school officials are urged to develop their own guidelines for the identification and reporting of sexually harassing behavior and to train all employees on how to identify harassing behavior and intervene on behalf of the victim using clear guidelines for reporting such behavior.

Mark Littleton

See also Bullying; *Davis v. Monroe County Board of Education;* Hostile Work Environment; Sexual Harassment, Quid Pro Quo; Sexual Harassment, Same-Sex; Title IX and Sexual Harassment

Further Readings

Lewis, J. E., & Hastings, S. C. (1994). *Sexual harassment in education* (2nd ed.). Topeka, KS: National Organization on Legal Problems in Education.

Office for Civil Rights, U.S. Department of Education. (2001). *Revised sexual harassment guidance: Harassment of students by school employees, other students, or third parties.* Available from http://www.ed.gov

Russo, C. J. (Ed.). (2006). *The yearbook of education law: 2006.* Dayton, OH: Education Law Association.

Legal Citations

Davis v. Monroe County Board of Education, 526 U.S. 629 (1999), *on remand,* 206 F.3d 1377 (11th Cir. 2000).

Title IX of the Educational Amendments of 1972, 20 U.S.C. § 1681.

Sexual Harassment, Quid Pro Quo

When harassment involves the exchange of sexual favors in exchange for desired benefits, it is typically referred to as "quid pro quo," literally, "this for that" sexual harassment. Quid pro quo harassment implies a power relationship between harassers and victims. Usually, quid pro quo harassment involves employees and supervisors, but the term may also be applied to students in educational settings who are involved with teachers or other staff members such as coaches. As an example in a school setting, it could be that a teacher, acting as harasser, awards a grade to a student on the provision that the victim grant sexual favors. Nonetheless, educational decisions based on the acquiescence to sexual demands may have alternate twists. For example, teachers may offer to withhold reports of poor grades to students' parents for the exchange of sexual favors.

Unlike hostile environment sexual harassment, quid pro quo harassment is more easily recognizable. Additionally, a single incident of quid pro quo harassment may well be sufficient to establish a sexual harassment claim, because individuals need not submit to demands for sexual favors in order for there to be violations. This entry looks at the law as it applies in educational settings.

Enforcement

Under Title VII of the Civil Rights Act of 1964, private and public institutions with 15 or more employees are liable for acts of supervisors and employees who sexually harass workers. Title VII is enforced by the Equal Employment Opportunity Commission (EEOC). Title IX of the Education Amendments of 1972 is an educational statute that prohibits disparate treatment of students in educational institutions on the basis of sex. The U.S. Supreme Court has yet to address a case of quid pro quo sexual harassment head-on in an educational setting.

While employee-to-employee sexual harassment is covered by Title VII, Title IX addresses employee-to-employee, employee-to-student, and student-to-student sexual harassment. Pursuant to Title IX, private and public institutions receiving federal funds may be liable for the sexual harassment of students or employees. Title IX is enforced by the Office for Civil Rights in the U.S. Department of Education.

Employer Liability

Unlike hostile environment sexual harassment, the courts tend to apply strict liability to supervisors of individuals who engaged in quid pro quo harassment. When supervisory employees in educational settings have primary or absolute authority to hire, promote, or terminate other staff members and they use their power to secure sexual favors, the courts are likely to find school boards strictly liable. In instances where supervisory employees have limited authority to hire, promote, or terminate the employment of their victim, then the courts are less likely to render boards strictly liable.

Prevention is the best tool to eliminate claims of sexual harassment. To this end, school boards and officials can take steps to reduce or prevent the occurrence of sexually harassing behavior by establishing, promulgating, and regularly updating their sexual harassment policies. Employees should be notified of the policies and trained on the content and intent of the policies. Appropriately devised policies include a commitment to eradicate and prevent sexual harassment, a definition of hostile environment sexual harassment, an explanation of penalties for sexually harassing conduct, an outline of the grievance procedures, contact persons for consultation, and an expressed commitment to keep all complaints and personnel actions confidential.

Additionally, once school officials are made aware of sexually harassing behavior by subordinates, it is incumbent on them to act and not to be deliberately indifferent to the plight of victims. Officials are likely to be identified as deliberately indifferent if they possess the authority to address the harassing behavior, have actual knowledge of the wrongdoing, and consciously disregard the behavior.

Providing educational training is crucial to identifying signs of sexual harassment. First, training should occur on sexual harassment complaint procedures. Part of this preparation should include information on how to file formal complaints, with whom charges should be filed, timelines for filing, and how to respond appropriately to such charges. Second, because most problems of sexual harassment do not follow formal complaint processes, all employees should be taught to identify potentially harassing behaviors. Regarding employee behavior that might lead to harassment charges, some behavior is fairly obvious, such as making sexually suggestive comments, giving inappropriate personal gifts, and sending intimate letters or cards. However, some behavior that is not so obvious includes flirting, lingering too long in a hug, engaging in playful exchanges, and leering ("elevator eyes"—staring at an individual with the eyes moving up and down the body). Clearly, dealing with issues of quid pro quo sexual harassment will help to improve conditions in schools for all, students and staff.

Mark Littleton

See also Equal Employment Opportunity Commission; Sexual Harassment; Sexual Harassment, Peer-to-Peer; Sexual Harassment, Same-Sex; Sexual Harassment of Students by Teachers; Title VII; Title IX and Sexual Harassment

Further Readings

Lewis, J. E., & Hastings, S. C. (1994). *Sexual harassment in education* (2nd ed.). Topeka, KS: National Organization on Legal Problems in Education.

Office for Civil Rights, U.S. Department of Education. (2001). *Revised sexual harassment guidance: Harassment of students by school employees, other students, or third parties.* Available from http://www.ed.gov

SEXUAL HARASSMENT, SAME-SEX

Sexual harassment is unwelcome conduct of a sexual nature, which is prohibited both by Title VII of the Civil Rights Act of 1964 as it applies to employees and Title IX of the Educational Amendments of 1972 when dealing with students. The genesis of sexual harassment legislation was to forbid employers from hiring and promoting employees on the basis of their gender and to prohibit the conditioning of employment in return for sexual favors.

The Law and Its Enforcement

According to Title VII of the Civil Rights Act of 1964, public school boards and nonpublic schools with more than 15 employees that receive federal financial assistance may be liable for sexual harassment claims. Title VII is enforced by the Equal Employment Opportunity Commission. Title VII addresses harassment only when the perpetrator and the victim are employees. On the other hand, Title IX of the Educational Amendments of 1972 covers employee-to-employee, employee-to-student, and student-to-student harassment. Under Title IX, public and nonpublic institutions receiving federal funds may be liable for sexual harassment of students and employees. The Office for Civil Rights in the U.S. Department of Education enforces Title IX claims.

The early sexual harassment litigation focused on male-female interactions in employment and educational settings. Yet, the U.S. Supreme Court expanded the parameters of prohibited sexual harassment in *Oncale v. Sundowner Offshore Services* (1998). In *Oncale,* the Court ruled that Title VII prohibits sexual harassment when the perpetrator and the victim are of the same sex. Subsequently, while the Supreme Court of Alabama (*H. M. v. Jefferson County Board of Education,* 1998) and Eighth Circuit (*Kinman v. Omaha Public School District,* 1999) agreed that Title IX prohibits the sexual harassment of students by teachers of the same sex, in neither instance had the plaintiffs presented actionable claims. Further, although not reaching the merits of the underlying claim, the Ninth Circuit pointed out that students had a clearly established right not to be harassed by peers based on their actual or perceived sexual orientations (*Flores v. Morgan Hill Unified School District,* 2003).

Same-sex sexual harassment manifests itself in various forms. Often, the harassment is in the form of bullying based on the victims' physical features or sexual orientation. For example, male students who possess delicate features or feminine characteristics may be verbally teased or physically assaulted by same-sex classmates because these characteristics do not portray the example of a "typical" male. Likewise, female students who possess more masculine features may be vilified by their more "typical" female contemporaries.

Students may be bullied because of their sexual orientation. Gay male students may be verbally teased, even ostracized, by their male heterosexual classmates;

on occasion, gay students choose to attempt or commit suicide to escape the emotional trauma. Often, the verbal abuse also leads to physical abuse. Reported abuse of openly lesbian students is less common than is abuse of their male peers.

Incidents of actual reported sexual assault by same-sex students are relatively rare. The few reports may be due to the lack of actual acts of sexual assault or the lack of reported behavior because of the embarrassment on the part of the victim. Same-sex sexual abuse is more common when perpetrators are school employees preying on students.

Avoiding Liability

As noted above, same-sex sexual harassment between students is often associated with bullying. Frequently, students are bullied because of their actual or perceived gay and lesbian sexual orientations. To this end, school boards and educational officials would be wise to establish appropriate preventative measures to avoid bullying behavior. As reflected by the Seventh Circuit's analysis in *Nabozny v. Podlesny* (1996), students who are subjected to harassment by peers due to their sexual orientation may receive significant protection via the Equal Protection Clause of the Fourteenth Amendment.

In addition to preventative measures, school boards should establish, and regularly revise, formal complaint procedures to address instances of bullying and harassing behaviors. At the same time, boards should inform teachers, staff, and students about appropriate behavior with regard to others so as to avoid sexual harassment. Insofar as sexually motivated harassment is frequently unreported, employees should be taught to identify harassing behavior. Same-sex harassment, particularly bullying behavior of students based on their sexual orientation, often begins with lewd gesturing and suggestive name calling, and unless educators intervene, it can quickly lead to physical violence.

Mark Littleton

See also Bullying; Equal Employment Opportunity Commission; Fourteenth Amendment; Hostile Work Environment; Sexual Harassment of Students by Teachers; Title VII; Title IX and Sexual Harassment

Further Readings

Lewis, J. E., & Hastings, S. C. (1994). *Sexual harassment in education* (2nd ed.). Topeka, KS: National Organization on Legal Problems in Education.

Office for Civil Rights, U.S. Department of Education. (2001). *Revised sexual harassment guidance: Harassment of students by school employees, other students, or third parties.* Available from http://www.ed.gov

Russo, C. J. (Ed.). (2007). *The yearbook of education law: 2007.* Dayton, OH: Education Law Association.

Legal Citations

Flores v. Morgan Hill Unified School District, 324 F.3d 1130 (9th Cir. 2003).

H. M. v. Jefferson County Board of Education, 719 So. 2d 793 (Ala. 1998).

Kinman v. Omaha Public School District, 171 F.3d 607 (8th Cir. 1999).

Nabozny v. Podlesny, 92 F.3d 446 (7th Cir. 1996).

Oncale v. Sundowner Offshore Services, 523 U.S. 75 (1998).

SEXUAL HARASSMENT OF STUDENTS BY TEACHERS

There is yet no definitive study indicating how prevalent teacher-on-student sexual harassment is. Even so, experts in the field estimate that a minimum of 10% of the student population experiences some form of inappropriate sexual activity with an educator at some time during their public education. Yet, due to the shame and guilt often experienced by students, these same experts suggest that the incidence of sexual misconduct is greater than what is actually reported. This entry briefly discusses legal cases and laws related to such harassment and preventive guidelines for educators.

There is no stereotypical perpetrator of sexual misconduct. Research indicates that teachers are the most common offenders, with others being coaches, administrators, and other school employees. Coaches, as well as others who spend extensive amounts of time with students in extracurricular settings, often develop close relationships with students. These relationships, combined with opportunity, enable the boundaries between educators and students to become blurred, leading to inappropriate sexual relationships. Offenders tend to be, but are not exclusively, males who have been deemed to be trustworthy, popular, and model educators. The perpetrators are seldom predators, meaning that they do not enter the profession to prey on the students. In retrospect, the perpetrators usually experience deep feelings of guilt and shame in light of their conduct.

Legal Cases

In *Franklin v. Gwinnett County Public Schools* (1993), a male high school teacher coerced a female student into sexual intercourse. In a landmark decision, the Supreme Court unanimously reasoned that Title IX of the Educational Amendments of 1972 was an appropriate vehicle for a student to pursue damages related to a sexual harassment claim. The Court specified that having a statute such as Title IX in place, yet not offering any remedy, would have left victims without redress. Subsequently, in *Gebser v. Lago Vista Independent School District* (1998), the Supreme Court essentially rejected the notion that a school board can be essentially strictly liable for the inappropriate sexual relationship that a teacher had with a student. The Court determined that an award of damages would have been inappropriate, because no school official with the authority to address the discrimination had knowledge of the act. As such, the Court was of the opinion that because there could not have been deliberate indifference to the Title IX violation, the board was not at fault.

Two federal statutes address incidents of sexual harassment. The first, Title VII of the Civil Rights Act of 1964, is an employment statute that prohibits discrimination on the basis of race, color, national origin, religion, and sex. Under Title VII, private and public institutions with 15 or more employees are liable for acts of supervisors and employees who sexually harass, and Title VII is enforced by the Equal Employment Opportunity Commission.

The second law, Title IX of the Education Amendments of 1972, is an educational statute that prohibits disparate treatment of individuals in educational institutions on the basis of sex. Under Title IX, private and public institutions receiving federal funds may be liable for the inappropriate actions of students and/or school personnel. Title IX is enforced by the Office for Civil Rights in the U.S. Department of Education.

Educator Guidelines

Identifying sexual misconduct is not an easy task, but there are some indicators that inappropriate behavior may be occurring. One indicator is overly affectionate behavior such as hugging or touching. Related indicating behavior is telling jokes of a sexual nature or using suggestive terms in conversation. Telephone visitation and conversations of an intimate nature between the educator and student are additional indicators of inappropriate relationships.

Unnecessary visitations beyond the school day are another sign. Those educators who extend their work days to assist students are often hard-working dedicated individuals seeking to make a difference in the lives of students. Yet, perpetrators frequently use this contact as a means of grooming the student for future sexual activity. Likewise, student-initiated contact may be an attempt to violate appropriate educator–student boundaries.

Finally, complaints and innuendos of an inappropriate relationship between an educator and student are indicative of sexual misconduct. These "rumors" should be taken seriously and be properly investigated. In some instances, consensual sexual activity occurs between an educator and a student who is of consensual age. The age of consent varies greatly from state to state, ranging from 15 to 18. Nevertheless, most states have laws or ethics codes that prohibit inappropriate sexual conduct between an educator and student regardless of the student's age.

In order to combat teacher-on-student sexual harassment, school officials should establish clear written policies that delineate and prohibit inappropriate relationships. Additionally, school personnel should be diligent in the scrutiny of prospective employees and should train employees on how to avoid inappropriate relationships and identify signs of misconduct. Finally, school board policymakers should identify individuals to serve as investigators of allegations and rumors. Although a sense of teacher guilt is imbedded in these recommendations, experts caution policymakers to avoid establishing a climate of suspicion. In such a climate, innocent teachers may believe that false accusations and vendettas against demanding teachers would become commonplace, although studies indicate that such accusations are rare.

Mark Littleton

See also *Franklin v. Gwinnett County Public Schools; Gebser v. Lago Vista Independent School District;* Hostile Work Environment; Sexual Harassment; Sexual Harassment, Quid Pro Quo; Sexual Harassment, Same-Sex

Further Readings

Fibkins, W. L. (2006). *Innocence denied: A guide to preventing sexual misconduct by teachers and coaches.* Toronto, ON, CA: Rowman and Littlefield Education.

Lewis, J. E., & Hastings, S. C. (1994). *Sexual harassment in education* (2nd ed.). Topeka, KS: National Organization on Legal Problems in Education.

Office for Civil Rights, U.S. Department of Education. (2001). *Revised sexual harassment guidance: Harassment of students by school employees, other students, or third parties.* Available from http://www.ed.gov

Shoop, R. J. (2004). *Sexual exploitation in schools: How to spot it and stop it.* Thousand Oaks, CA: Corwin Press.

Legal Citations

Franklin v. Gwinnett County Public Schools, 503 U.S. 60 (1992).

Gebser v. Lago Vista Independent School District, 524 U.S. 274 (1998).

SEXUALITY EDUCATION

Sexuality education is the curricular area that addresses human sexual development, identity, and orientation as well as sexual behavior across the life span. Historically, public school systems began offering sexuality education classes in the early 20th century, in Chicago. However, these early classes were generally limited to issues of personal health and what was called, at that time, "social hygiene." Explicit sexuality education did not become commonplace in the public school curriculum until the 1970s, even though many comparable programs were housed under the more neutral sounding titles of "health education" or "family life education."

By the late 1970s, a growing resistance mobilized against such programs. In addition to harboring hostility toward the civil rights movement and other social liberation movements, opponents focused on public school policies that they believed promoted godlessness and immorality. Given the opposition's deep unease with public discussions of sexuality in general and adolescent sexuality in particular, rescinding sexuality education classes became a favorite target for their activism. During the 1980s and 1990s, opposition activists launched a series of court challenges to these programs, but they found little success (see *Brown v. Hot, Sexy & Safer Productions,* 1995). Further, to date, no decisions from the U.S. Supreme Court directly address this point. Consequently, activists refocused their efforts in reshaping extant policies and procedures at all levels of governance, whether local, state, or federal.

Ironically, the HIV/AIDS pandemic indirectly assisted opponents of comprehensive sexuality education. Across the United States, public school districts without sexuality education programs, or those employing perfunctory curricula, embraced sexuality education as part of the larger public health response to HIV/AIDS. As a result, activists realized that they would not be able to remove sexuality education entirely from public school curricula. To this end, opponents of comprehensive sexuality education refocused their efforts by promoting "abstinence-only" sexuality education or curricula that focused on encouraging adolescents to refrain from sexual activity until marriage. While the efficacy of these programs has long been questionable at best, with a political change in the U.S. Congress in 1994, abstinence-only sexuality education found friendly, and national, political support. By 1996, then-President Clinton signed into law the first federally funded abstinence-only sexuality education program.

Currently, while the federal government continues to fund abstinence-only education, even if it is now doing so at reduced levels, there is wide public support for comprehensive sexuality education, not abstinence-only. Additionally, questions remain about whether the content of many of the federally funded abstinence programs is factually accurate. Moreover, the evaluation research regarding this federal program indicates that students who have participated fail to refrain from initiating sexual activity prior to heterosexual marriage and may be more likely to engage in high-risk sexual behavior, in particular, regardless of their sexual orientations or genders.

Citing the overwhelming public health evidence, local school boards can make strong legal arguments in support of comprehensive sexuality programs, particularly by invoking "compelling state interest" in reducing sexually transmitted diseases as well as unintended pregnancy. Additionally, there is evidence that some of the established abstinence-only programs may run afoul of the Establishment Clause in the First Amendment to the U.S. Constitution by invoking religious justifications for stressing sexual abstinence until heterosexual marriage. However, in some locales, the political risks for local board members and administrators of embracing comprehensive sexuality education would probably outweigh these legal considerations.

Catherine A. Lugg

See also Sexual Orientation

Further Readings

The content of federally funded abstinence-only education programs. Prepared for Rep. Henry A. Waxman. (2004, December). Washington, DC: United States House of Representatives Committee on Government Reform—Minority Staff Special Investigations Division.

Diamond, S. (1995). *Roads to Dominion: Right-wing movements and political power in the United States.* New York: The Guilford Press.

Santelli, S., Ott, M. A., Lyon, M., Rogers, J., Summers, D., & Schleifer, R. (2006). Abstinence and abstinence-only education: A review of U.S. policies and programs. *Journal of Adolescent Health, 38*(1), 72–81

Zimmerman, J. (2002). *Whose America? Culture wars in the public schools.* Cambridge, MA: Harvard University Press.

Legal Citations

Brown v. Hot, Sexy & Safer Productions, 68 F.3d 525, 539 (1st Cir. 1995) *cert. denied,* 516 U.S. 1159 (1996).

SEXUAL ORIENTATION

Sexual orientation is the proclivity or capacity for romantic love. All human beings have a basic sexual orientation, which can range from homosexual (individuals fall in love with people who are their same biological sex) to bisexual (individuals can fall in love with individuals of various biological sexes) to heterosexual (individuals fall in love with people who are of what is historically considered "the opposite sex"). According to the psychological research literature, individuals' sexual orientations are well established by the age of five and are highly resistant, if not impossible, to change. Individuals who have a nonheterosexual sexual orientation are currently understood to be lesbian, gay, or bisexual; collectively, the acronym is LGB.

Variations in human sexual orientation have existed across history and cultures. Even so, beginning in the late 19th century, officials in the United States criminalized sexual behavior that was nonheterosexual. By the 1920s, all states had made same-sex consensual sexual behavior a felony. This situation did not end until the 2003 U.S. Supreme Court's decision in *Lawrence v. Texas,* which ruled that all laws banning consensual sodomy, whether by cross-sex or same-sex couples, were unconstitutional.

Complicating this picture is that gender, or how individuals express their understandings of what it means to be male or female, has historically been used as a proxy for sexual orientation. Simply stated, if persons did not "do" their gender correctly, particularly effeminate men, the cultural assumption was that they were "queer" or homosexual, regardless of their actual orientation. Consequently, gender transgressors could be, were, and in some instances, still are fired from their jobs as well as harassed by their peers and law enforcement officials.

For educators working in public schools, the conflation of sexual orientation and gender meant that both male and female educators have had to adhere to rigid gender roles or face the loss of their positions. Additionally, because sexual orientation was equated with intrinsic criminality, states maintained bans on lesbian, gay, and bisexual school personnel. Heterosexual marriage was expected for male educators throughout the bulk of the 20th century. At the same time, many school boards actually banned married women from serving as teachers under the sexist logic that women could not satisfy both their husbands and their educational responsibilities. However, after World War II, a combination of greater awareness regarding human sexuality, rampant homophobia, particularly in the field of educational administration, and a dire need for public school teachers in light of the ongoing baby boom opened the doors wide to married female teachers. By the 1970s, female educators were expected to marry just like their male peers.

Since the 1970s, sexual orientation has served as a flashpoint in the politics of education. There have been numerous political battles at the local, state, and federal level as both a growing LGB civil rights movement and Protestant Right political activists have clashed over many aspects affecting public schooling policy.

Currently, the status of sexual orientation vis-à-vis American public schooling is dominated by policy incoherence. On the one hand, 20 states and Washington, D.C., outlaw discrimination based on sexual orientation, and another 6 jurisdictions have statewide policies that ban harassment and/or discrimination based on sexual orientation in public schools. On the other hand, 15 states provide no protection whatsoever regarding sexual orientation and public schooling. In addition, 8 states have "no promo homo" laws on the books. These laws prohibit the "promotion of homosexuality" by public school officials. Broadly construed and probably unconstitutional, no promo homo laws serve to stigmatize and silence individuals who have either a homosexual or bisexual sexual orientation. Until federal legislation is enacted, this policy incoherence involving sexual orientation and public schooling is likely to continue.

Catherine A. Lugg

See also Gay, Lesbian and Straight Education Network (GLSEN); Gay, Lesbian, Bisexual, and Transgendered Persons, Rights of; Sexual Harassment, Same-Sex

Further Readings

Blount, J. M. (2005). *Fit to teach: Same-sex desire, gender, and school work in the twentieth century.* Albany: State University of New York Press.

Human Rights Campaign. (n.d.). http://www.hrc.org

Lugg, C. A. (2003). Sissies, faggots, lezzies and dykes: Gender, sexual orientation and the new politics of education. *Educational Administration Quarterly, 39*(1), 95–134.

Legal Citations

Lawrence v. Texas, 539 U.S. 558 (2003).

SHELTON V. TUCKER

In *Shelton v. Tucker* (1960), the issue before the U.S. Supreme Court was whether a state statute requiring all public school educators to disclose every organization to which they belonged over a five-year period was unconstitutional. In its 5-to-4 ruling, the Court held that the broad requirements of the statute were unconstitutional, because it went beyond the scope of legitimate and substantial inquiries of teacher fitness and competency.

Facts of the Case

Shelton revolved around an Arkansas statute that required all public school teachers, administrators, and college faculty to make annual reports of their organizational affiliations for the preceding five years. Initially, plaintiffs filed two separate actions challenging the statute. One case went through the federal courts, while the other worked its way through state courts in Arkansas.

In the federal case, Shelton, a 25-year veteran teacher in the Little Rock public school system, did not file his affidavit that listed his organizational affiliations. As a result, the board chose not to renew his employment contract, and he filed suit. At trial, the evidence demonstrated that Shelton was a member of the National Association for the Advancement of Colored People and not a member of any subversive organization. The lower federal courts upheld the statute and declared it constitutional.

Similarly, at the state court level, a faculty member at the University of Arkansas and a public school teacher at Little Rock also declined to file the affidavits of organizational associations, and their contracts were not renewed. At trial, these plaintiffs also indicated that they did not have any affiliations with subversive organizations. As the case continued through the appellate process, the Arkansas Supreme Court upheld the statute and declared it constitutional. As the plaintiffs in both cases pursued further appeals, the litigation was eventually brought to the attention of the U.S. Supreme Court, which consolidated them as one case.

The Court's Ruling

In *Shelton,* the Supreme Court balanced the governmental interest in evaluating the fitness and competence of educators by means of knowing their organizational affiliations with the right of individuals to exercise their constitutional liberties. Providing a general rule of law, the Court declared that when the government has a legitimate and substantial interest, it may act to achieve those purposes. However, in achieving those purposes, the Court explained that the government cannot infringe on fundamental individual rights with the exercise of broad authority when narrowly tailored provisions could achieve their goals.

Applying established legal rules to *Shelton,* the Supreme Court recognized a fundamental problem with the Arkansas statute insofar as its scope was apparently limitless. In other words, the Court found that the statute was too broad, that it constrained liberties, and that it could be more narrowly written so as to not restrict more freedoms than necessary. The Court noted that many of the organizational affiliations that educators might report would have no connection to matters related to teacher fitness and competence. Moreover, the Court indicated that public disclosure of the reported affiliations might lead to pressures from groups outside the public schools to discharge a teacher if the teacher were affiliated with an unpopular organization.

Taking these reasons as a whole into consideration, the Court struck down the Arkansas statute. According to the Court, the statute violated the federal Constitution, because it was not narrowly tailored to achieve its goals; instead, the statute had an "unlimited and indiscriminate sweep" that resulted in infringement of individual rights.

Shelton does not remove school administrators' professional autonomy in the selection process of potential staff and in the evaluation process for existing staff.

Yet, it does demonstrate the need to balance governmental interests in legitimate inquiry with individual interests in associational affiliations. As the Supreme Court essentially reasoned in *Keyishian v. Board of Regents* (1967), and as many other judicial opinions subsequently emphasized, the protection of constitutional freedoms is nowhere more vital than within our schools.

Jeffrey C. Sun

See also First Amendment; *Keyishian v. Board of Regents;* Teacher Rights

Further Readings

Note: Less drastic means and the First Amendment. (1969). *Yale Law Journal, 78*(3), 464–474.

Legal Citations

Keyishian v. Board of Regents, 385 U.S. 589 (1967).
Shelton v. Tucker, 364 U.S. 479 (1960).

SINGLE-SEX SCHOOLS

Single-sex schools are gender-specific schools. While the existence of single-sex education in nonpublic schools, whether nonsectarian or religiously affiliated, especially in Roman Catholic schools, has always been legally permissible, the legality of publicly supported single-sex schools continues to be challenged actively and questioned in the courts. While the overall number of public single-sex schools in the United States is relatively small, it is growing, especially in the wake of the passage of the No Child Left Behind Act (NCLB) (2002). This entry discusses the related legal issues.

Background

According to the National Association for the Advancement of Single Sex Public Education (NASSPE), there are currently over 200 single-sex, public, K–12 schools operating in the United States. Thirty-three states presently have at least one public single-sex school, with Ohio and New York having the most with a total of 10 each. Founded in 1844, the oldest single-sex public school, Western High School, located in Baltimore, Maryland, is still in existence. A more recent and widely publicized public school endorsing gender separation in the schooling process, Young Women's Leadership School, was created in 1996 by former journalist Ann Rubenstein Tisch in New York City.

Advocates of public single-sex schools contend that there exists a sizable amount of scientific research that demonstrates that female students are extremely underrepresented in the subject areas of math and science. According to these advocates, single-sex schools would address current gender bias in mathematics and science while promoting female student achievement and entry into mathematics and science career paths. Other advocates have called for the creation of all-male academies in an attempt to limit school violence. On the other hand, opponents to public single-sex schools respond that the creation of such schools promotes sex-based segregation analogous to the race-based segregation that was outlawed in *Brown v. Board of Education of Topeka* (1954).

The central legal question surrounding single-sex schools is whether public school boards can create publicly supported, gender-specific schools as a means to improve student achievement. Since the passage of the NCLB, the controversy of the legality of public, single-sex schools has escalated. In 2004, the U.S. Department of Education released guidelines that would potentially endorse publicly supported single-sex schools if students attended them voluntarily. In its efforts to close the achievement gap by placing an increased emphasis on accountability, flexibility, and choice, the NCLB currently allows federal money to be used for innovative educational initiatives, including single-sex schools as a means of improving student achievement.

The two primary federal sources of legal authority that cover the issue of single-sex schools are the Equal Protection Clause of the Fourteenth Amendment of the U.S. Constitution and Title IX of the Education Amendments of 1972. Both the Equal Protection Clause and Title IX expressly prohibit discrimination on the basis of gender.

Supreme Court Statements

The only case to reach the U.S. Supreme Court directly on the issue of public, single-sex, K–12 schools was *Vorchheimer v. School District of Philadelphia* (1977). In *Vorchheimer*, a female high school honors student sued her school board under the Equal Protection Clause based on its refusal to admit her to a prestigious all-boys public high school. After a federal trial court ordered the student's admission, the Third Circuit reversed in the board's favor. The court was of the opinion that while the all-boys and all-girls high schools were separate, they were essentially equal in terms of educational quality. In a highly contentious, 4-to-4 split decision, with Chief Justice William Rehnquist not participating in the resolution of the case, the Supreme Court chose not to issue a written opinion.

Yet, insofar as the Court was deadlocked, its inability to reach a clear outcome meant that the earlier order denying the female admission to the all-boys public school remained in place. Conversely, in the context of higher education, in *United States v. Virginia* (1996), the Court ruled that the inability of officials at the Virginia Military Academy to justify the institution's policy of denying admission to women meant that it violated the Equal Protection Clause.

Until such time as the Supreme Court explicitly answers the question of whether public single-sex schools are legal, judicial controversies questioning their place in the current American public school landscape will undoubtedly continue. At the same time, the Equal Protection Clause and Title IX contain legal language suggesting that single-sex schools are constitutionally suspect and unlawful. Even so, the recent standards-based reform movement and its focus on enhancing student achievement along with accountability for educators has provided single-sex schools new opportunities to test their success at improving student achievement levels, especially for middle- and high-school-aged girls in the mathematics and science curriculum. The recent passage of the NCLB in conjunction with specific guidelines promulgated by the U.S. Department of Education allowing the possibility of voluntary, single-sex classrooms has fueled the climate for public school systems nationwide to experiment with single-sex schooling.

Kevin P. Brady

See also Catholic Schools; Equal Protection Analysis; No Child Left Behind Act; Nonpublic Schools; *United States v. Virginia*

Further Readings

Clark, S. G. (2006). Public single-sex schools: Are they lawful? *West's Education Law Reporter, 213,* 319–331.

Mead, J. F. (2003). Single-gender "innovations": Can publicly funded single-gender school choice options be constitutionally justified? *Educational Administration Quarterly, 39*(2), 164–186.

Russo, C. J., & Mawdsley, R. D. (1997). VMI and single-sex public schools: The end of an era? *West's Education Law Reporter, 114,* 999–1010.

Salomone, R. (2005). *Same, different, equal: Rethinking single-sex schooling.* New Haven, CT: Yale University Press.

Streitmatter, J. L. (1999). *For girls only: Making a case for single-sex schooling.* Albany: State University of New York Press.

Legal Citations

Brown v. Board of Education of Topeka I, 347 U.S. 483 (1954).
Brown v. Board of Education of Topeka II, 349 U.S. 294 (1955).
No Child Left Behind Act, 20 U.S.C. §§ 6301 *et seq.*
United States v. Virginia, 518 U.S. 515 (1996), *on remand,* 96 F.3d 114 (4th Cir. 1996).
Vorchheimer v. School District of Philadelphia, 532 F.2d 880 (3d Cir. 1976), *aff'd,* 430 U.S. 703 (1977).

Singleton v. Jackson Municipal Separate School District

Singleton v. Jackson Municipal Separate School District (1981) stands out as the culmination of a long-running dispute over setting an appropriate guide for integrating a school system. In this final iteration of the case, a federal trial court ruled that insofar as the school board met the criteria for achieving unitary status with regard to students, because it had been in compliance with its desegregation order since 1971, it was entitled to a release from its desegregation decree.

Facts of the Case

The dispute in *Singleton* began in 1963, when 10 school-aged children filed suit against their school board, asserting they had been irreparably injured by its failure to maintain unitary or desegregated schools. The plaintiffs alleged that the board ignored precedent from the U.S. Supreme Court directing school boards to create unitary school systems immediately (*Alexander v. Holmes County Board of Education,* 1969). The plaintiffs claimed that the board also ignored the six criteria that the Supreme Court declared should be used to determine whether school systems had achieved unitary status in *Green v. County School Board of New Kent County* (1968). These factors address the composition of a student body, faculty, staff, transportation, extracurricular activities, and facilities.

The trial court later found that the school board achieved unitary status with respect to five of the six established *Green* factors: faculty, staff, transportation, extracurricular activities, and facilities. Insofar as the remaining area of concern dealt with the desegregation of the student body, the board sent the court a new plan. The court accepted the plan for desegregating the secondary schools but not the elementary schools. In June of 1971, the court accepted a plan for desegregation of the elementary schools, and since that time, all parties agreed that the system had been desegregated. In 1981, when the board petitioned to have its desegregation order terminated, several persons opposed its request in order to assure continued protection for minority students.

The Court's Ruling

In resolving the dispute, the trial court noted the school board achieved unitary status in 1971 under the six *Green* factors. In the most significant aspect on one of the earlier rounds of litigation, and the proposition for which the Fifth Circuit's 1969 judgment in *Singleton* is remembered, the court was satisfied that the board demonstrated that it had desegregated its teaching faculty. At that time, the Fifth Circuit acknowledged that the board succeeded, to the fullest extent possible, in ensuring that students were taught by both Black and White teachers and that the ratio of Black to White teachers was appropriate. Additionally, the trial court reiterated the Fifth Circuit's holding that board officials proved that there was a racial balance in the distribution of administrative authority and that no one had mounted a successful challenge to the board's racial hiring practices in over a decade.

Turning to transportation and extracurricular requirements, the court pointed out that the Office of Civil Rights (OCR) had issued an order stating that the school board's policy of providing free transportation to all students who lived more than nine-tenths of a mile from their assigned schools was nondiscriminatory. The court also commented on the OCR's investigation of allegations of discrimination in the board's extracurricular programs, maintaining that there were no racial barriers for students who wished to participate.

The court next determined that the school board's facilities were desegregated and that its facility use policy, which required persons requesting use of facilities to agree, in writing, not to engage in or permit discriminatory activities, was nondiscriminatory. The court further observed that the board's commitment to desegregation was exemplified by its construction of four, new, fully integrated schools over the past 10 years.

Rounding out its judgment, the court added that while "desegregation plans are more optimistic than the actual result" (p. 909), the school board had met the standards for student assignments and accomplished its desegregation goals. At the same time, the court indicated that due to "White flight" and other demographic shifts, the board, on several occasions, found it necessary to alter its attendance zones. Insofar as the board adopted a policy of creating representative teams to make rezoning decisions, the court was satisfied that there were no claims of discrimination regarding school assignments and redistricting. To the extent that the board was able to demonstrate it met and continued to meet each of the six *Green* factors, the court concluded that it was no longer required to operate pursuant to a desegregation order.

Brenda R. Kallio

See also Dual and Unitary Systems; *Green v. County School Board of New Kent County;* White Flight

Legal Citations

Alexander v. Holmes County Board of Education, 396 U.S. 19 (1969).

Green v. County School Board of New Kent County, 391 U.S. 430 (1968).

Singleton v. Jackson Municipal Separate School District, 419 F.2d 1211 (5th Cir.1969), *cert. denied,* 396 U.S. 1032 (1970), 541 F. Supp. 904 (S.D. Miss. 1981).

SKINNER V. RAILWAY LABOR EXECUTIVES' ASSOCIATION

In *Skinner v. Railway Labor Executives' Association* (1989), the U.S. Supreme Court upheld the constitutionality of a drug-testing program for railroad employees in positions that had an impact on safety. Pursuant to *Skinner,* along with its companion case, *National Treasury Employees Union v. Von Raab* (1989), public employers may, under some circumstances, be able to require their employees to submit to suspicionless drug and alcohol testing. Although *Skinner* was not set in an educational context, it raises interesting questions about testing of school employees.

Facts of the Case

During the 1980s, the United States began fighting the "war on drugs." Consequently, all governmental agencies were charged with developing better safety standards and implementing new regulations to help in this battle in the workplace. In this context, the Federal Railroad Administration (FRA) in 1985 adopted regulations that subjected employees in safety sensitive positions to blood and urine tests either for "reasonable cause" or after they were participants in a variety of specified major train accidents that involved deaths or damages of more than $50,000 to railway property. The purpose of the testing program was to prevent further or future accidents that might have occurred due to empoyees' consumption of drugs or alcohol. Employees who refused to submit to testing were rendered unfit to work for 9 months but were entitled to hearings about their refusals to cooperate.

In response to the FRA's promulgation of the testing regulations, a group of employees challenged the drug and alcohol testing program. After a federal trial court in California upheld the program's constitutionality, the Ninth Circuit reversed in favor of the employees. At the heart of its analysis, the court deemed that the program violated the Fourth Amendment, because it tested for drugs and alcohol regardless of whether there was suspicion that employees engaged in the use of illegal drugs. On further review, the Supreme Court reversed in favor of the government.

The Court's Ruling

At the outset of its opinion, the Supreme Court acknowledged that the disputed program constituted a "search" within the meaning of the Fourth Amendment, insofar as the testing of railway employees was compelled as a result of a governmental initiative. Therefore, the Court was of the opinion that it was necessary to address the question of "reasonableness" in conducting the search. In other words, the Court sought to review the balance between the intrusiveness of any drug test against the legitimate governmental interest of promoting safety. In so doing, the Court relied on the concept of "special needs" outside normal law enforcement channels in finding that the testing program was designed to be used in situations wherein the probable cause and warrant requirements simply were not practicable. The Court further explained that while the Fourth Amendment's warrant requirement was designed to protect individuals' expectations of privacy, the regulations only required testing under clearly defined circumstances.

The Supreme Court reasoned that requiring railway officials to obtain warrants would have done little to advance the government's compelling interest in ensuring railway safety. In justifying its rationale, the Court pointed out that the employees knew not only that they were working in a highly regulated industry but also that the regulations were an effective means of deterring those who worked in safety sensitive positions from using drugs or alcohol. The Court decided that requiring the government, through the railway's

managers, to rely on individualized suspicion that employees engaged in drug or alcohol use would seriously impede them in carrying out their duty to obtain important information. The Court thus concluded that the government's compelling need to test employees under the circumstances described in the regulations outweighed any justifiable expectations of privacy that crews might have had to avoid testing.

Marilyn J. Bartlett

See also Drug Testing of Teachers; *National Treasury Employees Union v. Von Raab; O'Connor v. Ortega*

Legal Citations

National Treasury Employees Union v. Von Raab, 489 U.S. 656 (1989).
O'Connor v. Ortega, 480 U.S. 709 (1987).
Skinner v. Railway Labor Executives' Association, 489 U.S. 602 (1989).

SLOAN V. LEMON

Sloan v. Lemon (1973) was the last of three related church–state cases that the U.S. Supreme Court considered between 1971 and 1973. At issue in *Sloan* was whether the Commonwealth of Pennsylvania could reimburse parents for the tuition that they paid to send their children to religiously affiliated nonpublic schools. Based on its earlier judgment in *Lemon v. Kurtzman* (*Lemon I*) in 1971, in *Sloan,* the Court held that the statute permitting reimbursement was unconstitutional under the Establishment Clause of the First Amendment, because it impermissibly advanced religion. Knowledge of the facts in *Lemon I* is essential in understanding the Court's subsequent decision in *Sloan.*

In *Lemon I,* the Supreme Court first articulated its now-famous *Lemon* test, a three-pronged standard for use by the courts in adjudicating cases involving the issue of church–state separation. Under the *Lemon* test, a law or policy must have a secular purpose, must neither advance nor inhibit religion (i.e., it must be neutral), and must not foster excessive government entanglement with religion.

In *Lemon I,* the Court considered whether laws from Rhode Island and Pennsylvania authorizing state aid to nonpublic schools were constitutional. Both laws focused on improving secular education within nonpublic, primarily church-related elementary and secondary schools. The Rhode Island law provided state supplements for salaries of those teaching secular courses, while the Pennsylvania statute authorized state funding for various secular instructional costs. The Court declared both laws unconstitutional on the basis that they fostered excessive entanglement between government and religion because of the state bureaucracy that would have been necessary to ensure that public funds were used only to support secular instruction. *Lemon I* invalidated a number of contracts between religious schools and state governments that had been consummated in good faith prior to the final ruling.

Two years later, in *Lemon v. Kurtzman II* (1973) (*Lemon II*), the Supreme Court permitted the government to reimburse church-related schools for costs of secular instruction incurred prior to invalidation of the two state laws. The Court reached this outcome because it was satisfied that the plaintiffs had not sought interim injunctive relief, the related services had already been provided, denial of payment would have had serious financial consequences on private schools that relied on the state's formal agreement, and there was no possibility of continuing entanglement, because the contractual relationship legally could not continue beyond the final payments that the Court authorized for the 1970–1971 school year.

The Supreme Court handed down its opinion in *Lemon I* on June 28, 1971. On August 27, 1971, the Pennsylvania General Assembly, seeking to avoid the entanglement issue that doomed its previous aid statute, passed a new law authorizing direct reimbursements to parents for tuition expenses incurred in sending their children to sectarian and other nonpublic schools. The new statute specifically precluded any governmental control over policy determination, personnel, curriculum, or any other administrative function in the nonpublic schools. Further, the law imposed no restrictions or limitations on how the reimbursements could be used by qualifying parents. The intent, of course, was to distance public authority and oversight as far as possible from the operation of religious and other nonpublic

schools. Clearly, the General Assembly's intent was to disentangle church and state in accordance with the third prong mandate in the *Lemon* test. The plaintiffs challenged the new law immediately.

After considering the facts in *Sloan,* the Supreme Court concluded that Pennsylvania officials impermissibly singled out a class of citizens for special economic benefit and "whether that benefit [was] viewed as a simple tuition subsidy, as an incentive to parents to send their children to sectarian schools, or as a reward for having done so" (p. 832), the ultimate result was to preserve and support religious institutions. Ironically, while trying to avoid the church–state entanglement prohibited by the third prong of the *Lemon* test, the General Assembly passed a law that was interpreted as clearly advancing the cause of religion, a direct violation of the second prong of the test. In the end, the Court held that the statute was also unconstitutional under the Establishment Clause, not because it fostered entanglement, but because it had the impermissible effect of advancing religion. The Court concluded that the law was not severable so as to permit continuing tuition assistance to parents who send their children to private nonsectarian schools.

Robert C. Cloud

See also State Aid and the Establishment Clause; *Lemon v. Kurtzman; Walz v. Tax Commission of the City of New York*

Legal Citations

Committee for Public Education and Religious Liberty v. Nyquist, 413 U.S. 756 (1973).

Everson v. Board of Education of Ewing Township, 330 U.S. 1 (1947), *reh'g denied,* 330 U.S. 855 (1947).

Lemon v. Kurtzman I, 403 U.S. 602 (1971).

Lemon v. Kurtzman II, 411 U.S. 192 (1973)

Sloan v. Lemon, 413 U.S. 825 (1973).

Walz v. Tax Commission of the City of New York, 397 U.S. 664 (1970).

SMITH V. CITY OF JACKSON, MISSISSIPPI

Insofar as *Smith v. City of Jackson, Mississippi* (2005) involved a dispute over age discrimination in public employment, it should be of interest to educators. At issue in *Smith* was the nature of the relationship between the legal concept of "disparate impact" and the Age Discrimination in Employment Act of 1967 (ADEA). The Court's decision in *Smith* was such a narrow interpretation of the ADEA that it has placed the future of the law's viability in jeopardy as a tool to protect employees. *Smith's* importance rests in the fact that it calls on public employers, including school boards and other educational institutions, to offer valid explanations for practices that hint at having a disparate impact on older employees. *Smith* enabled the Court not only to consider whether documents can sustain claims but also to examine the extent to which disparate impact allegations depend on the proof requirements.

Facts of the Case

The dispute in *Smith* began in 1999 when a police department enacted a pay plan for its officers. On its face, the plan appeared logical by placing the officers on pay steps based on rank, time in service, and current salary. In an attempt to help keep its younger officers, the city paid them proportionally higher step raises than their older colleagues. As a result, 30 officers who were over the age of 40 filed suit under the ADEA, alleging disparate treatment and disparate impact.

A federal trial court in Mississippi granted the city's motion for summary judgment in pointing out that the officers failed to establish that officials acted with intent to discriminate. On appeal, the Fifth Circuit affirmed that a disparate impact claim is not cognizable under the ADEA. The U.S. Supreme Court agreed to hear a further challenge to resolve whether disparate impact could be made cognizable under the ADEA.

The Court's Ruling

On further review, the Supreme Court affirmed in favor of the city. As an initial matter, it is important to note the difference between disparate treatment and disparate impact, two legal theories of recovery in discrimination law. *Disparate treatment* pertains to actions taken by governmental agencies against individuals who are members of constitutionally protected groups or classes. In *Smith,* for example, the protected group was police officers over the age of 40. In addition, plaintiffs must be able to prove that defendants acted with intent to discriminate. On the other hand, *disparate impact* refers to policies that look fair on their face and have no apparent discriminatory intent but are discriminatory in actual practice. In *Smith,* the policy appeared to be fine, insofar as it was designed to give the younger police officers extra boosts in their pay to the detriment of the older police officers whose pay was sufficiently high. Yet, in practice, the older officers lost a tremendous amount of money. Disparate treatment claims may be filed under Title VII and the ADEA. Disparate impact claims are covered by Title VII, but until *Smith,* the Court did not recognize this claim under the ADEA.

In a plurality order, the Supreme Court was of the opinion that while disparate impact causes of action are cognizable under the ADEA, the plaintiffs failed to demonstrate their claim. In its analysis, the Court found that even though the older officers were able to show that they were being paid considerably less than their younger colleagues, they could not point to any employment procedures that would have explained the disparities. In addition, the Court reasoned that what appeared to be the disparate impact caused by the new payment plan could have been based on reasons other than age, such as seniority and position. To this end, the Court acknowledged that because city officials were trying to raise the level of wages of the younger police officers in order to remain competitive with the surrounding cities in an attempt to not lose the officers, the payment plan was justifiable.

Smith stands out as noteworthy, because it established what public employees need to prove in order to prevail in disputes involving claims of disparate impact under the ADEA. While the actual resolution of the legal question in *Smith* was as important as its outcome, equally significant is that it may make employers accountable for their actions and policies regarding creative pay systems.

Marilyn J. Bartlett

See also Age Discrimination in Employment Act; Teacher Rights

Further Readings

Benjes, S. (2005). Comment, *Smith v. City of Jackson*: A pretext of victory for employees. *Denver University Law Review, 83,* 231–257.

Sturgeon, J. (2007). *Smith v. City of Jackson*: Setting an unreasonable standard. *Duke Law Journal, 56,* 1377–1402.

Legal Citations

Griggs v. Duke Power Co., 401 U.S. 424, 432 (1971).
Hazen Paper Co. v. Biggins, 507 U.S. 604 (1993).
Smith v. City of Jackson, Mississippi, 544 U.S. 228 (2005).
Wards Cove Packing Co. v. Antonio, 490 U.S. 642 (1989).

Smith v. Robinson

The U.S. Supreme Court's judgment in *Smith v. Robinson* (1984) stands out as noteworthy because it spurred Congress to amend the Education for All Handicapped Children Act (EAHCA), now the Individuals with Disabilities Education Act (IDEA) substantively two years later. Under the legislative change, parents who successfully litigate their claims against their school boards can recover reasonable attorney fees.

Facts of the Case

Smith was the final chapter in a lengthy dispute between parents and school officials regarding the obligations of a school board under the IDEA. After the parents prevailed in their challenge in a federal trial court in Rhode Island, they requested that their school board reimburse them for attorney fees. The parents argued that they should have been able to recover those expenditures, because they would not have had to expend them had school officials met their obligation to their child in the first place. The federal trial court granted the parents' request for attorney fees, but the First Circuit reversed in favor of the school board.

The Court's Ruling

On further review, the U.S. Supreme Court affirmed in favor of the school board. While accepting that the EAHCA had no explicit language to guide the matter, the plaintiffs urged the Court to read an implied right to recovery for parents who prevailed in challenges

against local school officials. The Court was sympathetic to the parents' plight in *Smith* but adopted a narrow reading of the statute. Simply put, because the Court could not uncover a discussion in the text or legislative history of the EAHCA dealing with the availability of attorney fees as a remedy in the face of a finding that educators denied students their rights under the EAHCA, it refused to craft one judicially. Instead, the Court reasoned that only Congress could create the fee-shifting provision that the parents sought.

Acting in response to *Smith,* two years later, Congress modified the law with the passage of the Handicapped Children's Protection Act (HCPA). The sole purpose of the HCPA was to revise the EAHCA/IDEA to add a fee-shifting provision that explicitly allows parents to recover reasonable attorney fees from local school officials if they prevail in challenges under the statute. The amendments direct courts to ensure that fees are calculated according to local costs and allow judges the discretion to reduce recovery if parents protract proceedings by unreasonably refusing to accept good-faith settlement agreements. In essence, while parents must first prevail in order to recover fees, these provisions guarantee that if they are correct, they will not have to bear the financial burden of advocating for the rights of their children.

The provisions that the HCPA added remain in the current version of the IDEA. More recently, the Court was asked to consider their scope in *Arlington Central School District Board of Education v. Murphy* (2006). At issue was whether IDEA's fee-shifting provision allowed parents to recover the costs of experts if they prevailed in challenges brought under IDEA. Just as in *Smith,* the Court refused to find an implied right to recovery in the absence of explicit language to that effect. Whether Congress will follow the lead that it set in *Smith* and again amend the IDEA to revise the fee-shifting provision remains to be seen.

Julie F. Mead

See also *Arlington Central School District Board of Education v. Murphy;* Attorney Fees; Parental Rights

Further Readings

Huefner, D. S. (2007). The final regulations for Individuals with Disabilities Education Improvement Act (IDEA '04). *Education Law Reporter, 217*(1), 1–16.

Mawdsley, R. (2007). Attorney fees for partially successful IDEA claimants. *Education Law Reporter, 217,* 769–788.

Legal Citations

Arlington Central School District Board of Education v. Murphy, 548 U.S. 291 (2006).
Individuals with Disabilities Education Act, 20 U.S.C. §§ 1400 *et seq.*
Smith v. Robinson, 468 U.S. 992 (1984).

SOCIAL SCIENCES AND THE LAW

Muller v. Oregon (1906) is widely considered the earliest instance in which the Supreme Court used social science research to support its conclusions. In upholding the constitutionality of legislation that limited the number of hours women could work, the Court drew extensively from Louis Brandeis's brief, which reviewed social science and medical research to argue that long working hours had a negative effect on women's health. The Court's use of the arguments in the Brandeis brief marked an important turning point between 19th century and 20th century legal thought.

The dominant understanding of the law during the 19th century was that the law was a set of formal, neutral, and apolitical rules to be applied deductively to the issues in particular cases. Often described as legal formalism, this view was challenged in the early 20th century by legal realists who argued that law was a social activity and, as a result, social science evidence should be used to make law in instances when existing legal rules were inadequate for resolving legal questions.

Perhaps the most famous—or for some, infamous—use of social science research in judicial decision making is footnote 11 of the Supreme Court's opinion in *Brown v. Board of Education of Topeka* (1954). To support the contention that segregation was harmful to Black students, Chief Justice Earl Warren provided references to social science studies, which he described as "modern authority."

The NAACP's strategy of using social science research to build its case against school segregation developed slowly and was influenced in part by the case of *Mendez v. Westminster* (1946). In *Mendez,* a group of Mexican American parents won their suit, which contested the segregation policies of four Southern California school districts that required their children to attend different schools than White students attended. The Ninth Circuit upheld the trial court's ruling in *Westminster v. Mendez* (1947) after the school boards appealed. *Mendez* was significant for two reasons. First, it was widely interpreted as a sign that the doctrine of segregation was becoming less socially and legally tenable. Second, it was the first case in which social science evidence was used to challenge school segregation. Two expert witnesses for the plaintiffs argued that segregation was a form of discrimination that taught Spanish-speaking Mexican American students they were inferior to their White English-speaking peers. When the school districts appealed the lower court's decision, a number of prominent civil rights organizations filed amicus briefs in support of the Mexican American students and their families, including the NAACP and the American Jewish Congress (AJC). Both the NAACP and the AJC's briefs directly challenged the constitutionality of segregation using evidence from social science research to support their legal arguments.

After the Ninth Circuit Court's decision in 1947, the NAACP started to articulate a strategy for directly challenging the constitutionality of segregation. As the NAACP lawyers developed this tactic, with the assistance of other civil rights organizations, they started to marshal an extensive body of social scientific evidence against segregation. For example, as the case of *Sweatt v. Painter* (1950) was argued in the Texas courts in 1947, Thurgood Marshall used the testimony of anthropologist Robert Redfield to make the case that segregation has "irrevocably detrimental effects," even in the case of absolute equality of conditions between the "separate" school and the majority school.

The NAACP expanded its use of social science evidence against segregation in *Brown* and its companion cases as they were argued in the lower courts. Kenneth and Mamie Clark's doll experiments are the most famous of the studies that the NAACP used to challenge segregation. However, the Clarks were two among many expert witnesses appearing on behalf of the plaintiffs; 36 social scientists and educators provided testimony in support of the NAACP's legal arguments. This testimony was incorporated into the documentation provided to the Supreme Court as they considered the cases and debated in oral arguments. In addition, Kenneth Clark and fellow psychologists

Isidor Chen and Stuart W. Cook developed a summary of the social scientific evidence against segregation. Titled "The Effects of Segregation and the Consequences of Desegregation: A Social Science Statement" and signed by 32 prominent social scientists and physicians, the document synthesized the contemporaneous social science research on the social and psychological effects of segregation and the possible impact of desegregation. This document was filed as an appendix to the NAACP's brief in *Briggs v. Elliot.* Only five social scientists offered testimony on behalf of the defendant districts.

In the decades that followed, the Supreme Court's use of social science research in *Brown* was widely criticized. Some scholars argued that the Court should have reached the conclusion that segregation was unconstitutional solely on legal grounds. Others questioned the reliability of the social science evidence cited by the Court. Nonetheless, social science research continues to be an important influence on the legal arguments in desegregation, school financing, and affirmative action cases. For example, writing for the majority in *Grutter v. Bollinger* (2003), Justice Sandra Day O'Connor reaffirmed the use of diversity in school admissions, noting that the University of Michigan Law School's claim that enrolling a diverse student body serves important educational purposes was supported by "numerous expert studies and reports."

Jeanne M. Powers

See also Affirmative Action; *Brown v. Board of Education of Topeka* and Equal Educational Opportunities; School Finance Litigation

Further Readings

Carter, R. L. (1953). The effects of segregation and the consequences of desegregation: A social science statement. *The Journal of Negro Education, 22*(1), 68–76.

Hill, H., & Greenberg, J. (1955). *Citizen's guide to desegregation: A study of social and legal change in American life.* Boston: Beacon Press.

Jackson, J. P. (2001). *Social scientists for social justice.* New York: New York University Press.

Monahan, J., & Walker, L. (1986). Social authority: Obtaining, evaluating and establishing social science in law. *University of Pennsylvania Law Review, 134*(3), 477–517.

Legal Citations

Brown v. Board of Education of Topeka I, 374 U.S. 483 (1954).
Brown v. Board of Education of Topeka II, 349 U.S. 294 (1955).
Grutter v. Bollinger, 539 U.S. 306 (2003).
Muller v. Oregon, 208 U.S. 412 (1906).
Sweatt v. Painter, 339 U.S. 629 (1950).
Westminster v. Mendez, 161 F. 774 (9th Cir. 1947).

SOUTER, DAVID H. (1939–)

When President George H. W. Bush nominated David H. Souter for a seat on the U.S. Supreme Court, Souter's views on "hot button" issues were so unknown that the media labeled him the "stealth candidate." Unlike prior nominees such as Robert Bork, Souter had not made public pronouncements or written articles advancing controversial positions. Although he had been a lower court judge for years, Souter's opinions gave few clues as to how he would rule once he was sitting on the bench.

During his tenure on the Supreme Court, Souter has often defied prediction and continued to be a crucial swing vote. In his early days, Souter sided with Chief Justice Rehnquist in over 80% of cases. However, in recent years he has more closely aligned himself with Justices Stephen Breyer and Ruth Bader Ginsburg, voting with them over 60% of the time. On education law issues, Souter's voting record has generally been moderate to liberal, especially on issues concerning separation of church and state.

Early Years

David H. Souter was born on September 17, 1939, in Melrose, Massachusetts. As a child, he frequently visited his grandparents' farm in Weare, New Hampshire, a small town near the state capital at Concord. Souter's parents moved to Weare when he was 11, and he still resides there today when the Court is not in session.

Souter's teachers commented that he was an excellent student at an early age. While many people consider Souter to be quiet and unassuming, at Concord High School his classmates voted him "most sophisticated" as well as "most likely to succeed." Souter attended Harvard University, where he again excelled in his studies. He was elected to Phi Beta Kappa and graduated magna cum laude.

After graduating from Harvard, Souter won a Rhodes scholarship to attend Magdalen College at Oxford University, where he was awarded bachelor's and master's degrees in jurisprudence. On completing his studies at Oxford, he enrolled in Harvard Law School, where he did well but did not make law review. Much of his time was devoted to tutoring undergraduate students at a freshman dormitory. Souter later related how his experience advising students, although taking time away from his studies, broadened his perspective about the relationship between law and human social problems.

Following his graduation from law school, Souter returned to Concord, where he worked for the prominent local firm he had clerked for during the summer. Apparently, Souter grew restless with private practice and sought a career in public service law. He was first employed as an assistant attorney general in the criminal division of the state attorney general's office. It was there that Souter met future Senator Warren Rudman, who was to become both a close friend and mentor. For five years, he served as Rudman's deputy attorney general. Rudman admired both Souter's character and his legal ability, and upon leaving office, he recommended that Souter be named as his replacement. As New Hampshire's attorney general, Souter opposed the legislature's attempts to legalize casino gambling, prosecuted protesters at the Seabrook nuclear power plant, and defended the state's denial of Jehovah's Witnesses' requests to cover up the state motto—"Live Free or Die"—on their license plates.

On the Bench

Souter was next appointed as a judge in a position that required him to "ride the circuit" and hear a variety of cases throughout the state. As a trial court judge, he developed a reputation for fairness but also for being tough on crime. In 1983, Governor (and future White House Chief of Staff) John Sununu appointed Souter to a seat on the New Hampshire Supreme Court. On the bench, Souter demonstrated traits of independence and scholarly analysis that would come to the forefront when he was elevated to the U.S. Supreme Court. On the bench, he continued to show support for law enforcement.

New England values of civic duty and respect for tradition have influenced Souter's judicial decision making. His sense of civic responsibility has led him to serve as trustee on the Concord Hospital Board and for the New Hampshire Historical Society. Souter's respect for tradition is manifested in his reluctance as a judge to overturn precedent based solely on doctrinal disagreement with prior decisions.

With the backing of Rudman and Sununu, President Bush appointed Souter to the First Circuit, and the Senate unanimously approved his nomination. Not long thereafter, when Justice William Brennan retired from the Supreme Court, President Bush nominated Souter as his replacement. Close press scrutiny of Souter's background revealed only that he was a bachelor with a somewhat reclusive lifestyle. Souter's testimony impressed the Senate Judiciary Committee, and he easily won confirmation.

Supreme Court Record

To the consternation of conservatives, over the years, Justice Souter has moved to the left on many issues, especially in the field of education law, where he now frequently takes liberal positions on questions of separation of church and state and of minority and student civil rights. When Justice O'Connor was on the Court, Souter often was a key fifth vote for the majority in narrowly decided cases. With her replacement by Justice Samuel Alito, Souter may now likely find himself a dissenter in three- or four-member minorities.

On Religious Schools

Adherence to stare decisis was a factor in Souter's dissent in *Agostini v. Felton* (1997), wherein the Court permitted the on-site delivery of Title I remedial services for children who attended religiously affiliated nonpublic schools. He argued that the status of the law had not changed sufficiently to justify overruling the previous rejection of similar programs in the cases of *Aguilar v. Felton* (1985) and *School District of Grand Rapids v. Ball* (1985). Dissenting in *Zelman v. Simmons-Harris* (2002), Souter wondered how the Court could uphold Cleveland's voucher program in light of *Everson v. Board of Education of Ewing Township* (1947).

In First Amendment Establishment Clause cases, Souter has been a staunch supporter of separation of church and state as he has taken a "separationist" position. Souter dissented in all cases providing government assistance to religious schools. Even so, he joined the Court in *Lamb's Chapel v. Center Moriches Union Free School District* (1993), which found that denying a church's request to show a movie about family values from a religious perspective was "viewpoint" discrimination in violation of the First Amendment. Conversely, he dissented in *Good News Club v. Milford Central School* (2001), wherein the Court ruled that denying a Christian children's organization the use of public school classrooms for weekly meetings violated freedom of speech. Moreover, Souter authored the Court's opinion in *Board of Education of Kiryas Joel Village School District v. Grumet* (1994), determining that the state of New York could not create a separate school district for a village of Hasidic Jews so that they could send their special education students to a nearby school that would have honored their religious practices.

Other Religion Issues

In the most recent Supreme Court decisions involving displays of religious symbols on public property, *McCreary County, Kentucky v. American Civil Liberties Union of Kentucky* (2005) and *Van Orden v. Perry* (2005), Souter maintained that public displays of the Ten Commandments violated the Establishment Clause. He authored the Court's judgment in *McCreary*, striking down the Kentucky display. Souter dissented in *Van Orden*, which allowed a display on the grounds of the Texas state capitol because it was merely one of numerous other historical landmarks and monuments depicted.

In Free Exercise Clause cases, Souter voted to uphold the rights of religious minorities. In his concurring opinion in *Church of the Lukumi Babalu Aye v. City of Hialeah* (1993), he thought that a local ordinance that prohibited animal sacrifice was unconstitutional, and he urged the Supreme Court to return to the more lenient *Sherbert v. Verner* (1963) test. In *City of Boerne v. Flores* (1997), he dissented with the Court's decision to overturn the Religious Freedom Restoration Act.

Student Issues

His generally supportive attitude with regard to the state on criminal matters aside, Souter opposed allowing school officials to submit student-athletes to suspicionless drug testing in *Vernonia School District 47J v. Acton* (1995) and *Board of Education of Independent School District No. 92 of Pottawatomie County v. Earls* (2002).

In the only case involving student free speech during his time on the Court, Justice Souter sided with the student. He dissented in *Morse v. Frederick* (2007), which upheld a principal's right to discipline a student for displaying a sign that read "BONG HiTS [*sic*] 4 JESUS."

Justice Souter has supported the rights of racial minorities and the use of affirmative action programs. He dissented in *Adarand Constructors v. Pena* (1995), which struck down a program awarding preference to minority-based businesses in the construction industry. In the two University of Michigan cases, *Grutter v. Bollinger* (2003) and *Gratz v. Bollinger* (2003), Souter voted to uphold race-conscious admission policies for both undergraduate and law school students. He also dissented in the more recent case of *Parents Involved in Community Schools v. Seattle School District No. 1* (2007), wherein the Court invalidated race-conscious admissions plans for public schools.

Michael Yates

See also *Agostini v. Felton; Board of Education of Independent School District No. 92 of Pottawatomie County v. Earls; Board of Education of Kiryas Joel School District v. Grumet; Everson v. Board of Education of Ewing Township; Good News Club v. Milford Central School; Gratz v. Bollinger; Grutter v. Bollinger; Lamb's Chapel v. Center Moriches Union Free School District; Morse v. Frederic; Parents Involved in Community Schools v. Seattle School District No. 1;* Rehnquist Court; Roberts Court; *Vernonia School District 47J v. Acton; Zelman v. Simmons-Harris*

Further Readings

Yarbrough, T. E. (2005). *David Hackett Souter: Traditional Republican on the Rehnquist court.* New York: Oxford University Press.

Legal Citations

Agostini v. Felton, 521 U.S. 203 (1997).

Aguilar v. Felton, 473 U.S. 402 (1985).

Board of Education of Independent School District No. 92 of Pottawatomie County v. Earls, 536 U.S. 822 (2002), on remand, 300 F.3d 1222 (10th Cir. 2002).

Board of Education of Kiryas Joel Village School District v. Grumet, 512 U.S. 687 (1994).

Church of the Lukumi Babalu Aye v. City of Hialeah, 508 U.S. 520 (1993).

City of Boerne v. Flores, 521 U.S. 507 (1997).

Everson v. Board of Education of Ewing Township, 330 U.S. 1 (1947), reh'g denied, 330 U.S. 855 (1947).

Good News Club v. Milford Central School, 533 U.S. 98 (2001).

Gratz v. Bollinger, 539 U.S. 244 (2003).

Grutter v. Bollinger, 539 U.S. 306 (2003).

Lamb's Chapel v. Center Moriches Union Free School District, 508 U.S. 384 (1993).

McCreary County, Kentucky v. American Civil Liberties Union of Kentucky, 545 U.S. 844 (2005).

Morse v. Frederick, 127 S. Ct. 2618 (2007).

Parents Involved in Community Schools v. Seattle School District No. 1, 127 S. Ct. 2738 (2007).

School District of Grand Rapids v. Ball, 473 U.S. 373 (1985).

Sherbert v. Verner, 374 U.S. 398 (1963).

Van Orden v. Perry, 545 U.S. 677 (2005).

Vernonia School District 47J v. Acton, 515 U.S. 646 (1995), on remand, 66 F.3d 217 (9th Cir. 1995).

Zelman v. Simmons-Harris, 536 U.S. 639 (2002).

SOUTHEASTERN COMMUNITY COLLEGE V. DAVIS

Just six years after the enactment of the provision, the U.S. Supreme Court was called on to interpret the nondiscrimination guarantee provision of Section 504 of the Rehabilitation Act of 1973 in *Southeastern Community College v. Davis* (1979). Section 504 prohibits recipients of federal financial assistance from discriminating on the basis of disability in any of their programs. According to the act,

> No otherwise qualified handicapped individual . . . shall, solely by reason of his handicap, be excluded from the participation in, be denied the benefits of, or be subjected to discrimination under any program or activity receiving Federal financial assistance. (29 U.S.C. § 794(a))

The Court found that insofar as Southeastern Community College in North Carolina was operated by the state and accepted federal monies, it was bound by the requirements of Section 504 and its regulations.

Facts of the Case

The dispute arose when Francis B. Davis sought to enroll in the nursing program offered by Southeastern Community College. When school officials determined Davis had a severe hearing loss, they denied her request for admission. Officials reasoned that Davis's hearing loss made it impossible for her to complete the clinical portion of the program in a manner that was safe for patients. Moreover, insofar as Davis was unable to satisfy this requirement, officials were convinced that she could not reasonably have been adequately prepared to function in a professional nursing capacity. College officials considered modifications that might have allowed her to participate, but decided that making those accommodations would have altered the program to the extent that it would no longer have been beneficial to Davis.

Davis sued the college, alleging that officials only needed to have made reasonable accommodations for her hearing loss in order to avoid discriminating against her under Section 504. A federal trial court entered a judgment in favor of the college, but the Fourth Circuit reversed in favor of Davis.

The Court's Ruling

On further review, Justice Powell wrote the opinion for a unanimous Supreme Court that reversed in favor of the college. At issue was whether Davis was "otherwise qualified" for admission to the nursing program and if so, what "reasonable accommodations" the college was required to make in order to treat her in a manner comparable to that of her peers who were not disabled. After examining both the statute and its regulations, the Court, in an initial matter, ruled that "an otherwise qualified person is one who is able to meet all of a program's requirements in spite of his handicap" (p. 406)

The Supreme Court then turned to whether Davis could meet the requirements of the program with reasonable accommodations. The Court noted that the physical requirements of the course of study were adopted without any animus toward Davis or persons with disabilities generally. Rather, the Court pointed out that completion of the program required candidates to have the ability to understand and quickly react to spoken language when a speaker's face was unavailable for speech reading. While Davis was able to complete some tasks associated with nursing, the record reflected that she could not accomplish the goals of the college's program without substantial modifications. The Court was of the opinion that the accommodations contemplated by the regulations of Section 504 did not require officials to modify the program substantially. Accordingly, the Court concluded that because officials did not discriminate against Davis, they were under no obligations to make the modifications that she requested.

The precedent set by *Southeastern Community College v. Davis,* in particular its interpretation of "reasonable accommodations" as stopping short of "undue financial or administrative burdens" or modifications that would substantially alter the nature of programs, continues to guide interpretation of Section 504 today both in higher education and in K–12 schools.

Julie F. Mead

See also Rehabilitation Act of 1973, Section 504; *School Board of Nassau County v. Arline*

Further Readings

Clark, S. G. (2007). Making eligibility determinations under Section 504. *Education Law Reporter, 214,* 451–455.

Stone, K. L. (2007). The politics of deference and inclusion: Toward a uniform framework for the analysis of "fundamental alteration" under the ADA. *Hastings Law Journal, 58,* 1241–1295.

Legal Citations

Rehabilitation Act of 1973, Section 504, 29 U.S.C. § 794(a).

Southeastern Community College v. Davis, 442 U.S. 397 (1979).

SPENCER V. KUGLER

Spencer v. Kugler (1972), a relatively minor case that the Supreme Court did not address on its merits, involved a challenge to New Jersey's practice of aligning school district lines with municipal boundaries. The plaintiffs claimed that the practice led to schools with disproportionate numbers of Black students and was therefore a violation of the Equal Protection Clause of the Fourteenth Amendment and the Civil Rights Act of 1964.

In the initial round of litigation, the federal trial court in New Jersey refused to grant the relief sought by the plaintiff parents. The U.S. Supreme Court, with Justice Douglas dissenting, summarily affirmed the opinion of the three-judge panel, refusing to find that there was segregation of Black students from White students in the schools. The plaintiffs contended that the racial patterns in the schools adversely affected the quality of education afforded to the Black students. With no assurance that population factors would remain static, the plaintiffs' proposed relief would require the board to make racial reassignments on a term-to-term basis. The trial court was of the opinion that the patterns that the plaintiff parents objected to did not constitute a constitutional violation.

As part of its analysis, the trial court pointed out that New Jersey's constitution provided for a thorough and efficient system of public schools under which each municipality was a separate school system. Thus, according to the court, school district boundaries coincide with municipal boundaries. The court clearly noted that racially balanced municipalities were beyond the ken of both the legislatures and the courts.

Acknowledging that in *Brown v. Board of Education of Topeka* (1954) the Supreme Court required unitary school systems, absent any attempt by school officials in New Jersey to draw lines on racially discriminatory grounds, the trial court could not hold that basing district boundaries on municipal boundaries was unreasonable. Therefore, the court decided that the plaintiffs failed to present a cause of action for relief.

In its rationale, the court spent considerable time analyzing the requirements of *Swann v.*

Charlotte-Mecklenburg Board of Education (1971), a dispute that dealt with systems that had histories of creating dual school systems and then instituting freedom of choice plans that did little or nothing to achieve unitary status. In *Spencer,* the plaintiffs unsuccessfully alleged that de facto segregation was a violation of their constitutional rights. The court rejected the plaintiffs' claim that the de facto segregation that took place, even though there was no state action, was tantamount to de jure segregation.

The historical significance of *Spencer* is the fact that it hinged on de facto segregation. The net result of Spencer and similar litigation that remains in effect is that courts cannot devise plans to deal with de facto segregation.

J. Patrick Mahon

See also *Brown v. Board of Education of Topeka* and Equal Educational Opportunities; Civil Rights Movement; Fourteenth Amendment; *Swann v. Charlotte-Mecklenburg Board of Education*

Legal Citations

Brown v. Board of Education of Topeka I, 347 U.S. 483 (1954).
Brown v. Board of Education of Topeka II, 349 U.S. 294 (1955).
Spencer v. Kugler, 326 F. Supp. 1235 (D.N.J. 1971), *aff'd,* 423 U.S. 1027 (1972).
Swann v. Charlotte-Mecklenburg Board of Education, 402 U.S. 1 (1971).

Sports Programming and Scheduling

The scheduling of sports practice and competitions, whether at the pre-K–12 or postsecondary level, is largely the purview of controlling athletic organizations. Each state has a statewide association, in which membership is voluntary, that sets the policies and procedures for all extracurricular sports activity in pre-K–12 schools. For example, in Illinois, it is the Illinois High School Association (IHSA). These associations have counterparts at the collegiate level with the most well-known association being the National Collegiate Athletic Association (NCAA), which regulates everything from tournament entries to eligibility requirements for its member institutions.

For the most part, the courts have refused to become involved in evaluating whether specific policies promulgated by these voluntary athletic associations constitute state action or whether they are legally defensible. The most recent Supreme Court case on this issue is *Tennessee Secondary School Athletic Association v. Brentwood Academy* (TSSAA, 2007). Brentwood Academy ran afoul of the TSSAA's rules when one of its football coaches sent a letter to a student that invited him to football practice. The student was enrolled at Brentwood Academy, but he had not been in attendance for three days, and the TSSAA required that students attend a school for three days before a coach could invite them to practice. As a punishment, the school was excluded from football and basketball playoffs for two years. The school sued. In reviewing lower court rulings that found the TSSAA to be a "state actor," thereby granting Brentwood First Amendment protections, the Court held that the TSSAA's recruiting rule struck "nowhere near the heart of the First Amendment" (p. 2493). The Court maintained that although direct solicitation was not allowed, the school was still free to send brochures, post notices, and otherwise advertise their athletic programs. While joining the TSSAA could not necessitate that member schools give up their constitutional rights, the Court concluded that the recruiting rule was necessary to efficiently administer the state interscholastic athletic league.

There also exists federal statutory control of educational sports programming and scheduling through Title IX of the Education Amendments of 1972, according to which,

> No person in the United States shall, on the basis of sex, be excluded from participation in, be denied the benefits of, or be subjected to discrimination under any education program or activity receiving Federal financial assistance.

Title IX forbids gender discrimination in educational programs that receive federal funding.

Prior to the amendment of Title IX by the Civil Rights Restoration Act in 1987, the interpretation of the scope of Title IX was control by the U.S. Supreme Court case of *Grove City College v. Bell* (1984), which stated that the application of Title IX was program specific and did not provide blanket coverage to the institution as a whole. In order to rectify this interpretation, Congress amended Title IX to add the wording,

> For the purpose of this chapter, the term "program or activity" and "program" mean all the operations of . . . a local education agency, system of vocational education, or other school system . . . any part of which is extended Federal financial assistance.

With this amendment, it became clear that Title IX covers all actions of entire institutions.

The most recent case dealing with the issue of sports scheduling and Title IX is a case out of the Sixth Circuit, *Communities for Equity v. Michigan High School Athletic Association* (2006), in which concerned parents organized under the name Communities for Equity brought suit against the Michigan High School Athletic Association (MHSAA), alleging that its method of scheduling sports seasons discriminated against female athletes. The MHSAA scheduled the girls to play at disadvantageous, nontraditional seasons, thereby making it impossible for them to participate in the majority of tournament play. A federal trial court, entering a judgment in favor of the parents, was of the opinion that the MHSAA's actions did violate the Equal Protection Clause of the Fourteenth Amendment, the Civil Rights Act of 1964, and Michigan law. On further review, the Sixth Circuit affirmed that its disparate treatment in the scheduling of girls' sports at disadvantageous times was a violation of Title IX. Consequently, the court ordered the MHSAA to submit to it a compliance plan in which it demonstrated that it provided equal treatment to the scheduling of boys' and girls' sports.

Elizabeth T. Lugg

See also Equal Protection Analysis; High School Athletic Associations; Title IX and Athletics

Legal Citations

Communities for Equity v. Michigan High School Athletic Association, 459 F.3d 676 (6th Cir. 2006).
Grove City College v. Bell, 465 U.S. 555 (1984).
Horner v. Kentucky High School Athletic Association, 43 F.3d 265 (6th Cir. 1994).
Tennessee Secondary School Athletic Association v. Brentwood Academy, 127 S. Ct. 2489 (2007).
Title IX of the Education Amendments of 1972, 20 U.S.C. § 1681.

SPRINGFIELD TOWNSHIP, FRANKLIN COUNTY V. QUICK

Springfield Township, Franklin County v. Quick (1859) was the earliest U.S. Supreme Court case directly involving an educational issue. *Quick* arose in the context of a dispute related to the fact that provisions in the Northwest Ordinances set aside the 16th section of each township for school purposes for the benefit of township residents.

What the Supreme Court declared in *Quick* is that states do have the right to decide how to fund education within their own borders as long as they are not in violation of any federal laws to the contrary. Even though *Quick* was resolved in 1859, its legacy continues to today as witnessed by ongoing disputes over school funding. While the federal government involves itself in assuring equal opportunities for all students, it is still the duty of the states to determine how to divide the costs of education for the general population of their students.

Facts of the Case

At issue in *Quick* was a township's having sold its 16th section in 1836. Officials in the township took the sum of $7,423.36 that they received for the property, invested the money, and applied the interest to support the schools. Part of the argument in the litigation was whether the township was entitled to this money as well as to additional resources from a fund that accrued under the laws of the state of Indiana.

When Indiana adopted a new constitution in 1851, its eighth article established a school fund, derived from several sources, that was to be consolidated into a single fund. The first of these sources was the congressional township fund and any land still belonging to it. Ten other sources of funds were listed from which revenue was derived, and all of them were united into a common fund. The common fund was to be distributed among the counties according to the number of students that they had, with each county receiving an equal amount for each student, regardless of what officials provided for the students from their respective congressional townships funds. However, there was another section within article eight that specified that all of the trust funds that the state had were to be applied exclusively to the purposes for which each fund was created. In light of this provision, a suit in 1854 tested the validity of the new constitution.

The Supreme Court of Indiana ruled that selected funding provisions in the new constitution were null and void. Subsequently, when, in 1855 the Indiana legislature passed yet another new law providing for the distribution of the common fund, it inserted a provision that would not allow any township's congressional township fund to be diminished because of the distribution or to be diverted to any other township.

Officials in Springfield township filed suit, claiming that the township was entitled to both the interest from its own congressional township fund and to its distributive share of the common fund. The Supreme Court of Indiana decided against the Springfield township claim, because, according to the new law about the distribution, when a county disbursed funds to townships, officials were required to distribute the amounts given to each township equally, based on the number of students who resided there. At the same time, officials were supposed to take into consideration the amount of money that townships derived from their congressional funds, although county treasurers could not diminish the congressional funds or divert them to any other townships. The result was that in systems where the congressional fund was insufficient to cover expenditures for all students, the state would allocate funds to townships on the basis of need.

The Court's Ruling

On further review, a unanimous U.S. Supreme Court affirmed that the law was constitutional. While commenting that the state was obviously trying to get around the results of the former case, the Court held that legislators did nothing in violation of the allowable use of the congressional funds when they wrote the new law, because the funding of the schools within the state did come under the auspices of the state. To this end, the court acknowledged that Indiana law still allowed each township whatever money it was due from the congressional fund, but that townships were not entitled to an equal distribution of the common fund as well. The Court was thus of the opinion that legislators in Indiana were within their rights to decide how to distribute the common fund.

It is interesting to note that in *Quick,* the issue was one in which the state legislature was trying to be equitable to all residents by providing an amount from the common fund that would equalize how much money each school system got based on the number of students living within the system's boundaries. Officials in Springfield Township believed that they were due an equal share of the common fund as well as their own congressional fund. Similar issues of equity continue into the present day.

James P. Wilson

See also Federalism and the Tenth Amendment; School Finance Litigation

Legal Citations

Springfield Township, Franklin County v. Quick, 63 U.S. 56 (1859).

St. Martin Evangelical Lutheran Church v. South Dakota

St. Martin Evangelical Lutheran Church v. South Dakota, which reached the U.S. Supreme Court in 1981, helped to clarify both state and federal laws pertaining to the payment of unemployment compensation taxes by private, church-owned, church-managed schools. In sum, the Supreme Court did not have to address issues related to separation of church and state in *St. Martin*. Instead, the Court resolved the dispute on the interpretation of the intent of the original legislators and the wording of the Federal Unemployment Tax Act's (FUTA's) amendments. The end result of *St. Martin* is that the Court concluded that religious schools were still exempted from having to pay unemployment taxes under FUTA.

Facts of the Case

The facts revealed that St. Martin Lutheran Church operated a Christian elementary school that was not a separate legal entity from the church. The church not only financed the school but controlled it via a school board that was elected from within the congregation. When officials in South Dakota tried to impose an unemployment tax on the church for school employees, a referee in the Department of Labor rejected the church's challenge. After a state trial court reversed in favor of the church, state officials appealed.

The Supreme Court of South Dakota reversed in favor of the state in pointing out that FUTA included religious schools under its provisions and that its doing so did not violate either the Establishment Clause or the Free Exercise Clause of the First Amendment to the U.S. Constitution. On further review, the U.S. Supreme Court, in turn, unanimously reversed in favor of the church.

The Court's Ruling

At the outset of its opinion, the Supreme Court included an explanation of the development of the relevant laws. To this end, the Court pointed out that the federal laws for unemployment compensation taxes require that states include similar statutes to cover state-run unemployment plans even though, should they wish to do so, states may provide more benefits than the federal laws allow. In fact, the Court recognized that all 50 states have enacted statutes that are complementary to the federal laws pertaining to unemployment taxes.

At the same time, the Supreme Court noted that Congress amended FUTA in 1976 to narrow the definition of specified employers that were exempt from paying unemployment tax, such as church-related colleges and other schools. The Court observed that historically FUTA, which appeared originally as Title IX of

the Social Security Act of 1935 and called for a cooperative federal-state program to provide benefits to unemployed workers, had been fairly narrowly defined. Yet, through the ensuing years, the Court indicated that numerous amendments to FUTA provided coverage for more and more unemployed workers. The Court wrote that from 1960 to 1970, FUTA excluded all employees who worked for religious, charitable, educational, or any other businesses that are exempt from income tax under section 501(a) of the law. However, the Court conceded that a 1970 amendment narrowed the definition to include only those who were employed by religious organizations. The Court declared that a 1976 amendment further restricted those who were exempt from the unemployment tax to individuals whose duties were more directly related to church activities.

In *St. Martin,* the Supreme Court found that the definition of a church was not the building in which its activities took place but consisted of any church-run and church-supported activities. More specifically, the Court defined a church as "an organization which is operated primarily for religious purposes and which is operated, supervised, controlled, or principally supported by a church or convention or association of churches" (26 U.S.C. 3309(b), p. 774). The Supreme Court thus ruled that schools that are religious in nature and are owned or controlled by specific churches or association of churches could be considered Category I schools that are not covered by FUTA.

The Supreme Court added that schools that are controlled or operated by churches or association of churches, even if they were incorporated separately from the churches, fit into Category II, which is also exempt from FUTA. Another group of schools, Category III schools, are religiously affiliated but controlled by lay boards. These schools gained exemptions from FUTA in the later case of *Grace Brethren Church v. State of California* (1982), in which the Court maintained that these schools are exempt from unemployment taxes because such coverage would violate the First Amendment of the Constitution, not Section 3309(b)(1) of FUTA.

James P. Wilson

See also Nonpublic Schools

Legal Citations

Grace Brethren Church v. California, 457 U.S. 393 (1982).

St. Martin Evangelical Lutheran Church v. South Dakota, 451 U.S. 772 (1981).

STAFFORD ACT

The Robert T. Stafford Disaster Relief and Emergency Assistance Act of 1988 provides a means by which the federal government can assist local and state agencies, including public schools, when major disasters or emergencies threaten to overwhelm them. The Stafford Act authorizes the president of the United States to declare "a major disaster" or "an emergency," whichever is more appropriate in a given situation. In either case, the presidential declaration authorizes a wide range of federal services and resources to supplement limited local and state resources. In all instances, federal assistance is intended to augment state and local attempts to resolve the crisis, and federal funds may not be committed until the state and local agencies document maximum effort.

Last reauthorized in 2000, the Stafford Act includes procedures for requesting and obtaining a presidential declaration, defines the type and scope of federal assistance available in each case, and clarifies the conditions necessary to receive the aid. The Federal Emergency Management Agency, commonly referred to as FEMA, is responsible for coordinating federal support efforts under the Stafford Act through three major categories: individual and household, public, and hazard mitigation assistance. Within these categories, the federal government can provide direct grants for living expenses and funds for temporary housing, repair of public buildings, emergency communications systems, and other purposes.

Unless the major disaster or emergency occurs exclusively or predominately in the federal purview, the governor of an affected state must request assistance and a declaration by the president. Pertinent provisions regarding the two types of declarations are set forth in Section 401 of the Stafford Act, 42 U.S.C. § 5170, with respect to major disasters, and in Section 501, 42 U.S.C. § 5191, with respect to emergencies. The president may respond to a governor's request with a declaration of a major disaster, a declaration of an emergency, or a denial of the request altogether.

Major disasters are defined in the Stafford Act as

> any natural catastrophe including any hurricane, tornado, storm, high water, tidal wave, tsunami, earthquake, volcanic eruption, landslide, mudslide, snowstorm, or drought which in the determination of the President causes damage of sufficient severity to warrant major disaster assistance under the Act.

Accordingly, § 5170 of the act specifies that gubernatorial requests for major disaster declarations must prove that the disaster is of such magnitude that the state and local government cannot cope with the situation and that federal assistance is required. The state must execute its emergency plan, and state and local expenditures must comply with federal cost-sharing requirements before the federal government may intervene. Finally, the governor's request must demonstrate that federal assistance is necessary to supplement the resources and efforts of the state, local government, disaster relief organizations such as the American Red Cross and the Salvation Army, and compensation by private insurance companies for property loss. Only then may the president declare a major disaster under the Stafford Act.

When an incident that does not rise to the level of a major disaster occurs or threatens to occur, the governor of a state can request that the president declare an emergency. "Emergency" is defined in the Stafford Act as "any occasion or instance for which federal assistance is needed to supplement State and local efforts and capabilities to save lives and to protect property and public health and safety, or to avert the threat of a catastrophe." On occasion, the president may declare an emergency that is related to public schools and the educational process. Riots on college and university campuses and public school violence, such as the shootings at Columbine High School in 1999 or at Virginia Tech in 2007, are examples of emergencies that might trigger a presidential declaration. Governors requesting that a state of emergency be declared must show that an emergency actually exists, that state and local governments do not have the personnel or resources to resolve the problem, and that federal help is imperative.

Assuming that the president declares an emergency related to an incident or incidents at a public school or a college or university, the following federal relief services are provided to assist state and local agencies in resolving the emergency:

- personnel, equipment, supplies, facilities, and technical services to save lives, protect property and public health, and stabilize the situation;
- coordination of all emergency relief assistance;
- dissemination of health and safety information;
- provisions for campus security;
- investigation of the crime scene(s), if applicable;
- provision for temporary facilities to replace damaged school buildings;
- provision for continuation of essential community services;
- warning of further risks and hazards;
- repairs or restoration of state-owned facilities;
- crisis-counseling assistance and training; and
- legal services for injured parties and public school officials.

Through these and other strategies and services specified in the Stafford Act, the federal government has assisted state and local governments in reducing violence and increasing safety in American public schools.

Robert C. Cloud

See also School Board Policy; School Boards

Further Readings

Bazan, E. B. (2005, September 16). *Robert T. Stafford Disaster Relief and Emergency Assistance Act: Legal requirements for federal and state roles in declarations of an emergency or a major disaster* [report for Congress]. Washington, DC: Congressional Research Service.

Legal Citations

Disaster Mitigation Act of 2000, 42 U.S.C. §§ 5133 *et seq.*
Disaster Relief Act of 1974, 42 U.S.C. §§ 5121 *et seq.*
Stafford Disaster Relief and Emergency Assistance Act, 42 U.S.C. §§ 5121 *et seq.*

STARE DECISIS

Stare decisis represents the principle of doctrinal precedent underpinning American common law. (The term *stare decisis* is Latin for "to stand by things decided.") The doctrine of stare decisis encourages courts to resolve like cases alike, meaning that judges should follow earlier rulings when confronting issues that have been before them in prior litigation. Stare decisis is a basic principle of judicial interpretation of statutory law, common law, and constitutional law. Insofar as this doctrine is a fundamental aspect of judicial decision making, it strongly influences court actions in resolving any matters concerning education law or any other field of law.

In many instances, the U.S. Supreme Court has reviewed the multiple policy reasons for following stare decisis. The Court has repeatedly and consistently indicated that stare decisis is a fundamental aspect underlying the rule of law. This is because stare decisis, by placing the duty on the courts to follow prior precedent and decide like cases in a like manner, "promotes the evenhanded, predicable, and consistent development of legal principles," and accordingly adherence to this principle by courts "fosters reliance on judicial decisions, and contributes to the actual and perceived integrity of the judicial process" (*State Oil Co. v. Khan,* 1997, p. 20).

Insofar as the policy in favor of such reasons is so strong, the Court has explained that adhering to precedent is usually a wise policy, because in most matters it is more important that the applicable rule of law "be settled" than that "it be settled right" (*Agostini v. Felton,* 1997, p. 235, citing *Burnet v. Coronado Oil & Gas Co.,* 285 U.S. 393, 1932). Accordingly, the Court has maintained that it is willing to depart from stare decisis only where there is a compelling justification for doing so.

While stare decisis weighs heavy in judicial interpretation, it "is not an inexorable command because it 'is a principle of policy and not a mechanical formula of adherence to the latest decision'" (*Payne v. Tennessee,* 1991, p. 828, citing *Helvering v. Hallock,* 1940, p. 119). As such, where a prior decision has proven to be unworkable or badly reasoned, especially if it was reached by a narrow margin or with spirited dissent, the Supreme Court has not been constrained to uphold such judgments.

The Supreme Court has reasoned that the judicial interest in stare decisis is at its height in matters concerning property, contracts, and statutory interpretation. In the context of property and contracts, both of which can impact education law, the Court has determined that adherence to stare decisis is of heightened importance, because private reliance interests are highly involved in these areas. Stare decisis is significant in statutory interpretation for similar reasons. The legislature is thought to rely on consistent interpretation of the statutes it has enacted in taking, or refraining from taking, future action with respect to such statutes. For example, in *Hilton v. South Carolina Public Railway Commission* (1991), wherein Congress declined to alter a federal statute for three decades after the Court ruled on an interpretation of the law, the justices factored this implied reliance in its judgment not to tread on its previous interpretation.

At the same time, the Supreme Court observed that while it is always an important judicial interest, stare decisis is of its lowest importance in the area of constitutional interpretation. This is largely because such canon is more uniquely the domain of the courts, and because of the difficulty of passing a constitutional amendment, which might be the only possible legislative recourse (*Payne,* 1991, p. 828).

The Supreme Court's unwillingness to be bound by stare decisis is reflected perhaps no more clearly than in its striking down de jure segregation in public schools in *Brown v. Board of Education of Topeka* (1954). In *Brown,* the Court considered whether the provision of a public school education to children under racially segregated conditions violated the Equal Protection Clause of the Fourteenth Amendment to the U.S. Constitution. Regarding a similar question as applied to public transportation in *Plessy v. Ferguson* (1896), the Court had held that racial segregation did not run afoul of the Fourteenth Amendment so long as such services were "equal." In *Brown,* the Court examined the then-current state of public education and determined that inherent in the concept of racially segregated provision of public school education was an inequality that could not be remedied. The Court thus rejected its opinion in *Plessy. Brown* demonstrates the Court's willingness to confront and overturn its own precedent to correct fundamental flaws in previous decisions, particularly in the sphere of constitutional interpretation.

Alli Fetter-Harrott

See also Common Law; Rule of Law

Legal Citations

Agostini v. Felton, 521 U.S. 203 (1997).
Brown v. Board of Education of Topeka I, 347 U.S. 483 (1954).
Brown v. Board of Education of Topeka II, 349 U.S. 294 (1955).
Burnet v. Coronado Oil & Gas Co., 285 U.S. 393 (1932).
Helvering v. Hallock, 309 U.S. 106 (1940).
Hilton v. South Carolina Public Railway Commission, 502 U.S. 197 (1991).
Payne v. Tennessee, 501 U.S. 808 (1991).
Plessy v. Ferguson, 163 U.S. 537 (1896).
State Oil Co. v. Khan, 522 U.S. 3 (1997).

STATE AID AND THE ESTABLISHMENT CLAUSE

Over the past 60 years, the 16 words in the Establishment and Free Exercise clauses of the First Amendment rank among the most litigated language in the entire U.S. Constitution. Enacted as part of the Bill of Rights in 1791, the First Amendment declares that "Congress shall make no law respecting an establishment of religion, or prohibiting the free exercise thereof."

At the outset, it is worth noting that the goal of this entry is to provide an overview of Supreme Court litigation under the Establishment Clause in disputes involving state aid to K–12 religiously affiliated nonpublic schools and their students. For this purpose, it is unnecessary to engage in a full discussion of the different approaches to the Establishment Clause by undertaking what could be a lengthy examination of the attitudes of the jurists whose opinions have shaped the Court's First Amendment jurisprudence.

Instead, it is sufficient to note that the Court's judgments have largely been influenced by which of the two camps that have emerged in the majority on the bench at given points in time. The two perspectives that have tended to hold sway among the Court's members are those of the accommodationists and separationists. In the context of state aid, accommodationists believe that the Establishment Clause does not forbid the federal or state governments from providing some forms of assistance, under the legal construct known as the child benefit test, to children who attend religiously affiliated nonpublic schools. Conversely, separationists support the Jeffersonian metaphor that calls for preserving a "wall of separation" between church and state, language that is not in the Constitution; this is the perspective most often associated with the Supreme Court for the better part of the past half century.

Preliminary Cases

The U.S. Supreme Court extended the First Amendment so that it applied not only to Congress but also to the states in *Cantwell v. Connecticut* (1940). *Cantwell* was a dispute over solicitation of money for religious purposes that the justices resolved seven years before deciding the Court's first case on the merits of a claim involving education, the Establishment Clause, and state aid to religiously affiliated schools and their students in *Everson v. Board of Education of Ewing Township* (1947).

In the years prior to *Everson* and the development of its modern Establishment Clause jurisprudence, the Supreme Court examined two cases involving religiously affiliated nonpublic schools. In both instances, the Court relied on the Due Process Clause of the Fourteenth Amendment rather than the Establishment Clause.

In *Pierce v. Society of Sisters of the Holy Names of Jesus and Mary* (1925), the Supreme Court invalidated a statute from Oregon that would have essentially forced all nonpublic schools, religious and nonsectarian, to close. According to the law, parents could satisfy the state's compulsory attendance law for children, other than those who would today be classified as having disabilities, only by sending them to public schools. Even in striking down the law, the Court acknowledged that states could impose health, safety, and teacher qualification requirements on the schools as long as those requirements were no more rigorous than the requirements applied to public schools.

Cochran v. Louisiana State Board of Education (1930) dealt with a statute that made textbooks available for all students, regardless of where they attended school. A taxpayer unsuccessfully challenged the law as a private taking through taxation for a nonpublic

purpose. In unanimously affirming the judgment of the Supreme Court of Louisiana, the Court remarked that because students, rather than their schools, were the beneficiaries of the law, the statute served a valid secular purpose. This opinion set the stage for the child benefit test that would emerge in *Everson*. While the Court has consistently upheld similar textbook provisions, state courts have vitiated them under their own, more restrictive, constitutions.

Overview of Cases

The Supreme Court's modern Establishment Clause jurisprudence with regard to state aid in K–12 education evolved through three phases. During the first period, which began in 1947 with *Everson* and ended in 1968 with *Board of Education v. Allen*, the Court crafted the child benefit test, which permits state aid on the ground that it helps children rather than their religiously affiliated nonpublic schools. However, during this first stage, the Court helped to sow the seeds of later confusion in creating a two-part test in *Abington Township School District v. Schempp* and *Murray v. Curlett* (1963) to review the constitutionality of prayer and Bible reading in public schools. The Court later expanded this two-part test into the tripartite Establishment Clause standard in *Lemon v. Kurtzman* (1971), a dispute over state aid to religiously affiliated nonpublic schools in the form of salary supplements for teachers.

During the second stage, which started with *Lemon* in 1971 and culminated with *Aguilar v. Felton* in 1985, the Court largely refused to move beyond the limits it created under the child benefit test in *Everson* and *Allen*. When the Supreme Court applied the *Lemon* test in virtually all cases involving aid and prayer or other religious activity, its failure to explain how, or why, the justices applied this tripartite measure so widely created confusion. This situation was exacerbated because the Court developed the first two parts of the *Lemon* test in the context of cases involving prayer and Bible reading, not aid.

When dealing with aid, most programs passed *Lemon*'s first two prongs only to fail the amorphous excessive entanglement prong. Given the confusion that the *Lemon* test created, in *Agostini v. Felton* (1997), the Court modified it by reviewing only its first two parts—purpose and effect—while recasting entanglement as one element in evaluating a statute's effect.

The third, and most recent, phase with regard to aid to K–12 schools and their students began in 1993 with *Zobrest v. Catalina Foothills School District* (1993) and continues to the present day. During this time, the Court has reinvigorated the child benefit test by making it easier for governmental officials to use public funds to assist students who attend religiously affiliated nonpublic schools.

Against this backdrop, the remainder of this essay reviews the topics and cases involving state aid to religiously affiliated nonpublic schools. The essay examines the litigation primarily under the categories in which it can be placed rather than simply chronologically.

Different Forms of Aid

Transportation

Everson is the first Supreme Court case on the merits of the Establishment Clause and education. At issue in *Everson* was a statute from New Jersey that permitted local school boards to reimburse parents for the cost of transporting their children to religiously affiliated nonpublic schools. The Court affirmed the statute's constitutionality on the ground that the First Amendment did not prohibit states from extending general benefits to all residents without regard to their religious beliefs. In so doing, the Court placed student transportation in the same category as other public services such as police and fire protection.

In addition, *Everson* is noteworthy as the first case in which the Court applied the Jeffersonian metaphor into the lexicon of its First Amendment jurisprudence, writing that "the First Amendment has erected a wall between church and state. That wall must be kept high and impregnable" (p. 18). Following *Everson*, some states provide publicly funded transportation to students who attend religiously affiliated nonpublic schools while others refuse to do so under their constitutions.

The only other Supreme Court case involving transportation and religiously affiliated nonpublic schools was *Wolman v. Walter* (1977). In *Wolman*, the justices struck down that part of a statute from Ohio

that allowed public funds to be used to take students from religious schools on field trips. The Court held that the statute was unconstitutional, because the field trips were curricular-related insofar as they were instructional rather than nonideological secular services such as transportation to and from school.

Textbooks

Following the lead of *Cochran*, albeit on the basis of the First Amendment, rather than the Fourteenth, in *Board of Education v. Allen* (1969), the Supreme Court upheld a law from New York that required local school boards to loan books to children in grades 7 through 12 who attended nonpublic schools. Relying largely on the child benefit test, the Court observed that the law's purpose was not to aid religion or the religious schools, while its primary effect was to improve the quality of education for all students.

Allen represented the outer reach of the child benefit test prior to *Agostini v. Felton* (1997), discussed below. The Court upheld similar textbook provisions in *Meek v. Pittenger* (1975) and *Wolman v. Walter* (1977), both of which are discussed below.

Secular Services and Salary Supplements

In 1971, in its most significant case involving the Establishment Clause and education, *Lemon v. Kurtzman,* and in its companion case, *Earley v. DiCenso,* the Court struck down a statute that essentially provided salary supplements for teachers in religiously affiliated nonpublic schools. In so doing, the Court created the so-called *Lemon* test by adding a third test, on excessive entanglement, from *Walz v. Tax Commission of New York City* (1970) to the two-part test it created in *Abington Township School District v. Schempp*. In *Walz*, the Court upheld New York State's practice of providing state property tax exemptions for church property that is used in worship services. According to the *Lemon* test,

Every analysis in this area must begin with consideration of the cumulative criteria developed by the Court over many years. Three such tests may be gleaned from our cases. First, the statute must have a secular legislative purpose; second, its principal or primary effect must be one that neither advances nor inhibits religion; finally, the statute must not foster "an excessive government entanglement with religion." (*Lemon*, pp. 612–613, internal citations omitted)

In reviewing entanglement and aid, the Court explained that it had to take three additional factors into consideration: "we must examine the character and purposes of the institutions that are benefited, the nature of the aid that the State provides, and the resulting relationship between the government and religious authority" (*Lemon*, p. 615). As noted, the upshot is that until 1997 and *Agostini v. Felton*, discussed below, the Court struck down almost all forms of aid unless it was in the form of textbooks for students who attended religiously affiliated nonpublic schools.

Tuition Reimbursements to Parents

Two months after *Lemon*, the Pennsylvania legislature enacted a statute that granted parents whose children attended nonpublic schools the option of requesting tuition reimbursement. In *Sloan v. Lemon* (1973), the Supreme Court affirmed that the law impermissibly singled out a class of citizens for a special economic benefit. In distinguishing reimbursements from transportation and books, the Court indicated that since the former was unlike the latter, which were purely secular, the plan was unacceptable.

The Supreme Court expanded on *Sloan* in another case from New York, *Committee for Public Education and Religious Liberty v. Nyquist* (1973). In addressing the first of three issues in *Nyquist*, the Court decreed that even though the tuition grants in dispute went to parents rather than to school officials, they were unconstitutional since the parents would have used the money to pay for tuition with funds that could have been diverted for impermissible religious purposes.

Tax Benefits

On the second issue in *Nyquist*, the Supreme Court struck down a provision in the statute that granted parents of children who attended nonpublic schools income tax deductions as long as they did not receive tuition grants under the other part of the law. The

Court invalidated this provision because it was convinced that it had the effect of advancing religion since there was essentially no difference between a tax benefit and a tuition grant.

Ten years later, in *Mueller v. Allen* (1983), in an exception from its willingness to expand the parameters of the child benefit test, the Supreme Court upheld a statute from Minnesota that granted all parents state income tax deductions for the actual costs of tuition, textbooks, and transportation associated with sending their children to elementary or secondary schools. The Court distinguished *Mueller* from *Nyquist* primarily on the grounds that the tax benefit here was available to all parents, not only those whose children were in nonpublic schools, and that the deduction was one of many rather than a single, favored type of taxpayer expenditure. The Court concluded that the law passed all three parts of the *Lemon* test.

Reimbursements to Nonpublic Schools

In the third issue in *Nyquist* (1973), the Supreme Court struck down the statute's maintenance and repair provision for nonpublic schools since there were inadequate safeguards on how money could be spent. The Court wrote that since the government cannot erect buildings for religious activities, it cannot pay to have them renovated.

On the same day as it handed down *Nyquist*, in another case from New York, the Supreme Court applied essentially the same rationale in *Levitt v. Committee for Public Education and Religious Liberty* (1973), invalidating a statute that permitted the state to reimburse nonpublic schools for expenses incurred in complying with requirements for the administration and reporting of test results and other records. Insofar as there were no restrictions on the use of the funds, such that school could apparently be reimbursed for teacher-prepared tests on religious subject matter, the Court asserted that the aid had the primary effect of advancing religion.

Four years later in *Wolman v. Walter* (1977), the Supreme Court upheld a law from Ohio that allowed reimbursement for religious schools that used standardized tests and scoring services. The Court distinguished these tests from the ones in *Levitt* because the ones in the case at bar were neither drafted nor scored by nonpublic school personnel. In addition, the Court reasoned that the law did not authorize payments to church-sponsored schools for costs associated with test administration.

The Supreme Court revisited reimbursements in *Levitt* in *Committee for Public Education and Religious Liberty v. Regan* (1980) after the New York State legislature modified the disputed law from *Levitt*. The revised law granted reimbursements to nonpublic schools for the actual costs of complying with state requirements for reporting on students as well as for administering mandatory and optional state-prepared examinations. The Court explained that the new version of the statute passed all three parts of the *Lemon* test.

Loans of Instructional Materials

In *Meek v. Pittenger* (1975), the Supreme Court reviewed the constitutionality of loans of instructional materials, including textbooks and equipment, to religiously affiliated nonpublic schools in Pennsylvania. As in its previous judgments, the Court upheld the loan of textbooks but struck down provisions dealing with periodicals, films, recordings, and laboratory equipment as well as equipment for recording and projecting. The Court feared that loaning materials other than textbooks had the primary effect of advancing religion because of the nature of the participating schools.

Two years later, the Supreme Court reached similar results in another aspect of *Wolman* in upholding the part of the statute that specified that textbook loans were to be made to students or their parents, rather than directly to their nonpublic schools. Even so, the Court struck down a provision in the law that would have allowed loans of instructional equipment including projectors, tape recorders, record players, maps and globes, and science kits. The Court invalidated the statute's authorizing the loans in light of its concern that because it would be impossible to separate the secular and sectarian functions for which these items were to be used, the materials supported the religious missions of the schools.

In *Mitchell v. Helms* (2000), a case from Louisiana, the Supreme Court expanded the boundaries of the child benefit test. A plurality upheld the constitutionality of Chapter 2 of Title I, now Title VI, of the Elementary and Secondary Education Act, a federal law that permits the loans of instructional materials including library books, computers, television sets, tape recorders, and maps to nonpublic schools. Based on *Agostini v. Felton* (1997), discussed below, because the plaintiffs did not challenge the law's purpose, the plurality thought it necessary to restrict its analysis to the statute's effect. The Court concluded that Chapter 2 did not foster impermissible religious indoctrination, because the aid was allocated by using neutral secular criteria that neither favored nor disfavored religion, and the aid was available to all schools using secular, nondiscriminatory grounds for determining which schools were to receive it. At the same time, the plurality reversed those parts of *Meek* and *Wolman* that were inconsistent with the Court's new holdings on loans of instructional materials.

Auxiliary Services

In another aspect of *Meek*, the Supreme Court struck down a statute that allowed public school personnel to provide auxiliary services on site in religiously affiliated nonpublic schools. Moreover, the Court banned the on-site delivery of remedial and accelerated instructional programs, guidance counseling and testing, and services to aid children who were educationally disadvantaged. The Court asserted that it was immaterial that the students would have received remedial rather than advanced work, because the required surveillance to ensure the absence of ideology would have given rise to excessive entanglement between church and state.

Two years later, in yet another dimension of *Wolman*, the Court permitted the state to supply nonpublic schools with state-mandated tests, and it allowed public school employees to go to nonpublic schools to perform diagnostic tests to evaluate whether students needed speech, hearing, or psychological services. Further, the Court permitted public funds to be spent in providing therapeutic services to students from nonpublic schools but made it clear that this would be acceptable only if the services were not provided in the religiously affiliated nonpublic schools.

Zobrest v. Catalina Foothills School District (1993) ushered in the most recent era in the Supreme Court's Establishment Clause jurisprudence in K–12 schools. At issue was a school board's refusal to provide a sign-language interpreter, as required by the Individuals with Disabilities Education Act, for a deaf student in Arizona who wished to attend a Catholic high school. Reversing earlier judgments that denied the on-site delivery of services for students, the Court pointed out that an interpreter provided neutral aid to the student without offering financial benefits to his parents or school, and there was no governmental participation in the instruction, because the interpreter was only a conduit to effectuate the child's communications. The Court relied in part on *Witters v. Washington Department of Services for the Blind* (1986), wherein it upheld the constitutionality of extending a general vocational assistance program to a blind man who was studying to become a clergyman at a religious college. However, the Supreme Court of Washington later struck down the use of such public funds as being unconstitutional under the state constitution (*Witters v. State Commission for the Blind* (1989)).

A year later, the Court considered a case where the New York State legislature created a school district with the same boundaries as those of a religious community in an attempt to accommodate the needs of religious parents of children with disabilities. After all three levels of the state courts struck the statute down as violating the Establishment Clause, the Supreme Court, in *Board of Education of Kiryas Joel Village School District v. Grumet* (1994), affirmed. The Court invalidated the statute essentially because the state not only favored a specific religious group but also because officials failed to consider alternatives such as offering classes at public schools or neutral sites near one of the community's religious schools. While the state legislature sought to remedy the Establishment Clause problem, the state's high court again invalidated it for having the effect of advancing one religion (*Grumet v. Cuomo*, 1997; *Grumet v. Pataki*, 1999).

In 1974, the Supreme Court addressed the first of its three cases involving Title I of the Elementary and Secondary Education Act of 1965. In *Wheeler v. Barrera* (1974), the Court was of the view that because the question of whether officials in Missouri

could be required to provide remedial Title I instruction for students who were educationally disadvantaged on site in their religiously affiliated nonpublic schools was an issue of state law, the Court was unable to resolve the question. The Court indicated that officials had options available in meeting Title I's requirement that they provide eligible students with instruction at locations other than their religious schools.

Eleven years later, the Supreme Court revisited Title I in *Aguilar v. Felton* (1985). At issue was the constitutionality of permitting public school teachers in New York City to provide remedial instruction and materials for eligible students who were educationally disadvantaged on site in their religiously affiliated nonpublic schools. A divided Supreme Court affirmed earlier orders striking the law down as violating the Establishment Clause. The Court was satisfied that the program passed the first two parts of the *Lemon* test, because the school board developed safeguards to ensure that public funds were not spent for religious purposes. Yet, even though there were no allegations of impropriety, the Court invalidated the program in light of its fear that the monitoring system ran afoul of the third prong of the *Lemon* test, because it might have created excessive entanglement of church and state.

Decided on the same day as *Aguilar,* and more than a decade after the Supreme Court of Michigan upheld the state constitutional amendment on shared time, the justices struck down a dual-enrollment program in *School District of City of Grand Rapids v. Ball* (1985). The Court affirmed that the program was unacceptable, because it failed all three prongs of the *Lemon* test.

In *Agostini v. Felton* (1997), based on a change in the composition of the bench, the Supreme Court essentially repudiated its judgment in *Aguilar.* In a major shift in its jurisprudence, the Court reasoned that the Title I program was constitutional, because there was no governmental indoctrination, no distinctions were made among recipients based on religion, and there was no excessive entanglement. In a majority opinion that echoed her earlier dissent in *Aguilar,* writing for the Court, Justice O'Connor ruled that a federally funded program that provides supplemental, remedial instruction and counseling on a neutral basis to children who are disadvantaged was constitutional.

The Court upheld the practice, because the school board developed sufficient safeguards for the on-site delivery of services in religiously affiliated nonpublic schools. The most significant aspect of *Agostini* was the Court's modification of the *Lemon* test by reviewing only its first two parts, purpose and effect, while treating the third, entanglement, as one measure in evaluating a law's effect.

Vouchers

Controversy has arisen over the use of vouchers, as lower courts have reached mixed conclusions in disputes over their constitutionality. Yet, it was not until a dispute from Ohio made its way to the Supreme Court that vouchers garnered national attention.

Following several rounds of litigation in federal and state courts, in *Zelman v. Simmons-Harris* (2002), the Court upheld the constitutionality of a statute from Ohio that was designed to assist underprivileged children in Cleveland's failing public schools. In dealing with the most controversial part of the law, on vouchers, the Court relied on *Agostini* and began by considering whether the program had the purpose or effect of advancing or inhibiting religion. Insofar as there was no dispute over whether the program had a valid secular purpose, the Court was satisfied that it did not have the effect of advancing religion. The Court pointed out that the program was acceptable because it conferred aid under neutral secular criteria that neither favored nor disfavored religion, was available to both religious and secular recipients on a nondiscriminatory basis, and was offered directly to a broad class of persons who directed the aid to religious schools based on their own independent, private choices.

Post-*Zelman* litigation challenging vouchers focused on state constitutional grounds, because they are typically more stringent than those under the federal Constitution. Accordingly, the Supreme Court of Colorado (*Owens v. Colorado Congress of Parents, Teachers and Students,* 2004), the First Circuit (*Eulitt ex rel. Eulitt v. Maine, Department of Education,* 2004), the Eleventh Circuit (*Cooper v. Florida,* 2005), and the Supreme Court of Florida (*Bush v. Holmes,* 2006) all struck down voucher programs on the basis of state constitutional provisions.

Conclusion

Ongoing debate over the constitutional viability of state aid to religiously affiliated nonpublic schools under the child benefit test will undoubtedly continue for the foreseeable future as the Supreme Court's perspective shifts depending on the composition of the bench, and the issue is unlikely to be resolved any time soon. The acceptable limits of aid to religiously affiliated schools and their students is just one of the many important topics that bears watching as the Court's membership changes in the coming years.

Charles J. Russo

See also Child Benefit Test; Nonpublic Schools; Vouchers

Legal Citations

Abington Township School District v. Schempp and *Murray v. Curlett,* 374 U.S. 203 (1963).

Agostini v. Felton, 521 U.S. 203 (1997).

Aguilar v. Felton, 473 U.S. 402 (1985).

Board of Education v. Allen, 392 U.S. 236 (1968).

Board of Education of Kiryas Joel Village School District v. Grumet, 512 U.S. 687 (1994).

Bush v. Holmes, 919 So. 2d 392 (Fla. 2006).

Cantwell v. Connecticut, 310 U.S. 296 (1940).

Cochran v. Louisiana State Board of Education, 281 U.S. 370 (1930).

Committee for Public Education and Religious Liberty v. Nyquist, 413 U.S. 756 (1973).

Cooper v. Florida, 140 Fed. Appx. 845 (11th Cir. 2005).

Committee for Public Education and Religious Liberty v. Regan, 444 U.S. 646 (1980).

Eulitt ex rel. Eulitt v. Maine, Department of Education, 386 F.3d 344 (1st Cir. 2004).

Everson v. Board of Education of Ewing Township, 330 U.S. 1 (1947), *reh'g denied,* 330 U.S. 855 (1947).

Grumet v. Cuomo, 659 N.Y.S.2d 173 (N.Y. 1997); *Grumet v. Pataki,* 697 N.Y.S.2d 846 (N.Y. 1999), *cert. denied,* 528 U.S. 946 (1999).

Lemon v. Kurtzman, 403 U.S. 602 (1971).

Levitt v. Committee for Public Education and Religious Liberty, 413 U.S. 472 (1973).

Meek v. Pittenger, 421 U.S. 349 (1975).

Mitchell v. Helms, 530 U.S. 793 (2000), *reh'g denied,* 530 U.S. 1296 (2000), *on remand sub nom. Helms v. Picard,* 229 F.3d 467 (5th Cir. 2000).

Mueller v. Allen, 463 U.S. 388 (1983).

Owens v. Colorado Congress of Parents, Teachers and Students, 92 P.3d 933 (Colo. 2004).

Pierce v. Society of Sisters of the Holy Names of Jesus and Mary, 268 U.S. 510 (1925).

School District of City of Grand Rapids v. Ball, 473 U.S. 373 (1985).

Sloan v. Lemon, 413 U.S. 825 (1973).

Walz v. Tax Commission of New York City, 397 U.S. 664 (1970).

Wheeler v. Barrera, 417 U.S. 402 (1974).

Witters v. Washington Department of Services for the Blind, 474 U.S. 481 (1986), 771 P.2d 1119 (Wash.1989), *cert. denied*, 493 U.S. 850 (1989).

Wolman v. Walter, 433 U.S. 229 (1977).

Zelman v. Simmons-Harris, 536 U.S. 639 (2002).

Zobrest v. Catalina Foothills School District, 509 U.S. 1 (1993).

STATUTE

Statutes, in their most basic form, are the written laws that govern our daily lives and operations. These laws are written by legislative bodies at the state and federal levels, and, in the United States, are the most fundamental source of law. In its Latin root, *statute* is derived from the meaning of "it is decided." Thus, statutes reflect the decisions of law-making groups at various levels and may be based on long-standing customs or new groundbreaking changes. Although the legislatures of state or federal governments actually propose (as bills) and write statutes, the government's system of checks and balances allows the executive, legislative, and judicial branches to all have a hand in the development of the laws that govern everyday life. A bill sponsored by a legislator can be passed into law as a statute, which is then approved by the chief officer of the executive branch (the president of the United States or the governor of any state). From that point, judges interpret these laws as to their constitutionality and implementation.

All statutes are subject to interpretation by members of the judicial branch of government (i.e., the courts), and statutes put into place by a legislature can be found to be unconstitutional by a judicial body and then revoked. In essence, then, statutes are written by legislative bodies but are then interpreted by judicial bodies. In some cases, a statute might contain vague or unclear terminology that the courts must decipher

for practical purposes. Additionally, statutes can be modified or even rescinded by the same legislative body that established them. Statutes can also expire if such terms are written into the statute itself, or laws may be passed that automatically cancel a statute that has not been explicitly reauthorized by the legislature. Thus, although they represent binding law, statutes are neither permanent nor unalterable.

Because they are published in written form for use by such parties as citizens, lawyers, and judicial bodies, a group of statutes is typically organized by topic and published in volumes referred to as codes. Federal statutes compose the United States Code and are organized by topic into 50 sections called Titles; these Titles cover all areas of legal specificity including bankruptcy (Title 11), census (Title 13), education (Title 20), food and drug (Title 21), labor (Title 29), money and finance (Title 30), and war and national defense (Title 50). Most state codes are also divided by general subject areas such as a probate code (laws regarding wills, trusts, and other aspects of probate), education code (including but not limited to personnel, contracts, programs, discipline, organization of schools, school finance), family code (marriage, divorce, and child welfare issues), and criminal or penal code (violent crimes and punishments). The specific types of codes vary distinctly by state. The state of Texas, for example, publishes its state laws into 31 different codes, which can be purchased in book format or accessed online.

Insofar as education is a power granted to the states by virtue of the Tenth Amendment to the U.S. Constitution, statutes governing public schools are written and applied by state legislatures. Even the power of school districts to exist and operate must be granted by state statute or constitution, either explicit or implied. The degree of specificity regarding public schools found in statutes varies among states, with some being very specific in terms of what powers are expressly written and others being far more general. Still, federal statutes do have implications for public schools, even though education is a state responsibility. For this reason, most of the federal statutes influencing public education are carried out as part of the General Welfare Clause found in Article 1, Section 8 of the U.S. Constitution, which grants the U.S.

Congress the power to "pay the debts and provide for the common defense and general welfare of the United States." This clause grants the federal government the power to tax and spend monies for the general welfare of the country, which includes educational purposes. Any school or district that receives federal funds is thus bound by federal guidelines and statutes.

Likewise, the Commerce Clause, also found in Article 1, Section 8 of the Constitution, has been used to enforce federal statutes on public education. The Commerce Clause allows the U.S. Congress "to regulate Commerce with foreign Nations, and among the several States, and with Indian Tribes." Although the Commerce Clause would seem to rarely apply to public school functions, phrases within it such as the "advancement of society, labor, transportation, *intelligence,* care, and various mediums of exchange" allow this aspect of federal statute to impact public education at the state level.

Although a statute is simply a written law developed by a legislative body, it differs distinctly from other types of law such as common law or case law. From the time a statute is passed by the legislature, it is considered binding law until it is repealed by other legislation or overturned by a judicial decision.

Stacey L. Edmonson

See also Regulation; Stare Decisis

Further Readings

Best, A., & Barnes, D. (2007). *Basic tort law: Cases, statutes, and problems* (2nd ed.). New York: Aspen Press.

Cornell University Law School Web site. (n.d.). http://www.law.cornell.edu/uscode/#TITLES.

Statute. (n.d.). *'Lectric Law Library's Lexicon.* Retrieved October 26, 2007, from http://www.lectlaw.com/def2/s071.htm

Texas Legislature Online. (n.d.). http://tlo2.tlc.state.tx.us/statutes/statutes.html

U.S. Constitution. (1787). Retrieved February 1, 2007 from http://www.archives.gov/national-archives-experience/charters/constitution.html

Walsh, J., Kemerer, F., & Maniotis, L. (2005). *The educator's guide to Texas school law.* Austin: University of Texas Press.

STATUTE OF LIMITATIONS

A statute of limitations is just that: It is a type of statute that is passed by legislatures at both the state and federal levels that sets forth the specific time period within which causes of action must be filed or rights enforced. Statutes of limitation therefore represent legislative determinations as to the maximum period of time within which persons may file claims to enforce their rights. The fundamental premise behind statutes of limitation is to advance justice or fairness by barring old claims.

As the Supreme Court of the United States famously stated, statutes of limitation are

> designed to promote justice by preventing surprises through the revival of claims that have been allowed to slumber until evidence has been lost, memories have faded, and witnesses have disappeared. The theory is that even if one has a just claim it is unjust not to put the adversary on notice to defend within the period of limitation and that the right to be free of stale claims in time comes to prevail over the right to prosecute them. (*Order of Railroad Telegraphers v. Railway Express Agency,* 1944, pp. 348–349)

Statutes of limitation are essentially procedural in nature. In other words, statutes of limitation do not speak to the merit of a plaintiff's claim. Rather, defendants can raise the bar of the statute of limitations as a defense to claims by plaintiffs. Further illustrating the procedural rather than substantive nature of statutes of limitation, if defendants fail to assert the statute of limitations as a defense, a defense will be waived, and plaintiffs will be permitted to pursue even claims that are filed outside the applicable limitations periods. As alluded to earlier, legislatures at both the state and federal levels enact individual statutes of limitations. Accordingly, the application of statutes of limitations can vary from one jurisdiction to the next.

In general, statutes of limitation are classified by the types of actions or rights that are involved in litigation. For example, statutes of limitation for most tort actions are generally short, usually between one and two years. By contrast, statutes of limitation for contract actions are generally longer, usually between four and six years. Individual statutes may also include statutes of limitations that are embedded in the text of the statutes themselves and specific to the particular laws.

Also important to understanding the application of statutes of limitation is the concept of accrual. Statutes of limitation begin to run when a plaintiff's cause of action accrues. Put another way, accrual is the point at which the "statutory clock begins to tick." Traditionally, accrual has been said to occur when a defendant's wrongful act takes place or his or her obligation or liability arises. Thus, the statute of limitations is triggered by the conduct of defendants, not the subjective awareness of plaintiffs of their right to sue. However, this understanding of accrual has often led to harsh results.

The most famous illustration is that of a surgeon who leaves a sponge in a patient after surgery. Under the traditional understanding of accrual, the statute of limitations would begin to run at the moment of the doctor's negligence or wrongful conduct. Accordingly, if no complications or other ailments develop that would put the patient on notice of the doctor's error before the expiration of the statute of limitations, the unsuspecting patient may be barred from bringing suit.

In order to prevent this type of result, many jurisdictions have adopted the so-called discovery rule. Under the discovery rule, the statute of limitations begins to run once plaintiffs have notice or information that would put reasonable persons on notice of potential wrongdoings or causes of action. Importantly, under the discovery rule, plaintiffs need not have every specific fact necessary to file suit. Rather, the statute begins to run as soon as plaintiffs suspect that they may have been injured by a defendant's wrongful conduct. In the surgeon example, then, the statute of limitations would begin to run as soon as complications developed and the plaintiff had reason to believe that his or her injury was the result of negligence or wrongful conduct.

Insofar as statutes of limitation constitute complete defenses to suits, school boards, educational leaders, or even individual teachers can be expected to raise this defense any time they are met with stale or old claims. Moreover, as noted above, statutes of limitation may vary by jurisdiction; their application to schools and education-related claims will also vary depending on the state in which the suit are filed or on the types of claim that plaintiffs assert.

Christopher D. Shaw

See also Statute

Further Readings

Black, H. R. (1990). *Black's law dictionary* (6th ed.). St. Paul, MN: West.

Legal Citations

Jolly v. Eli Lilly & Co., 751 P.2d 923 (Cal. 1988).
Kinsinger v. Abbott Laboratories, 171 Cal. App. 3d 376 (Cal. Ct. App. 1985).
Order of Railroad Telegraphers v. Railway Express Agency, 321 U.S. 342 (1944).

STAY-PUT PROVISION

After students with disabilities are placed in special education programs, their placements may not be changed unless their parents are notified in writing of proposed changes and have been given opportunities to contest the actions of school officials (20 U.S.C. § 1415(b)(3)). Additionally, the Individuals with Disabilities Education Act (IDEA) provides that while administrative due process hearings or judicial actions are pending, students are to remain in their "then current placement" unless their parents and school boards agree to some other arrangement (20 U.S.C. § 1415(j)). This portion of the law has become known as the stay-put or status quo provision. The purpose of the stay-put provision is to provide educational stability and consistency (*Gabel ex rel. L.G. v. Board of Education of the Hyde Park Central School District*, 2005). Court cases related to this issue are described in this entry.

School Action

The program that students attended at the time that disputes arose is usually considered to be their then-current placement. One court described this concept as the operative placement actually functioning at the time the dispute first arose (*Thomas v. Cincinnati Board of Education,* 1990). According to this definition, a proposed placement that had never been implemented would not qualify as the stay-put placement. Thus, the stay-put placement generally is the placement that was last agreed upon by the parents and school board. If parents later withdraw their consent for a placement, it still remains the then-current placement (*Clyde K. v. Puyallup School District,* 1994).

On occasion, school personnel may make a placement that is meant to be temporary. When this is done, school officials are required to make their intentions clear. If school officials fail to make their intentions clear, then courts consider these placements to be the then-current placements. For example, in an early case, the staff at the private facility that a child attended called for his transfer to a residential school. The school board agreed to the new placement, but a year later notified the student's parents that inasmuch as school personnel saw no need for continued residential placement, the board would no longer assume financial responsibility for the placement. However, the trial court decided that the residential school was the student's then-current placement because board officials had assumed financial responsibility for it and gave no indication at the time that they intended to do so for one year only (*Jacobsen v. District of Columbia Board of Education,* 1983).

In a subsequent dispute, the same court determined that any limitation on a placement must be spelled out clearly and described in a settlement agreement (*Saleh v. District of Columbia,* 1987). In this case, the student was placed in a private school pending resolution of a placement dispute by mutual consent of the school board and parents. The board later claimed that the private school was an interim placement only. The court did not agree, ruling that it was the then-current placement, because its interim status had not been conveyed clearly. On the other hand, the District of Columbia Circuit affirmed that a private school placement ceased to be the then-current placement at the end of the school year, because a hearing officer's order clearly stated that it was to be for one year only (*Leonard v. McKenzie,* 1989). For similar reasons, the First Circuit wrote

that a settlement agreement between the parties calling for a temporary placement in a private school did not make it the child's stay-put placement (*Verhoeven v. Brunswick School Committee,* 1999).

Parent Action

A parentally made private school placement may be the stay-put placement if a school board failed to propose an appropriate program in a timely fashion. For instance, the federal trial court for the District of Columbia noted that where the school board had not proposed a program by a deadline established by a hearing officer, parents were justified in placing their child in a private school, which essentially became his then-current educational placement (*Cochran v. District of Columbia,* 1987).

Conversely, when parents unilaterally remove their child from a program, it does not cease to be the stay-put placement. The Eighth Circuit ruled that the placement a student attended when his parents removed him from the public schools was his then-current placement for IDEA purposes (*Digre v. Roseville Schools Independent School District No. 623,* 1988). Similarly, a federal trial court in Illinois insisted that the stay-put provision does not apply to students whose parents unilaterally place them in private schools (*Joshua B. v. New Trier Township High School District 203,* 1991).

When school officials believe that keeping students in their then-current placements presents a danger to them or others or a substantial disruption to the educational process, a change in placement order can be issued by a court or hearing officer in spite of the stay-put provision (*Honig v. Doe,* 1988; 20 U.S.C. § 1415(k)(3)(B)(ii)). Even so, the burden is clearly on school officials to show that a change is necessary.

Allan G. Osborne, Jr.

See also Due Process Hearings; Disabled Persons, Rights of; Free Appropriate Public Education; Least Restrictive Environment

Legal Citations

Clyde K. v. Puyallup School District, 35 F.3d 1396 (9th Cir. 1994).

Cochran v. District of Columbia, 660 F. Supp. 314 (D.D.C. 1987).

Digre v. Roseville Schools Independent School District No. 623, 841 F.2d 245 (8th Cir. 1988).

Gabel ex rel. L. G. v. Board of Education of the Hyde Park Central School District, 368 F. Supp. 2d 313 (S.D.N.Y. 2005).

Honig v. Doe, 484 U.S. 305 (1988).

Individuals with Disabilities Education Act, 20 U.S.C. §§ 1400 *et seq.*

Jacobsen v. District of Columbia Board of Education, 564 F. Supp. 166 (D.D.C. 1983).

Joshua B. v. New Trier Township High School District 203, 770 F. Supp. 431, (N.D. Ill. 1991).

Leonard v. McKenzie, 869 F.2d 1558 (D.C. Cir. 1989).

Saleh v. District of Columbia, 660 F. Supp. 212 (D.D.C. 1987).

Thomas v. Cincinnati Board of Education, 918 F.2d 618 (6th Cir. 1990).

Verhoeven v. Brunswick School Committee, 207 F.3d 1 (1st Cir. 1999).

STEVENS, JOHN PAUL (1920–)

John Paul Stevens was appointed as associate justice to the U.S. Supreme Court by President Gerald Ford in 1975. Although nominally a Republican, Stevens brought with him a reputation as a political moderate. On the Court, he demonstrated an independent streak, tending to be a pragmatic jurist who reached decisions on narrow factual and legal grounds rather than advocating a particular judicial philosophy. However, in recent years, as the Court has moved more to the right, Justice Stevens has frequently voted as a liberal in cases affecting education law.

Early Years

Stevens was born into a wealthy family in Chicago, Illinois, on April 10, 1920. His father owned the Stevens Hotel, which today is the Chicago Hilton. As a child, he grew up in a residential area near the University of Chicago campus, and he received his elementary and secondary education at the university's laboratory school. He then entered the University of Chicago, where he majored in English, edited the student newspaper, and graduated Phi Beta Kappa. After college, Stevens joined the U.S. Navy and was awarded the Bronze Star for his service during World War II as a code breaker in naval intelligence.

Returning home after the war, he enrolled in law school at Northwestern University. At Northwestern, Stevens was an outstanding student, serving as editor-in-chief of the law review, graduating first in his class, and earning the highest grades in the law school's history. On graduation from law school, he clerked at the U.S. Supreme Court for Justice Wiley Rutledge.

Following his clerkship, Stevens was hired as an associate with one of Chicago's most prestigious law firms. Three years later, he formed his own firm. In private practice, Stevens developed an expertise in the field of antitrust law. He taught courses on antitrust law at Northwestern University and at the University of Chicago. During this time, he also served as counsel for committees of the U.S. House of Representatives and U.S. attorney general's office studying monopolies and researching antitrust laws. Steven's reputation for integrity led to his appointment as chief counsel to a commission investigating alleged improprieties of state court judges in Illinois.

On the Bench

In 1970, on the recommendation of a college friend, U.S. Senator Charles Percy, Stevens was appointed by President Richard Nixon for a seat on the Seventh Circuit. During his tenure as an appellate court judge, Stevens authored over 200 opinions, many of which were quite lengthy and accompanied by detailed footnotes. His early writings provided a clue to his approach to judicial decision making, demonstrating a preference for narrowly tailored decisions rather than grand pronouncements on constitutional law.

In 1975, following the resignation of Justice William O. Douglas from the Supreme Court, Judge Stevens was on the short list of possible replacements. Edward Levi, U.S. attorney general and former dean of the University of Chicago Law School, was a strong supporter of Stevens and highly recommended him to President Gerald Ford. The American Bar Association gave Stevens its highest rating. In the aftermath of Watergate, President Ford nominated Stevens as a respected judge with moderate Republican leanings whose appointment would not create partisan political controversy. Judge Stevens's nomination was confirmed by a unanimous vote of the Senate.

On the Court, Justice Stevens proved to be less conservative than many of his initial backers might have hoped. During his first full term, he voted with liberal Justices William Brennan and Thurgood Marshall nearly 60% of the time. One of the biggest disappointments to conservatives has been Stevens's continued support in cases such as *Planned Parenthood of Southeastern Pennsylvania v. Casey* (1992) for upholding the principle of a woman's right to an abortion. In *Hill v. Colorado* (2000), he authored the majority opinion upholding a state statute prohibiting protestors at abortion clinics from approaching within 8 feet any person within a radius of 100 feet of a health care facility.

Supreme Court Record

Over the years, Justice Stevens established a record of what his supporters consider to be independence and his critics view as inconsistency. Cases involving race relations and affirmative action are illustrative. In *City of Richmond v. J. A. Croson Co.* (1989), Stevens concurred in the judgment of the Court striking down a 30% minority set-aside program in the local construction industry. However, he filed a dissenting opinion in *Adarand Constructors, Inc. v. Pena* (1995), where he voted to uphold a minority preference program in federal construction projects. Justice Stevens argued that adherence to precedent and principles of federalism justified distinguishing federal set-aside programs, which were permissible, and state set-aside mandates, which were not.

In cases involving race-conscious admission policies to colleges and universities, Justice Stevens authored a concurring opinion in the case of *Regents of University of California v. Bakke* (1978), concluding that the university's admissions policy violated Title VI of the Civil Rights Act of 1964 by discriminating on the basis of race in an institution receiving federal funding. However, in the two more recent cases involving the University of Michigan, *Gratz v. Bollinger* (2003) and *Grutter v. Bollinger* (2003), Stevens voted to uphold both the enhanced point system for minority undergraduate students and the law

school admissions policy allowing consideration of race as a factor in admissions.

Freedom of Expression

In cases involving First Amendment freedom of expression, Stevens typically has voted more out of pragmatic considerations than predisposed ideology. For example, in *Federal Communications Commission v. Pacifica Foundation* (1978), he wrote the majority opinion upholding sanctions of a radio station for broadcasting George Carlin's "Filthy Words" monologue at a time and in such a manner as could intrude into the privacy of a person's home or automobile.

Although he is the oldest member of the Court, Justice Stevens was among the first to master modern computer technology, and he authored the opinion of the Court in the case of *Reno v. American Civil Liberties Union* (1997) holding the Communications Decency Act unconstitutional. Notwithstanding the fact that the statute advanced the legitimate goal of protecting minors, its "indecency" and "patently offensive" provisions swept too far and abridged freedom of speech for adults, he wrote. In the case of *Texas v. Johnson* (1989), Stevens voted to uphold flag desecration legislation and dissented from the ruling of the Court that flag burning was a constitutionally protected form of symbolic expression.

Student Rights

In Fourth Amendment search and seizure cases, Justice Stevens has been more sympathetic to the protection of student rights than many of his colleagues. Although he concurred with the result of the Court's decision in *New Jersey v. T. L. O.* (1985) upholding the search of a student's purse by school officials, he dissented in part, arguing that the standard announced by the Court would permit school administrators to search students suspected of violating only the most trivial of school rules. Stevens dissented from the Court's decisions upholding random drug testing of student athletes and participants in extracurricular activities in *Vernonia School District 47J v. Acton* (1994) and *Board of Education of Independent School District No. 92 of Pottawatomie County v. Earls* (2002).

In cases concerning the rights of homosexuals, Justice Stevens's voting record has been very liberal. In *Boy Scouts of America v. Dale* (2002), he dissented from the Court's opinion holding that a private organization had a right to exclude homosexuals from membership. In *Bowers v. Hardwick* (1986), he dissented from the Court's opinion upholding the Georgia antisodomy statute. More recently, in *Lawrence v. Texas* (2003), he voted with the majority in striking down the state statute criminalizing homosexual conduct between consenting adults.

Establishment Clause

Justice Stevens has taken a strong separationist position on issues involving the First Amendment Establishment Clause. In two recent cases involving public displays of the Ten Commandments in Texas and Kentucky, he found both displays unconstitutional. Stevens has opposed almost all forms of public assistance to parochial schools, such as providing sign language interpreters, remedial instruction, audio visual equipment, and school vouchers. He has also voted against allowing religious groups access to public school facilities, writing forceful dissents in *Board of Education of Westside Community School v. Mergens* (1990) and *Good News Club v. Milford Central School* (2001).

Stevens has been criticized by religious fundamentalists for his opposition to prayer in public schools. He wrote the opinion of the Court in *Wallace v. Jaffree* (1985) holding an Alabama statute authorizing a moment of silence or voluntary prayer unconstitutional because it lacked a valid secular purpose, joined the majority in *Lee v. Weisman* (1992) declaring nonsectarian prayers at public elementary and secondary school graduation ceremonies unconstitutional, and authored the majority opinion in *Santa Fe Independent School District v. Doe* (200) striking down the practice of student-led prayers over the public address system at high school football games.

Indicative of Stevens's propensity to decide cases on narrow grounds is his opinion in *Elk Grove Unified School District v. Newdow* (2004), where a parent of an elementary school student alleged that a school district policy requiring willing students to recite the Pledge of Allegiance unconstitutionally violated the Establishment Clause because of the phrase "under God." The Court ruled that because the parent did not have legal custody of the student, he lacked prudential standing to sue.

In First Amendment Free Exercise Clause cases, Stevens has been less supportive of the rights of religious minorities. He cast a key vote in *Employment Division, Department of Human Resources of Oregon v. Smith* (1990), upholding the denial of unemployment benefits to Native Americans for their use of the illegal hallucinogenic drug peyote as part of a religious ceremony. He also voted with the majority in *City of Boerne v. Flores* (1997), striking down Congress's effort to overturn the *Smith* decision by enacting the Religious Freedom Restoration Act.

Special Education

One of the Court opinions authored by Justice Stevens that has had a tremendous impact on special education was the decision in *Cedar Rapids Community School District v. Garret F.* (1999), holding that the IDEA requires providing students with disabilities related services such as nursing care during school hours, even if the provision would strain the financial resources of the school district.

With the resignation of Chief Justice Rehnquist, Justice Stevens became the most senior member of the Supreme Court. In assessing Stevens's career, supporters cite his intellect, open-mindedness, and independence. During his long tenure on the Court, he has written more concurring or dissenting opinions than any of his contemporaries. Critics, especially conservatives, accuse him of lacking ideological consistency. Stevens has occasionally forged winning coalitions with centrists and liberals. However, some commentators feel that considering his sharp mind and personal charm, he should have exerted greater leadership. Now in his late 80s, Justice Stevens has recovered from cancer and is in relatively good health. His death or retirement could potentially shift the ideological balance of the Supreme Court.

Michael Yates

See also Cedar Rapids Community School District v. Garret
F.; Santa Fe Independent School District v. Doe;
Rehnquist Court; *Wallace v. Jaffree*

Further Readings

Manaster, K. A. (2001). *Illinois justice: The scandal of 1969
and the rise of John Paul Stevens.* Chicago, IL: University
of Chicago Press.

Urofsky, M. I. (Ed.). (2006). *Biographical encyclopedia of
the Supreme Court: The lives and legal philosophies of
the justices.* Washington, DC: C. Q. Press.

Legal Citations

Adarand Constructors, Inc. v. Pena, 515 U.S. 200 (1995).

*Board of Education of Independent School District No. 92 of
Pottawatomie County v. Earls,* 536 U.S. 822 (2002) *on
remand,* 300 F.3d 1222 (10th Cir. 2002).

*Board of Education of Westside Community School v.
Mergens,* 496 U.S. 226 (1990).

Bowers v. Hardwick, 478 U.S. 186 (1986).

Boy Scouts of America v. Dale, 547 U.S. 47 (2002).

Cedar Rapids Community School District v. Garret F., 526
U.S. 66 (1999).

City of Boerne v. Flores, 521 U.S. 507 (1997).

City of Richmond v. J. A. Croson Co., 488 U.S. 469 (1989).

Elk Grove Unified School District v. Newdow, 542
U.S. 1 (2004).

*Employment Division, Department of Human Resources of
Oregon v. Smith,* 494 U.S. 872 (1990).

Federal Communications Commission v. Pacifica Foundation,
438 U.S. 726 (1978).

Good News Club v. Milford Central School, G21 F Supp.2d
147 (N.D.N.Y. 1998); *aff'd,* 202 F.3d 502 (2d Cir. 2000,
rev'd); 533 U.S. 98 (2001).

Gratz v. Bollinger, 529 U.S. 244 (2003).

Grutter v. Bollinger, 539 U.S. 306 (2003).

Hill v. Colorado, 530 U.S. 703 (2000).

Lawrence v. Texas, 539 U.S. 558 (2003).

Lee v. Weisman, 505 U.S. 577 (1992).

New Jersey v. T. L. O., 469 U.S. 325 (1985).

Planned Parenthood of Southeastern Pennsylvania v. Casey,
446 U.S. 320 (1992).

Regents of University of California v. Bakke, 438 U.S. 265
(1978).

Reno v. American Civil Liberties Union, 521 U.S.
844 (1997).

Santa Fe Independent School District v. Doe, 530 U.S.
290 (2000).

Texas v. Johnson, 491 U.S. 397 (1989).

Vernonia School District 47J v. Acton, 515 U.S. 646 (1994).

Wallace v. Jaffree, 472 U.S. 38 (1985).

STONE V. GRAHAM

In *Stone v. Graham* (1980), the U.S. Supreme Court
addressed a Kentucky statute requiring that school
officials post a copy of the Ten Commandments, purchased with private contributions, on a wall in every
public classroom in the commonwealth. The Court
held that the law violated the Establishment Clause of
the First Amendment.

The Kentucky statute required that the following
notation was to be placed, in small print, at the bottom
of each display of the Ten Commandments: "The secular application of the Ten Commandments is clearly
seen in its adoption as the fundamental legal code
of Western Civilization and the Common Law of the
United States." Opponents of the statute filed suit
claiming that it violated the Establishment and Free
Exercise clauses of the First Amendment. In a per
curiam opinion, the Supreme Court used the *Lemon* test
to evaluate whether the statute was permissible under
the Establishment Clause. In *Lemon v. Kurtzman*
(1971), the Supreme Court held that to be permissible
under the Establishment Clause, (a) a statute must have
a secular legislative purpose; (b) its principal or primary effect must be one that neither advances nor
inhibits religion; and (c) the statute must not foster "an
excessive government entanglement with religion." No
consideration of the second or third criterion is necessary if a statute does not have a clearly secular purpose.

The Supreme Court held that the statute requiring
the posting of the Ten Commandments in public school
rooms violated the first part of the *Lemon* test in that it
had no secular legislative purpose and was therefore
unconstitutional. Accordingly, the Court thought it
unnecessary to proceed any further than *Lemon*'s secular purpose test, because it rejected arguments on behalf
of the commonwealth that a notation on the bottom of
the Ten Commandments, indicating that they are part of
"the fundamental legal code of Western Civilization
and the Common Law of the United States" (*Stone v.
Graham,* 1980, p. 41), was sufficient to indicate the
secular purpose of the posting. Moreover, the Court
was of the opinion that the main purpose for posting the
Ten Commandments on schoolroom walls was clearly
religious rather than educational.

The Court decided that posting the Ten Commandments violated the First Amendment because the Commandments were not integrated into the school curriculum, as is the case, for example, when a Bible may constitutionally be used to study subjects such as history, civilization, ethics, or comparative religions. Further, the Court maintained that the posted copies of the Ten Commandments were being used to induce schoolchildren to read, meditate upon, and obey the Commandments, which is not a permissible state objective under the Establishment Clause. The Court considered it to be irrelevant that the copies were purchased with private contributions, because the mere posting of the Commandments demonstrated official state support of their message. As such, the Court pointed out that the First Amendment protects the rights of citizens to post the Ten Commandments on private property and to engage in other kinds of private religious expression. There are many places in America where the Ten Commandments would be welcome and appropriate— houses of worship, private schools and universities, and private parks. It is only when public, state-supported property is used that the First Amendment becomes prohibitive of religious expression.

Stone v. Graham is most often cited for its importance with regard to the body of law that interprets teaching religious doctrine or displaying religious symbols as being sufficient to demonstrate government endorsement of their message. For example, even if school officials were to argue that the Ten Commandments could be viewed through a secular framework, their historically religious origin makes them irrefutably religious. This raises a question that the Supreme Court did not answer in *Stone v. Graham,* namely, the extent and manner in which religious themes, practices, or literatures may be presented in public contexts, when the First Amendment requires the separation of church and state, but the traditions of the country in many instances reflect and grow out of religious practices, such as Sunday "blue laws" or tax benefits for churches. Needless to say, this is an area that is ripe for future litigation.

Malila N. Robinson

See also First Amendment; Fourteenth Amendment; *Lemon v. Kurtzman;* Prayer in Public Schools; Religious Activities in Public Schools; State Aid and the Establishment Clause

Legal Citations

Abington Township School District v. Schempp and *Murray v. Curlett,* 374 U.S. 203 (1963).
Engel v. Vitale, 370 U.S. 421, 431 (1962).
Lemon v. Kurtzman, 403 U.S. 602 (1971).
Stone v. Graham, 449 U.S. 39 (1980).

STRIP SEARCHES

An unusual and highly controversial form of student search is the strip search. Strip searches are generally perceived to be among the most intrusive forms of searches and are typically administered when students are suspected of posing a considerable threat to school safety. While a legal framework for searching students was established decades prior, uncertainty remains with respect to particular aspects of administering searches, including the appropriateness of the type of search. This entry reviews a number of U.S. Supreme Court cases that have addressed the scope and rationale for strip searches.

The Supreme Court Speaks

In *New Jersey v. T. L. O.* (1985), the U.S. Supreme Court added clarity to discretionary powers of school officials administering searches of students. While it declared that searches of students require only a standard of reasonableness—a less rigid standard than probable cause—the Court also conveyed that students are entitled to legitimate expectations of privacy under the Fourth Amendment. Thus, students' rights are not relinquished entirely—a fundamental principle underlying former landmark students' rights cases.

The majority opinion, however, was far from absolute in addressing specific nuances of administering student searches. The Court offered little definitive and practical guidance with regard to the treatment of unlawfully seized evidence, the role of police in student searches, and the degree of privacy students have in government-owned storage.

Besides the provision that the scope of the search account for the sex, age, and maturity of the student, the majority failed to place any limitations on forms and types of searches allowable, including strip searches. Justice Stevens, in the dissenting opinion in

T. L. O., expressed concern about their use, stating that strip searches "[have] no place in the schoolhouse" (p. 382). With the exception of state laws that prohibit strip searching in schools, lower court cases reveal little consensus as to whether strip searches should be legally allowable.

Rulings in Favor of Schools

Cornfield v. Consolidated High School District No. 230 (1993) is a case that reflects the legal complexity of strip searching. *Cornfield* is also one of the more noteworthy and telling illustrations of judicial restraint in school administrative matters. Brian Cornfield, a 16-year-old high school student, was suspected of harboring illegal drugs in the crotch of his pants. He was subsequently strip searched by two male school officials. No drugs were discovered. Despite Cornfield's contention that his Fourth Amendment rights were violated, the court found the school's actions constitutional based on the two-part test created in *T. L. O.*

According to the Seventh Circuit in *Cornfield,* the search was reasonably justified based on two factors: the interest of school officials in maintaining order and safety and the student's problematic behavioral history. In reference to the scope of the search, the court upheld the use of the strip search as a reasonable means to "confirm or deny" suspicion of "crotching" drugs (p. 17). While it appeared that school officials may have exceeded legal boundaries of discretion with respect to intruding on the student's privacy, this case and others reflect an accommodating posture toward the strip search as a reasonable alternative if the legal criteria are met.

The Eleventh Circuit, in *Jenkins ex rel. Hall v. Talladega City Board of Education* (1996) illustrated again the effect of *T. L. O.*'s imprecise guideline regarding proper scope in student searches. In *Jenkins,* a student's accusation of theft of $7 from a backpack resulted in two second-grade girls being strip searched by a teacher and guidance counselor in a school restroom. Interestingly, the court disregarded the legality of the search and instead focused on the question of whether it had been established that the teacher and counselor were knowledgeable of the legal standards. Hence, the legality of the search itself was never decided, which in effect created more uncertainty as to what constitutes appropriate scope.

Unlawful Searches

At the same time, some courts have admonished school officials for failing to meet reasonableness requirements when administering strip searches, even when facts mirror aforementioned cases. In *Fewless v. Board of Education of Wayland Union Schools* (2002), school officials received a tip from four students scheduled to serve detention that another student was in possession of marijuana. Fewless, a 14-year-old special education student with a history of behavioral issues, was eventually strip searched. No drugs were discovered. The federal court ruled the search unlawful, as it was neither justified at its inception nor reasonable in scope. The court also noted that Fewless never gave consent to be strip searched.

In *Kennedy v. Dexter Consolidated Schools* (2000), the Supreme Court of New Mexico awarded punitive damages to two high school students who were strip searched because of a missing ring. Two students were subjected to searches while urinating and were later ordered to remove their undergarments. The court held that school officials both lacked individualized suspicion and exceeded lawful scope in administering a strip search.

In *Bell v. Marseilles Elementary School District* (2001), school officials and a municipal officer conducted a partial strip search of 30 to 35 students after 3 students reporting missing money after a gym class. A federal trial court in Illinois, in rejecting the board's motion for summary judgment, ruled that officials violated both parts of the *T. L .O.* analysis, namely justification and scope. According to the court, the police officer lacked reasonable suspicion to implicate the students in the missing money, and the strip searching of the students without a higher standard of suspicion was decidedly intrusive.

On the whole, the sample of cases presented here demonstrates varying and occasionally contradictory legal rationales employed to justify or censure strip searching. Some states, such as Wisconsin and California, have prohibited the use of strip searches in schools. Other states see strip searching as a crucial hedge against crime and violence in schools.

Nonetheless, its utility in public schools remains highly controversial.

Mario S. Torres, Jr.

See also In Loco Parentis; *New Jersey v. T. L. O;* Parental Rights

Further Readings

Mitchell, J. C. (1998). An alternative approach to the Fourth Amendment in public schools: Balancing students' rights with school safety. *Brigham Young University Law Review, 1998*(3), 1207–1241.

Spellman, R. (2002). Strip search of juveniles and the Fourth Amendment: A delicate balance of protection and privacy. *Journal of Juvenile Law, 22,* 159–179.

Stefkovich, J. A. (1994). Strip searching after *Williams*: Reactions to the concern for school safety? *West's Educational Law Reporter, 93,* 1107–1123.

Stefkovich, J. A., & Torres, M. T. (2003). The demographics of justice: Student searches, student rights, and administrator practices. *Educational Administration Quarterly, 39*(2), 259–282.

Legal Citations

Bell v. Marseilles Elementary School District, 2001 WL 818897 (N.D. Ill. 2001).

Cornfield by Lewis v. Consolidated High School District No. 230, 991 F.2d 1316 (7th Cir. 1993).

Fewless v. Board of Education of Wayland Union Schools, 208 F. Supp. 2d 806 (W.D. Mich. 2002).

Jenkins ex rel. Hall v. Talladega City Board of Education, 95 F.3d 1036 (11th Cir. 1996).

Kennedy v. Dexter Consolidated Schools, 10 P.3d 115 (N.M. 2000).

New Jersey v. T. L. O., 469 U.S. 325 (1985).

STUART V. SCHOOL DISTRICT NO. 1 OF VILLAGE OF KALAMAZOO

At issue in *Stuart v. School District No. 1 of Village of Kalamazoo* (1874) was whether a local school board had the authority to use its power to levy taxes on the general public in order to support high schools and to apply the funds to provide instruction for children in languages other than English, namely Latin and French. The Supreme Court of Michigan approved the board's decision to operate the high school and offer the language classes even though it lacked the express legislative authority to do so. The Court reasoned that the school board had the power to act, because nothing in the state's constitution, statutes, or policies restricted it from making such decisions in light of the voter approval that its members received when they were elected to represent their community. The Court added that insofar as the board was responsible for school operations, including course selections, it took 13 years before a group of disgruntled taxpayers challenged its actions. Because state officials had not objected to the board's action, the Court was satisfied that the claim against it was without merit.

Kalamazoo is most often cited for its importance with regard to the creation of free, tax-supported secondary schools. Even so, Kalamazoo is perhaps of even greater legal significance for local school boards, because it stands for the proposition that they have the implied authority to act as they deem appropriate in matters of educational policy, school governance, and educational programming. To this end, Kalamazoo stands out as the case that opened the door to granting local school boards the authority to set educational policy and standards for the students under their care.

Kalamazoo stands out as the earliest opinion on how the evolution of governance in American public education has been characterized by broad judicial interpretation of the implied powers of local school officials. More specifically, the Supreme Court of Michigan's decision in *Kalamazoo,* upholding the local board's extension of a common school system to include high schools, served as a bellwether that afforded other governing bodies the ability to extend their authority over educational programming. More recently, the U.S. Supreme Court recognized the viability of this long-held principle of board authority in *San Antonio Independent School District v. Rodriguez* (1973), wherein it found that local school boards have the authority to tailor educational programming to meet the needs of their specific communities.

Following *Kalamazoo,* judicial deference to local school boards has encouraged freedom and experimentation that is out of proportion to that suggested by the legal structure of public education. Creative boards typically introduce new practices in what may be described as exercises of their implied powers. If revolutionary educational practices are not challenged, or if they survive judicial scrutiny, then other school systems may adopt similar methodologies, thereby leading to their general acceptance. In the vast majority of cases involving new educational practices, local school boards have prevailed, usually on the basis that the adoption of innovative programming is a desirable way of achieving broad legislative and educational goals, especially because change is taking place at the local level.

Charles J. Russo

See also School Board Policy; School Boards

Legal Citations

San Antonio Independent School District v. Rodriguez, 411 U.S. 1 (1973).
Stuart v. School District No. 1 of Village of Kalamazoo, 30 Mich. 69 (Mich. 1874).

STUDENT SUICIDES

Suicide among adolescents has increased dramatically in the United States over the past 40 years. A 1991 Maryland case, *Eisel v. Board of Education of Montgomery County,* recognized a cause of action against a school district and its employees for failing to warn parents of a student's suicidal ideations. However, in the years since *Eisel,* most courts have ruled that school boards and their employees are not legally responsible for a student's death by suicide. This entry briefly examines the issue of student suicides and then looks more closely at education-related lawsuits.

A Rising Problem

Between the late 1960s and late 1990s, the teen suicide rate went up dramatically in the United States, particularly for adolescent males. According to a 1999 report from the U.S. surgeon general's office, suicide

is the third leading cause of death for teenagers, with adolescent boys about four times more likely to kill themselves than adolescent girls. The report noted that Hispanic high school students were more likely than other students to commit suicide and Native American male adolescents had the highest suicide rate in the nation.

Nevertheless, the problem of teen suicide may not be as bad as it is sometimes portrayed. Even though teen suicide is the third leading cause of death among teenagers, the suicide rate for young people is lower than the suicide rate for older Americans.

Legal Cases

Teenage suicides occasionally take place in the context of negative school events, but no court recognized the possibility of school district liability for a student's death until 1991, when Maryland's highest court issued its decision in *Eisel.* The Maryland court held that a school board could be held liable for a student's suicide if the district's professional employees knew the student was suicidal and failed to warn the parents or take other reasonable preventive action. According to the court, school counselors have a duty to use reasonable means to attempt to prevent a student from committing suicide if they are on notice of the student's suicidal intent.

Eisel was the first of a line of state and federal court decisions in which parents or guardians sued school districts and their professional employees, seeking to hold the schools and educators responsible for a child's suicide. One group of cases analyzed negligence claims against school districts arising from a student's suicide. A second group of cases considered constitutional claims.

Among the important cases is *Wyke v. Polk County School Board,* in which the Eleventh Circuit upheld a jury's negligence verdict against a school district and two other defendants arising from a student's suicide. The Eleventh Circuit ruled that a school can be liable for a student's suicide if the student attempted suicide at school and school authorities knew about the attempt and then failed to notify the student's parent or guardian. Nevertheless, in *Wyke,* the school board was liable only for approximately one-third of the damages that arose from the student's death. The jury concluded that the mother bore 32% of the responsibility and that the student's caretaker at the time of death was responsible for 35% of the total liability.

Another important decision in the area of school liability for a student's suicide is *Armijo v. Wagon Mound Public Schools,* a 1998 decision of the Tenth Circuit. Here the court recognized the possibility of a constitutional claim for a student's suicide based on the danger-creation theory. Even so, the court rejected plaintiffs' constitutional theory that the school board owed the suicide victim a duty to protect him against suicide based on a special relationship between the parties. The court also pointed out that the posture of the case required it to draw all inferences in favor of the plaintiffs and remanded the case back to the federal trial court for a consideration on the merits.

In 2004, Richard Fossey and Perry Zirkel surveyed all the cases on the issue of school district liability for student suicide that had been reported at that time. Fossey and Zirkel concluded that the courts, both state and federal, were inhospitable to plaintiffs seeking to hold educators legally responsible for a student's suicide. Courts relied on various legal theories to find in favor of defendants in these cases. In several cases, school districts prevailed on governmental immunity grounds. In some cases, plaintiffs' claims were defeated on the ground that the student's suicide was the result of some intervening cause, not the action or inaction of school authorities. Zirkel and Fossey acknowledged that *Eisel,* the case that had first recognized a cause of action against a school board arising from a student's suicide, had seldom been mentioned in the post-*Eisel* decisions, much less relied upon.

In a 2005 update of their 2004 article, Zirkel and Fossey reiterated their earlier conclusion that educators have little to fear from lawsuits arising from a student's suicide. The trend of litigation since the 1991 *Eisel* decision has not been favorable to plaintiffs in these cases. The authors maintained that school authorities may wish to adopt policies and programs to reduce the tragedy of student suicide based on professional and ethical concerns, but the risk of liability for these events is small.

Richard Fossey

See also Due Process; Negligence

Further Readings

Fossey, R., & Zirkel, P. A. (2004). Liability for student suicide in the wake of *Eisel. Texas Wesleyan Law Review, 10,* 403–439.

U.S. Surgeon General. (1999). *Mental health: A report of the Surgeon General.* Washington, DC: Author.

Zirkel, P. A., & Fossey, R. (2005). Liability for student suicide. *West's Education Law Reporter, 197,* 489–497.

Legal Citations

Armijo v. Wagon Mound Public Schools, 159 F.3d 1253 (10th Cir. 1998).

Eisel v. Board of Education of Montgomery County, 597 A.2d 447 (Md. 1991).

Wyke v. Polk County School Board, 129 F.3d 560 (11th Cir. 1997).

SWANN V. CHARLOTTE-MECKLENBURG BOARD OF EDUCATION

The U.S. Supreme Court's decision in *Swann v. Charlotte-Mecklenburg Board of Education* (1971) stands out for three reasons. First, *Swann* was the Court's last unanimous opinion in a major school desegregation case. Second, in *Swann,* for the first time, the justices considered the propriety of and upheld a court-ordered busing plan designed to end de jure segregation in public schools. Third, in *Swann,* the Court addressed other permissible means of achieving desegregation, including rezoning of attendance zones, limited use of racial quotas, and reassignment of educational personnel.

Facts of the Case

Swann began in 1965 when a group of plaintiffs unsuccessfully sued their school board over its geographic zoning and free transfer policy. A federal trial court in North Carolina ruled in favor of the school board on the basis that it had made progress toward desegregating the public schools. At the time, 66 of the district's 109 schools were entirely segregated. On appeal, in the initial round of litigation in 1966, the Fourth Circuit affirmed that the board had met its obligation to act without intent of enabling segregation. However, change was in the offing.

Two years later, in 1968, the Supreme Court found in *Green v. County School Board of New Kent County* that the county had to assume the burden of ending the historic patterns of segregation. The justices added that it was the federal trial court's duty to evaluate the plan's effectiveness and any alternatives that the school board submitted while maintaining jurisdiction until it was apparent that state-mandated segregation was completely eliminated. The plaintiff's attorney in *Swann,* Julius Chambers, thus viewed *Green* as providing a justification to seek further relief in expediting desegregation.

When *Swann* was relitigated in light of *Green,* the federal trial court determined that because the board's plan did not further desegregation, it had to develop a new, amended desegregation plan by the fall of 1970. The judge offered several remedies, including busing and rezoning. When the board's plan failed to impact school desegregation, the court appointed a special master to prepare a plan and, on receiving it, ordered its implementation. The board appealed to the Fourth Circuit, which directed the trial court to conduct hearings on the extensive use of busing elementary students and the reasonableness of the busing plan.

The trial court asserted that the plan was acceptable and again ordered its implementation as modified for junior and senior high schools; it accepted a so-called Finger Plan for rezoning elementary schools. The plan included faculty and student reassignments, closing of schools, and busing to achieve desegregation. After the Fourth Circuit approved the plan for the secondary, but not elementary, schools, the plaintiffs appealed.

The Court's Ruling

On further review, the Supreme Court ruled in favor of the plaintiffs in examining the duties of school officials along with the powers of federal courts to eliminate racially separate public schools. At issue in *Swann* was whether federal trial courts had the authority to craft solutions eliminating segregation when educational officials were unsuccessful in remedying the problem themselves. In response, the justices started by upholding the Finger Plan as a valid exercise of the district court's equitable powers that were consistent with *Brown v. Board of Education of Topeka* (1954).

At the same time, the Supreme Court identified other areas to address when remedial action is warranted. To this end, the Court noted that while it is not necessary for every school in a system to reflect a district's racial composition as a whole, a federal trial court may apply racial ratios or quotas as a starting point in shaping remedies; that one-race schools may be acceptable but should not result from past or present discriminatory actions; that attendance zones may not be laid down as rigid rules for all localities; and that it was possible to use busing as a tool in the fight to desegregate schools.

Further, the Court indicated that when constructing new schools as a remedy for de jure segregation, educational officials and the courts should not use location as a means of perpetuating dual systems. The Court concluded that once school systems have achieved unitary status, school boards did not have to make annual adjustments in the racial compositions of student bodies.

Darlene Y. Bruner

See also *Brown v. Board of Education of Topeka; Brown v. Board of Education of Topeka* and Equal Educational Opportunities; Dual and Unitary Systems; *Green v. County School Board of New Kent County;* Segregation, De Facto; Segregation, De Jure

Further Readings

Civil Rights Project, Harvard University. (n.d.). *Constitutional requirements for race-conscious policies in K–12 education.* Available from http://www.civilrights project.harvard.edu/policy/legal_docs/ked.pdf

Hunter, R. C. (2004). The implementation of Brown in achieving unitary status. *Education and Urban Society, 36*(3), 342–354.

Legal Citations

Brown v. Board of Education of Topeka I, 347 U.S. 483 (1954).

Brown v. Board of Education of Topeka II, 349 U.S. 294 (1955).

Green v. County School Board of New Kent County, 391 U.S. 430 (1968).

Swann v. Charlotte-Mecklenburg Board of Education, 402 U.S. 1 (1971).

SWEATT V. PAINTER

In *Sweatt v. Painter* (1950), the National Association for the Advancement of Colored People (NAACP) built a pivotal case in the history of school segregation. *Sweatt* represents the first time the Court ordered a traditionally White university to admit an African American student instead of sending him to an African American university. In a crucial finding, the Court held not only that facilities and their resources were unequal but also that the simple separation of the African American student from his White peers resulted in an unequal education opportunity.

The outcome in this and a related case formed the gateway to integration, as the Supreme Court ordered the admittance of African American students into traditionally White graduate and professional schools. In addition, *Sweatt*'s groundbreaking analysis became the basis for *Brown v. Board of Education of Topeka* (1954).

Facts of the Case

Heman Marion Sweatt, an African American postal worker, was denied admission to the University of Texas Law School despite his academic qualifications. Officials rejected his application, because a state law denied non-Whites access to the university. Instead, officials offered Sweatt a place at Prairie View University, the African American institution associated with Texas A&M University, which the state created and which, officials contended, met the constitutional "separate but equal" requirement mandated by *Plessy v. Ferguson* (1896).

The NAACP saw Heman Sweatt's situation as an opportunity for them to challenge the constitutionality of *Plessy*, which had been extended to education in *Gong Lum v. Rice* (1927). Insofar as the NAACP expected a general reluctance to overturn *Plessy*'s longstanding "separate but equal" doctrine, the

organization decided to focus on the inequalities of the separate school, anticipating that states would inevitably choose to desegregate rather than incur the expense of equalizing their separate facilities.

With this in mind, the NAACP filed suits calling for the improvement of facilities for African Americans, targeting the University of Texas Law School, in 1946. The NAACP thus recruited Heman Sweatt as their plaintiff, because he was an African American applicant who was rejected on the basis of his race even though he was otherwise qualified for admission. Sweatt unsuccessfully filed suit in state courts, claiming that officials violated his right to equal protection.

The Court's Ruling

On further review in *Sweatt v. Painter,* the U.S. Supreme Court examined whether the automatic rejection of an application based on race violated the Equal Protection Clause of the Fourteenth Amendment. Reversing in favor of Mr. Sweatt, a unanimous Court held that the Constitution required officials to admit him to the University of Texas Law School, because otherwise they would deny him the opportunity to obtain a legal education while granting it to others.

The *Sweatt* Court rejected *Plessy*'s notion that separate facilities could be equal, explaining that the separate law school for African Americans was not substantially equal to the University of Texas Law School. The Court reasoned that the separate law school was unequal based on tangible factors such as financial resources, size of faculty, number of library resources, number of students, and course offerings. The Court added that the African American law school was also inferior in intangible areas such as the reputation of the faculty, authority of alumni, and overall prestige.

In addition to the inequalities between the African American and White institutions, the Court pointed out that the isolation of these African American students was disadvantageous to their abilities to compete in the legal arena. Considering that Whites made up an overwhelming majority of the legal profession, the Court emphasized that the lack of contact and engagement with Whites due to the segregated system was problematic. According to the Court, such inequality resulting from this separation indicated that the separate African American school would never have been considered equivalent to the White school, regardless of how much money and prestige the African American school could accumulate.

While the Supreme Court was reviewing *Sweatt,* it simultaneously analyzed *McLaurin v. Oklahoma State Regents for Higher Education* (1950), which addressed the University of Oklahoma's separation of an African American student from his classmates in areas such as the classroom, cafeteria, and library. In *McLaurin,* handed down on the same day as *Sweatt,* the Court decided that isolating the plaintiff from his classmates hindered his academic experience by restricting his discussions and interactions with other students. Both *Sweatt* and *McLaurin* examined whether a racially segregated environment could produce equality in educational experiences, and both concluded that it could not, a direct challenge to *Plessy.*

Following *Sweatt* (and *McLaurin*), graduate and professional schools immediately admitted many more African Americans into their programs. Further, the NAACP's plan to end segregation in higher education transitioned into the battle in elementary and secondary schools, setting the stage for *Brown,* wherein the Supreme Court reasoned that separate schools based on race violated the Equal Protection Clause, because this resulted in unequal educational experiences. *Brown* struck down *Plessy*'s "separate but equal" doctrine in education, holding that desegregation was necessary to provide African American students with access to educational opportunities that were equal to those available to White students.

Wendy C. Chi

See also *Brown v. Board of Education of Topeka;* Equal Protection Analysis; Fourteenth Amendment; *Gong Lum v. Rice; McLaurin v. Oklahoma State Regents for Higher Education;* National Association for the Advancement of Colored People (NAACP)

Legal Citations

Brown v. Board of Education of Topeka I, 347 U.S. 483 (1954).
Brown v. Board of Education of Topeka II, 349 U.S. 294 (1955).
Gong Lum v. Rice, 275 U.S. 78 (1927).
McLaurin v. Oklahoma State Regents for Higher Education, 339 U.S. 637 (1950).
Plessy v. Ferguson, 163 U.S. 537 (1896).
Sweatt v. Painter, 339 U.S. 629 (1950).

TEACHER RIGHTS

Teachers enjoy rights in a variety of areas: freedom of speech, privacy, due process, and discrimination. This discussion of those rights involves primarily federal law. Even so, it is worth noting that there are state-level counterparts to nearly all of the principles covered, including freedom of speech and academic freedom, privacy, due process, and employment law.

Free Speech and Academic Freedom

A discussion of the expression rights of teachers involves the balance between the rights and responsibilities of public school employees and the institutions themselves. This balance is best met through an analysis of the capacities the speakers have taken to express their views. At one end of the balance, one must ask whether teachers are speaking as citizens, as employees, or as educators teaching in classrooms. At the other end, one must ask whether the interest of a school board in restricting teacher speech is inspired by its role as sovereign, employer, or educator, in the sense of being the leader of school curriculum. A series of U.S. Supreme Court cases illustrate this balance.

Teacher as Citizen

For purposes of free speech analysis, the difference between the role of teachers as citizens and as employee is often small. However, the judicial determination of what role speakers play is assuredly an important one, almost entirely dependent on one threshold question, asked most prominently in the landmark Supreme Court case of *Pickering v. Board of Education of Township High School District 205, Will County* (1968): Is the speech related to a matter of public concern? If the answer is "yes," the courts tend to favor speakers as citizens and restrict public employers' suppression of the expressive activities. If the answer is "no," the courts generally find in favor of the employers, allowing them wide latitude in the governance of their internal affairs.

In *Pickering,* a school board sought to dismiss a public school teacher after he wrote a letter to the editor of a local newspaper criticizing the board for its appropriation of funds and its handling of two failed tax levy campaigns. The board countered with accusations that the statements in the letter were false and had a negative impact on the efficient operation of the schools. In reality, the community and many of the teacher's coworkers greeted the letter with a good measure of apathy and disbelief. The letter itself was not directly critical of any particular board members or school administrators. The teacher unsuccessfully appealed his dismissal, but state courts in Illinois rejected his First Amendment claims.

On further review before the Supreme Court, the Court reversed in favor of the teacher. In an initial statement, the Court rejected the argument that public employees give up their constitutional rights as citizens on accepting government employment. According to the Court,

> The problem in any case is to arrive at a balance between the interests of the teacher, as a citizen, in commenting upon matters of public concern and the interest of the State, as an employer, in promoting the efficiency of the public services it performs through its employees. (*Pickering*, p. 568)

In striving to arrive at this balance, the Court weighed five factors: whether the subject of the speech was a matter of public concern, the closeness of the working relationships between speakers and those they criticized, whether there was a detrimental impact on the administration of the schools, whether employee performances suffered as a result of the expression and its response, and whether employees spoke in their professional capacity or as private citizens.

In applying these factors to the facts in *Pickering*, the Supreme Court was of the opinion that the letter to the editor dealt with a matter of public concern, namely, the use of taxpayer money in the operation of public schools. Insofar as the relationship between the teacher and the board members he criticized was not close on a daily basis, the Court ruled in favor of the teacher on the second factor as well. Compounded with that finding, the Court noted that there was no detrimental impact on the performances of either the board or the teacher. To this end, the Court pointed out that there was no levy on the ballot at the time of the letter, nor was there any evidence of disruption at the teacher's school.

Also significant to the speech issue in *Pickering* was the Court's discussion of the board's claim that the teacher's statements were false. To the extent that the statements were false, the Court had indicated that the statements must have led to some detriment on the part of the operation of the school board. The Court acknowledged that in *Pickering,* there was no detriment. Further, the Court observed that an accusation, even from one of its teachers, that the board was mismanaging funds reflected a difference of opinion on a matter of general public interest. "Absent proof of false statements knowingly or recklessly made by him, a teacher's exercise of his right to speak on matters of

public importance may not furnish the basis for his dismissal from public employment" (*Pickering*, p. 576).

Teacher as Employee

While the *Pickering* Court included among the other balancing factors the question of whether the speech related to a matter of public concern, the Supreme Court in *Connick v. Myers* (1983) placed special attention on that factor and made it a threshold question before applying a balancing test. In *Connick,* a district attorney (Connick) dismissed an assistant district attorney (Myers) for her refusal to accept an interoffice transfer and for then distributing a questionnaire to coworkers requesting opinions on transfers, office morale, the need for a grievance committee, the level of confidence in supervisors, and the pressure to work on political campaigns. The lower courts ruled in favor of the plaintiff, but the Supreme Court reversed in favor of the employer.

On the threshold question of whether the plaintiff's speech related to a matter of public concern, the Supreme Court reasoned that the First Amendment did not prevent the discharge of a state employee for speaking on matters of internal concern. According to the Court,

> When employee expression cannot be fairly considered as relating to any other matter of political, social, or other public concern, government officials should enjoy wide latitude in managing their offices, without intrusive oversight by the judiciary in the name of the First Amendment. (*Connick*, p. 146)

In answering the question of whether the speech related to a matter of public concern, the Supreme Court explained that it was necessary to look at the content, context, and form of the speech. The *Connick* Court recognized that with the exception of the questionnaire items dealing with political campaigns, the employee's speech constituted a matter of internal concern. Applying the *Pickering* balancing test, the Court ultimately decided that the employer's interest and the necessity in the efficient and successful operation of his office and the maintenance of close working relationships with superiors outweighed the public aspects of the employee's speech.

Related to both *Pickering* and *Connick* is another landmark decision by the Supreme Court in the area of public school teachers and free expression. In *Mt. Healthy City School Board of Education v. Doyle* (1977), an untenured public school teacher sued the school board, alleging that the nonrenewal of his contract was in retaliation for his constitutional exercise of free speech. Among the incidents the school board listed as reasons for not renewing the teacher's contract were his having had arguments with fellow teachers and staff members, making derogatory and obscene comments and gestures to students, and placing a telephone call to a local radio station to discuss the contents of a school district dress code for teachers. Ruling in favor of the board, the Court adopted a burden-shifting test. Under this test, employees must show that their conduct was constitutionally protected and that this conduct was the substantial motivating factor in the employer's decision. If employees satisfy this burden, employers must show that the employees would have been disciplined, such as being dismissed, regardless of whether they engaged in protected activities.

The school board in *Doyle* admitted that the phone call to the radio station was one of the reasons it chose not to renew the teacher's contract. Even so, the Supreme Court asserted that the mere fact that protected speech was used in the employment decision was not enough to warrant the teacher's reinstatement and/or granting an award of back pay. The Court explained that the board would have to demonstrate that it would have recommended the nonrenewal of the teacher's contract anyway, in light of the other incidents. Basically, the Court concluded that employees cannot use a free speech claim to overcome records of unsatisfactory performance justifying employers' adverse employment decision. The Court wrote,

> While a borderline or marginal employee should not have employment decisions weigh against him because of constitutionally protected conduct, that same employee ought not to be able to prevent the employer from reviewing his performance record by adding constitutionally protected conduct to it. (*Doyle.* p. 286)

On remand, the Sixth Circuit accepted the board's argument that it would not have renewed the teacher's contract regardless of whether he had placed the telephone call to the radio talk show.

In another case involving public education, *Givhan v. Western Line Consolidated School District* (1979), the Supreme Court posited that *Pickering* also applies to teachers who express themselves during private conversations with their supervisors. When school officials chose not to renew the contract of a nontenured teacher, she was told that this was partly because she did not get along well with her principal and because she complained about the school board's racially discriminatory employment practices. Although the Supreme Court refused to reinstate the teacher, it reasoned that the lower court was mistaken in finding that the board was justified in not renewing her contract. The Court was of the view that in applying *Pickering,* courts must consider not only the working relationships among employees but also the content of their speech in considering whether private communications are entitled to the protection of the First Amendment.

In *Waters v. Churchill* (1994), a nurse at a public hospital challenged her dismissal after her employers investigated negative comments to a colleague about her supervisor and department. A plurality of the Supreme Court indicated that regarding the regulation of speech, the government may treat its own employees differently than it does private citizens. The Court remarked as follows:

> The government's interest in achieving its goals as effectively and efficiently as possible is elevated from a relatively subordinate interest when it acts as sovereign to a significant one when it acts as employer. The government cannot restrict the speech of the public at large just in the name of efficiency. But where the government is employing someone for the very purpose of effectively achieving its goals, such restrictions may well be appropriate. (*Waters,* p. 675)

Effectively, *Waters* supports the view that even when adverse employment decisions are predicated on government employees' exercises of free speech, the interests of public institutions may outweigh the employees' free speech rights, particularly when the speech can reasonably be forecast to create a substantial disruption or material interference with workplace efficiency. Even when employee speech is on a matter of public concern, the plurality opinion in *Waters* granted the government, as employer, good-faith leeway in evaluating whether the speech is likely to be disruptive to its operations. In other words, *Waters* stands for the proposition that as long as public employers have reasonable beliefs that speech would disrupt their efficient operations, they may punish employees regardless of what they actually said. At the same time, it is important to note that the punishment must be based on the potential disruption and not in retaliation for the speech.

Garcetti v. Ceballos (2006) extends the argument against excessive judicial intrusion into governmental affairs, while emphasizing the role that employees/citizens play when making disputed statements. In *Garcetti,* a deputy district attorney examined an affidavit used to obtain a search warrant in a pending criminal case and determined that it was flawed; as a result, he authored a report outlining the misrepresentations and suggested that the case be dismissed. The prosecutor's office proceeded with the case, despite the recommendation. The attorney then claimed that he was subjected to a series of retaliatory employment decisions in violation of his First Amendment rights.

A closely divided Supreme Court in *Garcetti* disagreed with the employee on the basis that the controlling factor in such a situation was that he made his remarks as part of his regular job responsibilities. The Court held that "when employees make statements pursuant to their official duties, the employees are not speaking as citizens for First Amendment purposes, and the Constitution does not insulate their communications from employer discipline" (p. 1960). The *Garcetti* Court explicitly recognized *Pickering* as good law and reaffirmed that public employees do not lose their status as citizens merely because they are public employees.

Teacher as Educator

The right of school boards to restrict teachers' expression is at its highest when they wear the "educator hat." In this mode, the state is most concerned about the classroom speech of teachers. The Supreme Court case of *Hazelwood School District v. Kuhlmeier*

(1988) governs this part of the balance. In *Hazelwood,* a principal deleted two pages of a school-sponsored newspaper that contained controversial articles written by students as part of a journalism class that was a component in the school's curriculum.

In response to the students' First Amendment free speech claim, the Supreme Court upheld the principal's action, pointing out that school officials may exercise editorial control over the content and style of student speech in school-sponsored activities so long as their decisions are reasonably related to legitimate pedagogical concerns. Important to the outcome in *Hazelwood* was the fact that the Court treated school classrooms and other venues for school-sponsored expressive activities as nonpublic forums. Further, the Court thought it necessary to afford educational administrators broad discretion over school activities and events that bear the school's imprimatur.

There is little question that the *Hazelwood* decision applies beyond student speech to cover teacher speech. For example, a teacher's classroom speech in that nonpublic forum bears the imprimatur of the school. Consequently, school officials may restrict teachers' speech if they can cite legitimate pedagogical concerns for doing so.

In effect, *Hazelwood* helps to answer the larger question of the extent to which K–12 teachers have "academic freedom" in their teaching. In defense of academic freedom, teachers argue that it is their right to teach subject matter within their professional competence and without undue restraints or interference from school administration. Essentially, the teachers' position is that their purpose is to create an atmosphere in which knowledge and ideas may be freely exchanged. In response, school boards maintain that state and federal demands for academic accountability and curricular standards necessarily diminish the academic freedom of teachers. Boards are of the position that essentially, academic freedom is not a right that belongs to individual teachers. With heavy deference to the curricular authority of the state, academic freedom belongs not to individual teachers, but to the institutions that are charged with implementing mandated curriculum. This is not to say that teachers have no freedom to guide the content or style of their teaching.

From a legal perspective, courts have rejected a good number of First Amendment claims filed by teachers, instead upholding a wide range of board decisions, including dismissals, the nonrenewal of contracts, suspensions, reassignments, and reprimands, against teachers who crossed inappropriate lines in classrooms and at other school-sponsored events. In one such case, *Miles v. Denver Public Schools* (1991), the Tenth Circuit upheld the paid suspension of a teacher who used time in a ninth-grade government class to substantiate a rumor about two current students who were allegedly "making out" on a school tennis court. In an effort to apply the *Pickering* standard, the teacher asserted that the topic of the class discussion, the fact that the quality of the school and general society had declined in recent years, was a matter of public concern. However, the court applied *Hazelwood,* reasoning that since the classroom was a nonpublic forum, educational officials had legitimate educational grounds for imposing the suspension, namely, professionalism, ethics, and good judgment. Other examples in which courts upheld disciplinary sanctions that school officials imposed in light of teachers' classroom conduct and speech include discussions of current events at the expense of completing the curriculum; profanity by a teacher; showing R-rated movies that included profanity, sex, nudity, and drug use in violation of board or school policy; biology classes with too much talk of sex; biology and other public school science classes in which a teacher espoused creationism over evolution and allowed and/or used racial slurs.

On a few occasions, courts have ruled in favor of teachers who claimed First Amendment rights to free speech in the classroom. In such cases, it is important for teachers to gain support from their administration and to have strong pedagogical defenses for the curricular decisions they make, such as when a teacher engaged a fifth-grade classroom in a lesson on the industrial uses of hemp (*Cockrel v. Shelby County School District,* 2001) or when a high school teacher required her class to read and discuss *The Adventures of Huckleberry Finn,* despite Mark Twain's use of racially derogatory language (*Monteiro v. Tempe Union High School District,* 1998).

Teacher Privacy

Privacy rights for teachers generally are implicated in two circumstances: searches and seizure and personnel records. Search-and-seizure claims, which typically allege violations of the Fourth Amendment, arise in cases involving searches of classrooms, teachers' personal belongings, and vehicles and in cases involving drug testing policies. Suspicion-based searches of teachers must comport with a twofold reasonableness standard, following the Supreme Court decision in the student search case of *New Jersey v. T. L. O.* (1985): (1) whether the searches were justified at their inception and (2) whether they were reasonable in scope, in light of teachers' privacy expectations, the nature and severity of the alleged infraction, and the seriousness of the contraband that the searches targeted.

Following *O'Connor v. Ortega* (1987), a dispute involving the search of a doctor's locked office at a hospital, it is generally understood that school boards may search teachers' classrooms and other work areas without consent and without suspicion, as there would be little or no expectation of privacy in those areas. Like students' lockers, insofar as teachers' desks and classrooms belong to school boards, they may be searched at any time unless schools adopt policies to the contrary. However, suspicion-based searches of teachers' other property, such as briefcases, backpacks, purses, and cars, is typically held to the reasonable-suspicion standard.

In some circumstances, flowing from two other Supreme Court cases involving public employees, *Skinner v. Railway Labor Executives' Association* (1989) and *National Treasury Employees Union v. Von Raab* (1989), school boards may also adopt suspicion-based urinalysis drug testing policies. Suspicionless searches of teachers, usually in the form of drug-sniffing dogs in parking lots and urinalysis drug tests, are also lawful, just as they are for students. Often, the mandatory drug testing for teachers occurs only as part of the hiring process and later only upon suspicion. Moreover, at least one court has upheld random drug testing of teachers and other school employees who serve in safety-sensitive positions (*Knox County Education Association v. Knox County Board of Education,* 1998).

Similar to the law of search and seizure, the law of personnel records strives to balance individual teachers' rights to privacy with what is good for the whole organization and community. As with search and seizure, privacy is balanced most often with a measure of safety and security. More specifically, the balancing act involving personnel records involves employers' need to use full and valid information for important decision making and the public's right to know about the work of schools, particularly public schools, and their employees.

State and federal open records laws, including the federal Freedom of Information Act (FOIA), allow citizens to access public records and encourage openness in the operation of government agencies. While the FOIA applies only to federal agencies, states have similar laws allowing public access to records of state and local agencies. The definition of *public record* may vary from state to state, but is generally fairly broad.

With respect to personnel information, records usually contain employees' names, age, experiences, qualifications, dates of appointment, current positions, titles, salaries, promotions, suspensions, other changes of positions, and teaching evaluations. Whether any or all of these materials are publicly accessible varies by state. Medical information and other notes and informal materials related to employer decisions concerning individual employees are not accessible by the public.

As to privacy, generally, personnel information that would subject individuals to embarrassment, harassment, disgrace, or loss of employment is not subject to disclosure laws. When personnel records are deemed not to be public records, there may still be exceptions in which disclosure is determined to be in the public's best interest. Examples permitting disclosure include court orders and national security. Readers are strongly encouraged to check their state's statutes for the applicable definitions of *public record* and *personnel record.*

Due Process

Under the Fifth (as applied to the federal government) and Fourteenth Amendments, the government shall not deprive persons of life, liberty, or property without due process of law. For public school boards and public institutions of higher learning, which are regulated largely under state law, the Fourteenth Amendment applies. To make a successful due process claim against their boards, employees must show that they were deprived of one or more of these rights. When school boards make adverse employment decisions that impact their staff, such as when their contracts are not renewed or terminated or they are suspended, their actions particularly implicate persons' liberty and/or property interests. For schoolteachers and other staff, liberty interests include their reputations, good name, honor, standing in their communities, and opportunities to seek and obtain employment. Property interests are manifested in the provisions of persons' existing contracts, such as for salary and other benefits and/or legitimate claims or entitlements to continued employment.

Two leading Supreme Court decisions from the early 1970s illustrate the application of these principles. In *Board of Regents v. Roth* (1972), a nontenured college instructor sued his former employer after his 1-year contract was not renewed because he allegedly made statements critical of the university administration. In his suit, the instructor claimed that the university violated his rights to free speech and due process. On further review of judgments in favor of the instructor, the Supreme Court reversed in favor of the university, holding that individuals whose term contracts are not renewed have no legitimate claim or entitlement to continued employment. In effect, the Court pointed out that the instructor's property rights in the contract that was not renewed had expired. As such, the Court explained that absent evidence of a statute, contract, or institutional policy granting such rights, property rights will not extend beyond the terms of the contract under consideration. Similarly, the Court was of the opinion that the instructor was not deprived of liberty interests as there were no facts indicating that university officials acted in retaliation for the negative comments that he had made. The Court concluded that since there was no evidence that the instructor had lost his reputation or an opportunity to seek new employment, his claim should have been denied.

The facts of *Perry v. Sindermann* (1972) are similar to those in *Roth. Sindermann* involved a nontenured university employee who, while working under 1-year contracts, did not have his contract renewed after a year in which he made negative remarks about the state board of regents. However, the fact that there were significant differences between the two cases led to a different result such that the plaintiff in *Sindermann* prevailed in his claim. First, the Supreme Court acknowledged that the instructor was a 10-year employee in the state university system, most recently having worked under four successive 1-year contracts at another college. Second, the Court pointed out that the college's faculty handbook stated that faculty should "feel tenured" as long as their work is satisfactory and they have a positive attitude. In light of the plaintiff's longevity in the state college system and the guidelines in his college's faculty handbook, the Court decided that his lack of tenure did not defeat his due process claim. In fact, the Court thought that the college's policies and practices dictated that he receive some form of due process in advance of the nonrenewal of his contract.

Basically, *Roth* and *Sindermann* set up a due process inquiry that answers two questions. The first inquiry asks whether Fourteenth Amendment due process rights of life, liberty, and/or property are implicated when employers make decisions as to whether to dismiss, not renew the contracts of, suspend, or reprimand employees. According to the second inquiry, if the answer to the first is "yes," then the next question is what process is due. If the answer to the first question is "yes," then two types of due process must be afforded, procedural and substantive. Ultimately, any due process inquiry requires a balance of rights of the affected parties. On one hand, there are the employees' constitutional rights to life, liberty, and property. On the other hand, individual constitutional rights are not unlimited; courts must consider employers' interests in a safe, orderly, professional atmosphere with competent, satisfactory employees. Both procedural and substantive due process seek to strike an equitable balance between the rights of employees and employers while avoiding the risk of erroneous deprivations of rights.

Substantive due process asks whether an educational employer's exercise of authority was fair, reasonable, and appropriate in light of its power and the rights of the individual(s) under the circumstances.

Substantive due process checks governmental actors for abuse of discretion and/or arbitrary or capricious behaviors. No one doubts the authority that school boards have to enact and enforce reasonable rules and regulations for the management and operation of schools. However, substantive due process reinforces the notion that such authority is not without limits. At the same time, substantive due process is not meant to diminish rule-making and policy-making functions of schools. Rather, it is intended to curb abuses of power.

The purpose of procedural due process is to prevent governmental actors from depriving employees of life, liberty, or property without affording them an opportunity to contest the decision and to offer their side of the story. Usually spelled out in contracts, institutional policies, and statutes, procedural due process requires notice and an opportunity to be heard. The amount of due process that must be afforded varies from circumstance to circumstance, depending on the level of severity and deprivation. For example, in cases of teacher dismissal, individuals' due process rights would be higher than they are in cases of nonrenewal, suspension, or written reprimands. For written reprimands, the due process afforded is typically an opportunity for teachers to read them and offer written rebuttals, which are also to be placed in their personnel files. Under this circumstance, a formal hearing would follow. Due process for teacher suspensions varies by contract and depends on whether they are paid (no property interest affected) or unpaid (property interest affected). As *Roth* indicates, the nonrenewal of an individual's contract does not implicate property or liberty interests under the Fourteenth Amendment. To this end, individuals need to check their contracts, often collectively bargained via union processes, or state statutes. In several states, teachers whose contracts are not renewed are permitted to seek written statement of why their boards acted as they did and may request formal hearings to contest the decisions.

In cases where the contracts of tenured teachers are terminated and as reflected by the Supreme Court in *Cleveland Board of Education v. Loudermill* (1985), property and liberty interests are most assuredly affected, since existing contracts are being terminated before they expire. It is important to note that since tenured teachers have substantive due process property rights in their jobs, they are entitled to procedural due process; subject to state law and collective bargaining agreements, nontenured teachers typically do not have these rights. In such cases, procedural due process is at its most formal, lengthy, and costly. The procedural rights to notice and an opportunity to be heard often bring with them additional rights to be represented by counsel, to present evidence and subpoena witnesses, to cross-examine witnesses, and to appeal decisions.

Hearings that are conducted pursuant to procedural due process mandates vary in their formality but most often take place at local levels initially. Very rarely do teachers' due process claims go directly to a court. The idea is to keep the conflicts local and as simple and streamlined as possible. Only after at least one administrative hearing is there a right to judicial review. If teachers are ultimately successful in their claims against their school boards, they usually receive reinstatement (in case of nonrenewal or dismissal) and back pay (in cases where salary and benefits were cut or suspended unlawfully).

Discrimination and Harassment

Both state and federal law recognize several protected classes that grant individuals who have allegedly suffered illegal discrimination opportunities to seek redress from their employers, usually in the form of reinstatement (in cases of wrongful dismissal, nonrenewal, or demotion) and back pay (in cases where salary and benefits were suspended or terminated). Discrimination claims from teachers and applicants for teaching positions may arise on the basis of race, national origin, sex, sexual orientation, disability, religion, and age. With one exception, each of these classes is protected under state and federal law. Sexual orientation discrimination is not yet recognized under federal law, but it is in several cities, states, and individual school board policies. Insofar as many states' laws are patterned after federal laws, the present discussion is limited primarily to federal law.

Federal antidiscrimination laws can be divided into two broad categories: those prohibiting discrimination in employment and those prohibiting discrimination in programs or institutions receiving federal financial

assistance. The employment laws include Title VII of the Civil Rights Act of 1964, which prohibits discrimination on the bases of race, color, religion, sex, or national origin; the Age Discrimination in Employment Act (ADEA), which forbids discrimination against people 40 years of age or older; the Americans with Disabilities Act (ADA), which outlaws discrimination on the basis of disabilities in both employment settings and in public accommodations; and the Family and Medical Leave Act (FMLA), which allows employees extended leave for personal and family medical needs.

Federal antidiscrimination laws that target decisions made by entities receiving federal financial assistance include Section 504 of the Rehabilitation Act of 1973, which prohibits discrimination on the basis of disability; Title IX of the Educational Amendments of 1972, which forbids sex discrimination in educational settings; the Equal Pay Act of 1963, which outlaws wage discrimination on the basis of sex; and Title VI of the Civil Rights Act of 1964, which prohibits discrimination on the basis of race, color, or national origin.

Plaintiffs who file employment discrimination suits, either as applicants or as current employees, must typically show that they belong to a "protected class," meaning that they fit within a category of people protected by one or more law; that they were denied a benefit, such as a job, promotion, bonus, salary raise, or coaching contract, on the basis of membership in that category; that they were qualified for the benefit; and that someone outside of the protected class received the benefit. If plaintiffs succeed in stating claims, then employers can prevail if they can show nondiscriminatory reasons for their actions as long as they are not mere pretexts for discrimination. Successful defenses include, but are not limited to, offering the benefit to more qualified persons, reducing the workforce due to declining enrollment or poor financial circumstances, denying benefits due to poor work performance or violations of law or employer rules, rejecting job applicants for failure to meet substantive or procedural application requirements, and declining to make accommodations in cases involving disability or religion where doing so would cause undue hardship to employers.

Plaintiffs filing discrimination suits may claim that they have experienced (a) disparate impact by using evidence, such as statistics, from which judges or juries can infer discrimination or (b) disparate treatment by demonstrating employers' intent to discriminate. Sex discrimination, for example, can include discrimination on the basis of parental status, marital status, pregnancy, or sexual stereotyping, such as gender-based identity or expression.

Employers should be careful when they conduct job interviews so as not to discriminate against applicants. Interviewers may ask about former employment, motivation to work, job stability, initiative and innovation, ability to work with others, self-evaluation, and past accomplishments in academic and professional life. However, interviewers may not ask questions about parental status, marital status, child care issues, church attendance, religious affiliation (except a bona fide occupational qualification for a position in a religiously affiliated school), nationality, age, date of birth, or the nature or severity of disabilities. While employers cannot ask applicants about their disabilities, employees who need or wish to receive accommodations for their disabilities must provide such information.

Under Section 504 and ADA, employers are required to provide reasonable accommodations, such as physical accessibility, job restructuring, modified work schedules, reassignment to a vacant position, and provision of readers or interpreters, unless they would cause undue financial or administrative hardships on the employer. Even with these accommodations, though, employees must still be able to perform the essential functions of the job. Similarly, employers are required to offer reasonable accommodations for the religious beliefs and practices of their employees. Some limits may be placed on religious accommodation, such as imposing a maximum number of days of religious leave per academic year.

Most federal antidiscrimination laws, Title VI, Title VII, Section 504, and Title IX, apply not only in cases of employment discrimination but also in cases of alleged harassment. Harassment claims are most common in cases of alleged sexual harassment. Yet harassment on the basis of race, ethnicity, religion, and disability is also recognized. The standard of liability for the harassment varies, depending on the statute used. Under Title VII, victims of harassment can recover both compensatory and punitive damages, but employers are usually liable only in cases where there were tangible employment actions, such as dismissals or demotions. In cases lacking tangible employment actions, employers may show that they have policies against harassment, that they took actions to respond to known harassment, and that the alleged victims unreasonably failed to take advantage of the policy. Under Title VI (racial or national origin harassment) and Section 504 (harassment based on disability), the standard of liability is essentially the same. If educational employers act with deliberate indifference to known harassment, they are likely to be liable for damages under Title IX in cases in which employees have sexually harassed students. News stories abound involving school personnel as perpetrators of harassment, along with similar reports of students as perpetrators and victims. Even so, there is certainly an unfortunate prevalence of cases in which school personnel are victims under Title VII.

Patrick D. Pauken

See also Academic Freedom; Age Discrimination in Employment Act; *Board of Regents v. Roth;* Civil Rights Act of 1964; Collective Bargaining; *Connick v. Myers;* Due Process; Equal Employment Opportunity Commission; Equal Pay Act; Family and Medical Leave Act; *Hazelwood School District v. Kuhlmeier;* Highly Qualified Teachers; *Mt. Healthy City Board of Education v. Doyle; Perry v. Sindermann; Pickering v. Board of Education of Township High School District 205, Will County;* Reduction in Force; Sexual Harassment; Tenure; *Tinker v. Des Moines Independent Community School District;* Title VII

Further Readings

Mawdsley, R. D. (2006). Employee rights. In C. J. Russo (Ed.), *Key legal issues for schools: The ultimate resource for school business officials* (pp. 113–134). Lanham, MD: Rowman & Littlefield.

Legal Citations

Age Discrimination in Employment Act, 29 U.S.C. §§ 621 *et seq.*
Board of Regents v. Roth, 408 U.S. 564 (1972).

Civil Rights Act of 1964, 42 U.S.C. §§ 1971 *et seq.*

Cleveland Board of Education v. Loudermill, 470 U.S. 532 (1985), *on remand*, 763 F.2d 202 (6th Cir.1985), *on remand*, 651 F. Supp. 92 (N.D. Ohio 1986), *aff'd*, 844 F.2d 304 (6th Cir.1988), *cert. denied*, 488 U.S. 941 (1988), *cert. denied*, 488 U.S. 946 (1988).

Cockrel v. Shelby County School District, 270 F.3d 1036 (6th Cir. 2001).

Connick v. Myers, 461 U.S. 138 (1983).

Doyle v. Mt. Healthy City School District Board of Education, 670 F.2d 59 (6th Cir. 1982).

Equal Pay Act, 29 U.S.C. § 206(d).

Family and Medical Leave Act, 29 U.S.C. §§ 2601 *et seq.*

Freedom of Information Act, 5 U.S.C. § 552.

Garcetti v. Ceballos, 547 U.S. 410 (2006).

Givhan v. Western Line Consolidated School District, 439 U.S. 410 (1979).

Hazelwood School District v. Kuhlmeier, 484 U.S. 260 (1988).

Individuals with Disabilities Education Act, 20 U.S.C. §§ 1400 *et seq.*

Knox County Education Association v. Knox County Board of Education, 158 F.3d 361 (6th Cir. 1998).

Miles v. Denver Public Schools, 944 F.2d 773 (10th Cir. 1991).

Monteiro v. Tempe Union High School District, 158 F.3d 1022 (9th Cir. 1998).

Mt. Healthy City Board of Education v. Doyle, 429 U.S. 274 (1977).

National Treasury Employees Union v. Von Raab, 489 U.S. 656 (1989).

New Jersey v. T. L. O., 469 U.S. 325 (1985).

O'Connor v. Ortega, 480 U.S. 709 (1987).

Perry v. Sindermann, 408 U.S. 593 (1972).

Pickering v. Board of Education of Township High School District 205, Will County, 391 U.S. 563 (1968).

Rehabilitation Act of 1973, Section 504, 29 U.S.C. § 794(a).

Skinner v. Railway Labor Executives Association, 489 U.S. 602 (1989).

Title VI of the Civil Rights Act of 1964, 42 U.S.C. § 2000d.

Title VII of the Civil Rights Act of 1964, 42 U.S.C. § 2000e.

Title IX of the Educational Amendments of 1972, 20 U.S.C. § 1681.

Waters v. Churchill, 511 U.S. 661 (1994).

TECHNOLOGY AND THE LAW

Supreme Court justices argued more than a century ago that the progress of science, especially in the area of communication technology, made it imperative that America's attention shift to the spirit of the law to protect individuals against the privacy invasions of modern inventions. The technological landscape continues to change at a much faster pace than constitutional law, which has yet to deal efficiently with the latest scientific advances in sophisticated devices and computer communications using telephone or cable lines.

Most federal court judgments have been inconsistent during the growth in telecommunications technology. Many of the subsequent instruments of tele- communication networks, such as facsimile transmissions (or faxes) and electronic mail (e-mail), are based on the telephone and make use of the same underground cables, digital lines, radios, and satellite links to make connections between two or more users. The police and public have used telephones long enough to allow the development of a sizable body of legal code and case law. A discussion of communication technology, information technology, and related legislation follows.

Fax Communications

Facsimile communications are similar to other forms of protected wire communications in that they consist of digital signals transmitted over a traditional wired network. Facsimile transmissions, whether sent from computer to computer or fax machine to fax machine, run the risks of inadvertent misdialing and misdirection due to human error. Despite the absence of absolute security, a properly directed and received fax has the convenience of almost instant correspondence and provides the parties involved with a tangible paper record of every transaction and instance of communication. The case law on fax communications is meager on both state and federal court levels.

Electronic Mail Communication

E-mail presents the judiciary and lawmakers with a difficult area since it falls between a telephone communication and a written correspondence via postal mail. E-mail resembles telephone calls because it consists of intangible electronic signals traveling through wire systems and resembles first-class letters in that the data in the transmission contain nonvocal textual messages. Yet while e-mail is a cross between both, it is afforded the privacy protection of neither against government interception and acquisition. A revolution in telecommunications, e-mail allows computer users to send messages and data files across the country or the globe almost instantly and to keep an accurate and permanent record of this exchange for later reference on both the sender's and recipient's computers.

Like postal mail, every e-mail message is directed to a uniquely identifiable address and delivered to a password-protected electronic mailbox, where unread messages await the user to access the mailbox and open them. The development of e-mail, chat rooms, listservs, newsgroups, and instant messaging constitute even greater challenges to governments because these communications may be used for illicit or illegitimate purposes. Detection and prevention of these activities entails invading the privacy of the users by accessing and sometimes monitoring their e-mails.

Legislation Governing Copied Materials

The Copyright Act and "Fair Use"

As copiers became commonplace during the 1970s, articles, poems, and book excerpts were reproduced without legal repercussions. Widespread use of copying machines bred violations of copyright laws. In January 1976, Congress amended the original 1909 copyright laws by passing the Copyright Act, which includes photocopying and the educational use of copyrighted materials. Congress has subsequently modified this law by relying on testimony from librarians, publishers, authors, and educators in developing "fair use" guidelines, which allow the use of copyrighted materials without permission from the author under specific, limited conditions. Under the fair use principle, single copies of printed materials may be copied for the educator's personal use. No longer can materials be freely reproduced and distributed; the publisher or author of the work must grant permission and may charge a royalty fee for the material's use.

Copying for Educational Use

Videotapes, DVDs, computer software, and mixed media fall within the fair use guidelines of the copyright laws. Without a license or permission, educational institutions may not keep copyrighted videotapes and recordings for more than 45 days. The tape should not be shown more than once during this period, and then it must be erased.

Copyright and the Internet

Copyright issues involving the Internet have become an important concern as copyright holders have taken action to prohibit the unauthorized use of their materials on the World Wide Web and other platforms. The entertainment and software industries have worked with federal legislators to develop statutory protection that levies hefty penalties for possessing or distributing illegal electronic copies. The growing use of computers prompted Congress to amend the Copyright Act in 1998 and pass the Digital Millennium Copyright Act to protect materials published on the World Wide Web and allow copyright owners to prevent the downloading of their material without permission and a fee. Text, graphics, multimedia materials, and e-mail are protected by copyright laws and fair use guidelines must be applied when using information obtained.

The Future of Technology Law

In light of the vital role that the computer, the Internet and e-mail play in our society, a reinterpretation of various constitutional amendments and perhaps a new subfield of information technology law will develop. The keys to this new legal world may ultimately lie in the hands of the U.S. Supreme Court, which must strike the balance between promoting technology and protecting society. In developing this new body of law, the courts must remember that liberty, as a constitutional right, brought this country thus far and continues to propel it forward.

Doris G. Johnson

See also Copyright; Electronic Communication

Further Readings

Guirguis, M. (2003, December). Electronic mail surveillance and the reasonable expectation of privacy. *Journal of Technology Law & Policy, 8,* 135–145.

Sadker, D. M., Sadker, M. P., & Zittleman, K. R. (2005). *Teachers, schools, and society.* New, York: McGraw-Hill.

Legal Citations

Copyright Act, 17 U.S.C. §§ 101 *et seq.*
Digital Millennium Copyright Act, 17 U.S.C. § 512.

TENTH AMENDMENT

See FEDERALISM AND THE TENTH AMENDMENT

TENURE

Tenure provides educators with protection from dismissal due to arbitrary and capricious political and administrative actions. Educators are free to express their views in written and verbal commentary. The Association of University Professors (AAUP) as well as federal courts have emphasized the importance of academic freedom in a democracy. The concept of tenure has a long history, representing efforts to protect educators from job insecurity resulting from their verbal or written work. This entry reviews the origins of tenure, its evolution in the United States through the work of the AAUP, and its elaboration in U.S. Supreme Court rulings over the years. It also describes the function of tenure in various educational settings today, where it plays a central role in protecting academic freedom.

Tenure grants teachers and faculty protection from unfair dismissal. In 1245, Pope Innocent the IV granted exemptions to scholars in the University of Paris from appearing at ecclesiastical courts some distance from Paris. The following year, a Court of Conservation was founded to protect university faculty. Over time, universities were given autonomy from local, civil, and ecclesiastical officials. There were some limits to these protections when attacks were made on the prevalent dogma or authoritarianism, but the concept of autonomy provided insulation from excessive political encroachment. In the 1890s, Germany sought student protection through *Lernfreiheit,* or the freedom of university students to choose courses, move from school to school, and be free of dogmatic restrictions. Similarly, *Lehrfreiheit* stressed faculty rights to freedom of inquiry and freedom of teaching with the right to report on findings in an unhindered, unrestricted, and unfettered environment.

Through the founding of the American Association of University Professors (AAUP) in 1915, John Dewey and others sought to protect academics from interference with their employment by external persons or groups. During the early part of the 20th century, faculty members were often dismissed for offending powerful individuals or groups. Such political interference was frequent, and teachers had no recourse against unreasonable interference with their professional responsibilities.

In 1940, the AAUP issued a Statement of the Principles on Academic Freedom and Tenure. The principles included assumptions that tenure is a means toward freedom in teaching and research as well as in extracurricular activities. Tenure is important in recruiting and retaining qualified men and women in the teaching profession. Freedom and economic security were found to be indispensable to the success of an institution in meeting its professional obligations to students and society.

Thirty years later, in 1970, a committee of the AAUP and Association of American Colleges noted that the 1940 statement was not a static code, but rather a framework guiding future changes in the social, political, and economic climate. They noted that in *Keyishian v. Board of Regents* (1967), the Supreme Court reiterated that the United States is committed to safeguarding academic freedom to all citizens, not just teachers. That freedom is especially supported by the First Amendment. The AAUP uses censorship of institutions to encourage adherence to tenure and academic freedom guidelines.

In *Board of Regents v. Roth* (1972), the Supreme Court held that liberty and property rights are created by contract or state law and constitutionally protected. To acquire that protection, teachers are required to serve for a set period of time, often 4 years, before becoming permanent employees. During the probationary period, employees are not entitled to employment property rights. In *Perry v. Sindermann* (1972), the Court held that procedural due process safeguards are required for teachers who have a property or liberty interest in employment. Pretenure employees under probationary contracts do not have due process rights. States have different tenure provisions, but generally if there is a reduction in force, tenured faculty are dismissed last.

As citizens, educators have the freedom to express their beliefs and opinions and to engage in controversial debate and inquiry. However, they have obligations and responsibilities to be professional and ethical in their work, and tenure does not protect them if they fail to meet these requirements. They are also cautioned by AAUP guidelines to avoid persistent introduction of material that has no relation to the subject they are teaching. As noted in the 1915 AAUP Statement of Principles, when speaking as private citizens, educators have an obligation to inform listeners that they are not speaking as representatives of their educational institutions. This is sometimes difficult in teaching the humanities, where encouraging students to engage in critical inquiry often entails examining assumptions underlying policy decisions. Peer review has been used in recent years to ensure that faculty members are productive and current in their academic fields. Critics of tenure note that this may make it difficult to dismiss faculty members who are incompetent, nonproductive, underprepared, or not up to date in their fields. The enforcement of tenure is a function of individual schools and universities. Major institutions maintain administrative policies to ensure that faculty tenure rights are secure and followed throughout the organization.

Generally, administrators are not granted tenure. Although tenure is becoming less frequent in K–12 institutions, it is usually upheld in universities as a recruiting tool and for retention of top-flight productive scholars. Nontenured faculty who have continuing contracts for a length of time, generally 4 to 7 years, have certain property rights to employment but generally cannot receive de facto tenure absent an affirmative action by educational officials.

Tenure is a work in progress in distance learning institutions as the Internet involves new and emerging tools for teaching. Ethical codes for the use of the Internet are being developed and updated as technology advances. In recent years, there has been an increase in the number of contingency faculty without tenure protection. Since a growing percentage of faculty are contingency and/or part-time adjuncts, efforts are being made to include them in essential tenure protections. Indeed, the number of contingency (e.g., part-time and full-load nontenured faculty) exceeds the number of full-time tenured faculty. This may be a challenge for the future.

In *Sweezy v. New Hampshire* (1957), the Supreme Court noted the importance of tenure in academic freedom:

> The essentiality of freedom in the community of American universities is almost self-evident. . . . To impose any strait jacket upon the intellectual leaders in our colleges and universities would imperil the future of our Nation. No field of education is so thoroughly comprehended by man that new discoveries cannot yet be made. Particularly is that true in the social sciences, where few, if any, principles are accepted as absolutes. Scholarship cannot flourish in an atmosphere of suspicion and distrust. Teachers and students must always remain free to inquire, to study, to evaluate, to gain new maturity and understanding; otherwise, our civilization will stagnate and die. (p. 250)

This point has been reiterated by succeeding Supreme Court rulings through the years.

James Van Patten

See also *Board of Regents v. Roth; Keyishian v. Board of Regents; Perry v. Sindermann*

Legal Citations

Board of Regents v. Roth, 408 U.S. 564 (1972).
Keyishian v. Board of Regents, 385 U.S. 589 (1967).
Perry v. Sindermann, 408 U.S 593 (1972).
Sweezy v. New Hampshire, 354 U.S. 234 (1957).

TESTING, HIGH-STAKES

Generally, high-stakes tests are any measures whereby the results have important consequences for test takers and/or their schools. The prevalence of high-stakes tests has greatly increased since they were first used on a large scale during World War I to assign incoming soldiers to their duties. During the 1950s, colleges began widely using the Scholastic Aptitude Test (SAT) as an admissions test, a trend that currently leads almost all college-bound students to take it or other standardized measures, such as the American College Testing (ACT) examination. In addition, many states have recently developed high school exit examinations that prospective graduates must pass in order to receive their diplomas. Tests of this type are given in 22 states, in which 65% of the nation's student populations reside.

Legal challenges have not slowed the diffusion of high-stakes tests. As such, case law has shaped the way that high school exit examinations in particular are administered. The seminal case on the topic is *Debra P. v. Turlington* (1984), in which students in Florida brought a federal class action suit against the state for withholding diplomas from students who failed the test. On review, the Eleventh Circuit, following several rounds of litigation, held that tests can be used only if state officials can conclusively prove that they cover only material that was taught in the classrooms, that they are valid, and that students had received sufficient notice that they would have to take such examinations. Moreover, in acknowledging the higher failure rates of minorities than of nonminorities, the court instructed that the tests can be used only if officials can prove that their racially discriminatory impact was not due to the remnants of past segregation. As to notice, the court was of the opinion that students had to be given ample time to prepare themselves for the examinations.

In later cases, students with disabilities and those who were educated under unconstitutional tracking systems successfully challenged exit examination requirements as a prerequisite for receiving diplomas. A trilogy of cases from Texas demonstrates the nature of ongoing controversy with regard to graduation tests. On one hand, a federal and state court, respectively, agreed that tests could be used (*Williams v. Austin Independent School District,* 1992; *Edgewood Independent School District v. Paiz,* 1993). However, another federal trial court disagreed insofar as it allowed students who passed all of their required

courses but failed the state's competency test to participate in graduation ceremonies, on the basis that school officials could not impose new criteria on them without providing adequate notice and demonstrating that the examinations were sufficiently linked to the curriculum (*Crump v. Gilmer Independent School District,* 1992). At the same time, though, while the court granted the students' request for a preliminary injunction that enabled them to participate in the ceremony, it refused to direct educators to grant them their diplomas.

Successful litigation in opposition to high-stakes tests has pursued claims based on substantive and procedural due process violations. This has forced states and school officials to make adjustments in the implementation or designs of tests, but it has not foreclosed the legality of tests in their entirety. Courts have been willing to review state educational policies using a rational basis test that gives states wide discretion in its actions. Thus, states can proceed with policies that emphasize high-stakes tests as long as they satisfy students' procedural and substantive due process rights. Further, insofar as the Supreme Court refused to recognize education as a fundamental right in *San Antonio Independent School District v. Rodriguez* (1973), thereby meaning that it is unlikely to apply strict judicial scrutiny in challenges to testing, states and school systems will probably be able to continue to use high-stakes testing.

The enactment of the No Child Left Behind Act (NCLB) (2002) ushered in a new dimension in an era of increasing emphasis on high-stakes testing. Under the act's "adequate yearly progress" provisions, students must be tested every year in Grades 3 through 8 and once in 10th or 11th grade. This provision sets penalties, which include closing schools and dismissing staff members, for school systems that fail to improve test scores sufficiently. While it is certainly questionable whether states can, or will, impose such draconian measures, the NCLB gives a new meaning to high-stakes testing. Thus, although test scores, whether under state measures or the NCLB, are not always used as a basis for student promotions, the results of examinations create high stakes for teachers and administrators.

Gadeir Abbas

See also Adequate Yearly Progress; Equal Protection Analysis; No Child Left Behind Act; *San Antonio Independent School District v. Rodriguez*

Legal Citations

Crump v. Gilmer Independent School District, 797 F. Supp. 552 (E.D. Tex. 1992).

Debra P. v. Turlington, 730 F.2d 1405 (11th Cir. 1984).

Edgewood Independent School District v. Paiz, 856 S.W.2d 269 (Tex. Ct. App. 1993).

No Child Left Behind Act, 20 U.S.C. §§ 6301 *et seq.*

San Antonio Independent School District v. Rodriguez, 411 U.S. 1 (1973).

Williams v. Austin Independent School District, 796 F. Supp. 251 (W.D. Tex. 1992).

THOMAS, CLARENCE (1948–)

Clarence Thomas, who currently serves as an associate justice on the U.S. Supreme Court, is only the second African American to sit on the Court. Thomas is viewed as one of the most conservative members of the Court. This entry reviews his early life and career, his judicial appointments, and his record on the high court.

Early Years

Had someone suggested during his childhood that Clarence Thomas would one day sit on the U.S. Supreme Court, the idea would have seemed utterly absurd. Thomas was born in the segregated South in 1948, in a tiny, poor community of South Georgia known as Pin Point. His father deserted the family when Thomas was a small boy. When he was 6 years old, his family's house burned down, and his mother sent him to live in more comfortable circumstances with his grandfather in Savannah. Thomas attended Catholic schools and helped his grandfather with his business.

After high school, Thomas attended the Immaculate Conception Seminary in Missouri. After 2 years in seminary, he transferred to Holy Cross College, a small Catholic college in Massachusetts. During these tumultuous times, when American society was divided by the civil rights movement and the war in Vietnam, Thomas absorbed some of the ambient radicalism. He also grew disillusioned with Catholicism. After graduating cum laude from Holy Cross College, Thomas attended Yale Law School. He graduated from Yale in 1974.

Thomas began his legal career as an assistant attorney general for the State of Missouri. Three years later, Thomas joined the legal department of the Monsanto Corporation. He returned to government service in 1979, working for 2 years as a legislative assistant to Missouri Senator John C. Danforth. From there, Thomas rose rapidly through the ranks of the federal government. Thomas obtained an appointment as an assistant secretary for civil rights in the United States Department of Education. From 1982 to 1990, Thomas served as the chairman of the U.S. Equal Employment Opportunity Commission.

On the Bench

In 1990, President George H. W. Bush nominated Thomas to a federal appellate judgeship for the District of Columbia Circuit. One year later, President Bush nominated him to the U.S. Supreme Court, to fill the seat vacated by Justice Thurgood Marshall. At the time, Thomas was only 43 years old. His confirmation hearings were among the most bitter and hotly contested of any in history. A focal point of controversy involved the allegations from a former coworker, Anita Hill, that Thomas had sexually harassed her. Thomas vehemently denied these allegations and was narrowly confirmed in the Senate by a vote of 52 to 48.

Thomas returned to Roman Catholicism after his appointment to the Court. He married twice, the second time to Virginia Lamp, in 1987. He has one child from his first marriage.

Supreme Court Record

Justice Thomas has been a consistent vote on the Court's conservative wing. Thomas is often described as an originalist, someone who interprets the words of the Constitution as they were understood when it was originally drafted.

Another noteworthy feature of Justice Thomas's views is his skepticism of the doctrine of stare decisis, the practice of deferring to past decisions. In Justice Thomas's view, no matter how established a decision has become, if the decision is wrong, it must be corrected. In contrast, proponents of stare decisis take the view that stability in the law should be preserved, even if the decisions are flawed in some respect.

On the divisive issues of affirmative action and racial preferences, Justice Thomas has consistently voted to strike down such measures as unconstitutional. For example, in *Adarand Constructors v. Pena* (1995), the Court held that preferences for racial minorities in federal contracts would be reviewed under the demanding "strict scrutiny" test. The high bar of the "strict scrutiny" test means that in practice, it is very difficult to implement such programs. Justice Thomas agreed with the majority view but wrote separately to emphasize the following:

> Good intentions cannot provide refuge from the principle that under our Constitution, the government may not make distinctions on the basis of race. As far as the Constitution is concerned, it is irrelevant whether a government's racial classifications are drawn by those who wish to oppress a race or by those who have a sincere desire to help those thought to be disadvantaged. (p. 240)

Justice Thomas's views have subjected him to withering criticism, particularly from within the African American community.

With respect to specific constitutional provisions, Justice Thomas has taken a broad view of the First Amendment's Free Speech Clause. For example, in *McIntyre v. Ohio Elections Commission* (1995), Thomas concluded that a law banning anonymous campaign literature was unconstitutional. Thomas observed that the *Federalist Papers,* which were written by several founding fathers in defense of the federal Constitution, were published anonymously.

On the controversial issue of abortion, Justice Thomas has consistently opposed a federal constitutional right to an abortion. This is unsurprising, given Thomas's historical reading of the Constitution and his conclusion that established precedent is not necessarily entitled to deference.

Justice Thomas has also taken a narrow reading of the Commerce Clause, found in Article I, Section 8, which provides the authority for Congress "to regulate Commerce with foreign Nations, and among the several States, and with the Indian Tribes." Because the federal government is a government of limited powers, it must find authority within the Constitution to justify its actions. The Commerce Clause has been interpreted to authorize a wide range of activity by the federal government. Justice Thomas's narrow reading of that clause would curtail the scope of activities permitted to the federal government under the Constitution.

Another noteworthy aspect of Justice Thomas's presence on the Court is that he seldom asks questions during oral argument. Thomas has said that he learns more from listening than from interrupting.

Stephen R. McCullough

See also Affirmative Action; Rehnquist Court; Stare Decisis

Further Readings

Foskett K. (2004). *Judging Thomas: The life and times of Clarence Thomas.* New York: HarperCollins.

Gerber, S. D. (2002). *First principles: The jurisprudence of Clarence Thomas.* New York: New York University Press.

Thomas, A. P. (2001). *Clarence Thomas: A biography.* San Francisco: Encounter Books.

Legal Citations

Adarand Constructors v. Pena, 515 U. S. 200 (1995).

McIntyre v. Ohio Elections Commission, 514 U.S. 334 (1995).

THOROUGH AND EFFICIENT SYSTEMS OF EDUCATION

The term *thorough and efficient systems of education* refers to a standard of educational quality that is mandated by some, but not all, state constitutions. This term, along with similar ones, such as *thorough and uniform* and *thorough and efficient,* are key elements in school finance litigation. Specifically, courts must determine whether educational finance systems created by state legislatures provide sufficient funds to achieve the constitutionally mandated quality standard.

State constitutions contain "education clauses" mandating the establishment of free public education. Even so, the level of the duty imposed by these clauses varies a great deal. Although Grubb (1974) and Ratner (1985), working independently, recognized that the education clauses could be divided into four categories based on their language, Thro (1989) suggested the differences between education clauses are significant for school finance litigation. There are four categories of state education clauses.

First, at one end of the spectrum, are the 21 "establishment provisions" that simply mandate that a free public school system be established. These include the provisions in the constitutions of Alabama, Alaska, Arizona, Connecticut, Hawaii, Kansas, Louisiana, Massachusetts, Michigan, Mississippi, Missouri, Nebraska, New Hampshire, New Mexico, New York, North Carolina, Oklahoma, South Carolina, Tennessee, Utah, and Vermont. A typical example of an establishment provision clause is Tennessee's, which provides as follows: "The General Assembly shall provide for the maintenance, support and eligibility standards of a system of free public schools" (Tennessee Constitution, Article XI, § 12).

Second, there are 18 "quality provisions" mandating that educational systems of a specific quality be provided. These include the provisions from Arkansas, Colorado, Delaware, Idaho, Kentucky, Maryland, Minnesota, Montana, New Jersey, North Dakota, Ohio, Oregon, Pennsylvania, Texas, Virginia, West Virginia, Wisconsin, and Wyoming. A typical example is the Pennsylvania education clause that provides as follows: "The General Assembly shall provide for the maintenance and support of a thorough and efficient system of public education to serve the needs of the Commonwealth" (Pennsylvania Constitution, Article III, § 14). Generally, the specific quality is "thorough and/or efficient." As the West Virginia Supreme Court observed, Illinois, Maryland, Minnesota, New Jersey, Ohio, and Pennsylvania require "thorough and efficient" systems; Colorado, Idaho, and Montana require "thorough" systems; and Arkansas, Delaware, Kentucky, and Texas require "efficient" systems.

Third, there are six "strong mandate" provisions that establish a level of quality and that also provide a strong mandate to achieve it. These include California, Indiana, Iowa, Nevada, Rhode Island, and South Dakota. A typical example of both the purposive preamble and the stronger and more specific educational mandate is provided by the provisions of the California Constitution, which reads as follows:

A general diffusion of knowledge and intelligence being essential to the preservation of the rights and liberties of the people [purposive preamble], the Legislature shall encourage by all suitable means [stronger mandate] the promotion of intellectual, scientific, moral, and agricultural improvement. (California Constitution, Article IX, § 1)

Similarly, the Rhode Island education clause demands that the state legislature will "promote the public schools and . . . adopt all means . . . to secure . . . education" (Rhode Island Constitution, Article XII, § 1). The Indiana and Nevada provisions contain the "all means" language.

Fourth, at the far end of the spectrum are five "high duty provisions" which seem to place education above other governmental functions, such as highways or welfare. These provisions include Florida, Georgia, Illinois, Maine, and Washington. They are most clearly exemplified by the Washington State Constitution's education clause, which provides that "it is the paramount duty of the state to make ample provision for the education of all children residing within its borders, without distinction or preference on account of race, color, caste, or sex" (Washington Constitution, Article IX, § 1). Although other states have Category IV education clauses, Washington is apparently the only one that makes the duty "paramount" (*Seattle School District No. 1 v. Washington*, 1978). A second example is the Georgia provision that reads, "The provision of an adequate public education for the citizens shall be a primary obligation of the State of Georgia, the expense of which shall be provided for by taxation" (Georgia Constitution, Article VIII, § 1, ¶1).

William E. Thro

See also *Rose v. Council for Better Education; San Antonio Independent School District v. Rodriguez*; School Finance Litigation

Further Readings

Clune, W. (1992). New answers to hard questions posed by *Rodriguez*: Ending the separation of school finance and educational policy by bridging the gap between wrong and remedy. *Connecticut Law Review, 24,* 721–755.

Coons, J., Clune, W., & Sugarman, S. (1969). Educational opportunity: A workable constitutional test for state financial structures. *California Law Review, 57,* 305, 313–316.

Grubb, E. B. (1974). Breaking the language barrier: The right to bilingual education. *Harvard Civil Rights-Civil Liberties Law Review, 9*(1), 52–94.

Ratner, G. M. (1985). A new legal duty for urban public schools: Effective education in basic skills. *Texas Law Review, 63,* 777–864.

Thro, W. E. (1989). To render them safe: The analysis of state constitutional provisions in public school finance reform litigation. *Virginia Law Review, 75,* 1639–1979.

Thro, W. E. (1993). The role of language of the state education clauses in school finance litigation. *West's Education Law Reporter, 79,* 19–31.

Thro, W. E. (1994). Judicial analysis during the third wave of school finance litigation: The Massachusetts decision as a model. *Boston College Law Review, 35,* 597–617.

Thro, W. E. (1998). A new approach to state constitutional analysis in school finance litigation. *Journal of Law & Politics, 14,* 525–540.

Thro, W. E. (2005). The school finance paradox: How the constitutional values of decentralization and judicial restraint inhibit the achievement of quality education. *West's Education Law Reporter, 197,* 477–487.

Legal Citations

San Antonio Independent School District v. Rodriguez, 411 U.S. 1 (1973).

Seattle School District No. 1 v. Washington, 585 P.2d 71 (1978).

Serrano v. Priest, 487 P.2d 1241 (Cal. 1971), 557 P.2d 929 (Cal. 1976) *cert. denied,* 432 U.S. 907 (1977).

TIMOTHY W. v. ROCHESTER, NEW HAMPSHIRE, SCHOOL DISTRICT

At issue in *Timothy W. v. Rochester, New Hampshire, School District* (1989) was whether a school board was required to provide special education services to any students with disabilities regardless of the severity of their disabilities. In deciding that a board had to provide services, the First Circuit found that officials may not refuse to offer special education services on the basis that children are so severely handicapped that they are incapable of benefiting from special education. This now well-established rule from *Timothy W.* is commonly referred to as the "zero reject" principle.

Facts of the Case

Timothy W. was a multiply handicapped and profoundly mentally retarded child with complex developmental disabilities, spastic quadriplegia, cerebral palsy, seizure disorder, and cortical blindness. When Timothy was 4 years old, his local school board convened a meeting to determine whether he was qualified as "educationally handicapped" under the Education for All Handicapped Children Act (EAHCA), now the Individuals with Disabilities Education Act, and the corresponding New Hampshire statutes such that he would have been entitled to special education and related services.

At the meeting, Timothy's pediatrician and several other professionals reported that since he was capable of responding to sounds and other stimuli, he should have been provided with an individualized education program (IEP) that included physical and occupational therapy. However, two other pediatricians reported that Timothy had no educational potential. In response, school board officials maintained that Timothy was not "educationally handicapped," because the severity and complexity of his disabilities prevented him from being "capable of benefiting" from special education services. Accordingly, the board refused to provide educational services to Timothy for 2 years.

When Timothy was 7 years old, the school board convened another meeting to discuss his situation. Again, several professionals recommended an educational program that included physical therapy because they thought that Timothy could benefit from positioning and handling. Despite these recommendations, and even though a directive from the state education agency indicated that the board was not permitted to use "capable of benefiting" as a criterion for eligibility for special education services, local educational officials still refused to provide services to Timothy. Approximately 6 months later, in response to a letter from Timothy's attorney, the board's placement team met again and recommended special education services. Even so, the board refused to authorize the recommended placement and array of services. Timothy's attorney filed a complaint with the state education agency, which ordered the board to place him in an educational program. Again, the board refused.

The Court's Ruling

Timothy's attorney next filed suit in the federal trial court, alleging that the board had violated the EAHCA, New Hampshire special education statutes, Section 504 of the Rehabilitation Act of 1973, and the Equal Protection and Due Process Clauses of the constitutions of the United States and New Hampshire. Timothy's complaint sought monetary damages and an injunction to require the school board to provide educational services. The trial court denied the request for an injunction and abstained from addressing the damages claim in light of pending state administrative proceedings. Insofar as the state agency then pointed out that students' "capacity to benefit" was not an appropriate standard to determine their eligibility for special education, it directed the board to provide services for Timothy. The board appealed this order to the federal trial court, which reversed in its favor. The court held that the board was not obligated to provide Timothy with special education services. Timothy appealed to the First Circuit.

On further review, the First Circuit reversed in favor of Timothy. Looking to the plain language of the EAHCA, the court was of the opinion that any children with qualifying disabilities, especially those with severe disabilities such as Timothy, are entitled to special education and related services. To this end, the court explained that the fact that children may appear to be "uneducable" does not bar them from the protections of the EAHCA. To the contrary, the court ruled that the EAHCA gives priority to those children with the most severe disabilities. As such, the court reasoned that the EAHCA adopts a "zero reject" policy with respect to eligibility and that "capacity to benefit" from special education is not a prerequisite

for children to be eligible for services. In concluding, the court took an expansive view of what constitutes special education, noting that it includes fundamental skills, such as the development of motor and communication skills, as well as traditional cognitive skills.

Amy Steketee

See also Disabled Persons, Rights of; Individualized Education Program (IEP); Rehabilitation Act of 1973, Section 504; Zero Reject

Legal Citations

Individuals with Disabilities Education Act, 20 U.S.C. §§ 1400 *et seq.*
Rehabilitation Act of 1973, Section 504, 29 U.S.C. § 794(a).
Timothy W. v. Rochester, New Hampshire, School District, 875 F.2d 954 (1st Cir. 1989), *cert. denied*, 493 U.S. 983 (1989).

TINKER V. DES MOINES INDEPENDENT COMMUNITY SCHOOL DISTRICT

School officials are often confronted with difficult decisions when student attempts at expression result in disorder or the potential disruption of regular school activities. A fundamental case establishing the free speech and political rights of students in school settings is *Tinker v. Des Moines Independent Community School District* (1969). The results in *Tinker* leave school officials with some guidance for regulating student expression. School officials who wish to regulate student expression must be able to demonstrate that student expressive activities would result in material and substantial interference with the operations of the school or invade the rights of others. When school officials have specific facts that reasonably support predictions of disruption, they can regulate student expression, including banning specified activities.

Schools are considered limited public spaces. As such, students have fewer free speech rights in schools than they do on public streets. In schools, student free speech rights must be balanced against the obligation of school officials to protect student safety and privacy and to deliver a quality education. In general, student free speech rights extend only to expressions of a political, economic, or social nature that are not part of a school program. To this end, as the Supreme Court later ruled in *Hazelwood School District v. Kuhlmeier* (1988), school officials can regulate student writing in school newspapers with much less evidence of disruption than they can for student T-shirts or student discussions in the cafeteria. However, school officials can ban some forms of student expression of lewd or obscene natures, including student T-shirts, without any showing of potential disruption, since such speech has little or no educational value.

Facts of the Case

On December 16, 1965, a 13-year-old 8th grader, Mary Beth Tinker, and a 16-year-old 11th grader, Christopher Eckhardt, wore black armbands to school in protest of the Vietnam War. Mary Beth's older brother John, a 15-year-old 11th grader, wore an armband the following day. School officials suspended the students after they refused to remove their armbands. The protests followed a meeting at the Eckhardt house, where the parents of the students discussed ways to protest the Vietnam War.

On learning of the plan to protest the war, the principals of the Des Moines schools met on December 14, 2 days before the protest, and created a policy specifically prohibiting the wearing of armbands. The new policy said that students who wore armbands in protest of the war would be subject to out-of-school suspension and could return only after agreeing not to wear the armbands. The three students were suspended from school and did not return until after New Year's Day. The parents of these students filed suit in a federal trial court in Iowa seeking an injunction against the school board to prevent officials from disciplining the students.

The petitioners argued that wearing the armbands in school was within the students' constitutional rights to free speech. The trial court disagreed and dismissed the case, ruling that the board operated within its rights in suspending the students, although there was no finding that their actions created a substantial disruption of school activities. On further review, the Eighth Circuit affirmed without comment.

The Court's Ruling

The question presented to the U.S. Supreme Court was whether the First and Fourteenth Amendments to the Constitution allowed school officials to prohibit students from wearing symbols of political expression in school when the symbols are not "disruptive of school discipline or decorum." The petitioners argued that the students' wearing of the armbands was protected by the Free Speech Clause of the First Amendment and the Due Process and Equal Protection Clauses of the Fourteenth Amendment. The respondents countered that officials were within their rights to regulate student expression in the interest of maintaining an educational environment free from the disruption that the administration anticipated.

Justice Fortas, writing the majority opinion, penned the often-quoted line that neither teachers nor students "shed their constitutional rights to freedom of speech or expression at the schoolhouse gate" (*Tinker,* p. 506). Fortas reasoned that the wearing of armbands was akin to "pure speech" and was therefore protected by the Constitution. He contrasted the policy regulating armbands to other policies, such as dress codes, which previous court decisions upheld as constitutional. The difference, Fortas maintained, was in the intention of the message and the motivation of the administration in barring the expression. Fortas wrote that "undifferentiated fear" of disturbance was not enough to ban student expression. Fortas added that in seeking to limit student expression, "Where there is no finding and no showing that engaging in the forbidden conduct would 'materially and substantially interfere with the requirements of appropriate discipline in the operation of the school,' the prohibition cannot be sustained" (p. 509).

While agreeing in principle with the majority opinion, Justice Stewart, in his concurrence, qualified his agreement by noting his apprehension at the concept that First Amendment rights are "co-extensive" with those of adults. Stewart cautioned that in some cases, it is permissible to limit the rights of children.

The dissenting opinions of Justice Black and Justice Harlan focused on the need for school officials to establish discipline and an educational environment free from distracting and emotionally charged disruptions. Justice Black argued at length for the school, noting that the disruptions anticipated by the administration actually occurred and that the armbands took students' minds off their schoolwork. In a statement about the consequences of the court's decision, Justice Harlan dramatically warned,

> One does not need to be a prophet or the son of a prophet to know that after the Court's holding today some students in Iowa schools and indeed in all schools will be ready, able, and willing to defy their teachers on practically all orders. (*Tinker*, p. 525)

In sum, *Tinker* stands out as the first, and perhaps most important, case dealing with the free speech rights of students in American public schools.

Chad D. Ellis

See also *Bethel School District No. 403 v. Fraser;* Free Speech and Expression Rights of Students; *Hazelwood School District v. Kuhlmeier*

Legal Citations

Bethel School District No. 403 v. Fraser, 478 U.S. 675 (1986).
Hazelwood School District v. Kuhlmeier, 484 U.S. 260 (1988).
Tinker v. Des Moines Independent Community School District, 393 U.S. 503 (1969).

Tinker v. Des Moines Independent Community School District (Excerpts)

Tinker v. Des Moines Independent Community School District *stands out as the first Supreme Court case addressing the free speech rights of students. The Court concluded that unless it results in a reasonable forecast of material and substantial disruption, then school officials may not limit student free speech*

Supreme Court of the United States

TINKER

v.

DES MOINES INDEPENDENT COMMUNITY SCHOOL DISTRICT

393 U.S. 503

Argued Nov. 12, 1968.

Decided Feb. 24, 1969.

Mr. Justice FORTAS delivered the opinion of the Court.

Petitioner John F. Tinker, 15 years old, and petitioner Christopher Eckhardt, 16 years old, attended high schools in Des Moines, Iowa. Petitioner Mary Beth Tinker, John's sister, was a 13-year-old student in junior high school.

In December 1965, a group of adults and students in Des Moines held a meeting at the Eckhardt home. The group determined to publicize their objections to the hostilities in Vietnam and their support for a truce by wearing black armbands during the holiday season and by fasting on December 16 and New Year's Eve. Petitioners and their parents had previously engaged in similar activities, and they decided to participate in the program.

The principals of the Des Moines schools became aware of the plan to wear armbands. On December 14, 1965, they met and adopted a policy that any student wearing an armband to school would be asked to remove it, and if he refused he would be suspended until he returned without the armband. Petitioners were aware of the regulation that the school authorities adopted.

On December 16, Mary Beth and Christopher wore black armbands to their schools. John Tinker wore his armband the next day. They were all sent home and suspended from school until they would come back without their armbands. They did not return to school until after the planned period for wearing armbands had expired—that is, until after New Year's Day.

This complaint was filed in the United States District Court by petitioners, through their fathers, under s 1983 of Title 42 of the United States Code. It prayed for an injunction restraining the respondent school officials and the respondent members of the board of directors of the school district from disciplining the petitioners, and it sought nominal damages. After an evidentiary hearing the District Court dismissed the complaint. It upheld the constitutionality of the school authorities' action on the ground that it was reasonable in order to prevent disturbance of school discipline. The court referred to but expressly declined to follow the Fifth Circuit's holding in a similar case that the wearing of symbols like the armbands cannot be prohibited unless it 'materially and substantially interfere(s) with the requirements of appropriate discipline in the operation of the school.'

On appeal, the Court of Appeals for the Eighth Circuit considered the case en banc. The court was equally divided, and the District Court's decision was accordingly affirmed, without opinion. We granted certiorari.

I

The District Court recognized that the wearing of an armband for the purpose of expressing certain views is the type of symbolic act that is within the Free Speech Clause of the First Amendment. As we shall discuss, the wearing of armbands in the circumstances of this case was entirely divorced from actually or potentially disruptive conduct by those participating in it. It was closely akin to 'pure speech' which, we have repeatedly held, is entitled to comprehensive protection under the First Amendment.

First Amendment rights, applied in light of the special characteristics of the school environment, are available to teachers and students. It can hardly be argued that either students or teachers shed their constitutional rights to freedom of speech or expression at the schoolhouse gate. This has been the unmistakable holding of this Court for almost 50 years. . . . .

On the other hand, the Court has repeatedly emphasized the need for affirming the comprehensive authority of the States and of school officials, consistent with fundamental constitutional safeguards, to prescribe and control conduct in the schools. Our problem lies in the area where students in the exercise of First Amendment rights collide with the rules of the school authorities.

II

The problem posed by the present case does not relate to regulation of the length of skirts or the type of clothing, to hair style, or deportment. It does not concern aggressive, disruptive action or even group demonstrations. Our problem involves direct, primary First Amendment rights akin to 'pure speech.'

The school officials banned and sought to punish petitioners for a silent, passive expression of opinion, unaccompanied by any disorder or disturbance on the part of petitioners. There is here no evidence whatever of petitioners' interference, actual or nascent, with the

schools' work or of collision with the rights of other students to be secure and to be let alone. Accordingly, this case does not concern speech or action that intrudes upon the work of the schools or the rights of other students.

Only a few of the 18,000 students in the school system wore the black armbands. Only five students were suspended for wearing them. There is no indication that the work of the schools or any class was disrupted. Outside the classrooms, a few students made hostile remarks to the children wearing armbands, but there were no threats or acts of violence on school premises.

The District Court concluded that the action of the school authorities was reasonable because it was based upon their fear of a disturbance from the wearing of the armbands. But, in our system, undifferentiated fear or apprehension of disturbance is not enough to overcome the right to freedom of expression. Any departure from absolute regimentation may cause trouble. Any variation from the majority's opinion may inspire fear. Any word spoken, in class, in the lunchroom, or on the campus, that deviates from the views of another person may start an argument or cause a disturbance. But our Constitution says we must take this risk, and our history says that it is this sort of hazardous freedom—this kind of openness—that is the basis of our national strength and of the independence and vigor of Americans who grow up and live in this relatively permissive, often disputatious, society.

In order for the State in the person of school officials to justify prohibition of a particular expression of opinion, it must be able to show that its action was caused by something more than a mere desire to avoid the discomfort and unpleasantness that always accompany an unpopular viewpoint. Certainly where there is no finding and no showing that engaging in the forbidden conduct would 'materially and substantially interfere with the requirements of appropriate discipline in the operation of the school,' the prohibition cannot be sustained.

In the present case, the District Court made no such finding, and our independent examination of the record fails to yield evidence that the school authorities had reason to anticipate that the wearing of the armbands would substantially interfere with the work of the school or impinge upon the rights of other students. Even an official memorandum prepared after the suspension that listed the reasons for the ban on wearing the armbands made no reference to the anticipation of such disruption.

On the contrary, the action of the school authorities appears to have been based upon an urgent wish to avoid the controversy which might result from the expression, even by the silent symbol of armbands, of opposition to this Nation's part in the conflagration in Vietnam. It is revealing, in this respect, that the meeting at which the school principals decided to issue the contested regulation was called in response to a student's statement to the journalism teacher in one of the schools that he wanted to write an article on Vietnam and have it published in the school paper. (The student was dissuaded.)

It is also relevant that the school authorities did not purport to prohibit the wearing of all symbols of political or controversial significance. The record shows that students in some of the schools wore buttons relating to national political campaigns, and some even wore the Iron Cross, traditionally a symbol of Nazism. The order prohibiting the wearing of armbands did not extend to these. Instead, a particular symbol—black armbands worn to exhibit opposition to this Nation's involvement in Vietnam—was singled out for prohibition. Clearly, the prohibition of expression of one particular opinion, at least without evidence that it is necessary to avoid material and substantial interference with schoolwork or discipline, is not constitutionally permissible.

In our system, state-operated schools may not be enclaves of totalitarianism. School officials do not possess absolute authority over their students. Students in school as well as out of school are 'persons' under our Constitution. They are possessed of fundamental rights which the State must respect, just as they themselves must respect their obligations to the State. In our system, students may not be regarded as closed-circuit recipients of only that which the State chooses to communicate. They may not be confined to the expression of those sentiments that are officially approved. In the absence of a specific showing of constitutionally valid reasons to regulate their speech, students are entitled to freedom of expression of their views. As Judge Gewin, speaking for the Fifth Circuit, said, school officials cannot suppress 'expressions of feelings with which they do not wish to contend.'

In *Meyer v. Nebraska*, Mr. Justice McReynolds expressed this Nation's repudiation of the principle that a State might so conduct its schools as to 'foster a homogeneous people.' . . .

This principle has been repeated by this Court on numerous occasions during the intervening years. In *Keyishian v. Board of Regents*, Mr. Justice Brennan, speaking for the Court, said: "'The vigilant protection of constitutional freedoms is nowhere more vital than in the community of American schools.' The classroom is peculiarly

the 'marketplace of ideas.' The Nation's future depends upon leaders trained through wide exposure to that robust exchange of ideas which discovers truth 'out of a multitude of tongues, (rather) than through any kind of authoritative selection.'"

The principle of these cases is not confined to the supervised and ordained discussion which takes place in the classroom. The principal use to which the schools are dedicated is to accommodate students during prescribed hours for the purpose of certain types of activities. Among those activities is personal intercommunication among the students. This is not only an inevitable part of the process of attending school; it is also an important part of the educational process. A student's rights, therefore, do not embrace merely the classroom hours. When he is in the cafeteria, or on the playing field, or on the campus during the authorized hours, he may express his opinions, even on controversial subjects like the conflict in Vietnam, if he does so without 'materially and substantially interfer(ing) with the requirements of appropriate discipline in the operation of the school' and without colliding with the rights of others. But conduct by the student, in class or out of it, which for any reason—whether it stems from time, place, or type of behavior—materially disrupts classwork or involves substantial disorder or invasion of the rights of others is, of course, not immunized by the constitutional guarantee of freedom of speech.

Under our Constitution, free speech is not a right that is given only to be so circumscribed that it exists in principle but not in fact. Freedom of expression would not truly exist if the right could be exercised only in an area that a benevolent government has provided as a safe haven for crackpots. The Constitution says that Congress (and the States) may not abridge the right to free speech. This provision means what it says. We properly read it to permit reasonable regulation of speech-connected activities in carefully restricted circumstances. But we do not confine the permissible exercise of First Amendment rights to a telephone booth or the four corners of a pamphlet, or to supervised and ordained discussion in a school classroom.

If a regulation were adopted by school officials forbidding discussion of the Vietnam conflict, or the expression by any student of opposition to it anywhere on school property except as part of a prescribed classroom exercise, it would be obvious that the regulation would violate the constitutional rights of students, at least if it could not be justified by a showing that the students' activities would materially and substantially disrupt the work and discipline of the school. In the circumstances of the present case, the prohibition of the silent, passive 'witness of the armbands,' as one of the children called it, is no less offensive to the constitution's guarantees.

As we have discussed, the record does not demonstrate any facts which might reasonably have led school authorities to forecast substantial disruption of or material interference with school activities, and no disturbances or disorders on the school premises in fact occurred. These petitioners merely went about their ordained rounds in school. Their deviation consisted only in wearing on their sleeve a band of black cloth, not more than two inches wide. They wore it to exhibit their disapproval of the Vietnam hostilities and their advocacy of a truce, to make their views known, and, by their example, to influence others to adopt them. They neither interrupted school activities nor sought to intrude in the school affairs or the lives of others. They caused discussion outside of the classrooms, but no interference with work and no disorder. In the circumstances, our Constitution does not permit officials of the State to deny their form of expression.

We express no opinion as to the form of relief which should be granted, this being a matter for the lower courts to determine. We reverse and remand for further proceedings consistent with this opinion.

Reversed and remanded.

Citation: *Tinker v. Des Moines Independent Community School District,* 393 U.S. 503 (1969).

Title I

"Title I" is a shorthand reference for a federal statute designed to improve the educational achievement of poor students by providing federal funds to impoverished school districts. While the amount of funding has fluctuated over the decades, Title I remains the single largest federal educational program for elementary and secondary school children. It reaches millions of students and tens of thousands of school districts.

The Law and Its Context

For most of our nation's history, federal involvement in education was limited. A major shift occurred during the administration of President Lyndon B. Johnson. One of the components of President Johnson's "War on Poverty" included the Elementary and Secondary Education Act (ESEA), which Congress enacted in 1965. Title I of this act provided substantial funds to improve the education of financially disadvantaged school children. One purpose of this law was to alleviate the large disparity in funding between Black and White schools in the segregated South. Thus, Title I was a component of a broader body of civil rights measures.

Title I funds are allocated on the basis of complex formulas that depend on student enrollment, census poverty data, and other sources. The federal government allocates the money to state education agencies that, in turn, distribute it to local school districts. States must then account to the federal government for their use of the funds. Generally speaking, states are allowed considerable discretion in deciding how to use the funds.

Title I has evolved each time Congress has reauthorized the program. The first wave of change centered on ensuring that Title I funds were used to supplement rather than to replace local funds. Congress also sought to impose stricter enforcement of spending, to make sure the funds were being spent for proper objectives. President Ronald Reagan's more restrictive view of the role of the federal government and his skepticism about the effectiveness of federal programs led to spending cuts in Title I. However, the complex regulations were also simplified. Title I funding was gradually restored in later administrations.

Impact and Evolution

States' use of Title I funds in religious schools has proved controversial. For example, New York created a program to pay the salaries of teachers in religious schools, but those teachers could not teach religion or participate in religious activities. The state audited these schools for compliance. In *Aguilar v. Felton* (1985), the Supreme Court found that this program was unconstitutional because of the "excessive entanglement" of the government in religious affairs. Then, in 1997, in *Agostini v. Felton* (1997), the Court reversed itself and concluded that the New York program was, in fact, constitutionally permissible under the First Amendment's Establishment Clause.

Under President William Clinton, Congress amended Title I to require states to develop uniform standards for all students, including poor students, and to craft programs that will enable poor students to meet those standards. This package of reforms was known as the Improving America's Schools Act of 1994. These reforms reflected a shift from fiscal accountability, ensuring that the funds were properly spent, to academic accountability, ensuring that poor students actually improved their academic performance.

Another milestone in the movement to ensure better results for poor children was the passage of the No Child Left Behind Act (NCLB), signed into law in 2002 by President George W. Bush. The intent behind NCLB was to improve accountability and results for Title I funds. Among other things, NCLB requires Title I schools to make "adequate yearly progress" and seeks to ensure that teachers are properly qualified. A school that fails to make adequate yearly progress must allow parents to choose a different public school and also to prepare an improvement plan to correct the problems. Schools that do not make adequate yearly progress for 2 years are also required to provide tutoring assistance to certain students. NCLB has been criticized by some as unrealistic and unduly burdensome.

Following the passage of Title I, policymakers and educators had high expectations for improvement of the educational performance of poor children. They hoped that millions would be lifted out of poverty. Title I has fallen short of these lofty expectations. Nevertheless, many proponents of Title I link the program to improvements in academic performance for poor children.

Stephen R. McCullough

See also *Agostini v. Felton;* Civil Rights Movement; No Child Left Behind Act

Further Readings

McAndrews, L. J. (2006). *The era of education: The presidents and the schools, 1965–2001.* Chicago: University of Illinois Press.

Reese, W. J. (2005). *America's public schools: From the common school to No Child Left Behind.* Baltimore: Johns Hopkins University Press.

Legal Citations

Agostini v. Felton, 521 U.S. 203 (1997).

Aguilar v. Felton, 473 U.S. 402 (1985).

Improving America's Schools Act of 1994, 20 U.S.C. §§ 6301 *et seq.*

No Child Left Behind Act, 20 U.S.C. §§ 6301 *et seq.*

TITLE VII

The decade of the 1960s witnessed a broad congressional attack on discrimination in American society. Among targeted areas were housing, voting, education, and employment. Title VII of the Civil Rights Act of 1964, the first comprehensive federal employment discrimination statute, has provided an effective tool for litigants to challenge discrimination in the workplace and has altered employment practices in both public school and higher education in the United States. Title VII prohibits employment discrimination based on race, color, national origin, religion, and sex. In addition to basic hiring, dismissal, promotion, and demotion decisions, it extends to such wide-ranging employment issues as sexual harassment, pregnancy and maternity leave benefits, religious leave to observe one's religious holy days, and retaliation for exercising one's rights under Title VII. This entry reviews the general framework of Title VII in terms of the burden of proof required and the types of claims allowable. It then describes the mechanisms in place for administrative enforcement and judicial relief. Last, it discusses the use of Title VII with specific types of discrimination, including pregnancy and religious discrimination, harassment, and retaliation. In light of workers' reliance upon Title VII to challenge allegedly discriminatory practices in the job setting, the growing ethnic and racial diversity in the United States, and the continued push for social justice in all aspects of American life, Title VII will continue to be a vital piece of antidiscrimination legislation in the future.

Title VII outlaws employment discrimination by employers with 15 or more employees. When enacted in 1964, Title VII did not apply to public employers; a 1972 amendment extended coverage to political subdivisions, including public schools, colleges, and universities. Title VII prohibits an employer from discriminating against employees and prospective employees (applicants) in hiring, discharge, compensation, and "terms, conditions, or privileges of employment" on the basis of race, color, national origin, religion, and sex. It provides an exception for religious educational institutions in the hiring of employees of a particular religion to perform duties connected with the institution.

General Framework of Title VII

Burden of Proof

The burden in Title VII cases rests upon the employee or prospective employee to establish that the employer acted in an unlawfully discriminatory manner. To clarify the statutory process, the Supreme Court developed a three-step test of shifting burdens and order of proof in *McDonnell Douglas Corporation v. Green* (1973) and *Texas Department of Community Affairs v. Burdine* (1981). To prevail in a Title VII claim, the plaintiff must first establish a prima facie case that he or she (a) is a member of a protected group; (b) applied for a job for which he or she was qualified and for which the employer sought applicants; (c) was rejected; and (d) after the rejection, the employer continued to seek applicants of the plaintiff's qualifications. The burden then shifts to the employer, who must rebut the plaintiff by producing a legitimate, nondiscriminatory reason for the plaintiff's rejection. In the final stage, the plaintiff must establish that the employer's given reason was a pretext for actual impermissible discriminatory reasons. As the *Burdine* Court explained, at this step, the plaintiff can either show directly that the employer was more likely motivated by a discriminatory reason or indirectly that the employer's stated reason was not

credible. Courts adapt the basic *McDonnell Douglas-Burdine* test to fit charges of discriminatory dismissal, demotion or transfer, and denial of tenure.

Types of Claims

Plaintiffs may bring two types of claims under Title VII. Disparate-impact claims, infrequent in the education setting, challenge facially neutral employment policies or practices that on the surface appear nondiscriminatory but nonetheless disproportionately and significantly impact a protected group. An employer's primary defense is that such policy or practice is justified by business necessity. An example of a school disparate-impact case is *Thomas v. Washington County School Board* (1990), in which the Fourth Circuit ruled against the hiring practices of a school district with a predominantly White workforce. The court found the district's practices of hiring relatives of school district employees and posting vacancy notices in the district's buildings, while generally not advertising the vacancies, constituted a disparate-impact violation of Title VII. In another impact case, *United States v. South Carolina* (1977), a federal district court upheld South Carolina's use of National Teacher Examination (NTE) scores for certification and teacher salary purposes through the state aid formula, even though the NTE disqualified a greater proportion of Black test takers and applicants and placed them in disproportionately lower pay categories. South Carolina established a business necessity through a validation study that showed that the NTE scores were rationally related to the legitimate objective of selecting qualified teacher applicants.

More common in the education setting are Title VII disparate-treatment claims. In these cases, plaintiffs allege that school districts treated employees or job applicants differently and with unlawful intent. For example, a female teacher passed over for promotion to an administrative position might establish that the nonpromotion was unlawfully based on her gender. Or, in previous decades, Black applicants for teaching positions in a southern school district might have challenged the district's record of having never hired minority teachers as being an unlawful practice under Title VII.

Administrative Enforcement and Judicial Relief

Title VII created the federal Equal Employment Opportunity Commission (EEOC) to serve as an enforcement mechanism of Title VII. Before litigating, individuals must exhaust administrative remedies by filing a claim with the EEOC within 180 days after the alleged discrimination occurred. After notice is given to the employer, and absent a conciliation agreement between the parties or filing of suit against the employer by the EEOC, the agency notifies the aggrieved person, who then has 90 days to bring civil action.

When employees or prospective employees establish that employers intentionally engaged in unlawful employment practices, Title VII authorizes courts to award a wide range of equitable relief to the prevailing plaintiffs. Courts may issue affirmative injunctive relief ordering the employer to stop engaging in the unlawful discriminatory practice and to hire, reinstate, or take other equitable action. Court awards also may include attorneys' fees and back pay; awards of tenure, seniority, and front pay are possible but less common.

Specific Unlawful Employment Practices

Pregnancy

Congress enacted the Pregnancy Discrimination Act of 1978 (PDA) as an amendment to Title VII to clarify and protect the rights of pregnant employees. The PDA outlaws discrimination against employees or prospective employees based upon "pregnancy, childbirth, or related medical conditions." Further, employers must treat pregnant and maternity leave employees the same as employees suffering from other temporary disabilities in fringe benefits and leave policies that govern the length of leave, the use of leave for disabilities, and the conditions to return to work (such as medical and administrative clearance and notice requirements).

Harassment

Title VII prohibits harassment, which is generally defined as offensive words or actions, normally more than stray remarks or isolated behavior, that substantially annoy, alarm, or distress a person with no legitimate, official purpose. While harassment in the work- place can be religious, racial, or ethnic, most claims are gender based. The victim and harasser may be male or female, of the opposite or same sex. There are two basic types of sexual harassment. *Quid pro quo* (Latin for "something for something") harassment is when an employer makes employment decisions, including hiring, promotion, pay raise, nonfiring, or transfer, contingent upon sexual favors. A second type of harassment, a *hostile* (or abusive) work environment, exists when mistreatment based upon one's gender is so severe or pervasive that a reasonable person should not have to tolerate it or that it affects one's job performance. Examples may include offensive verbal (such as name-calling and "dirty" jokes) and physical (for example, leering or touching) conduct. The alleged victim must report the unwelcomed behavior to a school official who has the authority to take corrective or preventive action; liability exists if the administrator reacts to the actual notice of the alleged harassment with deliberate indifference.

Religion

In addition to Title VII's general ban against religious discrimination, a 1972 amendment, Section 701(j), states that "religion" includes the religious beliefs, observances, and practices of an employee or prospective employee. An employer must make reasonable accommodations for such workers unless doing so would cause an undue hardship on the operation of the organization. Supreme Court rulings have held that employers must offer a reasonable accommodation but not necessarily the employee's preferred choice and that an accommodation resulting in more than a de minimis cost to the employer constitutes an undue hardship.

In applying Title VII to the school setting, courts consistently hold that employees have a right to miss work to observe their religious holidays and to maintain their employment status when doing so. But an employer has no Title VII obligation to provide paid leave for an employee's absences for religious observances. For example, in 1984, the Tenth Circuit ruled that a school district had to allow a Jewish teacher to miss work to observe Yom Kippur and Rosh Hashanah, a total of 3 days; but if not fully covered by the district's leave policy, the district did not have to provide the teacher paid leave to cover all missed days.

Retaliation

Title VII protects from retaliation those individuals who challenge employment actions under the statute. Title VII outlaws an employer from retaliating against employees or prospective employees who oppose a practice made unlawful under the statute by filing a Title VII complaint or litigation or by participating in an investigation or proceedings under Title VII. Provided that the complainants acted in a good-faith belief that Title VII had been violated, they are protected from reprisal, whether successful or unsuccessful in their challenge. For example, a federal court in West Virginia in 1981 found that a school district transferred and removed coaching duties from a junior high school basketball coach because she filed state and federal agency charges challenging gender inequities in her district's athletic programs.

Ralph Sharp

See also *Ansonia Board of Education v. Philbrook;* Civil Rights Act of 1964; Disparate Impact; Equal Employment Opportunity Commission; *Griggs v. Duke Power Company; Harris v. Forklift Systems;* Hostile Work Environment; *McDonnell Douglas Corporation v. Green; Meritor Savings Bank v. Vinson; Oncale v. Sundowner Offshore Services;* Sexual Harassment; Sexual Harassment, Quid Pro Quo; Sexual Harassment, Same-Sex

Legal Citations

Ansonia Board of Education v. Philbrook, 479 U.S. 60 (1986).
Harris v. Forklift Systems, 510 U.S. 17 (1993).
McDonnell Douglas Corporation v. Green, 411 U.S. 792 (1973).
Meritor Savings Bank v. Vinson, 477 U.S. 57 (1986).
Pregnancy Discrimination Act of 1978, 42 U.S.C. § 2000e.
Texas Department of Community Affairs v. Burdine, 450 U.S. 248 (1981).
Thomas v. Washington County School Board, 915 F.2d 922 (4th Cir. 1990).
Title VII of the Civil Rights Act of 1964, 42 U.S.C. § 2000e.
United States v. South Carolina, 445 F. Supp. 1094 (D.S.C. 1977), *aff'd*, 434 U.S. 1026.

TITLE IX AND ATHLETICS

Title IX of the Education Amendments of 1972 prohibits public and private educational institutions that receive federal funds from discriminating due to gender in any aspect of their operations. The statute, which explicitly prohibits quotas, is coextensive with the prohibitions against gender discrimination provided by the Constitution's Equal Protection Clause. While there is no mention of intercollegiate or interscholastic athletics in the actual statute, the implementing regulations make it clear that athletics is covered by Title IX. The Office for Civil Rights (OCR) of the U.S. Department of Education is the agency charged with the enforcement of Title IX. Under the OCR's interpretation, which has been universally endorsed by the federal appellate courts, an institution must do one of three things to comply with Title IX in the context of athletics participation.

First, each gender's representation in varsity athletics must be substantially proportionate to its representation in the student body. The fact that the OCR expects a gender's representation among athletes to be "substantially proportionate" to that gender's representation in a student body necessarily begs the question of what is meant by "substantially proportionate." In 1996, the OCR clarified that athletic opportunities are

> substantially proportionate when the number of opportunities that would be required to achieve proportionality would not be sufficient to sustain a viable team, i.e., a team for which there is a sufficient number of interested and able students and enough available competition to sustain an intercollegiate team.

In plain English, the OCR first reviews how many additional participation opportunities must be offered to the underrepresented gender in order to achieve perfect proportionality. If this number is sufficient to field a viable team, then an institution is not considered substantially proportionate and must add a team. If it is not sufficient to field a viable team, nothing more is required.

To illustrate how the OCR test works, suppose a university is 55% female but offers 700 athletic participation opportunities. Men have 385 athletic participation opportunities, while women have 315 participation opportunities. This means women represent 45% of the athletes (315 divided by 700) though they represent 55% of full-time undergraduates. The first step is to consider how many opportunities must be added for women to achieve perfect proportionality of 55%. If male participation remains constant, which is the assumption employed by the OCR, the university must add 156 participation opportunities for women. If a university did so, it would have 471 female opportunities (315 current + 156 additional) and 385 male (all current). The second step is to address whether the number of new participation opportunities required, 156 in this example, is sufficient to field a viable team. Obviously, it is sufficient. In fact, the university could field seven or eight new women's teams with 156 additional opportunities.

Although the above example is purely hypothetical, the actual practice of the OCR yields similar results. In a letter dated August 24, 2000, OCR advised the University of Wisconsin that based on its deviation of 2.89 percentage points (involving an enrollment of women of 52.96% compared with their intercollegiate athletic participation of 50.07%), it failed to comply with its commitment in a plan submitted to OCR to meet the first prong of the three-part test. In this letter, OCR stated the deviation represented as many as 46 participation opportunities for women, which would be sufficient to sustain the addition of a viable women's team. In short, if one gender is 50% of the student body, its representation among varsity athletes must approximate 50%.

Second, if an institution has not achieved substantial proportionality, the institution may demonstrate that it has a continuing history of expanding opportunities for the underrepresented gender. In other words, it is acceptable for female representation among athletes to be substantially below their representation in the student body if the institution has consistently added new teams for women and intends to do so in the future. In evaluating "history," the OCR looks at the institution's record for adding teams, its record of increasing participants on existing teams, and its response to requests to add teams. In assessing "continuing practice," the OCR examines the institution's current policy for adding teams. In practical terms, this means that an institution must have consistently

added new teams for the underrepresented gender about every 3 to 4 years, must refrain from eliminating any teams for the underrepresented gender, and must have a plan for adding new teams in the future. To be sure, the fact that the OCR demands that teams be added in the future begs the question of when they may cease adding teams. Apparently, the answer is that an institution is excused from adding teams when it finally achieves substantial proportionality. Until that time, the institution must add teams at the rate of about once every 3 years.

Third, an institution may demonstrate that it is currently meeting all interests and abilities of the underrepresented gender. Because students are constantly entering and leaving the institution, survey data quickly become useless. Thus, if an institution is going to demonstrate that it is filling all needs and thereby meet the third prong, it must do surveys on a continuing basis. Presumably, this means that an institution must periodically survey the underrepresented gender and add a new team every time there is an indication of an unmet interest and ability until substantial proportionality is achieved.

As a practical matter, all three options eventually lead to substantial proportionality, the first option. Unless an institution has achieved substantial proportionality, it must either (a) add teams for the underrepresented gender periodically until such time as substantial proportionality is achieved, (b) cut opportunities for the overrepresented gender immediately so that substantial proportionality is achieved, (c) add a team every time there is an indication of an unmet interest and ability among the underrepresented gender until substantial proportionality is achieved, or (d) implement some combination of the first three options. The question is not *whether* the quota will be reached, but *when*.

In addition to mandating a particular level of participation, there are also regulations concerning the provision of athletic scholarships. As to athletic financial assistance, the regulation is specific. The regulation provides for athletic scholarships as follows:

1. To the extent that a recipient awards athletic scholarships or grants-in-aid, it must provide reasonable opportunities for such awards for members of each sex

in proportion to the number of students of each sex participating in interscholastic sports. (emphasis added)

2. Separate athletic scholarships or grants-in-aid for members of each sex may be provided as part of separate athletic teams for members of each sex to the extent consistent with this paragraph and § 106.41(c).

In effect, if 45% of the athletes are female, females should receive approximately 45% of total athletic financial assistance. Although, as in the case of the participation requirements, no level of permissible deviation from exact equality in scholarship aid has been established, OCR has issued a guidance letter that provides as follows:

> If any unexplained disparity in the scholarship budgets for athletes of either gender is 1% or less for the entire budget for athletic scholarships, there will be a strong presumption that such a disparity is reasonable and based on legitimate nondiscriminatory factors. Conversely, there will be a strong presumption that an unexplained disparity of more than 1% is in violation of the "substantially proportionate" requirement.

To be sure, the financial assistance regulation and the accommodating interests and abilities regulation work in tandem. As a gender's participation increases, its share of scholarship money must also increase. Thus, while adding some extra nonscholarship players may help the institution achieve substantial proportionality in the participation context, it may actually cause noncompliance in the financial context. Conversely, limiting nonscholarship players to achieve financial assistance compliance may cause the university to fail the substantial proportionality test. It is extremely difficult to meet both standards.

William E. Thro

See also Equal Protection Analysis; Title IX and Sexual Harassment

Further Readings

Snow. B. A., &. Thro, W. E. (1996). Still on the sidelines: Developing the non-discrimination paradigm under Title IX. *Duke Journal of Gender Law & Policy, 3,* 1–49.

Legal Citations

Cohen v. Brown University, 809 F. Supp. 978 (D.R.I. 1992), *aff'd,* 991 F.2d 888 (1st Cir. 1993), *remanded,* 879 F. Supp. 185 (D.R.I. 1995), *aff'd in part, rev'd in part,* 102 F.3d 155 (1st Cir. 1996).

Kelley v. Board of Trustees, 35 F.3d 265 (7th Cir. 1994).

Roberts v. Colorado State Board of Agriculture, 998 F.2d 824 (10th Cir. 1993).

Title IX of the Education Amendments of 1972, 20 U.S.C. § 1681.

TITLE IX AND SEXUAL HARASSMENT

Title IX of the Education Amendments of 1972, which prohibits gender discrimination by any educational institution, public or private, that receives federal funds, has been interpreted as prohibiting sexual harassment. In *Gebser v. Lago Vista Independent School District* (1998), the Supreme Court applied Title IX to sexual harassment of a student by an instructor. A year later, in *Davis v. Monroe County Board of Education* (1999), the Court extended that holding to sexual harassment of one student by another student.

In the context of faculty-student sexual harassment, discrimination by the school is demonstrated by showing that an "appropriate person" actually knew of the conduct and that the response of the school was deliberately indifferent. The first element, "knowledge by an appropriate person," refers to a school official who, at a minimum, has authority to address the alleged discrimination and to institute corrective measures on the school's behalf. In other words, "appropriate persons" are those who have the authority to address the misconduct by terminating or otherwise disciplining the offending party. The second element, "deliberate indifference," means that a school official knows of the conduct and, as a matter of official policy, has done nothing. Consequently, a school effectively causes a continuing violation. In other words, liability is imposed when the school knows of the harassment and affirmatively chooses to do nothing.

When the person engaging in sexual harassment is a student, rather than an instructor, additional requirements are imposed. In *Davis,* the Court stressed that the language of Title IX, coupled with the requirement that the recipient have notice of the proscriptions under the statute, requires that recipients subjected to liability have substantial control over the harasser and the environment in which the harassment occurs. As the Court noted, "Only then can the recipient be said to 'expose' its students to harassment or cause them to undergo it 'under' the recipient's programs" (*Davis,* p. 645). In reaching this conclusion, the Court relied in part on the requirement in Title IX that harassment occur under the operations of a funding recipient. The Court qualified the requirement involving control with respect to entities in higher education:

> A university might not, for example, be expected to exercise the same degree of control over its students that a grade school would enjoy [citation omitted], and it would be entirely reasonable for a school to refrain from a form of disciplinary action that would expose it to constitutional or statutory claims. (p. 649)

The Court imposed two additional conditions on its test for peer sexual harassment that were not addressed in *Gebser.* One provides a defense if the recipient can show that its response to harassment was not "clearly unreasonable." The Court distinguished this from a "mere 'reasonableness' standard," stating that in an appropriate case, "There is no reason why courts, on a motion to dismiss, for summary judgment, or for a directed verdict, could not identify a response as 'not clearly unreasonable' as a matter of law" (*Davis,* p. 649). The other condition, which is based on the attachment of Title IX to actions that occur under any program or activity, requires that damages be "available only where behavior is so severe, pervasive, and objectively offensive that it denies its victims the equal access to education that Title IX is designed to protect" (p. 652). Finally, the Court sought to avoid an overly expansive application of its holding to common behavior, particularly among children, involving things such as "simple acts of teasing and name calling" (p. 652).

The Court also stressed that it did not contemplate or hold that a mere decline in grades is sufficient to survive a motion to dismiss. The Court attempted to provide some general guidance as to when gender-oriented conduct rises to the level of actionable sexual harassment by stating that it "depends on a constellation of surrounding circumstances, expectations, and relationships, including, but not limited to, the ages of the harasser and the victim and the number of individuals involved" (*Davis,* p. 651). In both *Gebser* and *Davis,* the Supreme Court implicitly held that Title IX liability turned on a finding of intentional discrimination by the educational institution. In other words, before Title IX liability can be imposed, a party must demonstrate that officials at an educational institution made a conscious choice to discriminate. It is not enough to show that an employee or agent of the institution behaved improperly. Rather, a plaintiff must prove that an educational institution endorsed such conduct or failed to stop the harassment.

William E. Thro

See also *Davis v. Monroe County Board of Education; Gebser v. Lago Vista Independent School District;* Sexual Harassment; Sexual Harassment, Peer-to-Peer; Sexual Harassment of Students by Teachers

Further Readings

Snow, B. A., & Thro, W. E. (1996). Still on the sidelines: Developing the non-discrimination paradigm under Title IX. *Duke Journal of Gender Law & Policy, 3,* 1–49.

Snow, B. A., Thro, W. E., & Clemente, S. (2001). The problem of determining Title IX liability. *West's Education Law Reporter, 154,* 1–44.

Thro, W. E., & Snow, B. A. (2000). The subtle implications of *Gebser v. Lago Vista Independent School District. West's Education Law Reporter, 141,* 409–436.

Legal Citations

Baynard v. Malone, 268 F.3d 228, 239 (4th Cir. 2001).

Davis v. Monroe County Board of Education, 526 U.S. 629 (1999).

Floyd v. Waiters, 171 F.3d 1264, 1266 (11th Cir. 1999).

Gebser v. Lago Vista Independent School District, 524 U.S. 274 (1998).

Horner v. Kentucky High School Athletic Association, 206 F.3d 685 (6th Cir. 2000).

Kinman v. Omaha Public School District, 171 F.3d 607 (8th Cir. 1999).

Rosa H. v. San Elizario Independent School District, 106 F.3d 648 (5th Cir. 1997).

Title IX of the Education Amendments of 1972, 20 U.S.C. § 1681.

TRANSPORTATION, STUDENTS' RIGHTS TO

The duty of school boards and educational leaders to provide transportation for regular education students has become one of the most overwhelming tasks in the increasingly multifaceted world of educational leadership. At this point, suffice it to say that if students are entitled to transportation as part of their mandated related services under the Individuals with Disabilities Education Act, a variety of additional federal laws and regulations come into play.

Basic Requirements

Public school officials must sort through a seemingly endless array of state and federal statutes, rules, and regulations to arrange transportation for all categories of students designated by state statutes, as well as categories mandated by federal law and court judicial orders. For typical administrators, this range includes students who reside farther than the maximum walking distance, students from nonpublic schools who travel to schools within or outside of their districts, students with disabilities (as noted above), and students going to and from extra and cocurricular activities. In addition to scheduling issues, school officials may be called on to provide transportation to groups for which no state reimbursement is available.

Absent legislative or judicial mandates to provide student transportation, local school boards are free to decide whether to furnish transportation or to charge for making it available. Generally, if the provision of student transportation is truly optional, litigation seeking to force boards to provide service will fail either because the state has declared no clear legislative intent to provide transportation or because a state's constitution, legislature, or courts have declared no fundamental constitutional right to an education. In its only case

on point, *Kadrmas v. Dickinson Public Schools* (1988), the U.S. Supreme Court upheld the imposition of a fee to transport a student to school. Even so, previously, the Supreme Court of Utah permitted students to be transported at district expense if their presence was required in school-related activities (*Beard v. Board of Education of North Summit,* 1932). The court made a distinction between those who were participants in the extracurricular activities and those who were spectators. At the same time, the court added that the board could not at district expense furnish transportation to spectators of school activities. Subsequently, an appellate court in California found that a board's refusal to provide transportation for indigent students was an abuse of discretion (*Salazar v. Dawson,* 1992).

Most public school boards are responsible for providing safe and wide-ranging transportation plans for the majority of their students. For example, Ohio law requires school boards to provide transportation for students in kindergarten through eighth grade who live more than 2 miles from school. To this end, Ohio law provides clear evidence that a significant number of students, such as those who attend secondary school, are not required to be transported to and from school. While most boards do provide transportation for students K–12, they are not required to do so for all students. For example, an appellate court in Ohio held that a school board could eliminate high school busing due to financial constraints (*Russell v. Gallia County Local School District,* 1992).

Safety and Other Issues

As part of the process of providing transportation, school officials must recruit, employ, and train bus drivers who satisfy state standards and must frequently supervise and/or evaluate them to ensure that they operate buses in compliance with state and federal requirements. School boards that operate their own buses must regularly inspect the vehicles to establish that they conform to the state and federal safety standards.

The above operational decisions are played out against an environment of possible legal liability when students are injured as a result of the operations of school buses. Responsibility for student safety requires unending review of matters such as travel times, choice of pick-up and drop-off points, and alert attention to never-ending complaints. The prospect of troublesome behavior on buses may require contemplation of supervisory techniques, such as the use of videotaping or adult assistants on buses. Defenses, such as governmental immunity and contributory negligence, which may be available, do not offset the time and energy that must be invested to adequately defend a charge of negligence. In addition, even in the absence of legislative or constitutional mandates to furnish transportation, boards are not necessarily protected from litigation when students are injured in situations where arguably the presence of safe transportation would have prevented their being harmed.

Conflicts sometime develop concerning statutes that approve transportation but do not spell out the distance beyond which it must be supplied for students or circumstances under which it must be provided. In such a case, the Supreme Court of Appeals of West Virginia maintained that a school board violated the Equal Protection Clause of the Fourteenth Amendment in refusing to provide transportation to children who lived on a gravel road 2 miles away from school (*Shrewsbury v. Board of Education County of Wyoming,* 1980). Further, in a case in which a statute directed local boards of education to make transportation available to students wherever it was reasonable and desirable to so, parents of a small number of students sought transportation due to the existence of hazards between their dwellings and the school. Ruling in favor of the parents, the Supreme Court of Connecticut was of the opinion that a board had to furnish transportation (*Town of Waterford v. Connecticut State Board of Education,* 1961).

In addition to actually providing transportation, local school boards have the option of paying a mileage rate to parents who reside in out-of-the-way locations. Courts generally have upheld such arrangements as a reasonable means of satisfying the legal requirement of providing transportation for students. Even so, the mileage rates at which boards reimburse parents may well be subject to judicial review.

C. Daniel Raisch

See also Disabled Persons, Rights of; *Kadrmas v. Dickinson Public Schools;* Nonpublic Schools; Related Services; Rural Education; Year-Round Schools

Further Readings

Mawdsley, R. D. (1996). *Pupil transportation and the law* (2nd ed.). Dayton, OH: National Organization on Legal Problems of Education (now Education Law Association).

Legal Citations

Beard v. Board of Education of North Summit, 16 P.2d 900 (Utah 1932).
Individuals with Disabilities Education Act, 20 U.S.C. §§ 1400 *et seq.*
Kadrmas v. Dickinson Public Schools, 487 U.S. 450 (1988).
Russell v. Gallia County Local School District, 610 N.E.2d 1130 (Ohio Ct. App. 1992).
Salazar v. Dawson, 18 Cal.Rptr.2d 665 (Cal. Ct. App. 1992).
Shrewsbury v. Board of Education County of Wyoming, 265 S.E.2d 767 (W. Va. 1980).
Town of Waterford v. Connecticut State Board of Education, 169 A.2d 891 (Conn. 1961).

TRUANCY

Truancy, put simply, is the act of missing school. Truancy is identified as 1 of the 10 most important problems in schools. In fact, since student absenteeism has risen as high as 30% in some communities, this trend has had grave consequences for both children and their communities. This entry discusses causes and effects and some strategies for dealing with the problem.

Causes and Effects

Research has demonstrated that truancy is a reliable predictor of delinquency, gang involvement, substance abuse, and teen pregnancy. Further, insofar as many truants become dropouts, it also correlates with unemployment, low salary, imprisonment, and welfare.

Truancy affects communities by expending resources and time of family courts as well as juvenile justice systems, along with dealing with the rise in associated crimes. In addition, there can be a loss of state and federal education funding due to high absenteeism. This, in turn, could create either a rise in local property taxes or a reduction of educational resources, thereby impacting all students. Finally, insofar as truancy is correlated with unemployment and underemployment, it can have long-term effects for communities through lost tax revenues and expenditures on public assistance. Accordingly, it is in the interest of communities to reduce the rate of truancy.

The first set of factors correlated with truancy consists of student characteristics. Truant children tend to have low self-esteem and lack social competence. Further, drug and alcohol abuse, mental health issues, or poor physical health contribute to truancy. The second set of factors relate to families. These factors include lack of parental supervision, poverty, alcohol and drug abuse, domestic violence, and indifferent attitudes toward education. The third set of factors concern economic matters, such as parents having multiple jobs, students having to work to help support themselves and their families, the lack of affordable transportation and child care, single-parent households, and high mobility rates. The fourth set of factors includes school-based issues, such as perceived uncaring attitudes of teachers and administrators, school size, falling behind in schoolwork, boring and irrelevant curriculum, and bullying.

The legal definition of *truancy* varies from one state to the next. However, all definitions are connected with compulsory education laws that require children, generally between the age of 7 and 18 years, to continuously attend school. In general, school boards and educational officials have the authority to determine whether absences are excused. Even so, the number of unexcused absences required to make cases for truancy is set by state officials.

Approaches to Truancy

Jurisdictions also differ in their approach to truancy. Most states deal with truancy either through school-based intervention programs or via the mechanism of state law enforcement. In the court system, truancy is classified as a status offense because it would not be a violation if committed by an adult. Consequently, children can be categorized as status offenders in one state but be left alone by the legal systems of other jurisdictions.

The juvenile justice system, according to many scholars, is the least effective means of addressing truancy. The current emphasis on punishment in that system, rather than addressing the complexity of truancy, criminalizes truants. As such, children in the juvenile justice system tend to receive less rehabilitation and are more likely to become recidivists. Moreover, the adversarial nature of the juvenile justice system impedes its effectiveness in truancy cases. To this end, there is a tendency for parents and children to be set in opposition to one another, escalating rather than getting at the root of the problem.

Another justice system means of addressing truancy is to make parents liable for their children who are truant, often imposing fines or jail sentences. Parental liability statutes are typically incorporated in state tort and criminal laws. The logic behind these statutes is that since parents are responsible for their children, they must accept the consequences of the actions of their offspring. Advocates for this approach believe that this method gets parents' attention and compels them to focus more closely on the education of their children. Opponents respond that just like juvenile court, insofar as parental liability is adversarial, this approach exacerbates existing problems while possibly creating new ones.

Many jurisdictions choose school-based intervention programs in attempting to reduce truancy. The strength of this approach is that it works with children during the school day. This approach includes reorganizing the structure of middle schools to include assigning mentor teachers to individual or small groups of children; the ability to connect with teachers helps children feel less isolated and intimidated by middle school settings. School-based programs are more effective with early intervention.

Other alternatives to legal and school-based interventions are community-based programs to address truancy. Some of these programs work in concert with school officials, while others operate separately. In mentoring programs that work with school officials, educators provide mentors, either peers or volunteer members of communities. These mentors encourage the student to attend school by providing a support system. This approach may also promote students' interests in school by engaging them in extracurricular activities.

Mediation programs typically work outside of the school environment. In mediation, neutral third parties assist students and their parents to reach their own solutions. Mediators have no authority to impose solutions, but systematically help participants to identify the problems, work through the conflicts, agree on solutions, and develop plans of improvement. Advocates of mediation maintain that it has several advantages over using the court system to reduce truancy. First, supporters point out that mediation is a nonadversarial process, since parents and children are encouraged to work together to reach agreements on both problems and solutions. Second, proponents of mediation note that it focuses on rehabilitation, not punishment, thus promoting more durable change. Third, advocates of mediation explain that it enables participants to identify problems and produce more effective solutions. Finally, supporters maintain that mediation is a flexible process that can be tailored to the specific needs of the participants.

In sum, since the reasons for truancy are various and complex, it is important that educational officials work with the legal system in developing a multiplicity of programs to address the problems such behavior engenders.

Patricia A. L. Ehrensal

See also Compulsory Attendance; Juvenile Courts

Further Readings

Spaethe, R. (2000). Survey of school truancy intervention and prevention strategies. *Kansas Journal of Law & Public Policy, 9,* 689–702.

Stroman, J. (2000). Holding parents liable for their children's truancy. *UC Davis Journal of Juvenile Law & Policy, 5,* 47–66.

Trujillo, L. A. (2006). School truancy: A case study of a successful truancy reduction model in public school. *UC Davis Journal of Juvenile Law & Policy, 10,* 69–95.

Tuition Reimbursement

When school personnel fail to provide students with disabilities with the free appropriate public education (FAPE) called for in the Individuals with Disabilities Education Act (IDEA), the courts can grant appropriate relief (20 U.S.C. § 1415(i)(2)). One of the more common forms of relief is to provide tuition reimbursement to parents who may have obtained appropriate services privately.

The administrative and judicial proceedings concerned with contested placements under the IDEA can take months or even years before reaching final resolution of the underlying dispute. While these actions are pending, the IDEA requires that students remain in their current educational placements unless their parents and school board officials or states agree otherwise (20 U.S.C. § 1415(j)). Parents who are convinced that their child's current placement is inappropriate may not wish to have the child remain in that placement during the lengthy proceedings. Under these circumstances, parents may opt to remove their children from their current placements and enroll them in private facilities.

Under some circumstances, parents who succeed in showing that school board placements are inappropriate can be reimbursed for the cost of tuition and other expenses associated with their unilateral private placement. Initially, this relief was provided largely under case law, but the IDEA and its regulations now explicitly authorize judges and hearing officers to award tuition reimbursement (20 U.S.C. § 1412(a)(10)(C)(ii); 34 C.F.R. § 300.148).

The Supreme Court has delivered two important pronouncements regarding tuition reimbursement for parents who unilaterally place their children in private schools. In *Burlington School Committee v. Department of Education, Commonwealth of Massachusetts* (1985), the Court acknowledged that the IDEA allowed reimbursement as long as the parents' chosen placement was determined to be the appropriate placement for their child. The Court emphasized that when Congress empowered the courts to grant appropriate relief, it intended to include retroactive relief as an available remedy.

The Court articulated that reimbursement merely requires school boards to pay the expenses that they would have been paying all along if school personnel had developed proper individualized education programs (IEPs) from the outset. If reimbursement were not available, the Court observed, the rights of students to a FAPE and parental rights to participate fully in developing appropriate IEPs would be less than complete. On the other hand, the Court cautioned parents who make unilateral placements that they do so at their own financial risk, because they will not be reimbursed if school board officials can show that they proposed and had the capacity to implement appropriate IEPs.

In the Supreme Court's second case involving tuition reimbursement, *Florence County School District Four v. Carter* (1993), the justices unanimously affirmed that parentally chosen placements need not be in state-approved facilities for parents to obtain tuition reimbursements. In *Carter,* parents dissatisfied with the IEP that school officials developed for their daughter placed her in a private school that was not on the state's list of approved facilities. A federal trial court ruled that insofar as the school board's proposed IEP was inadequate, it was required to reimburse the parents for the cost of the private school placement.

On appeal, the Fourth Circuit affirmed. The court found that the private school provided an educational program that met the Supreme Court's standard of appropriateness as outlined in *Board of Education of the Hendrick Hudson Central School District v. Rowley* (1982), though it was not state approved and did not fully comply with the IDEA. The Fourth Circuit insisted that when a school board defaults on its obligations under the IDEA, reimbursement for a parental placement at a facility that is not approved by the state is not prohibited as long as the educational program provided at the school meets the *Rowley* standard.

The Supreme Court concurred, remarking that the IDEA is designed to ensure that all students with disabilities receive an education that is both appropriate and free. The Court emphasized that barring reimbursement under the circumstances in *Carter* would have defeated the IDEA's statutory purposes.

Naturally, parents are not entitled to be reimbursed for their private school tuition when school boards are successful in showing that they offered a FAPE. The most recent versions of the IDEA place some restrictions on a parent's ability to obtain a tuition reimbursement award, even when it is shown that a school board failed to provide a FAPE.

Under those provisions, at least 10 days before removing a child from the public schools, parents must notify school officials in writing that they are dissatisfied with the IEP of their child and afford educators the opportunity to take appropriate corrective action (20 U.S.C. § 1412(a)(10)(C)(iii)). Parents who fail either to challenge the IEPs of their children or to provide school officials with the written notice required by the IDEA prior to making unilateral placements are not entitled to reimbursements. Even prior to the inclusion of this provision in the IDEA, courts were hesitant to grant tuition reimbursement awards in situations in which school officials had not been given the opportunity to act.

At this writing, the Supreme Court has agreed to review yet another dispute involving tuition reimbursement. At issue in *Board of Education of the City of New York v. Tom F.* (2007) is whether parents who place their children in private schools are entitled to tuition reimbursement if the children have never attended the public schools.

Allan G. Osborne, Jr.

See also Free Appropriate Public Education; Individualized Education Program (IEP)

Legal Citations

Board of Education of the City of New York v. Tom F., cert. granted, 127 S. Ct. 1393 (2007), *aff'd*, 128 S. Ct. 1 (2007).

Board of Education of the Hendrick Hudson Central School District v. Rowley, 458 U.S. 176 (1982).

Burlington School Committee v. Department of Education, Commonwealth of Massachusetts, 471 U.S. 359 (1985).

Florence County School District Four v. Carter, 510 U.S. 7 (1993).

Individuals with Disabilities Education Act, 20 U.S.C. §§ 1400 *et seq.*

TUITION TAX CREDITS

Tuition tax credit policies fall into two broad categories. The older form allows a credit on state taxes for educational expenses, including private school tuition, incurred by parents or guardians. The second is a type of tuition tax credit policy more akin to vouchers; these are best described as "tuition tax credit vouchers." This entry describes these plans, their rationale, and some of the legal challenges they have faced.

Tax Credit for Expenses

In three states, parents who incur expenses for school books, tuition, or computers for their children may take credits on state taxes in order to serve as partial offsets against those expenses. These laws have existed in Minnesota and Iowa for decades; Illinois adopted such a policy in 1999. The U.S. Supreme Court upheld an earlier version of the Minnesota policy (one that allowed for an above-the-line deduction, rather than a tax credit) against an Establishment Clause challenge in *Mueller v. Allen* (1983).

Tuition Tax Credit Vouchers

Conventional voucher plans deliver state-allocated funds to schools through the private decisions of parents (see the "Vouchers" entry in this encyclopedia). In a roundabout way, this sort of voucher system can also be accomplished using tax credits. In 1997, Arizona became the first state to adopt this second type of tuition tax credit policy, one best described as "tuition tax credit vouchers." At that time, 5 years before the landmark *Zelman v. Simmons-Harris* (2002) decision, Arizona legislators were concerned about the legality of voucher legislation under the U.S. Constitution. They turned to tuition tax credits as a path toward the same goals. In a nutshell, the Arizona tax credit mechanism lets those who owe state taxes reallocate some of that money from the state general fund to a "scholarship-granting" organization (the legislation in Arizona and elsewhere refers to the voucherlike grants as scholarships).

Tuition tax credit voucher plans insert two intermediate steps into the conventional voucher process. First, the grants are issued by privately created, nonprofit organizations, rather than directly by the government. Second, state allocation is achieved through a tax credit given to donating taxpayers. The direct money pathway is from taxpayer to scholarship-granting organization to parent to school. The indirect part of the pathway is the forgone tax obligation given by the state government to the taxpayer.

Pennsylvania and Florida have followed Arizona and adopted tuition tax credit voucher policies in 2001, and Iowa and Rhode Island joined this group in 2006. These laws differ in various respects, most notably in whether the tax credit is full or for only a portion (e.g., 65% or 90%) of the donation and in whether the credit is available for private taxpayers, corporate taxpayers, or both. They also differ in whether they impose caps on individual donations and ceilings on overall donations and, if so, the amount of the caps and ceilings. They are described in a forthcoming publication by Welner.

Rationale for Tuition Tax Credit Vouchers

Tuition tax credit voucher systems are designed to provide government support for private schooling but to do so without any direct state payments. This is accomplished by having the tuition money pass through many sets of hands before making its way to private and parochial schools, but the overall policy effect is very much the same as with conventional vouchers. Arguably, this tax credit system still results in the government footing the tuition bill—through forgone tax revenues. Yet compared with voucher systems, control over funding decisions is largely delegated to two additional parties: (1) a subgroup of taxpayers, who can decide to which scholarship-granting organizations they will allocate the funds and (2) the scholarship-granting organizations, which are given the authority to decide grant recipients.

Legal Rulings on Tuition Tax Credit Vouchers

Arizona's law was challenged in state court but upheld in *Kotterman v. Killian* (1999). The Arizona Supreme Court decided that because the money never makes its way into the state general fund, there can be no state appropriation and thus no violation of the provisions in the state constitution that "No public money or property shall be appropriated for or applied to any religious worship, exercise, or instruction, or to the support of any religious establishment" (Arizona Constitution, Article II, §12) and that "No tax shall be laid or appropriation of public money made in aid of any . . . private or sectarian school" (Arizona Constitution, Article IX, §10):

> No money ever enters the state's control as a result of this tax credit. Nothing is deposited in the state treasury or other accounts under the management or possession of governmental agencies or public officials. Thus, under any common understanding of the words, we are not here dealing with "public money." (*Kotterman*, p. 618)

A federal court challenge was still ongoing at the time of this writing in 2007. However, the Supreme Court's holding in *Zelman*, grounded in a rationale of religious neutrality plus "genuine and independent private choice" (p. 648), is straightforwardly extendable from conventional vouchers to tuition tax credit vouchers. This permissive *Zelman* legal standard makes the new Arizona challenge difficult for the plaintiffs.

Research Findings

Research on the effects of tuition tax credit policies is scant. State reporting laws have been lax, as have official evaluations and audits. However, some basic, descriptive information is available. Perhaps the most noteworthy statistic is that more students receive tuition tax credit vouchers than receive conventional vouchers. As of 2004–2005, approximately 56,500 students received tuition tax credit vouchers in the three jurisdictions with the policy (Iowa and Rhode Island did not yet have the policy). The same year, fewer than 40,000 students received publicly funded traditional vouchers.

Research does point to some issues of equity. According to Glen Y. Wilson, in Arizona, when recipients are not means tested (i.e., they need not be low income), the state's wealthiest students appear to be receiving the vast majority of the law's benefits. The donor side of the equation also favors wealthier residents, since a taxpayer must itemize in order to receive the benefit. No research has yet been conducted on student-level outcomes, particularly achievement outcomes, resulting from tuition tax credit policies.

Kevin G. Welner

See also *Mueller v. Allen;* State Aid and the Establishment Clause; Vouchers; *Zelman v. Simmons-Harris*

Further Readings

Welner, K. G. (forthcoming). *Under the voucher radar: The emergence of tuition tax credits for private schooling.* New York: Rowman & Littlefield.

Wilson, G. Y. (2002). *The equity impact of Arizona's education tax credit program: A review of the first three years (1998–2000).* Tempe: Education Policy Research Unit, Arizona State University.

Legal Citations

Kotterman v. Killian, 972 P.2d 606 (Ariz. 1999).

Mueller v. Allen, 463 U.S. 388 (1983).

Zelman v. Simmons-Harris, 536 U.S. 639 (2002).

UNIONS

Unions are organizations specifically designed to protect and improve the social and economic welfare of their members. The primary responsibility of modern unions is to actively bargain with management officials regarding labor issues, such as wages, benefits, and the contractual terms and conditions associated with the employment of union members. Unions charge their members dues as a means of compensating union officials for the bargaining services they provide union members. Unions can also charge nonmembers fees, less than full dues, also known as agency fees, for the cost of representing their interests. This formal process of negotiating the contractual terms of employment, including salaries, working conditions, and fringe benefits between union officials representing employees and employers, is called the *collective bargaining process.* This entry looks at the historical background of teacher unions and important litigation related to union fees.

Growth of Public Employee Unions

While unions involved in private sector bargaining are governed primarily by federal law, unions working with public sector organizations, including public education, are governed by state law. In 1958, New York City Mayor Robert Wagner's Executive Order 49 permitted public employees to participate in collective bargaining for the first time. In 1959, Wisconsin became the first state to enact legislation authorizing unionization for public employees.

On the federal level, in 1962, President Kennedy's Executive Order 10988 gave national expression to the trend in establishing a policy recognizing governmental employees unions, thereby providing a major impetus for teachers' unions and collective bargaining. Subsequently, in 1970, President Nixon's Executive Order 11491 reinforced Kennedy's Executive Order by establishing a structure to administer federal labor relations.

A strike by public school teachers in April 1962, even though it just lasted for 1 day, led to the first collective bargaining agreement between a teacher association and a school board. Currently, the majority of states allow teachers to collectively bargain. At present, only a handful of states, including North Carolina, Texas, Utah, and Virginia, prohibit collective bargaining by employees of public school boards.

While private sector labor union membership has decreased over the past 30 years, public sector union membership, especially among teachers, has risen sharply over the same period. In education, the largest and most powerful unions representing educational employees are the American Federation of Teachers (AFT) and the National Education Association (NEA). The AFT was founded in New York City, partly as a result of the 1962 strike, and from its inception was a union organized by and composed of teachers. The AFT has more than 1.4 million members. In contrast, the NEA was originally founded as a professional organization for school administrators in the mid-19th century. However, over time, the NEA has grown to become one of the largest public sector unions in the United States, with a current membership of over 2.7 million members. Within the United States, current estimates indicate that over 80% of all public school teachers are members of the AFT, NEA, or local organizations affiliated with one of the two.

Agency Fees

One of the most litigated issues involving public sector unions has been whether they have the legal right to use nonunion member agency fees for political or ideological purposes unrelated to the union's collective bargaining responsibilities. *Agency fees* are fees that nonunion employees are required to pay in lieu of union dues paid by union members. In *Abood v. Detroit Board of Education* (1977), the U.S. Supreme Court ruled that a teachers' union could require nonmember teachers to pay agency, or service, fees to cover expenses associated with bargaining activities but could not require them to pay expenses associated with the support of the union's political or ideological activities. According to the Court, the First Amendment prohibits public sector unions from using nonunion members' agency fees for advancing unions' political or ideological causes that are unrelated to their collective bargaining duties and responsibilities.

Approximately a decade after *Abood,* the Supreme Court again addressed the issue of a union's use of agency fees imposed on nonunion employees, albeit not in a school setting. In *Communications Workers v. Beck* (1988), the Court reinforced *Abood*'s holding that unions have no legal right to use mandatory dues or fees to advance political or ideological endeavors. Yet under *Beck,* the responsibility of determining whether union officials were spending dues of nonmembers on political activities fell on the employees.

To provide more specific procedural guidelines in educational settings, in *Chicago Teachers Union, Local No. 1 v. Hudson* (1986), the Supreme Court reasoned that public sector unions must expressly inform nonunion employees specifically how much of their agency fees, or dues, are being spent on non-collective-bargaining-related activities and offer nonunion member employees a refund for that amount. As a direct result of *Hudson,* public sector unions must send all their nonunion member employees what are commonly referred to as "Hudson packets," informing them of their legal right to refuse permission to spend their agency fees on any noncollective bargaining activities.

Most recently, the Court dealt with the legal issue of agency fees for nonunion members in *Davenport v. Washington Education Association* (2007), wherein it found that states can legally require public sector unions to obtain permission from their nonunion members prior to spending agency fees on political or ideologically related activities. Collectively, *Abood, Beck, Hudson,* and *Davenport* emphasize the legal precedent that states have the legal right to prevent public sector unions, including teachers' unions, from mandating that nonmembers pay agency frees for noncollective-bargaining-related activities.

Kevin P. Brady

See also *Abood v. Detroit Board of Education;* Collective Bargaining; Contracts; *Davenport v. Washington Education Association*

Further Readings

Brady, K. P. (2006). Collective bargaining. In C. J. Russo & Ralph D. Mawdsley (Eds.), *Education law* (pp. 1–16). New York: Law Journal Press.

Brady, K. P. (2007). Bargaining. In C. J. Russo (Ed.), *The yearbook of education law: 2007.* (pp. 101–110). Dayton, OH: Education Law Association.

Brady, K. P. (2007). First Amendment rights, union dues, and politics. *School Business Affairs, 73*(9), 20–21.

Cresswell, A. M., & Murphy, M. J. (Eds.). (1976). *Education and collective bargaining: Readings in policy and research.* Berkeley, CA: McCutcheon.

Cresswell, A. M., & Murphy, M. J. (with Kerchner, C. T.). (1980). *Teachers, unions, and collective bargaining in public education.* Berkeley, CA: McCutcheon.

DeMitchell, T. A., & Cobb, C.D. (2006). Teachers: Their union and their profession. A tangled relationship. *West's Education Law Reporter, 212,* 1–20.

Legal Citations

Abood v. Detroit Board of Education, 431 U.S. 209 (1977).

Chicago Teachers Union, Local No. 1 v. Hudson, 475 U.S. 292 (1986), *on remand*, 922 F.2d 1306 (7th Cir. 1991), *cert. denied*, 501 U.S. 1230 (1991).

Communications Workers v. Beck, 487 U.S. 735 (1988).

Davenport v. Washington Education Association, 127 S. Ct. 2372 (2007).

UNITARY SYSTEMS

See DUAL AND UNITARY SYSTEMS

UNITED NATIONS CONVENTION ON THE RIGHTS OF THE CHILD

On November 20, 1989, the General Assembly of the United Nations noted under the Declaration of the Rights of the Child that "the child, by reason of his physical and mental immaturity, needs special safeguards and care, including appropriate legal protection, before as well as after birth." Asserting that a further articulation of those safeguards was necessary, the assembly ratified the Convention on the Rights of the Child (hereinafter "the Convention"), which came into force at the United Nations on September 2, 1990. The Convention specifically states that it does not take away from the rights stated in prior documents of the United Nations that deal with the protection of children.

All but two members of the United Nations have signed the Convention: the United States and Somalia. Thus, the Convention provides sovereign states and governments a standard for the treatment of all children based upon principles stated as rights and freedoms. The Convention and its relevance to education are discussed in this entry.

Key Convention Articles for Education

Under the Convention, there are four core principles: (1) nondiscrimination; (2) devotion to the best interests of the child; (3) the right to life, survival, and development; and (4) respect for the views of the child. Fifty-four articles articulate the civil, cultural, economic, political, and social rights of those less than 18 years of age and more specifically with respect to their health care; education; and legal, civil and social services. There are two optional protocols: Optional Protocol to the Convention on the Rights of the Child on the involvement of children in armed conflicts, adopted May 25, 2000, and entered into force on 12 February 2002, and the Optional Protocol to the Convention on the Rights of the Child on the Sale of Children, Child Prostitution, and Child Pornography, adopted May 25, 2000 and entered into force on 18 January 2002.

The Convention specifically refers to education in Articles 23, 28, and 29, while other articles that impact education include 33, 37, and 40. The Convention provides that all children, including those with mental and physical disabilities, have a right to a free education in the primary and secondary grades, one that develops their personality, talents, and both mental and physical abilities. School discipline is provided for, but it must ensure the dignity of the child and be in conformity with the Convention, which prohibits cruel, inhuman, or degrading treatment or punishment. The legal rights provided to adults in North America are provided to children, such as the right to be presumed innocent.

Application to Education

The application of the Convention as part of a country's domestic law has been problematic for several reasons. First, the Convention states the rights of individuals' vis-à-vis their own government, which is very different from state-to-state international law, as in the law of the seas. Second, the executive, not the legislative branch of government, ratifies the Convention; until the legislature affirms that decision, the Convention is not part of the country's domestic law. This is the case in Canada, Australia, and the United Kingdom, where the Convention has not been made domestic law through ratification by their legislatures. Nevertheless, the Convention has been considered as nonbinding legally but relevant to shaping the common law, to generating a reasonable expectation on the part of a litigant, or to being used for statutory interpretation when the domestic law is ambiguous or reflects the Convention's principles. The court, using a contextual approach, may refer to the values expressed in the Convention in interpreting the law.

In countries where ratification by the executive branch automatically makes such international treaties domestic law, as in Spain, Austria, and Romania, this difficulty does not exist. Thus, educational matters of corporeal punishment, rights of the disabled, and freedom of religion have been considered by various courts.

As noted, only two member countries of the United Nations are not signatories to the Convention: the United States of America and Somalia. However, the Convention has been cited by the Supreme Court of the United States, leading to a controversy regarding whether foreign law should be considered persuasive or conclusive, the areas of domestic law in which foreign law should apply (constitutional and private), and which foreign legal systems should be cited by American courts. In general, it is fair to say that although the Convention has not been signed by the United States administration nor brought into domestic law by the Congress of the United States, there are members of the U.S. Supreme Court (*Roper v. Simmons*, 2005) who perceive such international human rights principles as a "repository of wisdom," which, in a philosophical rather than persuasive or obligatory fashion, may be considered in the determination of human rights in domestic law. Even so, the view that foreign law may be cited in domestic cases is not unanimous among the justices of that Court and has been raised as a serious concern in the Congress of the United States.

Convention Remedies

There is no remedy for failure to abide by the Convention except in the case of jurisdictions in which the Convention is binding in domestic law. The United Nations provides, through its Committee on the Rights of the Child, for regular monitoring of the implementation of the Convention by signatories.

The United Nations Convention on the Rights of the Child provides an international standard with which countries can assess their performance in the tasks of the

protection and nurturing of those less than 18 years of age. Although it is not legally applicable or enforceable within a country unless through the operation of law of that country, it is nevertheless employed philosophically by courts in matters of principle and, in some cases, as a reference point for statutory interpretation.

J. Kent Donlevy

See also Universal Declaration of Human Rights

Further Readings

Chamberland, J. (2004, November, 18–20). *The application of the Convention on the Rights of the Child by Canadian courts since Baker: Coasting or speeding up?* Paper presented at "Making Children's Rights Work: National and International Perspectives," Montreal, Canada. Retrieved December 1, 2006, from htttp://www.Canadiancrc.com/ Chamberland_ eng_Nov04.htm

Harvard Law Review Association. (2005). The debate over foreign law in *Roper v. Simmons* (The Supreme Court, 2004 Term). *Harvard Law Review, 119,* 103–108.

United Nations Convention on the Rights of the Child. (n.d.). http://www.unhchr.ch/html/menu3/b/k2crc.htm

Legal Citations

Baker v. Canada (Minister of Citizenship and Immigration), [1999] (2 Supreme Court of Canada Reports) 817.

Hunter and Others v. Canary Wharf Ltd; Hunter and Others v. London Docklands Corporation [1997] UKHL 14 (House of Lords).

Minister of State for Immigration and Ethnic Affairs v. Ah Hin Teoh (1995) (Australian Law Reports) 128.

Roper v. Simmons, 543 U.S. 551 (2005).

UNITED STATES V. AMERICAN LIBRARY ASSOCIATION

United States v. American Library Association (ALA, 2003) is the most recent decision by the U.S. Supreme Court in a series of cases regarding the federal government's attempts to protect children from harmful online content. Although *ALA* concerned public libraries, it is generally presumed to also apply to public schools. In *ALA,* for the first time, the Supreme Court validated congressional attempts to protect students, via filtering software, from accessing indecent material on the Internet.

Facts of the Case

ALA is best understood by knowing the history of previous congressional attempts to regulate indecent Internet content. The first effort at legislation by Congress, the Communications Decency Act (CDA), was part of the Telecommunications Act of 1996. The act imposed criminal sanctions on anyone who behaves as follows:

> Knowingly (A) uses an interactive computer service to send to a specific person or persons under 18 years of age, or (B) uses any interactive computer service to display in a manner available to a person under 18 years of age, any comment, request, suggestion, proposal, image, or other communication that, in context, depicts or describes, in terms patently offensive as measured by contemporary community standards, sexual or excretory activities or organs.

The CDA also prohibited the transmission of materials that were "obscene or indecent" to minors under the age of 18.

The Supreme Court invalidated the CDA in *Reno v. American Civil Liberties Union* (1997), holding that the statute's indecency provisions violated the First Amendment. The Court struck down these provisions on the basis that they extended to commercial speech, did not define what "patently offensive" meant, and did not permit parents to decide for themselves the acceptability of online materials for their children.

Congress tried again in 1998 with the Child Online Protection Act (COPA), which required commercial online distributors to restrict access by minors to "harmful material" that showed sexual acts or nudity. In 2003, a federal trial court disallowed initial enforcement of COPA because the age verification procedures it required unduly hindered protected speech by adults. The Supreme Court upheld that judgment in 2004 in *Ashcroft v. American Civil Liberties Union,* ordering the case to go to full trial. The federal government lost at trial and, at this time, is in the process of appealing.

The third attempt by Congress was the Children's Internet Protection Act (CIPA). CIPA, which became

law in 2000, applies to schools and libraries that received funds or discounts under the federal "e-rate" program. CIPA requires these schools and libraries to operate "a technology protection measure with respect to any of its computers with Internet access that protects against access through such computers to visual depictions that are obscene, child pornography, or harmful to minors." CIPA had the same standards for adults but omitted the "harmful to minors" provision. In addition, CIPA allowed libraries to disable the technology protection measure for adults engaged in research or other lawful activity. In 2003, the U.S. Supreme Court agreed to accept *ALA* and decide the constitutionality of CIPA.

The Court's Ruling

Despite a lengthy lower court decision that found that because of the "severe limitations" of Internet filtering technologies, public libraries could not comply with CIPA without blocking "a very substantial amount" of speech that was constitutionally protected, the Supreme Court ruled that CIPA did not violate the First Amendment. The Court was satisfied that CIPA was constitutional insofar as librarians could unblock filtered material or disable Internet filtering software for adults who requested them to do so. At the same time, the Court also noted that public libraries were free to forgo their eligibility for e-rate funds if they wished to keep their computers unfiltered.

To the extent that the Court upheld the relative efficacy of Internet filtering tools, schools receiving e-rate funds must have an Internet filter in place or forgo the funds. Insofar as most schools that are eligible desperately need their e-rate funds to keep their computer networks current, few, if any, schools have opted out. Internet filters thus exist in the vast majority of K–12 schools, either because of CIPA or due to community pressure.

A number of analysts have expressed concern about both the under- and overblocking that occur with Internet filters. Even so, these filters will continue to serve as the primary mechanism for preventing student access to age-inappropriate Internet content in the near future. As an interesting side note, in the COPA appeal noted above, the federal government is arguing the ineffectiveness of the Internet filtering technologies for which it advocated in *ALA*.

Scott McLeod

See also Acceptable Use Policies; Children's Internet Protection Act; First Amendment; Free Speech and Expression Rights of Students; Technology and the Law

Legal Citations

Ashcroft v. American Civil Liberties Union, 542 U.S. 656 (2004).
Children's Internet Protection Act, 15 U.S.C. § 254.
Children's Online Privacy Protection Act, 15 U.S.C. § 6501.
Communications Decency Act, 47 U.S.C. § 230.
Reno v. American Civil Liberties Union, 521 U.S. 844 (1997).
United States v. American Library Association, 539 U.S. 194 (2003).

UNITED STATES V. LOPEZ

United States v. Lopez (1995), in which a student challenged a new federal law prohibiting the possession of guns in and around schools, reflects a textbook examination of the power of Congress under the Commerce Clause. *Lopez* reflects the Supreme Court's analysis of congressional authority in the limited context of school safety. The congressional action in this case was passage of the Gun-Free School Zones Act, part of the Crime Control Act of 1990. Congress used this legislation to address growing concerns about school violence, and the act was signed into law on November 29, 1990. The act provided that "it shall be unlawful for any individual knowingly to possess a firearm in a place that the individual knows, or has reasonable cause to believe, is a school zone." The maximum penalty was 5 years of imprisonment. While *Lopez* may be known as the case that invalidated the Gun-Free School Zones Act, it presents an insight into how the federal courts review federal legislation, including laws that impact schools.

Facts of the Case

Alfonso Lopez Jr. was a 12th-grade student in the San Antonio, Texas, schools. When on March 10, 1992,

Lopez was confronted by school officials based on an anonymous tip, he admitted that he was carrying an unloaded .38 caliber handgun. Lopez also had five bullets for the handgun. Lopez claimed that he brought the gun to school for delivery to a third party at the end of the school day in exchange for $40.

Lopez was charged with violating a Texas statute prohibiting the carrying of a firearm at school. The state charge was quickly dropped, and Lopez was charged with a violation of the Gun-Free School Zones Act of 1990. Lopez entered a plea of not guilty, and his attorneys moved to dismiss the charge on the grounds that Congress had exceeded its authority in adopting the Gun-Free School Zones Act.

A federal trial court in Texas denied the motion to dismiss on the basis that the act was a constitutional exercise of the well-defined power of Congress to regulate activities in and affecting commerce, finding that the business of elementary, middle, and high schools impacts on interstate commerce. Lopez waived his right to a jury trial. There was no material issue of fact, and Lopez was convicted on the basis of the undisputed evidence. He was sentenced to 6 months of imprisonment and 2 years of supervised release.

Lopez appealed his conviction to the Fifth Circuit, which reversed on the issue of congressional authority. The Fifth Circuit ruled that the law represented an impermissible extension of congressional power under the Commerce Clause.

The Court's Ruling

On further review, the Supreme Court in *United States v. Lopez* (1995) affirmed the order of the Fifth Circuit in a 5-to-4 judgment. Writing for the majority, Chief Justice Rehnquist held that the Gun-Free School Zones Act exceeded the congressional authority to regulate commerce among the several states. The chief justice spent a considerable time in his analysis discussing the development and meaning of the Commerce Clause. Rehnquist explained that the act was neither a regulation of the channels of interstate commerce nor an attempt to prohibit interstate transportation of a commodity through those channels.

Consequently, Rehnquist determined that if the Gun-Free School Zones Act were to withstand judicial scrutiny, it would have to be an activity that substantially affects interstate commerce. Rehnquist reviewed situations in which the court had upheld federal regulation when economic activity substantially affected interstate commerce. Rehnquist was of the opinion that regardless of how broadly one might seek to construe its terms, the Gun-Free School Zones Act was a criminal statute that had nothing to do with interstate commerce or economic activity. Consequently, Justice Rehnquist found that the act could not be sustained.

Rehnquist also reasoned that the Gun-Free School Zones Act did not contain any jurisdictional elements leading to a finding that it impacts on interstate commerce. Rehnquist noted a lack of congressional findings prior to the act's passage and noted that it did not include an element that would have limited its reach to firearms with a potential link to interstate commerce.

The government attempted to argue that possession of the gun in a school zone could result in a violent crime that would have the potential to impact on the national economy. The government claimed that the significant cost of insurance associated with violent crime affects the economy because the expense is spread throughout society. It also contended that the economy is harmed when the presence of violent crime limits the willingness of individuals to travel to areas they believe to be unsafe. The government suggested that the presence of guns in the schools presents a serious threat to the learning environment; this, in turn, could result in a less-educated citizenry, which would have an obvious adverse impact on the nation.

Rehnquist rejected the government's attempt to justify the congressional action. He pointed out that "if we were to accept the government's arguments, we are hard-pressed to posit any activity by an individual that Congress is without power to regulate" (*Lopez,* p. 564). Rehnquist noted that congressional authority under the Commerce Clause is subject to a degree of legal uncertainty for two main reasons. First, he stated that the enumerated powers of Congress have a judicially enforceable outer limit. Second, he noted that under the Constitution, Congress does not have the authority to enact virtually any type of legislation that it wishes. Rehnquist refused to follow earlier rulings that granted great

deference to Congress. In the end, Rehnquist and the majority affirmed the ruling of the Fifth Circuit and struck down the Gun-Free School Zones Act as an impermissible exercise of congressional power under the Commerce Clause. There were two concurrences (Kennedy and Thomas), and three dissents (Stevens, Souter, and Breyer), the latter of which essentially argued that the act fell within the sphere of congressional authority.

Jon E. Anderson

See also Gun-Free Schools Act

Further Readings

Martinez, R. (1995). S.O.S., Saving Our Schools: The constitutionality of the Gun-Free School Zones Act of 1990. *American Journal of Criminal Law, 22,* 491–514.

Russo, C. (1995). *Unites States v. Lopez* and the demise of the Gun-Free School Zones Act: Legislative over-reaching or judicial nit-picking? *West's Education Law Reporter, 99,* 11–23.

Legal Citations

Gun-Free School Zones Act of 1990, 18 U.S.C. §§ 921 *et seq.*
United States v. Lopez, 514 U.S. 549 (1995).

UNITED STATES V. MONTGOMERY COUNTY BOARD OF EDUCATION

At issue in *United States v. Montgomery County Board of Education* (1969) was a federal trial court's order regarding a desegregation plan to integrate the faculty of a school system in Alabama. The U.S. Supreme Court ruled that an earlier order was a reasonable step forward. It called for a ratio of 3 White to 2 African American teachers in order to have at least one teacher who was of a different race than the majority of teachers in a school; it also mandated that in schools with 12 or more teachers, at least 1 of every 6 teachers or staff members should be of a race different from that of the majority. *Montgomery* stands out as the first case on the merits of faculty desegregation.

Facts of the Case

Montgomery began in 1964 when African American children and their parents filed suit seeking desegregated schools. Based on the mandates established by the litigation in *Brown v. Board of Education of Topeka I* (1954) and *II* (1955), the trial court directed the school board of a formerly segregated district to establish a unitary system as soon as possible, while setting forth a plan including teacher ratios.

Moreover, the court indicated that it would annually review the board's progress toward achieving unitary status. When the board challenged the trial court's order, the Fifth Circuit modified it by changing the specific mathematical numbers and ratios to require only substantial or approximate ratios because it thought that the order was rigid and inflexible. The court also denied a request for a rehearing en banc.

The Court's Ruling

On further review, the Supreme Court reversed the decision of the Fifth Circuit and remanded with instructions to reinstate the original order from the trial court. At the outset of its analysis, the unanimous Court reiterated the findings of *Brown I* and *Brown II,* which held not only that segregation of the races was unconstitutional but also that the primary responsibility for abolishing segregated school systems rests with local authorities. The Court noted that as *Brown II* admonished, changes were to be made at the earliest practicable date "with all deliberate speed." Yet in *Montgomery,* the Court pointed out that its review of local circumstances revealed that state and school officials had done all they could to continue to maintain a dual system of racially segregated schools.

The primary issue before the Supreme Court related to the part of the trial court's order that involved the desegregation of faculty and staff. More specifically, the dispute focused on the specific numerical goals based on ratios of White-to-African American teachers, identified earlier in this entry, in order to move the district's goal to one of proportional representation in all schools as it existed in the entire school system. In rejecting the Fifth Circuit's belief that the trial court's order was rigid and inflexible, the justices were satisfied that it was not, because it was subject to annual review.

To this end, the Court reinstated the order requiring assignment of faculty and staff based on specific ratios to ensure that the ratio of minority-to-nonminority faculty in the schools was the same as in the school system, pointing out that it was not objectionable simply because it contained fixed mathematical ratios.

In recognizing that the school board had a history of noncompliance, the Court chided officials for operating as if *Brown I* and *II* had never been litigated. In upholding the trial court's order, the justices were strongly of the opinion that school officials had to adopt more aggressive and clear measures to move the district to unitary status in compliance with the dictates of the Fourteenth Amendment's requirement of equal educational opportunities for all children regardless of their race.

Deborah Curry

See also *Brown v. Board of Education of Topeka; Brown v. Board of Education of Topeka* and Equal Educational Opportunities; Dual and Unitary Systems; Equal Protection Analysis

Further Readings

Hunter, R. C., & Donahoo, S. (2004). The implementation of *Brown* in achieving unitary status. *Education and Urban Society, 36,* 342–354.

Russo, C. J., Harris, J. J., III, & Sandridge, R. F. (1994). *Brown v. Board of Education* at 40: A legal history of equal educational opportunities in American public education. *Journal of Negro Education, 63,* 297–309.

Legal Citations

Brown v. Board of Education of Topeka I, 347 US 483 (1954).
Brown v. Board of Education of Topeka II, 349 U.S. 294 (1955).
United States v. Montgomery County Board of Education, 395 U.S. 225 (1969).

UNITED STATES V. SCOTLAND NECK CITY BOARD OF EDUCATION

United States v. Scotland Neck City Board of Education (1972) dealt with a legislative act that allowed a city to establish its own school district while the county system was undergoing court-ordered desegregation. At issue in *Scotland Neck* was whether the creation of the new city district impeded the desegregation of the county school system. The U.S. Supreme Court ruled that implementing the statute would have created a new district out of an existing system in which 57% of the students were White and the other students were African American, while the other schools in the district were about 90% African American. The Court decided this was unconstitutional.

Facts of the Case

In *Scotland Neck,* the U.S. Justice Department instituted legal action to compel a county to create a unitary school system. Prior to 1965, the county school system was segregated. County officials subsequently developed a freedom-of-choice plan. Insofar as the plan produced very little desegregation, the Department of Justice moved to have the county create a unitary system "with all deliberate speed." However, before county officials could implement the new plan, the legislature of the state of North Carolina passed a law that allowed the city to create its own school district.

A federal trial court granted the Department of Justice's request to enjoin the implementation of the statute on the basis that it impeded the desegregation of the county schools. In response to an appeal by city officials and the legislature, the Fourth Circuit reversed in their behalf. On further review, the Supreme Court invalidated the statute.

The Court's Ruling

At the outset of its analysis, on a day when the Supreme Court resolved two desegregation cases with similar issues, it referred to its rationale in the other dispute, *Wright v. City Council of Emporia* (1972). In *Wright,* the justices refused to permit officials to carve city school districts out of segregated county systems, since doing so would have slowed down their shifts to unitary status. The difference between the two cases was that in *Wright,* the resistance came from city officials, while in *Scotland Neck,* it came from the state legislature.

As such, the Court noted that the law would have allowed the county and city to maintain the racially segregated identities in the schools in violation of the Equal Protection Clause of the Fourteenth Amendment. To this end, citing to its own precedent in *Swann v. Charlotte-Mecklenberg Board of Education* (1971), the Court explained that there was a presumption against desegregation plans that create schools with disproportionate racial compositions.

At the heart of its rationale, the Supreme Court was of the opinion that implementation of the statute would have impeded the creation of a unitary school system because it would have led to substantial disparity in the racial composition of the schools in the city and county. The Court next rejected the defendants' argument that the statute would have stemmed "White flight" from the public schools to private schools. The Court refused to give any weight to this argument, instead pointing out that the primary legal focus had to be on dismantling the dual school system.

Historically, *Scotland Neck* stands out as another example of states and school boards trying to avoid the mandate to create unitary school systems. Eighteen years after *Brown v. Board of Education of Topeka,* the Supreme Courts made it clear that it was in no mood to permit public officials to continue their evasive tactics with regard to implementing equal educational opportunities for all students.

J. Patrick Mahon

See also *Brown v. Board of Education of Topeka* and Equal Educational Opportunities; Civil Rights Movement; Dual and Unitary Systems; Fourteenth Amendment; *Swann v. Charlotte-Mecklenberg Board of Education;* White Flight

Legal Citations

Brown v. Board of Education of Topeka I, 347 U.S. 483 (1954).
Brown v. Board of Education of Topeka II, 349 U.S. 294 (1955).
Swann v. Charlotte-Mecklenberg Board of Education, 402 U.S. 1 (1971).
United States v. Scotland Neck City Board of Education, 407 U.S. 484 (1972).
Wright v. City Council of Emporia, 407 U.S. 451 (1972).

UNITED STATES V. VIRGINIA

United States v. Virginia (1996) is often called the "VMI" case because the U.S. Supreme Court had to determine whether the all-male Virginia Military Institute (VMI) unconstitutionally discriminated against women. In *United States v. Virginia,* the Court ruled that by operating the all-male military academy, the Commonwealth of Virginia violated the Equal Protection Clause of the Fourteenth Amendment of the U.S. Constitution.

Facts of the Case

VMI is a public college in Virginia, founded in 1839, which admitted only male applicants. VMI's mission was to produce citizen-soldiers. In order to meet its mission, VMI used what it called an "adversative teaching method." Under this methodology, to prepare citizen-soldiers, educators at VMI employed physical and mental stress, absence of privacy, and indoctrination into specified military values.

The dispute began in 1990 when the United States sued the Commonwealth of Virginia, arguing that the male-only admissions policy was a form of sex discrimination in violation of the Equal Protection Clause. After losing in the Fourth Circuit Court, Virginia chose to develop a new institution for women rather than change the VMI male-only policy. The Virginia Women's Institute for Leadership (VWIL), officials maintained, remedied any discrimination caused by the VMI's male-only admissions criteria. The United States disagreed and again filed suit arguing that Virginia violated the Equal Protection Clause. Ultimately, VMI went all the way to the Supreme Court, which held that Virginia violated the Equal Protection Clause.

The Court's Ruling

The Supreme Court began its analysis by noting that insofar as the VMI policy discriminated on the basis of sex, it was subject to scrutiny under the equal protection analysis. Over the years, the Court developed three tests to evaluate whether a public policy constitutes unconstitutional discrimination. *Strict scrutiny,* applied in cases in which race is at issue, is the most difficult test for a state (or commonwealth) to overcome because it requires a compelling governmental interest that is narrowly tailored. *Rational basis,* on the other hand, requires a state to demonstrate only that there was rational relationship to a legitimate state interest at stake, and it is usually very easy for a state to meet this burden. In sex discrimination cases, the court uses the *intermediate scrutiny test.*

Utilizing the intermediate scrutiny test, the Supreme Court had to evaluate whether the reasons Virginia officials gave for the male-only admissions policy were exceedingly persuasive. According to the Court, the burden is always on the state to prove that a policy is justified. As such, Virginia officials had to prove that the policy served an important government objective and that the means used were substantially related to achieving those objectives.

The Supreme Court first turned to a consideration of whether VMI's male-only admissions policy violated the Equal Protection Clause. Virginia argued that single-sex education provided important educational benefits and that having the VMI contributed to diversity in educational approaches. However, the Court found that there was no persuasive evidence that the VMI policy furthered the state's diversity mission.

Next, Virginia claimed that its teaching methods could not work if they were modified. The Court thought that VMI could still meet its mission of producing citizen-soldiers by utilizing its adversative teaching methods and that this was not inherently unsuitable for women. As such, the Court was of the opinion that Virginia unconstitutionally discriminated on the basis of sex.

The Supreme Court then had to evaluate whether Virginia remedied its violation of the Equal Protection Clause by establishing the VWIL. Commonwealth officials asserted that the separation of female and male students was justified because there are differences between the way men and women learn and develop psychologically. Yet the Court pointed out that even though VMI's methods might not have been appropriate for most women, this did not justify denying all women the opportunity to attend the VMI. The Court thus concluded that since VMI violated the

Equal Protection Clause, it had to admit qualified male and female applicants.

Utilizing the analysis that was first enunciated in *Mississippi University for Women v. Hogan* (1982), the Supreme Court's rationale in *United States v. Virginia,* the VMI case continues to provide insight into how the judiciary treats sex discrimination. Even so, it is important to keep in mind that Title IX also deals with sex discrimination in educational institutions. Title IX, for example, explicitly limits what types of educational institutions are allowed to have single-sex admissions policies. To this end, private undergraduate programs are generally exempt from Title IX's prohibition against single-sex admissions policies, as are religious institutions, if they have obtained waivers of its provisions. In sum, though, for most institutions, Title IX provides more guidance regarding sex discrimination and gender equity.

Karen Miksch

See also Civil Rights Act of 1964; Equal Protection Analysis; Single-Sex Schools

Further Readings

Russo, C. J., & Scollay, S. J. (1993). All male state-funded military academies: Anachronism or necessary anomaly? *West's Education Law Reporter, 82,* 1073–1085.

Legal Citations

Mississippi University for Women v. Hogan, 458 U.S. 718 (1982).
United States v. Virginia, 518 U.S. 515 (1996).

UNIVERSAL DECLARATION OF HUMAN RIGHTS

On December 10, 1948, the General Assembly of the United Nations adopted the "Universal Declaration of Human Rights" (hereinafter "the Declaration") in response to the carnage and barbarism of World War II. Although the statement is not legally binding upon member states, it expresses the moral conscience of the world and is based upon five principles:

respect for the rule of law, dignity of the person, fair and equitable treatment of individuals by governments, tolerance and acceptance of diversity, and the value of democratic participation.

The Declaration contains a preamble and 30 articles. Article 1 affirms the principle "that everyone is entitled to fundamental rights without regard to distinction of any kind, such as race, colour, sex, language, religion, political or other opinion, national or social origin." Together with the United Nations International Covenant on Civil and Political Rights and the International Covenant on Economic, Social, and Cultural Rights, the Declaration forms what is commonly called the "International Bill of Rights."

The Declaration has inspired the Dominion of Canada in the creation of its Charter of Rights and Freedoms, and organizations such as Amnesty International have referred to it in relation to the rights and freedoms claimed by individuals vis-à-vis their own and other governments. The U.S. Supreme Court has asserted that the Declaration has moral authority but does not grant citizens rights, nor does it bind the courts. In the United Kingdom, the courts have held that the Declaration may be consulted on human rights. Although the declaration has been incorporated in the constitutions of some countries in continental Europe, it does not create any new rights for Europeans. In Australia, the Declaration is given significant persuasive weight, but it is not part of domestic law. India gives great significance to the Declaration as an interpretive tool for its constitution, and South African courts use it as a reference on principles.

Article 26 of the Declaration speaks directly to education and provides, among other things, for free and compulsory elementary education that "shall be directed to the full development of the human personality . . . [to] promote understanding, tolerance and friendship among all nations, racial or religious groups." Individuals in various countries have used this article to argue for extra assistance in schools for disabled children, language testing, and religious programming in schools, independent religious schools, the right of a teacher to be associated with a Maoist organization, and the right of children not to be discriminated against in school due to the political convictions of their parents.

The United Nations Universal Declaration of Human Rights is a nonbinding international document that sets an international standard for the treatment of individuals and minority groups by member governments both internal and external to those governments. It was intended by the United Nations Commission on Human Rights to be the fountainhead from which would emerge specific further documents that would bind member states. Those two other documents, the International Covenant on Civil and Political Rights and the International Covenant on Economic Social and Cultural Rights, were adopted by the United Nations in 1966 and came into effect in 1976. However, in many countries, the documents must be ratified by legislative bodies to have effect, and this has not always been accomplished.

Nevertheless, the Declaration stands as an influential international document that can be referred to by most litigants in their jurisdictions as persuasive moral authority.

J. Kent Donlevy

See also United Nations Convention on the Rights of the Child

Further Readings

Canadian Human Rights Tribunal (Quebec). (1996). *Lisenko et al. v. Commisson Scolaire Saint-Hyacinthe Va-Monts.* Retrieved December 23, 2006, from http://www.canlii .org/qc/cas/qctdp/1996/1996qctdp131.html

United Nations. (n.d.). *Universal declaration of human rights.* Retrieved December 23, 2006, from http://www .un.org/Overview/rights.html

Legal Citations

A & Ors R. (On the application of) v. East Sussex County Council & Anor, (2003) England and Wales High Court 167.

Glasenapp v. Germany, (1986) European Court of Human Rights 9.

Islamic Academy of Education & Anr v. Vs, (2003) INSC 361 (Supreme Court of India).

In re Gauteng School Education Bill of 1995, (CCT39/95) 1996 (4) BCLR 537.

Peter Van Schaik v. Stephen Peter George Neuhaus, (1996) Australian Capital Territory Supreme Court. 37

Sosa v. Alvarez-Machain, 542 U.S. 692 (2004).

U.S. Department of Education

In 1980, Congress established the U.S. Department of Education (ED) in the Department of Education Organization Act. ED combined several offices from various federal agencies. It is now responsible for assisting the president and Congress in creating and implementing educational policy, along with administering and coordinating most of federal assistance programs for education.

In 1867, President Andrew Johnson signed legislation creating the first Department of Education. At the time, the department's primary task was to collect information and statistics on the nation's schools. However, people feared that it would exert too much control of the local school system and demanded its elimination. The department was reduced to the status of the Office of Education in 1868. Over time, the Office of Education was a part of several different federal agencies, including the Department of the Interior and the former Department of Health, Education and Welfare.

Increased federal funding for education in the 1950s and 1960s led to the creation of improved educational programs for poor students at every grade level through college. Federal legislation in the 1970s led to improved access to education for minorities, women, people with disabilities, and non-English-speaking students.

According to the ED, its mission includes ensuring access to equal educational opportunity for every individual; improving the quality of education through efforts of the states, local school systems, other state actors, the private sector, public and private nonprofit educational research institutions, community-based organizations, parents, and students; promoting participation of the public, parents, and students in federal education programs; advancing the quality and appropriateness of education through federally supported research, evaluation, and sharing of information; and improving the coordination, management, and accountability of federal education programs and activities to the public and the legislative and executive branches of government.

ED is involved in four major activities: establishing policies related to federal educational financial aid, its distribution, and monitoring; collecting data and overseeing research on schools and distributing the information to educators and the public; identifying problems in education and focusing attention on them; and enforcing federal statutes that prohibit discrimination in programs and activities that receive federal funding and ensuring equal access to education for all individuals.

Under the Tenth Amendment to the U.S. Constitution, the states are granted the authority to act in areas such as education as long as they are not prohibited from doing so in other sections of the Constitution. Insofar as education is not mentioned in the Constitution, the federal government has no power to act in this regard. Therefore, as a federal agency, ED is not permitted to exercise control in educational curricula, instruction, administration, or personnel at any educational institution, school, or school system. Individual states and municipalities have the power to establish schools and develop academic requirements.

Educational funding sources demonstrate the predominant role of the states and communities. The Department of Education (2002) states that a majority of educational expenditures are paid with state, local, and private dollars, with less than 9% coming from federal sources, such as ED, Department of Health and Human Services, and Department of Agriculture. When including secondary education, federal contributions, including student loans and other aid, make up only 12% of the total of all educational spending.

The Department of Education administers programs and initiatives in education across the United States. One of the most visible initiatives is the No Child Left Behind Act (NCLB), which reauthorized the Elementary and Secondary Education Act. The NCLB, which was signed into law in 2002 by President George W. Bush, is the primary federal law that affects elementary and secondary education. The NCLB is based on four general principles: increased accountability for states, school districts, and schools; greater choice for parents and students, especially for students attending poorly performing schools; more flexibility for states in using federal funds; and a stronger emphasis on reading.

ED is also involved in programs that are designed to improve math and science education, foreign-language studies, and high schools. In addition, ED supports the Teacher-to-Teacher Initiative, which provides technical support, professional development, and recognition for teachers of all grade levels.

Suzann VanNasdale

See also Federalism and the Tenth Amendment; No Child Left Behind Act

Further Readings

U.S. Department of Education. (n.d.). http://www.ed.gov

Legal Citations

Department of Education Organization Act, P.L. No. 96–88. No Child Left Behind Act, 20 U.S.C. §§ 6301 *et seq.*

U.S. SUPREME COURT CASES IN EDUCATION

To paraphrase Alexis de Tocqueville, an early writer on the American democracy, every educational issue eventually becomes a judicial question, and those judicial questions eventually reach the U.S. Supreme Court. Indeed, it seems that there is virtually not a single aspect of education that the Court has not addressed at some point in its history. In many instances, the foundations of modern constitutional law have been laid in education cases. Insofar as the Court hears approximately a half dozen cases per term that have a direct or indirect impact on education law, those who work in education law, whether as advocates or as academics, must constantly monitor its docket and decisions.

The Supreme Court's impact on education law has paralleled its influence on broader American society. During the 19th century, when the Court generally was disconnected from broader society, it was also disconnected from education. When the Court used the Due Process Clause to invalidate progressive economic regulations, it also used the clause to invalidate statutes designed to promote education. As the Court abandoned this mode of judicial activism in favor of blind deference to government officials, it also began to defer to education officials.

Following World War II, at which time the Supreme Court began to vigorously enforce the Bill of Rights and the Equal Protection Clause against the states, education cases were frequently the mechanism for that enforcement. When the Court attempted to transform American society, starting with *Brown v. Board of Education of Topeka* in 1954 through the 1970s, education cases, particularly the desegregation cases, were at the forefront. Similarly, as the role of the national government in education has expanded, the role of the Court, as the ultimate arbiter of federal law, has also expanded. Conversely, as the Court realized that the judiciary is not omnicompetent, education cases first signaled the retreat from micromanagement and broad societal transformation.

This entry explores the Supreme Court's education cases through the lens of its overall jurisprudence. To this end, it examines how the education cases, regardless of whether they confer landmark or minor decisions on technical points of statutory construction, contribute to and ultimately reflect developments in constitutional doctrine and the role of the Court. The text is divided into seven substantive sections, each of which deals with a specific period in American history, and ends with a brief conclusion.

From the Framing to the Twentieth Century (1789–1900)

During the first century of the American Republic, the Supreme Court did not regularly render decisions that affected the average American. However, when the Court did so, it spoke with a thunderclap. To be sure, a few cases from this initial era substantially changed America. *Marbury v. Madison* (1803) established the role of the Court in the American constitutional system as final arbiter in legal disputes. *McCullough v. Maryland* (1819) and *Gibbons v. Ogden* (1824) ensured that the national government, like the states, was a separate sovereign. *Dred Scott v. Sanford* (1857) arguably made the Civil War inevitable. The *Slaughterhouse Cases* (1872) rejected a natural law

reading of the post–Civil War amendments. *Plessy v. Ferguson* (1896), which institutionalized "separate but equal" in race relations, effectively nullified the Equal Protection Clause for half a century. Despite these landmarks, the Court's direct influence on education was minimal.

The Lochner Era (1901–1937)

During the first third of the 20th century, the Supreme Court, in a significant departure from the reasoning of the *Slaughterhouse Cases,* frequently used the Due Process Clause of the Fourteenth Amendment to nullify progressive social welfare legislation. Most famously, in *Lochner v. New York* (1905), the Court invalidated a statute from New York that regulated the maximum hours that bakers could work. The Court's rationale was that the statute violated the "Liberty of Contract" such that individuals were free to work for as long or under whatever conditions they wished and the state could not interfere. The Court employed similar rationales on occasion throughout the 1910s and 1920s to invalidate child labor laws and other economic legislation.

The *Lochner* substantive due process era reached its peak during the early years of the Roosevelt administration, when the Court, usually by narrow 5-to-4 majorities, consistently invalidated various portions of the New Deal legislation. Modern scholars almost universally regard the *Lochner* era as the epitome of judicial activism. The Court, without reference to the Constitution's text or structure, consistently substituted its judgment for that of the legislature.

During the *Lochner* era, the Supreme Court heard only two major education cases, applying the substantive due process approach in both. In *Meyer v. Nebraska* (1923), the Court invalidated a statute that prohibited teaching a foreign language to elementary school students. While one can debate the wisdom of such a policy, there is nothing in the Constitution's text, structure, or history that prohibits the pursuit of such a policy. Similarly, in *Pierce v. Society of Sisters of the Holy Names of Jesus and Mary* (1925), the Court invalidated an Oregon statute requiring parents to send their children to public schools. Although one could argue that the Free Exercise Clause arguably protects the right to send one's children to private religious schools, that Free Exercise argument applies only if religion motivates the choice. It would not apply if the parents simply believed that the educational benefits of private school were greater. While *Meyer* and *Pierce* have never been overruled, their reasoning must be regarded as suspect in light of the Court's subsequent repudiation of substantive due process analysis.

Judicial Restraint and Incorporation (1937–1953)

Beginning with *West Coast Hotel v. Parish* (1937), the Supreme Court retreated from its substantive due process analysis and began to defer to the judgment of government officials. This deference reached its height with *Wickard v. Filburn* (1942), wherein the Court held that growing crops for the benefit of one's own livestock constituted interstate commerce, and *Korematsu v. United States* (1944), wherein the Court refused to invalidate the forced internment of Japanese Americans. However, as the competing opinions in *Adamson v. California* (1947) demonstrate, the Court began to contemplate whether the Bill of Rights restrains the states.

Education cases followed these in trends. *Minersville School District v. Gobitis* (1940), which upheld a statute requiring students to pledge allegiance to the flag, is a classic example of deference to government officials. In *Gobitis,* the Court decided that the strong religious objections of Jehovah's Witnesses were insufficient to overcome the state's policy choice. Yet, 3 years later, *West Virginia State Board of Education v. Barnette* (1943), which reversed *Gobitis* on the same issue, represented one of the earliest and strongest statements of the civil liberties of minorities.

In *Everson v. Board of Education of Ewing Township* (1947), the Supreme Court applied the Establishment Clause to the states for the first time in a case involving education. While *Everson* approved of the state's efforts to provide transportation for parochial school students, *Illinois ex rel. McCollum v. Board of Education* (1948) invalidated voluntary religious instruction in the public schools. Conversely, *Zorach v. Clausen* (1952) upheld a program whereby children were released from the public schools to attend religious instruction. These cases foreshadowed the fundamental changes in religious jurisprudence that would come in the Warren and Burger Courts.

Warren Court (1953–1969)

Under the leadership of Chief Justice Earl Warren, the Supreme Court redefined its role in American life. When Warren took over as chief justice, there was serious debate about whether some provisions of the Bill of Rights even applied to the states. While the cases discussed next did not directly impact schools, the fact that they transformed American society eventually influenced much about life in the United States, including education.

As *Dennis v. United States* (1951) demonstrates, even when it was clear that constitutional provisions applied to the states, the Supreme Court gave them narrow interpretations. By the time Warren stepped down in 1969, there was no doubt that virtually the entire Bill of Rights applied to the states and, more important, that its provisions were interpreted expansively. Cases such as *Mapp v. Ohio* (1961), *Gideon v. Wainwright* (1963), and *Miranda v. Arizona* (1966) fundamentally altered how law enforcement and criminal trials work. *Baker v. Carr* (1962) and *Reynolds v. Sims* (1964) transformed state legislative elections, while ensuring that a "Senate-like" check would not exist at the state level. *Griswold v. Connecticut* (1965), which recognized a constitutional right to privacy, helped spark the "sexual revolution" and, more significantly, provided the cornerstone for the Court's abortion jurisprudence. *Katzenbach v. McClung* (1965) and *Loving v. Virginia* (1967) ensured that African Americans could be full participants in the everyday discourse of life. In short, the Warren Court fundamentally changed many aspects of constitutional law and, indirectly, everyday life.

As revolutionary as the changes were, the real impact of the Warren Court on American society came in the area of education. *Brown v. Board of Education of Topeka* (1954), along with *Marbury v. Madison* (1803) and *Ex parte Young* (1908), arguably is one of the three cornerstones of American constitutional law. *Brown's* significance, in constitutional, political, and societal terms, simply cannot be overstated. Although one can never diminish the contributions and moral leadership of Robinson, Parks, King, and others, *Brown* highlighted the harsh reality of segregation. Indeed, the Court's landmark judgments in *Baker, Katzenbach,* and *Loving* are at least tangentially the result of *Brown.* Moreover, *Brown's* progeny, *Brown II* (1955), *Cooper v. Aaron* (1957), and *Green v. County School Board of New Kent County* (1968), among others, forced the president, Congress, and the states to confront the problem of educational inequality.

The impact of the Warren Court's education cases was not limited to *Brown* and the problem of racial inequality. In *Engel v. Vitale* (1962), the Court held that the Establishment Clause precluded the recitation of state-authored prayers in public schools. A year later, in *Abington Township School District v. Schempp* and *Murray v. Curlett* (1963), the Court invalidated the practice of prayer and Bible reading in the public schools. *Epperson v. State of Arkansas* (1968) struck down a law prohibiting the teaching of evolution and so paved the way for the inclusion of ideas that are offensive to some religious groups. However, in *Board of Education v. Allen* (1968), the Court upheld the practice of lending textbooks for secular subjects to students who attended religiously affiliated nonpublic schools. Although the constitutional result of these cases was to remove mandatory religious expression from the public schools, the practical result was to generate a continuing controversy over how much voluntary religious expression is permitted in the public schools. Moreover, this controversy is not limited to the public schools, but extends to all aspects of the public square.

Finally, in *Tinker v. Des Moines Independent Community School District* (1969), the Supreme Court reasoned that students do not shed their constitutional rights to free speech at the schoolhouse gate. Accordingly, school officials may not discipline students for engaging in speech that does not materially and substantially disrupt the work and discipline of schools. *Tinker* directly prompted a wave of student speech litigation that continues four decades later. In fact, as explained in more detail below, the Court continues to struggle with the appropriate standard. Just as important, *Tinker* indirectly prompted students to raise other nonspeech claims.

The Warren Court era lasted only 16 years. Even so, it laid the foundation for all modern education law decisions. *Brown* ensured racial equality in the schools. The prayer cases abolished mandatory religious speech and put voluntary religious speech on the defensive. *Tinker* resulted in an expansion of student rights.

Burger Court (1969–1986)

The controversial decisions of the Warren Court were a major issue in the 1968 presidential election. Having announced his intention prior to the election, Chief Justice Warren stepped down in June 1969 and was replaced by Warren Burger. Within a period of 30 months, newly elected President Richard Nixon made three additional appointments: Justices Harry Blackmun, Lewis Powell, and William Rehnquist. Nixon and many conservatives thought that the Court would now turn substantially to the right and would reverse many of the Warren Court's landmark opinions. However, this belief was wrong.

The Burger Court did limit the implications of the Warren Court in several ways, but it also expanded those precedents and established new doctrines. Most significantly, in *Roe v. Wade* (1973), the Court recognized a constitutional right to abortion. That decision polarized the American public and helped to redefine American politics. Except for *Dred Scott v. Sanford* (1857), there has perhaps never been a more divisive Supreme Court decision. Yet the immediate impact of *Roe* was not nearly as great as some other Burger Court decisions.

After nearly two decades of delay and outright resistance to the mandate of *Brown,* the Supreme Court in *Swann v. Charlotte-Mecklenburg Board of Education* (1971) approved mandatory busing to eliminate the vestiges of de jure segregation. Following *Swann,* federal trial courts throughout the country began to implement mandatory transportation plans. The Court struck another blow for educational equality with *Plyler v. Doe* (1982), which required school boards to provide education to children whose parents were undocumented aliens. At the same time, the Burger Court restricted the scope of interdistrict remedies and mandatory busing in *Milliken v. Bradley*

(1974), in which it concluded that suburban districts that had not engaged in race discrimination could not be forced to participate. Moreover, in *San Antonio Independent School District v. Rodriguez* (1973), its only case on school finance, the Court rejected the notion that public education is a fundamental right and that wealth is a suspect class. Consequently, all school finance litigation shifted to state courts.

In *Regents of the University of California v. Bakke* (1978), the Supreme Court offered important, but ambiguous, guidance on the use of racial preferences in higher-education admissions. Justice Powell announced the judgment of the Court in an opinion that was joined in one part by a group of four justices, joined in another part by a different group of four justices, and had some parts that reflected Justice Powell's opinion alone. Only by closely parsing the various sections on Powell's opinion is it possible to obtain the Court's holding. Specifically, the Court ruled that while institutions cannot impose racial quotas, they can consider race as one factor in the admissions process.

Like the Warren Court before it, the Burger Court was skeptical of religion in the public schools. *Lemon v. Kurtzman* (1971) invalidated a program that provided financial assistance in the form of salary supplements to teachers in religiously affiliated nonpublic schools. More important, *Lemon* enunciated the Supreme Court's standards for evaluating Establishment Clause issues. Although the last three decades have seen consistent criticism of the *Lemon* test from many justices, the lower courts, and the academy, it continues to be applied in many religion cases. Under this standard, a practice is unconstitutional unless it has a secular purpose, has a principle or primary effect that neither advances nor inhibits religion, and does not foster "excessive entanglement" of religion. Yet despite the skeptical nature of *Lemon, Mueller v. Allen* (1983) upheld tax credits for parents who sent their children to private schools.

Continuing a trend that began in *Tinker,* the Supreme Court expanded the rights of students. According to *Goss v. Lopez* (1975), students were entitled to due process when facing significant disciplinary sanctions. However, in *New Jersey v. T. L. O.* (1985), while the Court noted that the Fourth Amendment applied in schools, it upheld an educator's search of a student. Further, *Wood v. Strickland* (1975) and *Carey v. Piphus* (1978) established that school boards may be liable financially when officials violate student rights. Nevertheless, the expansion of student rights was not absolute, since in *Ingraham v. Wright* (1977), the Court declined to extend *Goss* to corporal punishment. Also, in *Bethel School District No. 403 v. Fraser* (1986), while reaffirming *Tinker,* the Court allowed school officials to discipline students who engaged in vulgar speech.

Even as the Supreme Court was expanding the rights of students, it appeared to be limiting the rights of public school teachers and university professors. *Board of Regents v. Roth* (1972) and *Perry v. Sindermann* (1972) clarified when public employees were entitled to due process before dismissal. In *Mt. Healthy City School District Board of Education v. Doyle* (1977), the Court was of the opinion that teachers' constitutionally protected speech did not necessarily insulate them from dismissal if their school boards had independent reasons unrelated to the constitutionally protected conduct in acting. *Doyle* clarified the Burger Court's earlier judgment in *Pickering v. Board of Education of Township High School District* (1968) that teachers are free to comment on matters of public concern.

Finally, responding to new statutes designed to protect the disabled, the Burger Court was somewhat cautious. In *Southeastern Community College v. Davis* (1979), the Court maintained that a student who was deaf could be excluded from a nursing program. Moreover, *Board of Education of the Hendrick Hudson Central School District v. Rowley* (1982) adopted a relatively narrow interpretation of the Education for All Handicapped Children's Act, now the Individuals with Disabilities Education Act (IDEA), in refusing to require a sign language interpreter for a student who was deaf.

Rehnquist Court (1986–2005)

On the eve of the bicentenary of the Constitution, Chief Justice Burger resigned, and Associate Justice William H. Rehnquist was elevated to the center seat.

During this period, the Supreme Court was sharply divided along liberal and conservative lines. Between October 1986 and October 1991, the Court arguably had a liberal majority. From October 1991 until June 2005, the Court arguably had a conservative majority. However, in both of these eras, there were numerous circumstances in which one or more justices switched sides and rendered a liberal or conservative decision. Insofar as the Court was sharply divided and some justices had a tendency to "swing," it was difficult for the Court to reach clear and logical decisions. As such, the Rehnquist Court's jurisprudence, particularly in the last 5 years of its existence, could be characterized as embodying "split the difference" jurisprudence.

Despite the ambiguity of the Rehnquist Court's decisions, it did leave a significant legacy in one area, federalism. Prior to the Rehnquist Court, the principles of federalism, which is more appropriately called "dual sovereignty," were largely useless as a limitation on the powers of the national government. That began to change with *Gregory v. Ashcroft* (1991), wherein the Court determined that the states could impose mandatory retirement on state judges. A year later, in *New York v. United States* (1992), the Court indicated that Congress could not compel the states to enact specific legislation. Similarly, in *Printz v. United States* (1997), the Court observed that Congress could not compel state officials to enforce federal law. Beginning with *Seminole Tribe of Florida v. Florida* (1996) and extending through several other cases, the Court limited the power of Congress to abrogate the states' sovereign immunity, a development that is particularly important to states' litigation strategy. Yet the more significant federalism cases were those that limited the power of Congress over interstate commerce, such as *United States v. Lopez* (1995), a case involving guns in schools, and *United States v. Morrison* (2000), and those that limited congressional power to enforce the Fourteenth Amendment, *City of Boerne v. Flores* (1997) and *Morrison*.

The Rehnquist Court's legacy for education law was also significant. Like its jurisprudence in other areas, the Court largely "split the difference" in education law cases, including those involving race. Most obviously, in the University of Michigan racial preference cases,

Grutter v. Bollinger (2003) and *Gratz v. Bollinger* (2003), respectively, the Court upheld the law school admissions system that utilized race as one factor among many, but it invalidated the undergraduate admissions system that assigned a specific number of points based on race. In doing so, the Court decided that the achievement of the educational benefits of a broadly defined diversity was a compelling governmental interest that might justify the use of race. At the same time, the Court emphasized that a system in which race was the determining factor was not narrowly tailored. The practical effect of these cases is to adopt the diversity rationale offered by Justice Powell in *Regents of the University of California v. Bakke* (1978). Even so, these cases also impose significant limitations on how institutions may use race.

The Supreme Court also steered a middle course with respect to desegregation. Although the Court did not end judicially mandated court-ordered busing, it did substantially limit the power of the lower courts to employ it as a remedy. *Dowell v. Board of Education of Oklahoma City Public Schools* (1991) significantly narrowed the definition of unitary school systems, thereby making it substantially easier for boards to end federal court supervision. A year later, in *Freeman v. Pitts* (1992), the Court explained that school boards had no duty to remedy racial imbalances that were caused by residential housing patterns rather than acts of intentional discrimination. Further, in *Missouri v. Jenkins* (1995), the Court placed limits on the ability of federal trial courts to order broad desegregation remedies.

The Supreme Court followed the "split the difference" approach in religion cases involving education. On the one hand, the Court issued several judgments whereby the government favored religion, at least indirectly. In *Agostini v. Felton* (1997), the Court not only permitted the practice of allowing the delivery of federally funded remedial programs for disadvantaged children on-site in their religiously affiliated nonpublic schools; it also recrafted the *Lemon* test, in reviewing only its first two parts, purpose and effect, as it recast entanglement as one element in evaluating a statute's effect. In *Zelman v. Simmons-Harris* (2002), the Court ruled that Ohio could implement a school choice program, whereby parents choose to send their children to religiously affiliated nonpublic schools at public expense, using vouchers, because they made the choice to do so voluntarily and freely. The Court's rationale in *Zelman* was similar to its analysis in *Zobrest v. Catalina Foothills School District* (1993), wherein it found that a student in a religiously affiliated nonpublic school was entitled to receive special education services at public expense. *Board of Education of Westside Community Schools v. Mergens* (1990), *Rosenberger v. Rector & Visitors of the University of Virginia* (1995), and *Good News Club v. Milford Central School* (2001) all held that student religious clubs must be treated the same as nonreligious clubs. Further, in *Lamb's Chapel v. Center Moriches Union Free School District* (1993), the Court ensured that outside religious groups had the same access to school facilities as outside nonreligious groups.

On the other hand, there were instances in which the Supreme Court invalidated religious expression or assistance to religion. In *Lee v. Weisman* (1990), the Court rejected prayers by nonstudents at graduation ceremonies. Ten years later, in *Santa Fe Independent School District v. Doe* (2000), the Court struck down the practice of beginning high school football games with prayer. Further, in *Board of Education of Kiryas Joel Village School District v. Grumet* (1994), the Court invalidated the creation of a school district that was designed to benefit only a small religious sect.

The Supreme Court displayed its "split the difference" rationale in school sexual harassment cases. After *Franklin v. Gwinnett County Public Schools* (1992) established that school boards could be liable for damages under Title IX for instances of teacher-on-student sexual harassment, in *Gebser v. Lago Vista Independent School District* (1998), the justices clarified the circumstances under which boards can be liable when their employees sexually harass students. The Court limited liability to those situations in which school officials who had authority to act actually knew of the conduct but responded with deliberate indifference. In so ruling, the Court charged a middle course between absolute liability, the position of the plaintiff, and no liability whatsoever, the position of the school

board. A year later, in *Davis v. Monroe County School District* (1999), the Court essentially extended *Gebser* to sexual harassment of one student by another.

The Rehnquist Court's special education decisions reflect an expansion of disability rights. *Honig v. Doe* (1988) established that school officials could not expel or impose lengthy suspensions on students with disabilities if their misbehaviors were manifestations of their disabilities. Further, in *Cedar Rapids Community School District v. Garret F.* (1999), the Court was of the view that school boards can be required to provide related services, such as the attention of school nurses to students with disabilities while they attend class. Moreover, in *School Board of Nassau County v. Arline* (1987), the Court decided that school boards must accommodate the needs of teachers with disabling conditions.

Although the Rehnquist Court refused to overturn the student rights recognized in *Tinker* and *T. L. O.*, it did impose significant limitation on those rights. *Hazelwood School District v. Kuhlmeier* (1988) established that student expression in school-sponsored publications was not absolute and that officials could restrict their speech as long as their actions were rationally related to legitimate pedagogical concerns. Seven years later, in *Vernonia School District No. 47J v. Acton* (1995), the Court held that student athletes could be subjected to random drug tests. *Board of Education of Independent School District No. 92 of Pottawatomie County v. Earls* (2002) essentially extended its rationale to all students who participated in extracurricular activities.

Roberts Court (2005–Present)

Following the completion of the October 2004 Term, Justice Sandra Day O'Connor announced her retirement, and President George W. Bush nominated Judge John Roberts to take her place. Before Roberts's confirmation hearings could begin, Chief Justice Rehnquist died. The president then withdrew Roberts's nomination for the O'Connor seat and nominated him for chief justice. Justice O'Connor remained on the Court until January 2006, when she was replaced by Justice Samuel Alito. While the short tenure of the Roberts

Court makes it difficult to draw decisive conclusions regarding its general direction and ultimate place in history, it has already rendered significant education law decisions.

In *Parents Involved in Community Schools v. Seattle School District* (2007), a plurality of the Court ruled that the boards of public school systems that had not operated legally segregated schools or had been found to be unitary could neither classify students by race nor rely on such a classification in making student assignments to educational programming. At the same time, the Court acknowledged that achieving diversity was a compelling governmental interest only in the context of higher education. Effectively, *Parents Involved* precludes school boards from using race in the assignment of individual students. As a practical matter, *Parents Involved* makes it extraordinarily difficult for urban school districts to maintain racially balanced schools.

In *Morse v. Frederick* (2007), the Court decided that educators can act to limit student speech that can reasonably be regarded as encouraging illegal drug use; however, the Court left many unanswered questions regarding the exact scope of student free expression rights. However, *Morse* does provide clarity on speech that encourages illegal drug use.

In a little more than 2 years, the Roberts Court resolved three disputes involving special education. In *Schaffer ex rel. Schaffer v. Weast* (2005), the Court indicated that when parents and school officials cannot agree on the contents of student individualized education programs (IEPs) and placements of children, the objecting party, typically parents, bears the burden of proof in challenges unless state law imposes a different standard. A year later, in *Arlington Central School District Board of Education v. Murphy* (2006), the Court noted that the IDEA could not impose conditions such as requiring school boards to reimburse parents for the costs of paying for expert witnesses who help them to prevail in their disputes with educators, unless they were set out unambiguously in the statutory text. *Murphy* thus makes it more difficult for litigants to advocate expansive interpretations of the IDEA. Moreover, insofar as *Murphy* applies to all Spending Clause statutes, it should have significant ramifications for Title IX, Title VI, and Section 504 claims. Most recently, in *Winkelman ex rel. Winkelman v. Parma City School District* (2007), the Court expanded parental rights. In *Winkelman,* the Court interpreted the IDEA as conferring rights on the parents of students with disabilities that were separate and distinct from those of their children. As such, the Court maintained that since parents have their own rights, they may bring pro se actions.

In *Zuni Public Schools District No. 89 v. Department of Education* (2007), the Court upheld the Department of Education's standards for the distribution of federal impact aid monies. More specifically, the Court pointed out that the secretary of education could consider the population of individual school systems in evaluating whether states had programs that equalized expenditures among their districts.

Finally, in a case with implications for higher education, *Rumsfeld v. Forum for Academic and Institutional Rights* (2006), the Supreme Court reasoned that the Solomon Amendment is constitutional. *Rumsfeld* came after years of legal wrangling surrounding the question of military recruitment on college and university campuses. Many institutions had sought to exclude military recruiters from their campuses because they thought that the federal law concerning homosexuality in the military was offensive to their institutional values. Congress enacted the Solomon Amendment to override the actions of institutions that excluded military recruiters by requiring them to afford the military the same access provided to other recruiters or lose specified federal funds. The Supreme Court concluded that the Solomon Amendment's mandate was consistent with the First Amendment and did not violate the institutional freedoms of speech or association.

Conclusion

The Supreme Court's role with respect to education closely parallels its overall place in American life. At a time of judicial detachment from American life, the Court did not involve itself in education. When the Court used the Due Process Clause to second-guess legislative policy choices involving economics, it applied similar reasoning to education statutes. In an era when the Court deferred to government and began to incorporate the Bill of Rights in suits against the states, its education decisions reflected the same trends. As the Warren Court brought a revolution to American constitutional law, education cases such as *Brown* and disputes involving prayer in public schools led the way. While the Burger Court expanded some rights even as it limited others, its education jurisprudence was indicative of the overall jurisprudence. If the Rehnquist Court can be described as "split the difference" jurisprudence, its school-related cases illustrate this trend. Finally, the early days of the Roberts Court give some indication of how the justices may reshape education, but it is clearly a work in progress with much still to be determined.

William E. Thro

See also Burger Court; Rehnquist Court; Roberts Court; Warren Court

Legal Citations

Abington Township School District v. Schempp and *Murray v. Curlett*, 374 U.S. 203 (1963).

Adamson v. California, 322 U.S. 46 (1947).

Agostini v. Felton, 521 U.S. 203 (1997).

Arlington Central School District Board of Education v. Murphy, 548 U.S. 291, 165 L. Ed. 2d 526 (2006).

Baker v. Carr, 368 U.S. 186 (1962).

Bethel School District No. 403 v. Fraser, 478 U.S. 675 (1986).

Board of Education of Independent School District No. 92 of Pottawatomie County v. Earls, 536 U.S. 822 (2002), *on remand*, 300 F.3d 1222 (10th Cir. 2002).

Board of Education of Kiryas Joel Village School District v. Grumet, 512 U.S. 687 (1994).

Board of Education of the Hendrick Hudson Central School District v. Rowley, 458 U.S. 176 (1982).

Board of Education of Westside Community Schools v. Mergens, 496 U.S. 226 (1990).

Board of Education v. Allen, 392 U.S. 236 (1968).

Board of Regents v. Roth, 408 U.S. 564 (1972).

Brown v. Board of Education of Topeka I, 347 U.S. 343 (1954).

Brown v. Board of Education of Topeka II, 349 U.S. 294 (1955).

Carey v. Piphus, 435 U.S. 247 (1978).

Cedar Rapids Community School District v. Garret F., 526 U.S. 66 (1999).

City of Boerne v. Flores, 521 U.S. 507 (1997).

Cooper v. Aaron, 358 U.S. 1 (1957).

Davis v. Monroe County Board of Education, 526 U.S. 629 (1999).

Dennis v. United States, 341 U.S. 494 (1951).

Dowell v. Board of Education of Oklahoma City Public Schools, 498 U.S. 237 (1991), *on remand*, 778 F. Supp. 1144 (W.D. Okla. 1991), *aff'd*, 8 F.3d 1501 (10th Cir. 1993).

Dred Scott v. Sanford, 60 U.S. 393 (1857).

Engel v. Vitale, 370 U.S. 421 (1962).

Epperson v. State of Arkansas, 393 U.S. 97 (1968).

Everson v. Board of Education of Ewing Township, 330 U.S. 1 (1947), *reh'g denied*, 330 U.S. 855 (1947).

Ex parte Young, 209 U.S. 123 (1908).

Franklin v. Gwinnett County Public Schools, 503 U.S. 60 (1992).

Freeman v. Pitts, 503 U.S. 467 (1992).

Gebser v. Lago Vista Independent School District, 524 U.S. 274 (1998).

Gibbons v. Ogden, 22 U.S. 1 (1824).

Gideon v. Wainwright, 372 U.S. 335 (1963),

Good News Club v. Milford Central School, 533 U.S. 98 (2001).

Goss v. Lopez, 419 U.S. 565 (1975).

Gratz v. Bollinger, 539 U.S. 244 (2003).

Green v. County School Board of New Kent County, 391 U.S. 430 (1968).

Gregory v. Ashcroft, 501 U.S. 452 (1991).

Griswold v. Connecticut, 381 U.S. 479 (1965).

Grutter v. Bollinger, 539 U.S. 306 (2003).

Hazelwood School District v. Kuhlmeier, 484 U.S. 260 (1988).

Honig v. Doe, 484 U.S. 305 (1988).

Illinois ex rel. McCollum v. Board of Education, 333 U.S. 203 (1948).

Ingraham v. Wright, 430 U.S. 651 (1977).

Katzenbach v. McClung, 379 U.S. 294 (1965).

Korematsu v. United States, 323 U.S. 214 (1944).

Lamb's Chapel v. Center Moriches Union Free School District, 508 U.S. 384 (1993).

Lee v. Weisman, 505 U.S. 577 (1990).

Lemon v. Kurtzman, 403 U.S. 602 (1971).

Lochner v. New York, 198 U.S. 45 (1905).

Loving v. Virginia, 388 U.S. 1 (1967).

Mapp v. Ohio, 367 U.S. 643 (1961).

Marbury v. Madison, 5 U.S. (1 Cranch) 137 (1803).

McCullough v. Maryland, 17 U.S. 316 (1819).

Meyer v. Nebraska, 187 N.W. 100 (1922), 262 U.S. 390 (1923).

Milliken v. Bradley I, 418 U.S. 717 (1974).

Milliken v. Bradley II, 433 U.S. 267 (1977).

Minersville School District v. Gobitis, 310 U.S. 586 (1940).

Miranda v. Arizona, 384 U.S. 436(1966).

VACCINATIONS, MANDATORY

In efforts to protect the health and well-being of their citizens, all 50 states of the United States have enacted compulsory vaccination requirements as a condition for entry into public and private schools. These requirements are enacted as statutes, and in most cases, state legislatures delegate to their health departments the responsibility to implement and oversee the implementation of compulsory vaccination requirements. In addition, states are empowered, either by statute, regulation, or judicial interpretation, to exclude children who have not been vaccinated from school attendance and, if children lack valid exemptions, may initiate truancy or other proceedings against them and/or their parents. For various reasons, the enactment and enforcement of these requirements has resulted in litigation against the states and/or school boards by parents on behalf of their children who object to these requirements on multiple grounds, including those of health, philosophy, conscience, and/or religion. This entry summarizes the law and policy on school vaccination and describes some court challenges.

Law and Policy

Compulsory vaccination requirements in the United States date back some two centuries, with Massachusetts becoming the first state to enact a compulsory smallpox vaccination that gave its state health board the right to require citizens to be vaccinated when the board determined that the best interests of the public health and safety were served. Compulsory vaccinations as a condition for school attendance soon followed, with early legal challenges to these requirements occurring in the late 1800s.

While the 50 states set the requirements for compulsory vaccinations, the federal Center for Disease Control (CDC) currently recommends that children receive the following vaccinations on a recommended schedule between birth and 6 years of age: hepatitis B (HepB); rotavirus (Rota); diphtheria, tetanus, and pertussis (DTaP); *Haemophilus influenzae* type b (Hib); pneumococcal (PCV); inactivated poliovirus (IPV); influenza; measles, mumps, and rubella (MMR); varicella (VAR) (chicken pox); hepatitis A (HepA); and meningococcal (MPSV4). While compulsory vaccination requirements as a condition for school entry vary from state to state, all jurisdictions require the diphtheria, tetanus, measles, and rubella vaccinations, and nearly all states require the hepatitis B and varicella vaccines.

As compulsory vaccination policies have evolved, so have policies regarding exemptions to these requirements. Currently, all 50 states provide for either temporary and/or permanent medical exemptions, with all requiring a physician's verification that one or more vaccines would pose detrimental risks to a child's health; a few states allow for verification to come from a chiropractor. In addition, 48 states provide for religious exemptions; the requirements for seeking and gaining a religious exemption vary from state to state, with most states providing that students with religious exemptions may be excluded from attending school in times of epidemic. Depending on the source, 17 or 18 states currently provide exemptions based on reasons of philosophy, conscience, moral convictions, and/or personal beliefs, with the first such exemption enacted by Idaho in 1978 and the most recent by Arkansas in 2005. Finally, at least one state, Texas, provides an exemption for students who are currently on active duty in the U.S. armed forces.

Court Rulings

As noted above, legal challenges at both the federal and state levels date back to the late 1800s and early 1900s, with the decisions generally favoring the state and/or local school districts. Legal challenges at both the federal and state levels have generally centered on whether compulsory vaccination requirements or their exemptions are within the police power of the state to, among other things, regulate the health of its citizens, violate the Establishment and Free Exercise Clauses of the First Amendment to the U.S. Constitution, and/or violate the Due Process and Equal Protection Clauses of the Fourteenth Amendment to the U.S. Constitution.

In the earliest U.S. Supreme Court case, *Jacobson v. Commonwealth of Massachusetts* (1905), the justices upheld the Massachusetts compulsory smallpox vaccination requirement as within its police power to regulate the health of its citizens. Similarly, state courts have rejected challenges to the state's police power to regulate health by compelling vaccinations.

First Amendment Establishment and Free Exercise Clause challenges have also been largely unsuccessful, except in cases where objectors argued for religious exemptions that require objectors to be members of recognized churches whose teachings are specifically opposed to vaccinations. In these cases, some courts found that religious exemptions that favor such objectors over those who do not belong to organized churches violate the free exercise rights of nonchurch members. However, in many of these cases, the courts ruled that legislatures have written into statute provisions that sever religious exemptions

that are subsequently ruled constitutional, leaving religious objectors with no exemption at all.

As to the Due Process and Equal Protection Clauses of the Fourteenth Amendment, in a 1922 case from Texas, *Zucht v. King,* the Supreme Court rejected a challenge to a compulsory vaccination school attendance requirement on the grounds that the requirement did not deprive the child of liberty without due process of law and that the Equal Protection Clause was not violated merely because the requirement affected only schoolchildren. In the years since then, other courts have been of the opinion that compulsory vaccination requirements do not interfere with parents' due process rights to direct the upbringing of their children, nor do they violate equal protection rights of objectors, with the exception of the application of religious exemptions only to members of a recognized church.

In sum, despite continued legal challenges and the more recent formation of interest groups advocating for greater informed consent rights to decide whether children are vaccinated, the power of the states to regulate the health of its citizens by requiring, in pertinent part, compulsory vaccinations as a condition for school attendance is beyond dispute, as is the power of states to conditional school attendance on being appropriately vaccinated. With limited exceptions, the courts have upheld this power, and there is little evidence to suggest that this trend will be reversed.

David P. Thompson and Linda Carrillo

See also Compulsory Attendance

Further Readings

Carrillo, L. K. (2007). *Philosophical/conscientious exemptions to compulsory vaccination requirements.* Unpublished doctoral dissertation, University of Texas at San Antonio.
National Vaccine Information Center. (n.d.). http://www.nvic.org

Legal Citations

Jacobson v. Commonwealth of Massachusetts, 197 U.S. 11 (1905).
Zucht v. King, 260 U.S. 174 (1922).

VERNONIA SCHOOL DISTRICT 47J V. ACTON

The U.S. Supreme Court's judgment in *Vernonia School District 47J v. Acton* (1995) stands out as its first of two decisions on the important topic of drug testing of students. In *Acton,* the Court held that a school board's random drug-testing policy for student athletes was reasonable under the Fourth Amendment.

Facts of the Case

Acton began when, in response to parental concerns of increased drug use among students, a school board in Oregon instituted a drug-testing policy for student athletes. The policy focused on student athletes because they were leaders of the drug culture at their high school and there were at least two incidents wherein members of teams were injured due to the effects of drug use. The policy, which contained safeguards to protect the privacy rights of the student athletes, required all of those who wished to try out for interscholastic athletic teams to submit to urinalysis drug testing.

A seventh-grade student was suspended from interscholastic athletics because he and his parents refused to sign a consent form for drug testing, and they challenged his exclusion. A federal trial court upheld the policy, but the Ninth Circuit reversed on the basis that the policy violated both the Fourth and Fourteenth Amendments and the Oregon Constitution.

The Court's Ruling

On further review, the Supreme Court reversed in finding that the drug-testing policy did not violate the Fourth and Fourteenth Amendments. The Court stated that the Fourteenth Amendment does extend constitutional guarantee of the Fourth Amendment to searches and seizures by state officers, including public school officials. As an initial matter, the Court explained that since the collection and testing of urine under the policy was a search subject to the Fourth Amendment, it was necessary to turn to the question of its reasonableness. To this end, the Court pointed out that even though school officials are agents of the state, due to their custodial and tutelary relationship with students, they have the authority to act in loco parentis in safeguarding the children in their care. According to the Court, this relationship grants educators the ability to determine the appropriate nature and extent of children's constitutional rights in schools.

The Supreme Court then embarked on a three-part test in examining the policy's validity. First, the Court noted that student athletes have a lesser expectation of privacy than their peers who are not athletes. The Court indicated that this distinction stemmed from the communal of nature dressing, undressing, and showering in locker rooms, and the Court asserted that student athletes voluntarily subject themselves to a greater degree of regulation as well. The Court was satisfied that the policy was constitutional because student athletes expected intrusion on their normal rights to privacy.

Second, the Supreme Court observed that since there were sufficient safeguards in place to protect students' legitimate privacy interests, the policy did not violate their Fourth Amendment rights. Third, the Supreme Court was of the opinion that in light of the board's wish to deter drug use by student athletes, as well as to prevent harm to them, it articulated an important interest. As such, since the testing policy was an effective means of curbing drug use among students in general and student athletes in particular, the Court concluded that it passed constitutional muster.

Justice Ginsburg, in a concurring opinion, viewed *Acton* as a very narrow decision, applicable only to those students who volunteer to participate in interscholastic sports. She further asserted that random drug testing of all children who were compelled to attend public schools would be unconstitutional since they cannot avoid doing so.

Justice O'Connor dissented on the basis that the suspicionless testing required by the policy was unreasonable in light of the board's evidence. Instead, she suggested that the record demonstrated that suspicion-based drug testing of students who engaged in disruptive behavior consistent with drug use would have been more effective

Patricia A. L. Ehrensal

See also Board of Education of Independent School District No. 92 of Pottawatomie County v. Earls; Drug Testing of Students; In Loco Parentis

Legal Citations

Board of Education of Independent School District No. 92 of Pottawatomie County v. Earls, 536 U.S. 822 (2002), *on remand*, 300 F.3d 1222 (10th Cir. 2002).

Vernonia School District 47J v Acton, 515 U.S. 646 (1995), *on remand*, 66 F.3d 217 (9th Cir. 1995).

VIDEO SURVEILLANCE

Video surveillance is the use of video cameras to transmit signals to a specific, limited set of television monitors exclusively for the purpose of surveillance. Traditionally, video surveillance camera systems were used in locations where security is necessary, including airports, banks, and military installations. During the 1980s, video surveillance cameras were first placed on school buses as a deterrent to prevent vandalism and avoid litigation with parents. The installation of video camera surveillance systems has become one of the more controversial trends in monitoring school security. A primary legal concern of the use of video surveillance cameras in schools is balancing concerns for school safety with Fourth Amendment rights related to student, teacher, and staff privacy.

The Fourth Amendment of the U.S. Constitution protects individuals against unreasonable searches and seizures as well as unlawful invasions into an individual's privacy. In *New Jersey v. T. L. O.* (1985), the U.S. Supreme Court ruled that a search in the school environment is deemed reasonable only if that search is both justified at its inception and reasonably related in scope to the circumstances that originally justified the search.

Video Surveillance in the School Setting

In addition to monitoring student behavior, the use of video camera surveillance technology is increasingly being used by school officials to assist in the evaluation of teacher and school staff job performance.

In *Roberts v. Houston Independent School District* (1990), for example, an appellate court in Texas ruled that school officials did not violate a dismissed teacher's expectation of privacy by videotaping her classroom teaching performance. In general, the videotaping of a teacher's classroom teaching is legally permissible when used as an assessment tool in evaluating teaching performance.

In another case, *Crist v. Alpine Union School District* (2005), an appellate court in California found that officials did not violate the privacy rights of a school employee when they secretly placed video cameras in a shared office space among three employees. The cameras were placed secretly in the office in an effort to acquire visual evidence that one of the school employees was gaining unauthorized computer access. Here, the court held that the camera surveillance was permissible because school board officials had a legitimate reason for using the video surveillance that outweighed the employees' privacy rights.

Video Surveillance With Audio Capacity

Collecting audio data is generally prohibited under Title I of the Electronic Communications Privacy Act (2002). However, "silent video surveillance," or video surveillance without sound, is not covered under Title I of the act. Given recent technological advances in video surveillance, most modern video cameras have a zoom function that is often used as a substitute for audio communications.

Video Surveillance as an Educational Record

Under the Family Educational Rights and Privacy Act (FERPA), parents or legal guardians have the legal right to "inspect and review the educational records of their children." FERPA defines an educational record as "those records, files, documents, and other material which contain information directly related to a student."

Pursuant to FERPA, parents and legal guardians are usually legally entitled to access to videotapes of their children taken in a school setting. Even so, FERPA identifies five exceptions to the definition of *educational records.* Consequently, parents and legal guardians are usually not entitled to videotapes of their children of the following types:

- Records maintained by supervisory personnel
- Records maintained by administrative personnel
- Records maintained by instructional personnel
- Records maintained by a physician, psychiatrist, psychologist, or other recognized professionals
- Records maintained by law enforcement officers if the videotaping was conducted for law enforcement purposes

In most instances, the use of video surveillance without audio capabilities in public places, including schools, does not violate any constitutional principles, nor does it violate existing federal regulations, state statutes, or labor laws. Nevertheless, school officials need to be aware of the following guidelines when implementing a legally compliant video surveillance system:

1. The costs of implementing a video surveillance system can be high, and school officials need to weigh these costs against expected benefits.

2. Video surveillance cameras may be placed only in designated public or common areas of the school, such as school hallways, libraries, gymnasiums, cafeterias, and school parking lots. Under no circumstances may video surveillance cameras be placed in private areas, including school bathrooms, gym locker rooms, or student or staff lockers where individuals have a legally protected "reasonable expectation of privacy" under the Fourth Amendment.

3. Officials need to notify the general public through the use of prominent signs regarding the location of video surveillance cameras.

4. Officials should not record audio conversations on the video camera surveillance system. This is not only a potential violation of an individual's right to privacy under the Fourth Amendment but also a violation of federal law under Title I of the Electronic Communications Privacy Act.

5. Officials need to comply with FERPA. Under most circumstances, parents or legal guardians are entitled to access videotapes of their children taken in the school environment unless the videotapes are indispensable to the health and safety of a student or group of students in the school.

Legal scholars predict that an increasing number of Fourth Amendment legal challenges will require balancing the emerging uses of surveillance technologies with individual and workplace privacy and security. While privacy interests exist for students, teachers, and staff in the school environment, they are limited, even compared with other common public places, such as the workplace. These limitations in privacy explain the permissibility of video surveillance in many instances in schools.

Kevin P. Brady

See also Family Educational Rights and Privacy Act

Further Readings

Blitz, M. J. (2004). Video surveillance and the constitution of public space: Fitting the Fourth Amendment to a world that tracks image and identity. *Texas Law Review, 82,* 1349–1422.

Brady, K. (November 2005). Video surveillance in public schools: The delicate balance between security and privacy. *School Business Affairs, 71*(10), 24–26.

Legal Citations

Crist v. Alpine Union School District, 2005 WL 2362729 (Cal. Ct. App. 2005).

Electronic Communications Privacy Act, 18 U.S.C. § 2510 (2002).

Family Education Rights and Privacy Act, 20 U.S.C. § 1232g (2002).

New Jersey v. T. L. O., 469 U.S. 325 (1985).

Roberts v. Houston Independent School District, 788 S.W.2d 107 (Tex. Ct. App. 1990).

VILLAGE OF ARLINGTON HEIGHTS V. METROPOLITAN HOUSING DEVELOPMENT CORP.

At issue in *Village of Arlington Heights v. Metropolitan Housing Development Corp.* (1977) was whether the Village of Arlington Heights ("The Village") was motivated by racial discrimination when it denied the Metropolitan Housing

Development Corporation's (MHDC) request to rezone a 15-acre parcel of land from single-family to multiple-family classification. MHDC, a non-profit developer, planned to build 190 racially integrated, clustered units for low- and moderate-income tenants. When The Village denied MHDC's request for rezoning, MHDC brought suit alleging racial discrimination.

As the plaintiff, MHDC had the burden of proving that the decision of The Village officials to deny the rezoning request was motivated by an intention to discriminate. The Supreme Court found that MHDC did not fulfill that burden. Instead, the Court found that discriminatory purposes were not motivating factors in The Village's denial of MHDC's request.

Arlington Heights is one of the earliest cases involving an official action that, while appearing neutral in its nature, disadvantaged racial minorities. The Equal Protection Clause of the Fourteenth Amendment of the U.S. Constitution provides that "no state shall . . . deny to any person within its jurisdiction the equal protection of the laws." Previously, in *Washington v. Davis* (1976), the Supreme Court decided that an official action would not be found unconstitutional only because a racially disproportionate impact resulted. In *Arlington Heights,* the Court more specifically addressed the issue of proof and whether an Equal Protection Clause violation requires purposeful discrimination or solely a disproportionate, or "disparate," impact on a group of people.

Even though the Supreme Court ruled that a disparate impact alone is insufficient to prove a violation of the Equal Protection Clause, an unequal impact on any group may provide a starting point. The Court noted that a clear pattern of disproportionate impact, which can be explained only by discriminatory motivations, can become apparent even if a statute is neutral in its explicit language. The Court added that the impact of an official action may be so clearly discriminatory as to allow no other explanation other than it was adopted for discriminatory, and therefore unconstitutional, purposes. This inquiry into the motivating factor, the Court maintained, includes the circumstantial and direct evidence of the

intent or purpose of the action and can include a clear pattern unexplainable on grounds other than race; historical background, especially if it reveals official actions taken for invidious purposes; departures from the normal procedural sequence; and legislative or administrative history.

More specifically, the Court was of the opinion that looking to legislative or administrative history, such as contemporary statements made by members of the decision-making body and meeting minutes or reports, may reveal a proof of discriminatory motivating purpose. After considering these factors, in *Arlington Heights,* the Court agreed that there were acceptable reasons, other than discriminatory intent, for denying MHDC's zoning request.

Arlington Heights is most often cited for its importance with regard to claims involving the Equal Protection Clause and evaluating whether a discriminatory purpose was a motivating factor for a piece of legislation, a judicial order, or an official action. Supporters of the Supreme Court's decision in *Arlington Heights* contend that the Equal Protection Clause was intended to guarantee equal opportunities, not equal outcomes. Therefore, supporters assert that the focus should not be on trying to fix every racially disproportionate effect, but should focus only on remedying intentional intolerance.

Such an approach can be applied to public school policies that result in racial disparities. For example, in legislation such as No Child Left Behind (2002), it is apparent that closing the achievement gap among various subgroups of students is a national priority. No Child Left Behind requires states to set achievement standards, and student performance is measured through the use of standardized testing. Even so, controversy has arisen because various subgroups of students perform significantly lower than the general student population when taking both these standardized tests and other examinations.

Viewed in the light of *Arlington Heights,* as long as there are acceptable reasons to administer examinations other than intending to discriminate against a cultural, linguistic, ethnic, or socioeconomic group, the examinations can be considered constitutional, regardless of whether a specific group of students performs disproportionately in comparison to test takers.

Jennifer M. Hesch

See also Disparate Impact; Equal Protection Analysis; No Child Left Behind Act

Legal Citations

Brown v. Board of Education of Topeka I, 347 U.S. 483 (1954).
Brown v. Board of Education of Topeka II, 349 U.S. 294 (1955).
Plessy v. Ferguson, 163 U.S. 537 (1896).
Village of Arlington Heights v. Metropolitan Housing Development Corp., 429 U.S. 252 (1977).
Washington v. Davis, 426 U.S. 229 (1976).

VIRTUAL SCHOOLS

Virtual schools is the term used to describe schools that deliver instruction predominantly or exclusively through computer programs accessible via the Internet. Unlike traditional brick-and-mortar schools, virtual schools may have no physical place called "school," but create educational communities by linking students with teachers and classmates through the Internet. In virtual schools, students remain in their homes under the supervision of their parents, attending classes by means of their computers. In addition, virtual schools are referred to as "cyber schools," "online schools," "e-schools" and "Web-based schools." This entry looks at their development and related controversies.

Historical Background

As technology advanced, it is not surprising that computer-based learning began to be explored. Initially, virtual schools were used to help students obtain course work that was not available in their home schools. For example, if students at rural schools had wished to take advanced mathematics courses that were unavailable in their local schools,

their boards may have been able to provide them by means of online courses offered by other school systems, their states, or institutions of higher learning. This type of virtual learning remains popular today. In fact, a 2005 report for the National Center for Education Statistics said that asynchronous Internet-based courses were the most prevalent form of distance education used by urban and suburban school systems during the 2002–2003 school year.

In light of the success of course-by-course offerings, eventually, educators began to create whole "schools" that employed similar technologies. In fact, in 2004, the Education Commission of the States reported that the state educational agencies in 15 states operated some form of virtual schools.

Proponents of virtual schools note that in addition to offering flexible and individually tailored educational options, these schools provide an avenue to bring education to students for whom traditional class attendance may not have been possible, such as for students who are homebound due to illnesses, living in remote locations, or sentenced to juvenile or adult detention facilities. Some also note that virtual schools' attractiveness to students who are home-schooled allows states to bring children and families that exited the public education system back under state monitoring and support.

At the same time, virtual schools have been created as public charter schools. According to the Center for Education Reform's 2005 report, more than 80 virtual charter schools currently operate throughout the United States. While 40 states allow the authorization of charter schools, state charter statutes vary as to whether or not virtual schools are allowed under their provisions. For instance, some charter school laws preclude "home schools" as an option, and some of these states, though not all, view virtual schools as "home schools."

Related Controversies

Questions regarding whether virtual schools and home schools are synonymous or distinctive prompted considerable litigation in Pennsylvania. Courts there eventually determined that the two were separate entities and that although the charter school statute prohibited "home schools," virtual schools were permitted. Moreover, the litigation in Pennsylvania considered issues related to funding, oversight, and special education delivery. As a result, the Pennsylvania legislature amended the commonwealth's charter school law in 2002 to regulate this form of charter school. Now, only commonwealth officials may authorize virtual charter schools, describing requirements related to equipment and disclosure of operational practices; and statutory provisions limit their number, requiring that the schools' administrative offices be physically located in Pennsylvania.

Controversy about virtual charter schools has also occurred in California and Wisconsin. California, like Pennsylvania, amended its charter school law to place more explicit restrictions on virtual charter schools. When concerns arose that charter school operators were inappropriately profiting from virtual education, California instituted requirements that its virtual charter schools submit to independent audits and demonstrate that at least 50% of the funds received are used for direct costs of instruction. Schools unable to verify that level of expenditure face a reduction in state funds.

In Wisconsin, the state teachers union filed two suits challenging virtual charter schools. In the first claim, the union argued that since state statutes set geographical boundaries related to charter schools, it was improper for such schools to have enrolled students from distances through the statewide open-enrollment program. The court disagreed, finding in favor of the school board that operated the virtual charter. Current pending litigation raises a second challenge to virtual charter schools. The teachers' union alleges that such virtual schools should not be permitted to operate not only because they employ teachers who are not qualified but also because parents primarily have oversight over children during instructional time. No ruling has yet been made in this case.

As these examples illustrate, even though virtual schools appear to be growing in prevalence and popularity, they are not without controversy. These controversies seem to relate to three primary issues: concerns as to whether the instruction virtual schools provide is sufficiently similar to traditional schooling to satisfy states' definitions of "schools," worries about funding and the for-profit nature of some virtual education providers, and concerns about the ability of virtual schools to enroll students without regard to geographical boundaries and whether sufficient oversight of the educational programming of children can occur under those conditions.

Julie F. Mead

See also Charter Schools; Distance Learning; Homeschooling

Further Readings

Long, A. (2004). *Cyber schools.* Denver, CO: Education Commission of the States. Retrieved November 7, 2007, from http://www.ecs.org/clearinghouse/51/01/5101.htm

Mead, J. F. (2003). Devilish details: Exploring features of charter school statutes that blur the public/private distinction. *Harvard Journal on Legislation, 40,* 349–394.

Setzer, J. C., & Lewis, L. (2005). *Distance education courses for public elementary and secondary school students: 2002–03* (NCES 2005–010). Washington, DC: U.S. Department of Education, National Center for Education Statistics.

VOTING RIGHTS ACT

The Voting Rights Act was signed into law on August 6, 1965, during an era of rampant disenfranchisement of minorities, to enforce the Fifteenth Amendment to the U.S. Constitution. While the Fifteenth Amendment to the Constitution, ratified in 1870, already prohibited the denial or abridgment of the right to vote on account of color, race, or previous condition of servitude, various states circumvented its enforcement through such mechanisms as literacy tests, poll taxes, and gerrymandering.

There are two key sections of the Voting Rights Act: Section 2, which mostly tracks the language of the Fifteenth Amendment, and Section 5, which applies only to specified jurisdictions. While Section 2 is a permanent provision of the act, Section 5 must be renewed; in addition, while Section 2 addresses the impact of current voting practices on minority voting rights, Section 5 covers the impact of new voting practices on minority voting rights.

Section 2

Section 2 of the Voting Rights Act states as follows:

> No voting qualification or prerequisite to voting or standard, practice, or procedure shall be imposed or applied by any State or political subdivision in a manner which results in the denial or abridgement of the right of any citizen of the United States to vote on account of race or color. (42 U.S.C. §1973(a))

The Supreme Court's interpretation of Section 2 in *Mobile v. Bolden* (1980) as forbidding only voting practices founded on the "intent to discriminate" prompted Congress in 1982 to amend Section 2 to cover acts with discriminatory effect, not just intentionally discriminatory acts. In *Chisom v. Roemer* (1991), the Court described the 1982 amendment aptly: "Certain practices and procedures that result in the denial or abridgement of the right to vote are forbidden [under the Voting Rights Act] even though the absence of proof of discriminatory intent protects them from Constitutional challenge" (pp. 383–384).

In *Thornburg v. Gingles* (1986), in which a group of Black citizens sought to establish discrimination as a result of a White majority voting bloc, the Supreme Court set forth three requirements for minority groups seeking to establish a prima facie case under Section 2: (1) There must be a group that is sufficiently large and geographically insular enough to constitute a majority; (2) the group must be politically cohesive in support of its candidate(s); and (3) the majority must generally vote as a bloc so that it can usually defeat the preferred candidate of the minority group.

Further, the Supreme Court held that once the three requirements are established, the "totality of the circumstances" must be examined in order to determine whether there is a discriminatory practice. A nonexhaustive list of factors to be considered includes the extent of any history of discrimination in the state or political subdivision that has impacted the minority group's rights to register, vote, and participate in the democratic process; the extent to which voting in elections of the state or subdivision is racially polarized; the extent to which the state or political subdivision has voting practices or procedures that may lead to discrimination against minority groups; the extent to which minority groups suffer discrimination in education, employment, and health, hindering their ability to effectively take part in the political process; the extent of overt or covert racial undertones in political campaigns; the extent to which members of the minority group have been elected to public office in the state or political subdivision; whether there is significant unresponsiveness by elected officials to the needs of members of the minority group; and whether the policy underlying the voting practice or procedure is tenuous.

Section 5

Section 5 of the Voting Rights Act was renewed in July 2006 for 25 years with great bipartisan support. Since its enactment in 1965, it has been amended at various times and renewed four times, to provide remedies for minorities in states or political subdivisions with histories of discrimination. Those jurisdictions currently within the coverage of Section 5 include Alabama; Alaska; Arizona; parts of California and Florida; Georgia; parts of Michigan, New Hampshire, New York, North Carolina, South Dakota, and Virginia; Louisiana; Mississippi; South Carolina; and Texas. These jurisdictions must seek advance clearance from the Civil Rights Division of the Justice Department or the U.S. District Court for the District of Columbia before or immediately after making amendments to their election laws or procedures. The clearance must be sought to establish that the purpose or effect of the change in law, practice, or procedure is not the denial or abridgment of the right to vote on the basis of race, color, or language minority.

The Justice Department or the District Court for the District of Columbia must use a "nonretrogression" test in order to determine whether clearance should be granted. This test provides that to pass muster, those jurisdictions within the coverage of Section 5 have to "ensure that no voting procedure changes would be made that would lead to a retrogression in the position of racial minorities with respect to their effective exercise of the electoral franchise" (*Beer v. United States,* 1976, p. 141). The U.S. Supreme Court has held that the essence of Section 5 is not to maximize the voting strength of minorities, but rather to prevent retrogression.

Jurisdictions covered by Section 5 could get a declaratory judgment so as to get out of the section's coverage by establishing that within the 10-year period immediately preceding the action for declaratory judgment (a) there is no test or device being used in the state or political subdivision to deny or abridge the right to vote on the basis of race, color, and language; (b) no final judgment or consent decree has established denials or abridgment of the right to vote on the basis of race, color, and language within the jurisdiction, and no action is pending seeking to establish same; and (3) Section 5 has been complied with.

Unlike Section 2, where discriminatory effect suffices, parties who bring a case against a jurisdiction under Section 5 must establish that the change in election law or procedure has a discriminatory purpose. In essence, a violation of Section 2 is not necessarily a violation of Section 5 for the covered jurisdictions; even though a showing of a discriminatory result may suffice under Section 2, it can serve only as relevant evidence, not conclusive evidence, of discriminatory purpose required under Section 5.

Critics argue that Section 5 singles out specific southern states and that a number of the states included within Section 5's coverage no longer have a history of discrimination. Such criticism has persistently plagued Section 5 since 1970, when the Nixon administration campaigned to repeal it, but the Democratic majority in the Congress fought successfully against the repeal campaign. The renewal of Section 5 in 2006 enjoyed wide bipartisan support, to the surprise of critics.

Joseph Oluwole

See also *Brown v. Board of Education of Topeka;* Civil Rights Movement; Fourteenth Amendment; National Association for the Advancement of Colored People (NAACP)

Legal Citations

Beer v. United States, 425 U.S. 130 (1976).
Chisom v. Roemer, 501 U.S. 380 (1991).
Mobile v. Bolden, 446 U.S. 55 (1980).
Thornburg v. Gingles, 478 U.S. 30 (1986).
Voting Rights Act, 42 U.S.C. § 1973.

VOUCHERS

Publicly funded voucher policies are now established in jurisdictions throughout the United States, but the number of students receiving such vouchers remains very small. For the 2006–2007 school year, fewer than 57,000 vouchers were granted for all programs combined. This entry describes these policies, their effects, and their current legal status.

Each jurisdiction's voucher policy has its own unique characteristics, in terms of the targeted population and in terms of eligible private schools. In Florida, Georgia, and Utah, vouchers are available only for students receiving special education. In Arizona, voucher plans cover special education students as well as students in foster care. In Cleveland and Washington, D.C., voucher eligibility is limited to low-income students, and the same is true of Milwaukee's voucher program, the oldest and largest in the nation. In addition, a new statewide voucher program in Ohio targets students in schools under "academic watch" or designated as failing. Maine and Vermont have, for more than a century, allowed students in rural areas without public schools to use vouchers to attend nonreligious private schools. In addition, five states have "tuition tax credit vouchers" (see "Tuition Tax Credits" entry in this encyclopedia), which mirror conventional vouchers in most relevant aspects.

In 2002, when the U.S. Supreme Court upheld the constitutionality of Cleveland's voucher plan in *Zelman v. Simmons-Harris* (2002), the program at issue was one of only five publicly funded voucher plans in the nation; the other plans operated in Florida, Milwaukee, Maine, and Vermont. Many observers expected that *Zelman*'s lowering of the federal legal hurdle for vouchers would prompt the adoption of voucher policies in many more jurisdictions. In fact, only a limited expansion has thus far occurred. Voucher policies of one form or another have since become law in Colorado; Washington, D.C.; Arizona; Ohio; and Utah. As noted below, Colorado's law was thereafter found in violation of its state constitution, as was one of Florida's two voucher policies. Utah's 2007 voucher law was immediately withdrawn by voters, although an older plan for special education students remains.

Research on the effects of vouchers has explored several important policy issues. Regarding achievement, nonrobust findings of small and isolated gains have been reported for the privately funded voucher plan in New York City and the publicly funded voucher plan in Milwaukee. Overall, however, research has failed to associate these choice policies with increases in student achievement.

Regarding segregation, studies have tended to show that low-income students of color are well represented among voucher recipients, due to the fact that the largest existing voucher policies are means tested (i.e., recipient families must be lower income). However, parents of voucher students tend to have higher educational levels than other parents in their communities because choice programs select for parental involvement—a factor highly correlated with parental education.

Market principles suggest that voucher policies will generate responses by public schools that compete for the same students but those responses will not necessarily be focused on core educational concerns, such as curricular innovation. Instead, these responses may focus on marketing and promotion, and they may be targeted only at select, desired students. Overall, the evidence does not convincingly show substantial positive or negative public school effects of competition.

The legality of vouchers is now primarily a state court matter. Federal court challenges can still be pursued but will be governed by the *Zelman* precedent, meaning that the voucher policy will likely be upheld if it is structured so that the state funding makes its way to private, religious schools only through the intervening choices of parents. Challenges based on state constitutions, however, may have a greater chance of success. The Colorado Supreme Court, for example, stuck down

a voucher law in *Owens v. Colorado Congress of Parents* (2004) because it did not leave local school districts with substantial control over students instructed at those districts' expense. Similarly, the Florida Supreme Court struck down a voucher law in *Bush v. Holmes* (2006) because it impaired the state's ability to provide a single system of free public schools.

Other states may find that voucher laws run afoul of constitutional restrictions on education funding. Only 3 state constitutions (Louisiana, Maine, and North Carolina) include no such restrictions. The remaining 47 constitutions include one or both of two types of restrictions. Twenty-nine states prevent their governments from compelling individuals to financially support a church. Thirty-seven states prohibit the use of public funds to aid private, religious institutions (so-called Blaine Amendments). Even though these restrictions are often strongly worded, several state courts, including the court in Wisconsin's *Jackson v. Benson* (1998), which upheld the Milwaukee voucher plan, have interpreted them to require little or no more than the federal Establishment Clause. That is, under both the U.S. and the Wisconsin constitutions, voucher policies are allowed because aid is provided in a neutral and indirect way.

Most likely, state courts will vary considerably in how they interpret these provisions in their constitutions, with a resulting patchwork of voucher legality.

Kevin G. Welner

See also School Choice; State Aid and the Establishment Clause; Tuition Tax Credits; *Zelman v. Simmons-Harris*

Further Readings

General Accounting Office. (2001). *School vouchers: Publicly funded programs in Cleveland and Milwaukee.* Washington, DC: Author.

Gill, B. P., Timpane, P. M., Ross, K. E., Brewer, D. J., & Booker, K. (2007). *Rhetoric vs. reality: What we know and what we need to know about vouchers and charter schools.* Santa Monica, CA: RAND.

Lubienski, C. (2005). Public schools in marketized environments: Shifting incentives and unintended consequences of competition-based educational reforms. *American Journal of Education, 111,* 464–486.

McEwan, P. J. (2004). The potential impact of vouchers. *Peabody Journal of Education, 79,* 57–80.

Rouse, C. (1998). Private school vouchers and student achievement: An evaluation of the Milwaukee parental choice program. *Quarterly Journal of Economics, 113,* 553–602.

Legal Citations

Bush v. Holmes, 919 So. 2d 392 (Fla. 2006).

Colorado Congress of Parents v. Owens, 92 P.3d 933 (Colo. 2004).

Jackson v. Benson, 578 N.W.2d 602 (Wis. 1998).

Zelman v. Simmons-Harris, 536 U.S. 639 (2002).

WALLACE V. JAFFREE

At issue in *Wallace v. Jaffree* (1985) was whether a statute from Alabama could authorize a 1-minute period of silence in all public schools for meditation or voluntary prayer. The U.S. Supreme Court held that this law violated the First Amendment's Establishment Clause.

The original complaint, which did not mention the Alabama statute, alleged that the plaintiff brought the action to seek a declaratory judgment and an injunction restraining the defendants—members of the Mobile County School Board, various school officials, and the minor plaintiffs' three teachers—from maintaining or allowing the practice of regular religious prayer services or other forms of religious observances in the Mobile County Public Schools. The complaint alleged that this practice was in violation of the First Amendment, made applicable to states by the Fourteenth Amendment to the U.S. Constitution. The complaint further alleged that two of the petitioner's minor children had been subjected to various acts of religious indoctrination since the start of the 1981–1982 school year; that their teachers led their classes in saying certain daily prayers in unison; that the complainant's children were ostracized from their classmates if they did not participate in the daily prayers; and that the petitioner, Mr. Jaffree, repeatedly and unsuccessfully requested that the religious activities be stopped. The prime sponsor of the Alabama statute, State Senator Donald G. Holmes, admitted that his introduction of the statute at issue was an initial step toward his hope of returning voluntary prayer to the public schools in Alabama.

On its ruling, the U.S. Supreme Court stressed the fact that the initial ruling in the dispute, in a federal trial court in Alabama, mistakenly concluded that the Establishment Clause did not prohibit state officials from establishing a religion and that the Eleventh Circuit correctly reversed this misinterpretation. In rendering its judgment, the Court applied the so-called *Lemon* test in evaluating whether the statute violated the Establishment Clause. In *Lemon v. Kurtzman* (1971), the Court held that, first, a statute must have a secular legislative purpose; second, its principal or primary effect must be one that neither advances nor inhibits religion; and, finally, a statute must not foster an excessive government entanglement with religion. The Court ruled that no consideration of the second or third criteria is necessary if a statute does not have a clearly secular purpose.

In applying the *Lemon* test, the Supreme Court found that the enactment of the statute was not motivated by any clearly secular purpose. In fact, the Court specified that the statute did not have a secular purpose. The Court decided that the legislature had enacted the statute for the sole purpose of endorsing school prayer at the start of every school day, in violation of the established principle of government neutrality toward religion. Taking all of this into consideration, the Court struck the statute down not because it coerced students to participate in prayer, but insofar as the manner of its enactment conveyed a message of state-sponsored approval of prayer activities in public schools.

Wallace v. Jaffree is most often cited for its importance with regard to the body of law stating that public school administrators, teachers, students, and parents may neither mandate nor organize prayer at any time during school activities and events. Yet *Wallace* is perhaps of even greater significance to First Amendment precedent due to the Court's insistence that the freedom stipulated in the First Amendment embraces the right to choose to follow any religious faith, or none at all. Accordingly, school officials may not indoctrinate students into a particular religion or into any religious activity at all because children have the right to practice any religion they choose, or no religion at all.

Malila N. Robinson

See also First Amendment; Fourteenth Amendment; *Lemon v. Kurtzman;* Prayer in Public Schools; Religious Activities in Public Schools; State Aid and the Establishment Clause

Legal Citations

Lemon v. Kurtzman, 403 U.S. 602 (1971).
Wallace v. Jaffree, 472 U.S. 38 (1985).

WALZ V. TAX COMMISSION OF THE CITY OF NEW YORK

The precedent set in *Walz v. Tax Commission of the City of New York* (1970) is one of a constellation of opinions guiding judicial interpretation of the Establishment Clause of the First Amendment to the U.S. Constitution. The Establishment Clause refers to the maxim that governmental bodies "shall make no law respecting an establishment of religion." This provision and the First Amendment clause guaranteeing the right to exercise religion without governmental interference, the Free Exercise Clause, form the foundation for religious liberty in the United States. What actions result in the "establishment" of religion has engendered significant judicial interpretation during American history. *Walz* is a significant Supreme Court case, although it originated outside of education and contributed to current judicial interpretations of the First Amendment religion clauses.

Facts of the Case

The plaintiff in *Walz* took exception to a New York statute that granted tax exemptions to churches and other religious institutions. Religious groups were just one of a series of named beneficiaries of the exemption, which also applied to hospitals, libraries, historical societies, and patriotic groups, to name a few. The plaintiff argued that the exemptions provided to the religious institutions amounted to a requirement that he indirectly contribute to the religious groups, thereby violating his rights under the Establishment Clause.

After all three levels of the New York state courts upheld the statute's constitutionality, the plaintiff appealed to the U.S. Supreme Court. In turn, the Court agreed that the statute did not violate the Establishment Clause.

The Court's Ruling

Building on its opinion in *Everson v. Board of Education of Ewing Township* (1947), the Supreme Court considered the nature of the benefit afforded the religious groups that the statute aided. In a fashion similar to the transportation provided to children who attend religiously affiliated nonpublic schools in *Everson,* the Court viewed the tax exemption as a neutral state benefit that was available to a broad class of recipients without regard to religion. As such, the Court reasoned that such exemptions do not result in sponsorship or support of religion.

The Court next addressed whether the tax exemption would have resulted in excessive government entanglement with religion. In concluding that it did not, the Court explained that collecting taxes from churches would more likely have led to governmental entanglement with religion, while tax exemptions actually worked to create a separation by limiting the fiscal relationship between church and state, thereby insulating one from the other.

Finally, the Court engaged in a discussion of the purpose of the tax exemptions, observing that just as there was no sponsorship in the statute, likewise it could not discern any hostility to religion in the tax exemptions. The Court concluded its analysis by pointing out that while the Establishment Clause limited governmental involvement with religion, it did not require an absolute absence of contact between church and state.

Walz is an important Establishment Clause case that is most notable for its influence on the Supreme Court a year later, in the seminal case of *Lemon v. Kurtzman* (1971). In adding the excessive entanglement prong from *Walz* to the purpose-and-effect test that it created in *Abington Township School District v. Schempp* and *Murray v. Curlett* (1963), the Court created the oft-cited *Lemon* test, which requires that any policy or practice satisfy three criteria in order comport with the Establishment Clause: that the policy or practice (1) stems from a legitimate secular purpose (2) with a primary effect that neither advances nor inhibits religion nor (3) results in the excessive entanglement between government and religion. While the *Lemon* test has been the source of much discussion and speculation as to its ongoing vitality, it remains a guiding framework for Establishment Clause jurisprudence and, as such, continues the impact of *Walz*.

Julie F. Mead

See also *Abington Township School District v. Schempp* and *Murray v. Curlett; Everson v. Board of Education of Ewing Township; Lemon v. Kurtzman;* State Aid and the Establishment Clause

Further Readings

Green, S. K. (2006). Bad history: The lure of history in Establishment Clause adjudication. *Notre Dame Law Review, 81,* 1717–1754.

McCarthy, M. (2000). Religion and education: Whither the Establishment Clause? *Indiana Law Journal, 75,* 123–166.

Russo, C. J., & Mawdsley, R. D. (2001). The Supreme Court and the Establishment Clause at the dawn of the new millennium: "Bristl[ing] with hostility to all things religious" or necessary separation of church and state? *Brigham Young University Education and Law Journal, 2001,* 231–269.

Legal Citations

Abington Township School District v. Schempp and *Murray v. Curlett*, 374 U.S. 203 (1963).

Everson v. Board of Education of Ewing Township, 330 U.S. 1 (1947), *reh'g denied*, 330 U.S. 855 (1947).

Lemon v. Kurtzman, 403 U.S. 602 (1971).

Walz v. Tax Commission of the City of New York, 397 U.S. 664 (1970).

WARREN, EARL (1891–1974)

Chief Justice Earl Warren served on the U.S. Supreme Court from 1953 to 1969. Many legal analysts consider him to be the greatest chief justice of the 20th century. Warren's friend and colleague, Justice William Brennan, referred to him as "Super Chief." His influence on American jurisprudence was monumental, especially in the areas of civil rights and liberties. Warren will be forever known as the author of the Court's landmark decision in *Brown v. Board of Education of Topeka* (1954), in which it struck down the doctrine of "separate but equal" in public education. His admirers praise him for his commitment to the goals of protecting individual rights and liberties and promoting racial and political equality, while his critics assert that he was an unbridled judicial activist, creating new law by judicial fiat, substituting his own personal policy preferences and those of the Court for that of popularly elected legislatures.

Early Years

Warren was born in Los Angeles, California, on March 19, 1891, to Scandinavian immigrant parents. Shortly after his birth, his father, who was employed by the Southern Pacific Railroad, moved the family to Bakersfield, California. There, as a young man, Warren witnessed a city that was at the time best known for being vice ridden and for its corrupt city government. As he grew older, he worked for the railroad during summer vacations and saw firsthand the plight of the working poor and racial prejudice against Asian workers. These childhood experiences helped shape Warren's later views of the role of law and government in addressing societal ills.

Warren attended the University of California, Berkeley, from 1909 to 1914, earning his undergraduate and Juris Doctorate degrees. After brief stints working for an oil company and then a law firm, he enlisted in the U.S. Army during World War I, serving from 1917 to 1918, with the rank of first lieutenant; he never left the United States and did not engage in actual combat. After being discharged from the military, Warren worked in 1919 as clerk of the California State Assembly Judicial Committee. In 1920, he became deputy city attorney for Oakland and deputy district attorney for Alameda County; and in 1925, the same year he married his Swedish immigrant wife, Nina, he became district attorney for the county. The couple would have six children.

Some of Warren's detractors questioned his legal background. However, he was an experienced, aggressive, and successful prosecutor, never having had a conviction overturned. During his career, he professionalized the district attorney's office, and although he was regarded as a tough-on-crime prosecutor, he was also fair-minded about the rights of the accused and saw to it that indigents had public defenders. In 1932, Warren was voted the best prosecutor in the country.

Rise to the Bench

Warren, a Republican, was elected attorney general of California in 1938 and governor in 1942. In what is often viewed as a blemish on his record as a civil libertarian, while serving as governor he supported the internment of California's Japanese and Japanese American populations during World War II. Warren was so popular as governor that he won the Republican, Democratic, and Progressive primaries during his reelection campaign in 1946. After a failed bid for the vice presidency of the United States, as Thomas Dewey's running mate against Harry Truman in 1948, Warren became a national figure and a possible candidate for the 1952 Republican presidential nomination. At the national convention, seeing that he could not win the nomination over Dwight Eisenhower, he put his full support behind Eisenhower.

For his efforts in helping Eisenhower be elected as president, it seems that Warren was promised the first vacancy on the U.S. Supreme Court. The vacancy occurred in 1953, with the death of Chief Justice Fred M. Vinson. Eisenhower nominated Warren to fill the position of chief justice as a recess appointment in September 1953. The full Senate approved Warren's appointment in March 1954 by a voice vote.

Although many historians doubt that Eisenhower ever claimed that appointing Warren was his biggest mistake, he did prove to be more liberal than the president had expected. As chief justice, Warren led the Court through one of the most tumultuous periods in American history and used its decisions in an attempt to change society. The changes, especially those relating to race-based segregation, prayer in school, and the rights of accused criminals, upset critics enough that Warren faced demonstrations calling for his impeachment.

In addition, President Lyndon Johnson named Justice Warren to head what became known as the "Warren Commission," investigating the assassination of President John F. Kennedy. Although Warren was reluctant to accept the position, Johnson convinced him that it was for the good of the nation. The Warren Commission came to what is still considered by many to be a controversial conclusion that the shooter, Lee Harvey Oswald, acted alone.

Leading the Court

When Warren took his seat on the bench, he joined a Supreme Court that was divided along ideological lines and dominated by strong-willed personalities such as Hugo Black and William O. Douglas on the left and Robert Jackson and Felix Frankfurter on the right. Forging working coalitions among this group of contentious individuals would be a formidable task, challenging Warren's political as well as legal skills. His leadership ability was soon tried by a dispute that had carried over from the previous term and was in need of reargument: *Brown v. Board of Education of Topeka* (1954).

The *Brown Decision*

In *Brown,* the Court was asked to reconsider its prior ruling in *Plessy v. Ferguson* (1896), which upheld the constitutionality of the doctrine of "separate but equal" on public railway accommodations. Through force of conviction and personality, Warren accomplished the seemingly impossible task of carving out a unanimous judgment, reasoning that public schools segregated along racial lines were inherently unequal, in violation of the Fourteenth Amendment's Equal Protection Clause.

Most commentators praise *Brown* as a hallmark of justice, promoting fairness and equality for all Americans regardless of race. Critics, though, point out that Warren's opinion was based more on sociology and psychology than law, and not necessarily grounded in tight legal reasoning. In *Bolling v. Sharpe* (1954), writing for a still unanimous Court, Warren followed the logic of *Brown* in finding that racial discrimination in the public schools of the District of Columbia violated the Due Process Clause of the Fifth Amendment.

As widely accepted as *Brown* is today, it sparked controversy and, in some instances, open defiance, especially in the South. Enunciating a legal principle of racial equality was one thing, but implementing and enforcing it was another. Realizing that implementation would be difficult and could not occur overnight, the Court in *Brown v. Board of Education of Topeka II* (1955), in another unanimous opinion written by Justice Warren, announced that state and local officials should proceed with "all deliberate speed" in desegregating public schools. *Brown II* was meant to calm opposition, but in setting forth the responsibility of local federal trial courts for supervising its implementation of *Brown,* the justices placed federal courts in the role of arbiter of the nature and pace of school desegregation for the next 50 years.

Perhaps the greatest early challenge to *Brown* came in Arkansas, where the governor and state legislature refused to comply, asserting that the state had the authority to determine the constitutionality of the law and that the Supreme Court's decision was not legally binding. Rejecting this theory of "interposition," Warren secured a unanimous judgment in *Cooper v. Aaron* (1958), asserting in the strongest terms since *Marbury v. Madison* (1803) and *McCulloch v. Maryland* (1819) the supremacy of the federal judiciary in expounding the meaning of the Constitution.

Prayer in Schools

Equally controversial and perhaps initially even more unpopular than the Warren Court's desegregation opinions were its rulings involving prayer in public schools. In *Engel v. Vitale* (1962), the Supreme Court, with Chief Justice Warren joining the majority, decided that a purportedly nondenominational prayer composed by the New York State Board of Regents and recited by students at the beginning of each school day was an unconstitutional violation of the First Amendment's Establishment Clause.

The next year, in *Abington Township School District v. Schempp* and *Murray v. Curlett* (1963), the Court, with Warren again joining the majority, struck down the practice of beginning the school day with reading from the Bible and reciting the "Lord's Prayer" as unconstitutional. Severely criticized and misunderstood by much of the American public, these two cases prohibiting state-sponsored and teacher-led prayers in public schools provided a major impetus in the movement to impeach Warren.

Two of the most significant legal developments of Chief Justice Warren's jurisprudence were his broad interpretation of rights enumerated in the Bill of Rights and the extension of most of these constitutional protections to the states as well as the federal government. On a case-by-case basis, the Warren Court gradually "incorporated" under the Fourteenth Amendment Due Process Clause most of the provisions of the Bill of Rights and applied them to the states. This extension of protection of individual rights and liberties to actions by state and local government officials, such as school boards, teachers, and administrators, greatly expanded and enhanced the role of federal courts.

Defending Rights

Warren's most famous case in the area of criminal procedure, conceding that it did not have a direct impact on education, was in *Miranda v. Arizona* (1966), in which he authored the opinion of the Supreme Court in spelling out the rights of the accused, such as the right to remain silent and the right to an attorney in situations involving custodial interrogations by the police. Most Americans are familiar with the "Miranda warnings." Hailed by many as a check on abuse by the police and prosecutors of civil liberties, others criticized *Miranda* as "coddling" criminals and being "soft on crime."

The Warren Court placed further restrictions on law enforcement in the case of *Mapp v. Ohio* (1961), in which it highlighted the "exclusionary rule" and the principle that evidence that is gathered illegally may not be used against the defendant in court. Of significance to school-aged children, in *In re Gault* (1967), the Court maintained that juveniles accused of felonies must be accorded many of the same due process rights as adults. While the Court's judgment was condemned at the time, many law enforcement officials now recognize that the process of criminal investigation and interrogation is fairer because of this and other Warren Court rulings.

During Warren's tenure as chief justice, the Supreme Court expanded the First Amendment freedom of speech rights of students and teachers. In *Tinker v. Des Moines Independent Community School District* (1969), in which students were suspended for wearing black armbands protesting the war in Vietnam, the Court specified that students and teachers did not "shed their rights to freedom of speech or expression at the schoolhouse gate" (p. 506). In *Pickering v. Board of Education of Township High School District 205, Will County* (1968), in which a teacher was dismissed for writing a letter to the local paper criticizing the administration and its handling of school funds, the Court was of the view that teachers' free speech rights were constitutionally protected when making statements on matters of public concern.

Justice Warren was generally supportive of the right of freedom of speech. In the most prominent free speech case that the Warren Court resolved, *New York Times v. Sullivan* (1964), the Court declared that speech critical of public officials could not be libelous unless made with actual "malice," meaning that it was knowingly false or made with reckless disregard for the truth. However, there were limits on Warren's toleration for dissent. In *United States v. O'Brien* (1968), he authored the Court's opinion ruling that "draft card burning" in violation of the Selective Service Act was not a constitutionally protected form of symbolic speech.

Other Rulings

In an area indirectly affecting education, the Warren Court revolutionized the process of drawing up legislative districts in *Baker v. Carr* (1962), explaining that while issues of malapportionment were not nonjusticiable "political questions," best left to state legislatures, potential violations of the guarantees of equal protection of the law under the Fourteenth Amendment meant that it could intervene. In its analysis, the Supreme Court acknowledged that state gerrymandering of legislative and school district boundary lines had often been employed as a tool to preserve segregation.

In *Reynolds v. Simms* (1964), Warren authored the opinion of the Court in adopting the principle of "one person, one vote," a case that ultimately impacts school board elections. The Court indicated that not only congressional but also state legislative districts should be apportioned on the basis of population rather than geography. Warren considered the legislative apportionment decisions to be the most significant rulings of his career, ensuring fairness in representation and preventing the dilution of votes. Yet many critics viewed theses cases as infringing state sovereignty, unjustified legal intrusions by the federal courts into what are essentially questions of state and local politics.

The Legacy

In 1968, Warren informed President Lyndon Johnson of his decision to retire from the Supreme Court, hoping that he would be replaced by a successor who shared his judicial philosophy. Johnson nominated Justice Abe Fortas as Warren's replacement. Insofar as Johnson was considered to be a "lame duck," Senate Republicans preferred to hold the appointment over, waiting to see the outcome of the 1968 presidential elections. The Fortas confirmation hearings were acrimonious, with many of the complaints against Fortas being thinly veiled criticisms of the Warren Court. Eventually, facing allegations of off-the-Court ethical violations and charges of conflict of interest, Fortas withdrew his name from consideration. Richard Nixon, the newly elected president, named Warren Burger to fill the vacancy of chief justice. In 1969, Warren resigned from the Court. He died on July 9, 1974.

Chief Justice Warren led the Court through force of personality and great social and political skills. He made no pretense of being a legal scholar, and his opinions were not always carefully crafted. Warren, unlike his successors Chief Justices Warren Burger and William Rehnquist, seldom assigned the writing of the Court's opinion to himself. He preferred to establish the legal and policy tone, leaving the drafting of opinions to more intellectual colleagues such as Justices Hugo Black and William Brennan.

Warren formed an especially close working relationship with Justice Brennan, who shared both his judicial temperament and philosophy. In fact, Warren and Brennan often met to discuss cases before conferences. According to one analyst, Melvin Urofsky, they brought the perfect combination of political and intellectual gifts to the Court, with Brennan drafting legally rigorous opinions such as *Baker v. Carr,* which gelled with Warren's philosophical beliefs.

Warren left a lasting legacy and deeply influenced the course of American law. He fundamentally altered the role of the federal judiciary in the political and legal process, establishing the courts as institutions with the responsibility for protecting the rights of those whom he considered to be victims of the system and rendered powerless. Under Warren's leadership, all levels of government and other branches of the federal government were subjected to closer judicial scrutiny. His judicial activism was praised by liberals for bringing fairness and justice to the American system of government. However, liberals would not always constitute a majority of the Supreme Court.

In recent years, more conservative justices, who would probably argue that they engaged in a return to the status quo ante, used Warren's activist approach in support of policy and legal positions opposed to those of Warren. Still, Warren's most basic judgments regarding racial desegregation, prayer in public schools, rights of the accused, and legislative apportionment, though modified to some extent by the Court, have not been overruled. Warren's ability to lead a divisive Court on a new path in an era of great social and political upheaval earns him the distinction of being ranked as one its greatest chief justices.

Michael Yates and Randy L. Christian

See also *Abington Township School District v. Schempp* and *Murray v. Curlett*; Bill of Rights; *Bolling v. Sharpe; Brown v. Board of Education of Topeka; Cooper v. Aaron;* Fourteenth Amendment; *In re Gault;* Juvenile Courts; *Pickering v. Board of Education of Township High School District 205, Will County; Plessy v. Ferguson;* Prayer in Public Schools; U.S. Supreme Court Cases in Education; Warren Court

Further Readings

Kluger, R. (2004). *Simple justice: The history of Brown v. Board of Education and Black America's struggle for equality* (Rev. ed.). New York: Knopf.

Schwartz, B. (Ed.). (1996). *The Warren Court: A retrospective.* New York: Oxford University Press.

Urofsky, M. I. (Ed.). (2006). *Biographical encyclopedia of the Supreme Court: The lives and legal philosophies of the justices.* Washington, DC: CQ Press.

Warren, E. (1977). *The memoirs of Earl Warren.* Garden City, NY: Doubleday.

Legal Citations

Baker v. Carr, 368 U.S. 186 (1962).

Bolling v. Sharpe, 347 U.S. 497 (1954).

Brown v. Board of Education of Topeka I, 347 U.S. 483 (1954).

Brown v. Board of Education of Topeka II, 349 U.S. 294 (1955).

Cooper v. Aaron, 358 U.S. 1 (1958).

Engel v. Vitale, 370 U.S. 421 (1962).

In re Gault, 387 U.S. 1 (1967).

Mapp v. Ohio, 367 U.S. 643 (1961).

Marbury v. Madison, 5 U.S. 137 (1803).

McCullough v. Maryland, 17 U.S. 316 (1819).

Miranda v. Arizona, 384 U.S. 436 (1966).

New York Times v. Sullivan, 376 U.S. 254 (1964).

Pickering v. Board of Education of Township High School District 205, Will County, 391 U.S. 563 (1968).

Plessy v. Ferguson, 163 U.S. 537 (1996).

Reynolds v. Simms, 377 U.S. 533 (1964).

Tinker v. Des Moines Independent Community School District, 393 U.S. 503 (1969).

United States v. O'Brien, 391 U.S. 367 (1968).

WARREN COURT

Under the leadership Chief Justice Earl Warren, the U.S. Supreme Court engaged in judicial activism aimed at expanding civil rights. Hailed for his leadership in school desegregation, while vilified by diehard opponents,

Warren and the activist Court he shaped and led left a lasting legacy to the nation. He was committed to individual freedom, human rights, the First and Fourteenth Amendments, and Fourteenth Amendment due process and equal protection rights, and his leadership resulted in expanded social consciousness on freedom, civil rights, and human dignity. Warren also left an indelible mark on education and society, beginning with *Brown v. Board of Education of Topeka* (1954). While the issues that the Warren Court faced continue to be debated by succeeding courts, the framework for human rights was written in the opinions penned during its tenure. President Jimmy Carter posthumously awarded Warren the Presidential Medal of Freedom in 1981.

The *Brown* Decision

Shortly after his appointment as Chief Justice, Warren led a Bench of strong-willed, divided jurists to repudiate the 1896 *Plessy v. Ferguson* doctrine of "separate but equal" that led to segregation of races in public schools. *Brown v. Board of Education of Topeka* (1954), or *"Brown I,"* was a landmark opinion in correcting historical racial injustice in public schools.

Warren was a results-oriented jurist who often left the legal writing and articulation to the expertise of Associate Justices Black and Brennan. At the same time, Warren had a political touch, as reflected by his using fairness and justice to encourage his judicial colleagues to set aside their limited views of the Supreme Court's role.

As author of the Supreme Court's unanimous decision in *Brown I,* Warren asked whether segregation of children in public schools solely on the basis of race deprives them of equal educational opportunities. In answering his own question, Warren indicated that segregation causes children to experience feelings of inferiority, while retarding their social and intellectual development. He added that in the field of public education, the notion of "separate but equal" has no place, insofar as separate educational facilities are inherently unequal.

In 1955, in *Brown v. Board of Education of Topeka II,* under Warren's guidance, the justices delegated the job of carrying out desegregation with "all deliberate speed" to federal trial courts. Still, it took

time to implement desegregation fully, and the issue still confronts society.

Reactions to *Brown I* and *II* were formidable, especially in the American South. Disputes over the integration of Little Rock, Arkansas, eventually led President Eisenhower to call out federal troops to ensure safety of African American students entering Central High School. Further, the Supreme Court had to intervene in that dispute, in *Cooper v. Aaron* (1958). Other states supported private schools and in some cases closed public schools for short periods of time in order to avoid desegregation. Consequently, signs posted throughout the South and elsewhere called for Warren's impeachment.

The Chief Justice

Throughout his 16 years as chief justice, from 1953 to 1969, Warren led the Supreme Court to expand social and economic justice in the nation. Born in Los Angeles to Norwegian and Swedish immigrants, he attended the University of California, Berkeley, receiving his law degree in 1914. Warren had a unique ability to unite people.

Warren had a number of political positions before becoming governor of California. On most issues, he was a conservative Republican, tough on crime, a business supporter, and a persistent prosecutor. Influenced by patriotism of his era, he supported the decision, which he later regretted, to intern Japanese Americans during World War II.

In 1946, in a state that allowed individuals to run in any primary, Warren won the Republican, Democratic, and Progressive primary elections, running unopposed for governor in his first of three terms. As governor of California, Warren stood behind the faculty of the University of California during loyalty oath controversies in 1949 and 1950. He supported constitutional rights and principles of faculty academic freedom, defending the faculty from press attacks during political turmoil when Governor Ronald Reagan dismissed university President Clark Kerr. Warren ran as vice presidential candidate with Thomas E. Dewey of New York in 1948.

The death of Chief Justice Fred Vinson, on September 8, 1953, led to an opening for the position.

President Dwight Eisenhower appointed Warren to the Supreme Court, though he was troubled by Warren's social activism. In fact, Eisenhower is reported to have regarded his appointment of Warren as one of the biggest mistakes of his presidency.

Through political prowess and focusing on practical issues, Warren brought an often brilliant but divisive Supreme Court to consensus. Justices William O. Douglas, Felix Frankfurter, Hugo L. Black, Harold H. Burton, Tom C. Clark, Stanley Reed, Sherman Minton, and Robert H. Jackson made up the Warren Court in the early years of his service. There were seven Democrats and one Republican. Justices Jackson and Frankfurter advocated judicial restraint, while Justices Black and Douglas tended toward activism. Before Warren, the Vinson Court had been deeply divided.

Warren matured as a justice and moved the Supreme Court toward unanimity, especially in *Brown,* in framing issues in terms of individual rights and human dignity. Eighteen judges, including Brennan and Marshall, served on the high court during Warren's 16-year tenure. Warren's charismatic leadership led to a more unified court.

Other Education Rulings

In other education cases, the Warren Court touched off a firestorm of controversy in ruling that denominational prayers in public schools, in whatever form they took, were unconstitutional. In *Engel v. Vitale* (1962), the Court was of the opinion that the recitation of prayer in public schools was inconsistent with the Establishment Clause of the constitution. A year later, the Court struck down prayer and Bible reading in public schools in the companion cases of *Abington Township School District v. Schempp* and *Murray v. Curlett* (1963).

The Warren Court also upheld individual freedom of association. For example, in *Shelton v. Tucker* (1960), the Supreme Court pointed out that placing restrictions on the associational rights of teachers deprived educators of their rights to personal, associational, and academic liberty, which are protected by the Fourteenth Amendment. Moreover, the Warren Court was generally opposed to loyalty oath requirements for educators that emerged in response to fears of communism. As

such, in *Sweezy v. New Hampshire* (1957), the Court maintained that teachers must have academic freedom to inquire, study, and evaluate their subject matter in an atmosphere free of suspicion and distrust. Warren's opinion on behalf of the Court in *Sweezy* made it clear that every citizen has a right to engage in political expression and association, rights protected by the First Amendment and the Bill of Rights.

James Van Patten

See also *Abington Township School District v. Schempp* and *Murray v. Curlett; Brown v. Board of Education of Topeka; Brown v. Board of Education* and Equal Educational Opportunities; *Cooper v. Aaron; Engel v. Vitale;* Fourteenth Amendment

Further Readings

Newton, J. (2006). *Justice for all: Earl Warren and the nation he made.* Riverhead, MA: Putnam.

Spaeth, H. J. (1966). *The Warren Court.* San Francisco: Chandler.

Urofsky, M. I. (2001). *The Warren Court justices, rulings, and legacy.* Santa Barbara, CA: ABC-CLIO.

Legal Citations

Abington Township School District v. Schempp and *Murray v. Curlett,* 374 U.S. 203 (1963).

Brown v. Board of Education of Topeka I, 347 U.S. 483 (1954).

Brown v. Board of Education of Topeka II, 349 U.S. 294 (1955).

Cooper v. Aaron, 358 U.S. 1 (1958).

Engel v. Vitale, 370 U.S. 421 (1962).

Plessy v. Ferguson, 163 U.S. 537 (1896).

Shelton v. Tucker, 364 U.S. 479 (1960).

Sweezy v. New Hampshire, 354 U.S. 234 (1957).

WEB SITES, STUDENT

As the Internet has grown, situations in which students have been disciplined for the content of their personal Web sites have increased. Disciplining students for Web pages is a subset of disciplining students for out-of-school conduct. Students have constitutional rights, but these rights are not coextensive with the rights of adults. Also, schools have much greater latitude in disciplining students for at-school conduct than they have for off-campus conduct.

Most school boards now require students and/or their parents to sign acceptable use agreements. When students using school computers violate the terms and conditions of such agreements, they can be disciplined by school officials. Students may maintain Web sites that are purely personal, or they may host blogging sites that allow others to post comments. In general, students may not invoke their free speech rights when they create sites that defame others, contain obscenity, harass others, intentionally inflict emotional distress, violate copyrights, or invade the privacy of others. Students who have blogging sites may have additional legal considerations. This entry reviews legal cases related to student use of Web sites.

Free Speech

With a few notable exceptions, courts have come down on the side of the speech rights of students. Many of the disputes have been resolved out of court. Reported settlements on cases can be very expensive. Courts are reluctant to expand the authority of school officials to control off-campus conduct of students. In fact, educators fail in their attempts to impose discipline unless they can show the existence of a true threat and/or material and substantial disruption of school or interference with the rights of others. Courts will apply community standards when it comes to obscenity.

Buessink v. Woodland R-IV School District (1998) involved a Web site in which a student used vulgar language that was directed toward teachers, the principal, and the school's home page. After a friend saw the Web site at the plaintiff student's home, the student reported it to a teacher, who allowed other students to view the site. The court issued an injunction in favor of the student because there was no substantial disruption of school.

In *Killion v. Franklin Regional School District* (2001), a student wrote an e-mail that lampooned the school's athletic director, including comments about the teacher's eating habits and the size of his genitalia. The speech caused no disruption at school. A federal trial court decided that school officials did not have the authority to regulate such speech just because they

disliked what the student had to say. In addition, the court was of the view that school officials have much less authority to limit lewd and vulgar speech when it occurs outside of a school setting.

Coy v. Board of Education of North Canton City Schools (2002) raises an issue that commonly appears in these cases, namely, whether school disciplinary policies are vague and overbroad. Often, courts will find that the use of imprecise terms and definitions restricts the free speech rights of students. At trial, students must seek to show that they were disciplined for the content of their speech. At the same time, boards must attempt to prove that they disciplined students for breaches of acceptable use policy because they accessed a home page from a school computer.

Determining Threat

Legally, there are requirements for what constitutes a threat. For speech to constitute a threat, it must be communicated by the person making the threat. Next, a reasonable person would have to perceive the speech to be a threat. Finally, a reasonable person would have to believe that the person making the threat was capable of following through on it. Other people also look to see how the threat was perceived by the object of the threat. In one such case, *Latour v. Riverside Beaver School District* (2005), a federal trial court concluded that the rap songs on a student's Web site did not constitute a threat.

In *Emmett v. Kent School District, No. 415* (2000), when a student created a Web site that contained the mock obituaries of peers, the court held that the board could not discipline the student. The court explained that the Web site, having been designed and maintained out of school, did not create any threat of substantial disruption in the school and that the obituaries did not pose a threat to any students.

At issue in *Mahaffey ex rel. Mahaffey v. Aldrich* (2002) was a student's urging others to stab someone and then throw the victim over a cliff. A federal trial court pointed out that the statements did not constitute a threat and that the school policies were overbroad.

J. S. v. Bethlehem Area School District (2000) may be an anomaly. The court decided that school officials could take disciplinary action after a teacher targeted by the student's home Web site had to take a medical leave of absence. The court determined that no true threat existed; however, the student had accessed the Web site from a school computer, and this opened the door for disciplinary action. The speech on the Web site had disrupted the school under the analysis introduced in *Tinker v. Des Moines Independent Community School District* (1969). Further, in *Bethel School District 403 v. Fraser* (1986), the court concluded that the speech was vulgar and obscene; therefore, it had undermined the school's ability to inculcate civility.

It is incumbent on school officials to know when they can and cannot regulate the off-campus speech of students. As the Internet and student use of computers and other devices for electronic communications continue to grow, one can expect that litigation in this contentious area will continue.

J. Patrick Mahon

See also Bullying; Children's Internet Protection Act; Digital Millennium Copyright Act; Technology and the Law; *Tinker v. Des Moines Independent Community School District*

Further Readings

Hudson, D. L. (2005.). *Student expression in the age of Columbine: Securing safety and protecting First Amendment rights.* Available from http://www .firstamendmentcenter.org/PDF/First.Report.student .speech.pdf

Legal Citations

Bethel School District 403 v. Fraser, 478 U.S. 675 (1986).
Beussink v. Woodland R-IV School District, 30 F. Supp.2d 1175 (E.D. Mo. 1998).
Boucher v. School Board of the District of Greenfield, 134 F.3d 821 (7th Cir.1998).
Coy v. Board of Education of North Canton City Schools, 205 F. Supp.2d 791 (N.D. Ohio 2002).
Emmett v. Kent School District, 92 F. Supp.2d 1088 (W.D. Wa. 2000).
J. S. v. Bethlehem Area School District, 757 A.2d 412 (Pa. Commw. Ct. 2000).
Killion v. Franklin Regional School District, 136 F. Supp.2d 446 (W.D. Pa. 2001).
Latour v. Riverside Beaver School District, 2005 WL 2106562 (W.D. Pa. 2005).
Mahaffey ex rel. Mahaffey v. Aldrich, 236 F. Supp.2d 779 (E.D. Mich. 2002).
Tinker v. Des Moines Independent Community School District, 393 U.S. 503 (1969).

WEB SITES, USE BY SCHOOL DISTRICTS AND BOARDS

Web sites are a useful part of the Internet that can facilitate many of the information-sharing responsibilities of school boards and their staffs. Individual schools within systems often have at least one Web page; there may also be Web sites for entire districts that link to the Web sites of individual schools. Individual school Web sites are usually managed by teachers who have some expertise in technology. Administering duties are sometimes shared with students as part of computer and/or design classes. It is not uncommon for students to be given space to construct and maintain personal Web sites on school Web sites. While districtwide sites usually have Web site administrators who are dedicated to that task, this can vary depending on the size of a school system and its needs.

School boards typically use Web sites to share schedules; minutes from meetings; contact information of staff, including e-mail addresses; mission statements; staff bios, and other information. However, because Web sites are a part of the Internet, important legal issues can quickly arise that might catch unsuspecting school officials unprepared. Some of the Web site challenges in school settings include the scope of copyright protection, privacy issues, employee use, and Web site security. Boards can take preventive stands on these issues by first auditing their sites and then creating Web site construction policies. One way to address these issues is to conduct Web page legal audits. Tomas Lipinski, a noted authority on copyright law, refers to an audit as a series of cautions prompted by developing law or a checklist that school Web site content creators can use to audit their sites. Although an audit is not to be interpreted as legal advice, it can provide educational leaders with some basic knowledge that can reduce or prevent missteps.

Copyright does apply in cyberspace. As such, Professor Lipinski, among others, cautions district officials to check to see whether sites contain copyrighted work of students, staff, or the general public. In *Marcus v. Rowley* (1983), a teacher in California successfully sued a colleague for copyright infringement after the latter created an activity packet based primarily on her work. While the dispute dealt with printed hard copy rather than the Internet, it admonishes those with questions about fair use to start by considering four things: purpose, nature, amount, and market. Is the purpose of the use of the work nonprofit educational or commercial? The nature of the work is also important because fictional and poetic pieces that are not published tend to get more protection; the amount used comes into play, and this should be small relative to the size to the full work. Rowley, the defendant, used too much of the plaintiff Marcus's work. Further, the end user must consider whether the use of the material damaged a market for the author of the work.

Educators should ask such questions before they post the work of others on their own or district Web sites. Students may be inclined to post work of others that they like, such as lyrics to music, poems, or even literary works, and some staff members post their personal work. School board officials should be careful how they manage copyrighted work because they can be liable for the actions of their employees.

Another issue is the use of trademarks, which includes characters and logos. Even though logos tend to be popular with staff and students, school boards should avoid using them to make their sites more attractive and prohibit their use on district Web sites. A related question here is whether a logo is being used in an inconsistent manner with school product endorsement. Professor Abra Feuerstein, an expert in school governance issues, pointed out that more individual schools and systems are entering into endorsement deals with businesses in which, for example, in exchange for providing funds to buy large items such as scoreboards, businesses are allowed to put their names on the boards. Using a competitor's logo and displaying it prominently may violate a contract with one of these businesses and lead to legal issues for a district.

School boards should also include some text on links to commercial sites or social networking sites in their Web site construction policies. Social networking sites such as MySpace and Facebook are becoming increasingly popular with students. Unfortunately, though, they are also sometimes used for bullying and intimidation. School board policies would thus be wise to prohibit links to the sites.

In addition to these issues, school boards must be aware that sites and their content can be violated by hackers. One such incident occurred in New Jersey in 2000, when a hacker known as "Protokol" altered the content of a site on the anniversary of the Columbine, Colorado, school shootings and posted some terror-filled messages threatening to bomb the school. A 2002 account of the incident by J. D. Abolins, a computer expert in privacy and security issues, says the hacker added and replaced text, including this disturbing message: "Tuesday, May 2nd Columbine Relived!!!!!" Even though the site was restored the next day and no one was hurt at the school, it did cause a scare and raised the question about school Web site security. In response, U.S. Senator Robert Torricelli proposed the School Website Protection Act, federal legislation that sought to criminalize the activity of hackers. Torricelli's bill was criticized as being too broad because it criminalized protected activity, among other things. The bill failed to survive challenges in the Senate Judiciary Committee in 2001. Others advocated for education as a more viable approach to the problem.

Many schools and boards have now added a copyright notice to protect the work of their sites; it is worth noting that it is a good idea to have one, along with a privacy policy, as part of sites. Lipinski acknowledges that student privacy is not new, but the way it is viewed in the context of school Web sites is relatively new. This approach stems from the fact that information on the Web is truly global and can be used to exploit children. When it comes to student personal information, this is cause for caution for school officials. The Family Educational Rights and Privacy Act (FERPA) stipulates that federal funds may be withdrawn from educational agencies if they disseminate student information to third parties without permission of parents and eligible students. There are exceptions, such as directory information, but educators must give parents notice of the categories it wishes to make public. Schools should be especially vigilant in this area and must take precautions when releasing student information into that medium. Lipinski argues that parental notice and permission should be sought before any personal identifying information of students is posted on the school's Web site.

School officials should seriously consider conducting an audit and then creating a Web site construction policy as advocated here. While policies cannot end the risk of all litigation, they should help to put students and staff on notice and provide them with some safety guidelines when constructing school-related Web sites.

Mark A. Gooden

See also Acceptable Use Policies; Copyright; Cyberbullying; Electronic Communication; Family Educational Rights and Privacy Act; Technology and the Law

Further Readings

Abolins, J. D. (2002). The challenges of responding to Internet vandalism. *New Jersey Lawyer, The Magazine, 213,* 33–36.

Feuerstein, A. (2001). Selling our schools? Principals' views on schoolhouse commercialism and school–business interactions. *Educational Administration Quarterly, 37,* 322–371.

Lipinski, T. A. (1999). Designing and using Web-based materials in education: A Web page legal audit. Part I, intellectual property issues. *West's Education Law Reporter, 137,* 9–19.

Lipinski, T. A. (1999). Designing and using Web-based materials in education: A Web page legal audit. Part II, information liability issues. *West's Education Law Reporter, 137,* 21–34.

Legal Citations

Family Educational Rights and Privacy Act, 20 U.S.C. § 1232g (2002).

Marcus v. Rowley, 695 F.2d 1171 (9th Cir. 1983).

WEST VIRGINIA STATE BOARD OF EDUCATION V. BARNETTE

At issue in *West Virginia State Board of Education v. Barnette* (1943) was whether a school board could compel students to participate in the salute to the American flag or be disciplined if they refused to do so for religious reasons. Students who were Jehovah's Witnesses and their parents challenged a school policy on the basis that their religious beliefs prohibited them from recognizing or bowing down to any graven image. The plaintiffs filed suit due to their refusal to salute because they considered the flag to be a "graven image" within this religious precept. The Supreme Court decided that the state was acting unconstitutionally in a manner at odds with the Bill of Rights, in a case that continues to have influence today.

The Court's Ruling

Barnette arose amid controversy that had occurred in other states and shortly after the U.S. Supreme Court ruled in *Minersville School District v. Gobitis* (1940) that students were not free to excuse themselves from taking part in the flag salute. In *Barnette,* a local school board in West Virginia, enacted a policy compelling students to participate in the flag salute or be subjected to discipline. The local board policy was consistent with a mandate of West Virginia's legislature. At that time, the state legislature amended its laws to require that all schools conduct courses of instruction for the purpose of teaching, fostering, and perpetuating the ideals, principles, and spirit of Americanism and government.

On further review of an order enjoining the enforcement of the policy, the Supreme Court affirmed in favor of the plaintiffs. In reviewing the disputed policy, the Court held that the issue in *Barnette* was no less than a collision between individual rights conferred in the First Amendment's freedom of religion clauses and the rights of states to determine rules for their citizens. The Court found that while the state has the power to regulate public education, if its authority conflicts with an individual's religious views that are protected by the First Amendment, the constitutional rights apply to the states through the Fourteenth Amendment and protect citizens against such state action.

The Court found that fundamental rights such as those to life, liberty, and property as well as to freedom of religion, worship, and speech may not be submitted to a vote, nor can they be dependent on elections. The Court reasoned that one of the purposes of the Bill of Rights, which included all of these protections, was to separate specified rights from political controversy and place them beyond the reach of majorities and governmental officials. While states have important legitimate functions related to educating the young for citizenship, the Court was of the opinion that states cannot infringe on individual rights provided by the Bill of Rights.

The Supreme Court thus concluded that when the school board sought to compel students to salute the flag in contravention of their religious beliefs, it acted in a manner that contradicted the spirit and purpose of the First Amendment. As a result of *Barnette,* many school boards now make saluting the flag optional for students who believe that doing so violates their religion, and schools may not discipline them for acting in accordance with their beliefs.

Continuing Impact

When placing *Barnette* in the larger context, it becomes clear that issues related to the flag salute, the Pledge of Allegiance, and other nationalistic ceremonies are often proscribed in the context of national sentiment fostering patriotism in schools. Often, the rationales for having flag salute policies have related to encouraging national unity, educating children about government, informing students about citizenship, and furthering national loyalty to the United States.

While *Barnette* remains the law of the land, issues related to the flag salute and Pledge of Allegiance continue to surface. For example, in *Elk Grove Unified School District v. Newdow* (2004), the Supreme Court sidestepped the issue of whether an atheist noncustodial father could prohibit his daughter from reciting the Pledge of Allegiance because he objected to the words "under God." The Court noted that the noncustodial father could not challenge a local board policy because he lacked standing to sue. On remand, a federal trial court in California largely followed an earlier order of the Ninth Circuit in directing school officials not to allow the of Allegiance (*Newdow v. Congress of U.S.,* 2005).

Amid a national surge of patriotism following the terrorist attacks on the United States on September 11,

2001, many school boards have reinstated the daily Pledge of Allegiance and flag salute. Consistent with *Barnette,* school boards make the flag salute optional and without disciplinary consequences for students who refuse to participate for religious reasons.

Barnette stands as precedent for school boards on the issue of state action and efforts of the majority to use the machinery of the state to overcome individual constitutional rights. *Barnette* is thus often cited in cases involving Bible reading, prayer in public schools, and other disputes related to protecting student rights against encroachment by officials in public school. In sum, *Barnette* continues to guide school boards and officials on how to resolve conflicts when their policies intrude on the individual constitutional rights of students to the free exercise of religion.

Vivian Hopp Gordon

See also Bill of Rights; *Elk Grove Unified School District v. Newdow;* First Amendment; *Minersville School District v. Gobitis;* Pledge of Allegiance; Prayer in Public Schools; Religious Activities in Public Schools; State Aid and the Establishment Clause

Legal Citations

Elk Grove Unified School District v. Newdow, 542
    U.S. 1 (2004), *reh'g denied*, 542 U.S. 1 (2004).
Minersville School District v. Gobitis, 310 U.S. 586 (1940).
Newdow v. Congress of U.S., 383 F. Supp. 2d 1229
    (E.D. Cal. 2005).
West Virginia State Board of Education v. Barnette, 319
    U.S. 624 (1943).

WHEELER V. BARRERA

At issue in *Wheeler v. Barrera* (1975) was whether the parents of educationally deprived children who attended nonpublic schools were entitled to equitable relief regarding the distribution of federal funds for Title I programs in public and nonpublic schools. Title I of the Elementary and Secondary Education Act of 1965 was the first law to authorize federal funding of programs for educationally deprived children in both public and nonpublic schools. Title I's implementing regulations define *educationally deprived children* as those, including students with disabilities, who need special assistance as a result of poverty, neglect, delinquency, or cultural or linguistic isolation from the community at large in order to attain the educational level appropriate for their ages (45 CFR § 116.1 (i)).

While enacting President Lyndon Johnson's Great Society legislative package, Congress recognized that educationally deprived children attend nonpublic as well as public schools. Accordingly, Title I benefits were extended to eligible students in both types of schools.

Ultimately, the U.S. Supreme Court ruled that the plaintiffs were entitled to relief because of the failure of local and state officials to provide comparable Title I services for public and nonpublic school students. However, at the same time, the Court did not specify any particular form of service or accommodation to which parents were entitled. In summarizing its opinion, the Court emphasized that development of a plan to implement needed Title I services was the responsibility of state and local educational leaders, not the federal courts.

Facts of the Case

Parents of children attending nonpublic schools in Kansas City, Missouri, brought a class action suit, alleging that state school officials arbitrarily and illegally approved campus-based Title I programs for eligible public school children, such as the use of federally funded teachers during regular school hours, while depriving children in nonpublic schools of comparable services. Prior to *Wheeler v. Barrera,* the prevailing practice in Missouri was to provide comparable equipment, materials, and supplies to eligible students in nonpublic schools but to exclude providing federally funded teachers and support personnel on the campuses of nonpublic schools.

Among other things, the parents claimed that campus-based programs had to be provided for eligible children in nonpublic schools if such programs were routinely offered in the public schools. The plaintiff parents also claimed that Missouri's constitutional provisions prohibiting the use of public funds in nonpublic schools did not apply to Title I. The defendants countered that the parents' requests

exceeded Title I requirements and that Title I programs on nonpublic school campuses violated First Amendment provisions mandating separation of church and state.

Initially, a federal trial court denied relief and dismissed the case. On further review, the Eighth Circuit reversed, ruling that state officials had, in fact, violated Title I's dictates, which required them to provide comparable services to all children who were educationally deprived. In addition, the court found that if Title I programs were provided on public school campuses, officials had to offer comparable programs for children who attended nonpublic schools. The court added that the Missouri law barring use of public funds to support operations in nonpublic schools did not apply to Title I programs. Finally, the court declined to address the petitioners' (state officials') concerns about violating the Establishment Clause, because they had not implemented a formal plan for Title I instruction on nonpublic school campuses at the time. The petitioners sought further review, and the Supreme Court granted certiorari.

The Court Ruling

After reviewing the facts, the Supreme Court agreed that the parents and their children were due relief because of the failure of local and state officials to ensure the delivery of comparable services under Title I to their schools. However, the Court also decided that the plaintiffs were not entitled to any particular form of service because it was the responsibility of state and local officials, not the federal courts, to formulate suitable plans for relief. According to the Court, Title I clearly declared that state constitutional spending limitations could not be preempted as a condition of accepting federal funds. To this end, the Court determined that the Eighth Circuit had erred in ruling that federal law superceded state law in the authorization and expenditure of Title I funds. The Court emphasized that Title I did not call for identical services for educationally deprived children in public and nonpublic schools; instead, the Court explained that the law obligated state agencies to provide comparable services and that officials had various options in complying with this requirement.

In the end, the Supreme Court reasoned that public officials can provide on-campus Title I instruction for children in nonpublic schools. Yet the Court was of the opinion that if state officials choose not to use that method or if state law prohibits them from doing so, they have three alternatives: develop and implement plans that do not utilize Title I instruction on campuses of nonpublic schools but satisfy the act's comparability requirement; develop and implement a plan that eliminates on-campus instruction on all campuses and that uses other means, such as summer programs or neutral sites, to carry out congressional intent; or choose not to participate at all in the Title I program.

In light of *Wheeler v. Barrera,* government officials have administered Title I programs and services based on the three-pronged model that the Court suggested. In *Agostini v. Felton* (1997), the Court essentially affirmed *Wheeler* by upholding a public school board's assignment of publicly paid Title I teachers to inner-city, religiously affiliated nonpublic schools.

Robert C. Cloud

See also *Agostini v. Felton;* School Board Policy

Legal Citations

Agostini v. Felton, 521 U.S. 203 (1997).
Special District v. Wheeler, 408 S.W.2d 60 (1966).
Title I of the Elementary and Secondary Education Act of 1965, *as amended*, 20 U.S.C. §§ 241 *et seq.*, *currently codified at* 20 U.S.C. §§ 6301 *et seq.*
United States v. 93.970 Acres of Land, 360 U.S. 328 (1959).
Wheeler v. Barrera, 417 U.S. 402 (1975).

WHITE FLIGHT

Generally, "White flight" refers to the withdrawal of Whites from desegregating institutions, such as schools, school systems, or residential communities, due to the consideration and implementation of school desegregation plans. The concept of White flight is controversial because the loss of White students in school systems is fairly easy to document, whereas the reasons for their departures are not generally easy to identify or isolate. This entry reviews the phenomenon and scholarly discussion about its causes.

Early Research

During the 1960s and 1970s, city school systems in particular lost a large percentage of White students. According to researchers, the primary reason for White flight was dissatisfaction with the prospect of busing (Armor 1995; Coleman, Kelly, & Moore, 1975). The opposition of urban White families to school desegregation and busing motivated them to escape to private and/or religious schools or move to the suburbs.

At the same time, advocates of desegregation viewed the loss in White enrollments as being due to historical trends of suburbanization and demographic factors, especially the drop in the White birthrate (Orfield & Eaton, 1996; Pettigrew & Green, 1976). In a series of point-counterpoint academic articles, these researchers battled over the causes of declines in enrollment. While the researchers never agreed on the precise causes of White Flight, they did agree that metropolitan plans for school desegregation offered the best hope of minimizing White Flight because they included the White suburbs.

One study of school desegregation reported racial enrollment trends from 1968 to 1973 in the 67 largest central-city school districts in the nation (Coleman et al., 1975). The report concluded that Whites fled central cities not only for demographic reasons, such as the percentage of Blacks and size of school systems, but also due to school desegregation plans. As part of the process, White parents expressed concerns about declining educational quality, racial conflict, violence, value conflicts, and general disruption in the desegregation process. This study generated a host of follow-up analyses, including critical analyses that were summarized elsewhere (Robin & Bosco, 1976).

More Recent Studies

A great deal of quantitative empirical research on White Flight has taken place since the mid-1970s. One type of analysis, called "no-show" analysis, compares actual White enrollment, after the implementation of desegregation plans, to projected White enrollment. For example, one study of school desegregation litigation reported that the "no-show" rates were 45% in Boston, 42% in Savannah-Chatham County, 52% in Baton Rouge, and 56% in California, where Whites were assigned to formerly minority schools (Rossell, 1997). Put another way, this indicates that about half of Whites who were assigned to "Black" schools did not remain in public school systems immediately after the implementation of desegregation plans. The reports concluded that the percentage of minority students, not whether a plan involved metropolitan areas or urban districts, was the major factor affecting the extent of White Flight.

Analyzing a national probability sample of 600 school systems, another study found that school systems that had mandatory school desegregation plans lost one-third more White students than those that never had plans (Rossell & Armor, 1996). In addition, the study reported that districts with voluntary-only plans experienced less than 3% White enrollment loss, a rate that is not statistically significant. Similarly, the study noted that controlled-choice plans had enrollment loss almost as high as mandatory plans.

Still other researchers questioned whether "flight" should be characterized as simply "White" or as "middle class," because it may also include the Black middle class. This approach tries to explain why many Whites may flee school desegregation, when in surveys they indicate support for the principle of school desegregation. Various theories for this contradiction have been offered, including symbolic racism. While Whites have increasingly accepted the principle of desegregation, many White parents do not want to send their children to schools with a majority of Black students.

In another study, respondents in national surveys were asked whether Black and White students should attend the same or separate schools. In 1942, about one-third of the White respondents answered "same schools." This percentage has increased over time from 50% in 1956, to 75% in 1970, to 90% in 1980 (Armor, 1995). This study revealed that surveys in the 1990s in individual cities could identify fewer than 5% of White parents who selected the segregated-schools option. In like fashion, the study asked respondents whether they would object to sending their children to schools in which various percentages of Black children were enrolled. The percentage of Whites not objecting to sending their children to schools in which half of the students were White and

half were Black increased from 50% to over 75% from 1958 to 1983. The percentage of Whites not objecting to sending their children to majority Black schools rose from low-30s percentiles to the high 30s. In the eyes of many White parents, majority Black schools are not desegregated, regardless of the racial balance in the systems.

No Consensus

The passage of more than three decades since the original social science reports on White Flight has not led to consensus on its causes. If anything, one summary of the literature on White flight (Orfield & Eaton, 1996) offers a counterpoint to another (Rossell & Armor, 1996). The first study (Orfield & Eaton) argued that since Whites abandoned cities that did not have desegregation orders, such as Atlanta, New York, Chicago, and Houston, one cannot view school desegregation orders as the basis of flight. However, this same study accepts the notion that some school desegregation plans are more likely to accelerate flight than others, with metropolitan school desegregation plans as the most stable. A later statistical reanalysis of that data indicated that voluntary plans produced less White flight than mandatory plans (Rossell, 1997), regardless of whether they were metropolitan in scope.

Paul Green

See also Brown v. Board of Education of Topeka and Equal
    Educational Opportunities; Dual and Unitary Systems;
    Segregation, De Facto; Segregation, De Jure

Further Readings

Armor, D. J. (1995). *Forced justice: School desegregation
    and the law.* New York: Oxford University Press.
Coleman, J. S., Kelly, S. D., & Moore, J. A. (1975). *Trends in
    school segregation, 1968–1973.* Washington, DC: Urban
    Institute.
Orfield, G., & Eaton, S. E. (1996). *Dismantling
    desegregation: The quiet reversal of* Brown v. Board of
    Education. New York: New Press.
Pettigrew, T. F., & Green, R. L. (1976). School desegregation
    in large cities: A critique of the Coleman "White Flight"
    thesis. *Harvard Educational Review, 46,* 1–53.
Robin, S. S., & Bosco, H. S. (1976). Coleman's
    desegregation research and policy recommendations. In

F. H. Levinsohn & B. D. Wright (Eds.), *School desegregation* (pp. 46–57). Chicago: University of Chicago Press.

Rossell, C. H. (1997). An analysis of the court decisions in *Sheff v. O'Neill* and possible remedies for racial isolation. *Connecticut Law Review, 29,* 1187–1233.

Rossell, C. H., & Armor, D. J. (1996). The effectiveness of school desegregation plans, 1968–1991. *American Politics Quarterly, 24,* 296–302.

WIDMAR V. VINCENT

Widmar v. Vincent (1981) was the first Supreme Court decision to grant free speech protection to religious expression at an educational institution. In *Widmar,* the Court recognized that the Free Speech Clause provided a new and powerful counterweight to the Establishment Clause, requiring analysis of speech content. *Widmar* put public universities on notice that if they wanted to open their campuses to student expression but close them to religious expression, they must do so according to the requirements of the Free Speech Clause. This entry looks at the case, the ruling, and its impact.

Facts of the Case

In *Widmar,* a university-recognized student religious group (Cornerstone) challenged the University of Missouri at Kansas City's (UMKC) refusal to permit the organization to meet on university premises. For 4 years prior to filing a suit against UKMC, Cornerstone had sought unsuccessfully to gather on university premises, each year being rejected because of a UKMC board of curator's policy prohibiting the use of university buildings or grounds "for purposes of religious worship or religious teaching" (*Widmar,* p. 265). The student members of Cornerstone challenged UKMC's policy as violating their rights to free exercise of religion, equal protection, and freedom of speech under the First and Fourteenth Amendments to the Constitution.

A federal trial court in Missouri rejected the plaintiffs' claim, finding that their religious speech was entitled to less protection than other types of expression. The Eighth Circuit Court reversed, holding that "the Establishment Clause does not bar a policy of equal access" (*Widmar,* p. 266). On further review, the U.S. Supreme Court affirmed the judgment of the Eighth Circuit.

The Court's Ruling

In a broad rejection of UMKC's policy, the Supreme Court observed that the public university had created a forum generally open for use by student groups. Having done so, the Court reasoned that "the Constitution forbids a State to enforce certain exclusions from a forum generally open to the public, even if it was not required to create the forum in the first place" (*Widmar,* p. 267). The Court specifically found that generally open forums to engage in religious worship and discussion, as desired by student groups, were "forms of speech and association protected by the First Amendment" (p. 269). As a result, the Court maintained that the university's policy could survive constitutional scrutiny only if it "serve[d] a compelling state interest and . . . [was] narrowly drawn to achieve that end" (p. 270). The Court categorically rejected the university's compelling interest based on its interpretation of the Establishment Clause as requiring a "strict separation of church and State" (p. 270).

Analyzing UMKC's policy under the *Lemon v. Kurtzman* (1971) three-part test, the Court found that the university's open forum for student groups satisfied both the first (secular purpose) and third (no excessive entanglement) parts. Concerning the second part (effects) of the test, the Court that determined that "an important index of secular effect" (*Widmar,* p. 274) was the university's having created an open forum and extending the benefits of such a forum to a broad spectrum of groups.

In addition, the Court pointed out that the Free Speech Clause further restricted the university's compelling interest. The Court limited its holding to "content-based exclusion of religious speech" (*Widmar,* p. 276) and did not extend its rationale to "the capacity of the University to establish reasonable time, place, and manner regulations" (p. 277). To date, the Supreme Court has failed to indicate whether an educational institution's avoidance of an Establishment Clause violation will constitute a compelling interest to justify treating religious expression differently.

The Congress essentially extended *Widmar* to public secondary schools in enacting the Equal Access Act, which permits student-sponsored, noncurriculum groups to meet during noninstructional hours. Further, *Widmar* was a landmark case that set the scene 12 years later for *Lamb's Chapel v. Center Moriches Union Free School District* (1993), wherein the Supreme Court, in a rare unanimous decision, extended free speech protection for religious expression to the K–12 education level.

Until *Widmar,* the Court repeatedly invoked the *Lemon* test during the 1970s in concluding that state support for religious schools violated one or more of the tests (*Meek v. Pittenger,* 1975). *Widmar* represented a new genre of religion cases that did not fit the fact pattern that had characterized cases in the 1970s.

Ralph D. Mawdsley

See also *Board of Education of Westside Community Schools v. Mergens;* Equal Access Act; *Lamb's Chapel v. Center Moriches Union Free School District; Lemon v. Kurtzman;* Prayer in Public Schools; Religious Activities in Public Schools

Legal Citations

Equal Access Act, 20 U.S.C. §§ 4071 *et seq.*
Lamb's Chapel v. Center Moriches Union Free School District, 508 U.S. 384 (1993).
Lemon v. Kurtzman, 403 U.S. 602 (1971).
Meek v. Pittenger, 421 U.S. 349 (1975).
Widmar v. Vincent, 454 U.S. 263 (1981).

WINKELMAN EX REL. WINKELMAN v. PARMA CITY SCHOOL DISTRICT

The Individuals with Disabilities Education Act (IDEA) (2005) contains an extensive set of procedural due process safeguards for parents and their children. Yet the IDEA was unclear about the rights of nonattorney parents of students with disabilities who wished to file suit on behalf of their children. Consequently, there was a split among the federal circuits over whether nonattorney parents could intervene on behalf of their children in disputes with their school boards

over the delivery of a free appropriate public education (FAPE), which culminated in the Supreme Court's hearing an appeal in such a dispute, *Winkelman ex rel. Winkelman v. Parma City School District* (2007).

Winkelman began when parents in Ohio sued local school board officials in a fight over the educational placement of their son, who had autism spectrum disorder. After a federal trial court and the Sixth Circuit agreed that the board provided the child with a FAPE, the latter added that the IDEA did not permit the nonattorney parents to represent their son in judicial actions. The Supreme Court agreed to hear an appeal in order to resolve the dispute among the circuits.

As author of the Supreme Court's opinion in its 7-to-4 judgment, Justice Kennedy, joined by Chief Justice Roberts and Justices Stevens, Souter, Ginsburg, Breyer, and Alito, reversed in favor of the parents. In noting that the dispute was governed by the IDEA, Kennedy maintained that the IDEA allows parents to participate in developing the individualized education programs (IEPs) of their children and in dispute resolution procedures under which they can recover attorney fees if they prevail in litigation. As such, Kennedy viewed the IDEA as permitting parents to exercise their own rights once administrative proceedings are completed.

Kennedy indicated that unless the Court treated the word *rights* in the IDEA as referring both to parents and children, the law would not have made sense, since it presumably conferred such rights on parents. He thought that despite congressional unwillingness to address the issue explicitly, nothing in the law limited his view that the IDEA was supposed to grant parents independent, enforceable rights over the education of their children. Moreover, Kennedy pointed to language in the IDEA that allows parents to serve on the IEP teams of their children and to challenge their adequacy. According to Kennedy, the IDEA granted parents their own interest in its dispute resolution procedures because such an approach was consistent with the law's overall intent.

Justice Kennedy disagreed with the board's reliance on the Supreme Court's holding in *Arlington Central School District Board of Education v. Murphy* (2006). In *Arlington,* the Court interpreted the IDEA, which was enacted pursuant to the authority of Congress under the Spending Clause, in Article I,

Section 8, of the U.S. Constitution, as requiring "clear notice" before imposing new obligations on states and local school boards. Kennedy rejected the board's assertion that *Arlington* required Spending Clause legislation such as the IDEA to provide clear, unambiguous notice in refusing to permit parents to be reimbursed for the costs of fees for expert witnesses and consultants. In deciding that *Winkelman* did not impose extra substantive obligations on states, Kennedy determined that his rationale did not impact basic monetary recovery under the IDEA.

As to the school board's final contention that the Court's judgment would have increased the costs to states by requiring them to respond to litigation by nonattorney parents, Kennedy remarked that such an approach did not involve the Spending Clause. He also responded that states and local boards would not be defenseless in the face of increased cases since the IDEA permits courts to award attorney fees to prevailing educational agencies if, for example, parents needlessly increase the cost of litigation. Kennedy thus remanded for further consideration as to whether school officials provided the child with a FAPE.

Justice Scalia's dissent, which was joined by Justice Thomas, conceded that the IDEA confers some independently enforceable rights on parents. Even so, he observed that the Court went too far in creating a new set of parental rights, because there was no justification for its rationale in the IDEA. Rather, Scalia agreed with the board that by allowing nonattorney parents to represent themselves in challenges over the placements of their children, the Court opened the door to litigation that would unnecessarily tax the resources of school systems as they seek to defend themselves from baseless claims.

Charles J. Russo

See also Attorney Fees; Free Appropriate Public Education; Least Restrictive Environment

Legal Citations

Arlington Central School District Board of Education v. Murphy, 548 U.S. 291 (2006).

Individuals with Disabilities Education Act, 20 U.S.C. §§ 1400 *et seq.*

Winkelman ex rel. Winkelman v. Parma City School District, 127 S. Ct. 1994 (2007).

WISCONSIN V. YODER

Wisconsin v. Yoder (1972) was the third of three significant Supreme Court cases, following *Meyer v. Nebraska* (1923) and *Pierce v. Society of Sisters of the Holy Names of Jesus and Mary* (1925), that upheld the Fourteenth Amendment right of parents to direct the education of their children. However, because states had been made subject to the Free Exercise Clause of the First Amendment in *Cantwell v. Connecticut,* in 1940, *Yoder* also raised a free exercise claim. This entry looks at the case and the decision.

Facts of the Case

Yoder involved a criminal truancy charge against two Amish fathers who refused to enroll their children in public schools after they had completed the eighth grade in a one-room Amish school. The state of Wisconsin required, pursuant to its compulsory attendance law, that parents enroll their children in school between the ages of 7 and 16. In other words, this law would have required Amish children who had completed eighth grade at age 13 or 14 to attend public school until they reached the age of 16.

The fathers were found guilty of truancy, and each was fined $5. The Supreme Court of Wisconsin reversed the convictions, finding the application of the truancy law to the Amish to constitute a violation of the First Amendment's free exercise of religion provision.

The Court's Ruling

In a thorough and carefully reasoned opinion that explicated in a comprehensive manner the religious beliefs of the Amish, the U.S. Supreme Court upheld the decision of the state supreme court. In sum, the Court found three centuries of Amish religious beliefs and practice to be "inseparable and interdependent" (*Yoder,* p. 215). The Court was duly impressed with the Amish "life style [that had] not altered in fundamentals for centuries" (p. 217). The Court found the following conclusion inescapable:

> [That] secondary schooling, by exposing Amish children to worldly influences in terms of attitudes, goals, and values contrary to beliefs, and by substantially interfering with the religious development of the Amish child and his integration into the way of life of the Amish faith community at the crucial adolescent stage of development, [would] contravene the basic religious tenets and practice of the Amish faith, both as to the parent and the child. (p. 218)

According to the Court, to compel Amish children to enroll in public high schools past the eighth grade would have mandated that they "either abandon belief and be assimilated into society at large, or be forced to migrate to some other and more tolerant region" (*Yoder,* p. 218).

The Court rejected the state of Wisconsin's argument that "its interest in its system of compulsory education is so compelling that even the established religious practices of the Amish must give way" (*Yoder,* p. 221), finding instead that the absence of 1 or 2 additional years of education would neither make the children burdens on society nor impair their health or safety. During these 1 or 2 years, the Amish children were not inactive, and the Court remarked favorably on "the adequacy of the Amish alternative mode of continuing informal vocational education" (p. 235) on their farms.

Although the Supreme Court upheld the Amish way of life against a state compulsory attendance challenge, it was careful to explain that since only the parents' religious rights were litigated in *Yoder,* no one had determined what the rights of the Amish children might have been had they wanted to enroll in a public high school. In his dissent, Justice Douglas pointedly observed as follows:

> It is the student's judgment, not his parents', that is essential if we are to give full meaning to what we have said about the Bill of Rights and of the right of students to be masters of their own destiny. (*Yoder,* p. 245)

To date, no court has taken on the challenge of addressing a direct challenge between parents' and children's rights. The closest that courts have come is reflected in *Circle Schools v. Pappert* (2004), in which the Third Circuit upheld a student's free expression right to challenge a state Pledge of Allegiance statute, while rejecting the parents' claim based on their right to direct the education of their children. This parental right grounded in *Meyer* and *Pierce* is an entrenched judicial tradition in the United States, and although students in public schools have constitutional rights pursuant to *Tinker v. Des Moines Independent Community School District* (1969), courts have not yet been disposed to use student rights as a vehicle to detract from the rights of parents.

Ralph D. Mawdsley

See also *Pierce v. Society of Sisters of the Holy Names of Jesus and Mary; Tinker v. Des Moines Independent Community School District*

Legal Citations

Cantwell v. Connecticut, 310 U.S. 296 (1940).
Circle Schools v. Pappert, 381 F.3d 172 (3d Cir. 2004).
Meyer v. Nebraska, 262 U. S. 390 (1923).
Pierce v. Society of Sisters of the Holy Names of Jesus and Mary, 268 U.S. 510 (1925).
Tinker v. Des Moines Independent Community School District, 393 U.S. 503 (1969).
Wisconsin v. Yoder, 406 U.S. 205 (1972).

WOLMAN V. WALTER

At issue in *Wolman v. Walter* (1977) was a challenge to a statute from Ohio that provided a variety of types of aid to nonpublic, mostly religiously affiliated schools and their students; more specifically, 691 of the 720 charted nonpublic schools were religiously based. Among the benefits in dispute were textbooks for subjects in secular instruction, standardized testing and scoring services, diagnostic speech and hearing services, remedial services, an array of instructional materials, and the use of school buses for field trips for nonpublic school students. In the initial round of litigation, a federal trial court upheld the statute against all challenges.

On further review, a fractured U.S. Supreme Court, in a majority opinion by Justice Blackmun that resulted in six additional opinions from the justices, partially upheld the statute's constitutionality, relying largely on the *Lemon v. Kurtzman* (1971) test. Based on its own earlier decisions in *Board of Education v. Allen* (1968) and *Meek v. Pittenger* (1975), the Court allowed the state to provide textbooks for use in instruction in secular subjects. Further, to the extent that the law simply reimbursed the nonpublic schools for costs associated with keeping records required by state law and did not pay them for creating or scoring the tests or for costs associated with their being administered, Blackmun upheld the law's constitutionality. He was satisfied that the statute passed the *Lemon* test, because it included appropriate safeguards to make certain that public money was not diverted for the religious purposes of the schools.

Justice Blackmun next wrote that since providing diagnostic services on-site in the nonpublic schools did not create an impermissible risk of fostering ideological views, there was no need for state officials to engage in such excessive surveillance, as this would have created an impermissible entanglement between church and state. He added that providing health services to the students in the nonpublic schools did not have the primary effect of aiding religion. Blackmun found that there was little or no educational content, insofar as diagnosticians had limited contact with children, and so there was minimal risk that they would transmit their religious perspectives to students.

As to therapeutic, guidance, and remedial services, however, including those rendered in mobile units, Justice Blackmun was of the opinion that they could be offered only at sites that were not physically or educationally identified with the nonpublic schools, in order to avoid having the impermissible effect of advancing religion. By taking such an approach—having the services provided by employees of the public schools—he thought there was no risk of excessive entanglement.

Turning to the instructional materials, Justice Blackmun noted that the statute provided items such as projectors, tape recorders, record players, maps and globes, and science kits. Yet even though he acknowledged that the loans of instructional materials and equipment was ostensibly limited to neutral and secular items, he struck down this part of the statute because he feared that this arrangement had the inescapably primary effect of providing a direct and substantial advancement of sectarian education. Blackmun expanded his analysis by observing that since it was impossible to separate the secular educational function of the schools from their religious goals, the law was unconstitutional.

As to the statute's final provision, the use of public school buses for field trips, Justice Blackmun decided that this, too, was unconstitutional. He declared that this part of the law was unacceptable because officials in the nonpublic schools had the ability to control the timing and frequency of the field trips, meaning that the schools, rather than the students, were the recipients of the aid to further their religious goals. According to Blackmun, the close supervision that public school officials would have had to provide to ensure that the field trips were of a secular nature meant that there would have been excessive entanglement between the religious schools and the state, in violation of the *Lemon* test.

Wolman's viability is questionable in light of the Supreme Court's plurality judgment (less than the required five justices joined the opinion to make it binding precedent) in *Mitchell v. Helms* (2000). In *Mitchell,* a dispute from Louisiana, the Court upheld the constitutionality of a federal law that permits the loans of instructional materials, including library books, computers, television sets, tape recorders, and maps, to religiously affiliated, nonpublic schools. Although the plurality explicitly reversed those parts of *Wolman* that were inconsistent with its judgment in *Mitchell,* since the ruling was a plurality, the status of such loans remains uncertain.

C. Daniel Raisch

See also *Board of Education v. Allen; Lemon v. Kurtzman; Meek v. Pittenger; Mitchell v. Helms;* State Aid and the Establishment Clause

Legal Citations

Board of Education v. Allen, 392 U.S. 236 (1968).
Lemon v. Kurtzman, 403 U.S. 602 (1971).
Meek v. Pittenger, 421 U.S. 349 (1975).

Mitchell v. Helms, 530 U.S. 793 (2000), *reh'g denied*, 530
   U.S. 1296 (2000), *on remand sub nom. Helms v. Picard*,
   229 F.3d 467 (5th Cir. 2000).
Wolman v. Walter, 433 U.S. 229 (1977).

WOOD V. STRICKLAND

At issue in *Wood v. Strickland* (1975) was whether
school board members could be sued for monetary
damages in the context of school discipline and, if so,
under what conditions they may be financially liable.
In *Wood,* the U.S. Supreme Court found that board
members may be sued for monetary damages in school
disciplinary proceedings under civil rights law, particularly 42 U.S. Code, Section 1983, but only under
specified conditions.

The Basic Ruling

As a case of first impression, *Wood* focused on the procedural due process rights of students in Arkansas who
were subjected to long-term suspensions for the use of
alcoholic beverages at school. On further review of a
judgment of the Eighth Circuit, which indicated that
board members may be liable for depriving students of
their rights, the Supreme Court reversed and remanded
for further factual determinations.

In its analysis, the Supreme Court observed that
school board members must be afforded some degree
of financial immunity when administering student
discipline, since doing so would enable them to act in
the best interests of school communities without
intimidation or fear of senseless litigation. The Court
reasoned that in order to create safe school environments that are maximally conducive to learning,
school board members and, by extension, other educational officials must be afforded the authority to
administer discipline without tentativeness.

At the same time, the Supreme Court ruled that
school board members do not have complete immunity because under certain conditions, they can be
monetarily liable in school disciplinary proceedings.
The Court was of the opinion that if school board
members arbitrarily violate students' federal rights or
act with malicious intent in denying their rights or

cause them other injuries, they can be financially
liable. Consistent with the need for school officials to
exercise appropriate judgment and discretion in
school disciplinary proceedings, the Court softened
the impact of its ruling in specifying that students can
recover damages only when school board members
"acted with such an impermissible motivation or with
such disregard of the student's clearly established
constitutional rights that his action cannot reasonably
be characterized as being in good faith" (*Wood,*
p. 322). The Supreme Court remanded the dispute to
the Eighth Circuit, which returned the case to the trial
court for further consideration based on its determination that school officials violated the students' rights
to due process.

Impact of the Ruling

Wood is perhaps best known as setting a qualified
immunity standard for educational officials, including
school board members, meaning that they have a high
degree of, but not complete immunity from, financial
liability for their official actions. At the heart of its
analysis, the Court recognized that in the history of
public education, the administration of school discipline can be characterized as highly controversial,
particularly in light of the inherent risk that suspension and expulsion pose to the protected liberties of
students. Based on these risks and the frequent litigation associated with school discipline, *Wood* continues
to provide some degree of clarity on the degree to
which school officials may be liable for their actions.

Other courts frequently cite *Wood* for setting criteria
by which board members and other school officials
should be judged pursuant to the qualified immunity
standard. Prior to *Wood,* lower courts differed on
whether to apply subjective or objective criteria in
deciding the question of financial damages. Using subjective criteria, school officials would have to act with
malice or ill will toward students. On the other hand,
pursuant to objective criteria, educators could be liable
financially if they knew or should have known that their
actions violated students' federally protected rights,
regardless of whether they acted with malice or ill will.

In *Wood,* the Supreme Court explained that the
appropriate standard for judging the actions of school

board members and other educational official should contain elements of both: Officials can be liable even absent proof of malice or ill will, but "good faith" errors in the administration of discipline do not constitute a basis for such liability.

In later cases, the Supreme Court provided additional clarity on the extent to which plaintiffs can recover damages from school officials, for example, in *Carey v. Piphus* (1978); the Court also removed the subjective criterion from consideration in the non-school case of *Harlow v. Fitzgerald* (1982). In general, though, *Wood* set an enduring precedent that school officials have a great deal of latitude and protection from financial liability in the administration of school discipline. Even so, it is worth recalling that since the latitude and protection that educators enjoy is not absolute, they can be liable for intentionally violating the federally protected rights of students if they act with deliberate indifference to allegations of which they were aware.

M. Karega Rausch

See also *Carey v. Piphus;* Civil Rights Act of 1871 (Section 1983); Immunity; School Boards

Legal Citations

Carey v. Piphus, 435 U.S. 247 (1978).
Harlow v. Fitzgerald, 457 U.S. 800 (1982).
Wood v. Strickland, 420 U.S. 308 (1975), *on remand, sub nom. Strickland v. Inlow*, 519 F.2d 744 (8th Cir. 1975).

WYGANT V. JACKSON BOARD OF EDUCATION

Wygant v. Jackson Board of Education (1986) addressed Equal Protection Clause jurisprudence concerning the use of racial classifications as applied to public school teachers who lose their jobs as part of an agreed-on reduction in force. In *Wygant,* a plurality of the Supreme Court agreed that it is necessary to apply strict scrutiny even when integration, not segregation, is the state's goal and that general concerns about societal discrimination are an insufficient ground for employing racial classifications. As specifically applied to education, *Wygant* is also cited as a dismissal of a "role model" theory as justification for race-conscious practices. Most recently, *Wygant* was cited for these propositions in *Parents Involved in Community Schools v. Seattle School District No. 1* (2007).

Facts of the Case

Wygant involved a dispute over the application of the reduction-in-force, or layoff, provision of a collective bargaining agreement between the teachers' union and the Jackson (Michigan) Board of Education. According to the provision, "At no time will there be a greater percentage of minority personnel laid off than the current percentage of minority personnel employed at the time of the layoff" (*Wygant,* p. 270).

The facts revealed that the district had a history of racial tensions, although there was never a judicial declaration that the board engaged in discriminatory hiring practices. The provision was adopted as a necessary complement to the affirmative action hiring practices that the board adopted to create an integrated workforce.

In *Wygant,* the nonminority teachers who were affected by the layoffs challenged the provision as an improper use of a racial classification under the Equal Protection Clause and Title VII. A federal trial court dismissed most claims but ruled that the practice survived equal protection review. The Sixth Circuit affirmed that the school board had sufficiently justified the preferences used as necessary to redress societal discrimination in seeking to provide role models for minority students.

The Court Ruling

A sharply divided U.S. Supreme Court reversed in favor of the teachers. In a plurality, the justices found that since strict scrutiny applied, it was necessary to examine the facts in order to evaluate whether the school board's use of the racial classification was necessary and narrowly tailored to achieve a compelling state interest. In deciding that the provision failed both parts of the test, Justice Powell first explained, in perhaps the most cited quotation from the decision, that "societal discrimination, without more, is too amorphous a basis for imposing a racially classified remedy" (*Wygant,* p. 276).

At the same time, the plurality reasoned that the burden that the teachers who were released had suffered was too great to bear in furtherance of such a general goal. In contrast, the justices maintained that hiring preferences did not create the same effect and any burden was "diffused" among applicants generally.

Justice O'Connor, although agreeing with the outcome, wrote separately to express her view that the lower courts erred by not examining the propriety of the hiring goal. As such, she indicated that the school board's goal was improper because the number of minority teachers was tied to the number of minority students, when it should have been connected to the number of minority teachers available in the hiring pool. Justice White also concurred but wrote a short one-paragraph concurrence. He expressed his view that any policy that dismissed White teachers in order to add Black teachers should have been impermissible regardless of justification.

Justice Marshall penned a dissent in which he argued that the dispute should have been remanded because the trial court had not sufficiently explored the factual record. In addition, he thought that since the school board and the teachers' union voluntarily agreed to do so, they should have been permitted to adopt provisions that had the effect of preserving the benefits gained through preferential hiring practices. Justice Stevens filed a separate dissent, in which he asserted that the Court focused too heavily on the remedial justifications for the preferences that were used, while not sufficiently considering the prospective goals that the school board may have had in educating children for the future.

Julie F. Mead

See also Affirmative Action; Collective Bargaining; Due Process Rights: Teacher Dismissal; Equal Protection Analysis; Fourteenth Amendment; Reduction in Force; Title VII

Further Readings

Kang, J., & Banaji, M. R. (2006). Fair measures: A behavioral realist revision of "affirmative action." *California Law Review, 94,* 1063–1118.

The non-perpetuation of discrimination in public contracting: A justification for state and local minority business set-asides after *Wygant* (unsigned note). (1988). *Harvard Law Review, 101,* 1797–1815.

Legal Citations

Parents Involved in Community Schools v. Seattle School District No. 1, 127 S. Ct. 2738 (2007).

Wygant v. Jackson Board of Education, 476 U.S. 267 (1986).

YEAR-ROUND SCHOOLS

As the majority of American students are dusting off their backpacks, listening to their "iPods," and thinking about a new school year, others have been sitting in classes for much of the summer. It is not that these students have to go to summer school. Rather, they attend schools that have moved to a year-round schedule, another example of a reform that reflects how boards and legislatures are exercising their legal control over public education. This entry reviews the history of year-round education and considers the advantages and disadvantages of such a schedule.

The term *year-round schooling* is misleading in that it suggests an end to summer traditions such as summer camps or beach vacations. In reality, students in most U.S. year-round school systems spend about the same amount of days in class as peers in traditional calendar schools. The major difference is that calendars are arranged differently, with smaller, more frequent breaks. Year-round education essentially involves the reorganization of traditional school calendars so that long summer vacations are replaced by several smaller breaks, evenly spaced throughout the year.

Historical Background

Beliefs to the contrary notwithstanding, year-round schooling does not necessarily mean less vacation time for students and staff. The traditional school year calendar, with its early morning start times and 10- to 15-week summer breaks, was designed when most American families were earning a living by farming or running family businesses. At the time, school calendars revolved around the planting, cultivating, and harvesting of crops and working for the family farm or business so that children could be home to help during the busiest summer months. Schools retained this agrarian calendar after farming declined and the nation became more industrial, in part because it was difficult to conduct classes during the hot summer months without air-conditioning.

Beginning with *Stuart v. School District No. 1 of Village of Kalamazoo* (1874), the American legal system has recognized that local school boards, in addition to state legislatures, have the authority to engage in new educational initiatives. American schools began experimenting with a switch to year-round schedules on a larger scale during the early 1900s, and the idea began to take root in the 1970s and 1980s as studies demonstrated that American students were not scoring well on national and international tests.

According to the National Association for Year-Round Education (NAYRE), the trend is growing; more than 3,000 schools had year-round education programs during the 2006–2007 academic year. Previously, NAYRE reported that the number of year-round schools in the United States increased from just over 400 in the late 1980s to 2,880 during the 1999–2000 school year. While this represents less than 4% of all schools, it is 4 times the number of students in year-round schools only a few years ago.

Advantages

Interest in implementing year-round schools can be attributed to three acknowledged advantages of such a calendar: increased student achievement; greater satisfaction among parents, teachers, and students; and cost savings. The first two are often mentioned in conjunction with all year-round schools, while cost savings are typically associated only with multitrack, year-round schools, as they can help postpone the need to build new schools in areas experiencing significant population growth.

Year-round schooling became popular because some educational leaders believe that the practice can enhance student and teacher performance. One idea is that if students and teachers are refreshed by more frequent breaks, they are less likely to burn out as easily. Some teachers also complain that on traditional schedules, too much time is spent reviewing in the fall after many students have forgotten what they learned the previous year. Further, many English as a Second Language (ESL) children fall behind because they are not exposed to English during the long summer breaks. Also, students requiring academic intervention do not have to wait to go to summer school to get help. Instead, they can attend enrichment/remedial classes earlier in the year, to catch problems more quickly. Thus, year-round schooling is designed to alleviate these concerns.

Supporters say year-round systems improve academic performance. They point to Japan, where student scores are higher than those in the United States and children attend classes 220 days a year on average, as opposed to 180 days in U.S. schools. Even so, debate remains.

When many school systems in Texas adopted year-round calendars in the 1990s, nearly half switched back. School officials made the change back because insofar as the program did not improve academic performance substantially, they were unable to win the cooperation of parents. Put another way, educators found it simply too hard to fight tradition. Conversely, the Oxnard, California, district has a long record of successful year-round schooling, having done so since

1979. Further, a 9-year analysis of Oxnard revealed that student test scores improved significantly without changing the basic education program.

Of course, academic performance is not the only concern of school boards. By switching to a year-round schedule on a multitrack system, with several groups of students rotating, some overcrowded districts have avoided the expense of building new schools, even with increased maintenance costs and higher pay for teachers factored in the totals. In addition, moving to year-around may require legal changes, as boards may be required to bargain with the unions of their employees over various aspects of schedule changes, especially with regard to such key issues as providing transportation.

Disadvantages

Critics challenge the idea that year-round schedules improve grades and have raised other concerns. Especially for multitrack districts, they maintain that scheduling issues can harm families. For example, a family with children in different schools operating on different tracks could have a tough time scheduling day care or family vacations. Another problematic area is that sports teams in competing districts could have different schedules, so athletes may have games scheduled during breaks. It is difficult for everyone to coordinate practice times when some students participate in sports in multitrack schools while other team members follow different tracks. In an attempt to offset difficulties of this type, supporters of year-round schools recommend single-track systems as much as possible, urging that all schools in a district try to adhere to the same schedule.

Many school boards adopted year-round schooling only in the elementary schools, since most students have more complicated schedules as they get older. Also, educators have discovered that older students have a harder time adjusting to such a radical change, since they are accustomed to long summer breaks. In addition, many high school students worry that they would not be able to obtain summer jobs to earn income to make ends meet or to afford extra things such as clothing or car payments.

Year-round schooling continues to be controversial in most districts, even as school systems from New

York to Los Angeles have experimented with new calendars in the hope of making positive changes to improve student performance. It is difficult to project whether the idea will become more popular in the long term, as parents and administrators try to devise the best solution.

What the Research Says

Research has addressed the issue of the quality of time as it relates to student learning. Research on time on task and academic learning time have focused on the relationship between the amount of time students spend engaged in academic activities and how much they learn. Studies in this area have demonstrated that simply exposing students to classrooms and teachers is not sufficient to affect learning, implying that the educational quality of the activities and interactions that occur in those settings mediates the relationship between time and learning.

Reviews of the existing literature on year-round education generally agree that the outcomes are at least as positive as (or better than) those achieved under the traditional school calendar. However, the number of quality studies conducted and published in this area is limited.

Although researchers have not adequately addressed the reasons to explain why achievement may be slightly higher in year-round schools, one possibility is that this approach can use breaks to provide remediation and enrichment activities, thereby increasing students' exposure to curricula. Another possible explanation comes from a body of research that points toward a decline in achievement during the long summer vacations associated with the traditional school calendar. Year-round advocates claim that dividing the long summer vacation period into smaller pieces helps alleviate some of the academic loss that occurs over the summer in traditional school programs.

At least one study reported that while students who attend year-round schools may give up a few days of vacation, they gain a small advantage over their counterparts who take 10- to 15-week traditional breaks. Another study found that students lose on average 1 month of learning over a long summer break. Students in year-round schools tend to lose only about half that much, thereby lending support to those who say that evenly spaced vacations are better for students. At the same time, researchers caution that proponents of year-round schooling should not be too extravagant in their claims: Schedules do help achievement, but the studies supporting year-round schooling contain flaws and note that the impact of schedules is not large.

C. Daniel Raisch

See also Compulsory Attendance; School-Based Decision Making; School Choice; Transportation, Students' Rights to

Further Readings

Alcorn, R. D. (1992). Test scores: Can year-round schools raise them? *Thrust for Educational Leadership, 21*(6), 12–15.

Glass, G. V. (2002). *School reform proposals: The research evidence.* Tempe: Arizona State University, Education Policy Research Unit. Retrieved from http://epsl.asu.edu/epru/documents/EPRU%202002-101/epru-2002-101.htm

McMillen, B. J. (2006). *Academic achievement in year-round schools.* Raleigh: North Carolina Department of Instruction, Division of Accountability Services.

National Association for Year-Round Education. (n.d.). http://www.nayre.org

Wintre, M. G. (1986). Challenging the assumptions of generalized academic loss over summer. *Journal of Educational Research, 79*(5), 308–312.

Legal Citations

Stuart v. School District No. 1 of Village of Kalamazoo, 30 Mich. 69 (Mich. 1874).

Z

ZELMAN V. SIMMONS-HARRIS

At issue in *Zelman v. Simmons Harris* (2002) was the constitutionality of a program from Ohio that provided educational vouchers for children from poor families. Reversing earlier judgments to the contrary, the U.S. Supreme Court upheld the constitutionality of the program because it offered aid pursuant to neutral secular criteria that neither favored nor disfavored religion, was available to religious and secular beneficiaries, and was available to parents based on their own independent, private choices.

Background of the Case

The Supreme Court has generally interpreted the Establishment Clause of the First Amendment to the U.S. Constitution as preventing direct governmental funding of religious institutions. However, the government can provide indirect aid in a variety of ways. For instance, taxpayers can take deductions for donations to churches, and church property is tax-exempt. The federal courts, therefore, have long struggled to draw a line with regard to the types of public financial assistance that may be provided for K–12 education in religiously affiliated nonpublic schools. A key case in this area is *Zelman v. Simmons-Harris* (2002), wherein the Supreme Court upheld the Ohio Pilot Scholarship Program, a plan that provides vouchers for students from low-income families in Cleveland.

School voucher policies had been a point of academic debate ever since Milton Friedman put forward the concept of universal vouchers in 1955. Actual public voucher plans have been much less ambitious than Friedman proposed and have targeted needy students. In addition to Cleveland's plan, vouchers now exist in Milwaukee and Washington, D.C. (benefiting low-income families), as well as Florida and Utah (benefiting special-needs children). Arizona, Florida, Iowa, and Pennsylvania also have policies akin to vouchers, but implemented through a tax credit mechanism. All of these policies are effectively insulated from federal constitutional challenges due to *Zelman*.

When considering Establishment Clause issues, the predominant approach of the current Supreme Court focuses on the idea of governmental neutrality. Under this type of analysis, the Establishment Clause prohibits the government from acting nonneutrally; by preferring one religion over another; or by promotion of, or hostility to, religion generally.

The Court, applying this neutrality approach, allowed states to provide aid in supplying nonreligious textbooks for students in religiously affiliated nonpublic schools (*Meek v. Pittenger*, 1975); reimbursement to religious schools for the grading of tests that were prepared, mandated, and administered by the state (*Committee for Public Education & Religious Liberty v. Regan*, 1980); parental tax deductions for school expenses, including tuition (*Mueller v. Allen*, 1983); a sign language interpreter for a deaf student who attended a Roman Catholic high school (*Zobrest v. Catalina Foothills School District,* 1993); reading teachers for low-performing students eligible for Title I services, including for children who attended religious schools (*Agostini v. Felton,* 1997); and computers for students in religious and public schools (*Mitchell v. Helms,* 2000).

As applied by the majority in *Zelman,* the neutrality principle concerned the evenhandedness of the state's distribution of public funding in the voucher program. In so finding, the Court relied on the tenet it enunciated in *Everson v. Board of Education of Ewing Township* (1947), distinguishing between direct aid to religious institutions and indirect aid as part of a neutrally applied program whereby funding makes its way to religious institutions only through intervening choices of parents or other third parties.

The Court's Ruling

In *Zelman,* the Supreme Court stressed that the parents in Cleveland had a variety of nonreligious choices, including choices among public schools. Accordingly, the Court characterized the funding through the Cleveland voucher plan as offered to a broad class of citizens, not just to those seeking religious options. Further, the Court noted that parents could voluntarily choose among a selection of religious schools and some nonreligious private schools that participated in the program. For these reasons, the Court held that the program was neutral toward religion.

Even though the Supreme Court devoted considerable space to pointing out educational difficulties facing students in Cleveland's public schools, its eventual legal reasoning did not appear to rest on these troubles. Put another way, *Zelman*'s value as precedent appears to extend to laws providing vouchers to students in academically high-achieving school systems as well as struggling districts.

The Supreme Court's interpretation of the Establishment Clause remains in flux. Even so, it is likely that for the foreseeable future a majority of justices will continue to view government neutrality toward religion as the Court's guiding principle, at least in cases involving vouchers. Policymakers designing such plans should thus have approximate guidelines concerning how to craft statutes that can pass constitutional muster. Plans that grant benefits to students in religiously affiliated nonpublic schools beyond those available to their peers in public schools or otherwise favor religious institutions are likely to fall outside of these guidelines. Conversely, courts are likely to uphold plans that extend benefits to students in religiously affiliated nonpublic schools that are also offered to their peers in public schools. Advocates on both sides of the issue will, nonetheless, have plenty of room for argument concerning where on this continuum any given voucher or tax credit policy happens to fall.

Kevin G. Welner

See also *Agostini v. Felton; Everson v. Board of Education of the Ewing Township; Meek v. Pittenger; Mitchell v. Helms; Mueller v. Allen;* State Aid and the Establishment Clause; Tuition Tax Credits; Vouchers; *Zobrest v. Catalina Foothills School District*

Further Readings

Friedman, M. (1955). The role of government in education. In R. Solo (Ed.), *Economics and the public interest* (pp. 127–134). New Brunswick, NJ: Rutgers University Press.

Legal Citations

Agostini v. Felton, 521 U.S. 203 (1997).
Committee for Public Education & Religious Liberty v. Regan, 444 U.S. 646 (1980).
Everson v. Board of Education of the Township of Ewing Township, 330 U.S. 1 (1947), *reh'g denied*, 330 U.S. 855 (1947).
Meek v. Pittenger, 421 U.S. 349 (1975).
Mitchell v. Helms, 530 U.S. 793 (2000), *reh'g denied*, 530 U.S. 1296 (2000), *on remand sub nom. Helms v. Picard*, 229 F.3d 467 (5th Cir. 2000).
Mueller v. Allen, 463 U.S. 388 (1983).
Zelman v. Simmons-Harris, 536 U.S. 639 (2002).
Zobrest v. Catalina Foothills School District, 509 U.S. 1 (1993).

Zelman v. Simmons-Harris (Excerpts)

In Zelman v. Simmons-Harris, *the Supreme Court extended the boundaries of permissible state aid under the Establishment Clause in upholding a voucher program that allowed poor students to attend religiously affiliated nonpublic schools.*

Supreme Court of the United States

ZELMAN

v.

SIMMONS-HARRIS

536 U.S. 639.

Argued Feb. 20, 2002.

Decided June 27, 2002.

Chief Justice REHNQUIST delivered the opinion of the Court.

The State of Ohio has established a pilot program designed to provide educational choices to families with children who reside in the Cleveland City School District. The question presented is whether this program offends the Establishment Clause of the United States Constitution. We hold that it does not.

There are more than 75,000 children enrolled in the Cleveland City School District. The majority of these children are from low-income and minority families. Few of these families enjoy the means to send their children to any school other than an inner-city public school. For more than a generation, however, Cleveland's public schools have been among the worst performing public schools in the Nation. In 1995, a Federal District Court declared a "crisis of magnitude" and placed the entire Cleveland school district under state control. Shortly thereafter, the state auditor found that Cleveland's public schools were in the midst of a "crisis that is perhaps unprecedented in the history of American education." The district had failed to meet any of the 18 state standards for minimal acceptable performance. . . .

It is against this backdrop that Ohio enacted, among other initiatives, its Pilot Project Scholarship Program. The program provides financial assistance to families in any Ohio school district that is or has been "under federal court order requiring supervision and operational-management of the district by the state superintendent." Cleveland is the only Ohio school district to fall within that category.

The program provides two basic kinds of assistance to parents of children in a covered district. First, the program provides tuition aid for students in kindergarten through third grade, expanding each year through eighth grade, to attend a participating public or private school of their parent's choosing. Second, the program provides tutorial aid for students who choose to remain enrolled in public school.

The tuition aid portion of the program is designed to provide educational choices to parents who reside in a covered district. Any private school, whether religious or nonreligious, may participate in the program and accept program students so long as the school is located within the boundaries of a covered district and meets statewide educational standards. Participating private schools must agree not to discriminate on the basis of race, religion, or ethnic background, or to "advocate or foster unlawful behavior or teach hatred of any person or group on the basis of race, ethnicity, national origin, or religion." Any public school located in a school district adjacent to the covered district may also participate in the program. Adjacent public schools are eligible to receive a $2,250 tuition grant for each program student accepted in addition to the full amount of per-pupil state funding attributable to each additional student. All participating schools, whether public or private, are required to accept students in accordance with rules and procedures established by the state superintendent.

Tuition aid is distributed to parents according to financial need. Families with incomes below 200% of the poverty line are given priority and are eligible to receive 90% of private school tuition up to $2,250. For these lowest income families, participating private schools may not charge a parental copayment greater than $250. For all other families, the program pays 75% of tuition costs, up to $1,875, with no copayment cap. These families receive tuition aid only if the number of available scholarships exceeds the number of low-income children who choose to participate. Where tuition aid is spent depends solely upon where parents who receive tuition aid choose to enroll their child. If parents choose a private school, checks are made payable to the parents who then endorse the checks over to the chosen school. . .

The tutorial aid portion of the program provides tutorial assistance through grants to any student in a covered district who chooses to remain in public school. Parents arrange for registered tutors to provide assistance to their children and then submit bills for those services to the State for payment. Students from low-income families receive 90% of the amount charged for such assistance up to $360. All other students receive 75% of that amount. The number of tutorial assistance grants offered to students in a covered district must equal the number of tuition aid scholarships provided to students enrolled at participating private or adjacent public schools.

The program has been in operation within the Cleveland City School District since the 1996–1997 school year. In the 1999–2000 school year, 56 private schools participated in the program, 46 (or 82%) of which had a religious affiliation. None of the public schools in districts adjacent to Cleveland have elected to participate. More than 3,700 students participated in the scholarship program, most of whom (96%) enrolled in religiously affiliated schools. Sixty percent of these students were from families at or below the poverty line. In the 1998–1999 school year, approximately 1,400 Cleveland public school students received tutorial aid. This number was expected to double during the 1999–2000 school year.

The program is part of a broader undertaking by the State to enhance the educational options of Cleveland's schoolchildren in response to the 1995 takeover. That undertaking includes programs governing community and magnet schools. Community schools are funded under state law but are run by their own school boards, not by local school districts. . These schools enjoy academic independence to hire their own teachers and to determine their own curriculum. They can have no religious affiliation and are required to accept students by lottery. During the 1999–2000 school year, there were 10 startup community schools in the Cleveland City School District with more than 1,900 students enrolled. For each child enrolled in a community school, the school receives state funding of $4,518, twice the funding a participating program school may receive.

Magnet schools are public schools operated by a local school board that emphasize a particular subject area, teaching method, or service to students. For each student enrolled in a magnet school, the school district receives $7,746, including state funding of $4,167, the same amount received per student enrolled at a traditional public school. As of 1999, parents in Cleveland were able to choose from among 23 magnet schools, which together enrolled more than 13,000 students in kindergarten through eighth grade. These schools provide specialized teaching methods, such as Montessori, or a particularized curriculum focus, such as foreign language, computers, or the arts.

In 1996, respondents, a group of Ohio taxpayers, challenged the Ohio program in state court on state and federal grounds. The Ohio Supreme Court rejected respondents' federal claims, but held that the enactment of the program violated certain procedural requirements of the Ohio Constitution. The state legislature immediately cured this defect, leaving the basic provisions discussed above intact.

In July 1999, respondents filed this action in United States District Court, seeking to enjoin the reenacted program on the ground that it violated the Establishment Clause of the United States Constitution. In August 1999, the District Court issued a preliminary injunction barring further implementation of the program which we stayed pending review by the Court of Appeals. In December 1999, the District Court granted summary judgment for respondents. In December 2000, a divided panel of the Court of Appeals affirmed the judgment of the District Court, finding that the program had the "primary effect" of advancing religion in violation of the Establishment Clause. The Court of Appeals stayed its mandate pending disposition in this Court. We granted certiorari and now reverse the Court of Appeals.

The Establishment Clause of the First Amendment, applied to the States through the Fourteenth Amendment, prevents a State from enacting laws that have the "purpose" or "effect" of advancing or inhibiting religion. There is no dispute that the program challenged here was enacted for the valid secular purpose of providing educational assistance to poor children in a demonstrably failing public school system. Thus, the question presented is whether the Ohio program nonetheless has the forbidden "effect" of advancing or inhibiting religion.

To answer that question, our decisions have drawn a consistent distinction between government programs that provide aid directly to religious schools, and programs of true private choice, in which government aid reaches religious schools only as a result of the genuine and independent choices of private individuals. While our jurisprudence with respect to the constitutionality of direct aid programs has "changed significantly" over the past two decades, our jurisprudence with respect to true private choice programs has remained consistent and unbroken. Three times we have confronted Establishment Clause challenges to neutral government programs that provide aid directly to a broad class of individuals, who, in turn, direct the aid to religious schools or institutions of their own choosing. Three times we have rejected such challenges.

In *Mueller v. Allen*, we rejected an Establishment Clause challenge to a Minnesota program authorizing tax deductions for various educational expenses, including private school tuition costs, even though the great majority of the program's beneficiaries (96%) were parents of children in religious schools. . . .

That the program was one of true private choice, with no evidence that the State deliberately skewed incentives toward religious schools, was sufficient for the program to survive scrutiny under the Establishment Clause.

In *Witters* [*v. Washington Department of Services for the Blind*], we used identical reasoning to reject an Establishment Clause challenge to a vocational scholarship program that provided tuition aid to a student studying at a religious institution to become a pastor. . . .

. . . .

Finally, in *Zobrest v.* [*Catalina Foothills School District*], we applied *Mueller* and *Witters* to reject an Establishment Clause challenge to a federal program that permitted sign-language interpreters to assist deaf children enrolled in religious schools. . . . Looking once again to the challenged program as a whole, we observed that the program "distributes benefits neutrally to any child qualifying as 'disabled.' Its "primary beneficiaries," we said, were "disabled children, not sectarian schools."

. . . .

Mueller, Witters, and *Zobrest* thus make clear that where a government aid program is neutral with respect to religion, and provides assistance directly to a broad class of citizens who, in turn, direct government aid to religious schools wholly as a result of their own genuine and independent private choice, the program is not readily subject to challenge under the Establishment Clause. A program that shares these features permits government aid to reach religious institutions only by way of the deliberate choices of numerous individual recipients. The incidental advancement of a religious mission, or the perceived endorsement of a religious message, is reasonably attributable to the individual recipient, not to the government, whose role ends with the disbursement of benefits. . . .

We believe that the program challenged here is a program of true private choice, consistent with *Mueller, Witters,* and *Zobrest,* and thus constitutional. As was true in those cases, the Ohio program is neutral in all

respects toward religion. It is part of a general and multifaceted undertaking by the State of Ohio to provide educational opportunities to the children of a failed school district. It confers educational assistance directly to a broad class of individuals defined without reference to religion, *i.e.,* any parent of a school-age child who resides in the Cleveland City School District. The program permits the participation of *all* schools within the district, religious or nonreligious. Adjacent public schools also may participate and have a financial incentive to do so. Program benefits are available to participating families on neutral terms, with no reference to religion. The only preference stated anywhere in the program is a preference for low-income families, who receive greater assistance and are given priority for admission at participating schools.

There are no "financial incentive[s]" that "ske[w]" the program toward religious schools. Such incentives "[are] not present . . . where the aid is allocated on the basis of neutral, secular criteria that neither favor nor disfavor religion, and is made available to both religious and secular beneficiaries on a nondiscriminatory basis." The program here in fact creates financial *disincentives* for religious schools, with private schools receiving only half the government assistance given to community schools and one-third the assistance given to magnet schools. Adjacent public schools, should any choose to accept program students, are also eligible to receive two to three times the state funding of a private religious school. Families too have a financial disincentive to choose a private religious school over other schools. Parents that choose to participate in the scholarship program and then to enroll their children in a private school (religious or nonreligious) must copay a portion of the school's tuition. Families that choose a community school, magnet school, or traditional public school pay nothing. Although such features of the program are not necessary to its constitutionality, they clearly dispel the claim that the program "creates . . . financial incentive[s] for parents to choose a sectarian school."

Respondents suggest that even without a financial incentive for parents to choose a religious school, the program creates a "public perception that the State is endorsing religious practices and beliefs." But we have repeatedly recognized that no reasonable observer would think a neutral program of private choice, where state aid reaches religious schools solely as a result of the numerous independent decisions of private individuals, carries with it the *imprimatur* of government endorsement. The argument is particularly misplaced here since "the reasonable observer in the endorsement inquiry must be deemed aware" of the "history and context" underlying a challenged program. Any objective observer familiar with the full history and context of the Ohio program would reasonably view it as one aspect of a broader undertaking to assist poor children in failed schools, not as an endorsement of religious schooling in general.

There also is no evidence that the program fails to provide genuine opportunities for Cleveland parents to select secular educational options for their school-age children. Cleveland schoolchildren enjoy a range of educational choices: They may remain in public school as before, remain in public school with publicly funded tutoring aid, obtain a scholarship and choose a religious school, obtain a scholarship and choose a nonreligious private school, enroll in a community school, or enroll in a magnet school. That 46 of the 56 private schools now participating in the program are religious schools does not condemn it as a violation of the Establishment Clause. The Establishment Clause question is whether Ohio is coercing parents into sending their children to religious schools, and that question must be answered by evaluating *all* options Ohio provides Cleveland schoolchildren, only one of which is to obtain a program scholarship and then choose a religious school.

Justice SOUTER speculates that because more private religious schools currently participate in the program, the program itself must somehow discourage the participation of private nonreligious schools. But Cleveland's preponderance of religiously affiliated private schools certainly did not arise as a result of the program; it is a phenomenon common to many American cities. Indeed, by all accounts the program has captured a remarkable cross-section of private schools, religious and nonreligious. It is true that 82% of Cleveland's participating private schools are religious schools, but it is also true that 81% of private schools in Ohio are religious schools. To attribute constitutional significance to this figure, moreover, would lead to the absurd result that a neutral school-choice program might be permissible in some parts of Ohio, such as Columbus, where a lower percentage of private schools are religious schools, Likewise, an identical private choice program might be constitutional in some States, such as Maine or Utah, where less than 45% of private schools are religious schools, but not in other States, such as Nebraska or Kansas, where over 90% of private schools are religious schools.

Respondents and Justice SOUTER claim that even if we do not focus on the number of participating schools that are religious schools, we should attach constitutional significance to the fact that 96% of scholarship recipients have enrolled in religious schools. They claim that this alone proves parents lack genuine choice, even if no parent has ever said so. We need not consider this argument in detail, since it was flatly rejected in *Mueller*, where we found it irrelevant that 96% of parents taking deductions for tuition expenses paid tuition at religious schools. Indeed, we have recently found it irrelevant even to the constitutionality of a direct aid program that a vast majority of program benefits went to religious schools. The constitutionality of a neutral educational aid program simply does not turn on whether and why, in a particular area, at a particular time, most private schools are run by religious organizations, or most recipients choose to use the aid at a religious school. As we said in *Mueller*, "[s]uch an approach would scarcely provide the certainty that this field stands in need of, nor can we perceive principled standards by which such statistical evidence might be evaluated."

This point is aptly illustrated here. The 96% figure upon which respondents and Justice SOUTER rely discounts entirely (1) the more than 1,900 Cleveland children enrolled in alternative community schools, (2) the more than 13,000 children enrolled in alternative magnet schools, and (3) the more than 1,400 children enrolled in traditional public schools with tutorial assistance. Including some or all of these children in the denominator of children enrolled in nontraditional schools during the 1999–2000 school year drops the percentage enrolled in religious schools from 96% to under 20%. The 96% figure also represents but a snapshot of one particular school year. In the 1997–1998 school year, by contrast, only 78% of scholarship recipients attended religious schools. The difference was attributable to two private nonreligious schools that had accepted 15% of all scholarship students electing instead to register as community schools, in light of larger per-pupil funding for community schools and the uncertain future of the scholarship program generated by this litigation. Many of the students enrolled in these schools as scholarship students remained enrolled as community school students, thus demonstrating the arbitrariness of counting one type of school but not the other to assess primary effect. In spite of repeated questioning from the Court at oral argument, respondents offered no convincing justification for their approach, which relies entirely on such arbitrary classifications.

Respondents finally claim that we should look to *Committee for Public Ed. & Religious Liberty v. Nyquist* to decide these cases. We disagree for two reasons. First, the program in *Nyquist* was quite different from the program challenged here. *Nyquist* involved a New York program that gave a package of benefits exclusively to private schools and the parents of private school enrollees. Although the program was enacted for ostensibly secular purposes, we found that its "function" was "unmistakably to provide desired financial support for nonpublic, sectarian institutions." Its genesis, we said, was that private religious schools faced "increasingly grave fiscal problems." The program thus provided direct money grants to religious schools. It provided tax benefits "unrelated to the amount of money actually expended by any parent on tuition," ensuring a windfall to parents of children in religious schools. It similarly provided tuition reimbursements designed explicitly to "offe[r] ... an incentive to parents to send their children to sectarian schools." Indeed, the program flatly prohibited the participation of any public school, or parent of any public school enrollee. Ohio's program shares none of these features.

Second, were there any doubt that the program challenged in *Nyquist* is far removed from the program challenged here, we expressly reserved judgment with respect to "a case involving some form of public assistance (*e.g.*, scholarships) made available generally without regard to the sectarian-nonsectarian, or public-nonpublic nature of the institution benefited." That, of course, is the very question now before us, and it has since been answered, first in *Mueller*, then in *Witters*, and again in *Zobrest*. To the extent the scope of *Nyquist* has remained an open question in light of these later decisions, we now hold that *Nyquist* does not govern neutral educational assistance programs that, like the program here, offer aid directly to a broad class of individual recipients defined without regard to religion.

In sum, the Ohio program is entirely neutral with respect to religion. It provides benefits directly to a wide spectrum of individuals, defined only by financial need and residence in a particular school district. It permits such individuals to exercise genuine choice among options public and private, secular and religious. The program is therefore a program of true private choice. In keeping with an unbroken line of decisions rejecting challenges to similar programs, we hold that the program does not offend the Establishment Clause.

The judgment of the Court of Appeals is *reversed*.

It is so ordered.

Citation: *Zelman v. Simmons-Harris*, 536 U.S. 639 (2002).

ZERO REJECT

Zero reject is one of the key principles of the Individuals with Disabilities Education Improvement Act (IDEA), originally known as the Education for All Handicapped Children Act. IDEA requires states, through local educational agencies or school boards, to locate, evaluate, and serve all eligible students with disabilities aged 3 to 21. Zero reject mandates that school officials cannot exclude any students with disabilities from a free appropriate public education in the least restrictive environment. Pursuant to the contents of their individualized education programs, students with disabilities must be served at no cost to their families despite the nature or severity of their conditions or the potential of educational benefit. Further, school boards cannot cease services to students due to their expulsions, incarcerations, hospitalizations, or parental placement in nonpublic schools (although there are significant limitations when dealing with religious institutions). This entry describes how the principle developed and how it is applied.

Background

Prior to the enactment of a federal special education law in 1975, over 1 million children with disabilities were excluded from public schools or served inadequately. While many states attempted to serve students with mild disabilities, officials regularly denied services to those who had severe and multiple impairments. School codes often permitted the exclusion of students who were deemed "uneducable or untrainable," those who were judged as unable to benefit from further education, or those who did not have a mental age of a 5-year-old.

Officials in public schools often turned away students who were not yet toilet trained, and children were routinely placed on waiting lists or told to return when they could observe additional progress. In response to this widespread exclusion, the zero reject principle of the IDEA mandated that local educational agencies provide educations for every student with a disability, without conditions or exceptions. Even though the term *zero reject* is not used in the language of the IDEA, the concept is clearly embedded in the federal law as clarified by case law.

The seminal case involving zero reject arose in New Hampshire, where a local school board sought to stop paying expenses associated with providing services for a student in a residential facility who suffered from multiple profound disabilities. The board maintained that it should not have to pay for all of the child's expenses, because most had little, or nothing, to do with education. The board also believed that the child did not qualify for special education due to his inability to benefit from instruction and his limited learning capacity.

Reversing in favor of the student in *Timothy W. v. Rochester, New Hampshire, School District* (1989), the First Circuit clarified the reach of the concept of zero reject in ruling that that the severity of the student's handicapping conditions did not justify the denial of services. The court emphasized that the zero reject principle ensured that a student's potential for educational benefit could not be a prerequisite for enrollment or receipt of services.

Practice

As reflected by the principle of zero reject, the severity of students' disabilities simply cannot be a consideration for exclusion or the denial of services. Accordingly, all eligible students with disabilities must continue to receive services regardless of where they are placed. In fact, the denial of services to students with disabilities who have been expelled or are placed in any of the other array of settings is in direct violation of the zero reject principle.

The zero reject principle includes an additional responsibility for educational agencies under the IDEA's "Child Find" provisions. Child Find is an ongoing process that requires educational officials to provide public awareness campaigns and free referral and evaluation services to help identify young children with disabilities. Child Find services often develop and distribute information to the public that describes special education services, provides information for families concerned about their children's development, and assists families in accessing resources. The IDEA mandates this comprehensive Child Find system to ensure that all children who are in need of special education services are located, evaluated, identified, and served. In addition, the Child Find process requires states to report an accurate child count to the federal government each year that is consistent with the IDEA's principle of zero reject.

Kara Hume

See also Disabled Persons, Rights of; Free Appropriate Public Education; Inclusion; Individualized Education Program (IEP); Least Restrictive Environment

Further Readings

Katsiyannis, A. (1992). *Timothy W.:* The zero reject principle revisited. *Journal of Developmental and Physical Disabilities, 4,* 91–95.

Legal Citations

Individuals with Disabilities Education Act, 20 USC §§ 1400 *et seq.*
Timothy W. v. Rochester, New Hampshire, School District, 875 F.2d 954 (1st Cir. 1989), *cert. denied,* 493 U.S. 983 (1989).

Zero Tolerance

Zero tolerance policies have been established in virtually all schools in the United States. These policies originated in the Gun-Free Schools Act of 1994, which was established to further the goal of making schools safe—violence- and drug-free—under the Goals 2000: Educate America Act of 1994. According to the Gun-Free Schools Act, any school receiving funds under the Elementary and Secondary Schools

Act of 1965 must establish a zero tolerance policy for firearm weapons. Such policies, however, have been expanded to include drugs as well as some kinds of behavior. This entry discusses the policies, summarizes some related legal cases, and offers some assessments of effectiveness.

What Zero Tolerance Policies Say

When instituting zero tolerance policies, states expanded their scope to include all weapons. In addition, states included illegal drugs in their zero tolerance policies in an attempt to ensure that schools remain drug free. Further, many local school boards extended their zero tolerance policies to include look-alike drugs and weapons, as well as items that can be construed as weapons. After the shootings at Columbine High School, in Colorado, in 1999, many boards enacted zero tolerance policies for bullying and weaponless fights. Finally, many boards established zero tolerance policies for threatening language.

Controversy has surrounded zero tolerance policies from the start, not only because of their increasing scope but also because they carry punishments that range from short-term suspensions to permanent expulsions from school. Consequently, zero tolerance policies have raised various issues dealing with the due process rights of students.

In *Goss v. Lopez* (1975), the U.S. Supreme Court provided some guidance for due process in cases of short-term suspensions, 10 days or less. The Court ruled that since education can be an important property interest, it is covered by substantive due process, especially for exclusions of 10 days or more, even though it did not address these long-term exclusions.

In other words, especially when dealing with zero tolerance, before educators can deprive students of their right to schooling, officials must prove the existence of a compelling state interest while providing them with fair procedures. In *Goss,* the Supreme Court recognized that maintaining disciplined and orderly learning environments is a compelling state interest. Yet to balance this governmental need with students' property interests, the Court pointed out that students have the right to due process in school discipline cases. To this end, the *Goss* Court indicated that

procedural due process in school cases minimally must include oral or written notification of the specific violation(s) and the intended punishment, an opportunity to dispute the charges before a fair and impartial third-party decision maker, and an explanation of the evidence based on the record on which the charges are based.

The Court also explained that long-term suspensions may require more formal due process procedures but, again, did not offer guidance for these longer exclusions. Of course, the difficulty with zero tolerance policies is that they often do not provide many of these safeguards. To date, though, the Court has not addressed either zero tolerance policy or any long-term suspension case.

Limits Set by Courts

Courts have usually, but not always, ruled that zero tolerance policies are constitutional because they relate to schools' interest in maintaining safe and orderly learning environments. Even so, in addition to the due process issues raised by the punishments imposed under zero tolerance policies, concerns arise over issues of knowledge and intent. More specifically, controversies have arisen surrounding whether students can be suspended or expelled if they either did not know that they possessed items of contraband under zero tolerance policies or had no intention of using these objects. In litigation involving challenges to zero tolerance policies, as reflected by the following two cases, the courts sometimes reach divergent outcomes, based on unique factual circumstances, in addressing myriad legal questions under zero tolerance policies.

Seal v. Morgan (2000) involved a suspension of a student after school officials discovered a knife in the glove compartment of his vehicle. The facts reflected both that the knife did not belong to the student and that he was unaware that it was there. In ordering the student's reinstatement, the Sixth Circuit reasoned that suspending or expelling an otherwise innocent student for possessing a weapon that he did not know that he possessed did not rationally relate to any legitimate state interest.

In criticizing the underlying policy, the court made two important observations. First, the court remarked that the student could not possibly have harmed others with the weapon because he was unaware that it was in his possession. Second, because the student had no knowledge that he possessed the weapon, the court posited that he had no intent to violate the policy.

Ratner v. Loudoun County Public Schools (2001) concerned the suspension of a student after officials found a knife in his locker. The student explained to officials that he took the knife from a friend at school when she told him about the knife and said she intended to kill herself with it. The student maintained that he never intended to harm anyone with the knife and planned to tell both his parents and the parents of his friend after school.

In its analysis, the court focused on whether the student was aware of the policy and whether his actions violated it. The court was of the opinion that although the student's intention was to prevent his friend's suicide, he did knowingly violate the zero tolerance policy. The court thus concluded that since school officials provided the student with due process, they had the authority to suspend him from school.

Are Zero Tolerance Policies Effective?

The controversy surrounding zero tolerance policies also includes concerns over their efficacy, centering on two main issues. First, critics point out that school-associated deaths, which zero tolerance policies were meant to address, are relatively rare. Second, critics also note that in the 7 years after these policies were introduced, research data showed no significant effect of zero tolerance policies in reducing school violence.

At the same time, opponents criticize zero tolerance policies for being unfair and contrary to the developmental needs of children. Moreover, as minority and special needs students are disproportionately affected, questions can be raised as to whether zero tolerance policies violate students' rights to equal educational opportunity. A final concern about zero tolerance policies is that they have a tendency to criminalize children and their behavior.

In sum, it is clear that school officials need and parents support policies that afford them the opportunity to keep schools as safe and orderly learning environments.

Yet it is not evident that zero tolerance policies have, or are able to have, accomplished their stated goal of helping to ensure school safety.

Patricia A. L. Ehrensal

See also Goss v. Lopez

Further Readings

Ayers, W., Dohrn, B., & Ayers, R. (Eds.). (2001). *Zero tolerance: Resisting the drive for punishment in our schools.* New York: New Press.

Brady, K. P. (2002). Zero tolerance or (in)tolerance policies? Weaponless school violence, due process, and the law of student suspensions and expulsions: An examination of *Fuller v. Decatur Public School Board of Education School District. BYU Education & Law Journal,* 159–196.

Pelliccioni, C. D. (2003). Is intent required? Zero tolerance, scienter, and the substantive due process rights of students. *Case Western Reserve Law Review, 53,* 977–1007.

Russo, C. J. (1995). *United States v. Lopez* and the demise of the Gun-Free School Zones Act: Legislative over-reaching or judicial nit-picking? *Education Law Reporter, 99,* 11–23.

Legal Citations

Goss v. Lopez, 419 U.S. 565 (1975).
Ratner v. Loudoun County Public Schools, 16 Fed.Appx. 140 (4th Cir. 2001).
Seal v. Morgan, 229 F.3d 567 (6th Cir. 2000).

Zobrest v. Catalina Foothills School District

In *Zobrest v. Catalina Foothills School District* (1993), the U.S. Supreme Court found that under the Individuals with Disabilities Education Act (IDEA), a school board was required to provide the on-site services of a sign language interpreter to a hearing-impaired student in a private religious school. This entry describes the case and the Court's ruling.

Facts of the Case

The controversy in *Zobrest* began when the parents of a profoundly deaf student who attended a religious school asked officials on their local public school board to supply their son with a sign language interpreter for all of his classes, under the IDEA. After obtaining an opinion from the county attorney, the board refused that request but offered to provide a sign language interpreter within the public schools.

After the parents filed suit, the federal trial court in Arizona held that furnishing a sign language interpreter would have violated the First Amendment because the interpreter would have had the effect of promoting religious development at government expense. According to stipulations made by the parties, the interpreter would have been called on to interpret religious doctrine, since religious themes permeated classroom instruction.

A divided Ninth Circuit affirmed that providing a sign language interpreter would have violated the First Amendment because doing so failed the second part of the Supreme Court's test in *Lemon v. Kurtzman* (1971). The court decided that the interpreter would have been the instrumentality conveying the religious message and that by placing the interpreter in the religious school, the local board would have created the appearance that it was jointly sponsoring the school's activities. The court pointed out that while denying the interpreter placed a burden on the parents' free exercise rights, this burden was justified by a compelling state interest. The court explained that the government had a compelling state interest in ensuring that the First Amendment was not violated and there were no less restrictive means of accomplishing that goal.

The Court's Ruling

On further review, in a 5-to-4 decision, the Supreme Court reversed in favor of the parents. Chief Justice Rehnquist authored the majority's opinion, in which he ruled that the service of a sign language interpreter in this case was part of a general government program that distributed benefits neutrally to any child who qualified as disabled under the IDEA, without regard to whether the school attended was sectarian or non-sectarian, public or private. Rehnquist added that by giving the parents the freedom of choice to select a school, the IDEA ensured that a government-paid

interpreter would be present in a parochial school only as a result of the parents' private decision.

Rehnquist thus determined that the IDEA did not create any financial incentive for parents to choose a religious school and the interpreter's presence there could not be attributed to state decision making. The only economic benefit the religious school might have received would have been indirect, the chief justice wrote, and that would have occurred only if the school made a profit on each student, if the student would not have attended the school without the interpreter, and if the student's seat would have remained unfilled. Rehnquist reasoned that the provision of the interpreter would not have relieved the religious school of any costs that it would otherwise have borne. Rehnquist decided that aiding this student and his parents did not amount to a direct subsidy of the religious school because he, not the school, was the primary beneficiary of the IDEA. Further, Rehnquist was convinced that the task of a sign language interpreter was different from that of a teacher or guidance counselor insofar as a sign language interpreter would not add or subtract from the pervasively sectarian environment in which the student's parents had chosen to place him.

Justice Blackmun, in a dissenting opinion, indicated that the school board argued that the IDEA did not require it to furnish an interpreter at a private school as long as special education services were made available at a public school and that the IDEA's regulations prohibited the use of federal funds for religious worship, instruction, and proselytization. Blackmun believed that the case should have been vacated and remanded for decisions on those issues.

Moreover, Justice Blackmun remarked that a state-employed sign language interpreter would have been required to communicate the religious material in the religious and secular classes the student attended at the religious school. In an environment so pervaded by religious discussions, Blackmun was convinced that the interpreter's every gesture would have been infused with religious significance so that the sign language interpreter would serve as a conduit for the student's religious education, assisting the school in its mission of religious indoctrination.

Zobrest is significant because it signaled the beginning of the revitalization of the Child Benefit Test by allowing the on-site delivery of services for a student who attended a religiously affiliated, nonpublic school. As such, it set the stage for further rulings that allow public school districts to provide some educational services to students who attend sectarian schools. Specifically, 4 years after *Zobrest*, in *Agostini v. Felton* (1997), the Court made it clear that Title I remedial services could be provided on the premises of religiously affiliated nonpublic schools.

Allan G. Osborne, Jr.

See also *Agostini v. Felton;* Child Benefit Test; Disabled Persons, Rights of; *Lemon v. Kurtzman;* State Aid and the Establishment Clause

Further Readings

Mawdsley, R. D. (1998). Religious schools and the IDEA: An ongoing controversy. *West's Education Law Reporter, 125,* 595–610.

McCarthy, M. (1998). The road to *Agostini* and beyond. *West's Education Law Reporter, 124,* 771–785.

Osborne, A. G. (1994). Providing special education and related services to parochial school students in the wake of *Zobrest. West's Education Law Reporter, 87,* 329–339.

Legal Citations

Agostini v. Felton, 521 U.S. 203 (1997).

Individuals with Disabilities Education Act, 20 U.S.C. §§ 1400 *et seq.*

Lemon v. Kurtzman, 403 U.S. 602 (1971).

Zobrest v. Catalina Foothills School District, 509 U.S. 1 (1993).

ZORACH V. CLAUSON

In the 1952 case of *Zorach v. Clauson,* the U.S. Supreme Court upheld the practice of *released time,* whereby public school officials dismissed students during the school day so that they could go to other locations to participate in religious study off campus. In a 6-to-3 decision, the Court affirmed that school officials can accommodate a parental desire to have their children released from public school classes for the purpose of attending religious education classes.

Facts of the Case

Zorach involved a challenge to the constitutionality of a program in New York City that allowed its public schools to release students during the school day so that they could leave school grounds and participate in religious instruction and services at religious centers. Students could be released only with the written consent of their parents. Students who were not released remained in their classrooms. Unlike the practice that the Courts struck down as unconstitutional 4 years earlier, in *Illinois ex rel. McCollum v. Board of Education* (1948), the program did not involve the use of public funds or the use of public facilities.

Even so, a group of city taxpayers and residents filed suit, challenging the constitutionality of the law that allowed for the released-time program. The plaintiffs alleged that the program was unconstitutional because the weight and influence of the public schools were put behind religious instruction, public school teachers policed the program by keeping tabs on students who were released, all classroom activities came to a halt when students were released for religious instruction, and the schools provided a crutch for the churches to lean on for support of their religious training. Without the cooperation of the schools, the plaintiffs argued, the program would have been ineffective.

The initial suit was filed in state courts. Having lost there, the plaintiffs in *Zorach* appealed to the Supreme Court. On further review, the Supreme Court affirmed that the program was constitutional.

The Court's Ruling

Justice Douglas, writing the majority opinion, ruled that it took "obtuse" reasoning to inject any issue of the free exercise of religion into this case insofar as no one was forced to attend the religious classes and no one brought religious exercises or instruction into the public school classrooms. Rather, Douglas pointed out that the decision of whether students attended religious classes was up to them and their parents. The majority saw no evidence to support the contention that coercion was used to get public school students into religious classrooms.

According to Justice Douglas, in passing the law, the City of New York did not violate the Establishment Clause of the First Amendment. In fact, he offered that condemning the released-time law would have pressed the concept of separation of church and state to an extreme level. Instead, Douglas concluded that there was no constitutional requirement for government to be hostile to religion. In *Zorach,* he concluded that all the schools did was to accommodate their schedules to a program of external religious instruction.

Justice Black, in a dissenting opinion, asserted that the sole question before the Court was whether the state could use its compulsory education laws to help religious sects get attendees for their religious instruction classes. Black argued that the state made religious sects beneficiaries of its power to compel students to attend secular schools by manipulating compulsory education laws to help those sects get students. In another dissent, Justice Frankfurter added that there was all the difference in the world between letting students out of school and letting some students out of school to attend religious classes. As Frankfurter saw it, formalized religious instruction was substituted for other school activities, which those who did not participate in religious classes were required to attend.

In a more recent iteration of this issue, the Second Circuit rejected a challenge that a mother filed on behalf of her children (*Pierce ex rel. Pierce v. Sullivan West Central School District,* 2004). The court affirmed that New York's continuation of the program was acceptable because it passed Establishment Clause analysis insofar as it did not use public funds or on-site religious instruction, it was voluntary, and school officials did not coerce or pressure nonparticipants to engage in the activities.

Allan G. Osborne, Jr.

See also *Illinois ex rel. McCollum v. Board of Education;* Prayer in Public Schools; Released Time; Religious Activities in Public Schools

Further Readings

Mawdsley, R. D., & Mawdsley, A. L. (1988). Religious freedom and public schools: Analysis of important policy issues. *West's Education Law Reporter, 47,* 15–43.

Vacca, R. S., Hudgins, H. C., & Millhouse, L. M. (1997). Accommodation of religion without establishment of religion. *West's Education Law Reporter, 115,* 9–23.

Legal Citations

Illinois ex rel. McCollum v. Board of Education, 333 U.S. 203 (1948).

Pierce ex rel. Pierce v. Sullivan West Central School District, 379 F.3d 56 (2d Cir. 2004).

Zorach v. Clauson, 343 U.S. 306 (1952).

Zorach v. Clauson (Excerpts)

In Zorach v. Clauson, *the Supreme Court upheld the practice of releasing students from their classes in public schools so that they could attend religious instruction on the basis that doing so accommodated the religious wishes of their parents.*

Supreme Court of the United States

ZORACH et al.

v.

CLAUSON et al.

343 U.S. 306

Argued Jan. 31 and Feb. 1, 1952.

Decided April 28, 1952.

Mr. Justice DOUGLAS delivered the opinion of the Court.

New York City has a program which permits its public schools to release students during the school day so that they may leave the school buildings and school grounds and go to religious centers for religious instruction or devotional exercises. A student is released on written request of his parents. Those not released stay in the classrooms. The churches make weekly reports to the schools, sending a list of children who have been released from public school but who have not reported for religious instruction.

This 'released time' program involves neither religious instruction in public school classrooms nor the expenditure of public funds. All costs, including the application blanks, are paid by the religious organizations. The case is therefore unlike *McCollum v. Board of Education,* which involved a 'released time' program from Illinois. In that case the classrooms were turned over to religious instructors. We accordingly held that the program violated the First Amendment which (by reason of the Fourteenth Amendment) prohibits the states from establishing religion or prohibiting its free exercise.

Appellants, who are taxpayers and residents of New York City and whose children attend its public schools, challenge the present law, contending it is in essence not different from the one involved in the McCollum case. Their argument, stated elaborately in various ways, reduces itself to this: the weight and influence of the school is put behind a program for religious instruction; public school teachers police it, keeping tab on students who are released; the classroom activities come to a halt while the students who are released for religious instruction are on leave; the school is a crutch on which the churches are leaning for support in their religious training; without the cooperation of the schools this 'released time' program, like the one in the McCollum case, would be futile and ineffective. The New York Court of Appeals sustained the law against this claim of unconstitutionality. The case is here on appeal.

The briefs and arguments are replete with data bearing on the merits of this type of 'released time' program. Views pro and con are expressed, based on practical experience with these programs and with their implications. We do not stop to summarize these materials nor to burden the opinion with an analysis of them. For they involve considerations not germane to the narrow constitutional issue presented. They largely concern the wisdom of the system, its efficiency from an educational point of view, and the political considerations which have motivated its adoption or rejection in some communities. Those matters are of no concern here, since our problem reduces itself to whether New York by this system has either prohibited the 'free exercise' of religion or has made a law 'respecting an establishment of religion' within the meaning of the First Amendment.

It takes obtuse reasoning to inject any issue of the 'free exercise' of religion into the present case. No one is forced to go to the religious classroom and no religious exercise or instruction is brought to the classrooms of the public schools. A student need not take religious instruction. He is left to his own desires as to the manner or time of his religious devotions, if any.

There is a suggestion that the system involves the use of coercion to get public school students into religious classrooms. There is no evidence in the record before us that supports that conclusion. The present record indeed tells us that the school authorities are neutral in this regard and do no more than release students whose parents so request. If in fact coercion were used, if it were established that any one or more teachers were using their office to persuade or force students to take the religious instruction, a wholly different case would be presented. Hence we put aside that claim of coercion both as respects the 'free exercise' of religion and 'an establishment of religion' within the meaning of the First Amendment.

The only allegation in the complaint that bears on the issue is that the operation of the program 'has resulted and inevitably results in the exercise of pressure and coercion upon parents and children to secure attendance by the children for religious instruction.' But this charge does not even implicate the school authorities. The New York Court of Appeals was therefore generous in labeling it a 'conclusory' allegation. Since the allegation did not implicate the school authorities in the use of coercion, there is no basis for holding that the New York Court of Appeals under the guise of local practice defeated a federal right in the manner condemned by *Brown v. Western R. Co. of Alabama* and related cases.

Moreover, apart from that claim of coercion, we do not see how New York by this type of 'released time' program has made a law respecting an establishment of religion within the meaning of the First Amendment. There is much talk of the separation of Church and State in the history of the Bill of Rights and in the decisions clustering around the First Amendment. There cannot be the slightest doubt that the First Amendment reflects the philosophy that Church and State should be separated. And so far as interference with the 'free exercise' of religion and an 'establishment' of religion are concerned, the separation must be complete and unequivocal. The First Amendment within the scope of its coverage permits no exception; the prohibition is absolute. The First Amendment, however, does not say that in every and all respects there shall be a separation of Church and State. Rather, it studiously defines the manner, the specific ways, in which there shall be no concert or union or dependency one on the other. That is the common sense of the matter. Otherwise the state and religion would be aliens to each other—hostile, suspicious, and even unfriendly. Churches could not be required to pay even property taxes. Municipalities would not be permitted to render police or fire protection to religious groups. Policemen who helped parishioners into their places of worship would violate the Constitution. Prayers in our legislative halls; the appeals to the Almighty in the messages of the Chief Executive; the proclamations making Thanksgiving Day a holiday; 'so help me God' in our courtroom oaths—these and all other references to the Almighty that run through our laws, our public rituals, our ceremonies would be flouting the First Amendment. A fastidious atheist or agnostic could even object to the supplication with which the Court opens each session: 'God save the United States and this Honorable Court.'

We would have to press the concept of separation of Church and State to these extremes to condemn the present law on constitutional grounds. The nullification of this law would have wide and profound effects. A Catholic student applies to his teacher for permission to leave the school during hours on a Holy Day of Obligation to attend a mass. A Jewish student asks his teacher for permission to be excused for Yom Kippur. A Protestant wants the afternoon off for a family baptismal ceremony. In each case the teacher requires parental consent in writing. In each case the teacher, in order to make sure the student is not a truant, goes further and requires a report from the priest, the rabbi, or the minister. The teacher in other words cooperates in a religious program to the extent of making it possible for her students to participate in it. Whether she does it occasionally for a few students, regularly for one, or pursuant to a systematized program designed to further the religious needs of all the students does not alter the character of the act.

We are a religious people whose institutions presuppose a Supreme Being. We guarantee the freedom to worship as one chooses. We make room for as wide a variety of beliefs and creeds as the spiritual needs of man deem necessary. We sponsor an attitude on the part of government that shows no partiality to any one group and that lets each flourish according to the zeal of its adherents and the appeal of its dogma. When the state encourages religious instruction or cooperates with religious authorities by adjusting the schedule of public events to sectarian needs, it follows the best of our traditions. For it then respects the religious nature of our people and accommodates the public service to their spiritual needs. To hold that it may not would be to find in the Constitution a requirement that the government show a callous indifference to religious groups. That would be preferring those who believe in no religion over those who do believe. Government may not finance religious groups nor undertake religious instruction nor blend secular and sectarian education nor use secular institutions to force one or some religion on any person. But we find no constitutional requirement which makes it necessary for government to be hostile to religion and to throw its weight against efforts to widen the effective scope of religious influence. The government must be neutral when it comes to competition between sects. It may not thrust any sect on any person. It may not make a religious observance compulsory. It may not coerce anyone to attend church, to observe a religious holiday, or to take religious instruction. But it can close its doors or suspend its operations as to those who want to repair to their religious sanctuary for worship or instruction. No more than that is undertaken here.

This program may be unwise and improvident from an educational or a community viewpoint. That appeal is made to us on a theory, previously advanced, that each case must be decided on the basis of 'our own prepossessions.' Our individual preferences, however, are not the constitutional standard. The constitutional standard is the separation of Church and State. The problem, like many problems in constitutional law, is one of degree. In the *McCollum* case the classrooms were used for religious instruction and the force of the public school was used to promote that instruction. Here, as we have said, the public schools do no more than accommodate their schedules to a program of outside religious instruction. We follow the *McCollum* case. But we cannot expand it to cover the present released time program unless separation of Church and State means that public institutions can make no adjustments of their schedules to accommodate the religious needs of the people. We cannot read into the Bill of Rights such a philosophy of hostility to religion.

Affirmed.

Citation: *Zorach v. Clauson*, 343 U.S. 306 (1952).

Index

925

Bethel School District No. 403 v. Fraser, 1:67–72
  academic sanctions and, **1:**17
  acceptable use policies and, **1:**75
  Ambach v. Norwick and, **1:**70
  antigang policy and, **1:**370
  Justice William J. Brennan, concurring opinion in, **1:**72
  bullying and, **1:**131
  Chief Justice Warren E. Burger, majority
    opinion in, **1:**69–72
  Court's ruling in, **1:**68, **1:**341, **1:**358
  excerpts from, **1:**69–72
  facts of the case in, **1:**67–68
  FCC v. Pacifica Foundation and, **1:**68
  Ginsberg v. New York and, **1:**71
  Hazelwood School District v. Kuhlmeier and,
    1:419–426, **2:**560
  J. S. v. Bethlehem Area School District and, **2:**889
  lewd and vulgar attire issue in, **1:**358, **1:**366, **1:**370
  New Jersey v. T. L. O. and, **1:**71
  Chief Justice William H. Rehnquist, concurring opinion in, **2:**676
  student due process rights and, **1:**67–72
  student free speech rights and, **1:**67–68, **1:**75, **1:**259,
    1:341, **1:**358, **1:**366, **2:**560, **2:**561, **2:**563, **2:**564,
    2:676, **2:**679, **2:**889
  Tinker v. Des Moines Independent Community School District
    and, **1:**68, **1:**70, **1:**72, **1:**360
Bethlehem Area School District, J. S. v., **2:**888–889
BFOQ. *See* Bona fide occupational qualification (BFOQ)
Big Beaver Falls Area School District v. Jackson, **1:**192
Bilingual education, 1:72–74
  Adequate Yearly Progress for ELLs and, **1:**20–21,
    1:74, **2:**517
  Bilingual Education Act (1968) and, **1:**73, **1:**295
  Castaneda v. Pickard and, **1:**295, **1:**296
  Civil Rights Act of 1964, Section 601 and, **1:**73
  English as a second language and, **1:**294–296
  English immersion *vs.*, **1:**72–73
  English language learners and, **1:**74, **1:**294–295, **2:**516–518
  Equal Educational Opportunity Act and, **1:**304, **2:**493, **2:**517
  federal action regarding, **1:**73–74
  Fourteenth Amendment and, **1:**73
  historical context of, **1:**73
  immersion and English-only programs and, **1:**295–296
  Lau v. Nichols and, **1:**73, **1:**74, **1:**166, **1:**256, **1:**295, **1:**296,
    1:302, **1:**303, **2:**492–493, **2:**494, **2:**517, **2:**734
  laws, court rulings and, **1:**73–74
  legal reaction to, **1:**74
  limited English proficiency issues and, **2:**516–518
  Meyer v. Nebraska and, **1:**73, **1:**194, **2:**545–549, **2:**612
  NCLB (2002) and, **1:**74, **2:**517–518
  Office for Civil Rights (OCR) and, **1:**74
  program overview and, **1:**72–73
Bilingual Education Act (1968), **1:**73, **1:**295
Bilkin, Douglas, **1:**56
Bill of Rights, 1:74–77
  Articles of Confederation and, **1:**75–76
  Barron v. Baltimore and, **2:**529
  Bethel School District No. 403 v. Fraser and, **1:**67–72, **1:**75
  Board of Education of Independent School District No. 92 of
    Pottawatomie County v. Earls and, **1:**76, **1:**81
  common law and, **1:**191–192

Constitutional Convention and, **1:**75–76
corporal punishment and, **1:**76
cruel and unusual punishment protection and, **1:**76
Eighth Amendment and, **1:**76
English Bill of Rights and, **1:**75
Federal Bill of Rights and, **1:**75–76
The Federalist Papers and, **1:**75
Fifth Amendment and, **1:**76
First Amendment and, **1:**338–340
Fourth Amendment and, **1:**76
freedom of press and, **1:**75
freedom of speech and, **1:**75
freedom to assemble and, **1:**76
Hazelwood School District v. Kuhlmeier and, **1:**17, **1:**76
housing of troops and, **1:**76
individual freedoms guaranteed by, **1:**74, **1:**75–76
Ingraham v. Wright and, **1:**64, **1:**76
Lemon v. Kurtzman and, **1:**75
Magna Carta and, **1:**75
Miranda v. Arizona and, **1:**76
Morse v. Frederick and, **1:**75
New Jersey v. T. L. O., **1:**76
Ninth Amendment and, **1:**76
origins of, **1:**74–75
Pickering v. Board of Education of Township High School
  District 205, Will County and, **1:**75
In re Gault and, **1:**161, **1:**464–465
religious freedom and, **1:**75
right to keep and bear arms and, **1:**76
rule of law and, **2:**712–713
Second Amendment and, **1:**76
Seventh Amendment and, **1:**76
Sixth Amendment and, **1:**76
states' rights and, **1:**76, **2:**883
Tenth Amendment and, **1:**76
Third Amendment and, **1:**76
Tinker v. Des Moines Independent Community School District
  and, **1:**75
trial by jury in "suits at common law" and, **1:**76
trial by jury of peers and, **1:**76
U.S. v. Miller and, **1:**76
Vernonia School District 47J v. Acton and, **1:**76
Chief Justice Earl Warren and, **2:**883
Wheeler v. Barrera and, **2:**891–892
See also **Due process; Due process hearing; Due process**
  rights; *Lemon v. Kurtzman; specific amendment;*
  specific court case
BIP. *See* **Behavioral intervention plan** (BIP)
Birmingham Board of Education, Jackson v., **1:**473–474
Bishop v. Wood, 1:77–78
  constitutionally protected property rights and, **1:**77–78
  Court's ruling in, **1:**77–78
  facts of the case in, **1:**77
  reasons for dismissal issue and, **1:**77–78
Black, Hugo L., 1:78–79
  activist philosophy of, **2:**887
  Adamson v. California dissenting opinion and, **1:**79
  Burger Court and, **1:**136
  centrism of, **1:**111
  desegregation rulings and, **1:**135
  early years of, **1:**78

exceptions to the law and, **1:**195

Farrington v. Tokushige and, **1:**195

historical background regarding, **1:**194

kindergarten attendance and, **1:**487–489

mandatory vaccinations and, **2:**867–868

Massachusetts School Attendance Act (1852) and, **1:**194

Meyer v. Nebraska and, **1:**194

parent educational neglect charges and, **1:**194

Pierce v. Society of Sisters of the Holy Names of Jesus and Mary and, **1:**105–106, **1:**147, **1:**159, **1:**161, **1:**182, **1:**194–195, **1:**332, **2:**545, **2:**593, **2:**610, **2:**612, **2:**637–640, **2:**784

truancy and, **2:**839–841

Wisconsin v. Yoder and, **1:**135–136, **1:**137, **1:**195, **1:**256, **1:**439, **2:**506, **2:**610, **2:**612, **2:**637

year-round schools and, **2:**905–907

See also **Wisconsin v. Yoder**

Compulsory Education Act (Oregon), **1:**194–195

Conditional privileged information, **1:**235

Congress of the United States, Newdow v., **2:**643–644, **2:**892

Connecticut, Boddie v., **1:**177

Connecticut, Cantwell v., **1:**8, **1:**144–145, **1:**256, **1:**338, **2:**784

Connecticut, Griswold v., **1:**78–79, **1:**113, **1:**255, **1:**256, **1:**256x

Connecticut State Board of Education, Town of Waterford v., **2:**839

Connelie, Foley v., **1:**47

Connick v. Myers, 1:196–197

Court's ruling in, **1:**196–197

Elrod v. Burns and, **2:**654–655

facts of the case in, **1:**196

First Amendment free speech issue in, **1:**196–197, **1:**342, **2:**808–809

Garcetti v. Ceballos and, **1:**196, **2:**654

Mt. Healthy City School Board of Education v. Doyle and, **2:**809

Pickering balancing test and, **2:**808

Pickering-Connick test and, **2:**654

Pickering v. Board of Education of Township School District 205, Will County and, **1:**196, **2:**654

public concern issue in, **1:**196–197, **1:**342, **2:**808–809

time, place, and distribution manner issues in, **1:**196

Consent decree, 1:197–198

Adams v. California and, **1:**197

Brown v. Board of Education of Topeka and, **1:**197

definition of, **1:**197

desegregation rulings and, **1:**197

gender equity in interscholastic sports and, **1:**198

in higher education, **1:**197–198

Neal v. Board of Trustees of California State Universities and, **1:**198

Pennsylvania Association for Retarded Children v. Commonwealth of Pennsylvania and, **1:**197

special education rulings and, **1:**197

Consolidated High School District No. 230, Cornfield v., **2:**799

Consolidated Rail Corporation v. Darrone, **1:**350–352

Constitution Act, 1867 (Canada), **1:**141, **1:**241

Contracts, 1:198–200

arbitration and, **1:**51–53

basic requirements of, **1:**198–199

capacity to form agreements and, **1:**199

Cleveland Board of Education v. Loudermill and, **1:**176–180, **1:**200, **1:**272, **2:**813–814

closed shop and, **1:**180–181

collective bargaining and, **1:**183–185, **1:**200

definition of, **1:**198

Due Process Clause, Fifth and Fourteenth Amendments and, **1:**200

essential terms element of, **1:**199

impasse in bargaining and, **1:**457–458

legal subject matter requirement of, **1:**199

mediation and, **2:**538–539

motivation, behavior management and, **1:**199

objective manifestations of intent and, **1:**199

open shop and, **2:**605–606

reduction in force (RIF) and, **2:**666–667

school-related contracts and, **1:**200

specificity of terms element of, **1:**199

two party requirement of, **1:**199

unilateral *vs.* bilateral contracts and, **1:**199

valid consideration element of, **1:**199

written agreement preference and, **1:**199

Convention on the Rights of the Child. *See* **United Nations Convention on the Rights of the Child**

Cook, Stuart W., **2:**772

Coons, J. E., **1:**124

Cooperman, Board of Education of Plainfield v., **2:**700

Cooper v. Aaron, 1:200–201

Brown v. Board of Education of Topeka and, **1:**201, **2:**883, **2:**886

constitutional interpretation and, **1:**478, **2:**883

Court's ruling in, **1:**201

Justice William O. Douglas, concurring opinion in, **1:**256

facts of the case in, **1:**200–201

Fourteenth Amendment and, **1:**201

"one grade per year" desegregation plan issue in, **1:**200–201, **1:**256, **2:**709

Rogers v. Paul and, **2:**709–710

Chief Justice Earl Warren, unanimous Court's decision in, **2:**883

Cooper v. Florida, **2:**789

COPA. *See* Child Online Protection Act (COPA, 1998)

COPPA. *See* Children's Online Privacy Protection Act (COPPA, 1998)

Copyright, 1:201–203

acceptable use policies (AUPs) and, **1:**17

Copyright Act and, **1:**201–202, **1:**203, **1:**319, **1:**320, **1:**465–466, **2:**817

Copyright Law Revision (1976) and, **1:**202

Digital Millennium Copyright Act (1998) and, **1:**242–243

display in the course of teaching activities and, **1:**202, **1:**466

expiration of, public domain and, **1:**203, **1:**466

fair use exception factors and, **1:**202, **1:**319–321, **1:**466, **2:**817

library reproductions and, **1:**202

other accepted uses and, **1:**202–203, **1:**466

ownership issues and, **1:**203

Technology, Education, and Copyright Harmonization Act (202) and, **1:**202–203

technology and the law and, **2:**816–817

When U.S. Works Pass Into the Public Domain (Gasaway) and, **1:**203

"works for hire" concept and, **1:**203

Cordrey v. Euckert, **1:**315

Corley, Universal City Studios, Inc. v., **1:**243

Cornell, Drucilla, **1:**211

Cornfield v. Consolidated High School District No. 230, **2:**799

Coronado Oil & Gas Co., Burnet v., **2:**782

Corporal punishment, 1:203–205

American tradition of, **1:**204

Baker v. Owens and, **1:**204